P9-DHB-642

EINSTEIN ON PEACE

EDITED BY
OTTO NATHAN AND HEINZ NORDEN

PREFACE BY BERTRAND RUSSELL

SIMON AND SCHUSTER · NEW YORK · 1960

Published by Simon and Schuster, Inc.
Rockefeller Center, 630 Fifth Avenue
New York 20, N. Y.

First Printing

Library of Congress Catalog Card Number: 60–12583
Manufactured in the United States of America
By Kingsport Press, Inc., Kingsport, Tennessee.

CONTENTS

INTRODUCTION

DURING my last conversation with Einstein, only a few hours before his death, he talked about the embattled civil liberties in the United States since the end of the war and the rearmament of Germany, which he considered most unwise and a severe obstacle to the establishment of real peace in the world. A few days before, he had affixed the last signature of his life to a statement of nine scientists, in which the world was warned it would run the risk of universal annihilation unless the institution of war was abolished in the near future.

I was in London a few months later when that statement was released to the world. I discussed with Bertrand Russell the unique role Einstein had played in the fight against war, a fight which was now more crucial and urgent than ever before. It was then that I conceived of the project which is realized in this volume. Since Einstein himself could no longer speak to the world and was no longer able to struggle personally for peace on earth, I felt that the printed record of his ceaseless efforts against militarism and war might help in the fight for a saner world.

It seemed appropriate that the first collection of Einstein's writings to be published after his death should be a volume devoted to his activities in the cause of peace. Einstein's thirst for knowledge about the universe overshadowed everything else in his life. His curiosity about the laws of nature was first stimulated when, as a child, he was fascinated by a compass; and his interest in science was to dominate his thoughts until the end. Nothing else mattered as much as his scientific work; but I know from the experience gained in the many years during which I enjoyed his friendship and confidence that, except for his devotion to science, no cause was more important or closer to his heart than the determination that the institution of war be forever abolished. What were the roots of that determination? What were the forces that inspired him?

Einstein fought for the abolition of war not merely because he hated brutality and considered it unconscionable to seek solutions to international conflicts through killing of human beings; he was convinced that, as long as war existed as an accepted institution, the intellectual freedom of the individual—which he considered to be the foundation of human society—could not be realized. The existence of military institutions, the training of youth to serve as unthinking tools for the most flagrantly asocial purposes, the demoralizing effect of war preparations upon civilian life—Einstein considered all this incompatible with the dignity of free men.

Einstein was a socialist. He believed in socialism because, as a convinced equalitarian, he was opposed to the class division in capitalism and to the exploitation of man by man which he felt this system facilitated more ingeniously than any previous economic organization. He was a socialist because he was certain that a capitalist economy could not adequately perform for the welfare of *all* people and that the economic anarchy of capitalism was the source of many evils in contemporary society. And, finally, he was a socialist because he was convinced that, under socialism, there was a greater possibility of attaining the maximum degree of individual freedom compatible with the public welfare than under any other system known to man.

Einstein's socialism was a deeply felt human reaction to the inequities of the world in which he lived; it was not the result of methodical study, nor was it confined within the limits of an ideological creed. His free and unfettered mind, hostile to regimentation, would not have tolerated any restriction on his thoughts, acts or expressions. His mind having been trained in systematic reasoning, he believed in the necessity of a centrally planned economy which would provide orderliness of production and distribution and utilize the labor power of man in the interest of society as a whole. But he well realized the problems that may arise in a fully planned economy, which might, in fact, "be accompanied by the complete enslavement of the individual." Einstein was always apprehensive of concentration of power, regardless of the economic system under which such concentration would occur. His insistence on the development of real political democracy did not merely reflect his innermost feelings of equality and brotherhood toward his fellow man; he considered true democracy an indispensable antidote for the misuse of economic power, which appeared to him a constant threat to the welfare of society. It was this fear of concentrated power and the ambitions and drives to which such power might give rise that made it impossible for Einstein to hope that socialism would be a guarantee against war. He did not share the belief of other socialists that socialist countries would not go to war against one another; he was afraid that the power drives among them might become as forceful and disastrous as they had been among capitalist countries. Hence, the abolition of weapons and the institution of war was to Einstein, even in a world of socialist countries, an indispensable prerequisite to peace.

I have often felt that this rational analysis does not adequately explain Einstein's anxiety for a world in which man would live in total peace. It is difficult, if not impossible, to lay bare the inner motivations of an individual which, often unknown to the individual himself, cause him to act as he does or not to act as he might be expected to. Conscious of these difficulties, I should nonetheless like to record certain reflections which occurred to me when I tried to understand the phenomenon that was Einstein. He himself once said that his pacifism was not derived from any intellectual theory but was based on his deepest antipathy to every kind of cruelty and hatred. How did this deep antipathy originate which made him for over four decades a most passionate fighter against war—a fight to which he devoted much of the time and effort otherwise jealously guarded for his scientific work? Is it possible that this antipathy came to exist or grew more powerful because of his labors as a scientist? So far as could be established, he publicly expressed pacifist beliefs for the first time after the outbreak of war in 1914. Einstein had then already gained an outstanding reputation among the scientists of the world; his position in the history of science had been established. He was a deeply religious man—a religious unbeliever, as he once called himself—a man who revered nature with profound humility, who looked again and again in awe at the trees in front of his study, reflecting upon the richness and beauty of their branches and leaves and upon the minuscule understanding which man had acquired of the laws of nature in thousands of years of research and observation. When, in the summer of 1914, he rebelled against the war as "something unbelievable," when he lamented his belonging to the "rotten" species of man, I believe he must have felt that man's actions in war violated the sublime laws of the universe, that the willful killing of millions interfered with nature's course for which he, the scientist, had the deepest reverence. It appears that *this* was the real source of his antipathy to brutality, the motive power behind his passionate, devoted efforts to help abolish the very institution of war. It would seem that precisely because, as a scientist, he was engaged in the most abstract work of attempting to increase man's understanding of nature, he felt the compelling need to convince man not to flout nature's will, and decided to devote himself to the most concrete, even if at times visionary, objective of fighting for man's survival and creative fulfillment.

Those who challenged Einstein as naïve in political affairs, and too generous in lending his name to unorthodox causes, probably did not realize that he never supported a cause which might have violated the principles that guided him. While his basic political philosophy did not change throughout his life, he was far from being dogmatic or doctrinaire in his beliefs or their application to the practical problems as they occurred in his day. In the early years of Nazism in Germany, he announced that he was no longer able to advocate the policy of war resistance which he had so passionately promoted in the preceding years. He then came under particularly severe attack by the pacifist movement; but he himself never felt that he had forsaken the cause of pacifism, and continued to consider himself a convinced and devoted pacifist, one who was unable to adhere to a rigid policy in the face of changing circumstances. Pacifism meant to Einstein the realization of world institutions which would abolish war and safeguard international peace without resorting to arms and violence. But pacifism did not mean that countries should remain defenseless in the face of a nation such as Nazi Germany, which was then openly preparing for war and aggression. In fact, Einstein believed he served the cause of pacifism, as he understood it, when he called for the rearmament of the West against the menace of Nazism; he felt there was a better chance of avoiding war if Germany knew that the Western countries were militarily prepared in the event of conflict.

Einstein acted from similar premises when, in the fateful letter written in the summer of 1939, he advised President Roosevelt that the production of atomic bombs had become a distinct possibility, and when he recommended that the United States Government take an interest in supporting and accelerating the experimental work, then in progress, in regard to the production of atomic energy. Einstein made this suggestion to President Roosevelt not because he would have wanted the United States to use this monstrous weapon to spread death; rather, he hoped that the possession of atomic bombs by the United States might make the Germans more reluctant to explode such bombs, which Einstein feared they would succeed in producing before long. Both in 1933 and 1939, in the case of war resistance and atomic energy, Einstein acted from what he believed was a realistic appraisal of the forces which were marshaled for evil and destruction. He did not feel that the nakedness and peacefulness of unarmed nations would deter Fascist aggression; further, he knew that Fascist countries would never enter into, or abide by, international agreements for the protection of peace.

Einstein was by nature an internationalist; he disliked, to the extreme, nationalism and chauvinism, the excesses of which he held responsible for many evils in the world. He deplored the existence of political frontiers and their insidious and divisive impact upon mankind. As a scientist he was engaged in work which, more than anything else, is necessarily international despite the many efforts —sharply criticized by Einstein—toward scientific secrecy in the last two decades. Einstein hoped for intensification of cultural and scientific relations among the countries of the world when he advocated in 1914 a United Europe and when he welcomed in 1919 the establishment of the League of Nations and, in 1945, the United Nations. But his belief in the desirability of a world organization had been inspired even more by another consideration: Einstein had long since realized that the maintenance of international peace required the partial relinquishment of national sovereignty in favor of an international organization which would possess the administrative and judicial institutions necessary for the peaceful settlement of international conflicts and which alone would be entitled to maintain a military force; he hoped that the Covenant of the League of Nations and, later, the Charter of the United Nations would, in time, be so modified that an organization capable of maintaining world peace would emerge. Einstein's insistence on the need for an appropriate world organization gained momentum with the increase in the striking power of modern weapons. The production of the atomic bomb and its use over Japanese cities in 1945 made Einstein less tolerant than ever of token gestures toward peace. He had never believed that disarmament by small stages was a practicable policy against war, a policy which would ever lead to total disarmament and peace; he was convinced that a nation could not arm and disarm at the same time. He felt this even more strongly when, after 1945, the possibility of nuclear war threatened the annihilation of the human race. It was during those years of the postwar period that he became actively engaged in the movements for world government. He did not conceive of world government as an institution supplanting the primary functions of existing national governments; rather, he thought of an organization which would have circumscribed authority only in matters directly relating to the preservation of peace: any infringement upon the sovereign power of member nations would be limited by the world organization's obligations in the cause of international security. Einstein would have been the last to advocate the establishment of a huge power complex in excess of specific and immediate needs. He supported the establishment of a centralized, supranational body for the sole purpose of guaranteeing international security; otherwise, he was a strong advocate of decentralization.

The many documents assembled in this volume will reveal Einstein as a man with an almost obsessive drive to help in what he himself once called "the greatest of all causes—good will among men and peace on earth." This volume deals intentionally with only one aspect of Einstein's unusually rich and creative life—but his personality emerges as it would no matter which segment of his scientific or nonscientific interests might have been described. Einstein, as possibly no other man of his generation, enjoyed a singular reputation throughout the world: he was respected, admired, revered and loved. His name had an undefinable meaning for the mighty and the humble, partly because it had become a symbol of a scientific discovery of momentous significance, but possibly even more because of Einstein's innate humanity, which communicated itself to the world in a strange way. The world must have sensed what only personal contact with him would sufficiently reveal: the warmth and charm of his personality, the disarming informality with which he would greet friend and stranger alike, the utter lack of any air of superiority, so often characteristic of the mighty and famous, the absence of sentimentality, the candor of his conversation. The manner of his speech, clothing and food, the furniture in his study—all reflected the complete simplicity which characterized him and which is difficult of adequate description. He had no use for anything that was not necessary or essential to human existence; he had organized his own life with great economy in matter and time, avoiding the superfluous and concentrating on what seemed important, enriching or enjoyable. Simplicity characterized even his emotional life, as far as he allowed it to become known. Except for rare occasions there was, despite his warmth, an almost unbridgeable distance between him and the world outside. Although he eagerly sought and enjoyed the company of a few friends, Einstein was a lonely man who suffered from this loneliness and whose often sad eyes seemed to have a forlorn, faraway look, as if they wanted to pierce the mysteries of the universe. He was very conscious of the fact that, in an ironical way, the world had made his life lonely also in a physical sense. His unique reputation and universally known countenance had made him a virtual prisoner in his own house and its immediate surroundings; inconvenienced by the attention that was paid him everywhere, he could not live an everyday life as lived by millions, go where he might have liked to go, do what might have pleased him or mingle with whoever might have appeared congenial or interesting. It was touching to experience his bewilderment and joy when, on exceptional occasions, he would sit at the counter of a drugstore or indulge in some similar "activity" which forms the regular, inconspicuous routine of people everywhere.

Einstein knew of the reverence in which he was held. He could not explain it to himself and thought it was undeserved. However embarrassed he felt about it, he nonetheless recognized that his unique position in the community and the world offered him exceptional opportunities for action in behalf of individuals and society as a whole. He felt a deep responsibility to lend his efforts and influence whenever he hoped they might prove effective. He was ready, at any hour, to interrupt his scientific work, which mentally absorbed him even while he was otherwise occupied, to devote time and energy to individuals or public causes. He would receive visitors, study documents, prepare public pronouncements or render whatever service might be indicated. It was irrelevant whether he had been approached by a personality of great scholarly or public acclaim or by someone completely unknown to him and the world. He would act without delay, always sensitive to the feelings of anyone who communicated with him, however lowly his position in life might be.

The causes to which he lent support could not suffer any delay; they were all urgent: civil liberties, democracy, socialism, the Jewish problem, social and economic justice, and general education for a more productive and rewarding life. But as the years wore on, nothing became more compelling to Einstein than the struggle to abolish war. It was tragic that the great scientific discoveries, in which he had so prominent a part, were in his time primarily used not for the improvement of man's working and living conditions but for magnifying the means of terror and destruction. During the last few years of Einstein's life, military preparations multiplied and the preservation of world peace seemed more and more precarious. In the United States, the fight against war became increasingly difficult as advocates of peace became suspect of unpatriotic activities and were exposed to political persecution. As their numbers dwindled, Einstein deeply felt his increased isolation. He deplored the inaction of the academic community as well as the ignorance of many others who had fallen prey to nationalistic propaganda. He grew impatient at the lack of opposition to war preparations and the dominance of sheer insanity with regard to atomic weapons; yet, he never really despaired. I believe he did not despair because he never lost faith in the power of *reason*. He often suggested that a group of men, of indisputable achievement and distinction, appeal to the conscience of the world; he felt that the voices of men known to be reasonable could not remain unheard. That is why he was ready without hesitation to join Bertrand Russell and a small group of scientists in a challenging call to humanity to recognize and appreciate the magnitude of the disaster which threatened. This was in April 1955. As has been mentioned, it was Einstein's last act.

When I decided to prepare this volume, I hoped that the cumulative effect of Einstein's writings on peace would constitute still another appeal to reason. This is what I said in describing the project in the fall of 1955: "The world has now entered upon a period when it becomes increasingly clear that the struggle for peace must concentrate on the abolition of national armies, and of war itself; developments in the last few years have brought about not merely a quantitative but also a qualitative change in the international security problem. Disarmament negotiations of the traditional type no longer suffice if we are to cope with the momentous problem which faces mankind. The vision and steadfastness of Einstein, over four decades, evident in his writings, may serve to inspire men to engage in the kind of negotiations which have now become urgent and indispensable—negotiations to abolish war."

This, it seems to me, is as true now as it was when I wrote it almost five years ago. The real negotiations for a warless world have actually not yet begun. But mankind is spiritually better prepared and riper for such negotiations than at the time of Einstein's death. The forces of history, in a subtle way, make an impact upon men's reason; and the forces of history are moving in the direction of Einstein's vision: a world without war.

Otto Nathan

New York, August 1960

PREFACE

IT IS A VERY GOOD THING that Einstein's letters and writings on other than scientific subjects are being collected and printed. Einstein was not only the ablest man of science of his generation, he was also a wise man, which is something different. If statesmen had listened to him, the course of human events would have been less disastrous than it has been. It is the custom among those who are called "practical" men to condemn any man capable of a wide survey as a visionary: no man is thought worthy of a voice in politics unless he ignores or does not know nine tenths of the most important relevant facts. On this ground, no one listened to Einstein. In Germany, during Hitler's reign, the theory of relativity was condemned as a Jewish trick of which the sole purpose was to bewilder Aryans. It seems that Hitler and Himmler could not understand it and rashly inferred that *no* Aryan could. In the United States, where he lived after Germany had rejected him, he received, as a scientist, all that great measure of honor which was his due; but, when he allowed himself to say anything about political matters, what he said was, by most people, considered highly undesirable.

I was among those who almost always agreed with him. He and I both opposed the First World War but considered the Second unavoidable. He and I were equally perturbed by the awful prospect of H-bomb warfare. We agreed to make a joint pronouncement on this subject in conjunction with many eminent men of science who were willing to co-operate. I drew up a statement and sent it to Einstein. Before getting an answer from him, while traveling by air from Rome to Paris, I learned of his death. On arrival in Paris, I found his letter agreeing to sign. This must have been one of the last acts of his life.

We met from time to time, but I did not see much of him except while I was living in Princeton in 1943. At that time I used to go to his house once a week to discuss various matters in the philosophy of science with him and Pauli and Gödel. Pauli and Gödel are both very eminent in their respective fields, but Einstein was, of course, outstanding even among the most eminent. I found these informal discussions very illuminating and exceedingly valuable.

Einstein's attitude as regards the acceptance or rejection of a scientific theory was very different from that recommended by Francis Bacon. One must, of course, know the facts. But a theory, if it is to have any value, must not emerge from careful collection and collation of individual observations. It must emerge, rather, as sudden imaginative insight, like that of a poet or composer. When Eddington undertook to verify Einstein's predictions by observations of the eclipse of 1919, Einstein was much less interested in the result than Eddington was. I was reminded of the story about a female admirer of Whistler who told him that she had seen Battersea Bridge looking just as it did in one of his pictures, to which Whistler replied, "Ah, Nature's coming on!" One felt that Einstein thought the solar system was "coming on" when it decided to confirm his predictions. It is difficult to turn Einstein's method into a set of textbook maxims for the guidance of students. The recipe would have read as follows: "First acquire a transcendent genius and an all-embracing imagination, then learn your subject, and then wait for illumination." It is the first part of this recipe that offers difficulties.

Einstein was an extraordinarily satisfactory human being. In spite of his genius and his fame, he always behaved with complete simplicity and never seemed to be claiming any superiority. His work and his violin brought him, I believe, a considerable measure of happiness, but his wide sympathies and his concern with the destiny of mankind prevented him from acquiring an undue measure of serenity. I never saw in him any trace, however faint, of vanity or envy, which are vices to which even the greatest men, such as Newton and Leibnitz, are prone.

Einstein, throughout his life, cared for the individual and for individual liberty. He showed, himself, all the courage that his circumstances demanded and called upon others, often without success, to show equal courage. He had seen individual freedom lost in Germany with the advent of the Nazis, and he was quickly perceptive of any danger of a like disaster in other countries. He had small respect for the Big Battalions, and his attitude to governments was very like that of the Hebrew prophets. He was not only a great scientist but a great man, a man whom it is good to have known and consoling to contemplate.

BERTRAND RUSSELL

CHAPTER ONE

THE REALITY OF WAR

1914-1918

IN THE SPRING of 1914, Albert Einstein left Switzerland and, not without misgivings, settled in Berlin, the capital of Germany. He was then thirty-five years of age and had already achieved renown as a mathematical physicist throughout the scientific world. His Berlin appointment was in itself a signal honor. Famous scholars had come to Zurich to woo him away from the Institute of Technology, where he was then teaching. In his new position he was to be director of the newly created Institute of Physics in the Kaiser Wilhelm Society for the Development of the Sciences (Kaiser-Wilhelm-Gesellschaft zur Förderung der Wissenschaften), one of the top research organizations in Europe. He had also been elected a member of the famous Royal Prussian Academy of Sciences, a coveted distinction many savants twice his age failed to receive, and was appointed professor at the University of Berlin with all professorial privileges but without any teaching or administrative obligations. Adding the liberal salary he was to earn, this was indeed a unique opportunity for a man who even then closely fitted the popular notion of the unworldly scientist.

By both his temperament and the boldness of his scientific imagination, Einstein was a man set apart. Given to easy laughter, devoid of vanity or pretense, gentle and kind, he was, nevertheless, in his own words, an *Einspänner*, a man who goes by himself, drawing strength from solitude. Even as a boy, he had been deeply repelled by all evidence of authoritarianism, militarism, nationalism and bigotry. Writing of Einstein's early years, his lifelong friend Maurice Solovine, a fellow student and scientist, said that "what struck Einstein most forcibly and aroused his deep condemnation were the prejudices, injustices and reactionary ideas of those days." [1] But although Einstein was a pacifist before his arrival in Berlin, he had never, so far as is known, translated these sentiments into any form of organized protest. He had taken no stand on public issues, nor had he been engaged in civic affairs or political action.

The outbreak of the First World War, in August 1914, had a large impact not only on the belligerent countries, their people and the lives of their people but far beyond the confines of the conflict itself. The war not only created wholesale death and destruction, misery and pain, hunger and privation in the countries at war but caused a profound upheaval in human, political, cultural and scientific relationships throughout the world. Einstein was among those who were deeply shocked by the mere realization of what war actually was, that war was not only still possible but could, in fact, be waged on a huge scale. The experience of war was to change his life; not that his scientific work did not remain the very center of his existence, but in the sense that it was to make him a conscious citizen of the world, who henceforth was to consider the fight against war, the horrors of which were brought home to him every day, his most deeply felt concern until the hour of his death. Two letters, one written in the very first weeks of the war, the other a few months later, illustrate Einstein's thoughts and feelings in those days. Both letters were addressed to Paul Ehrenfest, a physicist teaching at the University of Leiden in Holland, one of Einstein's closest and dearest friends.[2] In his letter of August 19, 1914, Einstein said:

Europe, in her insanity, has started something unbelievable. In such times one realizes to what a sad species of animal one belongs. I quietly pursue my peaceful studies and contemplations and feel only pity and disgust. My dear astronomer Freundlich [Professor Erwin F. Freundlich of the Royal Observatory at Potsdam, Germany] will become a prisoner of war in Russia instead of being able there to observe the eclipse of the sun. I am worried about him.

Einstein's second letter to Ehrenfest was written early in December 1914 and included these remarks:

The international catastrophe has imposed a heavy burden upon me as an internationalist. In living through this "great epoch," it is difficult to reconcile oneself to the fact that one belongs to that idiotic, rotten species which boasts of its freedom of will. How I wish that somewhere there existed an island for those who are wise and of good will! In such a place even I should be an ardent patriot.

Germany's initial military success was facilitated by her violation of Belgium's neutrality, a violation so sharply in conflict with German cultural pretensions that it created a shock and uproar throughout the world. Even the Imperial German Government felt that some action was necessary. The result was a public declaration by intellectuals in a "Manifesto to the Civilized World." The Manifesto, issued early in October 1914, has long since become notorious.[3] The German word used in the title of the declaration was *Kulturwelt*, and this document, given wide publicity in the countries then at war against the Central Powers, went far toward lending the word *Kultur* the derogatory connotation that clung to it for many years.

The Manifesto made six negative points, all of them beginning with "It is not true that . . ." It disclaimed German war guilt. It denied charges of wanton violation of Belgium's neutrality, asserting that the Germans had merely anticipated the war plans of the Allies and that it would have been suicide to do otherwise. It denied that the Germans had committed atrocities in Belgium and specifically denied the alleged pillage of the Belgian city of Louvain. It denied that German methods of warfare defied the provisions of international law, citing instead the alleged Allied use of dum-dum (soft-nosed) bullets and the "shameful spectacle . . . of Russian hordes . . . allied with Mongols and Negroes . . . unleashed against the white race."

The final point was clothed in a negative formulation apparently to preserve the symmetry of the Manifesto but was in truth a defiant declaration to the world: "It is not true that opposition to our so-called militarism does not constitute opposition to our *Kultur*, despite the hypocritical allegations of our enemies." If this meant anything, it was that anyone who opposed German militarism necessarily opposed German "culture" as well. The thought is expressed in the concluding paragraphs:

> Were it not for German militarism, German culture would have been wiped off the face of the earth. That culture, for its own protection, led to militarism since Germany, like no other country, was ravaged by invasion for centuries. The German army and the German people today stand shoulder to shoulder, without regard to education, social position or partisan allegiance.
>
> We cannot wrest from our enemies' hand the venomous weapon of the lie. We can only cry out to the whole world that they bear false witness against us. To you who know us, who have hitherto

stood with us in safeguarding mankind's most precious heritage—to you we cry out: Have faith in us! Have faith in us when we say that we shall wage this fight to the very end as a civilized nation, a nation that holds the legacy of Goethe, Beethoven and Kant no less sacred than hearth and home.

In token whereof we pledge our names and our honor!

There were ninety-three signers to the Manifesto: artists, scientists, clergymen, poets, jurists, physicians, historians, philosophers and musicians, most of them prominent individually and some of international renown. Many had been identified with German nationalism, but there were others not usually so regarded—Ernst Häckel, the famous evolutionist; Wilhelm Röntgen, the discoverer of X rays; Paul Ehrlich, the great biochemist; Engelbert Humperdinck, the composer of *Hänsel und Gretel;* and even Max Reinhardt, the pioneer of the modern theater. Despite later halfhearted disavowals, the Manifesto undoubtedly expressed the dominant mood, not only among German intellectuals but among the German people at large.

Yet, within days after publication of the Manifesto, a noted German pacifist, Georg Friedrich Nicolai, composed a ringing challenge to it, a "Manifesto to Europeans." He circulated it among the faculty of the University of Berlin, where he held a chair in physiology. Nicolai was a distinguished physician, a cardiologist who already enjoyed a reputation for unorthodoxy. In the charged atmosphere then pervading Germany, so well illustrated by the Manifesto of the ninety-three, Nicolai's enterprise was hazardous indeed. Only three men joined him. One of them was Einstein. Here is the text of what may be assumed to be the first political document which Einstein signed:

Never before has any war so completely disrupted cultural cooperation. It has done so at the very time when progress in technology and communications clearly suggest that we recognize the need for international relations which will necessarily move in the direction of a universal, world-wide civilization. Perhaps we are all the more keenly and painfully aware of the rupture precisely because so many international bonds existed before.

We can scarcely be surprised. Anyone who cares in the least for a common world culture is now doubly committed to fight for the maintenance of the principles on which it must stand. Yet, those from whom such sentiments might have been expected—primarily scientists and artists—have so far responded, almost to a man, as though they had relinquished any further desire for the continuance of international relations. They have spoken in a hostile spirit, and they have failed to speak out for peace.

Nationalist passions cannot excuse this attitude which is unworthy of what the world has heretofore called culture. It would be a grave misfortune were this spirit to gain general currency among the intellectuals. It would, we are convinced, not only threaten culture as such; it would endanger the very existence of the nations for the protection of which this barbarous war was unleashed.

Technology has shrunk the world. Indeed, today the nations of the great European peninsula seem to jostle one another much as once did the city-states that were crowded into those smaller peninsulas jutting out into the Mediterranean. Travel is so widespread, international supply and demand are so interwoven, that Europe —one could almost say the whole world—is even now a single unit.

Surely, it is the duty of Europeans of education and good will at least to try to prevent Europe from succumbing, because of lack of international organization, to the fate that once engulfed ancient Greece! Or will Europe also suffer slow exhaustion and death by fratricidal war?

The struggle raging today can scarcely yield a "victor"; all nations that participate in it will, in all likelihood, pay an exceedingly high price. Hence it appears not only wise but imperative for men of education in all countries to exert their influence for the kind of peace treaty that will not carry the seeds of future wars, whatever the outcome of the present conflict may be. The unstable and fluid situation in Europe, created by the war, must be utilized to weld the Continent into an organic whole. Technically and intellectually, conditions are ripe for such a development.

This is not the place to discuss how this new order in Europe may be brought about. Our sole purpose is to affirm our profound conviction that the time has come when Europe must unite to guard its soil, its people, and its culture. We are stating publicly our faith in European unity, a faith which we believe is shared by many; we hope that this public affirmation of our faith may contribute to the growth of a powerful movement toward such unity.

The first step in this direction would be for all those who truly cherish the culture of Europe to join forces—all those whom

Goethe once prophetically called "good Europeans." We must not abandon hope that their voice speaking in unison may even today rise above the clash of arms, particularly if they are joined by those who already enjoy renown and authority.

The first step, we repeat, is for Europeans to join forces. If, as we devoutly hope, enough *Europeans* are to be found in Europe—people to whom Europe is a vital cause rather than a geographical term—we shall endeavor to organize a League of Europeans. This league may then raise its voice and take action.

We ourselves seek but to make the first move, to issue the challenge. If you are of one mind with us, if you too are determined to create a widespread movement for European unity, we bid you pledge yourself by signing your name.

Carefully worded as it was, this declaration might have affected the course of events had it received wide and representative support. One of the two men who, besides Nicolai and Einstein, were willing to sign was Wilhelm Förster, then already past eighty, the long-time head of the Berlin Observatory and a rueful signer of the Manifesto of the ninety-three intellectuals as well.[4] The other, Otto Buek, had come from Heidelberg to complete his studies in Berlin. This small group of heretics was not able to challenge successfully the so-called elite of German *Kultur;* the Manifesto to Europeans did not attract the signatures it would have needed to be effective and was not made public until several years later. This is how Nicolai described the experience with the Manifesto:

In circulating the Manifesto privately, we encountered much friendly approbation; but even those who approved were reluctant to sign. One objected to the passage about Greece as historically inaccurate; another said that the whole Manifesto was too late; still another said it came too early. One critic was against scientists' meddling in worldly affairs. Of those who saw the document, most were too cowardly, or they basically disagreed with its views. In those days even the best Germans were unwilling to be good Europeans, or dared not display their true feelings. Since the Manifesto could have value only if it were supported by the authority of recognized names, we dropped the plan.

Some forty years later Buek recalled that

the draft was discussed and approved in one of the university lecture halls and copies circulated among a large number of professors. Alas, we had overestimated the courage and integrity of German professors. The results of our efforts were pitiful. No more than three or four were prepared to sign. . . .

In the years to come—indeed, to the week of his death—Einstein was to sign a great number of public declarations drawn up by himself and by others. Since the Manifesto to Europeans foreshadows many of the ideals to which Einstein was to give lifelong devotion, it is important to know that he participated in its composition, as testified by Nicolai in a letter addressed to Einstein from East Prussia before the end of the war. It was written on May 18, 1918, only five weeks before Nicolai staged a dramatic escape by airplane from Germany to Denmark:

You slight yourself when you say that you "do not deserve mention in this connection"; for you did speak up, and the Manifesto to Europeans of which you are the co-author is nowhere forgotten. Indeed, without your participation, it might never have seen the light of day. At least I am inclined to believe, difficult as it is to determine such contingencies, that I should never have done anything alone.

There is another matter in which I think you do yourself an injustice. You are in no way to be "reproached" because you sit in Berlin and work. If anyone has the right, as a latter-day Archimedes, to cry out to the mercenaries of war, "*Noli tangere circulos meos*" [do not interfere with my work], it is *surely you!*

Finally, there is a third point on which you are not quite correct —at least, in my opinion. That is when you cite your Swiss citizenship. Citizenship is a second consideration here. You *are* German; indeed, you represent a portion of German culture all by yourself; and then you are European, a matter for particular emphasis today. I at least am today much more firmly convinced than I was at the time we wrote the Manifesto to Europeans that the impending cultural collapse can be avoided only if the idea of Europe, pure and simple, prevails. . . .

The world will not recover just because a few theoreticians stand up for such ideas. Mass support is necessary. And precisely because the danger is so great at the moment, I believe man's healthy common sense will grasp it instinctively and not tolerate that our fair earth be so shamefully violated. What we, a few isolated individuals, stand for today will, I believe, be the common property of all tomorrow. . . .

It is for the time to come, for the Europe to come, that we should do something. Perhaps you will consider whether, in an effort to rally and gain a hearing for all those hiding presently in lonely corners, you should not someday speak as a European to Europeans.

Even today we would meet with greater success than four years ago—even in Germany!

For Einstein, the war years count among the most creative periods of his life.[5] In 1915 he was able to announce his General Theory of Relativity, and all in all he published some thirty scientific papers from 1915 to 1918. His opposition to the war was no more diminished by the failure of the Manifesto than was Nicolai's. Nicolai himself, who originally had been a volunteer army physician with officer's rank, was degraded to private and made a hospital orderly.[6] While performing the menial tasks to which he was assigned, he found the leisure to write a remarkable book, *The Biology of War*, which analyzed the phenomenon of war on evolutionary grounds. Through this book, the Manifesto to Europeans, which was included in its introduction, with full credit to Einstein, did achieve a limited impact. However, plans to publish the book in Germany were defeated when the sheets, printed by a prominent German publishing house, were seized before publication. An earlier version, however, had been smuggled into Switzerland, where it was published as early as 1916. About 100 copies were smuggled back into Germany and clandestinely circulated. Before the end of the war, translations were published in French, Swedish, Danish, Finnish and English (both in England and the United States). According to Julio Álvarez del Vayo, later Foreign Minister of the Spanish Republic during the Civil War and an eyewitness to the outbreak of the First World War in Germany, the book became "a fundamental work in the clandestine literature of the time." [7]

Since the German pacifist organization and the Social Democratic party, the largest party in prewar Germany and the only political party with an outspoken antiwar position, were almost paralyzed by the outbreak of war, the need for a new and active peace movement made itself felt only a few weeks after the outbreak of hostilities. Discussions among a few imaginative personalities, who had been engaged for years in the fight against war and the movement for European co-operation, led, on November 16, 1914, to the formation of a new group, the Bund Neues Vaterland (New Fatherland League).[8] The purpose of the Bund was not only to fight for the prompt achievement of a just peace without annexations—a daring proposition in the chauvinist atmosphere of Germany in the early months of the war—but also for the establishment of a supranational organization after the war which it was hoped would make future wars impossible. The first pamphlet, which was published in October 1914, even before the actual formation of the group, was entitled *The Creation of the United States of Europe.*

The Bund included members of the aristocracy, retired diplomats and bankers, as well as journalists, constitutional lawyers and liberals. One of its early members was Ernst Reuter, who was to become mayor of West Berlin after the Second World War. Listed as a founder and active in support of the movement from the outset was Einstein. The Bund at once decided to publish a series of popular pamphlets to discuss its program and problems related to the war. Its frequent meetings were attended by Reichstag deputies. In a report on one of these meetings, held on March 21, 1915, Walther Schücking, Professor of International Law, observed:

> Also among those present was Professor Einstein, whose name I heard mentioned for the first time. His discovery of a law on the unity of time is said to be a scientific achievement of the first rank, and it is the reason why the Ministry of Education signed him for a Berlin position where he can devote himself to research without any teaching obligations.

Evidence that Einstein occasionally took the floor at these meetings also appears in the account of a Swiss woman student who had attended Einstein's first lecture at the Institute of Technology in Zurich:[9]

> At the outbreak of the First World War I happened to be in Berlin, where a committee had been organized to aid foreigners in need. There was a great deal to be done, and I soon became a kind of "maid of all work." Einstein's name was a very familiar one, for his eldest stepdaughter frequently came to the office with requests from him. He helped whomever he could, to the limit of his ability. Some of his requests caused me a good deal of trouble and called for considerable ingenuity, such as the procurement of for-

bidden pacifist literature for his like-minded friend, the biologist Professor Nicolai. . . . Einstein seemed to make an almost gleeful game of circumventing the authorities. He chortled every time he learned that we had succeeded in smuggling letters or books into a prison. But I was not always amused at his demands, which could be fulfilled only at the expense of great vigilance and dissimulation. He ignored these difficulties. He seemed to feel there could be no insurmountable obstacles if the will to help was strong enough. At the time, frankly, I thought this rather inconsiderate, for the risks were considerable and I myself had to answer repeatedly to a court-martial and was in danger of imprisonment. It was only much later that I was able to accept Einstein's view that no sacrifice is too great for those in need.

I met him personally at this time in a private socio-political club [probably the Bund Neues Vaterland], where many pacifist writers, scholars and politicians gathered every Monday night. . . . I was permitted to sit in a corner and listen. Einstein occasionally attended. When he spoke, it was always with great pessimism about the future of human relations. It was interesting to see how the celebrities crowded about him, while he always had an eye for the common man. I managed to get to him on one occasion, when I was depressed by the news of one German victory after another and the resultant intolerable arrogance and gloating of the people of Berlin. "What will happen, Herr Professor?" I asked anxiously. Einstein looked at me, raised his right fist, and replied; "*This* will govern!"

The most important action taken by the Bund during this early period was participation in an international meeting at The Hague in April 1915, arranged by the Dutch Anti-War Council in an effort to organize an international association to promote enduring peace. Four Germans, three of them members of the Bund Neues Vaterland, and one Austrian went to Holland with the unofficial blessing of the German Foreign Office, to explore possibilities of mediation with the Allies. Three members of the Bund's British counterpart, the Union of Democratic Control, also attended the meetings. It was planned that a high Dutch Government official should go to Berlin for preliminary official discussions. When news of the meeting leaked into the German press, it was denounced in German nationalist circles, and the German Foreign Office rejected the plan.

About the time of the Hague meeting in 1915, Einstein apparently offered a proposal for international action to his friend and mentor, the famous Dutch physicist and Nobel Prize winner H. A. Lorentz. The precise nature of the proposal is not known, but it was probably aimed at enlisting scientists from neutral countries in the cause of peace and may have been connected with the Hague endeavor, with which Lorentz was undoubtedly acquainted. On August 2, 1915, Einstein wrote to Lorentz: [10]

Your refusal of my proposal was not unexpected, since I already had indications of the sentiment among colleagues abroad. The situation in Berlin is strange. Professionally speaking, the scientists and mathematicians are strictly internationalist in outlook and go to great lengths to prevent any unfriendly step from being taken against colleagues in enemy countries. The historians and philologists, however, are for the most part chauvinist hotheads. The notorious "Manifesto to the Civilized World" is deplored by all persons of judgment here. Signatures were given carelessly, sometimes without the text having been read. Such, for example, was the case with [Max] Planck [physicist] and [Emil] Fischer [chemist], who have stood up forthrightly for the maintenance of international ties. I shall mention your suggestion to Planck, but I do not think these people can be persuaded to retract.

I must confess that I am bitterly disappointed at the narrow nationalist bias to be found even among men of great stature. I must also say that my once great respect for the politically advanced countries has much declined; I have realized that they all are in the grip of oligarchies which own the press, wield the power, and are able to do as they please. Some malicious wit has modified a fine old saying as follows: *Vox populi, vox idiocy*. If, in addition, one recognizes that those who are well informed and possess the power to act lack human compassion, it becomes apparent how sad is the thing which is worshiped as the "fatherland." Frontiers make little difference; it is much the same everywhere. Should relations, because of such an unreal concept of the State, really disintegrate among men who have come to esteem one another through personal and professional contact? I cannot possibly accept it; it would seem that men always need some idiotic fiction in the name of which they can hate one another. Once it was religion. Now it is the State.

To his friend, Paul Ehrenfest in Leiden, Einstein wrote on August 23, 1915:

The proposal I made to Lorentz was naïve. Impulse was stronger than judgment. I would so much like to do something to hold together our colleagues in the various "fatherlands." Is not that small group of scholars and intellectuals the only "fatherland" which is worthy of serious concern to people like ourselves? Should *their* convictions be determined solely by the accident of frontiers?

In March, and again in May 1915, six powerful German farm, industrial and middle-class groups had petitioned the German Chancellor, von Bethmann-Hollweg, opposing a premature peace treaty based on a compromise with the Allied Powers and advocating instead far-reaching territorial annexations. The Bund Neues Vaterland fought this petition with a comprehensive memorandum submitted in May 1915; it challenged the annexationist policies which had been suggested to the Chancellor. A briefer declaration of July 27, 1915, of similar content, aroused the fury of the German High Command since it had found its way into the world press. The statement was signed by ninety-one prominent Germans, including twelve members of the Bund Neues Vaterland, one of whom was Einstein. In a letter to Lorentz of September 23, 1915, Einstein expressed "his extreme satisfaction" over the "energetic declaration against annexations signed by many distinguished scholars." He remained, however, very doubtful as to whether he would succeed in convincing any of the signers of the infamous Manifesto to the Civilized World formally to denounce the Manifesto although it was increasingly recognized how ill advised the publication of the Manifesto had been. The Bund itself redoubled its peace efforts. During the summer of 1915 it sent a petition to the Reichstag, in which it demanded that the German Government make public its war aims and grant permission for a public discussion. It mailed out a collection of statements by British pacifists, such as Bertrand Russell, Arthur Ponsonby, George Bernard Shaw, and Fenner Brockway, all of whom Einstein was to come to know in later years. But the Bund was faced with increasing difficulties; from the very beginning it had suffered from official harassment, despite its excellent connections in high places. Its headquarters were raided, its officials grilled by the authorities; it was prohibited from publishing, and its members were forbidden to communicate with one another; two women secretaries were imprisoned. Finally, in February 1916, the Bund Neues Vaterland was enjoined from any further activity.

How anxious Einstein was to find support in the efforts to bring the war to an end is indicated in a letter which, a year earlier, on March 22, 1915, he dispatched to the great French writer and pacifist Romain Rolland,[11] who lived in neutral Switzerland and with whom he had not been acquainted before:

Through the press and through my association with the stalwart Bund Neues Vaterland, I have learned how valiantly you have committed yourself, heart and soul, to the cause of bridging the fateful misunderstandings between the French and German people. I am eager to express to you my deep admiration and respect. May your splendid example inspire other high-minded men to abandon the incomprehensible delusions that, like a malignant plague, have gripped even otherwise intelligent, able and sensible people.

When posterity recounts the achievements of Europe, shall we let men say that three centuries of painstaking cultural effort carried us no farther than from religious fanaticism to the insanity of nationalism? In both camps today even scholars behave as though eight months ago they suddenly lost their heads.

If you think I could be of any service to you—because of my present domicile or by virtue of my connections with scientists in Germany and abroad—I am at your disposal to the limits of my ability.

In a postscript, Einstein recommended his friend Dr. Heinrich Zangger, Professor of Forensic Medicine in Zurich, should Rolland either have need of someone familiar with conditions in Switzerland or simply wish to talk with "a refreshing, sincere person." Rolland replied immediately, on March 28, 1915,[12] on the letterhead of the Prisoner-of-War Agency of the International Red Cross in Geneva:

Your generous letter touched me deeply! This terrible crisis should have been a rude lesson for all of us European writers, thinkers and scientists. We should never have allowed ourselves to be taken so unawares. In the future we must be better armed against a repetition of such a calamity. We cannot flatter ourselves that this will be the last such folly of mankind; and we must at least see to it that the intellectual elite will never again take part.

From the outset of this upheaval it would have been up to those of us who, by virtue of age, are exempt from military service to delegate some of our number to gather in neutral territory and there to spread enlightenment in keeping with our views, to restrain impassioned outbursts in both camps, opposing them with the voice of reason—in a word, to function as the sane and lucid conscience of our nations.

Yes, we have sinned! We have lived far too much in the carefree and arrogant illusion that we are always strong enough to resist collective excesses. The events of recent months show us our errors and dictate our task. The indispensable task will be to organize ourselves later on a European or, better yet, a truly universal level. No doubt this will be more difficult after the war. Misunderstanding, rancor and bitterness will long endure. As a beginning, however, it will be enough if even a small group indicate their willingness to achieve such unity. The others will follow little by little. For the rest, I cling to the hope that the vast suffering and madness of these months will give way to a reaction in which the people will reawaken, ashamed, crushed and repentant.

In the meantime, we can only seek to maintain our faith and serenity amid the storm. Little by little, our spirit will spread. . . .

Later that year, on September 16, 1915, Einstein was able to visit Rolland at Vevey, Switzerland, and the two men laid the basis for an enduring friendship. Rolland recorded the visit in his diary: [13]

Albert Einstein came from Zurich (during a brief sojourn in Switzerland) to see me at Vevey, with his friend Dr. Zangger. We spent the whole afternoon together and had tea on the terrace of the Hotel Mooser, at the foot of the garden, amid swarms of bees pillaging the flowers.

Einstein is still a young man, not very tall, with a wide and long face, and a great mane of crisp, frizzled and very black hair, sprinkled with gray and rising high from a lofty brow. His nose is fleshy and prominent, his mouth small, his lips full, his cheeks plump, his chin rounded. He wears a small cropped mustache. He speaks French rather haltingly, interspersing it with German. He is very much alive and fond of laughter. He cannot help giving an amusing twist to the most serious thoughts.

Einstein is incredibly outspoken in his opinion about Germany, where he lives and which is his second fatherland (or his first). No other German acts and speaks with a similar degree of freedom. Another man might have suffered from a sense of isolation during that terrible last year, but not he. He laughs. He has found it possible, during the war, to write his most important scientific work. I ask him whether he voices his ideas to his German friends and whether he discusses them with them. He says no. He limits himself to putting questions to them, in the Socratic manner, in order to challenge their complacency. People don't like that very much, he adds.

He says the situation appears to him much less favorable than it was several months ago. The victories over Russia have revived German arrogance and appetite. "Greedy" seems to Einstein the word that best characterizes the Germans. Their power drive, their admiration of, and belief in, force, their firm determination to conquer and annex territories are everywhere apparent. The government is more moderate than the people. It has wanted to evacuate Belgium but could not do so; the officers threatened revolt. The big banks, industries and corporations are all-powerful; they expect to be repaid for the sacrifices they have made. The Kaiser is merely their tool, and the tool of the officers. He is decent, weak and in despair over a war which he never wanted and into which he was forced because he was so very easy to manipulate. All his unpredictable actions of the last few years and his disconcerting brusqueness were carefully plotted by pan-German cliques that manipulated him without his even suspecting it.

[Admiral Alfred von] Tirpitz [commander-in-chief of the German fleet] and [General Erich von] Falkenhayn [chief of the German general staff] are the protagonists of this deadly plot. Falkenhayn appears to be the more dangerous of the two. Tirpitz is more than anything else a powerful, impersonal machine. According to Einstein, the intellectuals in academic life are sharply divided into two groups: the mathematicians, physicists and pure scientists are tolerant; the historians and literary men are delirious with patriotic passion. As for the great mass of people, they are completely submissive and primarily interested in their own affairs —*domestiqué*—Einstein likes this expression by [Carl] Spitteler [the Swiss poet]. Einstein particularly blames the schools for this general servility. Education is wholly directed toward cultivating national pride and blind obedience to the state. He doesn't believe that this is a matter of race, since the French Huguenots, who have been refugees for two centuries, have acquired the same characteristics. The socialists are the one relatively independent element; but even among the socialists only a minority, grouped around [Eduard] Bernstein, has preserved any real independence. The Bund Neues Vaterland makes rather slow progress and does not enjoy wide support.

Einstein does not expect that Germany will be reformed under its own power. It lacks the energy, the bold initiative. He hopes for an Allied victory, which would destroy the power of Prussia and its dynasty. When I ask him whether such an ordeal will not rally the people even more closely to their ill-starred princes, the skeptical Einstein says that that is not their brand of loyalty; they stand in awe of their masters and respect power, but feel no affection. Once that power is broken, the Germans will behave like savage tribes who, after groveling before their idol, cast it into the fire when they realize it has been vanquished.

Einstein and Zangger dream of a divided Germany: on one side, southern Germany and Austria; on the other, Prussia. Such a defeat of the German empire, however, is more than doubtful. Everybody in Germany is convinced of victory. Official opinion is that the war will last at least another six months. Yet Einstein says that the well-informed know the situation is very serious and will worsen if the war lasts longer. The greatest shortages are not in food but in certain chemicals needed for war purposes. True, the altogether admirable ingenuity of German scientists is making good such shortages by means of new synthetics. Einstein says it is impossible to imagine the organizational skill which they have shown, encompassing every possible field. All the scientists teaching in the universities have been put in charge of military services or commissions. Einstein alone has refused such work.

Whatever the outcome of the war, France will be the major victim. Since all Germans know this very well, there is deep and widespread sympathy for France. (When I say that such German sympathy for France has always been somewhat contemptuous, Einstein and Zangger protest vigorously; they believe that this impression is created by German lack of sensitivity.) British political interests are becoming more and more obvious. Zangger, like all

German-Swiss, speaks of this with resentment. He seems well-informed and offers some little-known evidence of British speculations. England has prevailed on France to detain shipments, bound for Switzerland, arriving in the port of Marseilles (and the same has been done in the port of Genoa). Having arranged to have this merchandise surrendered to itself, England then resells it to Switzerland at twice or three times the original price. The war is indeed a fight between two monsters; France and Europe are crushed between them. Einstein, in spite of his lack of sympathy for England, still prefers that England win rather than Germany; England would know better how to let the rest of the world live.

We discuss the willing blindness and lack of psychology on the part of the Germans. Einstein tells me, bursting into laughter, that after each session of the Council of the University of Berlin the professors meet at a *Bierstube*, and each time the conversation among them starts with the same question: "Why are we so hated in the world?" Everyone then gives his reply, always careful not to blurt out the truth. Einstein also mentions a general meeting of the universities which took place secretly last July. Under consideration was the question whether the German universities should sever all ties with other universities and academies in the world. The motion was defeated by the universities of southern Germany which were able to command a majority. The University of Berlin, however, supported the motion. This university is the most representative and imperialistic of them all—all its professors are selected especially with that purpose in mind. . . .

On September 17, at eight o'clock in the morning, on the platform of the Vevey railroad station, I again see Einstein, bag in hand, departing for Berne. Once more we exchange a few words. He says that public sentiment has changed in Germany over the past fifteen years—ever since France and England started to move closer together. Until that time the military had not had the upper hand.

In observing Einstein I note that he, like that other small number of spirits who have remained free in the midst of the general servility of the intellectual, has reacted in such manner as to see the worst sides of his own people and to judge them with a severity akin to that of their enemies. I know more than one man in the French camp who could match his partiality for the other side. (It is noteworthy that Einstein is Jewish, which explains the internationalism of his position and the caustic character of his criticism.)

Switzerland was not the only neutral country Einstein was able to visit during the war. In the fall of 1916 he enjoyed the extraordinary privilege of a trip to Holland. On November 13, 1916, he wrote Lorentz: [14]

I am still entirely under the spell of my invigorating visit to Holland. What made it so refreshing was not merely meeting men whom I esteem so highly and who share my intellectual interests, but finding so much agreement in matters outside the realm of science. . . .

Lorentz was apparently still concerned about the Manifesto to the Civilized World or, possibly, as seems likely from various letters presented in the next chapter, about certain unanswered challenges to the Germans, from neutral sources, to accept impartial investigations of alleged war atrocities. Einstein reported having discussed the question with several colleagues with varying degrees of success; he was of the opinion that the matter would have to rest for the time being. Early in 1917 Einstein suffered a serious illness. By April 3, 1917, he was able to report to Lorentz that he was better and looking forward to another visit.[14] He was glad to learn that Planck had been in communication with Lorentz:

. . . The younger men are much worse. I am convinced we are dealing with a kind of epidemic of the mind. I cannot otherwise comprehend how men who are thoroughly decent in their personal conduct can adopt such utterly antithetical views on general affairs. It can be compared to developments at the time of the martyrs, the Crusades and the witch burnings. Only men of extraordinary independence of character seem able to resist the pressure of prevailing opinion. There does not seem one single man of that caliber in the Academy.

To his friend Ehrenfest in Leiden he wrote on June 3, 1917:

. . . The ancient Jehovah is still abroad. Alas, he slays the innocent along with the guilty, whom he strikes so fearsomely blind that they can feel no sense of guilt. Whence does he derive the right to punish and crush? Could it be from the possession of power?

I have grown much more tolerant though my basic views have not changed in the slightest. On the political side I see that those with the least restraint and the greatest thirst for power are often the very ones who, in private life, would not harm a fly. We are dealing with an epidemic delusion which, having caused infinite suffering, will one day vanish and become a monstrous and incomprehensible source of wonderment to a later generation.

Zangger had apprised Rolland of Einstein's regret that a forthcoming trip to Switzerland for recuperation could not include another visit to Rolland. Rolland voiced his own regrets in a letter to Einstein on August 21, 1917,[15] expressing the hope that the stay in Switzerland would help him withstand the rigors of another winter in wartime Berlin:

. . . I find it hard to believe that you should have lost the optimism which struck me so forcibly during your kind visit to me in Vevey two years ago, a visit which I cherish as a bright and stimulating memory.

As for me, my heart is heavy as I watch the West and, above all, my own France bleeding themselves white. Yet I remain optimistic about things as a whole and about the future progress of mankind. Nations may become weary and exhausted, as once happened to Spain. But mankind will continue its onward march with the help of new blood. I have faith that the future will bring a greater and richer civilization than we know today, a civilization in which the intellectual elements of Asia will offer a possibility for new developments to an impoverished Europe. . . .

I have read Professor Nicolai's remarkable book [*The Biology of War*] with passionate interest. I believe he is a friend of yours. Please let him know how much I liked his book. I have been virtually living with it these past months. It is a wonderful thing in these terrible times to come upon such a great, free and serene soul, an experience that serves as ample reward for the great folly that constitutes this second universal Deluge. But the Ark is afloat and will come ashore safely. . . .

What Rolland failed to mention in his letter is that he himself had written the foreword to Nicolai's book. The following day, August 22, 1917, Einstein replied from Switzerland:

I am touched by the warm interest you display in a man you have met but once. But for my uncertain health I would not, you may be sure, deny myself the privilege of visiting you. Unfortunately the smallest strain often exacts its toll. The dismal record of mankind has not made me *more* pessimistic than I actually was two years ago. Indeed, I find that the wave of imperialist sentiment that swept over leading circles in Germany has somewhat subsided. Yet, it would still be exceedingly dangerous, I believe, to come to an agreement with the Germany of today.

The victory of 1870 and the subsequent commercial and industrial success in that country have established a religion of power that found in [Heinrich von] Treitschke [German historian] an expression which is not in the least exaggerated. Virtually all men of education have become captivated by this powerful credo which has, in fact, supplanted the ideals of the era of Goethe and Schiller. I know people in Germany whose private lives are guided by utter altruism, yet who awaited the declaration on unrestricted submarine warfare with the utmost impatience. I am firmly convinced that only harsh realities can stem this confusion of minds. These people must be shown that they must respect non-Germans as equals and that, if they are to survive, they must earn the confidence of other countries. Neither by force nor breach of faith will they attain the goals they have set themselves.

I think it is hopeless to struggle against those goals with the weapons of the mind. Those who consider men like Nicolai to be utopians do so with honest conviction. Only facts can cure the misled masses of the delusion that we live for the state, and that the state should, at any price, concentrate all power in its own hands.

To my way of thinking, the best method of resolving this dreary dilemma would be to form an enduring military arbitration pact among America, Britain, France and Russia, with agreements on mutual aid and minimum and maximum limits of military preparedness. Such a treaty should include provisions for most-favored-nation treatment with respect to tariffs. Any nation should be allowed to join the treaty provided it has a democratically elected parliament in which the chief executive must command a majority. I shall not go beyond this brief outline.

If Germany, which is dependent on foreign markets for the sale of industrial products, were faced with such a stable situation, the view would soon prevail that the path it followed must be abandoned. However, so long as German statesmen are able to hope sooner or later for a shift in the balance of power, there can be no serious expectation that their policy will be changed. As evidence that everything remains as it has always been, I cite the manner in which the recent change in the German chancellorship was staged.

May you find solace in these gloomy times in your inspired creative work.

Rolland wrote again the following day, August 23, 1917:

. . . I am quite willing to believe that what you say about Germany is, unfortunately, true; but you do not know the sufferings of the "other side." The evil is contaminating; even as they fight one another, the nations pursue the same interests; and no one has yet found a way to halt, as one would an epidemic, the moral plague at the frontier. The war seems to me like a fight against a Hydra. For every head cut off, two others grow. That is why I do not believe in the efficacy of all those fine armies. I expect relief to come from other forces: from social forces. If this should not happen—well, God knows it would not be the first time that a powerful civilization collapsed. Life has a way of blossoming forth again even from the ruins.

Einstein was obviously not always as free of pessimism as mentioned in his letter to Rolland. Only a few months later, on December 18, 1917, he said in a letter to his friend H. A. Lorentz:

. . . I cannot help being constantly very depressed over the immeasurably sad things which burden our lives. It no longer even helps, as it used to, to escape into one's work in physics.

Despite outward unity and suppression of dissent, discontent with the war smoldered among the German people throughout 1916 and 1917, although it could not find an effective political expression. The

Russian surrender, toward the end of 1917, brought no relief; in fact, the situation steadily deteriorated during 1918, as Germany's resources dwindled and as American armed might came into play. Not until that year did it again become possible to talk peace openly in Germany. In reply to a letter from an academic correspondent, Einstein wrote on February 24, 1918:

I greatly admire your versatility and entertaining style although your ostentatious Teutonic muscle-flexing runs rather against my grain. I prefer to string along with my compatriot, Jesus Christ, whose doctrines you and your kind consider to be obsolete. Suffering is indeed more acceptable to me than resort to violence. History alone will teach us whither we shall be led by the attitudes exalted by you and so many of your contemporaries. Apart from the ultimate objectives, there can be no argument in matters of taste. Mine simply differs from yours.

Early in September 1918, with the Armistice still two months away, Einstein received a remarkable mimeographed document marked "Strictly Confidential" which invited him to attend a secret meeting of intellectuals to discuss the organization of a group that, when the time came, might be capable of negotiating the peace in place of the discredited German Government. It was signed by Kurt Hiller, a radical pacifist who indicated that *sub rosa* peace propaganda had been going on for some time. He appended a letter from a German front-line major who flatly stated that the war was lost. Einstein replied on September 9, 1918:

. . . Although I should be happy to attend your meeting, it does not seem proper for me, a citizen of Switzerland, to interfere in the political affairs of Germany.

Your pamphlet is brilliantly written, but your proposal seems to me too vague for realization. Were you to gather together a group of personalities in this country who have distinguished themselves through important intellectual achievements in various fields, you would merely assemble a collection of men who are interested in power politics. Assuming that they are honest in expressing their feelings, they would unite upon the principle that personal morality cannot be applied to international relations, that might makes right, and that man cannot exist without war. Any concessions these men might make to pacifism would be mere gestures to trap the innocent and unsuspecting. . . .

These people are but the children of their time. Their views are governed by their ambitions; and their ambitions, in turn, stem from that mass psychology which bears the stamp of Bismarck.

When the political principle just described was eloquently explained to a great scientist from a neutral country,[16] his comment was "Indeed, the world may be as you describe it, but I should not care to live in such a world." I am firmly convinced that the concept of a "world arrayed in arms against us" [a widespread German obsession in that period] has been forged by this reactionary outlook.

In my opinion, Germany's salvation lies only in a swift and radical process of democratization, similar to the democratic institutions of the Western powers. It is only through the creation of a democratic constitution, whatever shortcomings it may possess, that one can effect a sufficient degree of decentralization of power to prevent a recurrence of the events of 1914. The present regime no longer enjoys confidence anywhere abroad.

This, briefly stated, represents my convictions. As one who was a pacifist even before the war, I feel I have the right to voice my beliefs now.

Despite its official suppression, the Bund Neues Vaterland (p. 9) had clandestinely continued to exist; it again appeared in the open in October 1918. During that month, two public meetings were held in Berlin. At the second of these meetings a strongly worded declaration was adopted which received press coverage. In that declaration, the Bund reviewed its earlier activities and concluded:

Now that the consequences of power politics have become obvious to all and the government itself has adopted our program calling for a League of Nations, we demand forthwith: revocation of the state of siege, of censorship and protective custody; amnesty for all political prisoners; investigation into the question of war guilt; complete freedom of the press, speech and assembly; fight against militarism, especially in education. Further, the Bund calls for a complete change of the German constitution and government along democratic lines. For this purpose, a national constituent assembly should be elected by secret, equal and direct ballot, with both women and soldiers voting. Immediate implementation of these demands will spare the world a senseless final conflict.

It is likely, though not certain, that Einstein attended this meeting. At any rate, on October 26, 1918, his colleague Max Planck wrote him a letter explaining at length why he felt unable, despite his full agreement with the content, to sign the declaration Einstein had sent him; the declaration was probably the one just quoted. Planck added that his oath of allegiance to the Kaiser made it impossible for him to call for the Kaiser's abdication, but he expressed the hope that the Kaiser might take that step voluntarily.

On November 9, 1918, Kaiser Wilhelm II abdicated under revolutionary pressure, and the German Republic was proclaimed. Two days later, on the day of the Armistice, Einstein mailed two post cards to reassure his mother in Switzerland:

The great event has happened! I was afraid of a complete breakdown of law and order. Thus far, however, the movement has run its course in truly imposing fashion, the most tremendous experience conceivable. It is most curious to see how readily the people have accepted it. What a privilege to have lived through such an experience! No breakdown can be so severe that one would not willingly suffer it in return for so glorious a reward! Militarism and bureaucracy have been thoroughly abolished here.

Do not worry; everything has gone smoothly—indeed, impressively—so far. The present leadership seems thoroughly equal to its task. I am very happy at the way things are developing. Only now do I begin to feel at ease here. The defeat has worked wonders. The academic community regards me as a kind of archsocialist.

Einstein's basic political philosophy did not undergo any significant changes during his lifetime. He welcomed the revolutionary development of Germany in 1918 because of his interest in socialism and particularly because of his profound and unqualified devotion to democracy. Basic to his political thinking was the recognition of the dignity of the individual and the protection of political and intellectual freedom. In a great many utterances, spread over a large number of years, he continually voiced his deep concern for the democratic organization of society which alone, he felt, could guarantee the basic liberties of the individual.

That is why he greeted with so much enthusiasm the downfall of Imperial Germany and the establishment of a democratic republic. Nowhere did he express his profound belief in democratic ideals more succinctly than in some brief remarks made late in 1918. When radical students "deposed" the president of the University of Berlin and insisted upon other changes, Einstein, popular with students because of his curious blend of aloofness and geniality, was asked to intercede. With two colleagues, he went to the Reichstag building, where the revolutionary committees held their stormy sessions. After a period of waiting, he was permitted entrance and delivered the following remarks: [17]

Comrades!

Speaking as an old-time believer in democracy, one who is not a recent convert, may I be permitted a few words:

Our common goal is democracy, the rule of the people. It can be achieved only if the individual holds two things sacred:

First, willing subordination to the will of the people, as expressed at the polls, even when the majority is at odds with one's own personal desires and judgments.

How can we achieve this goal? What has been attained so far? What must still be done?

The old society of class rule has been abolished. It fell of its own sins and by the liberating acts of the soldiers. The councils which the soldiers swiftly elected, acting in concert with the Workers' Councils, must be accepted for the time being as the organs of the popular will. In this critical hour we owe them our unconditional obedience and must support them with all our power.

Secondly, all true democrats must stand guard lest the old class tyranny of the right be replaced by a new class tyranny of the left. Do not be lured by feelings of vengeance to the fateful view that violence must be fought with violence, that a dictatorship of the proletariat is temporarily needed in order to hammer the concept of freedom into the heads of our fellow countrymen. Force breeds only bitterness, hatred and reaction.

We must, therefore, unconditionally demand of the present dictatorial government, whose directives we must willingly follow, that, irrespective of party interests, it immediately prepare for the election of a constituent assembly, thereby eliminating all fears of a new tyranny as soon as possible. Only after such an assembly has been convoked and has satisfactorily completed its task—only then can the German people glory in the freedom they have won for themselves.

Our present social democratic leaders deserve our wholehearted support. Confident of the power of their ideals, they have already gone on record in favor of a constituent assembly. Thus they have shown that they respect democratic ideals. May they succeed in leading us out of the grave difficulties into which the sins and inadequacies of their predecessors hurled us.

Although in those years Einstein felt close to the Social Democratic party and occasionally may have attended some of its meetings, he probably never joined the party.[18] He was not a man of partisan political affiliations. When he perceived that the Weimar Republic was not fulfilling the great promise he had once seen in it, Einstein soon became disillusioned, and his disappointment grew with the passage of time. However, as his many writings testify over the years, his fundamental belief in democracy and socialism never changed.[19] In 1944, in a letter to his friend and colleague Max Born, he made some pertinent remarks which quite probably referred to the students' incident in the winter of 1918–19:

Do you recall the time, a little less than twenty-five years ago, when we took a trolley car to the Reichstag building, convinced that we could really help turn those fellows into honest democrats? How naïve we were, even as men forty years old! I can only laugh when I think about it. Neither of us realized how much more powerful is instinct compared to intelligence. We would do well to bear this in mind or the tragic errors of those days may be repeated.

CHAPTER TWO

REVOLUTION IN GERMANY: HOPE AND DISILLUSIONMENT | 1919-1923

ON SEPTEMBER 27, 1919, Einstein sent a post card to his mother in Switzerland:

> Good news today! H. A. Lorentz has wired me that the British expeditions have actually proved the light shift near the sun.

The telegram from Einstein's beloved friend Lorentz marked the beginning of a new phase in his life. Overnight he was to leap from purely scientific eminence to world-wide fame. Within weeks of the Armistice, British scientists had dispatched expeditions to faraway places to observe the eclipse of the sun, on March 29, 1919. One of the few observable phenomena, predicted by Einstein's theory, the bending of starlight as it passes through the sun's gravitational field, was brilliantly confirmed.[1]

Formal announcement of the news to a world to which real peace had not yet returned came in London on November 6, 1919, at a joint session of the Royal Society and the Royal Astronomical Society. Although few, other than scientists, understood the full significance of the scientific discovery, this act of international amity, coming so soon after the bitterness engendered by war, captured the imagination of people everywhere, as did Einstein's appealing and unconventional personality, which was fully described in the newspapers throughout the world.

Before the month was over, a friend relayed to Einstein a letter received from a British scientist: [2]

> The talk here is of almost nothing but Einstein, and if he were to come here now I think he would be welcomed like a victorious

Post card Einstein sent to his mother, September 27, 1919, about the first confirmation of his relativity theory. (See page 27) general. The fact that a theory formulated by a German has been confirmed by observations on the part of Englishmen has brought the possibility of co-operation between these two scientifically-minded nations much closer. Quite apart from the great scientific value of his brilliant theory, Einstein has done mankind an incalculable service.

Einstein's name began to blossom on the front pages of newspapers, and his maned head appeared on the covers of magazines. His every word and act was news. Yet, fame was a burden to Einstein, relieved only by the chance it gave him for lending effective expression to the causes he held dear. Even before he gained public renown, he had become involved in the cause of international reconciliation which was to occupy him increasingly in the years to come. As early as December 6, 1918, within weeks after the Armistice agreement, he wrote from Berlin to his friend Ehrenfest in Leiden:

. . . Within the next few days I expect to travel to Paris, by way of Switzerland, to plead with the Allies to save the famished German population from starvation. After so much deception it has become difficult to convince people of the bitter truth of conditions here. But I think they will trust *me* when I pledge my word of honor that I speak the truth. I must say, in passing, that the people here, once having gained some slight understanding of the causes of war, have borne the collapse with calm and dignity.

It was actually not until almost three and a half years later that Einstein visited France for the first time after the war. On March 22, 1919, he again wrote to Ehrenfest:

. . . At last I am once again passionately absorbed in a problem of General Relativity which gives me no peace day or night. As for politics, I have become deeply disillusioned. Those countries whose victory I had considered during the war by far the lesser evil I now consider only slightly less of an evil. Domestic politics here are utterly dishonest. Reaction is rife with all manners of excess, and dressed up in a repulsive revolutionary guise. One scarcely knows where to look in order to find any pleasure either in man or his pursuits.

In June 1919, months before his name was to become a symbol, Einstein signed an international appeal drawn up by Romain Rolland to which eventually more than 100 intellectuals lent their signatures: [3]

Brain workers, comrades, scattered throughout the world, kept apart for five years by the armies, the censorship and the mutual hatred of the warring nations, now that barriers are falling and frontiers are being reopened, we issue to you a call to reconstitute our brotherly union; but to make of it a new union firmly founded and more strongly built than that which previously existed.

The war has disordered our ranks. Most of the intellectuals placed their science, their art, their reason, at the service of the governments. We do not wish to formulate any accusations, to launch any reproaches. We know the weakness of the individual mind and the elemental strength of great collective currents. The latter, in a moment, swept the former away, for nothing had been prepared to help in the work of resistance. Let this experience, at least, be a lesson for us in the future!

First of all, let us point out the disasters that have resulted from the almost complete abdication of intelligence throughout the world, and from its voluntary enslavement to the unchained forces. Thinkers and artists have added an incalculable quantity of envenomed hate to the plague which devours the flesh and spirit of Europe. In the arsenal of their knowledge, their memory, their imagination, they have sought reasons for hatred, reasons old and new, reasons historical, scientific, logical, and poetical. They have worked to destroy mutual understanding and mutual love among men. So doing, they have disfigured, defiled, debased, degraded Thought, of which they were the representatives. They have made it an instrument of the passions; and (unwittingly, perchance) they have made it a tool of the selfish interests of a political or social clique, of a state, a country, or a class. Now, when from the fierce conflict in which the nations have been at grips the victors and the vanquished emerge equally stricken, impoverished, and at the bottom of their hearts (though they will not admit it) utterly ashamed of their excess of mania—now, Thought, which has been entangled in their struggles, emerges, like them, fallen from her high estate.

Arise! Let us free the mind from these compromises, from these unworthy alliances, from these veiled slaveries! Mind is no one's servitor. It is we who are the servitors of the mind. We have no other master. We exist to bear its light, to defend its light, to rally round it all the strayed sheep of mankind. Our role, our duty, is to be a center of stability, to point out the pole star, amid the whirlwind of passions in the night. Among these passions of pride and mutual destruction, we make no choice; we reject them all. Truth only do we honor; truth that is free, frontierless, limitless; truth that knows nought of the prejudices of race or caste. Not that we lack interest in humanity. For humanity we work, but for humanity as a whole. We know nothing of peoples. We know the People, unique and universal; the People which suffers, which struggles, which falls and rises to its feet once more, and which continues to advance along the rough road drenched with its sweat and its blood; the People, all men, all alike our brothers. In order that they may, like ourselves, realize this brotherhood, we raise above their blind struggles the Ark of the Covenant—Mind which is free, one and manifold, eternal.

Einstein spent most of the summer of 1919 in Switzerland. On his return to Germany he found two letters urging him to translate the Rolland appeal into action. To a liberal professor in Potsdam, Germany, he wrote on August 17, 1919:

. . . I was not among the authors who drafted the appeal. Being only too well aware of the bitterness prevalent in the various countries, I do not believe that such efforts toward international reconciliation hold out much promise of success at present. I gave my signature because it would have been worse to withhold it; but I was convinced that the appeal would not produce much of a response.

I must tell you frankly that I do not believe that collecting signatures here, as you suggest, will do much good, partly because of the painful absence of some who should be expected to sign, partly because of the likelihood of encountering opposition. For the time being, it might be better to cultivate our personal contacts abroad, thus quietly paving the way toward better relations. I also feel it would be salutary were we to spread information about the crimes which were committed by the German High Command in Belgium and France. This would help to create a better understanding among our own people of how the others feel. I belong to a small private group which is presently preparing a publication in this field. It seems to me of utmost importance to prevent the emergence of a spirit of vengefulness; otherwise the present miserable situation will only become worse.

That same day, Einstein wrote to another colleague in Breslau, Germany:

. . . I am afraid that any declaration coming from a large number of people who feel as we do may very well provoke a counter declaration which might have a very adverse effect upon the public at large. This would do our cause more harm than good.

Earlier that year, on April 26, 1919, Einstein had written Lorentz about the commission to investigate war crimes,[4] which he had joined:

You will surely recall the unhappy discussions about war atrocities which we had three years ago in Holland. My recollection of your very real concern in these dreadful events encourages me to submit the following to you.

A few private citizens here have formed a commission with the purpose of thoroughly examining those charges concerning Germany's conduct in the war which have become known abroad and are considered as proven. This is to be done with the help of official documents from here and, if possible, from abroad; the findings are to be published in this country. Besides myself, the commission consists of five people for whose absolute integrity and fairness I can vouch.

In order to gain access, as a starting point, to material dealing with such charges and to obtain, if possible, documentary proof, we must enlarge our commission to include members residing in neutral countries. We should be happy if you, dear colleague, were to join our commission; your great experience in human affairs and your reputation would greatly aid the cause. If, for some reason, you do not wish to do this, I should like to ask that you name some person in Holland whom you regard as willing and able to share in our work along the lines indicated.

I believe that only if the truth is fully uncovered will the intense hatred among nations eventually be mitigated. Here, many otherwise thoroughly honorable men regard these grave charges, insofar as they have had any inkling of them, as prejudiced lies. It is our aim to enlighten such people.

Lorentz replied almost immediately (May 4, 1919) and at considerable length. While he was disinclined to serve on the commission himself, he pledged the fullest co-operation. He promised to speak to a number of his fellow countrymen and also to certain Frenchmen and Belgians he was to meet during a forthcoming trip. Among Belgians he was

thinking particularly of Professor Massart, who, several years ago, demanded that the ninety-three German scholars and artists take the initiative in an effort like the one you are planning. Unfortunately, his request elicited virtually no response. . . . Depending on circumstances, I may try to make contact with representatives of the clergy and freemasonry. You probably know that these quarters have also challenged the Germans to take action, similar to that taken by M. Massart.

Lorentz also strongly suggested that Einstein make certain that the German Government would not only refrain from throwing obstacles in his way but assure him of its positive support; for he knew that non-Germans were unlikely to co-operate were they to suspect any official antagonism. Lorentz must have made good his promises, for on August 1, 1919, Einstein wrote him, from Switzerland, as follows:

Your generous help is invaluable to us. We are also grateful that the French and Belgian scholars named are prepared to assist us. At the time of my departure on June 28, we had not yet been able to gain access to the documents accumulated in Germany. There is open and, especially, clandestine resistance.

I understand the resentment over the famous Manifesto of the ninety-three, which, by the way, was drafted by Hermann Sudermann, the novelist and playwright. One day, while sitting beside him, I expressed myself about the Manifesto in terms that were anything but gentle and he, freely and without embarrassment, confessed to his authorship of it. He is a decent and unusually well-meaning man, as long as the red rag of "politics" is not waved in front of him.

As I say, I quite understand this resentment; it has for me a touch of the comic although hardly as much as the Manifesto itself and its doughty defenders. When a group of people suffer from collective delusions, one should try to deprive these people of any influence; but men of stature and vision cannot long be ruled by hate and passion, unless they themselves are sick. We must remember that, on the average, men's moral qualities do not greatly vary from country to country. Further, their actions are conditioned by the time and historic circumstance in which they find themselves; hence the seemingly wide variations in the conduct of men. To exclude for a period of several years German scholars from international social intercourse within the scientific community might perhaps teach them a useful lesson in modesty. It would do little harm and might even do some good, but it would be of little significance.

What does seem important is that Germans come to understand the attitude of the "enemy," lest the dreadful spirit of revenge, from which only new disaster can spring, gain ground. Our purpose is to work toward this modest goal.

Upon his return from Switzerland, on September 21, 1919, Einstein reported to Lorentz that the commission's first publication, concerned with alleged atrocities in Lille, France, during the war, had gone to press during his absence:

. . . When I received a printed copy a few days ago, I was quite startled. The preface was tactless. The documents used bore so little relationship to the issues under investigation that the pamphlet might have done more harm than good. There was no alternative but to withdraw the entire edition (fortunately small), with the intention to reprint it later on with additions and corrections. Because so much material is still available here and remains, as yet, unexamined, it seems premature to review the documents in Holland which so kindly have been made available to us. . . .

As for the judgment passed by colleagues abroad on scholars here, it seems to me overly harsh, despite the dreadful things that have happened. We should remember that, because the expression of public opinion was forcibly curbed for several years, most of them lack a clear picture of what has happened. It is hard for those who were outside to conceive how difficult it is to resist the power of mass suggestion. Even the bare facts have been presented here either not at all or incorrectly. That is why information and explanation are so badly needed.

It is, *a priori*, incredible that the inhabitants of a whole great country should be branded as morally inferior! The declaration of the ninety-three, foolish as it was, was neither conceived nor signed with any awareness of wrong. People whose passions have been whipped up to heights of bitterness by shrewd exploitation of all available means are not capable of examining the facts objectively. Now, after the fact, we seek to bring about an awareness of the deep wrong that was done—but what should these people do to purge themselves? Having now fallen themselves into utter impotence, they must assume that any declaration they could possibly make would be suspected of having been dictated by unconscionable opportunism. This is precisely the fear of the decent elements among them who up until now had thought that right was on their side. (Outside of Germany, at least those who are sober and calm should try to understand these circumstances.) It would do no harm, by the way, if these people here, as a result of being boycotted abroad, were made to recognize the true situation in which they now find themselves. This would help to eliminate whatever may still be left of their delusions of grandeur and their thirst for power, created by Germany's economic prosperity.

I am convinced that it was the historic conditions that facilitated the growth of "Prussians"; and I am afraid that in the greatly changed situation they now may be growing up somewhere else. I hope this fear will prove unfounded.

On January 12, 1920, Einstein was able to tell Lorentz:

. . . The new publication on Lille is in print and has already been sharply attacked. You will soon receive a copy. It is sad, indeed, that even men of high culture cannot rid themselves of narrow nationalism, not even in matters of right and wrong. The evil from the past continues to work its spell, and no end is in sight. . . .

Again, on March 18, 1920, he wrote:

. . . I am glad you were able to approve the pamphlet about Lille. It was signed only by those who actually examined the documents. The conviction is slowly gaining ground here that deep wrong was committed by the German Army and that the bitter hatred against Germany is justified. It is a pity that the efforts to punish war criminals are not being pursued on an international basis. Satisfaction over the act of justice to be achieved is impaired because only the German culprits will have to stand trial, even though dreadful things were also done to German prisoners by the French. The British are said to have behaved very correctly.

Conditions in Germany in the first postwar year were far from easy. Political passions ran high. Economic conditions were harsh. The food shortage, mainly due to the continued blockade by the victorious Allied Powers, was very severe. Einstein, with his comparative freedom of movement, was better off than most Germans at the time. But although, as he himself remarked to Lorentz, he did not suffer any real financial hardship, he was faced with certain difficulties resulting from heavy family responsibilities. In addition, he became increasingly exposed to political hatred and fanaticism. Under the circumstances, his Dutch friends were eager to get him out of Germany. In the fall of 1919 they were discussing the possibility of offering him a permanent position on the faculty of the University of Leiden. His German associates, on the other hand, especially Max Planck, urged him to stay in Berlin. In September 1919 Einstein wrote to Ehrenfest: [5]

. . . I promised him [Planck] not to leave Berlin until conditions should deteriorate to a point where he would regard such a step as natural and proper. . . . It would come in ill grace from me if, just when my political hopes are being realized, I were to walk out, without compelling necessity and perhaps, in part, for material advantage, on the very people who have surrounded me with love and friendship and to whom my departure at this time of alleged degradation would seem doubly painful. You have no idea with what warmth I am surrounded here and not merely by those who lick up the drops of oil my brain sweats out.

You see then how things stand with me. I can leave here only if future developments should make it impossible for me to stay. If such developments should not occur, my departure would be tantamount to a crude breach of my word to Planck. I would be breaking faith, and would certainly come to reproach myself later on. (I feel like some relic in an old cathedral—one doesn't quite know what to do with the old bones. . . .)

In forwarding Einstein's letter to Lorentz, Ehrenfest remarked that the awarding of the Nobel Prize would be one means of relieving Einstein's difficulties. Meanwhile, thanks to the considerable efforts exerted by his friends in his behalf,[6] he was able, in October 1919, to pay his first postwar visit to Holland. In the wake of this visit he was offered, and accepted, a visiting professorship at the University of Leiden. This enabled him both to maintain his position in Berlin and, from the fall of 1920 on, to make occasional brief visits to Holland.

During the fall of 1919 Einstein had also been instrumental in persuading the Bund Neues Vaterland (which, as indicated before, had resumed its militant activities shortly before the end of the war) to protest the so-called Allied "hunger blockade." On December 4, 1919, he complained to Ehrenfest:

. . . anti-Semitism is strong here [Berlin] and political reaction is violent, at least among the "intelligentsia." I noticed it especially in Rostock. Where will it all lead? They have not yet grasped the situation—namely, that something must give—nor do they seem likely to grasp it in the future. . . .

In December 1919, in a letter to his friend Max Born,[7] Einstein described the impressions of an anniversary celebration which he had attended at the University of Rostock, Germany:

. . . I listened to some pretty awful political demagogy and got some edifying glimpses of small-town politics. The funny part of it is that everyone knows everyone else so well that there are always subtle overtones to all the grandiloquence. The only meeting place available was the theater, which lent a further air of comedy to the celebration. The men of the old and the new governments sat separately in two proscenium boxes. The new men were needled in every possible way by the academic bigwigs, while the ex-grand duke received an almost interminable ovation. No revolution can prevail against this inborn serf mentality!

Despite the disillusionment reflected in his letter to Ehrenfest, Einstein addressed a meeting, held on December 16, 1919, under the auspices of the Bund Neues Vaterland. The meeting had been arranged in honor of Paul Colin, editor of *Art libre* and the first Frenchman to speak publicly in Berlin after the war. Einstein said:

On behalf of the men and women here assembled—men and women who bore aloft the ideal of the brotherhood of man even amid the terrors of war—I welcome you with all my heart, as the first Frenchman since the war to visit us in the sacred cause of international reconciliation.

The hour is grave and the tasks before us are stern. Everywhere, nationalist passions have been fanned into flame, and it is difficult to judge which is the more ominous—victory for your people or defeat for us. Both threaten to perpetuate a vendetta between neighboring countries. Yet, the root of the evil is not to be found in the present historic context, but rather in traditions which have been handed down by the educated classes in Europe from generation to generation, traditions which defy the Christian morality to which they pay lip service: he who commits rape and oppression will enjoy honor and glory; but one who experiences injustice will suffer shame and ignominy. These ancient and evil traditions threaten to seal the doom of our continent. We will oppose them with our passionate belief in the brotherhood of all men without which neither men nor nations can live in harmony with one another.

When the political doctrines of the German historian [Heinrich von] Treitschke were carefully expounded to him, a great Dutch colleague of mine [Lorentz] declared: "Indeed, the world may be as you describe it, but I should not care to live in such a world."

May the valiant and selfless efforts of our guest help this spirit strike roots on both sides of the Rhine!

Less than a month later, on January 6, 1920, Einstein appealed to the liberal journalist Hellmuth von Gerlach to initiate a petition to the German Government for the release of all political prisoners. He argued that the poor food situation in Germany rendered imprisonment particularly harsh.

In March 1920, the Kapp *Putsch* occurred in Germany, a counterrevolutionary rebellion by rightist and reactionary elements. It was suppressed by both the army and a general strike. In his letter to Lorentz of March 18, 1920, Einstein commented:

. . . We are very lucky that the recent reactionary *Putsch* failed so miserably. Life would have been intolerable under such people. Suffering is dreadful here. Many are dying from malnutrition. . . .

On April 7, 1920, Einstein wrote to Ehrenfest:

. . . Outward quiet has been restored here; but there is profound antagonism and hostility. The reckless use of force breeds only bitterness among the populace. Hunger and want ravage the city [Berlin]. Infant mortality is frightful. No one seems to know in what political direction we are headed. The government has sunk into utter impotence. . . .

On April 19, 1920, Einstein wrote to a noted German classical philologist: [8]

I understand that you are reluctant to be one of the sponsors of the Anglo-American Literary Aid Campaign for Central Europe, because you do not wish to appear on the same list with me, whom you describe as an Independent Socialist [the left-wing socialist group]. Particularly, since there may be some question as to whether I, a Swiss citizen, may properly take part in it, I should be glad to eliminate myself from this effort if anything could be accomplished by my withdrawal.

If I have thus far failed to do so, it is due to the thought that my close contacts in both neutral and former enemy countries might possibly prove useful to the cause of restoring international co-operation among scholars. Under the circumstances I suggest that we meet for a quiet talk during the next few days.

By mid-1920 the American Quakers were feeding more than half a million German children. Einstein was asked to comment on this program, and on July 11, 1920, he wrote:

Throughout these dark years of bitter disappointments, there has been no greater solace for me than to reflect on the magnificent welfare work of the American and British Quakers. With my own eyes I have seen them rescue worthy human beings who were in dire need. No matter how great the political disappointments which we have suffered and may yet have to suffer, we must not abandon hope for the realization of a just and rational world order, particularly when we realize the tremendous efforts that are being made for mankind as a whole in those two countries [England and the United States] which destiny has raised to supreme power.

More should be done to make the German people fully aware of the selfless Quaker aid; no other factor in public life is better qualified to restore mutual confidence among nations.

In the summer of 1920 Einstein visited Scandinavia. Soon afterward he was reminded of a promise to send a message to the Norwegian Student Union. On September 9, 1920, he wrote:

In grateful memory of the glorious summer days I was privileged to spend in Christiania [now Oslo] as a guest of the Norwegian students, I send you these warm greetings from my study in Berlin. Through you I came to know a student body that upholds our common cultural ideals and is free of narrow nationalism. Because of the many years which have elapsed since I was a student, it was a great joy to have you welcome me to your cheerful group, where I felt thoroughly at home. In addition to those objective and impersonal factors which bind together people of good will from all countries, the cause of healthy international relations calls for human beings who are warmhearted and freedom-loving. Because you possess these qualities and are students of a neutral country, it is to be hoped that you will make a significant contribution toward the recovery of Europe.

Einstein did not visit the United States until the following year; his fame, however, had preceded him. In May 1920, Columbia University awarded him its quinquennial Barnard Medal for Meritorious Service to Science. In his letter of acceptance he expressed the hope that this action was "a harbinger of better times, when a sense of international solidarity will help reunite scholars in different countries." In September 1920 a German Club for the Cultivation of Social and Scientific Relations in New York asked him for a contribution to a memorial volume on the occasion of its golden anniversary. The club posed the following questions to Einstein:

How can the intellectuals throughout the world, in the course of their everyday lives, help bring about true friendship among those nations which only recently were engaged in war against one another? How can they help create a spirit of brotherhood among men?

Einstein replied:

In my opinion, it is through their scientific contributions and artistic achievements that intellectuals can do most to advance international reconciliation and the brotherhood of man. Creative work lifts man above personal and selfish national goals. To concentrate on the problems and aspirations which all thinking men share creates a sense of comradeship that is eventually bound to reunite scholars and artists of all nations; it is unavoidable that, at times, political passions will divide those among them who are less broad-minded and lack the ability to think independently. Intellectuals should never tire of emphasizing the international character of mankind's cherished heritage. They must never allow themselves to be exploited in the service of political passions in their public declarations or any other public activity.

May I add that it would benefit the cause of international reconciliation if more young students and artists were to study in countries which were fighting each other during the last war. First-hand experience of this kind provides the most powerful antidote to the catastrophic ideologies created by the World War.

Einstein was still almost two years away from receiving the Nobel Prize when, on January 19, 1921, he addressed the Nobel Committee, endorsing the proposal of the Czech parliament to award the Peace Prize to President Thomas Garrigue Masaryk:

. . . Masaryk has earned wide renown as a protector of oppressed minorities, especially the Czechs and the Jews. He has never sacrificed lofty principles to political expediency, not even when the course he pursued must have seemed all but hopeless even to him. I am convinced that awarding him the Nobel Prize would represent a victory for international reconciliation, in the true spirit of the man who endowed the Peace Prize.

On January 31, 1921, in response to a request for an interview from the Berlin correspondent of the London *Observer*, Einstein wrote:

I cannot bring myself to accept your kind offer, not for lack of time but for other reasons. My views and opinions are currently being given far too much weight, and I have, therefore, grown reluctant to speak in public about subjects on which I possess no special competence. Further, there can be no doubt that there exists, here in Germany, considerable irritation with my pacifist and general political orientation; this irritation is intensified by Germany's troubled political situation. Given these circumstances, the remarks I would make are almost certain to be misinterpreted and might cause more harm than good.

On March 21, 1921, Einstein wrote [9] to Emmanuel Carvallo, mathematician and physicist at the École Polytechnique in Paris, thanking him for his letter:

I indeed consider it as one of my most sacred duties to do everything that can be done to improve relations among scholars. This is not easy for one who lives in the land of the vanquished. If one manifests a certain reserve, one is considered unfriendly by people abroad. If one is co-operative, those at home consider one disloyal. The situation looks worse than ever; daily events on both sides are interpreted in such a way as to prove that imperialism and violence are essential and indispensable. When will Europe realize that it is doomed should its political institutions fail to catch up with the development of technology? What is particularly unfortunate is the fact that personal contact among those peoples recently at war with one another has virtually ceased, thus allowing feelings of prejudice to achieve fantastic proportions. Even the commonplace truth that the character of individuals is not affected by frontiers has been forgotten.

By this time, Einstein had already become the center of considerable controversy in Germany.[10] The spectacle of a scientist taking an active part in public affairs was not in the old academic tradition. Further, pacifism, liberalism and internationalism were unacceptable to many Germans. Those who, like Einstein, publicly professed and acted upon such beliefs were risking blackmail, persecution and even attacks upon their lives, as evidenced by the many political assassinations of those years. The fact that Einstein was a Jew and that his work was baffling and incomprehensible to almost everybody made him an even more exposed target in nationalist and obscurantist circles. But the fire he drew did not emanate altogether from the ignorant and ill-willed; a number of respectable scientists and publicists joined the general attack upon him, an attack which at times took an organized, and even violent, form.

A nationalist student publicly, and with impunity, threatened to "cut the throat of that Jew." In a letter to his friend Max Born, written in December 1919, Einstein voiced one of his rare personal complaints. "The yellow press and other half-wits," he wrote, "are at my heels to the point where I can scarcely draw breath, let alone do any decent work." To Lorentz he wrote in the summer of 1920:

> . . . I have recently had to suffer a wide variety of attacks, chiefly from the newspapers. This is not altogether unwelcome, for it affords the opportunity of distinguishing one's true friends from the rest. Strange how every judgment in these times is based upon political criteria!

By fall the situation had grown so bad that Ehrenfest was again considering ways and means of getting Einstein out of Germany for good; and Lorentz felt constrained formally to reaffirm his confidence in Einstein when a major learned society attacked him. How Einstein felt about the nasty attacks about him is evidenced in a letter [11] which he addressed, on March 18, 1921, to an old friend who was then teaching in China:

> . . . I shudder when I think of all that has happened in the world since last we met, and of what may yet await us. It is almost cheering to think that someday it will be all over, one's own life as well.
>
> My troubles have been greatly exaggerated. My view of man is too objective, and my economic situation too secure for such things to disturb me. I live my life in my own way, unconcerned by outside criticism, and pursue my work to the extent that the rush of events allows me time. Discovery in the grand manner is for young people anyway and, hence, for me a thing of the past. I am on the verge of leaving for a two-month visit to America.

At about that time, Einstein was interviewed by Elias Tobenkin, correspondent for the *New York Evening Post*. The interview was published on March 26, 1921, two days before his departure for America.[12] Tobenkin had come to seek Einstein's views on the plight of German science, but Einstein's remarks ranged over a much wider field:

. . . Of course . . . science is suffering from the terrible effects of the war, but it is humanity that should be given primary consideration. Humanity is suffering in Germany, and everywhere in Eastern Europe, as it has not suffered for centuries.

Mankind . . . is afflicted with too strong and too narrow a conception of nationalism. The present wave of nationalism is a severe sickness. It takes but the slightest provocation or, at times, no provocation at all to be transformed into chauvinism.

The internationalism that existed before the war, in culture, commerce and industry, as well as in the broad sphere of ideas, was basically healthy. There can be no peace, nor can the wounds of war be healed until this internationalism is restored.

[Did this imply that he opposed the formation of small nations?]

Not in the least. . . . Internationalism, as I conceive the term, implies a rational relationship between countries, a sane union and understanding between nations, mutual co-operation for mutual advancement without interference with the particular customs of any nation.

[And how would he proceed to restore this internationalism that existed prior to 1914?]

Here . . . is where science, scientists, and especially the scientists of America, can be of great service to humanity. Scientists, and particularly the scientists of America, must be pioneers in this work.

In this matter of internationalism America is the most advanced among nations. It has what might be called an international "psyche." The extent of this internationalism was evidenced by the initial success of Wilson's ideas for a world organization as well as by the popular acclaim with which his ideas were greeted by the American people.

That Wilson failed to carry out his own ideas is beside the point.

What is important and indicative of the American state of mind is the enthusiastic response of the American people to those ideas. American scientists should be among the first to attempt to broaden and carry forward the idea of internationalism. The world, including America, must strive to restore friendship among nations. The work of peace cannot go forward as long as any government feels uneasy in regard to its international relations. Suspicion and bitterness do not provide the soil for progress; they should vanish. Intellectuals should be among the first to reject them.

Tobenkin was impressed with the simplicity of Einstein's study and noted the large number of books in English. The only pictures on the walls were two engravings of Newton. Einstein received Tobenkin "dressed in a pair of worn-out trousers and a sweater. If he had a collar on, the collar was very unobtrusive, for I cannot recall having seen it." When Einstein learned that the interview would be published only after Tobenkin's return to America, he said:

In that event, be certain that you do not omit to state that I am a convinced pacifist, that I believe the world has had enough of war. Some sort of international agreement must be reached among nations in order to prevent another war, for another war would mean the total destruction of our civilization. It is true civilization in Europe has been badly damaged and set back by the war; but the loss is not irreparable whereas the effect of another war may prove fatal.

During his frequent postwar European travels, Einstein was well received everywhere he went. In January 1921 he visited Austria and Czechoslovakia.[13] In February he went to Amsterdam with other German leaders (in the interest of what he described to Ehrenfest as a "quixotic political scheme") to attend an International Trade-Union Congress at which the subject of discussion was organized co-operation between labor and pacifist movements.

In 1921, Einstein made his first trip to the United States. He arrived in New York on April 2, 1921, in the company of Dr. Chaim Weizmann, leader of the Zionist movement. His pacifist activities were not widely known in America, and the trip had no political overtones. Its sole purpose was to raise funds for the projected Hebrew University in Jerusalem. Due in part to the generosity of the American medical profession, the endeavor proved successful.

Wherever he went in the United States, Einstein received an enthusiastic welcome, the only exception being a New York alderman who had never heard of him and balked at the decision of granting him the traditional "freedom of the city." [14] As for the American press, it was full of the mystique of Relativity. Einstein visited American institutions of learning and delivered scientific lectures at Princeton, where, on May 9, 1921, he received an honorary degree.[15] In his farewell speech made in New York late in May,[16] Einstein paid tribute to the internationalism of American science:

. . . The world, if it is to progress toward a brighter and nobler future, needs, as never before, the help of those great nations and men who are internationally minded. May I be permitted to express the hope that the spirit of internationalism which America has embraced with so much responsibility may very soon be extended to the sphere of politics. Without the active co-operation of the greatest country, the United States, all efforts toward a sane organization of international relations are bound to remain ineffectual.

By the time Einstein returned to Berlin in mid-1921, various efforts looking toward Franco-German reconciliation had been under way for some time; the Bund Neues Vaterland continued to take a leading role.[17] Late in 1921, and early in 1922, a number of outstanding German pacifists visited France for preliminary discussions. Einstein favored these efforts and followed them closely. However, when Romain Rolland's sister, Madeleine, in the name of the Women's International League for Peace and Freedom, asked him to sponsor an international summer seminar for young people in Italy, he replied, on February 15, 1922:

I scarcely need tell you how highly I esteem the movement to which you have dedicated yourself and how glad I was to receive an invitation to attend your meeting in Italy. If I find myself unable to accept, it is neither for lack of interest nor lack of courage to state my beliefs publicly.

The explanation lies in the fact that, ever since my theories have come to enjoy such astonishing popularity, I am the recipient of numerous invitations urging my personal support of causes all of which are worthy of dedication. But if I yielded to these pressures,

I would be unable, for the rest of my life, to devote myself to my quiet scientific pursuits. Hence, I find it necessary to absent myself from all large-scale social undertakings. . . .

In March 1922 the Bund Neues Vaterland, with its counterpart, the French League for Human Rights (the German group was shortly afterward to change its name to the German League for Human Rights), issued an appeal to democratic groups in France and Germany for "peace, security and reconciliation." Einstein's name appeared among the several hundred signers of the appeal. Another signer was Georg Friedrich Nicolai, who was thus joined with Einstein a second time in a manifesto urging peace and international brotherhood.

In March 1922, Einstein, not without some doubts about the desirability of the trip, ventured to Paris. The bitterness in Germany toward France was still so strong that Einstein considered it necessary formally to notify the Prussian Academy of Sciences of his intention to go to Paris. He advised them that he had received three separate invitations since the beginning of the year, the most recent one involving a series of lectures before the Collège de France. Although this last invitation had been extended in an attempt to pave the way for the restoration of relations among German and French scholars, he had at first politely declined, stating that he did so out of solidarity with his German colleagues:

. . . I could, however, not suppress the feeling [he wrote in his letter to the Academy on March 13, 1922] that in declining I followed the line of least resistance rather than the course dictated by my conscience. In the course of a discussion with [Foreign] Minister [Walther] Rathenau, this feeling ripened into deep conviction. I have, therefore, withdrawn my declination and accepted the invitation.

As a means to promote a Franco-German *rapprochement* in the intellectual sphere, Einstein's visit and his lecture on March 31, 1922, at the Collège de France, were successful. Although he was spirited from the Paris railway station to a secret residence to avoid threatened demonstrations, which never materialized, and although some French learned groups held aloof from him, Einstein was, on the whole, warmly received. An enthusiastic young French attorney wrote him afterward: [17a]

. . . You came like a messenger of peace, and many people, even politicians, viewed you in that light. One aged Deputy phrased it nicely in his newspaper:

"Einstein in Paris? It marks the beginning of a recovery from international madness. It is the victory of the archangel over the demon of the abyss. What am I saying? That it is a German who has been summoned, listened to, honored. . . . O Germany of Einstein! Germany of Goethe and Schiller, of Beethoven and Wagner! Is it really you who have come to us? . . ."

Recalling the visit many years later, Einstein's friend Maurice Solovine wrote: [18]

. . . He had several meetings with political figures, with whom he discussed methods of preventing future wars. . . . Everyone agreed that great efforts must be made to reduce the tension and savage hostility which exist between Germany and France. . . . However, the politicians with whom Einstein spoke held no official government positions; and the attitude of those who were in positions of influence was not at all conciliatory. France had been sorely tried and, psychologically speaking, it had not been easy to induce its people to forget their sacrifices and ordeals. . . . Einstein thought that constructive steps by intellectuals in all countries might foil the machinations of the politicians and others interested in war.

In a letter to his wife on April 9, 1922, Einstein wrote:

. . . You can scarcely imagine with what sympathy I have been greeted by the French people. Even as regards their attitude on the political scene I have found calm consideration coupled with a sincere desire for reconciliation—infinitely more promising than I had expected. Tomorrow I am off by car to visit some of the war ruins.

On Einstein's return trip to Germany, Solovine and two other friends accompanied him as far as Saint-Quentin. Here for the first time he came face to face with the frightful devastation of war. The sight made a deep impression on him, which Solovine described as follows:

. . . He talked to me a great deal and told me how aghast he was. . . . War is a terrible thing, he said repeatedly, and must be abolished at all cost. I said I did not think this could be accomplished either through propaganda or by the intentions of a few men in political life. Men of ignorance and evil intent, I said, were still too numerous; their doctrines were more readily accepted than the ideas put forth by groups of enlightened, well-meaning men. Alas, he said, what you say is very true and very frightening. . . . At this time Einstein had not yet conceived of any plan of political organization for putting an end to the scourge of war. He spoke of war from a purely humanitarian point of view.

Soon after his return, on April 19, 1922, Einstein wrote to Rolland,[19] apologizing that the rush of events had left no time to seek him out for a visit:

I am happy that my visit to Paris passed so harmoniously; I take pleasure in the thought that I may have helped to further intellectual co-operation between the two countries. I was particularly glad that the people I met displayed a sense of responsibility and did not show the arrogance or superiority born of victory. As I see it, our main difficulty is the rigid attitude which exists in our two countries toward the question of war guilt. Such an attitude is very hard to overcome and makes it difficult for the peoples of the two nations to establish personal contact. Yet, such contact is indispensable to restore sound relations between the two countries and eliminate the mutual distrust that now exists.

Rolland replied promptly, giving some details about a new liberal French journal, *Clarté*, soon to be launched with the co-operation of some of France's foremost writers. Einstein had already heard about the project in Paris. Some weeks later, Henri Barbusse, whose war novel *Le Feu* had earned him an international reputation, sent Einstein still further details about the journal and asked him to write a few lines about his visit to Paris. Einstein obliged, on July 11, 1922:

The days I spent in Paris will count among my finest experiences. I shall ever remember them with pleasure and gratitude. My colleagues in Paris received me as one would an old friend, without any of the reservations which, given the present dominance of nationalist sentiments, I would have expected. Common work and common interests promptly dispelled the shadows of the past. At our more intimate sessions we occasionally engaged in political discussions. What impressed me most was the fact that I nowhere noticed any hatred or intoxication with victory, but only concern and sorrow over what has happened.

With regard to the causes of the World War and the present political situation, a rather uniform attitude exists in France (as, incidentally, it does in Germany) which is honestly considered the only correct one. Differences of opinion that exist in the two countries are less concerned with the facts as such than with their evaluation. I do not expect that preoccupation with, and discussion of, the tragic events of the past can contribute much to the moral recovery of the two nations. Co-operation between them in rebuilding the devastated areas seems to me much more important.

Fruitful co-operation must be based on mutual confidence, and confidence can be created only by cultivation of personal relationships. The invitation extended to me by the faculty of the Collège de France was a first courageous step in this direction. I hope that similar gestures will be made in both nations.

An important step in that direction had been taken by the French a month earlier. A delegation of distinguished Frenchmen had come to Berlin to participate in a great Franco-German demonstration of amity organized by the German Peace Congress (Deutsches Friedenskartell), a group in which the German League for Human Rights had joined forces with fourteen other German pacifist groups. The tenor of the event was set by a French delegate, Victor Basch, professor at the Sorbonne in Paris, in a phrase about building a "Bridge across the Chasm." The main rally was held on the floor of the German Reichstag, whose presiding officer addressed it. Basch evoked thunderous applause when he pointed to Einstein, who sat in the audience, as living proof that, even after so frightful a war, the great men of France and Germany could work together. Einstein addressed the large meeting as follows:

Having listened to the inspiring words spoken here today, I should like to describe our present situation in the most sober terms, as though we were fortunate enough to witness the happenings on this miserable planet from the vantage point of the moon.

First, we might ask ourselves in what sense the problems of international affairs require today an approach quite different from that of the past—not just the recent past, but the past half-century. To me, the answer is quite simple: due to technological developments, the distances throughout the world have shrunk to one tenth of their former size. The production of commodities in the world has become a mosaic composed of pieces from all over the globe. It is essential and altogether natural that the increased economic interdependence of the world's territories, which participate in mankind's production, be complemented by an appropriate political organization.

The famous man in the moon would not be able to comprehend why mankind, even after the frightful experience of the war, was still so reluctant to create such a new political organization. Why is man so reluctant? I think the reason is that, where history is concerned, people are afflicted with a very poor memory.

It is a strange situation. The common man, exposed to events as they happen, has relatively little trouble adjusting himself to great changes, while the learned man who has soaked up much knowledge and serves it up to others faces a more difficult problem. In this respect, language plays a particularly unfortunate role. For what is a nation but a group of individuals who are forever influencing one another by means of the written and spoken word. The members of a given language community may scarcely notice it when their own peculiar outlook on the world becomes biased and inflexible.

In my travels through Holland, France and America, I was amazed to witness the rigidity of such language blocs. These distinctions of specific communities, cultivated by a common language and nationhood, are immensely difficult to bridge. They represent the evolutionary results of history over many centuries. We shall not deceive ourselves into believing that it will be easy to transcend these ingrained mental barriers. Yet unless we succeed, we cannot hope to achieve real political solidarity and co-operation among the nations of Europe.

I believe the condition in which the world finds itself today makes it not only a matter of idealism but one of dire necessity to create unity and intellectual co-operation among nations. Those of us who are alive to these needs must stop thinking in terms of

"What should be done for our country?" Rather, we should ask: "What must our community do to lay the groundwork for a larger world community?" For without that greater community no single country will long endure.

I believe that only he who is constantly aware of this fact, and strives to evaluate every situation in life by this criterion, will eventually be able to break through the frozen barriers that divide cultures. I consider it very important that, whenever there is an opportunity, men, speaking different languages and having different political and cultural views, communicate with each other across frontiers, not in expectation of private or national gain but in an attempt to bridge the gulf between different, relatively independent intellectual groups.

Only thus can we hope to achieve—in Europe, at least—the political unity that alone will enable us to survive and safeguard our intellectual heritage. Only then will life be worth living.

The French delegation was also given a warm reception in other parts of Germany. But the hopeful atmosphere thus achieved changed only two weeks later when, on June 24, 1922, Germany's Foreign Minister, Walther Rathenau, the exponent of the policy of international collaboration, was assassinated by reactionary opponents. Einstein knew Rathenau well. Writing to his mother on October 15, 1918, Einstein had characterized Rathenau as "eloquent and sparkling with spirit." Years later, he described his acquaintance with Rathenau at greater length: [20]

On several occasions, I spent hours in Rathenau's company discussing diverse subjects. These talks tended to be rather one-sided: on the whole, he spoke and I listened. For one thing, it was not easy to get the floor; and for another, it was so pleasant to listen to him that one did not try very hard.

Rathenau's real interests did not lie in the field of theoretical scientific thought. He was chiefly concerned with social problems and with art of any kind. His avowed allegiances were contradictory. He felt himself to be a Jew and thought along international lines, but at the same time, like many talented Jewish intellectuals of his generation, he was in love with Prussianism, its *Junker* class and its militarism. . . . After the war, it was Rathenau who strongly advised me to accept an invitation to Paris, a gesture which was then still considered quite risky. I clearly realized at that time how far removed he was from the narrow-minded nationalism that animated virtually all the German intellectuals I had come to know. Yet, strangely enough, he was a person inwardly dependent on the recognition of men much inferior to him in their human qualities. On the other hand, despite this curious dependence on others, he took pleasure in satirizing events and persons. These improvisations, in their droll simplicity, were often true works of art.

Einstein's files also contain the draft of a letter to an unidentified colleague, dated July 1, 1922,[21] in which he again speaks of Rathenau:

You ask my opinion about a memorial service at the university [of Berlin] on the occasion of Walther Rathenau's violent death. Here are my views: Ordinarily, in the case of the death of a cabinet member, such a service would not be appropriate. In this case, it is conceivable only as a protest demonstration by the university against political murder. In general, the intervention by a cultural institution into political affairs is to be condemned. But here, it is a question of *affirming a broad moral position*, of preserving those values that are above partisan strife. In my opinion, the university should unconditionally protest against political murder. (Both students and professors should speak.) The university must forthrightly denounce the despicable crime of premeditated murder in the service of politics; it must likewise affirm that any society which does not insist upon respect for all life must necessarily decay. I am convinced that a public meeting, at which such sentiments were expressed unanimously and outspokenly, could exert considerable influence on the formation of a sounder public opinion. On the other hand, silence on the part of the university might, in the present climate, be construed as an expression of sympathy with Rathenau's political enemies.

To Solovine, Einstein wrote on July 16: [22]

. . . There has been much excitement here ever since the abominable murder of Rathenau. I myself am being constantly warned to be cautious, have canceled my lectures and am officially "absent," although actually I have not left. Anti-Semitism is very widespread.

About ten days before, on July 6, 1922, Einstein wrote to Max Planck,[23] canceling a scientific lecture he had agreed to deliver:

. . . A number of people who deserve to be taken seriously have independently warned me not to stay in Berlin for the time being and, especially, to avoid all public appearances in Germany. I am said to be among those whom the nationalists have marked for assassination. Of course, I have no proof, but in the prevailing situation it seems quite plausible. . . . The trouble is that the newspapers have mentioned my name too often, thus mobilizing the rabble against me. I have no alternative but to be patient—and to leave the city. I do urge you to get as little upset over the incident as I myself.

Within weeks, however, Einstein had discarded whatever precautions he may have been persuaded to adopt. The occasion of his first public appearance was a "No More War" rally in one of the public parks of the German capital.[24] Ever since the end of the war, the anniversary of its outbreak, August 1, had been marked by such demonstrations which were attended, at times, by as many as 200,000 people. This time Einstein allowed himself to be paraded in a car during the rally, though he did not speak publicly.

On August 30, 1922, Einstein wrote to Lord Haldane of England (philosopher and statesman) and Paul Painlevé of France (mathematician and statesman), both of whom he knew personally. He urged them to give consideration to a plan whereby German reparations would be met in part by the sale abroad of shares in German industries.[25] He took pains to specify that his name not be publicly mentioned in this connection. Einstein's files indicate that only Haldane replied. Couched in noncommittal, though gracious language, Haldane implied having noticed the lack of enthusiasm on the part of those British Treasury officials with whom he had consulted.

Einstein's pacifist position at this period is best summarized in the article he contributed to *Die Friedensbewegung*, a German handbook of the pacifist movement, published in 1922: [26]

War constitutes the most formidable obstacle to the growth of international co-operation, especially in its effect upon culture. War destroys all those conditions which are indispensable to the intellectual if he is to work creatively. If he happens to be young and vigorous, his energies will be chained to the engines of destruction, while the older men will be trapped in an atmosphere of hate and frustration. Moreover, war leads to the impoverishment of nations and to long periods of economic depression. Hence, he who cherishes the values of culture cannot fail to be a pacifist.

What relation exists between science and the development of pacifism? Clearly, the influence of pure science on pacifist thinking has been but slight. Most of those representing the field of scientific endeavor which should be considered first—namely, the science of history—have certainly done little to foster the cause of pacifism. In fact, many historians, although not the best of them, have gone out of their way, particularly during the Great War, to make outrageously militaristic and superpatriotic pronouncements.

The natural sciences, on the other hand, are an altogether different matter. The natural scientist is receptive to pacifist objectives because of the universal character of the subject matter he deals with and his consequent dependence on international cooperation. This is also true of economists. Of necessity, they tend to regard war as a disruptive and disorganizing influence upon the economy.

However, what interests us most about the effect of science on the historical process are the material effects of science, rather than its effect on the minds of men. The development of technology, resulting from the work of scientists, has made the economies of the world interdependent: this is why every war must assume world-wide importance. Only when we come to appreciate the significance of this development shall we be able to muster the energy and good will needed to create an organization that will make war impossible.

Early in October 1922 Einstein departed from Marseilles on a six-month tour of the Orient, returning by way of Palestine and Spain. En route, aboard a Japanese steamer, he was plagued by intestinal pains, which a fellow passenger helped to relieve. Twenty-five years later, Einstein was to compose a touching epitaph for this Japanese physician and his wife (see p. 582).

Einstein kept a diary during the journey, but it contains little which bears on his views of war, peace or political affairs. On October 28, 1922, in Colombo, Ceylon, he noted:

. . . We rode in small one-man carriages drawn at a trot by men of herculean strength yet delicate build. I was bitterly ashamed to share responsibility for the abominable treatment accorded fellow human beings but was unable to do anything about it. These beggars of regal stature hurl themselves en masse at every tourist until he capitulates. They know how to beg and implore in a way which tears your heart. Along the streets of the native quarter one sees how these attractive people live their primitive lives. For all their nobility they give one the impression that the climate prevents them from thinking back or ahead more than a quarter hour. They live at ground level, amid great filth and a considerable stench, do little and need little. Their quarters are much too crowded to allow the individual any privacy. Half-naked, they exhibit beautiful and muscular bodies, with fine, patient features. There is no such hubbub as among the Levantines in Port Said, no brutality, no turbulence—only a quiet life of submissiveness, not without a certain serenity. Looking at these people closely, one loses one's appetite for Europeans, who are so much more degenerate and brutalized, look so much coarser and greedier—which, unfortunately, accounts for their superiority in practical affairs, their capacity to tackle big things and carry them through. I wonder whether we might not be like the Hindus, if we lived in this climate.

There is much activity in the harbor. Herculean workers with glossy black bodies load and unload the cargo. Divers engage in their daring performances. And always a smile on their faces when they sacrifice themselves for filthy money and for sated people who are mean enough to enjoy all that.

The high point of the journey was his extended visit to Japan, a country for which Einstein gained a deep and lasting affection. As he wrote to Solovine soon afterward (Whitsunday, 1923): [27]

The Japanese are marvelous—delicate manners, a lively interest in everything, a sense of art, intellectual naïveté accompanied by good sense—a wonderful people in a picturesque land.

It was in the course of this Far Eastern journey that Einstein learned he had been awarded the Nobel Prize in physics for 1921. By the time he returned, in the spring of 1923 (via Palestine and Spain), two events, of great significance both to himself and to the world, had taken place in Europe. Late in October 1922 Mussolini seized power in Italy; and early in January 1923 the French marched back into Germany's Ruhr district to enforce their demands for reparations from Germany. As Einstein expressed it in an autograph given to someone on October 12, 1923: [28]

Children do not avail themselves of the wisdom of their elders; nations do not listen to history. The bitter lessons of the past must ever be learned anew.

CHAPTER THREE

INTERNATIONAL CO-OPERATION AND THE LEAGUE OF NATIONS | 1922-1927

AFTER THE OUTBREAK of war in 1914, Einstein's views on the question of war and peace became increasingly crystallized; he had come to consider a supranational organization as a prerequisite to the abolition of war. Hence, it was to be expected that he would welcome the founding of the League of Nations in 1920. During the first years of its existence, he had no direct contacts with the League. In 1922, however, Einstein, together with Marie Curie, the eminent physicist, Henri Bergson, the French philosopher, and other personalities of world renown, was invited to become a member of the League's Committee on Intellectual Co-operation. Einstein accepted promptly: [1]

Although I am not clear at all as to the character of the work to be done by the committee, I consider it my duty to accept your invitation. In my opinion, no one, in times such as these, should refuse to participate in any effort made to bring about international co-operation.

The invitation to Einstein, which came four years before Germany's admission to the League, provoked a certain amount of controversy. Professor Gilbert Murray of Oxford, England, one of the prominent British leaders in the League of Nations movement, who later was to be chairman of the Committee on Intellectual Co-operation, stated shortly before his death in 1957: [2]

I was naturally eager to get Doctor Einstein made a member of the Committee on Intellectual Co-operation, partly because he would, in a sense, count as a German, and partly for his eminence, but there were two or three obstacles—some of my French colleagues objected to having a German so soon while some Germans argued that he was not a German at all but a Swiss Jew. Another difficulty was Einstein's own mistrust of the Committee on Intellectual Co-operation as merely a committee formed by the victors. A conversation with some leading members of the committee very soon satisfied him as to our real international and peaceful spirit. The German objection was not one that could be maintained; if he was a Swiss, the Germans had no ground for objecting to him.

Shortly after accepting the invitation to join the committee, Einstein had second thoughts about his own participation and had almost decided to withdraw. He sent word of his intention to Pierre Comert, Press Chief of the League and the only League official whom Einstein knew personally.[3] He remarked in a supplementary note that, while he himself had not been the object of hostile criticism by German intellectuals,

the situation here is such that a Jew would do well to exercise restraint as regards his participation in political affairs. In addition, I must say that I have no desire to represent people who certainly would not choose me as their representative, and with whom I find myself in disagreement on the questions to be dealt with. . . .

Mme. Curie and Gilbert Murray were among those who pleaded with Einstein not to withdraw. They apparently convinced him. Since he was unable to attend the committee's first meeting in Geneva in August 1922, he expressed his support in a telegram. The sentiments which doubtless helped him reach a positive decision with regard to membership in the committee are well expressed in a paper on the "Internationalism of Science" which he probably prepared at about the same time: [4]

When nationalism and political passions were reaching a climax during the war, Emil Fischer [the 1902 Nobel Prize winner in chemistry] remarked with emphasis at a session of the [Royal Prussian] Academy: "Whether you like it or not, gentlemen, science is and always will be international."

The great men among scientists have always known this and

felt it passionately, even in times of international conflicts when they stood alone amid their narrow-minded colleagues. During the war, the majority of voting members in every country betrayed their sacred trust. The International Association of Academies was destroyed. Congresses were, and still are being, held to which scholars from former enemy countries were not admitted. Political considerations, advanced with pompous solemnity, make it impossible for pure objectivity to prevail, without which great accomplishments cannot mature.

What can be done by well-meaning people who are immune to the emotional temptations of the moment, to restore health to the intellectual community? As long as the majority of intellectual workers remain so embittered, it will not be possible to arrange for an international congress of real significance. Moreover, psychological opposition to the restoration of international associations of scientific workers is still so formidable that the small number of broad-minded people cannot defeat it.

These more enlightened men can make an important contribution to the great task of reviving international societies by keeping in close touch with like-minded men and women the world over, as well as by steadfastly championing the cause of internationalism in their own spheres of influence. Real success will require time, but eventually it will undoubtedly come. I cannot let this opportunity pass without expressing my appreciation to the particularly large number of English colleagues who, throughout these difficult years, have never ceased to manifest a strong desire to preserve the international community of intellectuals.

The attitude of individual citizens is everywhere far superior to official pronouncements. Let men of good will bear this in mind rather than allow themselves to become exasperated or misled: *Senatores boni viri, senatus autem bestia* [the senators are honorable men, but the senate is a monster].

I am extremely hopeful for the progress of a general international organization. My feelings are based not so much on confidence in the intelligence and high-mindedness of scientists as on the inevitable pressure of economic developments. Since these developments are so largely dependent upon the work of even reactionary scientists, they too will have no choice but to assist in the establishment of an international organization.

Einstein's confidence in the ability of the League of Nations to achieve a peaceful solution to world problems was severely shaken when, in January 1923, the French Government refused to submit the problem of Germany's war-reparations payments to arbitration, and sent military occupation forces into the German Ruhr area. For once, Einstein found himself on the same side as the German nationalists, though for different reasons. Soon after his return from the Far East and the Mediterranean, in March 1923, he announced his resignation from the Committee on Intellectual Co-operation: [5]

I have become convinced that the League possesses neither the strength nor the sincere desire which it needs to accomplish its aims. As a convinced pacifist, I feel obliged to sever all relations with the League. I request that you strike my name from the roster of committee members.

The nature of the attacks made upon Einstein during this period is reflected in a note he himself addressed to the German Zionist organization in these very days. The note attempted to refute the charges made against him at meetings of the Nazi party, which was then still in its infancy:

. . . I authorize you to issue the following formal statement. Neither in Paris nor anywhere else have I ever denied that I was born in Ulm of German parents or that I later became a Swiss citizen by immigration. Further, may I say that I have never attempted to ingratiate myself in order to curry favor with anyone.

Gilbert Murray expressed his sorrow at Einstein's resignation from the League committee in a letter to Einstein, dated April 20, 1923: [6]

. . . I fully understand your action, and even feel the strongest sympathy with it, but I hope and believe that you are wrong. I am sure that the vast majority of the delegates present at the Assembly have the *good will* that is necessary. One cannot attend a meeting of the Assembly, or spend a few days at the Secretariat, without being convinced of this. But of course the *power* is another matter. We are faced in Europe with a military supremacy in the hands of one nation about as great as Napoleon's at the height of his power, and that makes all progress toward international justice extremely slow and difficult. Even those who, like myself, are deeply committed to the League sometimes find it difficult to keep our patience.

I am sorry that you definitely resigned. . . . I believe that the right line would have been for a number of us to say that it was impossible for the Committee on Intellectual Co-operation to function while the French were refusing to submit their case to arbitration and were creating practically a state of war in Europe. I believe that some other members of the committee would have been willing to take that line. The committee itself consists largely of people who have nothing particular to do with the League and are not, I fear, permeated with the League spirit. . . .

Einstein replied, on May 25, 1923:

It was only with the greatest reluctance that I decided to resign from the committee; and even I cannot be certain that I acted correctly. But once my faith in the League as a whole was shaken, it became impossible to participate further in any of its activities. Its chief defect is not the lack of real power behind it; rather, what I find most discouraging is that, by its silence and its actions, the League functions as a tool of those nations which, at this stage of history, happen to be the dominant powers. Thus, the League not only fails to uphold justice but actually undermines the faith of men of good will who believe in the possibility of creating a supranational organization.

I hope I have been able to convince you that my action has in no sense been determined by political bias, let alone chauvinism.

Because his resignation from the League's committee received wide publicity, Einstein felt obliged to offer a public explanation which appeared in the June 1923 issue of the German pacifist journal *Die Friedenswarte*.[7] He had considered it necessary to resign, he said,

because the activities of the League of Nations had convinced me that there appeared to be no action, no matter how brutal, committed by the present power groups, against which the League was willing to take a stand. I withdrew because the League of Nations, as it functions at present, not only fails to embody the ideal of international organization but actually discredits such an ideal.

I did so, however, with great reluctance, because the hope has not yet quite died in me that, within the shell of the League of Nations as it exists today, a better institution may develop in time. . . . May the League of the future prove my harsh words to have been mistaken.

That Einstein at no point renounced the principles of the League is made clear in a message he sent a mass meeting in Berlin.[8] The meeting, organized by the German League for Human Rights on July 17, 1923, was held in support of Germany's entry into the League of Nations:

I am glad about the opportunity to voice my conviction that the creation of a vigorous intergovernmental organization is vital to the survival of Europe. If the entry of the German Reich into the League of Nations will help promote that goal, it is our duty to work for Germany's entry.

Before the war, Einstein had played a prominent part in a series of international scientific conferences organized by the Belgian industrialist Ernest Solvay. These "Solvay Congresses" were now to be resumed, and on July 15, 1923, Lorentz had sounded out Einstein on the question of whether he wished to be invited. On August 16, 1923, Einstein replied that he had discussed the matter with a colleague, who had felt that

. . . it would be wrong for me to take part in a meeting from which my German colleagues are excluded on principle. I cannot help feeling that he is right. . . . I am convinced that politics should not be allowed to impinge upon scientific endeavors, nor should individuals be held responsible for the government of the country to which they happen to belong. Were I to take part in the Congress, I would, by implication, become an accomplice to an action which I strongly consider to be painfully unjust. This feeling becomes all the stronger when I think of the French and Belgians who have, of recent years, committed too many sins to continue to pose as the injured innocents. . . .

I should be grateful if you would see to it that I do not even receive an invitation to the Congress. I should like to be spared the necessity of declining—an action which might impede the good cause of gradually re-establishing friendly collaboration among the physicists of the various countries. . . .

Lorentz, on September 15, 1923, wrote that, while he understood Einstein's reasons, it was not quite true that German scientists were being excluded on principle.[9] The door was ajar and he hoped it would soon be fully opened. He also reported on his attendance as Einstein's successor at the first meeting of the Committee on Intellectual Co-operation:

. . . It was my impression that had you remained on the committee you would have been able to work well with its members. There exists, in these circles, a real desire for universal understanding, though it has not, as yet, asserted itself to the extent one might wish. . . .

In a letter to Mme. Curie, Einstein discussed in some detail both his resignation from the League committee and his disinclination to attend the Solvay Congress.[10] The letter, dated December 25, 1923, marked the occasion of the twenty-fifth anniversary of the discovery of radium. (Not until two and a half years later, when Einstein had won his point and Germans were no longer excluded on principle, did he accept the invitations to attend meetings of the Solvay Congress.) In his letter to Mme. Curie he remarked:

I realize that you will be annoyed with me, and justifiably so, for having resigned from the League committee and for having issued a sharply worded statement. After all, scarcely half a year earlier I myself had advised you to participate in the committee's work! I did not resign for base motives, nor because of pro-German sympathies. I had become convinced that the League (unlike the committee to which I belonged) functioned, despite a thin veneer of objectivity, as a willing instrument of power politics. Under the circumstances, I did not want to have anything to do with the League. I felt that a blunt statement to that effect could do no harm. Perhaps I was wrong, but such were my convictions at the time.

I have requested, furthermore, that I not be invited to Brussels [to attend the Solvay Congress of Physicists]. Although, psychologically speaking, I can well understand why Frenchmen and Belgians do not like to meet with Germans, it is certainly unworthy of men of true culture to treat one another according to their respective nationalities or by other superficial criteria as would the common mob, which is governed by mass suggestion. If that is the way of the world, I should choose to stay in my study rather than get upset over the conduct of people outside. Do not think for a moment that I consider my own fellow countrymen superior and that I misunderstand the others; that would scarcely be consistent with the Theory of Relativity. . . . But enough of that. I would not dare grumble to you in this fashion if I did not think of you as a sister in defiance, one who, somewhere in her soul, has always had some understanding of such feelings, and one to whom I have always felt particularly close.

The year 1923 was characterized by particularly turbulent and eventful developments affecting political and economic conditions in Germany. The occupation of the Ruhr by French troops served to hasten the complete collapse of the German currency, which had the most widespread political and economic repercussions. The survival of political democracy was at times in jeopardy. The Nazi movement gained strength. Nationalist passions grew apace. In November of that year Einstein abruptly departed for Leiden, Holland. Nationalist incitements, coincident with Hitler's unsuccessful Beer Hall *Putsch* in Munich on November 9, 1923, had once again aroused fears for Einstein's safety. So sudden was his departure that Max Planck, appearing at the Einstein home in response to an invitation, found his host gone and, in a state of great agitation, wrote him at once, pleading with him not to accept any of the tempting offers from abroad that would doubtless come his way. Whether or not Einstein again considered for a moment leaving Germany for good, he promptly reassured Planck of his decision not to do so, and returned to Berlin shortly thereafter.

On May 16, 1924, Gilbert Murray again wrote Einstein. The letter was marked "Confidential":

You have doubtless noticed from time to time the criticisms which I and others have made of the Committee on Intellectual Co-operation on the grounds of its one-sidedness. I think matters have now reached the point where, if you are willing to reconsider your attitude toward the committee, they would unanimously welcome your presence. I very much hope that you may consent to join us again.

There would be no inconsistency in this. You resigned as a protest after the invasion of the Ruhr and the subsequent embitterment of feeling between France and Germany, and your return to the committee would mark the beginning of that *rapprochement* to which we are all looking forward. I feel that at this moment when there seems a prospect of obtaining some final settlement of the reparations question and of getting the French out of Germany, good Europeans ought to do everything in their power to contribute to creating the right atmosphere, and your joining the League committee is just the sort of incident that would have an influence all through Europe. If you can give me a private assurance of your willingness to consider an invitation from the Council of the League to resume your place on the committee, I have very little doubt that the invitation will be forthcoming.

Einstein replied on May 30, 1924:

Upon my return from a trip of several weeks, I find your letter, which I sincerely appreciate and which has indeed made me very happy. It certainly deserves a very frank reply.

When I announced my resignation from the Committee on Intellectual Co-operation more than a year ago, I indicated that I did so not for lack of confidence in the work of the committee itself but because I had no faith in the League of Nations as a whole. I do not hesitate to tell you that my closest and most enlightened friends were the ones who expressed the deepest regret over my resignation. I myself have slowly come to feel that I was influenced more by a passing mood of disillusionment than by clear thinking. True, so far the League has often failed; but, at a time as saddening as this, it must still be regarded as that institution which offers the best promise of effective action to those who honestly work for international reconciliation. There is another factor which should be considered: those in this country who believe in a conciliatory policy should at this time do their utmost to assure that the spirit of European unity, so strongly manifest in the French people, be allowed to bear fruit.

I should like to advise you, therefore, that I would gratefully accept re-election to the committee and that I would do what I could to help the good cause. In the event that I were not elected, which would be quite understandable in view of what happened, I would be glad to work with the committee on any particular issue that might arise.

I cannot tell you [Murray replied on June 6, 1924] with what pleasure I have received your most generous and friendly letter of the thirtieth of May.

There is, of course, a certain delicacy in the situation, as some members of the committee will doubtless have resented your criticisms of it, just as, to a lesser degree, they resented mine; but I do not see how they can any longer maintain such resentment, even if anyone wished to do so, which I do not anticipate.

All the information which I get tends to show that there is to be a real and decided change in the direction of French policy, especially in matters connected with the League; and I cannot but feel that, when the Committee on Intellectual Co-operation eventually contains three savants of such world-wide importance as Mme. Curie, Bergson and yourself, it will at last strike the true note of international co-operation which has hitherto often seemed lacking. . . .

Only two weeks later, on June 21, 1924, Sir Eric Drummond, Secretary-General of the League of Nations, issued a formal invitation to Einstein:

I am desired by the President of the Council of the League of Nations to inform you that at its meeting on June 16, the Council decided to renew their invitation to you to serve as a member of the Committee on Intellectual Co-operation. . . .

May I, on behalf of the Council of the League of Nations, express the sincere hope that you may see your way to accept the invitation?

Einstein's acceptance was dated June 25, 1924.[11] On that same day he sent Pierre Comert a statement intended for the American press:

The fact that the League of Nations has again elected me to its Committee on Intellectual Co-operation is a reassuring indication of the generous sentiments that prevail within this body which I consider so important to the political organization of mankind; for I was re-elected despite the brusque resignation I submitted to the League early last year, under the depressing impact of the events taking place at the time. I am inspired by this capacity to understand and let bygones be bygones. Once forward-looking people everywhere will have prevailed on all countries to join, the League is sure to live up to its great mission of creating a world of peace.

The seriousness with which he appreciated his new responsibilities is revealed in a note Einstein addressed to Chaim Weizmann on July 19, 1924,[12] in which he explained his inability to attend an important Zionist meeting in London because it conflicted with the Geneva session of the Committee on Intellectual Co-operation:

. . . If I stay away [from Geneva] the feelings of the other committee members will be hurt. This is so because only a year ago I resigned from the committee in a big uproar, declaring publicly that the League was not doing its job. Now that the political situation has somewhat improved, I have been re-elected and am to attend my first session. I feel obliged to do so in order to avoid new misunderstandings. . . .

Thus Einstein at last became a functioning member of the League's Committee on Intellectual Co-operation.[13] Writing to his wife from Geneva on July 21, 1924, a few days before the session opened, he said:

The interior of the League of Nations building seems mysterious—a hotel with improvised furnishings that appears to have been transformed overnight, so to speak, into a scene for events never dreamed of before. People run about busily, speaking in soft voices.

Henri Bergson presided at the committee's meetings, with Gilbert Murray as vice-chairman. Prominent among the other members present were Mme. Curie, Robert A. Millikan, of the California Institute of Technology, and H. A. Lorentz, who, the year before, had been elected to the committee in Einstein's place. The official minutes for July 25, 1924, read:

. . . The committee also welcomed M. Einstein, both as an old and as a new colleague. He had been appointed a member of the committee, just as the other members had been, without requesting the appointment. He had returned to the committee at his own request, having wished to become a member of it. He therefore doubly belonged to it. The committee was happy and proud to count among its members a savant of world-wide reputation. . . . M. Einstein seemed, indeed, to have converted a part of humanity to [his] lofty speculations. It was hoped that he would be able to accomplish yet another conversion. Even during the war, and even before the war, his conception of the relations between peoples might not have been far away from the ideal of the League of Nations. If by his presence on a committee of the League of Nations he succeeded in attracting to this ideal all those who had been interested in his lofty speculations, he would have rendered a new and very great service to humanity.

The following day the committee considered an offer from the French Government to establish an International Institute of Intellectual Co-operation in Paris, to serve as the executive organ for the committee. Einstein's reaction to this proposal is summarized in the minutes as follows:

M. Einstein was of the opinion that the French proposal was of the highest importance and could only give rise to feelings of gratitude. The members of the committee were unanimous in their wish that all European countries should collaborate. Many persons in Germany were of the same opinion, but it must be remembered that many people there mistrusted the League of Nations and reproached it with not being inspired by a really objective and European spirit. There was reason to fear that the prospect of a transfer to Paris of the Committee on Intellectual Co-operation would prejudice the efforts of the committee and would prevent it from attaining those high aims which it pursued. Personally he did not share this fear and made no proposal, but he asked the committee to take account of existing circumstances and of the situation from a psychological point of view.

Einstein was assured that there was no intention of transferring the seat of the committee to Paris. It was ultimately decided to refer the plan to the League for action. Gilbert Murray, many years later, described Einstein's service on the committee:

. . . He was, in every way, a delightful colleague. He represented, completely, the true spirit of the committee. The only points on which we ever had differences were due to his special kindliness of disposition. There was one official, a Frenchman, whose conduct we considered to have been improper. Einstein, unwilling to condemn anyone, suspected that some of us were prejudiced against the man because of his very Left views, and had to be convinced that the charges against him were really sound.

It became a habit of the members of the committee to give an address to students of the Geneva University during sittings, but Einstein gave, instead, a violin recital which delighted his audience. . . .

During two of our annual meetings I happened to have breakfast every morning with Einstein, Mme. Curie and Eve Curie, the daughter who afterward wrote her mother's life. They were gay breakfasts, largely due to a pleasant stream of chaff between Eve Curie and Einstein, not quite like the solemnity often attributed to great savants. . . .

I may mention, too, that one day, when he was lunching with me at my house in England, he had been giving a very gloomy account of the international situation. When my wife exclaimed, "How is it, Dr. Einstein, that you can keep up such a cheerful spirit when you have this dark opinion of the world?" he answered, smiling, "We must remember that this is a very small star, and probably some of the larger and more important stars may be very virtuous and happy."

Einstein himself reported on the first session of the Committee on Intellectual Co-operation which he attended in the *Frankfurter Zeitung* of August 29, 1924:

I have just returned from the session of the League Committee on Intellectual Co-operation in Geneva and should like to convey some of my impressions to the German public. The object of the committee is to initiate or foster efforts which may promote international co-operation between the scientific and intellectual communities of various countries in the hope that national cultures, heretofore separated by language and tradition, may thereby be brought into closer communication. Rather than entertaining utopian schemes, the committee has initiated several modest but fruitful projects on a small scale, such as the international organization of scientific reporting, the exchange of publications, the protection of literary property, the exchange of professors and students among various countries, etc. Thus far, the greatest progress has been achieved in the sphere of international reporting.

While the specific projects just mentioned may be of little interest to the general public, much consideration should be given to the question of what attitude the German people and the German Government ought to adopt in principle toward the League of Nations. My personal impressions in Geneva are of interest only insofar as they involve this larger question.

All members of the committee were anxious at all times to emphasize the truly international character of the institution. Regardless of the question under discussion, Germany was always considered as though she were, in fact, a member of the League. It is true that the French mentality may unwittingly have dominated the proceedings to some extent, which is not surprising in view of the origin of the League and the nonparticipation of important nations; yet, I was happy to observe an honest desire to be objective. Such a spirit is bound to prove constructive in the future. I am convinced that the League of Nations is an institution which will make a real contribution toward the steady recovery of Europe's material as well as intangible resources. My experience has been that much can be accomplished when reason and unqualified sincerity are allowed to prevail.

While in Geneva, I also had the opportunity to discuss the question of Germany's entry into the League of Nations with various well-informed people, particularly Frenchmen. Without exception everyone was of the opinion that Germany should be treated like the other great powers and should be given a permanent seat on the League Council. It was also felt that Germany should join the League right after the successful termination of the London Conference. I fully concur in this view and believe, further, that Germany ought not attach any conditions or reservations to her entry into the League. Confidence begets confidence, and without confidence fruitful co-operation will not be possible. I hope that all those in Germany who believe in the necessity of international conciliation exert pressure so that the present favorable moment for Germany's entry into the League be effectively utilized.

Einstein further confirmed his favorable impression of the Committee on Intellectual Co-operation in a note to Solovine on October 30, 1924: [14]

. . . The League of Nations Committee is better than I thought. There is hope, after all, that things may improve in Europe.

Only the day before, October 29, 1924, he had replied to a French inquiry: *Les États-Unis d'Europe sont-ils réalisables?* [15]

There is no point in wondering whether a United States of Europe is feasible. It *must* become a reality if the significance and the human resources of Europe are to survive to any appreciable extent.

It was the established policy of the International Committee on Intellectual Co-operation to encourage the formation in various countries of affiliated national committees with at least semiofficial standing. Despite original doubts, Einstein apparently helped in creating such a national committee in Germany, an effort, however, that was not successful for several years. On December 16, 1924, he wrote to Lorentz:

. . . The other day I again spoke to [Max] Planck about the National Committee. He seemed somewhat at a loss to express himself and did not say either yes or no. He had no real conception of our aims and felt that mere assurances of brotherhood were of no practical value. I explained to him that the purpose of the committee was to find solutions to real problems, of which I mentioned a few. I also told him that the national committees were organs of the central [international] committee whose function it was to establish liaison with scholars and learned societies in the various countries. In my view this would be the moment when a letter from you might have a strong effect on his thinking. Should you be kind enough to write such a letter, please do not mention that I suggested it. . . .

Less than a month later, on January 9, 1925, Einstein again wrote Lorentz:

It is a difficult job to contribute in some way to the life of human beings in our world. . . . As you know, I asked Herr Planck . . . to organize, or at least keep a watchful eye on, a National Committee on Intellectual Co-operation. I noticed at once that my request made him unhappy, and the poor fellow has been searching his soul ever since. Whenever I inquired he said he had not as yet decided what he would do. Yesterday he himself brought the matter up and said he was unable to do what had been asked of him.

By way of justification he said something like this: "So long as Germans are excluded from international societies and meetings, they must properly hold aloof from all international events, even though they may continue to maintain cordial personal relations with individuals abroad." Of course I protested that international events could not all be lumped together. . . .

Despite the illogic of his reasoning, I did not think it wise to argue with him any further. The important thing is his basic attitude. His reasons are secondary and subject to change. If I judge Planck's position correctly, he himself would really like to co-operate, but loyalty to the social group to which he belongs makes this impossible for him. The political events of recent weeks, which have caused great bitterness here, have apparently tipped the scales in favor of his decision. How definite his decision is may be judged from his express request that I ask you not to write him on the matter.

I am quite unhappy about all this. The epidemic that afflicts Europeans is an emotional condition and, hence, cannot be combated with reason. I fear that at the present time we shall be unable to find anyone of sufficient prestige for a National Committee . . . someone who would be regarded by the intellectuals as one of their own and who would command their confidence. We shall have to await a resurgence of political awareness. . . .

Soon afterward, Einstein visited Lorentz and discussed his opposition to the establishment of an Institute of Intellectual Co-operation in Paris (see p. 69). Einstein, on the eve of an extended tour of South America from which he might not have returned in time to attend the next session of the committee, asked Lorentz to deliver a strongly worded declaration in his stead in which he would voice Einstein's particular objection to the appointment of a Frenchman as the institute's head.

Lorentz declined to co-operate. He felt that the appointment of Julien Luchaire was not only a foregone conclusion but an excellent choice. Further, by running counter to the majority view, Einstein would only weaken his influence within the committee.

Earlier in the year, on January 6, 1925, Einstein had supported a communist appeal for the release of political prisoners which appeared in the Berlin newspaper *Welt am Abend:* [16]

Every decent German must see the necessity of granting amnesty to political prisoners, if only because such an act will contribute to the cause of peace and progress. Men everywhere must feel a sense of shame that political justice is not, as yet, objective or free of prejudice. Political amnesty means fulfilling the elementary obligation of justice.

During this same period, Einstein sent the following message to Count Arco to express his good wishes for the successful work of a Russo-German society of which he was a board member.[17] Einstein said:

I am delighted to send you my warmest greetings, particularly since I am unable to accept the kind invitation to join you on your visit to Moscow. Scientific work, which I dare not interrupt at this time, makes it impossible for me to make the trip now.

May I take this occasion to express my pleasure at your efforts to re-establish, despite the current political struggles, broad cultural ties across the frontiers. I feel honored to be a member of your board and I wish your group the best of success.

In the spring of 1925 Einstein left for South America, a journey which was again without political purpose. He met statesmen, scientists and prominent members of the Jewish communities and was appropriately honored wherever he went. He ran into Otto Buek, who had signed the Nicolai Manifesto with him in 1914 (see p. 6) and who was now a correspondent for an Argentine newspaper.[18] A diary, kept by Einstein during part of the journey, records this entry made in Buenos Aires on April 17, 1925:

Strange people, these Germans. I am a foul-smelling flower to them, and yet they keep tucking me into their buttonholes.

In another entry, of April 30, 1925, he speaks of a visit to Montevideo and the resemblance of the Uruguayans to the Dutch and Swiss:

The devil take the large countries with all their conceit! Had I the power, I should divide them all into little ones.

In an interview which he gave to a *New York Times* correspondent in Berlin and which was published in *The New York Times* on May 17, 1925, Einstein spoke of the Far East: [19]

I think the coalition of Russia, Japan and China is quite natural. Because these countries are in a defensive position against the more advanced economies of Western Europe and the United States, they cannot do otherwise. In determining the conduct of nations, circumstances are stronger than political intentions; I feel certain that the development of the more advanced countries will be much endangered unless they pursue a cautious and farsighted policy.

The people of the Far East should not be deprived of the possibility of a decent standard of living. . . . Japan is now like a great kettle without a safety valve. She has not enough land to enable her population to exist and develop. The situation must somehow be remedied if we are to avoid a terrible conflict.

As for Russia, it seems to me that, in her economic conditions, she has made little progress under her present form of government and has little to show of a constructive nature. Industrial production has declined. But as to the future of Russia, it is, as in all things, difficult as well as unwise to prophesy.

Asked about the League of Nations, Einstein said:

Germany is mistaken in believing that the League of Nations is completely without merit. The League has admirable intentions, and some work of value has been accomplished. But I wish to emphasize my conviction that, unless the United States exerts its stabilizing influence, the League of Nations, as well as other international organizations, cannot continue to exist.

Contrary to his expectation, Einstein was able to go to Geneva for the Fifth Session of the Committee on Intellectual Co-operation,

July 27–30, 1925. His friend Lorentz was in the chair this time. Einstein warmly endorsed a plan which sought to establish an international university for the education of statesmen, diplomats, politicians, political writers, professors of political science and the like. The minutes contain a summary of his views:

. . . It was notorious that instruction in history was not at the moment conducted on sufficiently broad lines. Historians are not sufficiently free of prejudice and it seemed impossible to attain impartiality. It was necessary to establish some kind of institution which should be entirely free and to appoint men according to their qualifications and without regard to their opinions.

The committee, however, felt that the plan went beyond what it could then consider, though it authorized that the matter be further studied. Einstein also showed interest in the committee's work in "preventing the formation of erroneous opinions in regard to different countries," to be accomplished by direct exchanges among the National Committees on Intellectual Co-operation which the committee of the League had either recognized or helped to organize in various countries. It was considered particularly important to demand the modification of offensive passages in textbooks. Einstein took a more active part in the discussion of certain scientific projects of the committee, such as the proposal to create an international meteorological bureau as well as the project which sought to standardize scientific and archaeological terminology.

The treaties of Locarno between Germany and the victorious Allied Powers were concluded in the fall of 1925 and marked an important step toward international reconciliation; for the first time since the war, Germany met with the other Western Powers on an equal footing. Two months later the *New York Evening Post* and the *Philadelphia Public Ledger* asked Einstein to comment on these events for a special New Year's Day issue. Einstein replied: [20]

The Locarno Pact is proof that responsible government circles in Europe are now convinced of the need for a European organization on a supranational basis. The pact makes it obvious that traditional prejudices and war-born resentments have so weakened the population as to allow governments to dare take such a step. I hope and trust that the people themselves, once the blessings of this new understanding are felt, will follow suit and appreciate the astonishing progress that has been made.

The Institute for Intellectual Co-operation had meanwhile been authorized by the League and began to function late in 1925. As Lorentz had foreseen, its director-general was to be Julien Luchaire, a Frenchman, who had played an active role in establishing the committee as well as the institute. On October 24, 1925, Luchaire wrote Einstein asking his help in persuading the German Government to designate an official delegate to the institute.[21] The relationship between the committee and the institute was apparently not as clearly defined as some members, including Einstein, might have wished. This later became a matter of contention. Officially the institute was to be the committee's executive organ, but there was a gentleman's agreement that the director-general would always be a Frenchman; also, the institute's funds were in fact supplied by the French Government. When the institute was officially inaugurated in Paris on January 16, 1926, Einstein forthrightly voiced his misgivings in a banquet speech, which he delivered in halting French from German notes: [22]

For the first time during the past year, the leading statesmen of Europe have made a number of important decisions which clearly resulted from the realization that our continent cannot fully recover unless the latent power struggle among the existing countries comes to an end. The political organization of Europe must be strengthened, and an attempt must be made to abolish divisive tariff barriers. But these great objectives cannot be achieved merely by official treaties among the nations. What is particularly necessary is that the minds of the people be receptive to the concept of international co-operation. We must try to awaken in them a sense of solidarity that will not stop at the frontiers, as it has done in the past. It was with this end in mind that the League of Nations created the Committee on Intellectual Co-operation. This committee was meant to be decidedly an international and entirely nonpolitical agency for the purpose of restoring communication among the intellectuals in various countries who had become isolated by the war. It is a difficult task; for alas! it must be admitted that scientists and artists, at least in the countries with which I am familiar, are guided by narrow nationalism to a much greater extent than are men of affairs.

The committee has been meeting twice a year. To make its work more effective, the French Government has now decided to create and maintain a permanent Institute for Intellectual Co-operation. This generous act deserves the gratitude of all of us.

It is always an easy and satisfying job to praise things one approves of and to ignore those which one regrets or disapproves. But honesty is essential if our work is to progress. I shall not hesitate, therefore, to voice some criticism while, at the same time, expressing my good wishes on the establishment of the institute.

Almost every day I have had occasion to notice that the greatest obstacle to the work of our committee is lack of confidence in its political impartiality. Everything must be done to strengthen people's confidence and everything should be avoided that might impair it.

Now, when the French Government organizes and maintains, out of public funds, an institute as a permanent organ of the committee, with a Frenchman as its director, the detached observer can scarcely avoid the impression that French influence predominates in the committee. The impression is deepened by the fact that the chairman of the committee has so far also been a Frenchman. The men in question enjoy the highest reputation. They are esteemed and respected everywhere. Nevertheless, the impression of French predominance remains.

Dixi et salvavi animam meam [I have spoken and redeemed my soul]. I hope with all my heart that the new institute, by constant interaction with the committee, may succeed in promoting their common goals and may eventually gain the confidence and recognition of intellectual workers throughout the world.

Einstein, writing to his wife from Paris on January 17, 1926, spoke of an incident which involved an appointment to the board of the institute:

. . . Yesterday morning I had a furious battle with the Fascist member of the committee [Alfredo Rocco, Mussolini's Minister of Justice]. He will remember it as long as he lives. . . .

Rocco had been appointed to the committee and to the board of the institute in Paris on nomination by the League Secretariat, to succeed a known opponent of Mussolini. The members of the committee apparently had little voice in these appointments, and some of them, including Einstein and Mme. Curie, felt that political considerations played far too great a part. Mme. Curie opposed Rocco on the ground that members of the committee should be independent of their governments. Einstein's opposition was based on ideological reasons. Indeed, contrary to his habits, he went so far as to propose himself, in Rocco's stead, as a member of the board. But the opposition to Rocco collapsed when it became clear that Italy might threaten to withdraw from the League of Nations over the incident, and Rocco assumed a seat on the committee.

Romain Rolland's sixtieth birthday fell on January 29, 1926. Einstein was among those invited by Maxim Gorki, Stefan Zweig and Georges Duhamel to contribute to a *Liber Amicorum*, a "Book of Friends," to be presented to Rolland in celebration of his birthday.[23] Einstein prepared the following statement:

REVERED MASTER:

Only once did I see you in the flesh [see pp. 14 ff.]: you were still shaken by the initial impact of the European crisis, you appeared a lonely visionary amid the tortured masses, frustrated by your inability to bring them light and deliverance. You were never satisfied to use your rare creative talent to communicate only with the finer spirits; you have longed to help all human beings who are victims of self-inflicted misery.

The rude masses are driven by dark passions that dominate both them and the governments which represent them. They rant and rave, but succeed only in making one another yet more miserable. And, by and large, they seem to create all this misery without experiencing inner conflict. Those few who do not share in the coarse emotions of the masses and who, unaffected by such passions, cling to the ideal of brotherly love are faced with a more difficult situation. They will be rejected by their fellow men and persecuted like lepers unless they either act in a manner inconsistent with their conscience or cravenly conceal their real thoughts and feelings. You, revered master, have not kept silent. You have fought and suffered and given succor to those in distress, great soul that you are.

This age which has so deeply shamed us Europeans has made it

$$\frac{\partial^2 \varphi_{\mu\nu}}{\partial x_\alpha^2} = 0 \qquad \varphi_{\mu\nu} = \frac{\partial \varphi_\mu}{\partial x_\nu} - \frac{\partial \varphi_\nu}{\partial x_\mu}$$

$$\frac{\partial}{\partial x_\nu}(\Box \varphi_\mu) - \frac{\partial}{\partial x_\mu}(\Box \varphi_\nu) = 0 \quad \Big| \quad \Box \varphi_\mu = \frac{\partial \psi}{\partial x_\mu} \quad \Big| \quad \Box \overset{x}{\varphi} = 0 \quad \Box \psi = \psi$$

$$\boxed{\varphi_\mu = \overset{x}{\varphi_\mu} + \frac{\partial \psi}{\partial x_\mu}}$$

$$\frac{\partial \varphi_{\mu\nu}}{\partial x_\alpha} + \frac{\partial \varphi_{\nu\alpha}}{\partial x_\mu} + \frac{\partial \varphi_{\alpha\mu}}{\partial x_\nu} = \qquad \frac{\partial \varphi_{\mu\nu}}{\partial x_\nu} = \frac{\partial^2 \varphi_\mu}{\partial x_\nu^2} - \frac{\partial}{\partial x_\mu}\left(\frac{\partial \varphi_\nu}{\partial x_\nu}\right)$$

$$= \frac{\partial^2 \overset{x}{\varphi_\mu}}{\partial x_\nu^2} + \frac{\partial}{\partial x_\mu}(\Box \psi) - \frac{\partial}{\partial x_\mu}(\Box \psi) - \frac{\partial}{\partial x_\mu}\left(\frac{\partial \overset{x}{\varphi_\mu}}{\partial x_\mu}\right)$$

$$e_1 = -\mathcal{L}_{11}\frac{di_1}{dt} - \mathcal{L}_{21}\frac{di_2}{dt} + p_1 = 0$$

$$e_2 = -\mathcal{L}_{12}\frac{di_2}{dt} - \mathcal{L}_{22}\frac{di_2}{dt} + p_2 = 0$$

$$\overset{x}{\varphi_\mu} = \overset{xx}{\varphi_\mu} + \frac{\partial \chi}{\partial x_\nu}$$

$$\Box \varphi_\mu'' = 0 \qquad \Box \chi = 0$$

$$\Box \overset{x}{\varphi_\mu} = 0 \qquad \overset{x}{\varphi_\mu} = \psi_\mu + \frac{\partial \psi}{\partial x_\mu}$$

$$\varphi_{\mu\nu} = \frac{\partial \varphi_\mu^x}{\partial x_\nu} - \frac{\partial \varphi_\nu^x}{\partial x_\mu}$$

$$\frac{\partial g_{\nu\alpha}}{\partial x_\mu} + \frac{\partial g_{\mu\alpha}}{\partial x_\alpha} - \frac{\partial g_{\alpha\mu}}{\partial x_\mu} = 0$$

Verehrter Meister!

Ein einziges Mal habe ich Sie mit leiblichen Augen gesehen, als Sie noch unter dem ersten Eindruck der europäischen Katastrophe standen, ein Einsamer, Sehender, mit der grossen Masse unsäglich Leidender, unglücklich in dem Gefühl, nicht Licht schaffen und erlösen zu können. Nie haben Sie vollen Trost darin finden können, durch Ihre hohe Kunst und Ihr Wort auf die fein Organisierten zu wirken; Sie wollen der menschlichen Kreatur helfen, die in selbstgeschaffenem Elend schmachtet.

Die rohen Massen tun ihr Werk aus dunklen Leidenschaften heraus, und die sie verkörpernden Staaten, die sie völlig unterthan sind: Sie rasen in ihrem Wahn und treiben einander in tiefes Unglück. Aber sie vollbringen im Grossen Ganzen all diese Gräuel ohne inneren Zwiespalt. Die Wenigen jedoch, welche an den rohen Gefühlen der Massen nicht teilnehmen, sondern unbeeinflusst von diesen Leiden-

Einstein's original draft of his statement prepared for Romain Rolland's sixtieth birthday, January 29, 1926; he had used the sheet of paper before for scientific work. (See page 79) obvious that even noble minds may fall prey to barbaric sentiments. I do not believe that noble human attitudes flourish any better in the universities and academies than in the shops of the unknown, silent, common man.

There is one community, however, that counts you among its most illustrious luminaries. It is the community of those who are immune to the pestilence of hate, who seek to abolish war as the first step toward the moral regeneration of mankind and who view this task as incomparably more important than the special interests of their own particular state or nation.

The Eighth Session of the Committee on Intellectual Co-operation in Geneva, July 26–29, 1926, was probably a frustrating experience for Einstein. The minutes record a great deal of discussion but give little evidence of fruitful results. The question of correcting offensive passages in textbooks came up again, but it was decided that a national committee did not need to give any reasons when rejecting a request for such changes from any other national committee. Einstein agreed with the Rumanians, who suggested that copies of such requests by a national committee were to be sent regularly to the International Committee, which would assemble a reference file for consultation by any other national committee; however, for fear of treading on sensitive feelings, the Rumanian suggestion was not accepted. There was further inconclusive discussion as to whether it was compatible with the independence of a committee member to receive instructions from his government. Einstein's vote on the question was in the negative. There was equivocation on the earlier proposal to create an international school of higher political studies. Einstein pressed for a positive vote but was told that some of the major universities already had a somewhat international character and that the committee should limit itself to emphasizing such existing opportunities. Einstein also urged that action be taken to facilitate international travel by students and professors, who often encountered passport difficulties, but this was held to lie within the province of the national committees.

Even on purely scientific questions the committee was reluctant to take a forthright position. Despite Einstein's insistence on a clear-cut plan, the proposal for establishing an international bureau of meteorology was taken out of the hands of the subcommittee of which he was a member and referred to the League Council. The committee did little better with the plan to standardize scientific terminology, which Einstein had also supported.

In January 1927 the President of the Association of German Universities sent Einstein reprints of editorials about him that had appeared in the association's bulletin. He attempted to justify the republication of these press reports, all of them critical of Einstein, by explaining that it was the policy of the association to present all viewpoints, even when members were involved and mentioned by name. Further, the association did not necessarily identify itself with any of these statements. The letter received from the association bears Einstein's handwritten draft of a reply:

I am indifferent to what you publish about my person. I have repeatedly observed, however, that reports about international relations made to the academic community reveal a lamentable absence of objectivity. Unfriendly views expressed by foreign learned societies are recorded and friendly gestures are ignored, all of which only serves to foster a synthetic animosity among academic people. While responsible political leaders in Germany and France work for reconciliation, which they recognize as necessary in the interest of European culture and industry, the academic community continues to be paralyzed by petty considerations of prestige, thereby retarding the inevitable course of events. I hope this will soon change. It would, indeed, be unfortunate if the next academic generation were obliged to acknowledge the failure of our generation to comprehend the great task of its time.

Einstein, who had recognized the menace of Fascism at an early date, was keenly aware of the threat which its increasing strength presented to the peace of the world when Mussolini consolidated more and more his power over Italy and when Fascist tendencies became evident elsewhere in Europe. Whenever there was an opportunity, Einstein raised his voice against the Fascist menace. Early in February 1927, Henri Barbusse, the French writer, addressed himself to Einstein since he was "one of those who command attention among that group of great men of integrity who have risen to combat and arrest the encroaching barbarism of Fascism." Barbusse urged Einstein to become a contributor to a new international review, then in the process of development, and to sign a public appeal, which Einstein immediately consented to do. The appeal, called *Aux Esprits libres,* declared that, although eight years had passed since the end of war, the climate of war continued; that in almost every country basic freedoms were threatened by policies of violence; and that, because Fascism threatened to destroy all the freedoms gained during centuries of desperate struggle and sacrifice, the moment was ripe "for all those who have any intellectual and moral influence in the world community to unite in a committee whose aims will be to oppose and destroy the barbaric wave of Fascism."

Three months later, Einstein received an invitation from the Austrian Count R. N. Coudenhove-Kalergi, founder of the Pan-European Union movement, to attend and address the union's second congress, to be held in Brussels in October. Einstein replied on June 25, 1927: [24]

I am sure you know how very close to my heart is the cause of European unity; I am even more interested in all efforts to consolidate the various unity movements.

Partly because of lack of time and energy, partly because I would not have any original contribution to make to the cause you represent, I regret not being able to accept your invitation to participate in the Second Pan-European Congress.

May I take this occasion to suggest that you do all in your power to effect a merger of the two rival Pan-European movements. This would, without doubt, be a great step forward!

The rival movement to which Einstein referred was probably the Congress for a United States of Europe, which, under the auspices of the International League for Human Rights, had also convened in Brussels, just a year before. The formation of this congress was originally suggested by the German League for Human Rights, of which Einstein was still a member and which was instrumental in establishing the International League in 1922. It will be recalled that the Bund Neues Vaterland (as the German League for Human Rights was originally named) had been uncompromisingly in favor of a European Union ever since its inception in the fall of 1914.

Einstein attended the Ninth Session of the Committee on Intellectual Co-operation in Geneva, July 20–27, 1927. As he wrote to his wife from there:

. . . The committee is congenial, though predominantly oriented toward the French—a people I confess to liking better than "our people." I suppose I shall not live to see the merger of these diverse worlds; yet, it gives me pleasure to watch them both, without feeling that I belong to either. . . .

Einstein was appointed to represent the Geneva Committee on an Advisory Committee of Intellectual Workers established by the International Labor Office. He voiced reservations about the controlling position which had been given to the various National Committees on Intellectual Co-operation. He referred to the matter in a letter to Lorentz of September 13, 1927: [25]

. . . I am particularly troubled by a resolution which we adopted to the effect that in every sovereign state there should be but *one* national committee with which the Geneva Committee is to maintain continuing and official relations. There would be no objection, were it not for the fact that, unfortunately, in many countries a policy of oppression is practiced against national minorities. These minorities are excluded from the national committees and, thus, actually kept out of touch with the Geneva Committee. This fact renders us in Geneva guilty of complicity with regard to the existing policy of cultural oppression, the abolition of which we should consider one of our main tasks.

Perhaps you are unaware of how bad the situation is in many European countries. For your information, I am sending you a memorandum on the situation of oppressed Balkan peoples. I was deeply moved by it.

Do you think the committee might reverse its decision? The fact that the League is a representation of governments rather than of nationalities cannot justify a policy which recognizes only local committees that represent governments. Further, it should be mentioned in this connection that the members of our own committee are not representatives of governments. It is, therefore, quite logical that we should concede the right of every cultural group in every country to form local committees which would be in continuous and official contact with our committee. This would, undoubtedly, create many difficulties; but to overcome such difficulties would in itself be a great achievement. I believe the very existence of such representative organs might mitigate many hardships endured by the various persecuted minorities.

At the July session in Geneva, Einstein, supported by Mme. Curie, also took exception to the growing tendency of the institute in Paris to act without the prior approval of the Geneva Committee. The official record indicates that he proposed the following resolution:

The institute is requested to consult the opinion of the committee before concluding arrangements or undertaking work which in fact might limit the power of the committee to make decisions. . . .

Mr. Rocco agreed. It should not be forgotten, however, that the committee met only once a year. In the interval, the governing body represented it, and in cases of urgency it was indispensable to allow the governing body a certain latitude regarding decisions.

Mme. Curie replied that her proposal was of a peaceful nature [to facilitate a constructive solution]. Professor Einstein and she quite understood the necessity of allowing the institute a certain measure of initiative, but desired to avoid the repetition of certain incidents when the committee might be forced to adopt a disagreeable attitude toward the governing body and the institute. Her proposal was not in the least a formal summons to desist. She had merely desired to draw the attention of the institute to the necessity of acting with prudence.

Professor Einstein agreed. The proposal was designed merely to ask the institute to be prudent. It would have to be carefully interpreted, but the director of the institute was quite capable of doing this. . . .

Professor Murray pointed out that the misunderstandings which had arisen had not been due to any fault in the regulations but to a series of accidents. He thought there was no need for the committee to adopt a resolution which might appear ungracious toward the governing body and the institute. The committee might content itself with recommending that these organizations take the greatest precautions within the limits of the present regulations. . . .

The chairman [Lorentz] . . . thought that there was no necessity to amend the regulations, for the discussion which had taken place would constitute the authoritative interpretation of them.

Mme. Curie and Professor Einstein said that, in these circumstances, they could withdraw their proposal.

There were other difficulties as well. The committee had sponsored some work by the International Institute of Bibliography in Brussels. A document it had printed was found to contain many errors, and the preface was considered discourteous to the League. Einstein opposed a plan under which the document would have been distributed with a covering letter disavowing the committee's responsibility, and his recommendation to halt distribution was adopted. His general attitude on the committee's work was well expressed in a letter which he addressed, on November 12, 1927, to the Prussian Minister of Education, in reply to a communication received from that official:

> . . . All of the resolutions adopted [at the Geneva session in July] will be published by the League of Nations. As the proceedings themselves are not public, it is doubtful whether members are permitted to report on them. . . .
>
> The committee, especially under its present chairman, Professor Lorentz, endeavors to function merely as an intermediary. In other words, it seeks to *promote* the formation of international organizations and general co-operation in scholarly fields, without itself assuming the leading role in such efforts. It has attempted to persuade the Paris Institute to follow the same general policy. . . .
>
> With respect to the participation of learned societies in countries which formerly belonged to the Central Powers, the committee and its chairman have successfully maintained that *co-operation in fact* is more important than *formal membership* in international organizations. I feel this attitude is worth emphasizing since it implies that the committee desires to eliminate all considerations of mere prestige and seeks only to serve the common cause. . . .

A few months later, the German Government also created a national committee, the German Committee for Intellectual Co-operation, the members of which were to be appointed by the government itself. Einstein, who became a member of the German Committee on March 26, 1928, attended only one more session of the International Committee in Geneva, the session of 1930. At this session, several proposals were submitted by the German Committee; they were submitted over Einstein's protest (see p. 107). The question of an alternate to Einstein, which had been a matter of concern from the beginning of his participation, was settled in 1926, when Einstein agreed that Dr. Krüss, the director of the Prussian State Library in Berlin, be appointed as his permanent deputy, both on the Geneva Committee and at the institute in Paris. In 1933, Dr. Krüss succeeded to Einstein's seat on the committee.

Sometime during 1927, Einstein again visited Paris. The *Berliner Tageblatt* published the following account of an incident that took place during the visit: [26]

Our Paris correspondent has sent us the text of an interview which Professor Einstein granted to a representative of the Radical Socialist newspaper *L'Oeuvre*. Since it appeared to give a rather inaccurate version of Professor Einstein's views, we communicated with him, requesting an authoritative account of the statements which he had allegedly made. Professor Einstein advised our correspondent that he had indeed received the representative of *L'Oeuvre*, in the hope that such an interview would serve the cause of international amity. Unfortunately, his views had been greatly distorted. Here is the text of the statement he gave to our own correspondent:

"The oft-cited 'German war spirit,' I said, was frequently exaggerated. Contrary to the view widely held abroad, not only the German Left, but even Rightist circles, especially those who are responsible for political and economic decisions, were animated by a sincere desire to come to an understanding with France. True, the term *pacifism* was not well liked in Germany since it was frequently considered synonymous with an unrealistic political philosophy. Nevertheless, the desire for a *rapprochement* with France was widespread in every stratum of the population.

"Queried on my attitude toward the League of Nations, I said that, with regard to the great problem of world peace, it could not be denied that the League had been a keen disappointment to many and, further, that people everywhere had sensed its failure to act at decisive moments with courage and good will. Yet, I felt that all well-intentioned people should support this first attempt at restoring order in the sphere of international relations; for, despite the existence of the League of Nations, the outmoded and dangerous formula of the European balance of power still exercised a harmful influence.

"When I pointed out that France, like other countries, had not yet reached a courageous decision on the disarmament problem, the interviewer contended that European disarmament was inextricably linked with conditions in Russia, a country still outside the European community of nations. In reply, I stated my firm belief that Russia had no aggressive intentions against any European country and that, further, the European countries could in no way use this argument to account for their failure to promote disarmament."

On December 17, 1927, Einstein wrote a brief note to Captain Hellmuth von Beerfelde of the Berlin Peace Movement:

You need not try to win me over to the idea of an organized campaign for war resistance. I am already wholeheartedly devoted to that cause and shall do all I can to support it.

CHAPTER FOUR

WAR RESISTANCE I

1928-1931

THE BELIEF THAT WARS would become impossible if a considerable number of citizens in the various countries of the world refused military service may have been implicit in Einstein's pacifist views at an early time. Yet, not until around 1928 does he appear to have explicitly supported the organized movement for individual war resistance which had grown considerably since the First World War. For the next five years, until Hitler seized power in Germany, this form of militant pacifism dominated Einstein's political thinking.

One of his earliest statements on war resistance was contained in his reply to an invitation received from the Women's International League for Peace and Freedom asking him to attend a study conference on gas warfare to be held in Geneva simultaneously with a meeting of the League of Nations Disarmament Commission. Einstein declined the invitation but, on January 4, 1928, sent a statement to the Women's International League to be used in whatever way they considered most useful:

. . . It seems to me an utterly futile task to prescribe rules and limitations for the conduct of war. War is not a game; hence, one cannot wage war by rules as one would in playing games. Our fight must be directed against war itself. The masses of people can most effectively fight the institution of war by establishing, in time of peace, an organization for absolute refusal of military service. The efforts made in this direction in England and Germany appear rather promising. I believe that nothing your league could do would be more constructive than to utilize its resources to support such movements, even if so radical a policy were to lose you some of your members.

During the same period (January 1928) Einstein accepted election to the Board of Directors of the German League for Human Rights, which was then the most outstanding pacifist movement in Germany and a leader in the fight for civil liberties.[1] Einstein further crystallized his views on refusal of military service in four statements made during the latter half of 1928. Late in August 1928, a manifesto opposing military conscription was released; Einstein signed the manifesto together with almost seventy other outstanding pacifists from fifteen countries. To the No More War Movement in London,[2] the British section of the War Resisters' International, he sent a message on November 25, 1928:

I am convinced that the international movement to refuse participation in any kind of war service is one of the most encouraging developments of our time. Every thoughtful, well-meaning and conscientious human being should assume, in time of peace, the solemn and unconditional obligation not to participate in any war, for any reason, or to lend support of any kind, whether direct or indirect.

The American office of the League for the Organization of Progress, which had been founded in Paris in 1912 and was now located in Yellow Springs, Ohio, announced its intention of resuming publication of *Records of Progress,* a magazine that dated back to the Hague Conference of 1907. Einstein's contribution (of December 26, 1928) to the first issue was in reply to a request[3] that he answer the following question:

What institutions should actually be created to assure that the peaceful settlement of international conflicts, as provided for in the Kellogg Pact, will be more than a pious wish?

Einstein replied as follows:

Peaceful settlement of international conflicts will be possible only when all armies and all forms of compulsory military service are abolished. As a beginning, it would be most helpful if prominent citizens were to advocate the principle of refusing military service.

To the World Peace League in Geneva, Einstein contributed this statement for their "Golden Book of Peace":

No one has the moral right to call himself a Christian or a Jew if he is prepared to commit murder upon the instruction of a given authority, or if he permits himself to be used for the purpose of initiating or preparing such a crime in any way whatsoever.

In the spring of 1928 Einstein was afflicted by an illness which limited his activities for a number of months and made it impossible for him to attend the July session of the Committee on Intellectual Cooperation in Geneva. Yet, it was precisely during this period that Einstein was extremely active on behalf of the committee. As has been mentioned before, Einstein had been appointed the committee's representative on the International Labor Office's Advisory Committee of Intellectual Workers (see p. 85). When it was decided that German intellectuals should have a representative of their own on this body, Einstein's aid was sought in nominating a candidate of suitable stature. The question was one of some delicacy, since no less than three national organizations of intellectual workers existed in Germany, and agreement among them was essential; the wishes of the German Government also had to be considered.

Einstein himself was an honorary member of the smallest of the three organizations, which was socialist in orientation and the only one that could properly be termed a trade-union. This group promptly endorsed his nomination of a liberal Berlin economist, Professor Wichard von Möllendorff, who enjoyed international reputation. But the biggest of the three groups, a motley assemblage claiming almost half a million members, balked at this decision, and its ambitious head, the elderly Otto Everling, who was widely regarded as a reactionary, presented himself as a candidate. The situation was further complicated when Germany's Minister of Labor, a member of the Catholic Center party, advanced the candidacy of a college professor, a worthy but undistinguished friend and fellow party member.

During weeks of patient negotiation and correspondence with the government, the League of Nations, and union officials, which he conducted partly from his bed, Einstein was at first unable to compose these sometimes acrimonious differences. Circumstances, however, came to his aid. The Catholic Minister of Labor was succeeded by a socialist, and von Möllendorff was ultimately appointed by the International Labor Organization. But the victory proved to be only a temporary one; when von Möllendorff retired three years later, Everling succeeded him through back-door maneuvering, much to Einstein's dismay.[4]

The German League for Human Rights was by now publishing its own organ, *Die Menschenrechte.* Einstein wrote a special statement for the issue commemorating the tenth anniversary of the Armistice, November 11, 1928: [5]

The political apathy of people in time of peace indicates that they will readily allow themselves to be led to slaughter later. Because today they lack even the courage to give their signature in support of disarmament, they will be compelled to shed their blood tomorrow.

On December 20, 1928, he wrote to Edgar Ansel Mowrer, Berlin representative of the Chicago *Daily News,* presumably in response to a request for a New Year's statement:

I wish—

1. That the coming year may bring far-reaching international agreements for far-reaching disarmament on land and sea.
2. That the problem of international war debts may be solved in such a manner as to allow all European countries to exist without being compelled to sell their basic resources abroad.
3. That an honorable *modus vivendi* with the Soviet Union may be found, which would remove external pressure from that country and hence allow it to develop internally without interference.

The Women's International League for Peace and Freedom organized an International Conference on Modern Methods of Warfare and the Protection of Civil Populations which met in Frankfurt am Main, Germany, on January 4–6, 1929. Three hundred people attended, and papers were delivered by authorities from Germany, Sweden, Poland, Switzerland, England, France and Czechoslovakia. In agreeing to sponsor the conference, Einstein had written:

To me the killing of any human being is murder; it is also murder when it takes place on a large scale as an instrument of state policy.

Einstein's friend, the great physicist Paul Langevin of the Collège de France in Paris, drew up a declaration that was published with the conference proceedings and signed by many scientists, including Einstein: [6]

Science and technical skill are daily increasing the power of men to inflict injury on one another. By an automatic process, apparently beyond any partial regulation, scientific development has been used from its very beginning to perfect the art of killing. The Great War witnessed new methods of destruction, and, in the event of a new catastrophe, unprecedented horrors are involved because of the perfection of chemical and bacteriological weapons. This danger to civilization and the human race may very well throw doubt upon the moral value of scientific progress in the minds of people who were not revolted by the prospect of another war on the old lines.

The undersigned consider it their urgent duty emphatically to denounce the frightful danger threatening the whole of humanity, and in particular the more civilized nations, through these preparations for a new scientific warfare. As there can be no idea of limiting the development of science, the only alternative is to put a stop to war itself. It is indeed impossible to check the adaptation of thought to deed that life and a profound instinct impose increasingly upon us. Those who have devoted their lives to scientific research are grieved to see the results of their labors used for forwarding policies of violence. They, then, must be the first to fight against the danger that in spite of themselves they have helped to create.

Experience has shown that all international conventions that aim at limiting the application of science are inoperative: they introduce arbitrary distinctions, they do not go to the root of the evil; and nothing will prevent a nation from using all the resources that nature and science have put at its disposal.

The only efficacious action is to work for the suppression of war, to denounce the futility of seeking security in armaments, to proclaim with the utmost energy our conviction that the speedy establishment of international justice is a question of life and death for the human race. Public opinion must be convinced by organization and propaganda that peace and justice rest upon the common will of the peoples. Constant pressure must be exercised on the governments to create by agreement the necessary machinery.

For these reasons, and with this object in view, we, the undersigned, declare that our first duty is to protest against all war in principle, against the use that warfare makes of the best results of scientific work, and against the influence of all prejudices or interests which support the barbarous tradition of settling international difficulties by methods of violence.

On February 23, 1929, Einstein made the most concise and uncompromising of all his war resistance statements. It was in response to a request for a contribution to a symposium on the question, "What would you do if another war broke out?" sponsored by the independent Czech journal *Die Wahrheit:* [7]

I would unconditionally refuse all war service, direct or indirect, and would seek to persuade my friends to adopt the same position, regardless of how I might feel about the causes of any particular war.

More than a year later, in confirming the authenticity of this statement to a Dutch correspondent, Einstein wrote: "Although publication of the statement was suppressed in Prague by the censor, it found its way into newspapers of other countries. . . . I feel today exactly as I felt then and firmly believe that anyone who is serious about the preservation of our cultural values must adopt such a revolutionary position." This statement made Einstein the hero of militant pacifism throughout the world for years to come.

During all these years, Einstein ceaselessly pursued his scientific work. In February 1929, it was announced that he had formulated the first version of the Unified Field Theory,[8] in which the phenomena of electricity and magnetism were combined in a single set of equations, the reformulation and refinement of which were to occupy him until his death, more than twenty-five years later. On his fiftieth birthday, which came shortly after the announcement about the Unified Field Theory, on March 14, 1929, a profusion of gifts and good wishes were tendered him from all over the world. In New York, an Einstein Jubilee Committee held meetings to raise money for the Jewish National Fund. Einstein sent a message in which he said:

. . . Individuals do not matter. It is the work and the service of the community that count.

A draft of this message, which was found in his files and may not have been used, reads as follows:

You are celebrating a legend that bears my name. This is proof that, in spite of the catastrophic desire for power and luxury which characterizes our time, the eternal goals of the human spirit are not yet forgotten. This makes me very happy.

Einstein's files indicate again and again that not only was he approached by a great variety of people and causes but also that he lent his support freely, though not indiscriminately, as he was frequently accused of doing in later years. The following few examples, if not very significant in themselves, are nonetheless indicative of the multitude of causes in which he involved himself and also serve to illustrate the fact that he never lost sight of his main interests: peace, democracy and an independent homeland for the Jews.

In March 1929, Einstein agreed to serve on the board of the newly formed Jewish Peace League; and in April he prepared the following message for a special election issue of the British pacifist journal *No More War:*

The people *themselves* must take the initiative to see to it that they will never again be led to slaughter. To expect protection from their governments is folly.

On April 15, 1929, Einstein, with a number of other prominent Germans, protested the German Government's refusal to allow Leon Trotsky, exiled from the Soviet Union, to take up residence in Germany.[9] Two months later (on June 30, 1929), he wrote the Friends of the Soviet Union in Berlin:

Although I strongly disapprove of any anti-Soviet propaganda and of militarism, I cannot sign your appeal since it expresses political views which are in conflict with my own.[10]

Still later that year, on September 6, 1929, Einstein resigned his honorary chairmanship of the League against Imperialism and for National Independence, because it had attacked Jewish settlement work in Palestine.

In the early days after the First World War, Einstein had devoted much time (pp. 32 ff.) to attempts to seek objective clarification about the atrocities which the German Army allegedly committed during the war, chiefly in Belgium. At the time, the German Reichstag had appointed an investigating committee whose findings were published in 1927 in a five-volume White Book.[11] Since this publication actually amounted to an exoneration of the German Army, it prompted a retort from Professor Fernand Mayence of the University of Louvain, Belgium. In a pamphlet entitled *La Légende des Francs-Tireurs de Louvain,* Mayence sought to disprove the German contention that [in August 1914] Belgian civilians at Louvain had been summarily shot only because they had been caught sniping. After reading Mayence's pamphlet, Einstein spontaneously addressed a letter to him (October 29, 1928) and authorized its publication:

. . . I feel that you have made a great contribution to the cause of justice and international reconciliation by your attempts to offer precise information about those lamentable events to people who are of good will, but who have frequently been misled. I share your view that the bitterness which has accumulated for obvious reasons can be alleviated only by recognition of the truth, whatever it may be. I most sincerely hope that your work may make a serious contribution toward this noble objective.

Einstein's letter to Professor Mayence had repercussions in two different quarters. The secretary of the former Reichstag Investigating Committee protested mildly in a communication to Einstein, who tried to explain his own position in a personal meeting with him. On the other hand, Dom Norbert Nieuwland of the Abbey of Maredsous in Belgium, an eyewitness to the shootings at Dinant, Belgium, presented Einstein with additional material implicating the German Army. He advised Einstein that the German Post Office had banned Mayence's pamphlet from the mails, against which Einstein apparently filed an official protest. The outcome of these various contacts at first appeared hopeful. Einstein persuaded Professor Walther Schücking, a recognized scholar in international law and then teaching at the Institute for International Law at the University of Kiel, to meet with Dom Norbert for exploratory talks in May 1929, in Paris. A more formal meeting between German and Belgian Catholics, which took place a year later, was apparently inconclusive. In spite of affidavits signed by German eyewitnesses, the Belgians were unwilling or unable to concede that any Belgian had participated in the sniping. But, as Einstein said in a note to the secretary of the Reichstag Committee on March 31, 1931:[11]

. . . Although final clarification may not be attainable, common effort in that direction will help to improve the general atmosphere.

In July 1929 the editor of the *Christian Century* called on Einstein, who expressed deep admiration for Gandhi. Asked about his own pacifist views, Einstein said: [12]

My pacifism is an instinctive feeling, a feeling that possesses me; the thought of murdering another human being is abhorrent to me. My attitude is not the result of an intellectual theory but is caused by a deep antipathy to every kind of cruelty and hatred. . . .

Among the cases around which the German League for Human Rights conducted broad public campaigns was that of Josef Jakubowski, a Russian prisoner of war who had stayed on in Germany as a farm hand. In 1925, Jakubowski was sentenced to death for the murder of his own child, a crime allegedly committed to evade payment of alimony. After his execution, the League, in the course of a long and bitter struggle, proved that Jakubowski was innocent and that his trial had been marked by prejudice. The real culprits were ultimately brought to justice. In July 1929, Einstein, together with Heinrich Mann, Arnold Zweig and other notables, headed a public campaign to raise funds for a Jakubowski Fund to enable the League to continue fighting against miscarriages of justice and, particularly, against capital punishment.[13]

During that same month (July 11, 1929), Einstein addressed a confidential letter to Germany's Foreign Minister, Gustav Stresemann, which indicated that his early misgivings about the International Institute for Intellectual Co-operation in Paris (see pp. 69 ff.) had not been allayed.

. . . The fact that neither Germany nor England participate [in financing the institute] cannot fail to overemphasize the influence of France, a fact which is not conducive . . . to international solidarity.

I am convinced that, were Germany to contribute annually an amount of about 40,000 marks, the institute would promptly appoint a German assistant director who might exert considerable influence . . . if someone could be found whose ability and interest in promoting the idea of international solidarity were such that he would gain the confidence and respect of the institute . . . England would feel obliged to follow Germany's example, particularly in view of the present political constellation there.

It appears from Einstein's files that his suggestion was not acted upon by the German Government. As early as 1922, Einstein was invited to become a member of the board of the République supranationale, a pacifist group seeking to establish a new kind of minorities law under which anyone could renounce his citizenship without losing the privilege to live and work in a given country. The purpose of this group is not very clearly described in the material available. But Einstein seems to have been well informed about it. When the invitation to join its board was received in 1929, he replied as follows (August 19):

The policy suggested by the République supranationale does not appeal to me. States are not organized merely for the purpose of waging wars. They constitute local organizations which attempt to find solutions to highly important economic and cultural problems. If it were really possible, formally and legally, to separate the majority of the people in a given area from the state which is established there it would result either in the destruction of basic organizational values or in complete disfranchisement of the majority. This seems to me almost like advocating universal castration to prevent the transmission of hereditary diseases.

Einstein's friend, the French mathematician Jacques S. Hadamard (himself an avowed pacifist), in a letter dated September 16, 1929, took sharp issue with the decision for complete nonparticipation in wars which Einstein had announced in his statement for the Czech journal *Die Wahrheit* earlier that year. Hadamard cited a good deal of historical evidence to show that countries refusing to defend themselves against aggression did not thereby prevent aggression, and that aggressors were not deterred either by opposition in their own country or by the pressure of world opinion. And what about the League of Nations? Should it also be restrained from using force? Hadamard considered the Geneva Protocol of 1924, in which an attempt was made to define aggression, a significant step on the road to peace. Reluctant to oppose Einstein on such an important problem, he had withheld from publication an article written even before he had known about Einstein's declaration, pending clarification of their disagreements. On September 24, 1929, Einstein mailed a reply to which he sometimes referred in later years, after the change in his pacifist view caused by the Nazi victory in Germany:

I was very glad to receive your letter, first because it came from you, and then because it displays the great earnestness with which you are considering the grave problems of Europe. I reply with some hesitation, because I am well aware that, when it comes to human affairs, my emotions are more decisive than my intellect. However, I shall dare to *justify* my position. But let me first make a qualification. I would not dare preach to a native African tribe in this fashion; for the patient there would have died long before the cure could have been of any help to him. But the situation in Europe is, despite Mussolini, quite different.

The first point I want to make is this: In a Europe which is systematically preparing for war, both morally and materially, an impotent League of Nations will not be able to command even moral authority in the hour of nationalist madness. The people in every country will insist that their own nation is the victim of aggression and will do so in perfectly good faith. . . . You cannot educate a nation for war and, at the same time, make its people believe that war is a shameful crime.

My second point: I admit that the country which decides not to defend itself assumes a great risk. However, this risk is accepted by society as a whole, and in the interest of human progress. Real progress has never been possible without sacrifices.

My third point: While the risks are great, they are not necessarily fatal. Since Germany, after four years of exhausting warfare, did not suffer more permanent damage than she actually has, a European country which does not even engage in war will certainly not suffer more than Germany actually did.

My fourth point: As long as nations systematically continue to prepare for war, fear, distrust and selfish ambitions will again lead to war.

My fifth point: We cannot afford to wait until the governing classes in the various countries decide voluntarily to accept interference with the sovereign power of their nation. Their lust for power will prevent them from doing so.

My sixth point: Public declarations by prominent personalities, who enjoy the respect of the man in the street, to the effect that their country should not engage in any warlike or even military action, will constitute an effective weapon against the war spirit.

My seventh point: To wage war means both to kill the innocent and to allow oneself to be innocently killed. . . . How can any decent and self-respecting person participate in such a tragic affair? Would you perjure yourself if your government asked you to do so? Certainly not. How much worse, then, to slaughter innocent men?

To tell the truth, this last argument is, in my opinion, the strongest; at least, this is the way it affects me. As far as I am concerned, the welfare of humanity must take precedence over loyalty to one's own country—in fact, over anything and everything.

In November 1929, the two men met in Paris and discussed the issues on which they so seriously disagreed. Hadamard then prepared a statement which he submitted to Einstein before publication. He had narrowed down the area of disagreement to some extent. He quoted Einstein as having admitted it might well be that he was ahead of his time, but that there are things that must be said before their time in order to pave the way to the future. On the other hand, Hadamard stuck to his point that the very possibility of a country's gaining a victory without firing a shot would merely serve to advance despotism. Responding to a second request by Hadamard for an expression about the draft publication, Einstein wrote on August 9, 1930:

Of course, I read your statement at the time and had no objection to its publication. . . . But my views have not changed. If, in the event of war, it is possible to declare the government of a given country "guilty," certainly those are not guilty who must risk their lives. I remain as convinced as ever that the only hope lies in rejecting the concept of war as a means of settling disputes. If those who, by their accomplishments, are considered leaders of their nations should publicly proclaim their unconditional opposition to war, such an attitude would swiftly spread among the whole population. I do *not* believe that, given the present circumstances, the risks which must be accepted in order to attain that objective would be too great.

A businessman and veteran of World War I wrote Einstein from a small German town in November 1929, suggesting that the growing drift toward nationalism among continental veterans' organizations might effectively be counteracted by a solemn meeting on the old battlefields of groups of veterans from various countries. Under the impact of a remarkable book, by the Englishman Ralph H. Mottram, *The Spanish Farm*, which eloquently exposed the futility and monstrosity of war, the correspondent merely restated a proposition which he had originally made five years earlier.[14] Einstein replied on November 28, 1929:

I believe that your suggestion is wonderful and capable of realization. . . . I shall try indirectly to establish certain contacts which may help in the execution of your plan. You will hear from me again; please feel free to call on me.

Einstein replied to a further letter from the veteran on January 1, 1930:

I believe you did well in addressing yourself to [H. G.] Wells, indicating that both [R. N.] Coudenhove [-Kalergi; see p. 84] and myself had approved of your scheme. I should not like to see the matter placed in the hands of a general. . . . I wish your endeavor every success.

Whether this initiative ultimately led to the formation of an international veterans' organization has not been established.

On January 16, 1930, Einstein formulated answers to three questions about disarmament, submitted to him by the editor of the Transocean News Agency at Berlin.[15] Einstein's statements were published in *The New York Times* of January 21, 1930, in a special dispatch over his own name:

Q: Do you believe that a country, by adopting total or partial disarmament, would act irresponsibly or may even endanger its very existence?

A: It is generally recognized that the policy of maintaining large armaments, pursued by all powers, has proven most harmful to humanity. I assert, moreover, that, under existing conditions, no country would run any real risk by adopting unilateral disarmament. If this were not so, countries which are now inadequately armed or not armed at all would be in an extremely dangerous and precarious situation. This, however, is not the case. I am convinced that those who have a selfish economic or political interest in armament production and in the expansion of the military establishment are using their alleged concern over the armaments of other countries merely as a tactical pretext.

Q: Do you believe that any progress toward disarmament achieved by the countries participating in the present London Naval Conference would set an example to mankind?

A: I am convinced that the first really successful step toward disarmament would exert a profound educational influence and would make it incomparably easier to take the second and third steps. For such an initial arrangement among the participating nations would make it more difficult for them to intimidate members of parliament by voicing concern over national security, as has been done in all countries in the past.

Q: Do you believe that armaments are economically advantageous and that countries would suffer economic hardship by disarmament?

A: Production of armaments can never be an economic asset to a country as a whole. It always implies the unproductive use of human and material resources. Besides, conscription for military service of men in their productive years curtails the productive potential of the country's economic sector, not to mention the moral damage which a people suffers from material and spiritual preparation for war.

Leo Szilard, a physicist who worked with Einstein in Berlin and who, in 1939, was to be associated with Einstein in the initial steps toward the production of atomic bombs (see Chapter IX), had conceived of an international scheme for peace. It was submitted to H. Noel Brailsford (journalist and author) in England in the spring of 1930. The new group contemplated by Szilard was to be an international organization of intellectuals, chiefly scientific workers, prepared to act together, across frontiers, to realize peace and disarmament through international government. Brailsford was uncertain about the merits of Szilard's project and inquired of Einstein about the extent of his own support of the scheme. Einstein replied on April 24, 1930:

. . . Szilard is associated with a group of decent and able young men, mostly physicists, who sympathize with his ideas. But as yet no organization of any kind has been created . . . I consider Szilard a fine and intelligent man who is ordinarily not given to illusions. Like many people of that type, he may be inclined to exaggerate the significance of reason in human affairs. . . . I am not clear about the prospects for Szilard's plan. More importantly, there does not seem to exist a powerful, cohesive element which could make a group of such select individuals really effective. However, one should not remain completely inactive in the face of such vital issues while those who are greedy and obsessed by power increasingly ravage the face of our planet.

When Einstein was asked to attend and address a World Congress for International Peace through Religion, at Berne, Switzerland, he declined, not without adding some outspoken comments (May 23, 1930): [16]

I regret not being able to attend your congress. I should have been particularly anxious to attend since I keenly feel that the co-operation of religious organizations in the work for peace should be obtained. . . . Had I been able to address your congress, I would have said that, in the course of history, the priests have been responsible for much strife and war among human beings; they have much to atone for. They have usually been the slaves of the organized powers of hate to which they only rarely offered any resistance. I would not have pleaded with them; I would merely have reminded them of their plain duties as human beings. . . .

When, in May 1930, the No More War Movement in England asked for a contribution to its organ, *The New World*, Einstein wrote:

You have asked me how I feel about the relationship between science and war. Science is a powerful instrument. How it is used, whether it is a blessing or a curse to man, depends on man himself and not on the instrument. A knife is useful to the lives of human beings, but it can also be used to kill.

The solution of our problems cannot come from science; it can only come from man himself. As long as human beings are systematically trained to commit crimes against mankind, the mentality thus created can only lead to catastrophe again and again. Our only hope lies in refusing any action that may serve the preparation or the purpose of war.

A few months later, in another statement on the same theme, Einstein said: [17]

Science ennobles anyone who is engaged in it, whether a scholar or merely a student. The technological applications of science, moreover, serve to liberate man from monotonous physical labor. Indeed, only science has made it possible to abolish slavery.

Yet science cannot liberate us from the scourge of war. Science is a powerful instrument that can enhance or destroy life. Nothing can save us from the horrors of war but man's firm resolve to abolish it, and his unconditional refusal to allow his energies to be misused for an evil cause. Let us be mindful of Luther's dictum:

"There is no measure but that ye must be reasonable."

On May 30, 1930, the Women's International League for Peace and Freedom, following the ratification of the Kellogg-Briand Pact outlawing war as an instrument of national policy, published a manifesto for world disarmament.[18] Einstein was one of the first signers, together with Bertrand Russell, Stefan Zweig, Thomas Mann, Jane Addams and Ivan Pavlov. The English text read:

Scientists and technicians throughout the world have brought evidence:

That scientific methods of warfare have rendered national defense and protection of civilian populations illusory; and

That a new war would mean simultaneous annihilation of a large part of the population by fire, poison gas and chemicals.

Whole nations are in peril!

Do you know the meaning of a new war which would use the means of destruction science is ceaselessly perfecting?

Do you know that in the future war will no longer be profitable to anyone, since not only arms, munitions and food depots but all important industrial centers would be targets of attack? This would bring about total destruction of industries.

Do you know that bombing squadrons could simultaneously destroy cities like London, Paris, New York and Berlin?

Do you know that poison gas can destroy not only the human organism, instantly or after unspeakable suffering, but that it can penetrate the depths of the earth, poisoning soil and water for long periods of time?

Do you know that fire bombs, by means of chemical processes, can achieve temperatures of 3,000° C., thus destroying all life that might have escaped before the effects of poison gas?

Despite official assurances of peace, the danger of war throughout the world has never been more serious nor the problems involved more complex. Will people allow their governments to prepare for such wars of annihilation?

Peoples of the world: unite and testify to your desire for peace by demanding universal disarmament!

War is already renounced [this is a reference to the Kellogg Pact]; let us now demand the renunciation of armaments.

The undersigned men and women, whether in political parties or outside of them, are convinced:

That the present armament policies do not furnish any safety to the peoples of the world and, in fact, lead all nations to economic disaster;

That this policy makes a new war inevitable;

That in the future every war will be a war of extermination;

That the declarations of peace in behalf of governments remain futile as long as these governments keep on delaying disarmament, which should be the logical sequel to renouncing war.

The undersigned therefore demand universal and total disarmament and urgently request their governments to give their delegates to the next disarmament conference formal instructions to critically examine all proposals for disarmament, already made or newly received, originating from any source whatsoever; and to take all measures to ensure the swift realization of world disarmament.

The denial of American citizenship to Rosika Schwimmer, Hungarian-born pacifist who refused to swear that she would bear arms, provided Einstein with an occasion to state his views even more forcefully than he had done before. On July 3, 1930, he wrote to the Women's International League for Peace and Freedom: [19]

I feel that Mrs. Schwimmer has made a valuable contribution by the position she adopted and that she deserves the full support of all true humanitarians.

While it is true that governments represent the will of the people, the people are still under the spell of outmoded traditions of military duty. World peace, so urgently needed, will never be achieved unless the best minds actively oppose the organs of authority and the real forces behind authority. Those who are convinced that this step is necessary have the duty publicly to announce and defend their convictions even if they thereby incur the ill will of the existing authorities. Success will come only when a sufficient number of influential people have the moral courage to adopt such an attitude.

It is a revolutionary attitude. But men have never freed themselves from intolerable bondage, frozen into law, except by revolutionary action. Such action is inevitable in this case also. Much credit must be given Mrs. Schwimmer for having realized this and for having had the courage to accept the consequences of her actions.

Earlier in the year Paul Painlevé, President of the Governing Body of the International Institute for Intellectual Co-operation in Paris, had written to Einstein expressing serious concern over certain sweeping recommendations from the German Committee on Intellectual Co-operation, of which Einstein was a member. Einstein replied on April 9, 1930:

I am very glad that your letter provides me with the welcome opportunity to offer my views on the proposals of the German National Committee. To my deep regret and despite the express disapproval of the German Foreign Office, the proposals were adopted by the National Committee during a session at which only about half a dozen members of the board were present. The proposals are the work of Herr Krüss [see p. 87]; we were not advised of their content beforehand.

First, ahead of all concrete issues must come the firm desire to foster international co-operation and mutual trust which is essential to fruitful collaboration. The initiative taken by the German National Committee is not at all calculated to promote a spirit of mutual trust. Had they really desired to influence the future work of the institute, they should have sought some initial confidential discussions with the French staff, in clear recognition of the fact that the burden of the institute has so far rested almost exclusively on the shoulders of France. Such a gesture would have been all the more appropriate since, thus far, the contribution of the German group to the work of the International Committee on Intellectual Co-operation has been rather insignificant.

As for the substance, I know that, while I agree with certain critical remarks you voiced regarding the German proposals, I nonetheless feel compelled to *adhere uncompromisingly to the view that the institute must remain an indivisible unit*. Once segments of the institute are relocated in various countries—unfortunately, there is already one precedent—the significance of the institute as a body which is meant to further the development of a true international spirit becomes impaired. If the Committee on Intellectual Co-operation is to remain true to its high mission, we must not make any concessions to national vanity and jealousy, those evil hereditary maladies of European history.

I wish to use this opportunity to make one other remark: I have always regretted the fact that the institute was established in Paris and financed exclusively by French funds. Doubtless, this was done for noble reasons, but, in a time of so much political restlessness, it seems to me it was bound to give rise to strong suspicions. Even Mr. Luchaire, conducting the work of the institute in a truly exemplary spirit of international impartiality, could not altogether dispel these suspicions.

In my view, the cause of international friendship would be greatly served if the French group were to present the following proposal: to move the institute *in toto* to Geneva and have all countries contribute to its financial support under a quota system. In view of the great sacrifices France has made, such a proposal should not come from our side. However, were the French to make it themselves, I believe that such an act of self-abnegation would be gratefully welcomed and viewed by everyone as an important contribution to the cause of internationalism. However, such a proposal is likely to be accepted only in the course of time. Right now, I believe the most urgent task is the preservation of the institute's integrity.

The minutes of the last session in Geneva of the Committee on Intellectual Co-operation which Einstein attended, on July 23–29, 1930, make but scant reference to the bitter struggle over reorganization that must have taken place. Because Einstein was unable to attend the meetings of the executive committee, Herr Krüss, the alternate German member, substituted for him. Apparently to prevent Herr Krüss' membership on that committee, Mme. Curie consented, with Einstein's support, to be elected as Einstein's successor. Plans to reorganize the work of the institute were the subject of protracted discussions in which Einstein took the same position as in his letter to Painlevé. The propositions of the German National Committee were apparently not accepted in their entirety.

The only occasion on which Einstein took the floor for a lengthy statement came during the discussion of Painlevé's proposal that the committee concern itself with the question of elementary education. "The committee would not be fulfilling the hopes of public opinion if it did not interest itself in this question. While cognizant of the difficulties which would be encountered from political quarters, M. Painlevé was of opinion that they should be approached courageously. . . ."

M. Einstein strongly supported the observations of M. Painlevé and Mme. Curie on elementary education [the minutes continue].[20] A consideration of the program of work drawn up by the Committee of Enquiry gave the impression of a house in flames when, in endeavoring to save the furniture, no care had been taken to choose the most valuable pieces. In reality, to state it most simply, the problem in question was whether education as a whole should be considered as a means of furthering pacifist ideas.

M. Einstein was convinced, and his view was based on very reliable information, that, in studying this problem, the committee would have the support of the various member states. He believed that the committee should go forward without fear of being stopped even if it might be stopped later. In any case, do not let it give up before it has begun. This was the most important problem that could be studied. Were success obtained on this point alone, work of great importance would have been accomplished.[21]

In regard to the "problem of different cultural groups coexisting in the same territory," it was evident from an examination of the actual situation of European, and not only from extra-European, peoples that the different levels of culture in the ethnic minorities constituted presently one of the most serious problems and were detrimental to European relations. M. Einstein believed it to be the committee's duty to bring this point to the attention of all of

Europe. If the committee put everything else aside and dealt only with this problem and the problem of elementary education, it would have embarked upon a program of considerable size. . . .

Despite the fact that his views had prevailed to some extent, Einstein left Geneva apparently quite disillusioned about the work of the committee. To Albert Dufour-Feronce, a League undersecretary who previously had been an official of the German Foreign Office, he wrote: [22]

. . . If I have decided to go no more to Geneva, it is because experience has taught me that, unfortunately, the committee as a whole seems to lack the determination necessary to achieve real progress toward improving international relations. From my observations it would seem that the committee has merely wanted to create a semblance of activity. In this respect, I feel, it has on the whole been even worse than the League.

It is precisely because of my profound desire to give whatever help I can toward the establishment of an international arbitrating and regulative authority that I feel compelled to resign from the committee.

By creating "national committees" which would form the only channel of communication between the Geneva Committee and the intellectual community in each country, the committee gave, in fact, its blessing to the policy of oppression of cultural minorities. This constitutes a deliberate denial of its function: that of lending moral support to all national minorities in their struggle against cultural oppression.

In the matter of combating chauvinist and militarist trends in education in the various countries, the attitude of the committee has been so halfhearted that one can no longer expect any serious effort in this vitally important sphere.

Further, the committee has steadfastly refused to give moral support to those personalities and organizations which have pledged their wholehearted support to help create an international order based on law and directed against militarism. The committee has never made an attempt to resist the appointment of members whom it knew to advocate the very opposite of the principles which it should be their duty to support.

Since you will surely appreciate my decision well enough from these few remarks, I shall not want to bore you with further arguments. It is certainly not my responsibility to draw up an indictment; I merely wished to explain my position. Had I seen any hope at all in the committee, you may be sure I would have acted otherwise.

Apparently this letter was not considered an official resignation; almost two years later, on his return from America, Einstein found letters inviting him to sessions of the committee and institute sessions to be held in July 1932 in Geneva. He replied, on April 20, 1932, that he had assumed his term of office had expired in 1931, adding that he did not believe he was the person to do useful work on the committee.

Before Dr. Krüss was to replace him, Einstein was to have one further, important association with the International Institute of Intellectual Co-operation in Paris, an open exchange of letters with Sigmund Freud. Despite his disappointment at the time of his resignation from the committee, the occasion of the League of Nation's tenth anniversary in 1930 prompted Einstein to make the following statement: [23]

I am rarely enthusiastic about what the League of Nations has accomplished or has not accomplished, but I am always thankful that it exists.

Many years later he described the Committee on Intellectual Cooperation to one of his biographers in these terms:

Despite its illustrious membership, it was the most ineffectual enterprise with which I have been associated.

In October 1930, under the title of "The World As I See It," Einstein published another statement of his *Weltanschauung*, in the *Forum and Century*.[24] Only one paragraph of this widely reprinted statement is of interest here, the paragraph in which Einstein describes his attitude toward militarism:

. . . This brings me to the worst outgrowth of herd life, the military system which I abhor. I feel only contempt for those who can take pleasure marching in rank and file to the strains of a band. Surely, such men were given their great brain by mistake; the spinal cord would have amply sufficed. This shameful stain on civilization should be wiped out as soon as possible. Heroism on command, senseless violence and all the loathsome nonsense that goes by the name of patriotism—how passionately I despise them! How vile and contemptible war seems to me! I would rather be torn limb from limb than take part in such an ugly business. I happen to think highly enough of mankind to believe the specter of war would long since have disappeared had the sound common sense of the people not been systematically corrupted by commercial and political interests operating through the schools and the press. . . .

Romain Rolland wrote to Einstein on September 30, 1930, soliciting a contribution to a "Golden Book" to be presented to the Hindu poet Rabindranath Tagore on the occasion of his seventieth birthday the following May. Tagore had recently visited Einstein, and the two had held a widely publicized philosophical colloquy.[25] Einstein replied on October 10, 1930:

I shall be glad to sign your beautiful text and to add a brief contribution. My conversation with Tagore was rather unsuccessful because of difficulties in communication and should, of course, never have been published. In my contribution, I should like to give expression to my conviction that men who enjoy the reputation of great intellectual achievement have an obligation to lend moral support to the principle of unconditional refusal of war service. . . .

On October 12, 1930, Rolland replied that the contribution suggested by Einstein seemed very appropriate. However, the people ought to be told that refusal of war service might entail great sacrifice and martyrdom. "In our harsh society," wrote Rolland, "martyrdom is almost always a necessary stage through which reason must pass in order to advance. . . ."

During the years of his active life, Einstein signed a number of manifestoes which he did not draft himself. These documents not only illustrate some of the public issues in which Einstein was vitally interested; they are also an indication of the many efforts to achieve a saner world by the most illustrious minds in the interwar period. Einstein lent his support probably to none of those documents with greater enthusiasm than to the manifesto that was released on October

12, 1930, and represented an appeal against conscription and the military training of youth. It was signed by Einstein, Tagore, Romain Rolland and many other fighters against wars, including Jane Addams, John Dewey, Upton Sinclair, Sigmund Freud, Auguste Forel, Thomas Mann, Stefan Zweig, Selma Lagerlöf, H. G. Wells and Bertrand Russell. It was sponsored by the Joint Peace Council, a loose confederation or advisory committee embracing the Quakers, the Fellowship of Reconciliation, the War Resisters' International, the Women's International League for Peace and Freedom and several other pacifist groups. The manifesto read as follows: [26]

The governments of all countries have at long last officially acknowledged that the peoples of the world are entitled to peace. In the Paris [Kellogg-Briand] Pact those governments have repudiated war as an instrument of national policy.

Nevertheless preparation for war continues. There is a particularly stark contrast between the peace declarations of governments and the maintenance and extension of military training of youth.

Military training takes two forms: In many countries legal conscription exists; in others, while nominally voluntary, training is imposed on a wide scale by moral or economic pressures. Furthermore, all governments claim in the name of national defense the ultimate right to demand war service from their citizens, men and women.

We believe that everybody who sincerely wants peace should demand the abolition of military training of youth and should help abrogate the right of governments to impose conscription upon their citizens. Conscription places the individual entirely at the mercy of military powers. It is a form of slavery. The peoples' unquestioning acceptance of this slavery only illustrates its insidious effect.

Military training is the education of the mind and body in the technique of killing. It is education for war. It is the perpetuation of the war mentality. It thwarts the growth of man's will for peace. The older generation commits a grave crime against the younger generation if in schools, universities, official and private organizations, youth are educated, often under the pretext of physical training, in the science of war.

Under the terms of peace treaties, the defeated countries were enjoined to abolish military training as well as conscription. It is time that the peoples themselves, not only in the defeated countries but throughout the world, took at last the initiative to do away with both military training and conscription.

If governments fail to recognize the depth of man's revulsion to war, they must be prepared to face the opposition of those for whom loyalty to their own conscience and to mankind is supreme. Let the peoples of all countries adopt as their goal: "No more militarization! No more conscription! Education for humanity and peace!"

On November 30, 1930, Einstein left Berlin on the first of what were to be three successive yearly visits to the California Institute of Technology at Pasadena. The ocean voyage afforded him some welcome rest, despite the fact that even aboard ship he was besieged by the press as never before. In a fragmentary but outspoken diary he commented on his princely stateroom:

December 2, 1930 . . . The excessive and pretentious attention makes me uncomfortable. By accepting so much unnecessary consideration I feel like an indirect exploiter of labor. . . .

December 3, 1930 . . . Every member of the crew behaves with such dignity and simplicity that one feels odd about one's own unpolished manners. Once again, Southampton impressed me with England's might. Everything goes on quietly and serenely. . . . Even the reporters practice reserve! Honor to whom honor is due. A single "no" is enough. The world can learn much from them—but not I who still dress carelessly, even for the holy sacrament of dinner. . . .

As the ship drew nearer to America, Einstein noted:

December 10, 1930 . . . Countless telegrams, giving the ship's radio operators a hectic time. The fat jolly Dutchman translates everything into English. . . .

The "fat jolly Dutchman" was Hendrik Willem Van Loon, American historian and artist, whom Einstein met on board. The arrival in New York the following day is described as:

. . . worse than the most fanciful anticipation. Just off Long Island hordes of reporters swarmed aboard. . . . Then a host of photographers rushed at me like hungry wolves. The reporters asked particularly inane questions to which I replied with cheap jokes that were received with enthusiasm. I almost forgot about the two broadcasting companies. One carried my message to the American people. For the other I improvised a pretty little parable: I was Jacob and not quite sure whether I had got the right wife (broadcasting company). Thus I pleased them both and, thanks to Else's [Mrs. Einstein's] shrewd management, earned $1,000 for the welfare fund. By noon I was dead. . . .

This was the message Einstein broadcasted from shipboard in New York harbor: [27]

As I am about to set foot again on United States soil, after an absence of ten years, the thought uppermost in my mind is that this country, today the most influential on earth because of the peaceful work that is being done here, constitutes a bulwark of the democratic way of life. Here, everyone stands up proudly and jealously for his civil rights. Everyone, irrespective of birth, has the opportunity, not merely on paper but in actual practice, to develop his energies freely for the benefit of the community as a whole.

Your country has demonstrated, by the work of its heads and its hands, that individual freedom provides a better basis for productive labor than any form of tyranny; whenever men are inspired by a healthy pride in their society, they feel a responsibility to make sacrifices for its sake. The sense of solidarity one finds in the American people is the basis for your firm belief in a great international community of all nations and cultures. This belief has led to the creation of cultural institutions whose blessings extend to all countries of the world.

Your country possesses the power to help defeat the specter that menaces our age: militarism. Your political and economic position is so powerful today that, if you are serious in your endeavors, you can break the tradition of war from which Europe has suffered throughout its history and from which the rest of the world has also suffered, even if to a lesser degree. Destiny has placed this historic mission in your hands. By fulfilling that mission you will build an enduring monument to your country and your generation.

Inspired by these hopes, I salute you and the soil of your country. I eagerly look forward to renewing old friendships and to broadening my understanding in the light of what I shall see and learn while I am among you.

During the next five days Einstein was subjected to an intense round of speech-making, press conferences, meetings, ceremonies, sight-seeing, visits to estates, operas and concerts.[28] He met philosophers, publishers, politicians, scientists, and Jewish and Zionist leaders. He was taken to see his sculptured head on the portal of New York's Riverside Church. He received the keys of the city at a crowded City Hall ceremony at which Mayor James J. Walker and President Nicholas Murray Butler of Columbia University spoke. He delivered an address at a mass meeting in Madison Square Garden in celebration of the Jewish festival of Hanukkah. He shook hands with Arturo Toscanini, Fritz Kreisler and Rabindranath Tagore. Hindu visitors bowed their heads to the ground before him, Zionists exclaimed, "You belong to us," singers kneeled before him. He was glad to be able to spend the nights in his quiet quarters on board ship, where guards protected him from importunities.

A climactic point in Einstein's career as a militant pacifist came on December 14, 1930, when he spoke at a meeting in New York's Ritz-Carlton Hotel, under the auspices of the New History Society. The speech was delivered extemporaneously,[29] and when the interpreter originally designated proved unequal to the task, Mrs. Rosika Schwimmer (see p. 106) volunteered to translate Einstein's remarks into English:

When those who are bound together by pacifist ideals hold a meeting they are usually consorting only with their own kind. They are like sheep huddled together while wolves wait outside. I believe that pacifist speakers face this difficulty: they ordinarily reach only their own group, people who are pacifists anyhow and hardly need to be convinced. The sheep's voice does not reach beyond this circle and is, therefore, ineffectual. That is the real weakness of the pacifist movement.

Genuine pacifists, those whose heads are not in the clouds but who think in realistic terms, must fearlessly endeavor to act in a manner which is of practical value to the cause rather than remain content merely to espouse the ideals of pacifism. Deeds, not words, are needed; mere words get pacifists nowhere. They must initiate action and begin with what can be achieved now.

As to what our next step should be, I should like you to realize that under the present military system every man is compelled to commit the crime of killing for his country. The aim of all pacifists must be to convince others of the immorality of war and rid the world of the shameful slavery of military service. I wish to suggest two ways to achieve that aim.

The first has already been put into practice: uncompromising war resistance and refusal to do military service under any circumstances. In countries where conscription exists, the true pacifist must refuse military duty. Already, a considerable number of pacifists in many countries have refused and are refusing, at great personal sacrifice, to serve a military term in peacetime. By doing so, it becomes manifest that they will not fight in the event of war.

In countries where compulsory service does not exist, true pacifists must publicly declare in time of peace that they will not take up arms under any circumstances. This, too, is an effective method of war resistance. I earnestly urge you to try to convince people all over the world of the justice of this position. The timid may say, "What is the use? We shall be sent to prison." To them I would reply: Even if only two per cent of those assigned to perform military service should announce their refusal to fight, as well as urge means other than war of settling international disputes, governments would be powerless, they would not dare send such a large number of people to jail.

A second line of action for war resisters, which I suggest, is a policy which would not involve personal involvement with the law. That is, to try to establish through international legislation the right to refuse military service in peacetime. Those who are unwilling to accept such a position might prefer to advocate legislation which would permit them, in place of military service, to do some strenuous or even dangerous work, in the interest of their own country or of mankind as a whole. They would thereby prove that their war resistance is unselfish and merely a logical consequence of the belief that international differences can be settled in ways other than fighting; it would further prove that their opposition to war could not be attributed to cowardice or the desire for personal comfort or unwillingness to serve their country or humanity. If we declare our willingness to accept work of a dangerous nature, we shall have advanced far on the road to a more peaceful world.

I further suggest that pacifists of all countries start raising funds to support those who would want to refuse military service but who cannot actually do so for lack of financial means. I, therefore, advocate the establishment of an international organization and an international pacifist fund to support the active war resisters of our day.

In conclusion, may I say that the serious pacifists who want to accomplish peace must have the courage to initiate and to carry on these aims; only then will the world be obliged to take notice. Pacifists will then be heard by people who are not already pacifists; and once they are listened to, their message is bound to be effective. If they are too restrained, their voices will continue to reach only those in their own circle. They will remain sheep, pacifist sheep.

Einstein's speech was greeted by pacifists with great enthusiasm, first in America and then throughout the world. Indeed, it established him as one of the outstanding international heroes of pacifism. He received many congratulatory messages, and in the ensuing months buttons with the legend "2%" began to blossom from the lapels of young men on American streets and campuses.

Einstein's "Two-Per-cent Speech" drew one reaction that may not have come to his attention. On February 16, 1931, H. Runham Brown, Honorary Secretary of the War Resisters' International in England, addressed an inquiry to Einstein's friend Romain Rolland:

1. Do you share Einstein's view that refusal to accept any war service constitutes a practical means for abolishing war?

2. Do you feel that those who personally refuse such service should receive the support of all who wish to put an end to war?

In his reply to H. Runham Brown, on February 20, 1931, Rolland stated[30] his belief that refusal of all participation in war, direct or indirect, was an "obligation of conscience" and that he entirely agreed with Einstein, as his actions during the First World War had demonstrated.

. . . But if you raise the question as a practical matter rather than as a moral obligation, I think Einstein's approach is indeed controversial. War will by no means be abolished if "two per cent of the population of the world refuse to fight." Einstein seems to overlook the fact that the technique of war has changed since 1914, and is still changing. The tendency has been to employ small armies of technicians who know how to run air squadrons armed with gas and bacteriological torpedoes and other weapons of mass destruction. In such circumstances it becomes a matter of complete indifference to governments whether two or ten per cent of the population refuses military service. Governments would not even need to throw war resisters into jail. Soldiers and noncombatants alike would be subjected to the deadly rain. . . .

Rolland went on to support social revolution as the only method for "abolishing the system that begets war." He did not abandon the principle of nonviolence and voiced words of high praise for Gandhi and for individual war resisters; but he felt that organized action on a large scale was necessary. He believed that isolated action would prove powerless to stay the danger of war already on the horizon.

In a farewell message to New York from shipboard on December 16, 1930, Einstein expressed satisfaction for having "had the opportunity to accomplish something of social value." Three days later the ship touched at Havana, Cuba, and he noted in his diary:

December 19, 1930 . . . Revolution, but no visible sign of it. Crisis on account of falling cane-sugar prices. Fine Spanish buildings. Academy, Geographic Society, always the same. Luxurious clubs side by side with naked poverty, mainly affecting the colored people. They huddle in windowless wooden shacks. But mild climate and bananas, happy faces despite severe unemployment. There is real suffering only when people are separated from the soil in rough climate. . . .

The passage through the Panama Canal impressed him deeply although he soon complained that "the passengers are becoming more and more annoying. There is no end to the business of taking photographs." And three days later: "Everyone has to have his picture taken with me. . . . The autograph business for the benefit of charity is flourishing. . . . They make a dreadful fuss over me [*haben einen Narren an mir gefressen*]. Where will it all end?"

Einstein was fascinated by California: "Everyone has a car . . . but some of the cars are positively antediluvian. Today I saw a wretched old rattletrap offered for $25! The shops are magnificent.

Everyone serves himself and pays for the things he has gathered in his basket. The packaging is ingenious, especially the cartons for eggs. Everyone recognizes me on the street and smiles at me." The cottage rented by Einstein as his residence he described as a "shingled gingerbread house."

On January 8, 1931, Einstein paid a visit to Hollywood, where a special screening of the motion picture *All Quiet on the Western Front*, based on the famous German novel by Erich Maria Remarque, was held for his benefit. "A fine piece," he commented, and expressed indignation that it was suppressed in Germany.[31]

> The suppression of this film [he said] marks a diplomatic defeat for our government in the eyes of the whole world. Its censorship proves that the government has bowed to the voice of the mob in the street and reveals so great a weakness that a reversal of policy must be emphatically demanded.

Later that year Einstein's statement played a part in the successful campaign which the German League for Human Rights waged to have *All Quiet on the Western Front* shown in Germany. On January 9, 1931, Einstein noted in his diary:

> Visit to Upton Sinclair. A splendid idealist and at the same time a man with a gay temperament. Favorable opinion of Russia because, he says, they educate the masses and bring them to life. . . .

On January 22, 1931, Sinclair, a resident of Pasadena, took Einstein to see the Russian director Sergei Eisenstein's film about Mexico; the bullfighting sequences filled Einstein with loathing.

Toward the end of the month Sinclair sent Einstein "some Russian statistics which have just come to me." He also pleaded for a statement on the occasion of the twenty-fifth anniversary of the *New Leader*, a socialist weekly magazine published in New York. Here are Sinclair's questions and Einstein's answers, given on February 3, 1931:[32]

> Q: What would you say is the duty of American workers in relation to the growing peril of armaments and the war danger?
>
> A: The United States is today the most powerful nation on earth. Hence, the success of the fight against militarism and the threat of war depends very considerably on how Americans react to these problems. This is especially true of the socialist parties;

it is hardly necessary to say why they should be particularly interested in the active struggle against war.

Q: Will you tell the American workers what you think about the spectacle of misery and starvation in a land which has such enormous powers of production as the United States? As you know, we are able to produce more food than we can market, and we run our factories at only a small percentage of their capacity; and yet many millions of people are in need of food and other primary necessities.

A: The present grave crisis in consumption is, in my opinion, a clear indication that the existing economic organization, as far as one can call it an "organization," is not suitable to provide adequately for the needs of the population. This statement, however, should not be considered an indictment; it should rather cause us to endeavor to organize the economy in such a way that the very existence of people will no longer be threatened by economic crises.

Einstein's reference to the political influence which the United States could and should enjoy in the world was not an isolated remark. It was a problem with which Einstein was obviously preoccupied in those days and which he emphasized frequently during his visit to America. His views seem best summarized in the last paragraph of an article which he prepared about the impressions gained while in the United States.[33] The statement, which was released in America on March 29, 1931, after his return to Europe, reads as follows:

The United States is today the most powerful among the technologically advanced countries of the world. Its potential influence on the development of the international political situation is almost incalculable. But America is a large country and its people so far have not taken much interest in the great international problems, chief among which is the problem of disarmament. This must change, if only in America's own interest. The last war made it obvious that there are no longer any barriers between the continents and that the destinies of all countries are closely interwoven. The people of this country must hence come to realize that they bear a great responsibility for the political development in the world. The role of the idle spectator is unworthy of America. In the long run it would be disastrous for all of us.

On February 2, 1931, the *Yale Daily News* published Einstein's answers to a long series of questions relating to the field of science.[34] Only one of the questions touched upon politics. In his reply, Einstein once again emphasized the view that science in itself could have no direct influence in building the international organization that was necessary if world chaos were to be avoided; man's determination alone could solve that problem.

On February 16, 1931, Einstein addressed several hundred students at the California Institute of Technology: [35]

. . . I could sing a hymn of praise about the progress made in the field of applied science; and, no doubt, you yourselves will promote further progress during your lifetime. I could speak in such terms since this is the century of applied science, and America is its fatherland. But I do not want to use such language. . . . Why does applied science, which is so magnificent, saves work and makes life easier, bring us so little happiness? The simple answer is that we have not yet learned to make proper use of it.

In times of war, applied science has given men the means to poison and mutilate one another. In times of peace, science has made our lives hurried and uncertain. Instead of liberating us from much of the monotonous work that has to be done, it has enslaved men to machines; men who work long, wearisome hours mostly without joy in their labor and with the continual fear of losing their pitiful income.

You may feel that this old man before you is singing an ugly song. I do it, however, for the purpose of making some suggestions to you. If you want your life's work to be useful to mankind, it is not enough that you understand applied science as such. Concern for man himself must always constitute the chief objective of all technological effort, concern for the big, unsolved problems of how to organize human work and the distribution of commodities in such a manner as to assure that the results of our scientific thinking may be a blessing to mankind, and not a curse.

Never forget this when you are pondering over your diagrams and equations!

On his way east, en route back to Europe, Einstein was greeted in Chicago by a peace delegation. He spoke to the group from the rear platform of his train (March 3, 1931): [36]

I am very glad that you have given me this opportunity to make a few remarks about the problem of pacifism. The developments of the last few years have once more indicated that we are hardly justified in assuming that the struggle against armaments and the spirit of militarism can be safely left in the hands of governments. Even the creation of pacifist organizations with large memberships will not bring us much closer to our goal.

I am convinced that the only way to be effective is through the revolutionary method of refusing military service. We need organizations in different countries to give material and moral support to all those who have the courage to resist war. This is the only way to make pacifism a vital issue and to inaugurate a vigorous campaign that will attract men of strong character. It is a fight not sanctioned by law, but one which must be fought if people are to have the right to resist the demands of governments that they perform criminal actions.

Many who consider themselves good pacifists will not want to participate in such a radical form of pacifism; they will claim that patriotism prevents them from adopting such a policy. But, in an emergency, such people cannot be counted on anyhow, as we learned so well during the World War.

The next day, March 4, 1931, was another sixteen-hour ordeal for Einstein.[37] He was continually in the limelight, from his early arrival in New York to the midnight sailing for Europe. The Einstein party went straight to the ship, where a delegation from the War Resisters' League was waiting. Einstein repeated his Chicago statement, interpolating the following remarks:

The evidence of the last disarmament conferences shows that the governments are either unwilling or unable to obtain real disarmament. It is the people who must express their desire for disarmament if they really want it.

The pacifist movement in general is not dramatic enough in peacetime to attract great numbers of people. However, the fight against military service will have a dramatic impact because it will inevitably create a conflict by providing a direct challenge to our opponents.

If, in time of peace, members of pacifist organizations are not ready to make sacrifices by opposing authorities at the risk of imprisonment, they will surely fail in time of war when only the most steeled and resolute person can be expected to resist.

The socialist leader Norman Thomas was present at the shipboard reception and sought to elicit Einstein's impressions of America, which was then in the grip of an economic depression. Einstein replied:

It is easier to win over people to pacifism than to socialism. Social and economic problems have become much more complex, and it is necessary that men and women first reach the point where they actually believe in the possibility of peaceful solutions. Once this has been accomplished, they may be expected to approach economic and political problems in a spirit of co-operation. I would say that we should work first for pacifism, and only later for socialism.

In the afternoon Einstein moved to a hotel where he received an unending stream of callers, including Helen Keller. Reporters noted that he had greatly gained in poise and in the ability to handle himself as a celebrity. "Gone was the flustered and bewildered German scientist," one of them wrote, "who early in December first met a crowd of newsgatherers and cameramen . . . and then fled from them in dread. In his place today was a gentleman who was smilingly at ease." Even after speaking at a fund-raising dinner at the Astor Hotel given by the American Palestine Campaign, at which Rabbi Stephen S. Wise hailed him as a "monarch of the mind," Einstein's day was not over. More than seventy-five representatives of antiwar youth groups, many of them carrying signs, had gathered on the pier to honor him when he boarded ship. The formation of a Youth Peace Federation emerged later from this demonstration, and Einstein cabled:

I wish you favorable progress in the radicalization of pacifism. Only resistance to military service can bring success to the pacifist movement.

In a farewell telegram, President Herbert Hoover expressed his hope "that your visit to the United States has been as satisfying to you as it has been gratifying to the American people." On March 14, 1931, from Berlin, Einstein cabled a message of gratitude to the

American people. It appeared in *The New York Times* the following day:

As little as a fish understands water until removed from its element, just so little is man able to understand the peculiarity of his daily surroundings until he has sought contact with an environment where the existing customs, standards and aspirations are very different from those which he encounters in his daily routine.

To me the United States revealed itself as just such a new world of commanding interest. It is a world of confraternity, of co-operation, just as our Europe is one of individualism. In America, every man finds the sphere in which he can effectively function. . . .

Far more sympathy and esteem than I deserve awaited me in the United States—indeed, more than any one individual might be worthy of—and I gladly seize this opportunity of recording my appreciation and gratitude.

During his visit to the United States, Einstein granted an interview to George Sylvester Viereck of New York, a spokesman for German causes. The thoughts which occupied him so much in those days are well summarized in that interview. Einstein is reported to have said: [38]

There is enough money, enough work and enough food, provided we organize our resources according to our necessities rather than be slaves to rigid economic theories or traditions. Above all, we must not permit our minds and our activities to be diverted from constructive work by preparations for another war. I agree with the great American Benjamin Franklin, who said that there never was a good war or a bad peace.

I am not only a pacifist but a militant pacifist. I am willing to fight for peace. Nothing will end war unless the peoples themselves refuse to go to war.

Every great cause is first championed by an aggressive minority. Is it not better for a man to die for a cause in which he believes, such as peace, than to suffer for a cause in which he does not believe, such as war? Every war merely enlarges the chain of vicious circles which impedes the progress of mankind. A handful of conscientious objectors can dramatize the protest against war.

The masses are never militaristic until their minds are poisoned by propaganda. I agree with you that we must teach them to resist propaganda. We must begin to inoculate our children against militarism by educating them in the spirit of pacifism. The trouble with Europe is that her people have been educated on a wrong psychology. Our schoolbooks glorify war and conceal its horrors. They indoctrinate children with hatred. I would teach peace rather than war, love rather than hate.

The textbooks should be rewritten. Instead of perpetuating ancient rancors and prejudices, we should infuse a new spirit into our educational system. Education should begin in the cradle. Mothers throughout the world have the responsibility of sowing the seeds of peace into the souls of their children.

It may not be possible in one generation to eradicate the combative instinct. It is not even desirable to eradicate it entirely. Men should continue to fight, but they should fight for things worth while, not for imaginary geographical lines, racial prejudices and private greed draped in the colors of patriotism. Their arms should be weapons of the spirit, not shrapnel and tanks.

Think of what a world we could build if the power unleashed in war were applied to constructive tasks! One tenth of the energy that the various belligerents spent in the World War, a fraction of the money they exploded in hand grenades and poison gas, would suffice to raise the standard of living in every country and avert the economic catastrophe of world-wide unemployment.

We must be prepared to make the same heroic sacrifices for the cause of peace that we make ungrudgingly for the cause of war. There is no task that is more important or closer to my heart.

Nothing that I can do or say will change the structure of the universe. But maybe, by raising my voice, I can help the greatest of all causes—good will among men and peace on earth.

CHAPTER FIVE

WAR RESISTANCE II

1931-1932

EINSTEIN GAVE MORE than moral support to the pacifist cause. On many occasions he translated his convictions on peace and other social issues into concrete action. In 1929, when death sentences were pronounced against anti-Jewish Arab rioters in Palestine, he supported the War Resisters' International in its effort to have the sentences commuted and cabled a plea to that effect directly to the High Commissioner for Palestine.[1] When later that year a young Finn, Arndt Pekurinen, was jailed for refusing military service, Einstein signed, jointly with others, a letter of protest to the Finnish authorities which the War Resisters' International had drafted.[2]

Einstein's support of this protest led to further correspondence which illustrates how persistent he was in the pursuit of a cause to which he had become devoted. When the Finnish Minister of Defense advised Einstein that the conscription law allowed the government to employ conscientious objectors for nonmilitary work under civilian control, Einstein replied as follows, on February 20, 1930:

> I thank you for your detailed letter of February 7, 1930. It shows that Finland has solved in truly dignified and exemplary fashion the difficult problem which confronts the state when an individual refuses military service.

Apparently this letter received wide publicity in Finland. It prompted a communication from Felix Iverson, Professor of Mathematics at the University of Helsingfors (Helsinki) and President of the Finnish Peace League, who suggested that Einstein had been misinformed by the Minister of Defense. Pekurinen had been given no choice but to be employed in work that directly or indirectly served military purposes. His actual assignment had been to serve in the Finnish Army's fire department, where he was charged with safeguarding large military installations and stores. On March 6, 1930, Einstein dispatched a third letter to the Finnish Defense Minister:

Friends in Finland have advised me that the letter in which I expressed my appreciation to you was based on false assumptions. Morality and fairness make it necessary that those who object to military service be employed only in work that has no close connection with military purposes. This was not true in the case of one of your citizens, A. Pekurinen. Hence the imposition of dishonorable punishment for his refusal of military service cannot be regarded as morally justifiable.

At about the same time, a number of defendants were hailed into court in Sofia, Bulgaria, for antiwar propaganda. They proposed Einstein as a witness for the defense, and he promptly wrote to the president of the court, on February 20, 1930:

. . . Of course the danger of war is ever present and will continue until we succeed in creating international guarantees against war. One specific source of danger today arises from the well-known conflict of interests that exists between certain circles and governments on the one hand and Russia on the other.

The fight against war is legal in all those countries which have any claim to true civilization, and it is always a worthy struggle. The persecution of war resisters is a shameful practice for any modern state; it can only mean that the state actually supports militaristic goals.

The manuscript draft of this letter contains a sentence that apparently was not included in the version actually dispatched:

I hereby declare that I myself have engaged in antiwar propaganda.

On August 5, 1930, Einstein submitted for publication a communication to the editor of the Copenhagen newspaper *Politiken* in which he advised the Danish people of his decision to award two special gifts, placed at his disposal, to war resisters: [3]

As you may know, the memory of the Danish composer Viktor Bendix and his wife, Rigmor Stampe, is honored each year by means of a "commemoration gift." This gift of 1,000 kroner is to be used for purposes or causes which these two personalities supported, regardless of whether single individuals or groups of people are involved. While the sum is modest, the symbolic meaning of the gesture, as an expression of protest, should not be underestimated.

The award should be given in instances where the state and society are considered guilty of neglecting human values—for example, their failure to develop outstandingly talented young people, or to pay tribute to an important social action which did not come to the public's attention; or when state and society are found to coerce their citizens, particularly through military and war service. From the point of view of unwritten moral law, such coercion must be considered illegal because it is incompatible with the conscience of a steadily increasing number of people of high ethical stature.

My views on this grave and burning issue are sufficiently well known, since I have made no secret, either privately or publicly, of my sense of outrage over officially enforced military and war service. I regard it as a duty of conscience to fight against such barbarous enslavement of the individual with every means available. I assume that the Bendix awards for 1929 and 1930 were placed in my hands because of a belief that I would make certain to have them used in the service of antimilitarist propaganda. The awards should encourage those who have announced their determination never to participate in any war, offensive or defensive, directly or indirectly; they should also be used in support of those who have actually been subject to persecution because of their refusal of military service. It has, therefore, been a particularly great satisfaction for me to give emergency assistance to two war resisters who, because of the strength of their conviction, served a harsh sentence of six years' hard labor, and help rebuild their shattered lives.

Through this gift, offered in the name of two high-minded personalities, a good cause may be served and, possibly, even greater things may be accomplished. I should like to let the Danish public know about it.

In his speech at the Ritz-Carlton Hotel in New York in December 1930 (see p. 116) Einstein made it a point to appeal for funds in support of war resisters, an appeal which did not go unheeded. The War Resisters' International immediately offered to set up an "Einstein Fund," [4] which Einstein made official in a message he sent to a meeting of the War Resisters' International held at Lyon, France, in August 1931. When Einstein, returning from the West Coast, passed through Chicago in March 1931, $200 was raised.[5] Yet, on May 11, 1931, Mrs. Einstein, in acknowledging a contribution from Mrs. Schwimmer, wrote:

. . . I could wish we had a larger fund. Every day or so, people who have gotten into trouble by refusing military service come to us for help. Word has gone around that we have a small fund for such purposes. Unfortunately, it has all been distributed, except for a few marks.

The effect of my husband's speeches in America is truly inspiring. The movement has made great strides.

Einstein entertained great admiration for the father of the Czechoslovak Republic, Thomas G. Masaryk, whose nomination for the Nobel Peace Prize he had endorsed nine years earlier. When the Czech journal *Die Wahrheit* asked Einstein for a statement to be included in a special issue on the occasion of Masaryk's eightieth birthday, he wrote:

Professor Masaryk is the living example of how one's love for one's own people can indeed be in perfect harmony with the outlook of a world citizen.

On April 13, 1931, Einstein wrote to President Masaryk directly:

After years of soul-searching and disillusionment over the failure of the disarmament conferences, I have become convinced that the world can be delivered from the scourge of war only by self-sacrificing men who refuse any and all military service. I consider it my duty to give such men whatever help I can and to try to organize an international association of like-minded people for their support.

The superior court of Brünn in your country has sentenced to a long prison term Mr. Přemysl Pitter, a man of high moral character who shares the antiwar sentiments just described.

Because of my deep admiration for you, whose great moral stature has so magnificently withstood the test of adversity, I feel impelled to suggest that you exercise your powers of executive clemency in this case. The esteem in which you are held by free men throughout the world stems from your human qualities rather than from your position as head of state; your action, therefore, would render a great service to the cause of justice and humanity.

Einstein received only a routine acknowledgment from the President's Chancellery; but a year later, a four-page handwritten letter arrived from Masaryk, which, unfortunately, was lost, apparently when the Einstein summer home near Berlin was raided by the Nazis in 1933.[6] Einstein's reply to Masaryk's letter is dated September 5, 1932:

I am deeply moved to learn how conscientiously you are wrestling with the knotty problem of resistance to military service. It is indicative of your deep feeling for humanity that you were good enough to write me on the subject at such length in your own hand. If all countries enjoyed the leadership of men such as yourself, the movement to abolish war would not appear as hopeless as, alas! it does today.

I find it hard to understand why so few people seem to regard it as shameful and unworthy of governments to coerce people into performing the very acts which the religions, taught and professed by those same governments, consider most evil—acts, moreover, that seriously imperil the very survival of world civilization.

Your letter was a rewarding experience and I thank you for it.

As a result of the bombing of the San Francisco Preparedness Day Parade in 1916, a California labor leader, Thomas J. Mooney, was sentenced to death, a sentence later commuted to life imprisonment. His case (and the similar one of Warren K. Billings) became a prominent issue among liberals, many of whom believed the two men innocent. Einstein became acquainted with the case while he was in California. After his return to Germany he sent Mooney the following message, dated March 18, 1931:[7]

I know full well what strange judicial conditions exist in California and how arbitrarily persons are treated who are repugnant to certain influential groups. I am also aware of the heroic struggle of a small minority in your country, where wealth wields even more power over public authorities than in Western Europe.

I am convinced that the energy of the American people will overcome this grave condition once the ill-informed masses become aware of its existence.

On June 2, 1931, Einstein followed this up with a direct appeal to Governor James Rolph of California in which he said:

I am deeply convinced that you, Mr. Governor, would perform a real service to the cause of justice if you were to grant these two men absolute pardon now that they have served fifteen years of grief.

Einstein also took part in the world-wide protest in the *cause célèbre* of the eight Scottsboro boys convicted in April 1931 in Alabama of having allegedly raped two women (one of whom later retracted the accusation). When he was advised that doubts had been voiced in America as to whether he had actually supported the convicted men, he wrote to the German economist Alfons Goldschmidt, on July 25, 1931:

. . . By way of documenting my participation in the protest on behalf of the eight Scottsboro Negroes, I hereby confirm that . . . I requested and authorized you to affix my name to the protest. . . .

Another case that engaged Einstein's attention in 1931 was the assassination of Dr. Milan Sufflay, a Croat scholar. Although the identity of the murderers was known, the Yugoslav Government apparently closed its eyes to the situation. Einstein, along with Heinrich Mann, the famous writer, signed a letter of protest under the auspices of the German League for Human Rights.[8]

A particularly famous case with which Einstein associated himself at this time in Germany revolved on the surface around the issue of academic freedom but had its roots in the pacifist movement and in the fight against war. The central figure in this case was Professor Emil J. Gumbel of Heidelberg University. Gumbel was an outspoken liberal and active pacifist. Since the end of the war Gumbel had been fighting, on the side of the truly democratic and republican elements in Germany, for faithful compliance with the Versailles Treaty and against the many reactionary *revanche* movements that had sprung up in those years. He became particularly well known through the publication of several books and pamphlets in which he documented the secret rearmament activities undertaken by Germany in violation of its treaty obligations, as well as the existence of Ku-Klux-Klan-like *Vehme* courts. These "courts" were secret tribunals, without any standing in law, which had been responsible for the murder of many liberals and pacifists who opposed a renaissance of reaction and war. Gumbel's activities in defense of the Republic were the cause of nationalist attacks upon him and his academic position for many years. In 1925, the Department of Philosophy of Heidelberg University, of which he was a member, adopted a resolution censuring Gumbel. Thereafter, the efforts to oust him from the university never ceased. His promotion, long overdue, was withheld. When finally, in 1931, the government took a hand in the affair and gave Gumbel a minor promotion, nationalist faculty and student elements, claiming that the government's action constituted a violation of academic self-government, were responsible for violent demonstrations. The case attracted international attention. In April 1931, the German League for Human Rights called a mass protest meeting in Berlin, in which Einstein participated. Here is the address which he had prepared, but which he did not find it possible to deliver: [9]

Although many academic chairs exist, wise and high-minded teachers are few and far between. There are many large lecture halls, but there are not many young people who genuinely thirst for truth and justice. Nature is generous in producing the average and mediocre man, but only rarely does she create someone who is distinguished by superior talents.

We are aware of this; there is little use to complain. Has this not always been the case, and will it not always be so? No doubt, this is true; and we have no choice but to acquiesce in what nature does. But there is also such a thing as the spirit of a given time, the mentality characteristic of a particular generation, passed on from one man to another, which places its distinctive mark on a community. Each of us must make an effort toward modifying that mentality to some extent.

Compare the spirit that animated youth in our universities a century ago with the spirit that prevails today. They believed in the betterment of human society; they had respect for honest opinion, and they possessed the kind of tolerance for which our great minds lived and fought. In those days men strove for that larger political unity called Germany. Then it was the students and the teachers at the universities in whom these ideals burned brightly.

Today, too, there exist people who are eager for social progress, who believe in tolerance and freedom of thought and who strive for a larger political unity of what is now called Europe. But, today, it is no longer the college students and university professors who embody the hope and ideals of men. Whoever observes men and times in a sober and dispassionate way must arrive at the same conclusion.

We are assembled today to take stock of ourselves. The occasion for our meeting is the case of Professor Gumbel. Inspired by an uncompromising sense of justice, Professor Gumbel publicized the details about a number of political crimes that have gone unavenged. He did so with devoted industry, high courage and exemplary fairness, performing through his books a signal service to our community. Yet this is the man whom the student body and a good many faculty members of his university are doing their best to expel.

Political passion must never be allowed to go to such lengths. I am convinced that anyone who reads Gumbel's books with an open mind will share my own impression of his work. Men like him are indispensable if we are ever to build a sound political framework for our society.

Let every man judge for himself, by what he himself reads, not by what others tell him! Then the case of Professor Gumbel, after so inglorious a beginning, may yet bear fruitful results.

In a letter to a colleague, Einstein gave still another estimate of the case: [10]

As a person I respect [Gumbel] even more highly. Both his political activities and his publications are characterized by a high sense of ethics. The conduct of the students toward him is one of the saddest symptoms of our time, which has little respect for the ideals of justice, tolerance and truth. What shall become of a people who brutally persecute contemporaries such as Gumbel and whose leaders offer no opposition to the common mob? . . . It is dreadful to mislead inexperienced young people out of selfish motives. If things continue in this way, we shall witness the red terror after having lived under Fascist tyranny.

Upon the suggestion of the War Resisters' International Einstein tried to help five Polish war resisters, showing once more his firm belief in the cause of refusal of military service. He addressed himself to military courts in the Polish cities of Brest and Warsaw (on November 6, 1932):

As a friend of justice and of human progress I feel compelled to appeal to you on behalf of several Polish citizens who, following the voice of conscience, have refused to do military service in your country. . . .

I am convinced that it is unworthy of a modern state to expose men to long and cruel persecution purely because of their refusal to accept obligations which, for good reasons, they consider immoral. There are some countries where such men, who are usually guided by the highest moral principles, are offered a possibility of complying with the dictates of their conscience without violating the laws of the land. England, even during the war, served as a shining example in this respect.

For the sake of justice and for the sake of Poland I implore you to see to it that prosecution of these men be dropped.

Throughout 1931, Einstein continued to issue public statements in support of war resistance. One such statement, dated April 17, 1931, was addressed to the German magazine *Jugendtribüne:*

Governments are far too dependent on the economic beneficiaries of the war machine to expect from them a decisive step toward the abolition of war in the near future. I believe serious progress can be achieved only when men become organized on an international scale and refuse, as a body, to enter military or war service. The peoples of the world must be made to realize that no government is justified in expecting its citizens to engage in activities which traditional morality considers criminal. What the Quakers have achieved on a religious basis must become the common conviction of all serious human beings.

On the eve of his departure for a month's stay in England, Einstein wrote to the Swedish Information Bureau on Questions of Peace and International Co-operation (April 30, 1931):

I am firmly convinced that a powerful international organization which systematically upholds the right to refuse military service and gives moral and material support to those who courageously practice such refusal would serve one of the most worthy causes in which human beings can be engaged in our time.

On the same day Einstein wrote to Kirby Page, editor of *The World Tomorrow* in New York,[11] who had reported to him on a poll of 19,000 American clergymen:

It speaks well for the American clergy that fifty-four per cent of those who answered your questionnaire indicated they would not participate in any future war. Only by taking such a radical position can we be of any help to the world, since governments are used to designating any war started by them as a war of defense.

It would be a big step forward if an international association of clergymen were organized which would publicly advocate refusal of military service and whose members would pledge themselves to act accordingly in the event of war. Considering the great moral influence of the United States in the world, an effort to organize such an association does not appear at all hopeless; it might lead to results of historic significance and would be a great tribute to those who initiated such a movement.

How seriously Einstein took this proposal may be judged from a coincident entry in the diary he kept during his visit to England:

. . . Resolved: I will attempt to unite the clergy of all nations behind the goal of legalizing the right to refuse military and war service.

Einstein apparently did not know that, for the past three years, an International Union of Antimilitarist Clergymen and Ministers had already existed. The union was one of several constituent groups of the Joint Peace Council with which Einstein later co-operated. A letter received soon after his return from England from Rabbi Leo Baeck of

Berlin provided Einstein with further opportunity to make his views known. Dr. Baeck advised Einstein that a letter from the World Conference for International Peace had requested him to ask Einstein to address a conference in Geneva, scheduled for August 1931, on the subject of religion and pacifism. Einstein replied to Baeck on July 10, 1931:

I scarcely need tell you how heartily I welcome any effort to mobilize the clergy for the pacifist movement. Nevertheless, to my sincere regret, I shall not be able to present to the conference the address requested of me. It has become impossible for me to attend such functions. There are too many, all of them important, for me to single out any one. For example, I am unable to attend the eminently important Congress of the War Resisters' International which will take place in Lyons this year. I must limit myself strictly to what can be accomplished at my desk.

Please excuse that I am not able to accept the invitation.

The following year, Einstein had extensive dealings with the International Union of Antimilitarist Clergymen and Ministers.

The visit to Oxford, England, in May 1931, for the purpose of delivering a number of lectures, was a stimulating experience in a new, sometimes alien environment. There were many meetings, dinners, banquets and the award of still another honorary degree. Yet he found time to engage in intimate contacts with his colleagues and to pursue his own scientific problems. Nor were world affairs neglected, as some of his diary notes indicate:

May 20, 1931: . . . In the evening, student meeting under the auspices of the League of Nations Association. For two hours they shot questions at me about Russia and the internal political situation in Germany.

May 23, 1931: . . . Met at long last pacifist students in a cozy old private home. One finds great political maturity among the British. How inadequate are *our* students by comparison!

May 26, 1931: . . . In the afternoon, visit by the War Resisters' International. Discussion about effect and dissemination of my speeches in America. The thing holds great promise. I must put all my energy behind it. Wonderful fellows; the basis is the English religious tradition. . . .

Another diary entry is reminiscent of a mishap that occurred to Einstein during his visit to Japan, when he borrowed a top hat so small that he had no choice but to carry it in his hand all day. On May 15, 1931, he noted:

> . . . My dress shirt simply would not button properly, with the result that my hairy chest peeked out almost every time I moved. I ransacked my bachelor's quarters, discovered needle and thread, and sewed up the thing to the point where I could just slip into it; and my appearance was now decent. . . .

Soon after his return from England Einstein, together with eight other prominent German pacifists, gave (on June 2, 1931) his consent and signature to a statement strongly opposing the Swiss militia system which was then being considered in other parts of Europe: [12]

> We the undersigned, active supporters of the German peace movement, view with concern the growing tendency within the international peace movement to drop the demand for the limitation of trained reserves, leading to the abolition of conscription, and to favor, instead, the principle of reducing the period of military training; the adoption of this principle would lead to a general acceptance of the Swiss militia system.
>
> We urgently request that, before recommending this course of action, you make a careful study of a system, such as the Swiss, which makes a soldier of every able-bodied citizen from his eighteenth year to the end of his life and provides every household with a gun. Our Swiss pacifist comrades, in the enclosed letter to the delegates of the League of Nations Assembly in 1928, contend that "to judge by the Swiss experience with the militia system, its introduction all over the world would simply mean a renewal of the war spirit among the nations and would make disarmament impossible. No more subtle way of preventing disarmament altogether could be found by an enemy of peace."
>
> The fact is that the shorter the period of military training, the bigger the number of recruits who can and will be subjected to it. This means that the militarization of the mind of a nation will be carried on to an extent hitherto unknown and will render illusory any hopes concerning progress toward peace. Besides, it is to be feared that the Central Powers will not acquiesce for any length of

time in the coexistence of the double system. Already the Austrian Parliament has adopted a resolution demanding that the Austrian Government take steps toward obtaining the permission of the Allied Powers to introduce military conscription in the form of a militia. We in Germany, who know conscription not only as a wartime measure but as a permanent institution with a decisive influence on the mind and life of the nation, would especially urge you, our British comrades, not to desert us in a struggle against a system which, though already shaky, may be riveted once more on the protesting masses. It is well to remember that it is not the peoples but the governments who wish to maintain it and that there is ample evidence of increased opposition to it as a system incompatible with the Kellogg Pact and its implications.

On June 13, 1931, Einstein wrote to an academic correspondent in Germany, in response to a communication which is not available in his files. Einstein's reply is so characteristic that it is meaningful even without reference to the nature of the inquiry:

Your purpose is excellent, your method totally inappropriate. In moral causes there is no such thing as organization, nor can there be any. That is why Buddha and Christ never founded any clubs.

One of the members of the War Resisters' International delegation that had visited Einstein at Oxford in May was its chairman, the British Member of Parliament A. Fenner Brockway. He published his impression of the meeting with Einstein in the July 1931 issue of *The New World:* [13]

. . . Professor Einstein agreed that it is the refusal of military service which is the important thing, but argued that if exemption can be obtained as a normal right in return for an offer of civil service, the tyranny of conscription would be broken.

As he sees the problem, there are two ways of resisting war—the legal way and the revolutionary way. The legal way involves the offer of alternative service, not as a privilege for a few, but as a right for all. The revolutionary way involves uncompromising resistance, with a view to breaking the power of militarism in time of peace or the resources of the state in time of war. The general conclusion of Professor Einstein was that both tendencies are valuable, and that certain circumstances justify the one and certain circumstances the other.

Professor Einstein surprised me by the strength of his conviction that the only peace societies that are worthy of support today are those which oppose all war without qualifications and insist upon complete disarmament by their own government, whatever other nations may do.

"There are so many fictitious peace societies," he exclaimed. "They are prepared to speak of peace in time of peace, but they are not dependable in time of war. Advocates of peace who are not prepared to stand for peace in time of war are useless. To advocate peace and then to flinch when the test comes means nothing—absolutely nothing. . . .

"A government can always present a case for war in such a way that the people believe that they are protecting their homes from an invader, or a would-be invader. You must make up your minds that under no circumstances whatever will you support war. . . ."

Professor Einstein urged that a great effort should be made to secure the support of men and women of influence in every country. He admitted that it is difficult for men holding official positions or university posts to declare themselves openly as war resisters. . . . But despite the difficulties, the recruitment of the "intellectuals" on the side of peace must be attempted. "If a sufficient number of men and women of intellectual standing would declare themselves openly in favor of war resistance, the impression that only impractical idealists are war resisters would be removed. . . ."

A group of Americans visited Einstein at his country house near Berlin in July 1931. Einstein's opinion was sought on a proposal to organize a Kellogg League that would appeal to all people opposed to war. Einstein is reported to have said: [14]

Gathering a list of names is not enough. What is needed are practical efforts to inspire the people with sufficient enthusiasm to make them convince others to join. No great ideal will cause conditions to improve unless people are ready to make sacrifices for their beliefs. What sacrifice is there in joining a list of names?

It is not enough that men in prominent positions are suffering because they have espoused pacifism. I do not believe that national governments would even heed a declaration of prominent individuals unless there were a great number of them. In any event, if a formal declaration against war is the only requirement for membership, the league will remain a scrap of paper.

The people of all countries must absorb pacifism in a cultural and social way. I fear very much that of those who, in a formal sense only, join in the renunciation of war in time of peace, many will become weak-kneed when the threat of war becomes a reality.

You will have to devise a cult that will initiate new members and practice the ideals of pacifism through weekly social gatherings and cultural programs in which peace is especially emphasized. Only in this way can the ideal of world peace get under the skin of the common people. The aim of pacifism, therefore, must be to function in the daily life of the people.

The meeting of the War Resisters' International at Lyons, France, about which Einstein had recently written to Rabbi Baeck took place August 1–4, 1931. This was Einstein's message: [15]

You represent the movement most certain to end war. If you act wisely and courageously, you may become the most effective body of men and women involved in the greatest of all human endeavors. The people of fifty-six countries whom you represent have a potential power far mightier than the sword.

All the nations of the world are talking about disarmament. You must teach them to do more than just talk about it. The people must take this matter out of the hands of statesmen and diplomats. Only they themselves can bring disarmament into this world.

Those who think that the danger of war is past are living in a fool's paradise. We are faced today with a militarism more powerful and more dangerous than that which brought on the World War. That is what the governments have accomplished! But among the peoples of the world the idea of war resistance is growing. You must fearlessly accept the challenge and aggressively spread the idea of war resistance. You must convince the people to take disarmament into their own hands and to declare that they will have no part in war or in the preparation for war. You must call on the workers of all countries to unite in refusing to become the tools of interests that war upon life. Today, in twelve countries, young men are resisting conscription and refusing military service. They are the pioneers of a warless world. Every true friend of peace must support them and help them in rousing the conscience of the world to the evils of conscription.

I appeal especially to the intellectuals. I appeal to my fellow scientists to refuse to co-operate in research for war purposes. I appeal to the clergy to seek truth and renounce national prejudices. I appeal to all men of letters to announce publicly their support of our position.

I ask every newspaper that prides itself on supporting peace to encourage its readers to refuse war service. I ask editors to challenge men of eminence and influence by asking them bluntly: Where do you stand on the question of peace? Are you afraid to identify yourself with those who are refusing war service? Must you wait for everyone else to disarm before you put down your weapons and hold out the hand of friendship?

This is not the time for temporizing. You are either for war or against war. If you are for war, then go ahead and encourage science, finance, industry, religion and labor to exert all their power for the arms build-up, to make weapons as deadly as possible. If you are against war, then challenge everyone to resist it to the limits of his capacity. I ask everyone who reads these words to make this grave and final decision.

Let this generation be the one to take the greatest step forward ever made in the history of mankind. Let it leave to future generations the inestimable heritage of a world from which the brutalities of war have been banished forever. We can do this if we are determined. It merely requires that all who hate war shall have the courage to say that they will not tolerate war.

I appeal to all men and women, whether they be eminent or humble, to declare, before the World Disarmament Conference convenes at Geneva next February, that they will henceforth refuse to give assistance to any war or preparations for war. I ask them to inform their governments in writing of that decision and to confirm the decision by advising me about it.

I shall look for many thousands of responses to this appeal. They should be addressed to me at the headquarters of the War Resisters' International, 11 Abbey Road, Enfield, Middlesex, England. I have authorized the establishment of the Einstein War Resisters' International Fund. Contributions to this fund should be sent to the Treasurer of the War Resisters' International.

The message made a deep impression on the people assembled at Lyons. On September 15, 1931, H. Runham Brown, of the War Resisters' International, wrote Einstein that his message had received wide and favorable publicity in most countries, except in Germany, where only the *Friedensfront*, the organ of the German War Resisters' section, carried the full text of the message, and some of the important newspapers published scanty excerpts from the message, omitting Einstein's call to action. Only a few letters were received in response to Einstein's request, and the contributions to the War Resisters' International Fund were insignificant.

Despite his clear and forthright position on war resistance, Einstein was still criticized for not going far enough. In an open letter to *Die Weltbühne*, a widely known radical and pacifist weekly of pre-Hitler Germany, the publicist Kurt Hiller (see p. 22) suggested, under the title "Go One Step Further, Einstein!" that pacifism, to be effective, should advocate social revolution. Einstein, who privately characterized Hiller's piece as "rather stupid," wrote him on August 21, 1931:

I have entered into a public discussion of political matters only because of inquiries and challenges I could not ignore. I agree with you that, because of the development of our economy, more planning has become necessary in many parts of the economy. I am not very hopeful concerning revolutions in countries with democratic institutions. I am not convinced that those who would gain power through an action that is revolutionary and is based on some slogan would operate in accord with my ideals. I also believe that the fight for peace must be pushed energetically, far ahead of any efforts to bring about social reforms. . . .

On August 15, 1931, Einstein wrote to a Swiss war resister:

. . . Let me express my respect for your courage and integrity. One man who is brave enough to refuse military service serves mankind better than thousands who do what they conceive to be their normal duty. A man like yourself acts as a grain of sand in a machine. It is my hope that by means of such grains of sand the war machine will be destroyed or, at least, the degrading system of conscription will be abolished. . . .

To a New York college teacher who intended to organize the teachers for active opposition to war plans, Einstein replied on August 21, 1931:

I believe the movement which you are organizing is of great importance. The school, more than any other institution, has a considerable influence in shaping the political views of the coming generation. It is, therefore, of great significance to cultivate and keep alive pacifist ideas among teachers. If you are at all successful in winning teachers over to pacifism in America, you will set a useful pattern for other countries since teachers are well organized everywhere. Particularly valuable would be a campaign to purge textbooks of chauvinist tendencies. . . .

More than 100,000 Belgians of Flemish origin gathered at Dixmude, Belgium, on August 23, 1931, in an annual pilgrimage to the monument commemorating their fellow countrymen who fell in the First World War. Einstein sent the following message: [16]

I consider myself very fortunate to know about the great peace demonstration which the Flemish people have undertaken. To all who had any part in it I wish to say, in the name of all men of good will who are concerned about the future: In this hour of reflection and awakening conscience we feel a deep sense of solidarity with you.

We must realize that the present miserable world situation is unlikely to improve unless we fight hard to change it; the handful of those who are dedicated to militant action is small when compared to the many who are undecided and misled. Moreover, those who have an interest in keeping the machinery of war going wield much power; they will stop at nothing to make public opinion serve their deadly aims.

It would appear that the leading statesmen of today sincerely endeavor to bring about an era of enduring peace. But the ceaseless piling-up of armaments shows only too clearly that they are unequal to the task of coping with the hostile forces preparing for war. In my opinion, deliverance will come only from the power of the people themselves. If they wish to avoid the degrading slavery of war service, they must declare themselves, in no uncertain terms, in favor of total disarmament. As long as armies exist, any serious conflict may lead to war. Any pacifist movement that does not actively fight for disarmament is necessarily condemned to impotence.

May the conscience and common sense of the people be awakened, so that we may bring about a new era in the life of nations, from which we shall one day look back on war as an incomprehensible aberration of our forefathers!

On September 17, 1931, the day before the Japanese invasion of Manchuria began, Einstein wrote to the Dutch journal *Nieuw Europa*:

In these times of crisis the belief has gained much strength that a worthwhile future for the nations of Europe is necessarily linked to the achievement of comprehensive disarmament. It cannot be emphasized too strongly that disarmament can be successful only when every country is assured that the mandates of an international court of arbitration will actually be carried out. Those who are in earnest about peace should see to it that each country assumes the obligation to take action, to the limits of its capacity and in concert with all the other nations, against any country which violates a verdict of the international court.

During that same month, Einstein addressed a letter to the editor of the *Vorwärts*, the central organ of the German Social Democratic party, to suggest publication of an article on war resistance which had been prepared by a conscientious objector. Einstein wrote:

It is an open secret that the Social Democratic party suffered a loss of prestige and confidence by compromising with militarism. This is most regrettable because this development will not help the necessary improvement of political conditions; but the damage is not irreparable. The restoration of international solidarity can reinvigorate socialism, but such solidarity is possible only on the basis of sincere pacifism. . . .

The editor of the *Vorwärts* declined Einstein's suggestion for publication of the article.[17] Individual war resistance was relatively unimportant, he felt; it would be far more significant to expose the terrible insanity of a future war. Besides, propaganda by the Social Democratic party recommending the refusal of military service even in peacetime might lead to complications with neighboring countries which, unlike Germany, practiced military conscription. The difference between the party and Einstein was one of method rather than principle. Would not Einstein state his own views in the *Vorwärts?* Apparently, Einstein was unwilling to engage in a debate on these terms.

The Disarmament Conference scheduled to meet early in 1932, which Einstein had already mentioned in his message to the Congress of the War Resisters' International at Lyons, increasingly occupied his thoughts. *The Nation*, a magazine published in New York, on September 23, 1931, carried the following article by Einstein: [18]

The fruits of man's inventive genius over the past century might well have made life carefree and happy, had our institutions been able to keep up with the advance of technology. As it is, these hard-won achievements are, in the hands of our generation, as dangerous as a gun wielded by a toddler. Possession of our wonderful means of production has generated want and famine, and not freedom.

Technological progress is most pernicious when it serves to destroy human life and the hard-won products of human labor, as we of the older generation witnessed to our horror in the World War. But more terrible even than this kind of destruction is, to my mind, the abject servitude which war forces upon the individual. What could be worse than to be compelled, by society, into actions which all of us as individuals regard as heinous crimes! And how few had the moral courage to resist. In my eyes they are the true heroes of the World War.

There is, however, one ray of hope. It seems to me that the responsible leaders of the nations today do, in the main, sincerely wish to abolish war. Resistance to this absolutely necessary measure centers in the unfortunate traditions of the various nations. These traditions are passed on, through the machinery of the educational system, like a hereditary disease from generation to generation. The principal villains in perpetuating these traditions are military training, its glorification and, equally, that sector of the press which is controlled by heavy industry and the military. Without disarmament there can be no enduring peace. Conversely, continuation of the arms race at the present pace will inexorably lead to new disasters.

That is why the Disarmament Conference of 1932 will be of crucial importance to this generation and the next. When one considers how pitiable, on the whole, have been the results of past conferences, it becomes obvious that all thoughtful and responsible people must do all they can to alert the public to the tremendous importance of this conference. Only if the statesmen have powerful support for a policy of peace from a majority of their people can they hope to attain their great goal. To help shape public opinion in that direction by words and deeds is the responsibility of all of us.

The doom of the conference would be sealed if the delegates arrived with rigid policy instructions, the realization of which would at once become a matter of national prestige. This danger, it seems, is being recognized on all sides. During the recent series of bilateral conferences, statesmen have endeavored to prepare the ground for the Disarmament Conference. This seems to me a very promising device; two men or two groups of men can usually thrash out their differences more reasonably, honestly and dispassionately when no third party is listening in, in the presence of whom they must be careful about what they say. Only if the conference is being prepared in this painstaking manner, if surprise maneuvers are thus ruled out and if an atmosphere of confidence is created through genuine good will, can we hope for a successful result.

In such affairs of state success is not a matter of brilliance, still less of shrewdness; rather, it is a question of sincerity and trust. Sheer intelligence, thank heaven, cannot be a substitute for moral integrity.

The individual observer cannot afford merely to wait and criticize. He must serve the cause as best he can. The world's fate will be the one it deserves.

To a correspondent in Maine, Einstein wrote on September 30, 1931:

I do not accept the theory that wars are made solely or even primarily by capitalists. I believe the problem of removing existing grave economic injustices is even more important than the pacifist problem. But I am convinced we must not make the solution of the latter contingent upon the solution of the former since, even today, conditions are ripe for creating an organization that will abolish war.

I am further convinced that refusal of military and war service will have the effect of causing governments to be more sympathetic to the concept of collective enforcement of decisions resulting from international arbitration.

Mrs. Schwimmer submitted to Einstein certain proposals for mass action in connection with the forthcoming Disarmament Conference. Einstein replied the same day:

In my opinion your proposals do not have enough substance. In particular, one cannot simply and categorically demand disarmament without acquainting the threatened countries with the arrangements through which they would become secure from aggression. . . .

Einstein also regretfully withdrew his permission, previously granted through Mrs. Schwimmer, to allow someone to search his files for antiwar statements, a collection of which was then in preparation: [19]

On further reflection I have abandoned this plan. We could do the cause only harm by trumpeting trivial stuff, even though it may emanate from His Worship—namely, myself. . . .

On October 8, 1931, Einstein sent a message to a meeting of the German section of the War Resisters' International, the Bund der Kriegsdienstgegner: [20]

In this land, where the ideology of violence and professional militarism is unfortunately still so firmly rooted in the people, even among the most highly educated groups, it takes unusual courage and independence to stand up for a principle which to the uncorrupted mind is accepted as a matter of course: That no authority, not even the state, has the right to require citizens to perform acts which the generally recognized moral code brands as criminal.

When the moral power of man deteriorates, science and technology will debase him and nothing, not even our established institutions, will be able to protect him. Only the strong and unbending will to promote international justice can provide an effective basis for successful disarmament efforts.

Let us never forget that compromise has often destroyed the greatest human endeavors from which mankind might otherwise have derived untold blessings. If we are firm and defiant, we shall win the enlightened to our cause, and eventually even the vacillating masses.

The leaders of the Swedish Committee for a People's Parliament for Disarmament intended to call mass meetings throughout the world to coincide with the forthcoming Geneva Conference. They submitted to Einstein a proclamation to be issued for that purpose. His reply, written on Armistice Day 1931, contains his first reference to the Japanese "incident" in Manchuria.

I am glad to learn that you are working so vigorously in Sweden for the success of the Disarmament Conference. . . . But let me say that it is not sufficient to exert pressure upon nations in an effort to compel them to disarm; for I am convinced that the obligations already assumed by various countries with respect to international arbitration do not provide an adequate basis for disarmament. The position of France on this question is quite justified. Individual governments will be able to risk disarmament only when all countries agree to enforce the decisions reached in Geneva or The Hague—that is, by joining in economic and, if necessary, even military sanctions against any offender.

I am further convinced that all sincere opponents of the military system must lend vigorous support to such a program. That such a course is necessary is amply proven by Japan's recent action [the invasion of Manchuria]. Today the cry of disarmament is heard from the lips of even those who are actually unwilling to renounce military adventures.

The editor of the French journal *Paix Mondiale*, recalling the frequent appeals for a revision of the Versailles Treaty and, particularly, the unilateral war-guilt clause imposed on the Central Powers, posed three questions to which Einstein replied as follows (on November 17, 1931):

Q: Are you in favor of a revision of the Treaty of Versailles? If yes, in what form?

A: I am convinced that in certain respects the peace treaty is unfair and unreasonable. At the present juncture, however, revision does not appear appropriate, particularly since international relations can be much improved, even without formal revision, if the various nations honestly so desire.

Q: Can substantial disarmament be brought about without prior moral disarmament?

A: It is certainly important to strive for moral disarmament. But this alone is not sufficient. Substantial disarmament will become possible only when countries are offered guarantees against aggression. The need for such guarantees is once again clearly demonstrated by Japan's invasion of Manchuria. If all countries had been obligated to join in an economic boycott against the aggressor, Japan would certainly have had to forego its adventure.

Q: Under present conditions, is not the Disarmament Conference of 1932 headed for certain failure with all its tragic consequences?

A: I believe the conference should take place in any event; at very least, it will help to clarify the situation and focus attention on this important problem.

In an article which appeared in *The New York Times*, November 22, 1931, Einstein said: [21]

Let me begin with a confession of political faith: that the state is made for man, not man for the state. This is true of science as well. These are age-old formulations, pronounced by those for whom man himself is the highest human value. I should hesitate to restate them if they were not always in danger of being forgotten, particularly in these days of standardization and stereotype. I believe the most important mission of the state is to protect the individual and make it possible for him to develop into a creative personality.

The state should be our servant; we should not be slaves of the state. The state violates this principle when it compels us to do military service, particularly since the object and effect of such servitude is to kill people of other lands or infringe upon their freedom. We should, indeed, make only such sacrifices for the state as will serve the free development of men. To Americans this may all seem self-evident, but not to Europeans. Hence we may hope that the fight against war will find powerful support among Americans.

And now, about the Disarmament Conference. Ought one to laugh, weep or hope when one thinks about it? Imagine a town inhabited by hot-tempered, dishonest and aggressive citizens. Life is in constant peril and normal activity impossible. The city fathers seek to remedy this dreadful state of affairs, but the citizens insist on their right to carry a knife. After years of futility the city council at last brings to the floor an ordinance that would regulate the length and sharpness of the knives which citizens are allowed to carry.

Of course, things will go on in the same old way, as long as the possession and use of knives are not outlawed and the laws continue to be enforced by the courts and the police. Regulating the length and sharpness of knives will only help the strongest and most pugnacious and leave the weaker at their mercy.

I am sure all of you understand the moral of this parable. It is true that we have a League of Nations and an International Court of Arbitration. But the League is not much more than a meeting place and the International Court has no means of enforcing its judgments. These institutions offer no protection to any country in the event of aggression. If one bears this in mind, the attitude of France in refusing to disarm without adequate security must be judged less harshly than is usually the case.

Unless all countries can agree to limit their national sovereignty by assuming responsibility for joint action against any government that openly or covertly evades a judgment of the International Court of Arbitration, we shall never emerge from our present state of universal anarchy and terror. By no sleight of hand can unlimited sovereignty of individual states be reconciled with security against aggression. How many more disasters will be necessary to induce the nations to commit themselves to help enforce the decisions of the recognized international court? Developments in the past hardly justify much hope for improvement in the near future. All who cherish civilization and justice must exert every effort to convince their fellow citizens of the need for subjecting all countries to an international obligation of this kind.

It will be argued, not without some justification, that this approach overestimates the efficacy of organizational machinery and neglects the psychological, or rather the moral, factor. Moral disarmament, people insist, must precede material disarmament. They say further, and rightly so, that the greatest obstacle to international order is the monstrously exaggerated spirit of nationalism that goes by the appealing but misused name of patriotism. During the last century and a half, this false idol has everywhere attained a sinister and exceedingly pernicious influence.

To gauge the real significance of this argument, one must realize that man's institutions and his state of mind affect one another. Institutions depend on traditional emotional attitudes to which they owe their origin and survival and, in turn, they exercise a powerful influence on those emotional attitudes within nations.

Nationalism, presently grown to such excessive heights, is in my opinion intimately associated with the institution of compulsory military service or, to use a euphemism, the militia. Any state that demands military service of its citizens is compelled to cultivate in them a spirit of nationalism, in order to lay the psychological foundation for their military usefulness. The state must idolize this instrument of brute force to the students in its schools, exactly as it does with religion.

The introduction of compulsory military service is, to my mind, the prime cause for the moral decay of the white race and seriously threatens not merely the survival of our civilization but our very existence. This curse originated, together with great social blessings, with the French Revolution and soon swept over all other nations.

Whoever seeks to cultivate an international mentality and wants to combat chauvinism must take his stand in opposition to compulsory military service. The severe persecution to which conscientious objectors to military service are subjected is as shameful to society today as was the persecution to which religious martyrs were exposed centuries ago. And how dare the Kellogg Pact outlaw war while leaving the individual in each country to the tender mercies of the war machine!

If, at the Disarmament Conference, we do not want to limit ourselves to technical problems of organization, but also wish to consider, for educational reasons, the psychological aspects of disarmament more directly, then we must try to create international legal means by which men may refuse to serve in the army. Such measures would undoubtedly produce a powerful moral effect.

Let me summarize my views: Mere agreements to limit armaments confer no protection. Compulsory arbitration must be supported by an executive force which is guaranteed by all the participating countries and which is ready to proceed against any aggressor with military and economic sanctions. Compulsory military service, the chief source of unhealthy nationalism, must be combated; most important of all, protection on an international basis must be provided for conscientious objectors.

The manuscript of Einstein's article contained several important passages which were omitted in the article as published by *The New York Times*. One of the omissions was Einstein's recommendation of a recently published book by Ludwig Bauer, *War Again Tomorrow*, which Einstein felt treated the questions discussed in his article "acutely, without prejudice and with great psychological understanding." Also omitted was a long passage in which Einstein quoted Professor D. Holde of Berlin, one of the major figures in the protest action on behalf of Gumbel (see p. 132), and author of the following concrete proposal for legalizing war resistance:

In the Kellogg Pact, government representatives throughout the world have morally outlawed war, denouncing it as a dishonorable and inadmissible tool for settling whatever differences may come to exist among the various nations. A minimum proposition for the forthcoming Disarmament Conference logically results from this action. . . .

All signers of the Kellogg Pact, in the name of their governments and before the whole world, should solemnly assume the obligation never to compel any of their citizens or nationals, by force, moral coercion or other pressure, to participate, against their ethical or religious convictions, or against their moral conscience, in any act of war, directly or indirectly, nor to support any such acts in any way, directly or indirectly.

For example, not even clergymen, of whatever denomination, and whether performing religious services in the field or elsewhere, should be enjoined to bless the arms of soldiers or other persons taking part in war; nor to implore God for victory of their nation. Such actions, in the light of the outlawry of war, must be regarded as dishonorable and contrary to the spirit of brotherhood.

Passage of such a resolution would represent another highly important obligation on the part of the governments which signed the Kellogg Pact. It would solemnly codify, before all the world, the fundamental moral and legal commitments which these governments assumed under the pact, and would thus help facilitate general world disarmament.

The difficulties of clearly delineating the relationship between the state and the individual occupied Einstein throughout much of his life. The problem is alluded to both in the above article contributed by him to *The New York Times* and in Professor Holde's proposition for legalizing war resistance. During the same period, Einstein addressed a letter to the Italian Minister of Justice, Alfredo Rocco. He asked Rocco to approach Mussolini with the suggestion that Italian men of science be spared the humiliation of a compulsory loyalty oath. Einstein continued: [21a]

. . . However much our political convictions may differ, I know that on one basic point we are in agreement: We both admire the outstanding achievements of the European intellect and see reflected in it those values we most cherish. They could only have developed in a society where freedom of conscience and teaching prevails and in which the search for truth took precedence over all other considerations. . . .

I do not propose to argue with you the question of whether, and to what extent, man's liberty may ever have to be restricted in the interest of the state. However, I feel there cannot be any doubt that the pursuit of truth and scientific knowledge ought to be treated as sacred by every government, and that it serves the highest interest of society as a whole to respect the freedom of those who sincerely seek truth and scientific knowledge. . . .

In an unpublished draft of a letter to *The New York Times*, which was probably prepared after Einstein's arrival in Pasadena for his second visit, Einstein recommended a pamphlet by John H. Dietrich, *Shall the Nations Disarm?* published under Unitarian auspices:

. . . Its dissemination may well have a crucial effect on public opinion in America and throughout the world, thus favorably affecting the results of the Disarmament Conference. Is there not, somewhere in America, a person of rank or distinction who might arrange for wide distribution of this work, thereby performing an enduring service to our imperiled civilization? At this juncture such an action might well be of historic significance to the entire world.

On December 2, 1931, Einstein once again set sail for America, this time on a small ship that took him directly to California. Mrs. Einstein wrote to Mrs. Rosika Schwimmer on February 3, 1932, from Pasadena: "We avoided traveling by way of New York; my husband is unequal to the heavy demands made on him there." Einstein's preoccupations at this time may be gauged from the following diary entry made on shipboard December 6, 1931:

. . . I decided today that I shall essentially give up my Berlin position and shall be a bird of passage for the rest of my life. Gulls are still escorting the ship, forever on the wing. They are my new colleagues, although, heaven knows, they are more efficient than I. They know more about geography too. How dependent man is on external things, compared to such creatures! . . .

A few months earlier, Einstein had obviously still intended to stay in Germany although he was considering the possibility of abandoning his German citizenship. In a letter to Professor Max Planck (of the Prussian Academy of Sciences), drafted on July 17, 1931, but apparently never mailed, Einstein gave expression to the insecurity which he felt as a result of the increasing effect of Nazi activities on public and political affairs in Germany:

I feel impelled to call your attention to a matter which is closely related to the conditions of my employment. You will surely recall that after the war I declared my willingness to accept German citizenship, in addition to my Swiss citizenship.[22] The events of recent days suggest that it is not advisable to maintain this situation. Therefore, I should be grateful if you saw to it that my German citizenship were revoked, and to advise me whether such a change will permit me to maintain my position in the Academy of Sciences (which I sincerely hope).

Concern for the many people who are financially dependent on me, as well as a certain need for personal independence, compels me to take this step. I very much hope that you will understand and that you will not interpret this request as an act of ingratitude toward a country and an institution which have granted me enviable living and working conditions during the best years of my life. So far, I have always rejected offers from abroad, however tempting, which would have forced me to leave the scene of my work. I hope I shall be able to maintain this attitude also in the future.

Einstein, avoiding contact with his fellow passengers, enjoyed the leisure of the ocean voyage. With ironic reference to an anonymous letter which he had recently received in Berlin, he noted on December 9, 1931:

. . . Only one thing is lacking. There are never any anonymous letters. Too bad, for in such letters even the clumsiest lies are, so to speak, sincere—that is to say, they express the writer's true personality.

At Porto Moios on the Pacific coast of Central America, he was taken on a tour of the banana plantations. He found the American type of colonization to be exemplary, but noted, on December 20, 1931:

. . . I learned that the Indians, who resemble the Eskimos, are dying out. They cannot endure the rigors of work and, without working, they starve in the hills. In the tropics the struggle for existence seems, for man, animal and plant, even more naked and brutal than with us. Our own struggle has become intensified through the modern corporation which has organized it systematically and whose actions are motivated by the hunger for dividends of the unknown, the nameless. What an edifying spectacle! Yet there is no way out. Dog eat dog, for no purpose and with no end in sight.

On the day of his arrival in Los Angeles, December 30, 1931, Einstein noted that "ten per cent of the people are unemployed in Pasadena," and on January 9, 1932: ". . . Pretty precarious conditions here. Hoover refuses to receive a delegation representing the unemployed."

On that same day the magazine *Liberty* published a flattering portrait of John D. Rockefeller, Jr., by George Sylvester Viereck. During Einstein's visit to New York a year earlier, Viereck had arranged a meeting between Einstein and Rockefeller. The passages in Viereck's article in regard to Einstein are brief but significant and obviously constitute part of the discussion between Rockefeller and Einstein which took place at their meeting in New York: [23]

. . . Professor Einstein argued that the strict regulations laid down by his [Rockefeller's] educational foundations sometimes stifled the man of genius. "Red tape," the Professor exclaimed, "encases the spirit like the bands of a mummy!" Rockefeller, on the other hand, pointed out the necessity for carefully guarding the funds of the foundations from diversion to unworthy ends or individuals who are not meritorious. Standing his ground against the greatest mind in the modern world, he ably defended the system under which the various foundations were conducted.

"I," Einstein said, "put my faith in intuition."

"I," Rockefeller replied, "put my faith in organization."

Einstein pleaded for the exceptional man. Rockefeller championed the greatest good of the greatest possible number. Einstein was the aristocrat, Rockefeller the democrat.

Each was sincere; each, without convincing the other, persuaded the other man of his sincerity.

The conversation drifted to economic problems. Einstein advocated the paring down of working hours to give a chance to the unemployed, and suggested the desirability of prolonging the school years to keep children from competing with their elders.

"Does not such an idea," asked Rockefeller, "impose an unwarranted restriction upon individual freedom?"

Einstein countered with the statement that the present economic emergency justified measures similar to those taken by all governments in wartime.

Einstein voiced his opposition to war. While John D. Rockefeller, Jr., is equally opposed to it, his feet are too firmly planted upon realities to permit him to share in their entirety the views of the more extreme pacifists. "War," Einstein exploded, "can be ended only if men refuse to bear arms!"

In the February 1932 issue of *The Crisis*, organ of the National Association for the Advancement of Colored People, Einstein wrote: [24]

It seems to be a universal fact that minorities, especially when their individuals are recognizable because of physical differences, are treated by the majorities among whom they live as inferiors. The tragic part of such a fate, however, lies not only in the automatically realized disadvantages suffered by these minorities in economic and social relations, but also in the fact that those who meet such treatment themselves for the most part acquiesce in this prejudiced estimate because of the suggestive influence of the majority, and come to regard people like themselves as inferior.

This second and more important aspect of the evil can be met through closer union and conscious educational enlightenment among the minority, and so an emancipation of the soul of the minority may be attained. The determined effort of the American Negroes in this direction deserves every recognition and assistance.

"This year my husband is again working effectively for disarmament and peace," Mrs. Einstein wrote to Mrs. Schwimmer in a letter of February 3, 1932; "he recently delivered, for this purpose, a speech at Whittier College, the great Quaker school. I have the impression that our cause has made great strides since last year." Einstein's remarks in that address about the implications of a possible failure of the Geneva Disarmament Conference are almost prophetic. As a guest in the United States, he probably would not have been so candid and outspoken about America's responsibilities in the world, had he not viewed the international situation with the gravest concern: [25]

Americans today are deeply disturbed about economic conditions in their own country. Their responsible leaders are primarily concerned with remedying the serious unemployment at home. There is even less awareness than exists in normal times of the interdependence of conditions in the United States and the rest of the world and, particularly, in Europe, the mother of America.

However, the present economic system, based on free enterprise, will not be able to overcome these difficulties on its own power. Regulations by the state are needed to arrange for an equitable distribution of manpower and consumer goods; without such government regulation, the economy, even of the richest country, will not be able to function adequately. The fact is that, through improved technology, the amount of work required to satisfy man's needs has been considerably curtailed; and the "free" economy is no longer able to provide employment for all those who want to work. Specific regulatory measures have become necessary if everyone in the country is to benefit from technical progress and nobody is to be harmed.

If the economy requires careful regulation to operate in orderly fashion, how much more necessary is such regulation in the sphere of international relations! Relatively few people persist in the belief that acts of violence, in the form of wars, present a satisfactory solution to international problems—that is, one that is compatible with human dignity. But we have failed to be sufficiently consistent and vigorous in our efforts to prevent war—the savage and inhuman relic of an age of barbarism. Some serious reflection is necessary to understand the problem sufficiently; and we need courage if we are to serve the cause of peace resolutely and effectively.

Whoever genuinely seeks to abolish war must resolutely insist that his own country surrender a portion of its sovereignty to international institutions; he must be ready, in the event of an international dispute, to make his own country abide by the decision of an international court. He must uncompromisingly support universal disarmament as is actually provided for in the miserable Treaty of Versailles. Unless we cease indoctrinating the masses of people with militarism and aggressive nationalism, we cannot possibly hope for progress.

Nothing in recent years has been more shameful for the major powers than the failure of the various disarmament conferences; and this failure is not merely attributable to the intrigues of ambitious and unscrupulous statesmen; it is also due to the indifference and apathy of people everywhere. Unless these circumstances change, we are bound to destroy our great cultural heritage.

I believe that the American people are not fully aware of their responsibility in this matter. Perhaps they think: "Let Europe perish if the malice and discord of its peoples destroy it! The good seed sown by President Wilson has produced very little in the sterile soil of Europe. We are strong and secure and in no hurry for new foreign entanglements."

Such an attitude is neither noble nor realistic. America is not without responsibility for the difficulties that beset Europe. By ruthlessly pressing her claims, she in fact hastens the economic and moral decline of Europe; she has contributed to the Balkanization of Europe and must, therefore, share in the responsibility for the breakdown of political morality and the emergence of the spirit of revenge which feeds on despair. This spirit will not stop short at the gates of America; indeed, I might almost say that it has already affected America. I say to you: Be circumspect and be on your guard!

Let us be outspoken and straightforward: the Disarmament Conference presents the final opportunity to you, no less than to us, to preserve the best that humanity has produced. It is toward America, the strongest and, relatively speaking, healthiest among the nations, that the eyes and hopes of all mankind are directed.

Two days after the Whittier address, on January 20, 1932, Einstein records in his diary: "Talk by [Jacob Gould] Schurman [former U.S. Ambassador to Germany] on present-day Germany; discussed structure of her political parties with some irony; superficial because of his timidity concerning the economic situation." On January 25, 1932, Einstein, Schurman and Charles A. Beard, the historian, were all guests of honor at a dinner given by the California Institute of Technology. Einstein, after paying tribute to Schurman's academic and diplomatic career, said: [26]

I cannot forego discussing another subject; to ignore it would be to risk the suspicion of willful silence. The basis of European-American civilization has been badly shaken; in the face of the sinister, intangible power that threatens, a sense of perplexity and fear grips all of us. While we are richer than any generation before us, both in consumer goods and in the means of production, a great part of mankind continues to suffer from dire want. Production and consumption decline more and more, and confidence in public institutions has sunk lower than ever before. It seems as if, everywhere, the whole economic organism were incurably diseased.

There has been much speculation about the causes of the disease, and it would seem that purely technical remedies might effect a cure. The optimist may ask, why should it not be possible to restore the balance between production and consumption through appropriate measures? The pessimist, however, raises a different question: Why should our civilization not perish from inner decay exactly as civilization did under the Roman Empire? Who, then, is right? And where do we stand?

Let me try to answer the question from a historical perspective. Our civilization has always been predicated upon the maintenance and improvement of our culture. It is a culture which has been nourished by two sources. The first derives from the spirit of ancient Greece, renewed and supplemented by the Italian Renaissance. It challenges the individual to think, observe and create. The second derives from Judaism and primitive Christianity. It is characterized by the motto: Protect your conscience by selfless service to mankind. In this sense we may speak of our culture as having evolved from both creative and moral sources. Down until the end of the Middle Ages cultural life derived its strength solely from the second, or moral, source. What resulted was a meager but stable culture. During the Renaissance, when the wellsprings of man's creativity began to flow more freely, an ever more richly burgeoning culture ensued which, from generation to generation, down to our own day, has provided an unending source of inspiration. The consequence of this exciting evolution has been the creation of a powerful civilization and technology, together with very large increases in population and a rising physical and intellectual standard of living.

We had apparently forgotten that the moral source remains vital to our existence. Now, however, we are dismayed to realize that this source has lost much of its power and that, without it, we are hopelessly doomed. The more powerful the tools which the creative ability of past generations delivered into our hands, the greater must be man's moral powers to use them wisely. Man does not lack the intelligence to overcome the evils in society; what is lacking is his selfless, responsible dedication to the service of mankind.

Must I argue this at length? Do we not witness how, every day, in almost every land, the people's sense of justice is too weak to force the reversal of judicial verdicts that are felt to be miscarriages of justice? Is it not true that nations continue to honor treaties whose economic impracticability has long since been recognized even if not officially acknowledged? And is it not also true that nations still engage in material and psychological preparation for war although there can be no doubt that another war would be disastrous to mankind and is antithetical to the moral law we officially profess to honor? One can forever keep on asking such questions, receiving but a skeptical smile in reply. It was Heinrich Heine who sang the bitter song: Only a fool waits for an answer.

Let me conclude with grateful acknowledgment of the free and hospitable institutions of your country that make it possible for me to address this large group with this much candor.

In his letter to Einstein of October 4, 1931, Arnold Kalisch, editor of *Die Friedensfront* (p. 143), had asked Einstein to support the nomination of H. Runham Brown, Honorary Secretary of the War Resisters' International, for the Nobel Peace Prize. Since nominations had to be submitted before February 1, 1932, Kalisch renewed his request in a letter that reached Einstein in California. Kalisch enclosed a draft of a letter to be sent to a group of German professors in an effort to have them endorse the nomination.

In his letter to the Nobel Committee (January 1932), Einstein said:

. . . I believe Mr. Runham Brown has done more for the cause of peace than any other active pacifist. He has generously contributed to this most worthy cause his time, his boundless energy and his great personal courage. With no resources other than his own modest means, he has managed to make war resistance into an organized movement, thus rendering much more effective the activities of those who assume the grave personal risks and sacrifices involved in refusing military service.

But Einstein had no illusions concerning the popularity of either the man or his cause among the German academic community. As he wrote to Kalisch:

I believe it would be unwise as well as futile to ask German professors by letter to support the nomination. Since it is a delicate matter, their support should be sought only through personal contacts and not by a round-robin letter. Similarly, I do not wish that my statement supporting the nomination be made public or enclosed in a circular letter. It would only engender unpleasant repercussions. You may, of course, show my statement to those people whom we would expect to react favorably. We must avoid giving premature publicity to the matter, lest we provoke an immediate campaign which would be calculated to antagonize many people, possibly even members of the Nobel Committee.

The Nobel Peace Prize for the year 1932 was not awarded.

On February 1, 1932, Einstein addressed a meeting at Pasadena under the auspices of the Los Angeles University of International Relations, a school for diplomats and economists which was affiliated with the University of Southern California. Mrs. Einstein, in her letter to Mrs. Schwimmer two days later, complained that "the affair was not only lacking in seriousness but was treated as a kind of social entertainment. It was embarrassing to have to listen to the chairman crack jokes. . . . The main speaker, however, was a former Naval officer who treated his topic very well." Einstein echoed these sentiments in his diary and added: "I too gave a speech, but alas! this was hardly a responsive audience. The propertied classes here seize upon anything that might provide ammunition in the struggle against boredom. One must not mistake their real motive for serious interest. It is a sad world in which such people are allowed to play first fiddle. . . ."

This was Einstein's speech: [27]

The greatest obstacle to disarmament has been the inability of most people to appreciate the enormity of the problem. Most objectives are accomplished in small steps. Think, for example, of the transition from absolute monarchy to democracy! But we are here concerned with an objective that cannot be attained slowly, step by step.

So long as the possibility of war exists, nations will continue to insist on the fullest possible military preparedness to insure their victory in a future war and will find it unavoidable to educate the young people in warlike traditions and narrow nationalist vanities. The glorification of the war spirit will proceed as long as there is reason to believe that situations may arise where that spirit will need to be invoked for the purpose of waging war. To arm means simply to approve and prepare for war, not for peace. Hence, disarmament cannot come in small steps; it must come about at one stroke or not at all.

To accomplish so profound a change in the life of nations, a mighty moral effort and a deliberate rejection of deeply ingrained traditions are required. Anyone who is unwilling to let the fate of his country, in the event of a conflict, depend without qualification upon the decisions of an international court of arbitration, and who is not prepared to see his country enter into treaties that provide for such a procedure without any reservations, is not really resolved to abolish war. This is a case of all or nothing.

It should be emphasized that previous attempts to insure peace have failed only because they were directed toward compromise solutions that were inadequate to cope with the task. Disarmament and security cannot be separated; they must come about simultaneously. Security will be achieved only when all nations commit themselves to abide by the decisions of an international authority.

We are at present at a crucial crossroad in history. It is for us to determine whether a way to peace shall be found or whether man shall continue along the old road of brute force, so unworthy of our civilization. If we choose the way of peace, freedom for the individual and security for society await us; if we do not, slavery of the individual and the annihilation of civilization threaten us. Our fate will be the one we deserve.

To a citizens' mass meeting held the following day, February 2, 1932, in the courthouse at Santa Barbara, California, Einstein sent a message in which he reiterated his well-known views on disarmament and international arbitration and in which he once more urged the United States to become more active in the fight for peace: [28]

It is of the greatest importance that the citizens of America take an active part in the problem of disarmament. The United States could be the most influential factor in international affairs today, provided its citizens really wanted it. . . .

Two days later, on February 4, 1932, Einstein listened to a speech by Jacob Gould Schurman on the Japanese invasion of Manchuria. His comment was: "Clever and amoral. Hence, how unfortunate. . . ." On February 27, 1932, Einstein himself addressed a meeting organized in Pasadena by representatives of eleven universities in Southern California to stimulate public attention to international affairs.[29] In some respects, Einstein's remarks anticipated by more than five years President Franklin D. Roosevelt's speech, "Quarantine the Aggressors": Einstein stressed the danger to society of unlimited economic freedom and emphasized the need for a planned economy to solve the complicated problems of production and distribution under modern conditions. If unrestrained *sacro egoismo* led to dire consequences in economic life, it was even more destructive to international relations; highly mechanized warfare threatened our very survival, but thus far our efforts to prevent war had been wholly inadequate. In advocating once more disarmament, international arbitration and collective security, Einstein made these ideas more alive by referring to the acute situation in the Far East:

> Suppose that the American, British, German and French governments enjoined the Japanese Government to cease immediately its acts of war in China, under threat of an airtight economic boycott. Do you believe any Japanese government would risk plunging its country into the perilous adventure of defying such a threat? Then why is such pressure not exerted? Why should men and nations live in a world where they must fear for their very survival? The answer is that they pursue a certain course for their own miserable and temporary advantage and are unwilling to subordinate their selfish aims to the well-being and prosperity of society as a whole. . . .

Einstein, who a few days later, on March 4, 1932, sailed back to Europe, concluded the address with an appeal to the young generation to work toward a fundamental change of the conditions facing mankind: "We, the older people, look to the young and hope that they will strive with all their might to achieve the better world that was denied our generation."

CHAPTER SIX

THE EVE OF FASCISM IN GERMANY | 1932-1933

THE YEAR 1932 was the last year before night fell over Germany and, later, over almost the entire continent of Europe. Ever since the Nazis achieved their unexpected and sweeping victory in the Reichstag elections of September 1930, the menace of Fascist dictatorship overshadowed every other political problem in Germany. Because many political leaders, who had been sworn to protect the democratic institutions of the country, directly or indirectly co-operated with the Fascists and since the political Left was disunited, confused, without sufficient understanding of the real nature of Fascism, and hence ineffective, Nazism became a reality in 1933.

The year 1932 was one of increasing anxiety and apprehension for all those who knew that a Nazi dictatorship would mean not only the end of decency, law and freedom, but also the thorough militarization of the German people and active preparation for war. Einstein was one of the relatively small minority who had no illusions about the nature and magnitude of the threat hanging over the country. In addition, he was deeply troubled over the particular catastrophe which would befall the Jewish part of the population in the event of Nazi rule. The hope for a saner organization of the world, for which he had struggled so vigorously since the end of the First World War, both alone and in co-operation with others, seemed to be in jeopardy. His decision to accept a position in America and to leave Germany, which he had strenuously refused to do over the years, must have been partly due to the realization that even he could do extremely little, if anything at all, to stem the relentless tide of hate, oppression and militarism which was enveloping the German nation. And yet, to the very last, Einstein continued to labor for the abolition of war and for international understanding. In fact, during the last year before Nazism took hold of Germany, which also happened to be his last full year in Europe, Einstein, in addition to his many customary activities in public affairs, participated in several large and important projects: his demonstrative one-day visit to the Disarmament Conference in Geneva, his co-operation in efforts to establish an international peace center, his involvement with a highly controversial Peace Congress in Amsterdam and, finally, his exchange of public letters with Sigmund Freud on the problem of war.

Einstein's concern with mobilizing the clergy for peace on an international scale had been mentioned before (pp. 104, 136). Soon after his return to Europe in the spring of 1932, he received a letter from the Reverend J. B. Th. Hugenholtz, of Ammerstol, The Netherlands, a guiding spirit and delegate to the Joint Peace Council of the International Union of Antimilitarist Ministers and Clergymen. Hugenholtz asked Einstein's support and attendance at a meeting which the Joint Peace Council planned to hold in Geneva in May 1932.

Complaining bitterly of the financial stringencies that beset the peace movement, Hugenholtz spoke of a fund-raising plan which he proposed to submit to Einstein. On April 16, 1932, Einstein replied:

> I can scarcely find words to tell you how important I consider it to organize the clergy for the purpose of combating the military spirit in the different countries. Thus far, most ministers of all denominations have been meek servants of the state, on which, in many countries, they are economically dependent. They have been servile even when the demands of the state were in complete contradiction to the most elementary laws, to say nothing of the moral principles, taught by all religious groups. The conduct of the clergy during the World War was shameful; if it were possible to effect a radical change in their attitude, it would be a big step forward.

At the end of another visit to Oxford University, in May 1932, Einstein went to Geneva on behalf of the Joint Peace Council, although he had originally declined Hugenholtz' invitation. The long-awaited Disarmament Conference was finally in session in Geneva and had been meeting for many weeks. Endless discussions took place, but the chances for swift and decisive action grew slimmer and slimmer. Pacifists were bitterly disappointed. To focus public attention on the threatened failure, the Joint Peace Council made a dramatic effort in which Einstein participated. On Sunday, May 22, 1932, he and Lord Ponsonby, a former Member of Parliament and one of Britain's leading pacifists at the time, left London for Geneva, where they held a press conference the next day; it was attended by some sixty correspondents.

Ponsonby presented a brief declaration on behalf of himself, Einstein, Romain Rolland and the distinguished French novelist and militant pacifist Victor Margueritte:

Since it has become apparent that the negotiations in Geneva are not progressing in such a way as to lead to a practical disarmament program which would be essential if the world is to be saved from the horror of a new war, we believe the time has come for the peoples of the world to take the matter into their own hands. They must insist on complete disarmament within five years, and on the immediate renunciation of war under any circumstances. At the same time, they must request the abolition of conscription and the immediate cessation of the military draft and of the production of arms and munitions.

The peoples of the world must be prepared to achieve these goals by refusing, both individually and collectively, to perform military service or to participate in the production and transportation of war materials.

Einstein then spoke as follows: [1]

I came here to speak to you because friends convinced me that it was my duty to do so. I should like to make a few, simple remarks concerning my impressions of the situation. I need hardly mention that I agree with my friend here in every detail.

To begin, I should like to say that, if the implications were not so tragic, the methods used at the Disarmament Conference could only be called absurd. One does not make wars less likely to occur by formulating rules of warfare. One must start with the unqualified determination to settle international disputes by way of arbitration. What is involved are questions of morality and good will; it is not a problem for the so-called technical experts.

I do not intend to deal at length with the methods which should be employed, since my friend and associate has already described them briefly. I would rather restrict myself to answering questions.

[What was his opinion of moral disarmament?]

The question of whether material or moral disarmament should come first reminds me of the question of which came first, the chicken or the egg. Of course, moral disarmament is essential; but as long as governments are preparing for war, they will not be capable of honestly promoting moral disarmament.

Moral disarmament, like the problem of peace as a whole, is made difficult of solution because men in power never want to surrender any part of their country's sovereignty, which is exactly what they must do if war is to be abolished. I am convinced, therefore, that the solution to the peace problem cannot be left in the hands of governments; rather, we must see to it that people who are intellectually and morally independent pool their influence and resources in fighting militarism. That is how we must counteract the doubt and disillusionment which are currently undermining the all-important influence of intellectual leaders.

In reply to the question as to whether he believed in the possibility of arbitration to guarantee international security, Einstein repeated his oft-repeated position on the peaceful solution of international disputes.

[What did he think of the Geneva Protocol outlawing aggression, which was never fully ratified?]

We must not yield one iota. The greatest crime is to compromise in order to gain a small point. We must continue to fight for the ratification of the Geneva Protocol.

[What about the role of women and the working class in the fight against war?]

Both are important. I have in mind the International Women's Co-operative Guild, the Women's International League for Peace and Freedom and others that could greatly help us to bring about real progress. Similarly, working-class organizations and parties should be keenly interested in the peace movement. They should realize, however, that there is real danger in accepting those compromises which sacrifice the ultimate goal for the sake of temporary sham accomplishments, such as "humanization of war, social patriotism," etc. People must be persuaded to refuse all military service. Only concrete actions such as this will make a real impression.

I am absolutely convinced that we should use every possible means to strengthen the war resistance movement. Its moral significance cannot be overestimated. Unlike anything else, this movement, at one and the same time, inspires individual courage, challenges the conscience of men, and undermines the authority of the military system. I have the greatest admiration for the 78,000 French teachers who have refused to teach along chauvinist lines.

[If he did not believe that a compromise were possible, was he not sounding the death knell of the Disarmament Conference?]

That, indeed, is my intention. In my opinion, the conference is working in the direction of a bad compromise. Any agreement that may now be reached as to which type of arms would be permissible in war will not be kept when it comes to the test of war. War cannot be humanized. It can only be abolished.

When Lord Ponsonby was reminded that in many countries the press was controlled by the government, and that, therefore, a press conference, such as the one they were holding, might not be very effective, he agreed and said: "Perhaps we have not accomplished very much here today, but we are both determined to keep on working ceaselessly."

There were others who had reservations about the visit. Romain Rolland recorded some irritation in his diary [2] because the invitation to attend the Geneva Conference or to sign the Ponsonby-Einstein declaration reached him only on the day on which Ponsonby and Einstein left London for Geneva. But he immediately advised Einstein that he would be a signatory to the declaration:

. . . I associate myself with you in insisting vigorously on the necessity of appealing not only to public opinion, which is diffuse and divided, but also, clearly and sharply, to the masses of workers in the armament industry and in transportation. They must work and strike against any effort either to unleash or facilitate a war. The key to the solution of the situation lies in their hands. . . .

And in further emphasis he wrote at the bottom of the declaration:

I believe firmly that the last point of the declaration should be the first. "God (which means, in this case, the various governments and the League of Nations) helps those who help themselves!" It is up to the peoples to impose peace and not to wait for action by their governments, which have only contempt for them and will continue to do so until the peoples' will manifests itself unmistakably.

A French journalist who attended the press conference complained to Rolland that Einstein had sat in his armchair, replying to meaningless questions with generalities. No real plan of action had been proposed; and both Einstein and Ponsonby had departed quickly, without waiting for further developments. Rolland disagreed with the journalist's interpretation that Einstein was merely an instrument of other forces, such as the War Resisters' International; but he did note that Einstein tended to become impractical once outside the scientific field.

That Einstein's brief appearance in Geneva made a greater impression than Romain Rolland was led to believe is indicated in an article about the Geneva Conference called "The Comedy of Peace." The article, prepared by Konrad Bercovici, a Rumanian-American novelist, was published in the February 1933 issue of the magazine *Pictorial Review*. Bercovici's account of Einstein's Geneva visit, while possibly exaggerated, suggests, nonetheless, the universal and instinctive appreciation of Einstein's personality.[2a]

. . . All the newspapermen left the conference chambers when the news spread that Einstein had arrived in Geneva. Even some of the delegates decided that a look at the great man was worth more than listening to bacteriological and aerial discussions.

He had no official standing at the Peace Conference. He was no delegate of any power. He was not even an accredited newspaperman. And yet no one . . . questioned his right to be there. No one, except a Balkan delegate, disputed his supreme right to be there:

"Who sent for him?" he asked. "What does he represent? Whom does that Jew represent?"

The Balkan delegate was hushed up. An American correspondent actually hit the fool on the mouth with the paper pad in his hand.

It was curious to see the silvery-haired, heavy-set man walking up the broad stairs of the Peace Palace, with hundreds of people following him at a respectful distance. Years of interviewing had not given the newspapermen that familiarity with Einstein which they assume even with crowned heads. . . .

They all stopped two or three steps below him, ranging themselves quietly when he turned, smiled, and said that he would talk to them later on. A young reporter almost fainted with excitement when Einstein asked him for his lighter to rekindle the cigar he was smoking.

He walked into the conference room. The technician of the Aerial Committee, reading a paper at that moment, stopped for a second, then continued. That brief second, however, was an acknowledgment, a more marked acknowledgment of the greatness the man radiated than if all had stopped everything they were doing and applauded him. All eyes were turned toward Einstein. Where he was the world was. . . .

A little later Einstein appeared in the pressroom. And again the newspapermen stood aside at a respectful distance. They did not crowd him, shout at him or hurl questions at him. It was the first real sensation these people had had since they had come to Geneva. . . .

On Sunday, July 10, 1932, Einstein received Corder Catchpool of the Friends Service Council (the British section of the Quaker movement) at his summer home in Caputh, near Berlin. Catchpool prepared a detailed record of the interview: [3]

. . . Einstein's little stone and timber villa . . . stands between lake and forest, looking over the waters of the Schwielow-See, and backed behind by the ubiquitous pines. . . . The white sand of the long strip of garden glared in the brilliant sunshine as I ascended the path. . . . It was intensely hot. . . . The Professor was sitting in the only shady spot, under the broad gable eaves . . . The whole front of the house seemed to be open. . . .

[On the subject of Einstein's thesis that refusal of military service by as few as two per cent of those subject to conscription would make war impossible] I got in a serious question. Couldn't a dictatorial government, in Russia, for instance, easily shoot off the two per cent, and go on as before? "Yes, the two per cent or even ten per cent. It wouldn't work in Russia and some other countries." But partial inapplicability, he felt, is no real criticism of the principle; there remain plenty of countries where it would work and should be made to work. Professor Einstein came back over and over again to the importance of personal refusal to take part in war as the most essential and practical step in the process of abolishing it. "Because in this way so few can make so big an impression. You don't need many men, but they must be determined." This thought of a great crusade against war by personal resistance is his central message. "Nothing is to be expected from the Disarmament Conference—let us hope that when this has been generally realized, men's minds will turn to more radical methods. . . ."

The peoples of the world must learn to place their confidence in treaties upon which the community of nations rests. Such a community of nations (*Völkergemeinschaft*) must have the power to implement its will. The peoples of the world must recognize that a supranational controlling power exists; otherwise they will again fall prey to national war psychology and again fail to revolt against it. The Professor has formed a fairly clear idea of what this supranational force should be like. Germany's Versailles army of 100,000 might be taken as what constitutes a reasonable national unit. Smaller countries might have a rather larger quota in proportion to their population. While those armies would be composed of professional soldiers, they should be regarded as a police force, and should, so far as possible, *not* be stationed in their own land. . . .

We are up against the great problem that mere refusal to participate in war service may be too negative for youth. . . . A heroic pacifism is certainly possible. I raised the question whether it is not asking too much of youth to refuse military service in, for example, a country like France. "Emphatically no!" said the Professor. "On the contrary, the difficulty in Germany today is that while we have no compulsory service, there exists a strong military spirit. To this spirit of militarism youth readily falls prey when lacking the pacifist backbone which a great conflict over conscription might engender. . . ."

I asked what should we do with the youth once we have abolished war? "It is a very important question, but there is time enough to think about it." Youth is attracted by everything that makes great personal demands, especially when risk is attached. . . . Professor Einstein has no hesitation in welcoming . . . governmental schemes of alternative service. Difficult problems are no doubt involved, but they are outweighed by the great moral impression that must be made by the fact that men can no longer be compelled to become murderers. "That is more horrible than anything."

I did not ask upon what fundamental principle Professor Einstein's opposition to war is based; but I think that we have it here, and that we find him standing very near to the Quaker position. . . .

[Einstein commented on a number of other points.]

The Polish Corridor: "I should not have created it, but there is no purpose in altering it now. The mere fact of the physical separation of East Prussia from the rest of Germany does not constitute a sufficient argument against the existence of the corridor. Many a state consists of two or more separate islands. A situation such as the corridor problem presents a strong argument in favor of a superstate."

Manchuria and Sanctions: If at the outset England and America had closed their harbors, Japan would have given way at once. During a recent visit to the United States, Professor Einstein inquired why this had not been done, and was struck by the naïveté of the answer: that with so many commercial interests at stake such a step was obviously out of the question.

Russia and Japan: The danger of war is real, though capitalism is not the sole cause of it, as the Marxists claim. In Professor Einstein's view the psychological factor is of even greater importance.

Gandhi and Nonviolence: While Gandhi's economic views are questionable, his *Satyagraha* is very important, and could be applied to Europe's problems. . . .

I began to leave, but on the way down the garden, the conversation continued on a fresh fact: peace and education. The teaching of science is all right, but history! Since it is taught from a nationalist standpoint, it creates grave and dangerous problems. "I once put it this way: 'The peoples suffer from their own memories. . . .'" The merry laugh broke out, accompanying my departure as it had welcomed my arrival. . . .

A witness to this interview was the Reverend J. B. Th. Hugenholtz, the Dutch pacifist minister with whom Einstein had been in correspondence earlier in the year and who was a weekend guest at the Einstein summer home. Hugenholtz had sought this occasion to submit to Einstein a plan for the establishment of an International Peace House at The Hague, to be financed independently of the existing pacifist organizations for which it would provide office space, library and meeting facilities. The groups to be approached for moral support were the War Resisters' International, the Women's International League for Peace and Freedom, the International Fellowship of Reconciliation and the International Antimilitaristic Bureau. On July 25, 1932, Einstein acknowledged the outline of the Hugenholtz plan:

I am in full agreement with the text of your outline and hope you will succeed in gaining the approval and unconditional co-operation of the organizations mentioned. Please keep me informed of the success of your efforts.

I am returning your proposal with my signature. I agree to everything except the suggestion that I serve as chairman of the executive committee. That office should be filled by someone who will really do the work rather than merely serve as "window dressing." In general, I incline to the view that the groups concerned should be consulted about the details of the new organization. Every effort should be made to avoid the impression of domination by a small inner circle. I have full confidence in your tact and discretion in this respect.

Hugenholtz accepted Einstein's suggestions and sent him copies of the letters he had written to the various pacifist groups. He reported that a peace congress, to be held in Amsterdam late in August, with Henri Barbusse playing a prominent role, had fallen under Communist domination and that the groups in the Joint Peace Council had reluctantly decided not to participate. A few months later Hugenholtz wrote again. The pacifist groups did not seem to understand his plan for an International Peace House. The War Resisters' International and the International Antimilitaristic Bureau had declined to lend their support, and the other groups had not replied. The Amsterdam Antiwar Congress had been "a failure," and he was now engaged in organizing a "real" antiwar congress. He felt that the work of establishing the International Peace House should proceed without further delay. Would Einstein perhaps help raise money for the project in America "when you are in Princeton"? Einstein's final letter in the exchange is dated October 26, 1932:

I made my participation in your undertaking dependent on the approval and co-operation of the most important pacifist groups. If this cannot be fully achieved, I should regard it as a serious error to go ahead with the project, and I could not participate in it. The worst thing we pacifists could do is to offer the militarists the spectacle of discord.

I also regard it as a serious error to convoke, so soon after the Amsterdam Congress, another congress for the same purpose. I should not wish to participate in any way. Much as I deplore the errors made by M. Barbusse in connection with the congress he sponsored, I am convinced that the pacifist movement must avoid anything that could possibly be considered a counteraction. I beg, indeed, I implore you not to do anything that might harm our cause. At the moment it is more important to restrain oneself than to display initiative. Please continue your patient efforts to achieve full unity among the militant pacifist organizations, even if this means relinquishing some of your own personal desires.

Long before he received Hugenholtz' communication, Einstein had known a great deal about the World Antiwar Congress. As early as April 19, 1932, Barbusse had wired him from Paris asking him to be a sponsor of the congress which was originally conceived in connection with the situation in the Far East. The Japanese invasion of Manchuria in September 1931 was followed, in January 1932, by incidents in Shanghai that led to widespread bloodshed. Barbusse, like many others, viewed the Japanese action as ultimately directed against the Soviet Union. Einstein promptly replied to Barbusse, on April 20, 1932:

I would never take part in such a congress, which would be pathetic in its impotence. It would be something like holding a congress to keep volcanoes from erupting or to increase the rainfall in the Sahara Desert.

Ever since Japan embarked on its Manchurian adventure, it has been clear to me that it was supported by powerful, invisible allies. While I have no direct evidence as to their identity, I feel they are the same forces which are sabotaging the disarmament effort. I believe, moreover, that they exist in France rather than in England. Militarists and munitions industrialists are skillful in exploiting for their own purposes the fears that have haunted the French people ever since the war. To avoid the necessity of adopting the economic measures that would be required to cope with economic crises, governments have always resorted to military adventure, and everywhere the unquenched thirst for dividends is a powerful force behind the scene. . . .

My warmest thanks for your new book on the great French champion of justice [Zola].

Einstein's letter crossed one in which Barbusse set forth the plans for the congress at greater length. It was to be held originally in Geneva on June 28, the eighteenth anniversary of the assassination in Sarajevo of the heir to the Austrian throne, which had been the initial cause of the First World War. The congress was supposed to rise above all partisan debate and to rally the moral and intellectual forces of the world against the folly of an imperialist war. By integrating the scattered pacifist movements that had grown up since the war, it was to operate on the broadest possible basis. Sponsors, in addition to Einstein and Barbusse, were to be Mme. Sun Yat-sen, Theodore Dreiser, Upton Sinclair, John Dos Passos, Heinrich Mann, Maxim Gorki, George Bernard Shaw, H. G. Wells, Romain Rolland and Paul Langevin. Einstein replied on April 26, 1932:

Your letter of April 20 convinced me that I had misinterpreted your telegram and was mistaken about the character of the congress which you suggested. I was under the impression that all you intended was to make a rather impotent protest in the hope of affecting the war policy which Japan is pursuing at the moment. I realize now that you are aiming at a much larger target: to help create a more effective antiwar movement than has thus far existed. In such an endeavor I should be glad to participate as fully as possible.

I am convinced that only one policy will prove effective: All member states of the League of Nations and, in addition, the United States must accept the unconditional obligation to carry out all decisions of the League and the International Court of Arbitration at The Hague.

If we succeeded in convincing the more educated groups in the various countries of the necessity of so far-reaching a renunciation of national sovereignty, we would actually be accomplishing something that would be useful. Had we been able to accomplish this in the past, Japan's insolent action could have been prevented by the imposition of a boycott of all Japanese goods and ships.

During the spring Einstein received a number of messages from Barbusse reporting sponsorship by many other prominent persons as well as steady progress in the organization of the congress. Attached to a letter dated May 18, 1932, was the text of an appeal, to be signed by all the sponsors, which was to serve as a public announcement. The appeal pointed out that the war unleashed in China by Japan was unmistakably directed at the Soviet Union "with the approval and connivance of the great imperialistic powers." The thought was particularly emphasized in the first paragraph of the appeal: "While the Disarmament Conference is in full swing in Geneva, Japan has hurled itself against the Asiatic mainland. It has slaughtered countless innocent people in Chapei. It has occupied Manchuria. Crudely camouflaged as an independent republic, Manchuria is clearly to serve as a strategic base for any war against the Soviet Union. For fifteen years the Soviet Union has striven to build a new world order based on a co-operative community of workers, a reasonable distribution of national income, the pursuit of common welfare, and the abolition of exploitation and oppression of man by his fellow man: in short, on principles diametrically opposed to the anarchy of the capitalist system. The Soviet Union, dedicated to its great task of socialist and human construction, has for months heroically resisted Japanese provocation. . . ."

Early in June 1932, from Caputh, Einstein replied to Barbusse's suggestion to sign the appeal:

On my return from England I received your letter enclosing the draft of an appeal. Because of the glorification of Soviet Russia which it includes, I cannot bring myself to sign it. I have of late tried very hard to form a judgment of what is happening there, and I have reached some rather somber conclusions.

At the top there appears to be a personal struggle in which the foulest means are used by power-hungry individuals acting from purely selfish motives. At the bottom there seems to be complete suppression of the individual and of freedom of speech. One wonders what life is worth under such conditions.

This, however, does not cause me to consider the intrigues of Japan and the powers behind her any less damnable than you do. I have on various occasions hinted at the possibility of an international economic boycott against Japan, only to find that nothing could be achieved, obviously because of the powerful private economic interests that are involved! If you could bring yourself to rephrase the first paragraph of your appeal along more objective lines, omitting any glorification of conditions in the Soviet Union, I would certainly sign it.

In one of his letters, Barbusse had mentioned that his journal, *Monde*, which Einstein had helped him launch some four years before, was in financial difficulties. He had requested a few lines from Einstein, emphasizing the importance of its survival. Einstein obliged with this statement:

We live in a time of moral decay. Reverence for life and respect for truth has been deteriorating. The blatant idol of brute force obtrudes itself everywhere. Those whose obligation it is to guard our spiritual heritage have yielded to weary skepticism. They stand idly by watching our moral impoverishment.

In France, those who are in power pursue goals of personal ambition and greed, feeding and exploiting the popular fears which survived the World War.

Monde is a solitary voice of humanity, seeking to rouse the dormant conscience of the indolent and exposing, honestly and fearlessly, the origin and evil implications of recent developments in the world.

In a letter which was mailed before the receipt of Einstein's refusal to sign the appeal, Barbusse advised Einstein that he had not felt able to wait for the signatures of all the suggested sponsors and had hence published the appeal over his and Rolland's names alone. In a later letter Barbusse reported that the appeal had been well received. He suggested that Einstein's own experience in trying to promote the idea of an economic boycott against Japan was proof of capitalism's role in fomenting war. As for conditions in the Soviet Union, he considered them the subject of much gross calumny and urged Einstein to visit Russia and judge for himself. Einstein replied from Caputh, on June 17, 1932:

You are undoubtedly aware that I agree with you on all essential points. Everything must be done to prevent any external threat to the development of Russia. In my criticism of the appeal I merely sought to avoid glorification of the internal situation in Russia. I do not wish to discuss the matter at length at this time. But I am rather convinced that if Barbusse happened to be in Russia, he would be somewhere in prison or exile, if indeed his life had been spared.

In any event, in the interest of the extraordinarily important cause of peace I should like to urge that, at the Geneva Congress, all peace efforts be supported with great energy, but without any expression in favor of Bolshevism. Otherwise ugly controversies will be inevitable among the most sincere and most devoted people, and your project will probably have even less practical success than it, unfortunately, anyhow has.

It is my conviction that the cause of peace can be effectively served only if the principle of the inviolability of life and the individual is not made the subject of political controversies. We must never forget that the most courageous fighters against militarism come from a religious group, from among the Quakers.

As the congress took shape during the ensuing weeks, its locale shifted from Geneva (where the authorities deemed it subversive), to Brussels and finally to Amsterdam, where it opened on August 27, 1932.[4] Before that date Einstein was to receive five more letters from Barbusse urging his active participation. The German economist Alfons Goldschmidt also appealed to him from Moscow in the hope that he might participate, as did Willi Münzenberg, the German Communist leader and Reichstag Deputy. Barbusse gave glowing accounts of many additional sponsors and hundreds of local committees which supported what had now come to be called the "International Congress against Imperialist Wars." Its letterhead listed Einstein's name among twenty-six other sponsors. Einstein's apprehension that the congress might split the pacifist ranks proved to be well founded. On August 22, 1932, Barbusse wired Einstein from Paris:

Your presence antiwar congress Amsterdam August 26 of crucial importance stop absence would be interpreted vote of nonconfidence stop implore you come Amsterdam stop Romain Rolland Paul Signac Maxim Gorki wiring.

On the back of the telegraph blank Einstein scribbled the following message, with many corrections and interlineations:

When Japan invaded Manchuria, the conscience of the civilized world was not strong enough to prevent this injustice. The economic interests of the war industries proved more powerful than the peoples' desire for justice. Now it has become clear to everyone that one of the purposes of the Japanese adventure was to weaken Russia by military attack and to obstruct its economic development.

All supporters of a healthy development of international legal institutions, regardless of their political or economic ideology, must do all in their power to insure that brute force and the unrestrained lust for profits be replaced by institutions which will make just and considerate decisions. Everyone who stands by idly while our culture is so gravely threatened must share in the guilt.

When, in the leading countries of the world, the desire for justice is strong enough, justice will be achieved. I hope that this congress will help to mobilize public opinion in such a way as to compel governments of the great powers to take the measures necessary to avert the impending disaster.

On September 11, 1932, Barbusse advised Einstein that his message had been warmly applauded. Yet a contemporary account in a German pacifist magazine noted that, in contrast to the enthusiasm that greeted Communist orators, Einstein's message had been received "with extraordinary coolness." On September 23, 1932, a German "Committee against Imperialist Wars," an offshoot of the Amsterdam Congress, notified Einstein that he had been elected a member, not only of this group, but also of a World Antiwar Committee. He replied on September 29, 1932:

I have carefully considered your invitation to become a member of your committee, but I feel unable to accept this invitation. I have long since come to regret my membership in the International Committee which prepared the Amsterdam Congress, although I was in complete accord with the congress about the aims it pursued. I objected, however, to the fact that the congress was entirely under Russian-Communist domination. Also, its resolution is styled in the phraseology customary to the Communist movement. Prominent Social Democrats were excluded from the congress committee. Militant pacifists pleaded with me not to participate in the congress in view of its intolerant political attitude. Had I known in advance about the political position of the congress leadership, I should never have allowed myself to be elected to the Amsterdam Committee; it is important for me to retain a position of political neutrality. Failure to do so might jeopardize my chances of serving the cause of militant pacifism.

On the same day Einstein replied to a similar invitation to sponsor another offshoot of the Amsterdam Congress, a Physicians' Antiwar Committee:

. . . It would be splendid if the medical profession were to become concerned with the cause of active political pacifism. But I believe all such endeavors should be scrupulously free of partisan auspices. This was certainly not true of the Amsterdam Congress, which turned into a Soviet project, pure and simple. That is why so many active pacifists withdrew from it. I am sure Romain Rolland would not have lent his name to the congress had he been properly informed of its political character. Nor would I have done so. If you should want to become active in the cause of peace, I urge you to avoid any identification with the Amsterdam Congress.

The chairman of the main German committee replied that Einstein's objections were without merit. Only six per cent of the presiding committee of the Amsterdam Congress had been Communists. Not only had Social Democrats not been excluded, they had actually been welcomed. The resolution had been drafted by a commission on which Communists represented only a very small minority; indeed, Communists had criticized the resolution for not being strong enough. Many non-Communist pacifists had, in fact, declared that the congress proved that it was possible to collaborate with Communists. Einstein concluded this exchange with the following letter on October 13, 1932:

My information [concerning the Amsterdam Congress] came from unexceptionable sources in whom I have full confidence. One of my informants is a militant pacifist of great merit and absolute integrity. Since I am anxious to avoid partisan ties, I cannot join your organization although I approve fully of your aims. I am, however, prepared to co-operate with you in special situations.

Einstein was not the only one who was disillusioned with the Amsterdam Congress. Victor Margueritte, the French writer, who stood further to the left than Einstein, sent Einstein a copy of his sharply phrased letter of withdrawal from the Amsterdam Committee. Einstein replied on October 19, 1932:

You are quite right . . . Barbusse is a fine man but unfortunately a poor performer. He allowed himself to be so completely taken in by the Bolshevists that the congress lost its suprapartisan character. I am sure that Romain Rolland must also have been greatly dissatisfied with the leadership of the congress but finds it perhaps difficult to withdraw gracefully. I believe that the cause of peace can best be served by creating a militant pacifist organization composed of eminent artists and scholars. Such a group, which would undoubtedly exert great influence, could be assembled if the project were handled with sufficient skill.

Margueritte replied promptly and with enthusiasm. He himself had been thinking of precisely such a group and would have broached the plan to Einstein during a visit to Berlin in May 1932, had not Einstein been away in England. A forthcoming meeting in Paris of the International League against Anti-Semitism might be just the forum for launching such a Committee of Vigilance. Einstein wrote again, suggesting that Margueritte see Langevin, whom Einstein apparently suggested as the prospective head of such a group. Einstein may have discussed the scheme with Langevin in person, or in letters of which no copies were kept. On November 20, 1932, he wrote to his friend Maurice Solovine in Paris: [5]

Tell M. Langevin once again how grateful I am to him and urge him to answer my letter soon. I wrote him about the formation of an international association of leading intellectuals, of dependable pacifist orientation, that should seek, through the press, to exert political influence in matters of disarmament, security, etc. Langevin should be the central figure of such a group, because he is a man not only of good will but also of good political sense.

That same day, Einstein wrote to Chaim Weizmann in London: [6]

. . . I believe you are entirely right in your remarks about the danger of war and the futility of efforts made by political leaders. For some time I have attempted to help assemble an effective group of independent individuals whose prestige derives from their intellectual achievements and whose objectivity and honesty are unquestioned. The purpose of the group would be to support or influence all efforts directed toward international co-operation, disarmament and security, by issuing public announcements on the important questions of the day. [Count] Coudenhove [-Kalergi] [founder and head of the Pan-European Union] would not qualify for this group, because his reputation is not based on achievements in a nonpolitical field; further, his political orientation—for example, his sharp attack on Russia—might jeopardize the effectiveness of such a group. It is indeed doubtful whether any professional politician should be an official member of the organization. . . .

Apparently the plan made no headway, for the following year (July 1, 1933), Einstein wrote to a Frenchwoman who had suggested a similar plan:

The plan which you have advanced closely resembles one which I have repeatedly discussed with Langevin. It appears to be exceedingly difficult to find people who have achieved eminence solely by virtue of their moral qualities. That is why we have tried to form a group of some thirty persons who, in addition to their moral qualities, have gained world-wide reputation through their intellectual achievements. Moral qualities alone would be no guarantee that the group could really become effective.

The project has made no progress because I have received no further news from Langevin, who is a very busy man. Perhaps you will have an opportunity to reawaken his interest. It is possible that the recent political events in Germany have deterred him. Yet it is conceivable that, even now, such an international group might enjoy enough prestige to protect its members against persecution by chauvinist governments.

If you wish to help, you could best do so by discussing the project with Langevin and then reporting back to me in detail. Please tell him that I am prepared to come to Paris just as soon as my health permits.

Einstein's growing apprehension of a Nazi victory in Germany and the resulting increase in the danger of war led him to look everywhere for co-operation and assistance in his fight for sanity. This seems the reason why, in 1932, he addressed himself twice to another intellectual giant, Sigmund Freud. His attitude toward Freud's work had been sympathetic, but not altogether favorable; yet it seems that Einstein made a distinction between Freud the father of psychoanalysis and Freud the social philosopher. It is chiefly in the latter capacity that Einstein approached Freud in his attempt to assemble a group of intellectual leaders and, subsequently, suggested that Freud engage with him in a public discussion about how mankind could be delivered from the menace of war.

Einstein and Freud met personally on at least two occasions. Except for the two letters on the problem of war, their correspondence, so far as can be established, was almost completely limited to the exchange of interesting messages on birthdays and other special occasions. Freud was well aware of Einstein's reservations about his work. In a letter to George Sylvester Viereck of November 6, 1929, he had written: [7]

> . . . You have strikingly isolated the real, true, almost naïve elements that make up the greatness of this rare man, his freedom from countless human foibles. . . . I was already familiar with Einstein's position on psychoanalysis. Several years ago I had a long talk with him during which I realized, to my amusement, that he knows no more about psychology than I do about mathematics. Indeed, I believe I am even ahead of him; while I fully appreciate the *raison d'être* of mathematical thinking, he denies the justification of psychology. . . .
>
> In praising my style and skill in presentation, Einstein merely proves how well-meaning a man he is. He would like to give me credit for the content of my writings. But lacking the necessary understanding, he praises at least my style. . . .

By 1931, Einstein's views had not greatly changed. On December 6 of that year, en route to America, he noted in his diary:

> . . . I understand Jung's [Carl Gustav Jung, a Swiss psychiatrist and disciple of Freud] vague, unprecise notions, but I consider them worthless: a lot of talk without any clear direction. If there has to be a psychiatrist, I should prefer Freud. I do not believe in him, but I love very much his concise style and his original, although rather extravagant, mind. . . .

Einstein's views on psychoanalysis were later modified. When, on April 21, 1936, he addressed Freud on the occasion of his eightieth birthday, he remarked that, until recently, he had found it difficult to have a definite opinion about the validity of Freud's theories. This had now changed since a few cases of which he had heard left no doubt at all in that respect. "This," Einstein wrote, "I considered a blessing; it is always a blessing when a great and beautiful conception is proven to be in harmony with reality." In the last communication Einstein sent Freud, on May 4, 1939, only a few months before Freud's death, he once again expressed his admiration for Freud's literary excellence and said that one must be satisfied if one is able to understand the structure of thoughts in a field of science in which one is not an expert oneself.

The letter which Einstein addressed to Freud, concerning the projected organization of intellectual leaders, was sent in 1931, or possibly 1932, and read as follows: [8]

I greatly admire your passion to ascertain the truth—a passion that has come to dominate all else in your thinking. You have shown with irresistible lucidity how inseparably the aggressive and destructive instincts are bound up in the human psyche with those of love and the lust for life. At the same time, your convincing arguments make manifest your deep devotion to the great goal of the internal and external liberation of man from the evils of war. This was the profound hope of all those who have been revered as moral and spiritual leaders beyond the limits of their own time and country, from Jesus to Goethe and Kant. Is it not significant that such men have been universally recognized as leaders, even though their desire to affect the course of human affairs was quite ineffective?

I am convinced that almost all great men who, because of their accomplishments, are recognized as leaders even of small groups share the same ideals. But they have little influence on the course of political events. It would almost appear that the very domain of human activity most crucial to the fate of nations is inescapably in the hands of wholly irresponsible political rulers.

Political leaders or governments owe their power either to the use of force or to their election by the masses. They cannot be regarded as representative of the superior moral or intellectual elements in a nation. In our time, the intellectual elite does not exercise any direct influence on the history of the world; the very fact of its division into many factions makes it impossible for its members to co-operate in the solution of today's problems. Do you not share the feeling that a change could be brought about by a free association of men whose previous work and achievements offer a guarantee of their ability and integrity? Such a group of international scope, whose members would have to keep contact with each other through constant interchange of opinions, might gain a significant and wholesome moral influence on the solution of political problems if its own attitudes, backed by the signatures of its concurring members, were made public through the press. Such an association would, of course, suffer from all the defects that have so often led to degeneration in learned societies; the danger that such a degeneration may develop is, unfortunately, ever present in view of the imperfections of human nature. However, and despite those dangers, should we not make at least an attempt to form such an association in spite of all dangers? It seems to me nothing less than an imperative duty!

Once such an association of intellectuals—men of real stature—has come into being, it might then make an energetic effort to enlist religious groups in the fight against war. The association would give moral power for action to many personalities whose good intentions are today paralyzed by an attitude of painful resignation. I also believe that such an association of men, who are highly respected for their personal accomplishments, would provide important moral support to those elements in the League of Nations who actively support the great objective for which that institution was created.

I offer these suggestions to you, rather than to anyone else in the world, because your sense of reality is less clouded by wishful thinking than is the case with other people and since you combine the qualities of critical judgment, earnestness and responsibility.

The high point in the relationship between Einstein and Freud came in the summer of 1932 when, under the auspices of the International Institute of Intellectual Co-operation, Einstein initiated a public debate with Freud about the causes and cure of wars. Einstein's official letter is dated July 30, 1932; it was accompanied by the following private note of the same date:

I should like to use this opportunity to send you warm personal regards and to thank you for many a pleasant hour which I had in reading your works. It is always amusing for me to observe that even those who do not believe in your theories find it so difficult to resist your ideas that they use your terminology in their thoughts and speech when they are off guard.

This is Einstein's open letter to Freud, which, strangely enough, has never become widely known: [9]

DEAR MR. FREUD:

The proposal of the League of Nations and its International Institute of Intellectual Co-operation at Paris that I should invite a person, to be chosen by myself, to a frank exchange of views on any problem that I might select affords me a very welcome opportunity of conferring with you upon a question which, as things now are, seems the most insistent of all the problems civilization has to face. This is the problem: Is there any way of delivering mankind from the menace of war? It is common knowledge that, with the advance of modern science, this issue has come to mean a matter of life and death for civilization as we know it; nevertheless, for all the zeal displayed, every attempt at its solution has ended in a lamentable breakdown.

I believe, moreover, that those whose duty it is to tackle the problem professionally and practically are growing only too aware of their impotence to deal with it, and have now a very lively desire to learn the views of men who, absorbed in the pursuit of science, can see world problems in the perspective distance lends. As for me, the normal objective of my thought affords no insight into the dark places of human will and feeling. Thus, in the inquiry now proposed, I can do little more than to seek to clarify the question at issue and, clearing the ground of the more obvious solutions, enable you to bring the light of your far-reaching knowledge of man's instinctive life to bear upon the problem. There are certain psychological obstacles whose existence a layman in the mental sciences may dimly surmise, but whose interrelations and vagaries he is incompetent to fathom; you, I am convinced, will be able to suggest educative methods, lying more or less outside the scope of politics, which will eliminate these obstacles.

As one immune from nationalist bias, I personally see a simple way of dealing with the superficial (i.e., administrative) aspect of the problem: the setting up, by international consent, of a legislative and judicial body to settle every conflict arising between nations. Each nation would undertake to abide by the orders issued by this legislative body, to invoke its decision in every dispute, to accept its judgments unreservedly and to carry out every measure the tribunal deems necessary for the execution of its decrees. But here, at the outset, I come up against a difficulty; a tribunal is a human institution which, in proportion as the power at its disposal is inadequate to enforce its verdicts, is all the more prone to suffer these to be deflected by extrajudicial pressure. This is a fact with which we have to reckon; law and might inevitably go hand in hand, and juridical decisions approach more nearly the ideal justice demanded by the community (in whose name and interests these verdicts are pronounced) insofar as the community has effective power to compel respect of its juridical ideal. But at present we are far from possessing any supranational organization competent to render verdicts of incontestable authority and enforce absolute submission to the execution of its verdicts. Thus I am led to my first axiom: The quest of international security involves the unconditional surrender by every nation, in a certain measure, of its liberty of action—its sovereignty that is to say—and it is clear beyond all doubt that no other road can lead to such security.

The ill success, despite their obvious sincerity, of all the efforts made during the last decade to reach this goal leaves us no room to doubt that strong psychological factors are at work which paralyze these efforts. Some of these factors are not far to seek. The craving for power which characterizes the governing class in every nation is hostile to any limitation of the national sovereignty. This political power hunger is often supported by the activities of another group, whose aspirations are on purely mercenary, economic lines. I have especially in mind that small but determined group, active in every nation, composed of individuals who, indifferent to social considerations and restraints, regard warfare, the manufacture and sale of arms, simply as an occasion to advance their personal interests and enlarge their personal authority.

But recognition of this obvious fact is merely the first step toward an appreciation of the actual state of affairs. Another question follows hard upon it: How is it possible for this small clique to bend the will of the majority, who stand to lose and suffer by a state of war, to the service of their ambitions? (In speaking of the majority I do not exclude soldiers of every rank who have chosen war as their profession, in the belief that they are serving to defend the highest interests of their race, and that attack is often the best method of defense.) An obvious answer to this question would seem to be that the minority, the ruling class at present, has the schools and press, usually the Church as well, under its thumb. This enables it to organize and sway the emotions of the masses, and makes its tool of them.

Yet even this answer does not provide a complete solution. Another question arises from it: How is it that these devices succeed so well in rousing men to such wild enthusiasm, even to sacrifice their lives? Only one answer is possible. Because man has within him a lust for hatred and destruction. In normal times this passion exists in a latent state, it emerges only in unusual circumstances; but it is a comparatively easy task to call it into play and raise it to the power of a collective psychosis. Here lies, perhaps, the crux of all the complex factors we are considering, an enigma that only the expert in the lore of human instincts can resolve.

And so we come to our last question. Is it possible to control man's mental evolution so as to make him proof against the psychosis of hate and destructiveness? Here I am thinking by no means only of the so-called uncultured masses. Experience proves that it is rather the so-called "intelligentsia" that is most apt to yield to these disastrous collective suggestions, since the intellectual has no direct contact with life in the raw but encounters it in its easiest, synthetic form—upon the printed page.

To conclude: I have so far been speaking only of wars between nations; what are known as international conflicts. But I am well aware that the aggressive instinct operates under other forms and in other circumstances. (I am thinking of civil wars, for instance, due in earlier days to religious zeal, but nowadays to social factors; or, again, the persecution of racial minorities.) But my insistence on what is the most typical, most cruel and extravagant form of conflict between man and man was deliberate, for here we have the best occasion of discovering ways and means to render all armed conflicts impossible.

I know that in your writings we may find answers, explicit or implied, to all the issues of this urgent and absorbing problem. But it would be of the greatest service to us all were you to present the problem of world peace in the light of your most recent discoveries, for such a presentation well might blaze the trail for new and fruitful modes of action.

Yours very sincerely,
A. EINSTEIN

Leon Steinig, a League of Nations official who did much to inspire this correspondence, wrote Einstein on September 12, 1932:

. . . When I visited Professor Freud in Vienna, he asked me to thank you for your kind words and to tell you that he would do his best to explore the thorny problem of preventing war. He will have his answer ready by early October and he rather thinks that what he has to say will not be very encouraging. "All my life I have had to tell people truths that were difficult to swallow. Now that I am old, I certainly do not want to fool them." He was even doubtful whether [Henri] Bonnet [Director of the Institute of Intellectual Co-operation in Paris] would want to publish his pessimistic reply. . . .

Einstein replied to Steinig four days later saying that even if Freud's reply would be neither cheerful nor optimistic, it would certainly be interesting and psychologically effective.

Freud's reply, dated Vienna, September 1932, has also never been given the attention it deserved:

DEAR MR. EINSTEIN:

When I learned of your intention to invite me to a mutual exchange of views upon a subject which not only interested you personally but seemed deserving, too, of public interest, I cordially assented. I expected you to choose a problem lying on the borderland of the knowable, as it stands today, a theme which each of us, physicist and psychologist, might approach from his own angle, to meet at last on common ground, though setting out from different premises. Thus the question which you put me—what is to be done to rid mankind of the war menace?—took me by surprise. And, next, I was dumfounded by the thought of my (of *our*, I almost wrote) incompetence; for this struck me as being a matter of practical politics, the statesman's proper study. But then I realized that you did not raise the question in your capacity of scientist or physicist, but as a lover of his fellow men, who responded to the call of the League of Nations much as Fridtjof Nansen, the polar explorer, took on himself the task of succoring homeless and starving victims of the World War. And, next, I reminded myself that I was not being called on to formulate practical proposals but, rather, to explain how this question of preventing wars strikes a psychologist.

But here, too, you have stated the gist of the matter in your letter—and taken the wind out of my sails! Still, I will gladly follow in your wake and content myself with endorsing your conclusions, which, however, I propose to amplify to the best of my knowledge or surmise.

You begin with the relations between might and right, and this is assuredly the proper starting point for our inquiry. But, for the term *might,* I would substitute a tougher and more telling word: *violence.* In right and violence we have today an obvious antinomy. It is easy to prove that one has evolved from the other and, when we go back to origins and examine primitive conditions, the solution of the problem follows easily enough. I must crave your indulgence if in what follows I speak of well-known, admitted facts as though they were new data; the context necessitates this method.

Conflicts of interest between man and man are resolved, in principle, by the recourse to violence. It is the same in the animal kingdom, from which man cannot claim exclusion; nevertheless, men are also prone to conflicts of opinion, touching, on occasion, the loftiest peaks of abstract thought, which seem to call for settlement by quite another method. This refinement is, however, a late development. To start with, group force was the factor which, in small communities, decided points of ownership and the question which man's will was to prevail. Very soon physical force was implemented, then replaced, by the use of various adjuncts; he proved the victor whose weapon was the better, or handled the more skillfully. Now, for the first time, with the coming of weapons, superior brains began to oust brute force, but the object of the conflict remained the same: one party was to be constrained, by the injury done him or impairment of his strength, to retract a claim or a refusal. This end is most effectively gained when the opponent is definitely put out of action—in other words, is killed.

This procedure has two advantages: the enemy cannot renew hostilities, and, secondly, his fate deters others from following his example. Moreover, the slaughter of a foe gratifies an instinctive craving—a point to which we shall revert hereafter. However, another consideration may be set off against this will to kill: the possibility of using an enemy for servile tasks if his spirit be broken and his life spared. Here violence finds an outlet not in slaughter but in subjugation. Hence springs the practice of giving quarter; but the victor, having from now on to reckon with the craving for revenge that rankles in his victim, forfeits to some extent his personal security.

Thus, under primitive conditions, it is superior force—brute violence, or violence backed by arms—that lords it everywhere. We know that in the course of evolution this state of things was modified, a path was traced that led away from violence to law. But what was this path? Surely it issued from a single verity: that the superiority of one strong man can be overborne by an alliance of many weaklings, that *l'union fait la force.* Brute force is overcome by union; the allied might of scattered units makes good its right against the isolated giant. Thus we may define "right" (i.e., law) as the might of a community. Yet it, too, is nothing else than violence, quick to attack whatever individual stands in its path, and it employs the selfsame methods, follows like ends, with but one difference: it is the communal, not individual, violence that has its way. But, for the transition from crude violence to the reign of law, a certain psychological condition must first obtain. The union of the majority must be stable and enduring. If its sole *raison d'être* be the discomfiture of some overweening individual and, after his downfall, it be dissolved, it leads to nothing. Some other man, trusting to his superior power, will seek to reinstate the rule of violence, and the cycle will repeat itself unendingly. Thus the union of the people must be permanent and well organized; it must enact rules to meet the risk of possible revolts; must set up machinery insuring that its rules—the laws—are observed and that such acts of violence as the laws demand are duly carried out. This recognition of a community of interests engenders among the members of the group a sentiment of unity and fraternal solidarity which constitutes its real strength.

So far I have set out what seems to me the kernel of the matter:

the suppression of brute force by the transfer of power to a larger combination, founded on the community of sentiments linking up its members. All the rest is mere tautology and glosses. Now the position is simple enough so long as the community consists of a number of equipollent individuals. The laws of such a group can determine to what extent the individual must forfeit his personal freedom, the right of using personal force as an instrument of violence, to insure the safety of the group. But such a combination is only theoretically possible; in practice the situation is always complicated by the fact that, from the outset, the group includes elements of unequal power, men and women, elders and children, and, very soon, as a result of war and conquest, victors and the vanquished—i.e., masters and slaves—as well. From this time on the common law takes notice of these inequalities of power, laws are made by and for the rulers, giving the servile classes fewer rights. Thenceforward there exist within the state two factors making for legal instability, but legislative evolution, too: first, the attempts by members of the ruling class to set themselves above the law's restrictions and, secondly, the constant struggle of the ruled to extend their rights and see each gain embodied in the code, replacing legal disabilities by equal laws for all. The second of these tendencies will be particularly marked when there takes place a positive mutation of the balance of power within the community, the frequent outcome of certain historical conditions. In such cases the laws may gradually be adjusted to the changed conditions or (as more usually ensues) the ruling class is loath to rush in with the new developments, the result being insurrections and civil wars, a period when law is in abeyance and force once more the arbiter, followed by a new regime of law. There is another factor of constitutional change, which operates in a wholly pacific manner, viz.: the cultural evolution of the mass of the community; this factor, however, is of a different order and can only be dealt with later.

Thus we see that, even within the group itself, the exercise of violence cannot be avoided when conflicting interests are at stake. But the common needs and habits of men who live in fellowship under the same sky favor a speedy issue of such conflicts and, this being so, the possibilities of peaceful solutions make steady progress. Yet the most casual glance at world history will show an unending series of conflicts between one community and another or a group of others, between large and smaller units, between cities, countries, races, tribes and kingdoms, almost all of which were settled by the ordeal of war. Such war ends either in pillage or in conquest and its fruits, the downfall of the loser. No single all-embracing judgment can be passed on these wars of aggrandizement. Some, like the war between the Mongols and the Turks, have led to unmitigated misery; others, however, have furthered the transition from violence to law, since they brought larger units into being, within whose limits a recourse to violence was banned and a new regime determined all disputes. Thus the Roman conquest brought that boon, the *pax Romana*, to the Mediterranean lands. The French kings' lust for aggrandizement created a new France, flourishing in peace and unity. Paradoxical as its sounds, we must admit that warfare well might serve to pave the way to that unbroken peace we so desire, for it is war that brings vast empires into being, within whose frontiers all warfare is proscribed by a strong central power. In practice, however, this end is not attained, for as a rule the fruits of victory are but short-lived, the new-created unit falls asunder once again, generally because there can be no true cohesion between the parts that violence has welded. Hitherto, moreover, such conquests have only led to aggregations which, for all their magnitude, had limits, and disputes between these units could be resolved only by recourse to arms. For humanity at large the sole result of all these military enterprises was that, instead of frequent, not to say incessant, little wars, they had now to face great wars which, for all they came less often, were so much the more destructive.

Regarding the world of today the same conclusion holds good, and you, too, have reached it, though by a shorter path. There is but one sure way of ending war and that is the establishment, by common consent, of a central control which shall have the last word in every conflict of interests. For this, two things are needed: first, the creation of such a supreme court of judicature; secondly, its investment with adequate executive force. Unless this second requirement be fulfilled, the first is unavailing. Obviously the League of Nations, acting as a Supreme Court, fulfills the first condition; it does not fulfill the second. It has no force at its disposal and can only get it if the members of the new body, its constituent nations, furnish it. And, as things are, this is a forlorn hope. Still we should be taking a very shortsighted view of the League of Nations were we to ignore the fact that here is an experiment the like of which has rarely—never before, perhaps, on such a scale—been attempted in the course of history. It is an attempt to acquire the authority (in other words, coercive influence), which hitherto reposed exclusively in the possession of power, by calling into play certain idealistic attitudes of mind. We have seen that there are two factors of cohesion in a community: violent compulsion and ties of sentiment ("identifications," in technical parlance) between the members of the group. If one of these factors becomes inoperative, the other may still suffice to hold the group together. Obviously such notions as these can only be significant when they are the expression of a deeply rooted sense of unity, shared by all. It is necessary, therefore, to gauge the efficacy of such sentiments. History tells us that, on occasion, they have been effective. For example, the Panhellenic conception, the Greeks' awareness of superiority over their barbarian neighbors, which found expression in the Amphictyonies, the Oracles and Games, was strong enough to humanize the methods of warfare as between Greeks, though inevitably it failed to prevent conflicts between different elements of the Hellenic race or even to deter a city or group of cities from joining forces with their racial foe, the Persians, for the discomfiture of a rival. The solidarity of Christendom in the Renaissance age was no more effective, despite its vast authority, in hindering Christian nations, large and small alike, from calling in the Sultan to their aid. And, in our times, we look in vain for some such unifying notion whose authority would be unquestioned. It is all too clear that the nationalistic ideas, paramount today in every country, operate in quite a contrary direction. Some there are who hold that the Bolshevist conceptions may make an end of war, but, as things are, that goal lies very far away and, perhaps, could only be attained after a spell of brutal internecine warfare. Thus it would seem that any effort to replace brute force by the might of an ideal is, under present conditions, doomed to fail. Our logic is at fault if we ignore the fact that right is founded on brute force and even today needs violence to maintain it.

I now can comment on another of your statements. You are

amazed that it is so easy to infect men with the war fever, and you surmise that man has in him an active instinct for hatred and destruction, amenable to such stimulations. I entirely agree with you. I believe in the existence of this instinct and have been recently at pains to study its manifestations. In this connection may I set out a fragment of that knowledge of the instincts, which we psychoanalysts, after so many tentative essays and gropings in the dark, have compassed? We assume that human instincts are of two kinds: those that conserve and unify, which we call "erotic" (in the meaning Plato gives to Eros in his Symposium), or else "sexual" (explicitly extending the popular connotation of "sex"); and, secondly, the instincts to destroy and kill, which we assimilate as the aggressive or destructive instincts. These are, as you perceive, the well-known opposites, Love and Hate, transformed into theoretical entities; they are, perhaps, another aspect of those eternal polarities, attraction and repulsion, which fall within your province. But we must be chary of passing overhastily to the notions of good and evil. Each of these instincts is every whit as indispensable as its opposite, and all the phenomena of life derive from their activity, whether they work in concert or in opposition. It seems that an instinct of either category can operate but rarely in isolation; it is always blended ("alloyed," as we say) with a certain dosage of its opposite, which modifies its aim or even, in certain circumstances, is a prime condition of its attainment. Thus the instinct of self-preservation is certainly of an erotic nature, but to gain its end this very instinct necessitates aggressive action. In the same way the love instinct, when directed to a specific object, calls for an admixture of the acquisitive instinct if it is to enter into effective possession of that object. It is the difficulty of isolating the two kinds of instinct in their manifestations that has so long prevented us from recognizing them.

If you will travel with me a little further on this road, you will find that human affairs are complicated in yet another way. Only exceptionally does an action follow on the stimulus of a single instinct, which is *per se* a blend of Eros and destructiveness. As a rule several motives of similar composition concur to bring about the act. This fact was duly noted by a colleague of yours, Professor G. C. Lichtenberg, sometime Professor of Physics at Göttingen; he was perhaps even more eminent as a psychologist than as a physical scientist. He evolved the notion of a "Compass-card of Motives" and wrote: "The efficient motives impelling man to act can be classified like the thirty-two winds and described in the same manner; e.g., *Food-Food-Fame* or *Fame-Fame-Food*." Thus, when a nation is summoned to engage in war, a whole gamut of human motives may respond to this appeal—high and low motives, some openly avowed, others slurred over. The lust for aggression and destruction is certainly included; the innumerable cruelties of history and man's daily life confirm its prevalence and strength. The stimulation of these destructive impulses by appeals to idealism and the erotic instinct naturally facilitate their release. Musing on the atrocities recorded on history's page, we feel that the ideal motive has often served as a camouflage for the lust of destruction; sometimes, as with the cruelties of the Inquisition, it seems that, while the ideal motives occupied the foreground of consciousness, they drew their strength from the destructive instincts submerged in the unconscious. Both interpretations are feasible.

You are interested, I know, in the prevention of war, not in our theories, and I keep this fact in mind. Yet I would like to dwell a little longer on this destructive instinct which is seldom given the attention that its importance warrants. With the least of speculative efforts we are led to conclude that this instinct functions in every living being, striving to work its ruin and reduce life to its primal state of inert matter. Indeed, it might well be called the "death instinct"; whereas the erotic instincts vouch for the struggle to live on. The death instinct becomes an impulse to destruction when, with the aid of certain organs, it directs its action outward, against external objects. The living being, that is to say, defends its own existence by destroying foreign bodies. But, in one of its activities, the death instinct is operative *within* the living being and we have sought to trace back a number of normal and pathological phenomena to this *introversion* of the destructive instinct. We have even committed the heresy of explaining the origin of human conscience by some such "turning inward" of the aggressive impulse. Obviously when this internal tendency operates on too large a scale, it is no trivial matter; rather, a positively morbid state of things; whereas the diversion of the destructive impulse toward the external world must have beneficial effects.

Here is then the biological justification for all those vile, pernicious propensities which we are now combating. We can but own that they are really more akin to nature than this our stand against them, which, in fact, remains to be accounted for.

All this may give you the impression that our theories amount to a species of mythology and a gloomy one at that! But does not every natural science lead ultimately to this—a sort of mythology? Is it otherwise today with your physical sciences?

The upshot of these observations, as bearing on the subject in hand, is that there is no likelihood of our being able to suppress humanity's aggressive tendencies. In some happy corners of the earth, they say, where nature brings forth abundantly whatever man desires, there flourish races whose lives go gently by, unknowing of aggression or constraint. This I can hardly credit; I would like further details about these happy folk. The Bolshevists, too, aspire to do away with human aggressiveness by insuring the satisfaction of material needs and enforcing equality between man and man. To me this hope seems vain. Meanwhile they busily perfect their armaments, and their hatred of outsiders is not the least of the factors of cohesion among themselves. In any case, as you too have observed, complete suppression of man's aggressive tendencies is not in issue; what we may try is to divert it into a channel other than that of warfare.

From our "mythology" of the instincts we may easily deduce a formula for an indirect method of eliminating war. If the propensity for war be due to the destructive instinct, we have always its counter-agent, Eros, to our hand. All that produces ties of sentiment between man and man must serve us as war's antidote. These ties are of two kinds. First, such relations as those toward a beloved object, void though they be of sexual intent. The psychoanalyst need feel no compunction in mentioning "love" in this connection; religion uses the same language: Love thy neighbor as thyself. A pious injunction, easy to enounce, but hard to carry out! The other bond of sentiment is by way of identification. All that brings out the significant resemblances between men calls into play this feeling of community, identification, whereon is founded, in large measure, the whole edifice of human society.

In your strictures on the abuse of authority I find another suggestion for an indirect attack on the war impulse. That men are divided into the leaders and the led is but another manifestation of their inborn and irremediable inequality. The second class constitutes the vast majority; they need a high command to make decisions for them, to which decisions they usually bow without demur. In this context we would point out that men should be at greater pains than heretofore to form a superior class of independent thinkers, unamenable to intimidation and fervent in the quest of truth, whose function it would be to guide the masses dependent on their lead. There is no need to point out how little the rule of politicians and the Church's ban on liberty of thought encourage such a new creation. The ideal conditions would obviously be found in a community where every man subordinated his instinctive life to the dictates of reason. Nothing less than this could bring about so thorough and so durable a union between men, even if this involved the severance of mutual ties of sentiment. But surely such a hope is utterly utopian, as things are. The other indirect methods of preventing war are certainly more feasible, but entail no quick results. They conjure up an ugly picture of mills that grind so slowly that, before the flour is ready, men are dead of hunger.

As you see, little good comes of consulting a theoretician, aloof from worldly contact, on practical and urgent problems! Better it were to tackle each successive crisis with means that we have ready to our hands. However, I would like to deal with a question which, though it is not mooted in your letter, interests me greatly. Why do we, you and I and many another, protest so vehemently against war, instead of just accepting it as another of life's odious importunities? For it seems a natural thing enough, biologically sound and practically unavoidable. I trust you will not be shocked by my raising such a question. For the better conduct of an inquiry it may be well to don a mask of feigned aloofness. The answer to my query may run as follows: Because every man has a right over his own life and war destroys lives that were full of promise; it forces the individual into situations that shame his manhood, obliging him to murder fellow men, against his will; it ravages material amenities, the fruits of human toil, and much besides. Moreover, wars, as now conducted, afford no scope for acts of heroism according to the old ideals and, given the high perfection of modern arms, war today would mean the sheer extermination of one of the combatants, if not of both. This is so true, so obvious, that we can but wonder why the conduct of war is not banned by general consent. Doubtless either of the points I have just made is open to debate. It may be asked if the community, in its turn, cannot claim a right over the individual lives of its members. Moreover, all forms of war cannot be indiscriminately condemned; so long as there are nations and empires, each prepared callously to exterminate its rival, all alike must be equipped for war. But we will not dwell on any of these problems; they lie outside the debate to which you have invited me. I pass on to another point, the basis, as it strikes me, of our common hatred of war. It is this: We cannot do otherwise than hate it. Pacifists we are, since our organic nature wills us thus to be. Hence it comes easy to us to find arguments that justify our standpoint.

This point, however, calls for elucidation. Here is the way in which I see it. The cultural development of mankind (some, I know, prefer to call it civilization) has been in progress since immemorial antiquity. To this *processus* we owe all that is best in our composition, but also much that makes for human suffering. Its origins and causes are obscure, its issue is uncertain, but some of its characteristics are easy to perceive. It well may lead to the extinction of mankind, for it impairs the sexual function in more than one respect, and even today the uncivilized races and the backward classes of all nations are multiplying more rapidly than the cultured elements. This process may, perhaps, be likened to the effects of domestication on certain animals—it clearly involves physical changes of structure—but the view that cultural development is an organic process of this order has not yet become generally familiar. The psychic changes which accompany this process of cultural change are striking, and not to be gainsaid. They consist in the progressive rejection of instinctive ends and a scaling down of instinctive reactions. Sensations which delighted our forefathers have become neutral or unbearable to us; and, if our ethical and aesthetic ideals have undergone a change, the causes of this are ultimately organic. On the psychological side two of the most important phenomena of culture are, firstly, a strengthening of the intellect, which tends to master our instinctive life, and, secondly, an introversion of the aggressive impulse, with all its consequent benefits and perils. Now war runs most emphatically counter to the psychic disposition imposed on us by the growth of culture; we are therefore bound to resent war, to find it utterly intolerable. With pacifists like us it is not merely an intellectual and affective repulsion, but a constitutional intolerance, an idiosyncrasy in its most drastic form. And it would seem that the aesthetic ignominies of warfare play almost as large a part in this repugnance as war's atrocities.

How long have we to wait before the rest of men turn pacifist? Impossible to say, and yet perhaps our hope that these two factors —man's cultural disposition and a well-founded dread of the form that future wars will take—may serve to put an end to war in the near future, is not chimerical. But by what ways or byways this will come about, we cannot guess. Meanwhile we may rest on the assurance that whatever makes for cultural development is working also against war.

With kindest regards and, should this exposé prove a disappointment to you, my sincere regrets,

Yours,
SIGMUND FREUD

Einstein was apparently not disappointed when Freud's reply was received. He addressed the following letter to Freud on December 3, 1932:

You have made a most gratifying gift to the League of Nations and myself with your truly classic reply. When I wrote you I was thoroughly convinced of the insignificance of my role, which was only meant to document my good will, with me as the bait on the hook to tempt the marvelous fish into nibbling. You have given in return something altogether magnificent. We cannot know what may grow from such seed, as the effect upon man of any action or event is always incalculable. This is not within our power and we do not need to worry about it.

You have earned my gratitude and the gratitude of all men for having devoted all your strength to the search for truth and for having shown the rarest courage in professing your convictions all your life. . . .

By the time the exchange between Einstein and Freud was published in 1933, under the title *Why War?*, Hitler, who was to drive both men into exile, was already in power, and the letters never achieved the wide circulation intended for them. Indeed, the first German edition of the pamphlet is reported to have been limited to only 2,000 copies, as was also the original English edition.

Besides the four major projects in 1932 that were just recorded, some of the messages, replies to inquiries, and similar statements which Einstein prepared during that same period give evidence of the increasing political tensions of those days. On April 20, 1932, he submitted to the Russian-language journal *Nord-Ost*, published in Riga, Latvia (then still an independent country), a contribution to a symposium on "Europe and the Coming War":

As long as all international conflicts are not subject to arbitration and the enforcement of decisions arrived at by arbitration is not guaranteed, and as long as war production is not prohibited, we may be sure that war will follow upon war. Unless our civilization achieves the moral strength to overcome this evil, it is bound to share the fate of former civilizations: decline and decay.

To Arnold Kalisch, editor of the magazine *Die Friedensfront*, who asked him to sponsor a book against war by a Czechoslovakian physician, Einstein wrote on April 26, 1932:

No doubt you know how anxious I am to support anything that could effectively help combat the militaristic orientation of the public. But I have reservations . . . about this book. If war psychosis could be regarded as an illness like, say, paranoia, then any panic in a meeting would likewise have to be considered a sickness. It appears to be quite normal for people to raise little resistance to the emotional attitude of their fellow human beings. . . . In the case of war, to describe the psychosis that may then exist as an illness does not bring us one single step closer to solving the problem of wars. . . .

Coudenhove-Kalergi of the Pan-European Union asked Einstein to sponsor a congress planned for the fall of 1932. Einstein replied on July 6, 1932:

Although I believe without any qualification in the idea of a United Europe, I cannot bring myself to join your committee. Here is my reason:

The Pan-European movement is identified with your name. In a special publication you have taken an outspokenly hostile position against present-day Russia, at a time when devious efforts were made to bring about a suppression of that country through military force. In these circumstances, to join your committee would imply that I align myself with a position which I do not share. I certainly do not approve of much that is taking place in Russia, but I approve even less of the violent methods that are being used to suppress the only serious attempt to create a just and rational economic order.

To Maxim Gorki, the great Russian writer, who was approaching his sixty-fifth birthday, Einstein wrote on September 29, 1932:

I understand that you are celebrating the anniversary of your excellent creative artistry. I feel the need to tell you on this occasion how greatly I rejoice that there is such a man as you in the world. Few creative masters of the first rank have remained, to the degree that you have, both servants of their own society and fighters for the improvement of mankind's lot. May your work continue to ennoble men, whatever form their political organization may take. Destiny will always be decided by what the individual feels, wills and does. That is why, in the long run, the education of man will always be far more the task of creative minds than of political leaders.

To a Berlin newspaper that asked him to state his position on the freedom of the press, Einstein wrote on October 13, 1932: [10]

A country that restricts or even suppresses freedom of opinion and criticism on political matters, spoken or written, is bound to deteriorate. A citizenry that tolerates such restrictions testifies to, and thereby further increases, its political inferiority.

To the German journalist Rudolf Olden, who urged him to sponsor a demonstration of intellectuals for freedom of the press, speech, assembly and teaching, Einstein replied on October 12, 1932:

I am firmly convinced that any country whose citizens surrender any of those rights should not be considered a civilized nation, but merely a state of powerless subjects. It is unworthy of an independent individual to belong to such a state if there is any way he can avoid it. . . . I sympathize with your efforts; to support them is the compelling duty of all those who comprehend the significance of what is involved and who value the welfare and dignity of their community.

On November 18, 1932, commenting on certain disarmament proposals (including the establishment of an international police force) made by Édouard Herriot, the new French Premier, Einstein issued the following statement: [11]

I am convinced that Herriot's plan represents an important step forward with regard to how, in the future, international disputes should be settled. I also consider Herriot's plan to be preferable to other proposals that have been made. In striving for comprehension, the way a given problem is defined is always crucial. That means, the question to be asked is not under what conditions are armaments permissible and how wars should be fought. Rather, the point of departure must be the following resolution:

"We are prepared to submit all international disputes to the judgment of an arbitration authority which has been established by the common consent of all of us. To make this possible it is necessary that certain conditions be satisfied which will guarantee our security. The problem is to reach agreement among ourselves about these conditions."

The renunciation of unlimited sovereignty by individual nations is the indispensable prerequisite to a solution of the problem. It is the great achievement of Herriot, or rather of France, that they have announced their willingness, in principle, for such a renunciation.

I also agree with Herriot's proposal that the only military force that should be permitted to have truly effective weapons is a police force which would be subject to the authority of international organs and would be stationed throughout the world.

My main objections to Herriot's plans are these: The police formations should not be composed of national troop units which are dependent on their own governments. Such a force, to function effectively under the jurisdiction of a supranational authority, must be—both men and officers—international in composition.

There is a second important point of disagreement with the French plan—namely, its support of the militia system. A militia system implies that the entire population will be trained in military concepts. It further implies that youth will be educated in a spirit which is at once obsolete and fateful. What would the more advanced nations say if they were confronted with the request that every citizen must serve as a policeman for a certain period of his life? To raise the question is to answer it.

These objections should not appear to detract from my belief that Herriot's proposals must be gratefully welcomed as a courageous and significant step in the right direction.

The following statement of Einstein was made, probably sometime in 1932, on behalf of the Reichsbanner, the semimilitary formation organized for the defense of the Weimar Republic by liberals and the non-Communist left of Germany in the last few years of the Weimar Republic: [12]

Unquestionably the *Reichsbanner,* because of its systematic work of informing and advising the public and thanks to its independence from any one political party, is most capable of counteracting the dangers of Nazi propaganda. I, therefore, believe that at a time when political self-discipline has everywhere deteriorated, every thoughtful citizen who possibly can should support the *Reichsbanner* in order that a great economic debacle may be averted and confidence in law and order restored, both at home and abroad.

When it became known that Einstein intended to pay another visit to the United States during the winter of 1932–1933, a group of patriotic American women protested, to the Department of State, the granting of a visa to a person whom they described as a Communist and a member of the War Resisters' International. Einstein replied with the following statement: [13]

Never before have I been so brusquely rejected by the fair sex; at least never by so many of its members at once!

How right they are, those vigilant, civic-minded ladies! Why open one's door to someone who devours hard-boiled capitalists with as much appetite and gusto as the Cretan Minotaur devoured luscious Greek maidens in days gone by; one who is wicked enough to reject every kind of war, except the inexorable war with one's own spouse!

Give ye therefore heed to your prudent and loyal womenfolk and remember that the Capitol of mighty Rome was once saved by the cackling of her faithful geese.

Possibly, the ladies had been nettled by another statement of Einstein about "patriotic women": [14]

It seems to me that the patriotic women rather than their menfolk ought to be sent to the front in the next war. It would at least provide a novelty in this desolate domain of infinite confusion. Besides, why should heroic impulses on the part of the fair sex not find a more romantic outlet than attacks on a defenseless civilian?

Einstein departed for America on December 10, 1932. His stay in Pasadena was marked by less public activity than on the two previous visits there. On January 22, 1933, he again addressed a group of students of the California Institute of Technology: [15]

It is heartening to see California youth take such a deep interest in the maintenance and strengthening of peace, which is, indeed, one of the most important problems challenging mankind today.

Americans, without doubt, enjoy a particularly favorable position: under no conceivable circumstances could their country be seriously threatened by military aggression. Nevertheless, as a nation they have an abiding interest in the creation both of an international arbitration tribunal for the settlement of international disputes, and of a machinery for the enforcement of the judgments of such a tribunal. The World War has made obvious how closely the destiny of nations is interwoven. The fact that economic crises have occurred throughout the world at about the same time teaches the same lesson.

The principal conclusion is that American youth must make its influence felt in the direction of having the United States participate in every effort to create an international organization. Understandably, the experiences of the war and postwar years have deterred many Americans; but if the United States continues its traditional isolation, all mankind, including the United States, will suffer.

It seems to me that, at the present time, the most urgent task for pacifist organizations is to campaign with all their energy for the abolition of compulsory military service throughout the world. Only then can a conciliatory spirit gain ground among the nations of the world. We all know that Germany is demanding a military status equal to that of other nations, and the request for such equality is obviously justified. However, the real question is on what basis this equality should be restored. If we do not now succeed in abolishing compulsory military service on an international scale, then it will undoubtedly be restored in Germany, creating a situation every bit as menacing as that which existed before the war. The most important task of pacifists today is to awaken the peoples of the world to the dangers of the situation while, at the same time, making energetic efforts leading toward international abolition of compulsory military service.

Another statement along similar lines, probably prepared for a pacifist meeting in California, was made around the same time: [16]

I warmly welcome you assembled fighters for peace. You well know that the situation in the world has not improved in recent years. Everywhere the depression has strengthened reactionary forces which, in turn, are exploiting blind nationalism for their own ulterior purposes. While more and more countries prepare to introduce compulsory military service, freedom of speech and of the press is being curtailed. Man's sense of freedom, dignity and justice is deteriorating.

Remember that while society has a right to count on your cooperation for the common good, it has no jurisdiction over your bodies and your souls. There is no power on earth from which we should be prepared to accept an order to kill or to be trained for killing.

Let us pledge ourselves to do our best to spread this spirit of war resistance. Above all, let us vow that this shall be the spirit in which we shall rear our children.

To an American educator who had visited him in Caputh in 1931 Einstein wrote on February 1, 1933: [17]

Men of stature among generations past fully recognized the importance of securing international peace. The growth of technology in our day has made this ethical postulate a matter of life and death to civilized mankind. Active participation in solving the problem of peace is a question of conscience which no man of good will can evade.

We must be clear that the powerful industrial groups of all countries, which participate in the production of arms, are trying to sabotage efforts to obtain a peaceful settlement of international disputes. Governments will achieve this important goal only when they can count on the active support of the majority of the people. In an age such as ours, when we live under democratic forms of government, the fate of nations is dependent on the people. It is important that we be conscious of this at all times.

The malevolent attacks on Einstein did not cease after his arrival in the United States. Perhaps the most telling refutation to such attacks was offered in a Concurrent Resolution of the legislature of the State of New Jersey, adopted January 30, 1933,[18] the very day Hitler became Chancellor of Germany:

WHEREAS, Announcement has been made that the New Institute of Advanced Studies, situated in the State of New Jersey, has invited the eminent scientist, Professor Albert Einstein, to become a member of its faculty; and

WHEREAS, It is further announced that the said Professor Albert Einstein has accepted the invitation; and

WHEREAS, The outstanding scientific ability of Professor Einstein is universally acknowledged and commended; and

WHEREAS, The addition of the said Professor Albert Einstein to the faculty of a New Jersey institution of learning brings with it honor to the State of New Jersey and to its people; and

WHEREAS, We, the members of the New Jersey Legislature, are cognizant of the high position of eminence occupied in the scientific world by the said Professor Albert Einstein and of the honor that is conferred upon our state by his accepting membership in the faculty of one of our institutions within the state; now therefore

Be it resolved, That the Legislature of the State of New Jersey do, and it does hereby welcome the said eminent Professor Albert Einstein to the State of New Jersey, to his new scene of scientific activities; and

Be it further resolved, That an invitation be extended to Professor Albert Einstein to address the members of the legislature in the very near future; and

Be it further resolved, That a copy of this resolution be forwarded to the said Professor Albert Einstein and to the New Institute of Advanced Studies, in New Jersey.

Despite the official honor conferred upon him by this resolution, Einstein was bitterly attacked by a Princeton alumnus as a "foreign spouter of doctrines inimical to our Constitution, history and social life" who should be barred from lecturing at Princeton "because of his Communistic and pacifistic doctrines." Since attacks from other sides also continued, Einstein found himself obliged, on July 7, 1933, to send the following letter to both *The Times* (of London) and *The New York Times:*

I have received a copy of a circular issued by the Better America Federation, containing alleged photographs of me purporting to show that I am connected with the Third [Communist] International.

I have never had anything to do with the Third International, and never have been in Russia.

Furthermore, it is manifest that the pictures purporting to be my photographs do not resemble me. The pictures are probably an attempted forgery inspired by political motives.

Hitler's ascent to power on January 30, 1933, certainly did not come as a great surprise to Einstein. He decided not to return to Germany at all; his plans for the immediate future were still vague, as is indicated in a letter which he sent from Pasadena to a friend on February 27, 1933: [19]

. . . I dare not enter Germany because of Hitler. . . . We leave here on March 10, and I shall have days of work requiring great exertion in Chicago and New York before the passage. . . . I have already canceled my lecture at the [Prussian] Academy [of Sciences]. . . . I leave on March 25 for Switzerland to meet my son. . . . Subsequently, I shall go either to Lake Lugano or to Belgium, or Holland. . . .

"I am not going home," Einstein announced in an interview on the eve of his departure from Pasadena, as reported by Evelyn Seeley in the *New York World-Telegram* of March 11, 1933. He pronounced his decision in a statement which has become widely known: [20]

As long as I have any choice in the matter, I shall live only in a country where civil liberty, tolerance and equality of all citizens before the law prevail. Civil liberty implies freedom to express one's political convictions, in speech and in writing; tolerance implies respect for the convictions of others whatever they may be. These conditions do not exist in Germany at the present time. Men, among them leading artists, who have made a particularly great contribution to the cause of international understanding, are being persecuted there.

Just as an individual may become mentally ill when subject to stress, so a social organism is equally subject to disease when faced with profound problems. Nations usually survive such difficulties. It is my hope that a healthier atmosphere may soon be restored in Germany. I also hope that, in days to come, Germany's great men, such as Kant and Goethe, will not only be celebrated from time to time, but will be ever honored—in public life, in the minds of the people, and by the living observance of the great principles for which they stood.

"We shall probably go to Switzerland," Einstein told Miss Seeley. "My citizenship is a strange affair. Although my real citizenship is Swiss, I am a German citizen on account of my official position.[21] However, for an internationally minded man citizenship of a specific country is not important. Humanity is more important than national citizenship."

Einstein had to hurry away from the interview to attend a scientific seminar. Miss Seeley relates: "As he left the seminar, walking across the campus, Dr. Einstein felt the ground shaking under his feet. Los

Angeles was being visited by the worst earthquake in its history, but Dr. Einstein went calmly home."

In Chicago, on March 14, 1933, his fifty-fourth birthday, Einstein was honored at a luncheon [22] that included many prominent persons, such as the Governor of Illinois, attorney Clarence Darrow, and physicist Arthur Holly Compton of the University of Chicago, who introduced him. "Einstein spoke in a small, hesitant voice, occasionally asking someone near him for a word," says the account in *The New York Times*. He spoke of the problem of "finding a method of distribution which would work as well as that of production" and of "how to organize international affairs in such a manner as to abolish war."

The turn of events in Germany lent added significance to Einstein's visit to New York. The several busy days he spent in the city in mid-March of 1933 were once again a great personal triumph. On March 17, Mrs. Rosika Schwimmer and Alfred Lief, whose anthology of Einstein's pacifist writings, *The Fight Against War*, was to be published later that year, arranged a reception for him at the Waldorf-Astoria Hotel.[23] It was attended by many notables. In the course of the reception, a number of questions were addressed to Einstein. When asked whether the United States should appropriate money for a budget for peace, as it did for war, Einstein said he favored the idea. However, it was important to make sure that the right people would decide how to spend the money appropriated for peace. Otherwise, it might do no more good than the money spent for "peace" by the Carnegie Foundation. Einstein reiterated his conviction that partial disarmament could not prevent wars; its only function would be to save some money.

Mrs. Rosika Schwimmer inquired whether, in his opinion, anything could be done in America to ease the political tension in Europe. Einstein felt it would be a mistake to minimize the potential influence of the American press; but whatever might be done should not be done by "direct" action. American sympathy with the German people and American grief at the turn of political events in Germany should be expressed in a dignified manner, not by calling the Germans fools. He said it was shameful of the German Academy of Art to behave in such a way that a writer like Heinrich Mann and an artist of the eminence of Käthe Kollwitz should find it necessary to resign. Pacifists in Germany were now officially considered enemies of the state.

On March 20, 1933, the Nazis raided the Einstein summer home at Caputh, near Berlin, on the pretext that arms might be hidden there. Einstein, on the high seas en route to Europe, issued the following statement:

The raid on the home of my wife and myself in Caputh by an armed crowd is but one example of the arbitrary acts of violence now taking place throughout Germany.

These acts are the result of the government's overnight transfer of police powers to a raw and rabid mob of the Nazi militia.

My summer home has often in the past been honored by the presence of guests. They were always welcome. No one had any reason to break in.

Einstein did not go to Switzerland. Instead he retreated for several months to the little Belgian seaside resort of Le Coq-sur-mer. The Nazi seizure of power posed grave problems of conscience to him, as it did to many other pacifists. It took him some time to adapt his views to the new situation. That the transition was not made immediately is shown in a note which he sent as late as May 1, 1933, to the Viennese author of a book defending the Jews against the charge of cowardice: [24]

I shall not object should you decide to dedicate your book to me. But I cannot bring myself to write a preface. As an antimilitarist I am not in the least interested in how Jews behave as soldiers. I can assure you that I should have taken advantage of any and all means for evading military service, had anyone ever tried to press me into it. If one desires to be a hero, one should do so by accepting the consequences that will result from refusing military service.

But the incisive change in Einstein's position was to come shortly.

CHAPTER SEVEN

ADVENT OF NAZISM AND ADVOCACY OF MILITARY PREPAREDNESS. DEPARTURE FROM EUROPE | 1933

NAZISM'S ADVENT TO POWER in Germany on January 30, 1933, cast a shadow over Einstein's life which was not to disappear to the end of his days. He was never able to forget that it was Germany, the land of his birth, that brought war and immeasurable suffering and misery to the world and that, in its satanic desire for the annihilation of all Jews, attained a degree of bestiality and barbarism which not even one possessed of the wildest imagination could have anticipated. Einstein was so deeply wounded that he remained completely aloof from Germany and, with a consistency that few others have shown, rejected all the many attempts of *rapprochement* made to him after the end of the war.

The threat of war, which Nazism constituted from its very inception, the war itself and, after the war, the remilitarization of Germany and the world preoccupied Einstein constantly and influenced, if not determined, many of his actions and decisions in public affairs. He never wavered in his profound abhorrence of war, nor in his conviction that only the creation of a supranational organization would safeguard the peace of the world; but the seizure of unlimited power in the heart of Europe by a political constellation that defied all moral and ethical laws and openly glorified war caused Einstein to abandon his support of war resistance and advocate rearmament in the West—a radical departure from his previous views which appeared to him inescapable in the face of the mortal danger confronting the world.

Einstein possessed the moral strength to reverse himself in view of compelling circumstances. But he never failed to distinguish between strategy and principle. It is true that, when the Nazi monster threatened the peace of Europe, Einstein acknowledged and, in the face of severe attacks by pacifist friends, publicly advocated the necessity of military preparedness; it is equally true that he never ceased to advocate the establishment of a machinery for the settlement of international disputes through peaceful means. Throughout the twenty-two years that elapsed from the time Nazism took hold of Germany in 1933 until his death in 1955, Einstein seized every opportunity to fight for the abolition of war, whatever temporary policy he might advocate at a given time. He fought against war with particular vigor in the early years after the end of the Second World War. But he grew increasingly pessimistic about the chances for early success in this fight; more and more, he refused to support what he considered to be half measures or actions which he could not possibly conceive as effective in terms of the ultimate aim—that of abolishing war.

The counterrevolutionary upheaval in Germany imposed other changes in Einstein's life. Although, in the summer of 1932, before the actual advent of Nazism to power, he had accepted an invitation to become the first faculty member of the new Institute for Advanced Study in Princeton, New Jersey,[1] he had not planned to leave Europe altogether. He intended to maintain his membership in the Prussian Academy of Sciences and to spend summer semesters in Berlin. These plans now became impossible. While his emigration to the United States did not mean any change in his scientific work—even his assistant came with him to America—his daily life differed in many respects from what it had been in Berlin. What he missed most, and for which he never found a substitute, was his association in Berlin with an unusual group of outstanding scientists whose stimulating friendship he greatly enjoyed. There were also scientists outside Berlin who, like Langevin and Marie Curie in Paris, and Ehrenfest in Holland, had been particularly close to him and who, after his departure from Europe in the fall of 1933, were of necessity no longer part of his immediate life.

Upon his return from the United States to Europe on March 28, 1933, he officially resigned from the Prussian Academy, which almost certainly would have expelled him within the next few days. His resignation led to an exchange of communications between the academy and himself.[2] He declared that he did not want to live in a country where not all citizens enjoyed equality before the law, while the academy accused him of having participated in the spreading of atrocity stories about Germany in foreign countries when, the academy claimed, it would have been his obligation to defend Germany against those absurd allegations. In his final letter, dated April 12, 1933, Einstein said:

. . . To give such "testimony" as you request of me would be a denial of all the principles of justice and liberty for which I have stood all my life. Such testimony would not have been, as you suggest, a demonstration in behalf of the German people; rather, it would only have furthered the cause of those who seek to destroy the very ideals and principles that have earned the German people a place of honor in the civilized world. Had I issued such testimony in the present circumstances, I would have contributed, if only indirectly, to moral corruption and the destruction of all existing cultural values. . . .

The Bavarian Academy of Science, of which Einstein was a corresponding member, emphasized its solidarity with the Prussian Academy and asked him the leading question on April 8, 1933, as to what he himself thought his future relationship with the Bavarian Academy ought to be in view of his break with the Prussian Academy. Einstein replied on April 21, 1933:

[My reasons for resigning from the Prussian Academy] would not necessarily imply severance of my relations with the Bavarian Academy. If, nevertheless, I desire my name to be stricken from the roster of its members, it is for other reasons.

The primary object of an academy is to protect and enrich the scientific life of a country. Yet to the best of my knowledge, the learned societies of Germany have stood by passively and silently while substantial numbers of scholars, students and academically trained professionals have been deprived of employment and livelihood. I do not want to belong to any society which behaves in such a manner, even if it does so under pressure.

That Einstein had not been mistaken about the sentiments of his colleagues in the Prussian Academy and that his resignation did not come a day too early became very clear in the several letters which his friend Max Planck addressed to him during the month of March 1933. These letters did not reach him until early in April, a number of days after he had mailed his resignation. It must have been very painful to him to gather from Planck's letter that even he—the same man who, twenty years before, had urged Einstein to resign from his position in Zurich and to accept membership in the academy—appeared to be affected by the hate campaign in the German press against

Einstein and considered Einstein's resignation the only way in which his removal from the academy could have been accomplished "honorably"—a way, Planck said, which "spared Einstein's friends immeasurable grief." This undoubtedly implied that his "friends" had been prepared to approve of his expulsion had his resignation not been received before. Einstein replied to Planck's letters on April 6, 1933:

. . . I have never taken part in any "atrocity-mongering." I will give the academy the benefit of assuming that it made these slanderous statements only under outside pressure. But even if that should be so, its conduct will hardly be to its credit; some of its more decent members will certainly feel a sense of shame even today.

You have probably learned that these false accusations were used as an excuse for the confiscation of my property in Germany. My Dutch colleagues joined in an effort to help me over the initial financial difficulties. It was fortunately not necessary for me to accept their help since I had been careful to prepare for such an emergency. It will certainly be easy for you to imagine how the public outside of Germany feels about the tactics employed against me. Surely there will come a time when decent Germans will be ashamed of the ignominious way in which I have been treated.

I cannot help but remind you that, in all these years, I have only enhanced Germany's prestige and never allowed myself to be alienated by the systematic attacks on me in the rightist press, especially those of recent years when no one took the trouble to stand up for me. Now, however, the war of annihilation against my defenseless fellow Jews compels me to employ, in their behalf, whatever influence I may possess in the eyes of the world.

That you may better appreciate my feelings, I ask you to imagine yourself for the moment in this situation: Assume that you were a university professor in Prague and that a government came into power which would deprive Czechs of German origin of their livelihood and at the same time employ crude methods to prevent them from leaving the country. Assume further that guards were posted at the frontiers to shoot all those who, without permission, attempted to leave the country that waged a bloodless war of annihilation against them. Would you then deem it decent to remain a silent witness to such developments without raising your voice in support of those who are being persecuted? And is not the destruction of the German Jews by starvation the official program of the present German Government?

If you were to read what I actually said (not distorted accounts), you would doubtless realize that I expressed myself in a thoughtful and moderate way. I say this not to apologize but to demonstrate vividly the ignoble and ignominious manner in which the German authorities have behaved toward me.

I am happy that you have nevertheless approached me as an old friend and that, in spite of severe pressures from without, the relationship between us has not been affected. It remains as fine and genuine as ever, regardless of what has taken place "on a lower level," so to speak. The same holds true for Laue, for whom I have the very highest respect.

P.S. I have chosen a somewhat formal form of address to make sure that the letter will not be opened or seized en route.

How deeply Einstein was shaken by the events in Germany is revealed in a communication which he sent to Max von Laue, another German physicist who had been a close and loyal friend for many years. Von Laue, Nobel Prize winner in 1914, was one of the relatively few people who defended Einstein during the early twenties when he was subject to vicious political attacks. Von Laue was also one of the few scientists who remained in Germany after 1933 without paying any allegiance to the Nazi regime. Einstein wrote to him on May 26, 1933, during a brief visit to Oxford:

. . . I do not share your view that the scientist should observe silence in political matters, i.e., human affairs in the broader sense. The situation in Germany shows whither such restraint will lead: to the surrender of leadership, without any resistance, to those who are blind or irresponsible. Does not such restraint signify a lack of responsibility? Where would we be, had men like Giordano Bruno, Spinoza, Voltaire and Humboldt thought and behaved in such a fashion? I do not regret one word of what I have said and am of the belief that my actions have served mankind. Do you think that I regret not being able to stay in your country under present circumstances? It would have been impossible for me, even if they had wrapped me in cotton. But my feeling of warm friendship for you and a few others in Germany remains strong. I hope we will meet again in happier times. . . .

Einstein expressed his feelings also in communications to several other physicist friends. In one of his frequent letters to Paul Ehrenfest, his intimate friend in Holland, Einstein said on April 14, 1933:

I am sure you know how firmly convinced I am of the causality of all events. You are hence well aware that I never act out of blind passions. I have come to regard developments in Germany in the following way:

A small group of pathological demagogues was able to capture and exploit the support of a population which is completely uneducated politically. This group is now moving in a direction that will become increasingly destructive. There is the danger that even countries outside of Germany will be contaminated, particularly since those belonging to this group in Germany are masters of propaganda. This is why I felt it absolutely necessary to do what I could in order to mobilize some decent individuals outside of Germany, and I have done so with great caution insofar as I did not say anything for which I would not have been willing to assume responsibility. If powerful moral and economic pressure had not been brought to bear so quickly, the Jews would have suffered even more than they actually have. Our friends in Germany need not do anything to protect me; in fact, such action would needlessly endanger them. However, it must be said that, in general, the lack of courage on the part of the educated classes in Germany has been catastrophic. Let me remind you of how pitifully the Academy of Arts conducted itself in the cases of Heinrich Mann and Käthe Kollwitz. Another case in point is the stupid attitude of the Secretary of the Prussian Academy, who permitted the release of the calumnious press notice about myself. . . .

Among the many physicists in foreign countries who were appalled by the attitude of the Prussian Academy was Hans Thirring, Professor of Physics at the University of Vienna, a philosopher and an active fighter against war. He voiced his dismay at the academy's treatment of Einstein in letters to Planck and to Professor Erwin Schrödinger, another physicist at the University of Berlin. On May 3, 1933, Einstein replied to a letter from Thirring in which Thirring had expressed sympathy and admiration for him:

In these times it requires much courage to say those things which ought to be taken for granted and to act accordingly; there are few indeed who actually possess that courage. You are one of the few. I wish to shake your hand; it is the hand of someone whose entire way of thinking is very similar to my own. The future will be on our side unless the revolution from below will destroy all intellectual values.

It should be clear by now that much more is involved than merely the Jews. The Jews have become victims only because they occupy an exposed position both as individuals and intellectuals. The representatives of the scientific world have failed in their duty to defend intellectual values because they have completely lost their passionate love of them. This is the only reason why vicious individuals of inferior intellect have been able to seize power and indoctrinate the population with their contemptible ideas.

While things have not yet reached this point everywhere, it would be disastrous not to realize that we must fight and convince those whose values have remained uncorrupted that they, like us, must not abstain from the struggle.

Among the European physicists, one of Einstein's most beloved friends was Paul Langevin in Paris. Einstein wrote him on May 5, 1933:

Dear Friend:

Since we met at Antwerp, far-reaching and serious events have taken place which endanger our civilization and, most particularly, the security of Europe. As was the case during the war, we have once again become used to reading every day about dreadful acts of terror, although we should be aware that many of these crimes never become known to the public. A group of armed bandits in Germany has successfully silenced the responsible segments of the population and imposed a kind of revolution from below which will soon succeed in destroying or paralyzing everything that is civilized in society. That which, today, threatens our cultural values will, in a few years, become a grave military menace unless the countries still living under a parliamentary system eventually decide to take vigorous action. Such action, today, could still be of a purely economic character. It is unfortunate that the danger confronting us is not sufficiently recognized or, if there is adequate information, the initiative for energetic action is missing, although less than fifteen years have passed since the last horrible experience of war. I am convinced that, today, it is still possible to defeat the German menace by imposing a commercial blockade.

The superb attitude which the French Government and my French colleagues have displayed toward me has been a great satisfaction. Since official notification of my election to the Collège de France has so far not reached me, I have not yet been able officially to express my gratitude.

I now find myself in a kind of dilemma which is just the reverse of that which confronts many of my fellow Jews who have been driven out of Germany. I accepted an appointment arranged for in Princeton by Abraham Flexner at the Institute for Advanced Study for the entire winter (about five to six months). I have also been invited to spend one month during each of the next five years at Christ Church College in Oxford. In addition, Spain has offered me a kind of professorship at the University of Madrid. I accepted the position and promised to go there next April, before I received the French offer. . . . And finally, during this present month, I agreed to give a series of lectures at the Franqui Foundation in Brussels. Since I cannot do any of these things during the summer vacation, it is not clear to me when and for how long I could come to Paris. I gave the French Consul detailed information about all of this when, at the direction of the French Minister, he discussed the French project with me for the first time.

You may feel that it would have been my duty not to accept the Spanish and French offers since my actual abilities are hardly in proportion to what is expected of me. Under the existing circumstances, however, such a refusal might have been misinterpreted since both invitations were, at least to some extent, political demonstrations which I considered important and did not want to spoil. . . . Maybe events will make it possible that one day we shall once more live close to each other. This would be a great joy to me. . . .

Although Einstein was assured of the position at the Institute for Advanced Study in Princeton and although, as his letter to Langevin revealed, famous universities in several countries were bidding for his services, his personal situation remained quite precarious. He was without a permanent home; members of his immediate family were still in Germany. Nor was life in Le Coq-sur-mer without its vicissitudes. There were rumors that the Germans had placed a price on his head and that attempts would be made to kidnap or assassinate him. Further, there came a constant stream of visitors, many of them seeking aid. Nevertheless, Einstein carried on much as he had before. On April 29, 1933, he wrote to Thomas Mann:

I am anxious to tell you something that is really quite obvious: The responsible and conscientious attitude shown by you and your brother [2a] has been, in the recent past, one of the few cheerful events in an otherwise dark Germany. Many others who could have provided intellectual leadership had neither the courage nor the strength of character necessary to draw a clear demarcation between themselves and those who, through resorting to violence, have made themselves the representatives of the state. Their failure to act has resulted in strengthening the power of those catastrophic elements; they have done incalculable harm to Germany's good name. In addition, they run the risk of being contemptuously ignored by the very mob they now seek to flatter.

Once more, it becomes clear that the fate of a community is primarily determined by the level of its moral standards. Any leadership worthy of the name will crystallize and develop only on the basis of the values and ideals which you and your brother represent. Even if you should not live to see such leadership materialize, this hope should give you real solace in these cruel times and in the bitter days yet to come.

To the German writer Wilhelm Herzog, Einstein wrote on May 5, 1933:

. . . The great task [of German intellectuals in exile] is to impress upon those countries that still adhere to the ideals of culture and freedom, the living conviction that it is terribly dangerous to witness events as passive spectators. Today it is still possible to crush those who have usurped power in Germany; it could still be done, without bloodshed, by economic means. Otherwise, within a few years, much sacrifice of human life will be unavoidable, and, even then, there will be no certainty of a favorable outcome. I have the impression that the enormity of the present danger is not properly appreciated abroad and that people are lulled by the hope that the specter will one day disappear of its own weight. . . .

While at Oxford, Einstein also wrote to an old Zionist friend, Stephen S. Wise, Rabbi of the Free Synagogue in New York and one of the earliest and most active fighters in America against Nazism. At the time, Rabbi Wise was under heavy attack by Jewish groups in the United States who feared that any bitter denunciations of Hitlerism by American Jews might provide an excuse for the German Government to intensify its campaign of persecution against the Jews in Germany. Wise had stated these difficulties and controversies in a letter to Einstein of May 9, 1933. Einstein replied on June 6, 1933:

First of all, I should like to thank you for having stimulated me to write to Mr. Holmes [John Haynes Holmes, Minister of the Community Church in New York and an intimate friend of Rabbi Wise's]. I did so immediately upon reading your letter, which means today. I can assure you that I have not been lazy these days, but I have simply not been able to do all that I should have liked to do.

I have thought about the disagreements between yourself and Mr. Cyrus Adler [President of the Jewish Theological Seminary of America], which are revealed in the correspondence you sent me. I am sure you are surprised to learn that I have not come to an unequivocal position.

Those activities of Jews outside Germany which become public knowledge may, on the one hand, make an impression upon the German Government; on the other hand, they may serve as pretext for their anti-Semitic provocations and as justification for the reign of terror against German Jews. Nevertheless, it is quite possible that demonstrations of protest by American Jews may be an important factor in mobilizing the sentiments of non-Jews in America so that they too may oppose those who are now in power in Germany. . . .

However, I have no doubt that it is much more important to carry on *well-organized* activities behind the scenes, directed particularly toward American government authorities and the American press. The simple truth must be emphasized again and again that the Germans are secretly arming at a great pace. Factories are working day and night, some of them in Sweden (airplanes, bombs, tanks and heavy artillery). Millions of men are being trained clandestinely; anyone who would dare denounce these violations of the Versailles Treaty would be punished as a traitor; silence is being enforced by all means of terror. The desire for revenge among the educated segments of the population explains their failure to oppose the contemptible and criminal regime, as well as their failure to act at a time when they could have done so successfully. The price which will have to be paid, even if the present government is allowed to stay in power but one year, will be the sacrifice of a terrifying number of human lives and untold destruction. . . .

Were the leaders in America to realize that, under these conditions, any policy of toleration is a crime, particularly a crime against France, for which a heavy penalty will have to be paid, they would certainly not hesitate to adopt a policy of careful supervision of the entire German industry and would find means to stop further criminal developments. Were the American authorities correctly appraised of the nature of the German menace, they would undoubtedly be more willing to arrange, via Geneva, some effective protection of the Jewish population in Germany.

The public must be made aware, through the press, of the German military danger. They must be informed of the consequences which a new European war would entail, particularly in view of the threat posed by Japan, a threat which would greatly increase were Europe to become paralyzed through war.

Although he continued to emphasize how important it was for individuals to refuse military service, Einstein had for some time been wavering in his view that the use of force was never justified; the notion of an international police force composed of citizens of different nations appealed to him increasingly to secure world peace. He had taken up the idea with the War Resisters' International during his visit to America the preceding winter. In response, Lord Ponsonby reaffirmed the position of that group in a letter, dated February 6, 1933, to H. Runham Brown, its honorary secretary. A copy of Ponsonby's letter was forwarded to Einstein on April 10, 1933. Ponsonby used uncompromising language:

> . . . Professor Einstein's . . . views are, of course, worthy of close consideration. . . . But I am inclined to think that, in our desire to be what people call practical, we may commit ourselves to some halfway house which would be in conflict with our extreme view. This would certainly alienate support from us. Our strength lies in our uncompromising attitude. . . .
>
> I am quite sure we should avoid advocating anything like new forms of military organization. Professor Einstein's mention of the fusing of small professional armies and the eventual establishment of an international police force reminds me of the French proposals and is a policy advocated here by Lord Davies and others. I personally have always strongly opposed it for two main reasons:
>
> 1. It is undesirable, because it is an admission that force is the factor which can resolve international disputes.
>
> 2. It is impracticable, because the League of Nations, which cannot even get complete agreement about an abstract resolution or protest, would never get anything like agreement about the action and movements of an international force.
>
> . . . If I allow a crack of the door to be opened, I cannot logically or rationally hold my ground against those who will easily force the door wide open. I refuse to be deprived of my locks and bolts. I cannot forge them to be strong enough yet, but posterity will do so—sooner than people expect.

Lord Ponsonby's negative response to the suggestion concerning an international police force obviously did not affect Einstein's own views. In fact, with Hitler's advent to power and the subsequent complete change in the international political situation, Einstein became increasingly impressed with the desirability of organizing military power on an international basis. He discussed the matter in renewed correspondence with Reverend Hugenholtz and Otto Lehmann-Russbüldt. To these two militant pacifists, however, the creation of an International Peace House (see p. 174) still seemed the most important task. Einstein did not reject the idea of such a peace center, which he hoped would sometime result from a merger of the existing peace organizations, but balked at lending his name to the ambitious plans of his two pacifist friends. He wrote, on July 1, 1933:

. . . I must confess freely that the time seems inauspicious for further advocacy of certain propositions of the radical pacifist movement. For example, is one justified in advising a Frenchman or a Belgian to refuse military service in the face of German rearmament? Ought one to campaign for such a policy? Frankly, I do not believe so. It seems to me that in the present situation we must support a *supranational* organization of force rather than advocate the abolition of all forces. Recent events have taught me a lesson in this respect. . . .

The following day Einstein sent a statement to the *Biosophical Review*, published by the Spinoza Center in New York. Once more he emphasized his belief in a supranational court as the only possible solution to the peace problem, and said that he also considered an international police force a necessary instrument to secure peace.[3]

During his springtime visit to England, Einstein had met Lord Davies in Glasgow, and had apparently decided that the position of the New Commonwealth Society, which Lord Davies headed, was close to his own. On July 20, 1933, he sent Davies this statement for publication:

In my view your books are the best and most effective publications in their field. I could not have expressed my own position as well or as completely as you have:

No disarmament without security.

No security without a mandatory international court of arbitration and an international standing army.

You have proved these points impressively, and I fervently hope your labors will attract the serious attention they deserve.

The following month, Einstein accepted election as a "foundation member" of the New Commonwealth Society and, upon the request of Lord Davies, prepared a statement in which he characterized the international army as a "police force" and included these remarks:

This goal, so essential if we are to avert the menace of utter annihilation, unfortunately cannot be attained little by little. Renunciation of competitive armaments by individual countries will be possible only when the problem of security is completely solved. Such a program requires that the participating countries voluntarily renounce a part of their sovereignty. At present, such renunciation meets resistance due to the vain nationalism especially of the great powers.

The statesman who can bring into being such international arrangements will have rendered mankind as great a service as any man has ever performed.

The question Einstein pondered most deeply during these disturbing months at Le Coq-sur-mer concerned the wholehearted support he had given in the past to the idea of individual war resistance. He could no longer postpone making a decision on the principle involved: in June, Alfred Nahon, a young French pacifist then living in Belgium, fervently implored him to appear for the defense at the forthcoming trial of two conscientious objectors, Day and Campon, who were at the time held prisoners in Brussels. Einstein's possible intervention in the case was apparently also of interest to the Belgian Court. Early in July a lady, close to the court, wrote him that "the husband of the second fiddler would like to see you on an urgent matter." This was a reference to King Albert of Belgium, whose wife, Queen Elizabeth, had played second fiddle to Einstein's first during several informal string quartet sessions.[4] The meeting took place; the discussion with the King apparently helped Einstein to come to a decision on the crucial matter of war resistance. This is indicated in a letter which he addressed to the King on July 14, 1933, and which was obviously meant to state with great precision what had been said before orally at the meeting:

YOUR MAJESTY:

The matter of the conscientious objectors is constantly on my mind. It is a grave question, far transcending the special case before me.

I have already indicated why, despite my close association with the War Resisters' movement, I shall not intervene:

1. In the present threatening situation, created by the events in Germany, Belgium's armed forces can only be regarded as a means of defense, not an instrument of aggression. And now, of all times, such defense forces are urgently needed.

2. If anyone is to intervene in the case, it should not be one who enjoys your country's hospitality.

I should like to venture some additional remarks, however. Men who, by their religious and moral convictions, are constrained to refuse military service should not be treated as criminals. Nor should anyone be permitted to sit in judgment on the question of whether such a refusal is rooted in deep conviction or in less worthy motives.

In my view there exists a more dignified and more effective way of testing and utilizing such men. They should be offered the alternative of accepting more onerous and hazardous work than military service. If their conviction is deep enough, they will choose this course; and there will probably never be many of such people. As substitute work I have in mind certain types of mine labor, stoking furnaces aboard ships, hospital service in infectious-disease wards or in certain sections of mental institutions, and possibly other services of a similar nature.

Anyone who voluntarily accepts such service without pay is possessed of remarkable qualities and really deserves even more than merely being accepted as a conscientious objector. Certainly, he should not be treated as a criminal. Were Belgium to enact such a law or merely establish such a custom, it would constitute noteworthy progress toward true humanity.

With respect and cordiality,
ALBERT EINSTEIN

King Albert's reply, sent from Ostend on July 24, 1933, was exceedingly friendly, but noncommittal:

MY DEAR PROFESSOR:

I have received with great pleasure the letter you have so kindly written me, and I send you my warmest thanks.

I am most responsive to what you say about Belgium and the sincerity of its foreign policy.

The Belgian Government intends to stay out of the conflicts that are taking place in or among its neighbor countries; under no circumstances will it consent to discriminatory practices which the great majority of Belgians consider unacceptable. As you have said it so well, our army is defensive in character. To serve in it means to serve the will of a free people intent on maintaining the place which is legitimately theirs in the society of nations.

We are delighted that you have set foot on our soil. There are men who by their work and intellectual stature belong to mankind rather than to any one country; yet the country they choose as their asylum takes keen pride in that fact.

The Queen joins me in sending you best wishes for a pleasant stay in Belgium. Please accept my expression of high esteem.

ALBERT

Even before he had received this reply, Einstein had taken the step that was to disappoint many of his pacifist admirers. On July 20, 1933, he wrote to Alfred Nahon, the French anti-militarist in Belgium who had requested Einstein's intervention on behalf of two imprisoned conscientious objectors: [5]

What I shall tell you will greatly surprise you. Until quite recently we in Europe could assume that personal war resistance constituted an effective attack on militarism. Today we face an altogether different situation. In the heart of Europe lies a power, Germany, that is obviously pushing toward war with all available means. This has created such a serious danger to the Latin countries, especially Belgium and France, that they have come to depend completely on their armed forces. As for Belgium, surely so small a country cannot possibly misuse its armed forces; rather, it needs them desperately to protect its very existence. Imagine Belgium occupied by present-day Germany! Things would be far worse than in 1914, and they were bad enough even then. Hence I must tell you candidly: Were I a Belgian, I should not, in the present circumstances, refuse military service; rather, I should enter such service cheerfully in the belief that I would thereby be helping to save European civilization.

This does not mean that I am surrendering the principle for which I have stood heretofore. I have no greater hope than that the time may not be far off when refusal of military service will once again be an effective method of serving the cause of human progress.

Please bring this letter to the attention of your friends, especially the two who are now in prison.

Repercussions came even before the letter was published in *La Patrie humaine* on August 18, 1933. The French Secretary of the Defense Committee of the League of Conscientious Objectors (affiliated with the War Resisters' International) wrote Einstein an outraged letter, repeating an earlier request that he serve as a sponsor. Surely the rumors could not be true! The high priest of war resistance could not desert his faithful followers! Einstein replied on August 28, 1933:

Several years ago, corresponding with Professor Hadamard [see p. 99], I defended refusal of military service in about these words: "I admit that for certain Negro tribes in Africa, renunciation of war might involve the gravest danger; but it is altogether different with the civilized nations of Europe. . . ."

Since I made this statement, my views have not changed, but the European situation has—it has come closer to conditions in Africa. So long as Germany persists in rearming and systematically indoctrinating its citizens in preparation for a war of revenge, the nations of Western Europe depend, unfortunately, on military defense. Indeed, I will go so far as to assert that if they are prudent, they will not wait, unarmed, to be attacked. . . . They must be adequately prepared.

I take little pleasure in saying this, for in my heart I loathe violence and militarism as much as ever; but I cannot shut my eyes to realities.

If you can suggest any other way in which those nations that have remained free can protect themselves, I should be glad to learn about it. As for me, I can conceive of no alternative (other than military preparedness) until the present perilous situation is overcome. However, if we realize that actually no other alternative exists, we must be honest enough to admit it.

Lord Ponsonby, with whom Einstein had journeyed to Geneva less than a year before, also wrote him concerning his present views on military service. Ponsonby's letter, written in German, is dated August 21, 1933: [6]

. . . I am sure you will not take it amiss if I express deep disappointment over the change in your attitude on war resistance. I understand only too well your distress and despair at the events in Germany. However, no matter how provocative a government may be, this fact is not, in my view, a sufficient justification for denying the reasonableness and effectiveness of refusing military service. Hitler's methods may be insane and criminal, but I am firmly convinced he is not such a fool as to think he could gain anything for Germany by waging war against another country. He would have all of Europe arrayed against him, and utter defeat would be inevitable. Besides, he has neither money nor arms and is much too concerned with his own security to become involved in such stupid ventures. Belgium's security, now and in the future, hinges solely on a policy of disarmament. All who work toward that goal, by refusing any kind of participation in war, deserve our unswerving respect and encouragement. Refusal of military service is not only a desirable policy in time of peace; it should enlist our full support at all times, particularly in time of crisis. My belief in the necessity of war resistance remains firm and unshaken. I venture to express the hope that, although the present cruel and oppressive measures adopted in Germany may have shaken your faith, you will not allow your change in viewpoint—a temporary change, I feel sure—to become public knowledge, at least not until you have given the matter mature reconsideration. Should your views be made known, you can be sure that every chauvinist, militarist and arms merchant would delight in ridiculing our pacifist position.

Einstein replied on August 28, 1933:

Under circumstances such as prevailed in Europe until late last year, refusal of military service was, in my opinion, an effective weapon in the struggle for reason and dignity. Now, however, the situation has changed; I hope it will not remain so for long.

Can you possibly be unaware of the fact that Germany is feverishly rearming and that the whole population is being indoctrinated with nationalism and drilled for war? Do you believe for a moment that Germany's overlords will be any easier on the French than they have been on their own fellow citizens who are not willing tools? What protection, other than organized power, would you suggest?

I loathe all armies and any kind of violence; yet I am firmly convinced that, in the present world situation, these hateful weapons offer the only effective protection. I am certain that, if you yourself held today a responsible high office in the French Government, you would feel obligated to change your views in the face of the prevailing danger.

In response to many inquiries, the War Resisters' International, late in September 1933, circulated among its sections Einstein's exchange with Ponsonby, with the injunction that it be kept strictly confidential. "At the moment there is no possibility of obtaining any retraction from Professor Einstein. It is a great blow to our cause," wrote H. Runham Brown, the secretary of the War Resisters' International. Another official of the War Resisters' International said: "I am afraid there is nothing more we can do just now but to emphasize publicly our renewed determination to work for the principle of war resistance and to point out that this failure does not mean that our principle is unsound but that humanity is, after all, very weak."

The consternation in pacifist circles regarding Einstein's letter to Nahon is illustrated in an article in the *Press Service* of the International Antimilitaristic Commission, which was published in Haarlem, Holland. The story, dated September 7, 1933, reprinting and discussing Einstein's letter, appeared under the title "Einstein an Apostate," and contained these unfriendly remarks:

> . . . At a very critical moment Einstein takes the part of militarism. . . . He now thinks he can save European civilization by means of fire bombs, poison gas and bacteria. . . . The apostasy of Einstein is a great victory for German National Socialism. . . . Einstein's action has done unutterable harm to the fight against militarism.

Another bitter reaction, of which Einstein could not have been aware, was expressed by Romain Rolland in a diary note of September 1933.[7] Rolland recalled his earlier opposition to Einstein's "puerile assurances" and "deceptive promise" that the refusal of some thousands of determined men to accept military service could prevent war (see p. 118). Now Einstein was refusing to support the very objectors he had encouraged in their disobedience, thus repudiating the creed he had once preached.

> Such weakness of spirit is indeed unimaginable in a great scientist, who should weigh and express his statements carefully before putting them in circulation. It is even more incredible coming from the author of the Theory of Relativity. Had it never occurred to him that circumstances might develop, circumstances such as those that prevail today, which would make it dangerous to practice conscientious objection which he espoused? It is a joke, a kind of intellectual game, to advocate the idea at a time when no

risks are involved; on the other hand, one has assumed a particularly serious responsibility for having indoctrinated blind and confident youth without sufficient consideration of all implications. It is quite clear to me that Einstein, a genius in his scientific field, is weak, indecisive and inconsistent outside it. I have sensed this more than once.

One can imagine the homicidal fury of the Hitlerites when they learned that a German had sounded the call to arms to other nations against Germany. Nothing could have been more fatal to the cause of the Jews in Germany. Einstein did not anticipate this. I am afraid that he may now find it quite difficult to justify himself. His constant about-faces, hesitations and contradictions are worse than the inexorable tenacity of a declared enemy. . . .

The letters of protest kept coming. The International League of Fighters for Peace inquired as to the authenticity of Einstein's changed viewpoint, which they regarded as a radical departure from his earlier declarations that had become the veritable credo of pacifists. Einstein replied on September 7, 1933:

I have indeed made the two statements in question; they do express my conviction. I cannot imagine that any sensible person would wish France and Belgium to become helplessly exposed to a probable German invasion. However, the present situation leaves no doubt that were these countries to remain defenseless, invasion would be inevitable. If the international situation is restored to what it was even a year ago, I shall resume my previous position, but certainly not any earlier.

Two days later, on the eve of his departure for England, he wrote to a Belgian War Resisters' Committee:

It is quite true that I hold to the view that in the present circumstances refusal of military service is inappropriate in those countries that have adhered to democratic institutions. As long as no international police force exists, these countries must undertake the defense of culture. The situation in Europe has changed sharply within the past year; we should be playing into the hands of our bitterest enemies were we to close our eyes to this fact.

Einstein, indeed, felt obliged to issue a general statement, dating from this period in Le Coq-sur-mer:

My ideal remains the settlement of all international disputes by arbitration. Until a year and a half ago, I considered refusal to do military service one of the most effective steps to the achievement of that goal. At that time, throughout the civilized world there was not a single nation which actually intended to overwhelm any other nation by force. I remain wholeheartedly devoted to the idea that belligerent actions must be avoided and improved relations among nations must be accomplished.

For that very reason I believe nothing should be done that is likely to weaken the organized power of those European countries which today represent the best hope of realizing that idea.

Before his departure for England, Einstein also gave an interview to Leo Lania, himself an exile from Germany.[8]

I rely with assurance on one fact which seems to me to imply the swift and inevitable collapse of the Nazi dictatorship [Lania quoted him]. It is not the strength or the virtues of the adversaries of Nazism on which I count. It is on the stupidity of the Nazis themselves. . . .

It has been said that the existence of a stage of siege permits the worst imbeciles to govern a land. It is not true. Without some intelligence not even a dictator flanked by bayonets can maintain his rule indefinitely. Hitler and his minions lack even that minimum degree of intellectual ability required by a dictatorship under modern conditions. . . .

I am a convinced democrat. It is for this reason that I do not go to Russia although I have received very cordial invitations. My voyage to Moscow would certainly be exploited by the rulers of the Soviets to the profit of their own political aims. Now I am an adversary of Bolshevism just as much as of Fascism. I am against all dictatorships.

I could never live in Italy under the shadow of the Fasces, nor in Russia under the rule of the secret police, and, naturally, still less in Germany, assuming it were possible for me to go there. I want nothing to do with Germany today. . . . It is beyond me why the entire civilized world has failed to join in a united effort to make an end to this modern barbarism. Can it be that the world does not see that Hitler is dragging us into war? . . .

Before leaving for America, Einstein arrived in England on September 9, 1933, for a month's stay. The following day he complained to Helene Dukas, his secretary, who had stayed behind in Le Coq-sur-mer:

. . . The antimilitarists attack me as being an evil renegade. These fellows wear blinders; they refuse to acknowledge their expulsion from "paradise."

Letters urging him to clarify his change of views followed him to England and even America. Professor G. C. Heringa of the University of Amsterdam was another pacifist who could not believe the published reports. On September 11, 1933, Einstein wrote him from Cromer, England:

I assure you that my present attitude toward military service was arrived at with the greatest reluctance and after a difficult inner struggle. The root of all evil lies in the fact that there is no powerful international police force, nor is there a really effective international court of arbitration whose judgments could be enforced. All the same, antimilitarists were justified in refusing military service as long as the majority of the nations of Europe were intent upon peace. This no longer holds true. I am convinced that developments in Germany tend toward belligerent acts similar to those in France after the Revolution. Should this trend meet with success, you may be sure that the last remnants of personal freedom on the continent of Europe will be destroyed.

While it is quite true that the deterioration of conditions in Germany is partially attributable to the policies of neighboring countries, there seems little purpose at this juncture in blaming them for these policies. The plain fact is that the gospel of force and repression, currently prevailing in Germany, poses grave threats to the Continent of Europe and the independence of its inhabitants. This threat cannot successfully be combated by moral means; it can be met only by organized might. To prevent the greater evil, it is necessary that the lesser evil—the hated military—be accepted for the time being. Should German armed might prevail, life will not be worth living anywhere in Europe.

I believe, nonetheless, that even now it is not too late to avert war by preventing German rearmament through diplomatic pressure. *But such pressure will require absolute military superiority on the part of Germany's neighbors.* To destroy such superiority or to prevent its achievement is tantamount to betraying the cause of European freedom.

You cannot compare French militarism to German militarism. The French people, even those at the top, have remained preponderantly pacifist in outlook and are maintaining an army merely for the defense of their country. This is even more true of the Belgian people.

To summarize: In the present circumstances, realistic pacifists should no longer advocate the destruction of military power; rather, they should strive for its internationalization. Only when such internationalization has been achieved will it be possible to work toward the reduction of military power to the dimensions of an international police force. We do not cause the danger to disappear by merely closing our eyes to it.

During his stay in England, Einstein held conversations with a number of leading British statesmen, in an effort to convince them of the threat posed by German rearmament. He saw Winston Churchill, Sir Austen Chamberlain and Lloyd George. To his wife he wrote:

. . . Today I visited Churchill. He is an eminently wise man; it became very clear to me that these people have made their plans well ahead and are determined to act *soon*. . . .

Einstein made his first major public appearance since the Nazis had come to power on October 3, 1933, in London. The occasion was a mass meeting at the Royal Albert Hall, organized by the Refugee Assistance Fund, in which a number of relief agencies, including the Quakers, had joined for the purpose of providing aid for scholars exiled or soon to be exiled from Germany. Because Scotland Yard had received a tip that a plot was afoot to assassinate Einstein, the hall was heavily guarded. Apparently Einstein remained unaware of the danger, although, according to some accounts, threats of a similar nature had been a factor in his decision to go to England. At the meeting, an audience of 10,000 listened to speeches by Einstein, Sir Austen Chamberlain (former British Foreign Secretary), Sir James Jeans (physicist and astronomer), Lord Rutherford (physicist) and Sir William Beveridge (economist and educator). Einstein's address was as follows: [9]

I am glad you have given me an opportunity of expressing to you my deep sense of gratitude as a man, a good European and a Jew. Through your well-organized program of relief you have rendered great service, not only to those scholars who have been the innocent victims of persecution, but to all of humanity and to science. You have shown that you, and the British people as a whole, have remained faithful to the tradition of tolerance and justice which your country has proudly upheld for centuries.

It is precisely in times of economic distress, such as we experience everywhere today, that we may recognize the effectiveness of the vital moral force of a people. Let us hope that, at some future time, when Europe is politically and economically united, the historian rendering judgment will be able to say that, in our own days, the liberty and honor of this continent were saved by the nations of Western Europe; that they stood fast in bitter times against the forces of hatred and oppression; that they successfully defended that which has brought us every advance in knowledge and invention: the freedom of the individual without which no self-respecting individual finds life worth living.

It cannot be my task to sit in judgment over the conduct of a nation which for many years counted me among its citizens; it is perhaps futile even to try to evaluate its policies at a time when it is so necessary to act. The crucial questions today are: How can we save mankind and its cultural heritage? How can we guard Europe from further disaster?

There can be no doubt that the present world crisis, and the suffering and privation which it has engendered, are in large measure responsible for the dangerous upheavals we witness today. In such times discontent breeds hatred, and hatred leads to acts of violence, revolution and even war. Thus, we see how distress and evil beget new distress and evil.

Once again, as was the case twenty years ago, leading statesmen are faced with a tremendous responsibility. One can only hope that, before it is too late, they will devise for Europe the kind of international treaties and commitments whose meaning is so completely clear that all countries will come to view any attempt at warlike adventures as utterly futile. However, the work of the statesmen can succeed only if they are backed by the sincere and determined will of the people.

We are concerned not only with the technical problems of securing and maintaining peace but also with the important task of enlightenment and education. If we are to resist the powers that threaten intellectual and individual freedom, we must be very conscious of the fact that freedom itself is at stake; we must realize how much we owe to that freedom which our forefathers won through bitter struggle.

Without this freedom there would be no Shakespeare, Goethe, Newton, Faraday, Pasteur or Lister. There would be no decent homes for the mass of people, no railways or radios, no protection against epidemics, no low-priced books, no culture, no general enjoyment of the arts. There would be no machines to relieve people of the drudgery required to produce the necessities of life. Were it not for these freedoms, the majority of people would lead lives of oppression and slavery, as they did under the great ancient despotisms of Asia. Only in a free society is man able to create the inventions and cultural values which make life worth while to modern man.

Without doubt the present economic difficulties will bring forth some legislation to the effect that an adjustment between supply and demand of labor as well as between production and consumption will always be brought about through government control. But these problems too must be solved by free men. In the search for a solution we must be careful not to be driven into a kind of slavery which would impede any healthy development.

I should like to give expression to an idea which occurred to me recently. When I was living in solitude in the country, I noticed how the monotony of a quiet life stimulates the creative mind. There are certain occupations, even in modern society, which entail living in isolation and do not require great physical or intellectual effort. Such occupations as the service of lighthouses and lightships come to mind. Would it not be possible to place young people who wish to think about scientific problems, especially of a mathematical or philosophical nature, in such occupations? Very few young people with such ambitions have, even during the most productive period of their lives, the opportunity to devote themselves undisturbed for any length of time to problems of a scientific nature. Even if a young person is fortunate enough to obtain a scholarship for a limited period, he is pressured to arrive as soon as possible at definite conclusions. Such pressure can only be harmful to the student of pure science. In fact, the young scientist who enters a practical profession which earns him a livelihood is in a much better position, assuming, of course, that his profession affords him sufficient time and energy for his scientific work.

Should we merely lament the fact that we live in a time of tension, danger and want? I think not. Man, like every other animal, is passive by nature. Unless goaded by circumstance, he scarcely takes the trouble to reflect upon his condition and tends to behave as mechanically as an automaton. I think I am old enough to be able to say that, as a child and a young man, I passed through such a phase. One thought only of the trivialities of one's personal existence, slicked back one's hair, and strove to talk and act like one's fellows. Only with difficulty did one perceive what lay behind the conventional mask of behavior and speech. It protected the real person as though he were wrapped in cotton wool.

How different it is today! In the stark lightning flashes of these tempestuous times, one is able to see human beings and human values in all their nakedness. Every nation and every human being now clearly exposes his virtues and weaknesses, aims and passions. In the rush of contemporary events, ordinary behavior becomes meaningless; conventions fall away like dry husks.

Men in distress become aware of the inadequacies of economic institutions and the need for supranational political commitments. Only when subjected to peril and social upheaval do nations feel induced to adopt progressive measures; one can only hope that the present crisis will lead to a better world.

But over and above this rather abstract approach, we must not lose sight of those supreme and everlasting values which alone lend meaning to life and which we should strive to pass on to our children as a heritage purer and richer than that which we received from our own parents. Noble endeavors such as yours will serve this end.

Apparently, Einstein was persuaded to omit in the delivery of the address two paragraphs that followed the third paragraph in his original draft. They read as follows:

The seizure of power, which results from preaching doctrines of hate and vengeance in a great country, constitutes a serious menace to world peace, regardless of whether or not the usurpers consciously seek war. Europe's history offers many examples of such a development. Even if we did not hear stories of clandestine German rearmament and other disquieting trends, the present situation in Europe would still give cause for alarm.

However, it is still time to avoid a dangerous conflagration. If I may express a hope, I should like to suggest that the fire department be consulted rather than the courts, and that we appreciate above all the opinions and wishes of those neighbors whose homes are most directly exposed.

As a matter of fact, Einstein appears to have written two entirely different drafts of this speech. The second draft served as the basis for a pamphlet, *Europe's Danger—Europe's Hope*, which was published in London, in 1933, by the Friends of Europe and also contained several portions of the Albert Hall speech. Here is the original version of the manuscript used in the pamphlet: [10]

When I speak of Europe, I do not mean the geographical concept of Europe but, rather, a certain attitude toward life and society which has grown up in Europe and is characteristic of our European civilization. I speak of that spirit which was born in ancient Greece and which, more than a thousand years later, at the time of the Renaissance, spread from Italy to the whole Continent of Europe—the spirit of personal liberty and respect for the rights of the individual.

To what do we owe our knowledge of the laws of nature and the heretofore unparalleled technological possibilities for improving our human condition if not to the realization of bygone days that only the individual is truly capable of creating what is new and worth while? That is why the individual must be guaranteed the freedom to grow, to communicate and to worship and—insofar as it is compatible with the welfare of society—the freedom of action.

Few would deny that the basis for a dignified human existence is endangered by the present world situation. There are forces at work which seek to destroy the European heritage of freedom, tolerance and human dignity. Fascism, nationalism, militarism and Communism, while constituting diverse political institutions, all lead to the subjugation and enslavement of the individual by the state, and put an end to tolerance and personal liberty.

All who cherish a more dignified and satisfying human existence and who believe that they understand the underlying causes of the present menace should feel obligated to raise their voice in protest and warning. If we do not act with energy, we shall be doomed to a way of life indistinguishable from that under ancient Asiatic despotisms. Indeed, it will be even worse, for the modern despots, while no more reasonable than their ancient predecessors, have at their disposal far greater technological means for inflicting violence, as well as psychological weapons, such as schools, radio and the press, against which ordinary mortals are defenseless.

The essence of despotism lies not only in the fact that one man with virtually unlimited authority holds power, but that society itself becomes an instrument for enslaving the individual. This is why I consider the servitude to the state as the main enemy of the European spirit. It means that the state, rather than being what it ought to be—an instrument in the hands of its citizens—comes to hold the population unconditionally in its power. The Germans express this concept when they use the term *Menschenmaterial* (man power) rather than "the people."

What factors convert the free European into a slave of the state? My simple answer is: the necessity for military organization on the part of each separate state or, in other words, the existing anarchy in international law. I believe the Germans have been reduced to helpless victims of the state due to the fact that the geographic location of Germany exposes that country to attack and therefore makes it most dependent on rigid military organization. Such military organization demands that the individual be degraded to the status of an obedient pawn, devoid of will. It demands that youth be trained to give automatic and unquestioning obedience to their "superiors." In short, it means the total renunciation of personal liberty and human dignity.

The inferior men who govern Germany today owe their power

mainly to the fact that former generations were taught to be servile, an attitude diametrically opposed to the sense of personal responsibility that marks the true European character.

If it is true that individualism, the recognized basis of European civilization, is more seriously threatened by the military organization of various countries than by anything else, then there can be no doubt as to how the danger should and must be overcome: every country must be given an effective guarantee of security from its neighboring countries. Planned disarmament is impossible without security guarantees from the entire community of nations; war is not a parlor game played according to definite rules. On this fundamental principle I unequivocally share the French point of view.

I am further convinced that even a collective guarantee of national security by the community of nations is by no means sufficient. The military establishments of the individual countries must be internationalized—that is, transformed into an international police force subject to the authority of a supranational body.

If the reader considers this utopian, let him, for purposes of comparison, imagine a country in which there are no courts and no police. Instead, the law compels every citizen to come to the defense of a fellow citizen whenever a third party is guilty of illegal acts against that citizen. Do you believe for a moment that the citizens of such a country would ever want to be without arms? I doubt it.

The serious nature of the official efforts that led to the recent Disarmament Conference in Geneva indicates that a general awareness exists of the danger hovering over us. Its failure, thus far, to achieve disarmament is not difficult to understand. There are problems, such as the problem of war, that cannot be solved piecemeal. Either the security of individual countries is guaranteed through international arrangements, in which case the need for countries to maintain their own military establishment will no longer exist, or there is no such guarantee and each nation will continue to arm to the teeth.

Nationalism, in my opinion, is none other than an idealistic rationalization for militarism and aggression. Fascism is that form of government which is wholly adapted to military purposes. This is manifest in the fact that a *Fuehrer* can hold on to power only by acting aggressively, at least to outward appearances. He must forever dangle before the eyes of his people the objectives, real or imaginary, for which they are being asked to sacrifice their freedom.

A few months after Einstein had settled in America, Rennie Smith, the Secretary of the Friends of Europe, sent him a set of the group's pamphlets and asked his help in securing their wide distribution in the United States. It was also suggested that he might be able to assist in raising funds for the purpose, first, of providing "accurate information about what is happening in Germany with special regard to external relations and, second, of encouraging the effective cooperation of people and governments for the prevention of war." Mr. Smith asked Einstein to give permission for the reprint of his pamphlet by an American newspaper, obviously not knowing that such a republication had already taken place. Einstein replied on February 13, 1934:

The *New York Herald Tribune*, on February 4, without consulting or even notifying me, has published an article over my name [using the contents of the pamphlet] . . . omitting any mention of the Friends of Europe. I do not think we should silently tolerate this sort of mischief, but I have no time to pursue the matter myself.

The publication of my article was quite appropriate in the collection of the Friends of Europe, a publication which is designed for a specific group of people. I would not, however, have authorized a republication in newspapers because of the unfavorable consequences such publication might have for the Jews and liberals still living in Germany. Those who wield tyrannical power in Germany look on me as an apostate German and will hold innocent people responsible for my actions. . . .

CHAPTER EIGHT

ARRIVAL IN AMERICA, REARMAMENT AND COLLECTIVE SECURITY | 1933-1939

On October 17, 1933, Einstein arrived in America, never to return to Europe. He assumed his position at the Institute for Advanced Study at Princeton, which became his permanent and last residence. During the next six years, until the outbreak of war in Europe, Einstein made fewer public statements about the problems of war and peace than at any other epoch since the end of the First World War. His relative silence cannot be attributed to his physical separation from Europe and his old friends, nor was this due to any change in his basic beliefs; the explanation was rather the complete change in the international situation resulting primarily from the change of the political constellation in Europe. Einstein never doubted that Nazism in Germany would mean war unless the other Western nations adopted in time appropriate measures to avert the danger. This is the reason why Einstein now urged less frequently than before the establishment of international peace through international law, which he knew to be difficult of accomplishment at any time and certainly impossible to achieve as long as Hitler and Mussolini were in power.

As is revealed by his writings during that six-year period, Einstein was often severely criticized for no longer promoting war resistance by individuals and for advocating rearmament of Western nations. Time and again, he patiently sought to explain the reasons for this change by emphasizing the dreadful meaning of Fascism and calling attention to Nazism's fanatic drive toward war; it would be a crime against the pacifist ideal, he once said, to close one's eyes to those unfortunate facts. He was convinced that the methods of achieving peace must necessarily be adapted to changing circumstances. He urged the United States to relinquish isolation and enter into the League of Nations, which he hoped would be much strengthened by American membership. Even before 1933 he had considered whether it might not be necessary to promote the establishment of an international police force to safeguard international security, although his pacifist associates frowned upon the idea. Possibly because of the catastrophic developments in Germany, Einstein had now become convinced that an international military force was an indispensable prerequisite to the abolition of war. Had it already existed, he would have much preferred such an international military organization to the rearmament of individual nations, which he now suggested as a possible antidote for German aggression.

Einstein's feelings about his new surroundings in America are reflected in a letter which he addressed to his friend, Queen Elizabeth of Belgium, on November 20, 1933:

DEAR QUEEN:

I should have written you long since, and would have, were you not the Queen. Yet, I am not quite clear why this fact should be an obstacle. But such questions lie more within the province of a psychologist. Most of us prefer to look outside rather than inside ourselves; for in the latter case we see but a dark hole, which means: nothing at all.

Since I left Belgium I have been the recipient of many kindnesses, both direct and indirect. Insofar as possible I have taken to heart the wise counseling of those who urged me to observe silence in political and public affairs, not from fear for myself, but because I saw no opportunity for doing any good. . . . Princeton is a wonderful little spot, a quaint and ceremonious village of puny demigods on stilts. Yet, by ignoring certain social conventions, I have been able to create for myself an atmosphere conducive to study and free from distraction. Here, the people who compose what is called "society" enjoy even less freedom than their counterparts in Europe. Yet, they seem unaware of this restriction since their way of life tends to inhibit personality development from childhood. Should civilization in Europe collapse as it did in Greece, the intellectual desolation that will result will be as profound as it was then. The tragic irony is that the very quality which is the source of the unique charm and value of European civilization—that of the self-assertion of the individual and of the various nationality groups—may also lead to discord and decay. . . .

Einstein probably did not really intend, nor would he have been able, to stay completely out of public affairs. The unrest about his changed attitude on war resistance persisted. To the several inquiries that reached him almost as soon as he arrived in America he responded with the general statement he had drafted before his departure from Belgium (see p. 234). On October 22, 1933, Professor F. M. Hardie, under whose presidency the famed Oxford Union Society had adopted the motion "That this House will in no circumstances fight for its King and Country," addressed a letter to Einstein that, in essence, could be reduced to a one-syllable question—"Why?" A pacifist, said Professor Hardie, places peace even above justice: "To be consistent the pacifist should say that even to be ruled by a Hitler is better than to fight." Einstein replied in November 1933:

I shall gladly attempt to answer your question. I share your belief that the avoidance of war is the most important task facing mankind today. Yet, in the hope of avoiding war, I cannot go so far as to accept the permanent destruction of all our intellectual and political traditions.

Until the Hitler regime came into being, I was of the opinion that the refusal of military service was a justifiable and effective weapon in the fight against war. In those days, no country attempted to impose its will by force and at the expense of other countries. Conditions, unfortunately, have changed. In Germany, today, an entire population is being systematically indoctrinated in the spirit of militarism and war. While I strongly disagree with those who feel that this fact justifies a preventive war, I do believe that those countries which have maintained democratic institutions must do all within their power to stop this perilous trend through vigilance and negotiation. Such an approach can be successful only when the German usurpers become convinced that a policy of armed adventure would prove hopeless to them. Germany will not recognize this fact unless the rest of Europe is militarily strong and united. Hence, in the present situation, I do not believe it either benefits Europe or the cause of peace to pursue a policy that might weaken the military strength of the democratic nations of Europe.

The clamor among pacifists persisted. On December 3, 1933, in response to a troubled inquiry from the Philadelphia branch of the Women's International League for Peace and Freedom, Einstein restated his position at length: his belief in the necessity of limiting national sovereignty and in the importance of a really effective international arbitration authority; but also his conviction that war resistance, in the face of the threat of Hitler, was an incorrect policy:

. . . Of course, this does not mean that I have in any sense become a proponent of war. On the contrary, I consider military preparedness in these [democratic] countries [of Europe] the most effective means, in times such as these, of making progress toward the goals of pacifism. I need hardly emphasize that, rather than a policy of rearmament on a national basis, I should much prefer the creation of a sufficiently strong international military or police force.

Together with Nobel Prize winners Sinclair Lewis (literature), Frank Kellogg (peace) and Irving Langmuir (chemistry), Einstein was guest of honor at a dinner given in New York, on December 18, 1933, by World Peaceways to commemorate the hundredth anniversary of the birth of Alfred B. Nobel. The thesis of the main address delivered by Frank Kellogg, former U. S. Secretary of State and father of the Kellogg-Briand Pact, did not seriously differ from Einstein's beliefs, except that Kellogg considered a policy of gradual disarmament possible and advocated giving somewhat more limited authority to an international arbitration court than Einstein suggested in those days. Einstein's own remarks dealt primarily with the personality of Nobel: [1]

We are gathered here today to express our gratitude to the magnanimous creator of the Nobel Foundation. We can perhaps accomplish this most effectively, I believe, by attempting to understand his [Nobel's] motivations. What may have happened inside this man to make him decide on so unique a last will?

I believe the answer to this question may be found in the fact that the attainment of economic power is rarely based on productive ability or creative achievement. Inventiveness and organizational ability derive from altogether different talents and are seldom combined in one person. Schopenhauer was not wrong in considering the will and the intellect as mutually antagonistic.

Probably, Nobel was primarily a creative mind. While his talent for organization predestined him to the attainment of dominating power, what really concerned him was the development of the creative spirit and the cultivation of a rich personality. Love of personal and intellectual freedom necessarily leads to a passionate preoccupation with the problem of peace since there exists no greater menace to personal freedom than war and militarism.

That Nobel's chief creative achievements benefited the very powers which he considered most evil and destructive may well have caused him much distress. Thus we should view his testament as a heroic effort on his part to insure that the fruits of his lifework would serve good and life-giving purposes, and in this way to resolve the painful contradiction in his personality. Thus the testament amounts to an act of the noblest self-emancipation.

It is men like Nobel who will help us to find solutions to the burning social and economic problems that beset us today—men to whom economic achievements are but tools to serve the development of *human* values.

Einstein resumed his practice of sending messages to antiwar meetings, though the emphasis was now more and more on the necessity of building a genuine international organization. On March 22, 1934, he wrote to the Antiwar Committee at New York University:

I am gratified to learn that students of New York University plan to commemorate the seventeenth anniversary of the United States' entry into the World War by holding a meeting which will be devoted to the problems of peace. Because of America's important political influence in the world, it is of great significance that the younger generation is taking an interest in this most important issue of our time. We can never forget that it was Woodrow Wilson, America's great son, who was responsible for the creation of the League of Nations.

Resolutions in favor of peace and disarmament are not enough. As many people as possible must be made to realize that these great goals can be attained only by the establishment of an international organization which embraces all the major powers and has at its disposal an adequate executive force.

I believe, further, that your meeting should support President

Nicholas Murray Butler's suggestion that there be co-operation between the United States and Great Britain in this matter. It should also be most desirable if co-operation between American and British students would be initiated, particularly since unquestionably similar trends are noticeable in British student groups.

Einstein drafted the following address for an official reception given by the State of New Jersey in March 1934:

I am most anxious to express to all of you my satisfaction and appreciation of your demonstration of cordiality. This gratifying occasion convinces me once again that the most rewarding moments in life come to us by the grace of destiny rather than through acts of merit. Our most memorable experiences derive from the affection and sympathy of our fellow human beings. Such sympathy is a gift from God which is even more gratifying when it seems undeserved. Sympathy should always be accepted with cheerful gratitude and with that modesty which flows from a sense of one's own inadequacy; it arouses the desire to return to others what one has received oneself in such rich measure.

I am anxious to thank you also because this meeting in which you participate seeks to support a selfless project of human charity. I have often had an opportunity to admire the spirit of brotherhood which is one of the finest traditions in the United States. Surely, no other country has created so many and so powerful institutions devoted to the improvement and welfare of mankind throughout the world.

Was it not also this same spirit of supranational brotherhood which inspired your Wilson to participate in the creation of the League of Nations after the Great War? Disillusionment over the lack of international spirit in the rest of the world may have caused America to withdraw, for the moment, behind its own walls; yet I hope and believe that this country, infused as it is with the spirit of brotherhood, may one day again participate in the work of an international organization the establishment of which is so vital to the future of mankind. Some of the policies of your present President seem to justify this hope. . . .

To a Rochester rabbi, Einstein addressed the following letter on April 5, 1934:

I am today as ardent a pacifist as ever before. Nonetheless, I believe that, until the military threat to the democracies, posed by the existence of aggressive dictatorships, has ceased, we are not justified in advocating the weapon of war resistance in Europe. Any attempt to weaken the military preparations of Germany's neighbors would be disastrous to European civilization. While the goals of pacifism remain unchanged, the methods of achieving peace must necessarily be adapted to changing circumstances. The goal of pacifists today must be to create a community of action among those powers that have not been affected by dictatorial methods.

Einstein's ideas concerning the role which the United States ought to have played in those days, particularly in regard to the League of Nations, are cogently expressed in an address which was probably prepared for a New Jersey State Conference on "The Cause and Cure of War," held in Princeton in April 1934. After having emphasized the need for compulsory arbitration to settle international disputes, Einstein continued:

To the convinced pacifist the League of Nations is a promising beginning for a truly international organization and should receive our sincere support. Yet, one should never forget that the League, as presently constituted, offers no real protection to its members. This explains why its member states find it impossible today to reduce their armaments and why all efforts made in the past in that direction were bound to fail.

The recent withdrawal from the League of two great powers with large military establishments [Germany and Japan] does not, in my view, weaken the organization. Both countries, because of their aggressive policies, were likely to do more harm than good to the League and its efforts to develop along pacifist lines. Moreover, the danger posed to the rest of the world by these two countries provides an incentive to countries remaining in the League to further close ranks. If the League is to withstand the challenges that may threaten peace in the years ahead, it must develop into a more effective instrument of mutual aid among its member nations.

In my opinion, American pacifists should consider it their primary task to influence the United States into joining the League of Nations, an organization which owes its very existence to a famous American, President Wilson. It now lies within the power of the United States to make the League an effective instrument of international security; any condition which the United States might attach to its entry into the League would, undoubtedly, be accepted. The events of the past twenty years have made it obvious that the destiny of the United States is closely interwoven with that of the Old World. Therefore, its nonparticipation in the existing international organization may constitute the partial surrender of control over its own destiny.

Despite the perilous international situation and the consequent militarization of certain great nations, pacifists, if they energetically pursue the struggle for peace, may face the future with confidence. They have a powerful ally in the widespread recognition of the devastating effects that would be caused by another war. In the United States, England, France and Russia, the most urgent quest of people is for security and stability. Today more than ever before, the pacifists of those countries have the opportunity to bring about the transformation of the League of Nations into an effective instrument for peace.

On the occasion of Brotherhood Day, April 29, 1934, sponsored by the National Conference of Christians and Jews, a message from Einstein was among many included in a nation-wide radio broadcast: [2]

Organized religion may retrieve some of the respect that it lost in the last war if it dedicates itself to mobilizing the good will and energy of its followers against the rising tide of reaction.

To an antiwar meeting called on May 26, 1934, at Teachers College, New York, under the auspices of the American League against War and Fascism, Einstein wrote:

It is reassuring to know that American intellectuals are so deeply interested in the problem of peace. On this occasion we remember with gratitude the high-minded leadership of President Wilson, who succeeded in taking the first step toward creating an international organization for the peaceful settlement of international conflicts. May American intellectuals do their share in persuading the United States, one of the two principal factors of power, to emerge from its isolation and throw its support in the direction of an effective international organization.

Support of international solidarity also happens to constitute the best defense against Fascism, which poses such a grave threat to our cultural life.

Einstein was invited to speak on "Educators and World Peace" at a conference of the Progressive Education Association held in New York on November 23, 1934, which was also to be addressed by the Soviet Ambassador to the United States, Alexander Troyanovsky. Here is Einstein's message, read to the meeting: [3]

The United States, by virtue of its geographical location, is in the fortunate position of being able to teach a rational type of pacifism in its schools, without having to fear for its security. Since there exists no serious danger of foreign aggression, there is no need to indoctrinate American youth with the spirit of militarism. Real danger exists, however, that the problem of peace may be approached from a purely emotional point of view. . . .

However, it should be made clear to young people that the United States may nevertheless be drawn into military involvements at any time, although a direct attack upon the country is very unlikely; this can easily be demonstrated by referring to America's participation in the First World War. Thus, even Americans can hope to enjoy true security against military involvement only when a satisfactory solution is found to the problems of peace as a whole. We must guard against the view that a policy of political isolation will make the United States really secure. On the contrary, America's youth must be made to realize the importance of finding an international solution to the problem of peace. Moreover, it must be made clear to them that American politicians have incurred a grave responsibility by their failure to support Wilson's bold peace plans, thereby impairing the effectiveness of the League of Nations.

It must also be pointed out that the mere demand for disarmament is futile, as long as great nations exist which are prepared to use military force. France, therefore, is eminently reasonable in suggesting that the security of individual nations must be guaranteed by international institutions. To achieve such security, international treaties for common defense against an aggressor, while necessary, are not sufficient. In addition, military defense resources must be internationalized in such a way that it will no longer be possible for a country to employ, for its own exclusive purposes, the military forces stationed on its territory.

These vital problems should be brought home to young people if the various nations are to build a basis for the effective protection of peace. Also, the spirit of international solidarity must be strengthened and chauvinism combated. In the schools, history must be taught as the evolution of progress and human civilization, rather than a glorification of the use of force and military successes to the young generation. In my opinion, H. G. Wells's *Outline of History* would be excellent for this purpose.

Of considerable, if less immediate, importance to the promotion of pacifism is the teaching of geography and history in such a way as to foster sympathetic understanding for the national characteristics of the different countries in the world, especially of those whom we are in the habit of describing as "backward."

Also dating back to 1934 is the draft of a speech which, while not delivered, was clearly intended for an organization to aid the victims of Nazism:

. . . How is it possible that one of the most civilized nations has sunk so low as to wage such a cruel and unjust campaign against a small and defenseless minority, a minority, moreover, which has made great contributions to civilization and which cannot be accused of having done anything to provoke such hostility?

The great Spinoza said that man should be neither hated nor despised because of his conduct; rather one should endeavor to understand him. Only by understanding the motivations underlying man's conduct can we hope to prevent the dreadful disasters men may inflict on one another.

The tendencies to love and hate, joyfully create and cruelly destroy are intimately bound together in the soul of every man. When law and order exist in a society, this inconsistent and conflicting inner structure of man does not become obvious since, under normal circumstances, these destructive drives are suppressed and remain dormant in the average human being. Only in congenital criminals do these dark aspects of human nature erupt despite the counteracting influences of society.

But there are times when neither the state nor society exert a counteracting influence or, if so, they do so only very imperfectly. Their failure to act occurs in time of war or when a politically influential group seeks to exploit man's destructive tendencies. Under such circumstances social taboos against cruelty and barbarity become inoperative, and those aspects of human nature that are ordinarily carefully concealed or disguised are free to do their dreadful work. Only a very few who, with great difficulty, succeeded in gaining real independence and isolation will be unwilling to participate in mass crime.

Is there hope that we shall learn to avoid such disasters? I do not believe that there can be complete protection in that respect, particularly since we have little or no power to change human nature. However, if we were to act upon Wilson's exciting plan for world law and order, we should arrive closer to the goal. An effective League of Nations such as Wilson envisioned would prevent war and thus weaken nationalism, which feeds mainly on a war mentality. Moreover, the decline in nationalism, which would thus take place simultaneously with the increase in real security for individual countries, would eliminate one of the main causes of degenerative processes in society, such as we are witnessing at present in Central Europe.

For the time being, our only satisfaction must come from the knowledge that the fight against evil will strengthen the forces working toward greater decency in society.

A particularly detailed statement of Einstein's changed position on war resistance and of his thoughts on the international security problem was presented in his article "A Re-examination of Pacifism." It appeared in the January 1935 issue of the little magazine *Polity* and was prepared in response to an article (November 1934), "Speak, Einstein, for the Peace of Europe," prepared by Brent Dow Allinson, a very active pacifist. Einstein's article read as follows: [4]

Mr. Allinson has, in a courteous way, placed me on the defendant's bench. I am happy about it since it gives me a welcome opportunity of expressing publicly certain ideas which I feel should become known.

Mr. Allinson's accusation, put briefly and plainly, is something like this: "A few years ago you publicly urged refusal of military service. Now—although the international situation has become unexpectedly worse and more acute—you keep silent or, what is worse, you even retract your former statements. Is this because your understanding or your courage, or possibly both, have suffered under the pressure of the events of the last few years? If not, then show us without any delay that you still belong to the brotherhood of the upright."

Here is my answer. I am convinced of the principle that a real solution to the problem of peace can be achieved only by the organization of a supranational court of arbitration which, unlike the present League of Nations in Geneva, would have at its disposal the means of enforcing its decisions; an international court of justice with a permanent military establishment or a police force. This conviction is excellently stated in Lord Davies' book *Force* (London, Ernest Benn, Ltd., 1934), which I strongly recommend to everyone who is seriously and genuinely concerned with this fundamental problem of mankind.

Starting from this basic conviction, I favor any measure which I consider likely to bring mankind closer to the goal of a supranational organization. Up to a few years ago, the refusal to bear arms by courageous and self-sacrificing individuals *was* such a measure; however, it can no longer be recommended as a course of action, at least not to European countries. As long as democratic governments of a similar character existed in the larger nations, and as long as none of these countries based their plans for the future on a policy of military aggression, the refusal of military service on the part of a fairly large number of citizens might well have induced the governments of these nations to become more favorably disposed toward the concept of international arbitration of conflicts between nations. Moreover, refusal of military service was likely to educate public opinion toward genuine pacifism and make obvious the unethical, immoral aspects of compulsory military service. In such a context, refusal of military service constituted a constructive policy.

Today, however, you must recognize that several powerful nations make it impossible for their citizens to adopt an independent political position. These nations have succeeded in misleading their citizenry through an all-pervasive military organization and through dissemination of false information by means of an enslaved press, a centralized radio service and a system of education oriented toward an aggressive foreign policy. In those countries, refusal of military service means martyrdom and death for those courageous enough to adopt such an attitude. On the other hand, in those countries which still respect the political rights of their citizens, refusal of military service is likely to weaken the ability of the healthy sections of the civilized world to resist aggression. Therefore, today, no intelligent person should support the policy of refusing military service, at least not in Europe, which is particularly endangered. Under present circumstances, I do not believe that passive resistance, even if carried out in the most heroic manner, is a constructive policy. Other times require other means, although the final goal remains unchanged.

These are the reasons why, in the present political context, a convinced pacifist must seek to promote his beliefs in ways different from those of earlier, more peaceful times. He must work for closer co-operation among the peaceful nations in order to minimize, as much as possible, the chances of success on the part of those countries whose adventurous policies are based on violence and brigandage. In particular, I am thinking of well-considered and sustained co-operation between the United States and the British Empire, including possibly France and Russia.

It is conceivable that the existing threat to peace will tend to facilitate such a *rapprochement* and bring about a peaceful solution of international problems. This is the only hope in the present dark situation; all efforts which aim specifically at influencing public opinion in the right direction can make an important contribution to the maintenance of peace.

Apparently, even this detailed pronouncement did not completely dispel the uneasiness created by Einstein's changed position on war resistance. Since he was obviously anxious to establish as much clarity as possible about his position on a problem so important to him, he issued yet another, briefer statement:

The seeming inconsistency of my statements concerning the policies which appear desirable in the pursuit of the pacifist ideal can be explained by the far-reaching changes in Europe's political situation. When my earlier pronouncements were published, refusal of military service was a practical possibility in all the major countries; this was no longer the case when my article in the magazine *Polity* appeared. In times such as these, any weakening of the democratic countries caused by a policy of refusing military service would actually be tantamount to a betrayal of the cause of civilization and humanity; only organized co-operation on the part of the democracies will bring us closer to the pacifist goal. In Fascist countries any activity in behalf of pacifism is altogether out of the question.

On February 16, 1935, Einstein again wrote to the Queen Mother of Belgium:

. . . Among my European friends I am now called "The Great Stone Face" [*Der grosse Schweiger*], a title I well deserve for having been so completely silent. The gloomy and evil events in Europe have paralyzed me to such an extent that words of a personal nature do not seem able to flow any more from my pen. Thus I have locked myself into quite hopeless scientific problems —the more so since, as an elderly man, I have remained estranged from the society here. . . .

He added a few feelingly warm words about the death of King Albert, who had lost his life the year before in a mountain-climbing accident, and expressed the hope that the Queen would find solace in her work as an artist.

. . . The effect of such work on us I know from my own scientific endeavors. Tension and fatigue succeed each other as they do if one is strenuously climbing a mountain without being able to reach its peak. Intense preoccupation with things other than human factors makes one independent of the vicissitudes of fate; but it is a harsh discipline which reminds us again and again of the inadequacy of our abilities.

At times I think back longingly to the happy hours of the past and am tempted to visit Europe; but so many obligations would await me there that I seem unable to find the courage for such a project. . . .

To a New York correspondent who had chided him for saying there were no German, Russian or American Jews—only Jews—Einstein wrote in early April 1935:

In the last analysis, every one of us is a human being, whether American, German, Jew or Gentile. If this position, the only dignified one, were generally accepted I should be the happiest of men. I find it sad, indeed, that in the world we live in, differences of nationality and cultural traditions separate people to such a large extent; but since this is the inescapable reality, one cannot refuse to recognize it. . . .

In the spring of 1935, antiwar demonstrations took place in many American colleges, partly under the leadership of a National Student Strike Committee, which represented a number of radical and religious youth groups. To one of those demonstrations, held at Temple University in Philadelphia, Einstein sent, on April 9, 1935, a statement which apparently was also read to a similar demonstration at Princeton University several days later: [5]

It is a promising sign that America's academic youth addresses itself so zealously to the most important problem of the day, the preservation of peace. The creation of a serious attitude of good will is the first indispensable step toward this goal. The second step, equally indispensable, is a clear recognition of the means by which this goal may be attained. For these reasons, I cannot urge you strongly enough to acquaint yourselves with the New Commonwealth Society in London, which was organized by Lord Davies. The books of this lucid and politically seasoned author seem to me to present the problem of achieving peace convincingly and exhaustively. Fundamental to his approach is the concept of an international court of arbitration, coupled with an international police force.

Do not be satisfied with merely expressing fine sentiments and pretty words about peace. You should approach the problem as a practical task of great magnitude and should lend your support to whatever organization seems to understand the problem most clearly and knows what methods should be employed toward its solution.

Einstein was one of several prominent men who were asked to comment on a ruling passed at Connecticut State College which stated that "any formal public agitation or formal public discussions on the campus promoted by individuals of the college staff or individual students which reflect upon the college military instruction or training will subject such individuals to cause for removal." To Professor Walter Landauer at Storrs, Connecticut, Einstein wrote on April 29, 1935:

While from a purely legal point of view, a university administration may have the right to impose on the faculty functions which have nothing to do with the real purpose of an institution of higher learning, from the point of view of education such measures seem ill-advised; they will have an unfortunate effect on the selection of the academic staff. Men of weak character will be prone to any compromise, while men of convictions and integrity will be deterred from entering the teaching profession. Those, however, who are compelled by necessity to submit to regulations which they consider morally objectionable will be assailed by a sense of impotent frustration that deprives them of the love and devotion to their work—qualities incomparably more important to the achievement of great contributions than silent acquiescence to formal loyalty.

On June 18, 1935, from Old Lyme, Connecticut, Einstein wrote to an Ohio organization which called itself SOS ("Stop Organized Slaughter"). The organization, which pledged itself to defend America in case of invasion, sought to work for peace by drastically eliminating all profits derived from war industries and by drafting wealth as well as men.

Just as the United States is able to prevent internal struggles only through its legislative, judiciary and executive institutions, so peace in the world can be secured only by the establishment of corresponding international organs. Half measures offer no prospect of success. . . .

In an interview with Robert Merrill Bartlett, appearing in the magazine *Survey Graphic*, August 1935, under the title "Peace Must Be Waged," Einstein is quoted as saying: [6]

. . . War is on the way. I doubt that it will come this year—or the next; the stage is not yet ready. But in two or three years' time it is going to come. Germany is rearming rapidly now, and the contagion of fear is sweeping Europe. England might have checked this disastrous trend two years ago if she had taken a firm position against Germany's rearming; but she failed to do so. In Nazi Germany there still are some intellectuals who oppose the military-nationalistic policies, but most of those who might have voiced such opposition were exiled or have been suppressed. Of course, I have now been away from Germany for two years and, therefore, cannot accurately sense public feeling there. Certainly, many who suffered from 1914 to 1918 do not want another war. But there are many young, restless people, the victims of troubled conditions, who are being exploited by the present regime. Germany is still war-minded, and conflict is inevitable. The nation has been on the decline mentally and morally since 1870. Many of the men with whom I associated in the Prussian Academy have not proven of high caliber in the nationalistic years since the World War.

[Did he still believe in vigorous personal resistance to war? Did he still believe that, if two per cent of the people in a nation refuse to fight, war can be averted?]

Intellectual resistance of this type is not sufficient in view of the circumstances which we now face. Pacifism defeats itself under certain conditions, as it would in the case of Germany today. Anyone who resists the military program will be quickly eliminated.

We must educate the people and work toward creating a public sentiment to outlaw war. I believe there are two features in this program of action: First, create the idea of supersovereignty: men must be taught to think in world terms; every country will have to surrender a portion of its sovereignty through international cooperation. If we want to avoid war, we must try to make aggression impossible through the creation of an international tribunal having real authority. Both the League and the World Court lack the power to enforce their decisions. Although these institutions may be unpopular now, the trend is toward world organization; institutions of this type are inevitable. . . . Military training and competition in armaments will never avert war. . . .

Second, we must understand the economic causes of war. The

fundamental difficulty lies in the selfish desire of people who put profit before humanity. There are those who refuse to adopt liberal ideas; they remain provincial, self-satisfied and content as long as they are sure of their monetary profits. We suffer from the ills of economic nationalism and war because those people will not suppress their passion for more and more wealth. Romain Rolland may not be far wrong in considering social revolution the only means of ending the war system. Since I do not know what exactly his present position on communism is, I could not say whether or not I agree with him. But he is no doubt correct in attacking individual greed and the national scramble for wealth as factors that tend to make war inevitable. There is at least one change in the economy we must strive for, and that is the control of the munitions industry. . . .

This is not to imply that I wish to reduce life, as some people do, to the interplay of economic forces. There is a persistent emotional element in all human relations that must be coped with. Each national group tends to feel differently from any other and often permits its conduct to be controlled by prejudice. We need to be made conscious of our prejudices and learn to correct them. . . .

[Shall we ever be able to abolish war?]

Yes, I believe so; in fact, I am certain of it. Our hope lies in educating the youth to a saner view of life. . . . To bring beauty and brotherhood into life is the chief aspiration of man and the highest happiness. This will be accomplished, not through fear, but by challenging what is best in human nature.

[Whom did he consider the most significant leader in the world today?]

I doubt that there has been a true moral leader of world-wide influence since Tolstoi. He remains in many ways the foremost prophet of our time . . . there is no one today with Tolstoi's deep insight and moral force. I admire Gandhi greatly but I believe there are two weaknesses in his program: while nonresistance is the most intelligent way to cope with adversity, it can be practiced only under ideal conditions. It may be feasible to practice it in India against the British but it could not be used against the Nazis in Germany today. Then, Gandhi is mistaken in trying to eliminate or minimize machine production in modern civilization. It is here to stay and must be accepted.

[He had made a real sacrifice in taking issue with the Nazi Government and leaving Germany. Would he take the same steps again?]

I have made no sacrifice. I have done only what any thinking man would do under the circumstances. . . . One must not avoid taking a firm position on certain big issues. I claim no credit for my action; there was no other course to take.

. . . I am very happy with my new home in this friendly country and with the liberal atmosphere of Princeton. . . . Many a day I sit in my study for hours with a sheet of paper before me. During that time I may write down only a few little figures of some sort. . . .

On October 22, 1935, twenty days after Italy had invaded Ethiopia, Einstein and Alfred E. Smith, former Governor of New York, spoke over a nation-wide radio network on the occasion of a dinner given in New York by two groups devoted to aiding political and non-Jewish refugees from Germany. Here is Einstein's script: [7]

The process of cultural disintegration, which has assumed such dangerous proportions in Central Europe during the past few years, must alarm anyone who is sincerely interested in the welfare of humanity. Because neither the establishment of an international organization nor the sense of responsibility among nations has progressed sufficiently to allow joint action against the disease, efforts in two different directions are being made to protect our cultural values from the danger that threatens them.

The first and most important of these efforts must be an attempt to bring about a consolidation, within the framework of the League of Nations, of those nations which have not been directly affected by recent developments in Europe. Such a consolidation should have as its aim the common defense of peace and the establishment of military security. The second effort is to help those individuals who have been compelled to emigrate from Germany, either because their lives were endangered or their livelihood was taken away from them. The situation of these people is particularly precarious because of the economic crisis throughout the world and the high level of unemployment in almost all countries, which has frequently led to regulations prohibiting the employment of aliens.

It is well known that German Fascism has been particularly violent in its attack upon my Jewish brothers. We have here the spectacle of the persecution of a group which constitutes a religious community. The alleged reason for this persecution is the desire to purify the "Aryan" race in Germany. As a matter of fact, no such "Aryan" race exists; this fiction has been invented solely to justify the persecution and expropriation of the Jews.

The Jews of all countries have come to the assistance of their impoverished brothers as best they could and have also helped the non-Jewish victims of Fascism. But the combined forces of the Jewish community have not nearly sufficed to help all these victims of Nazi terror. Hence, the emergency among the non-Jewish emigrants—that is to say, people of partly Jewish origin, liberals, socialists and pacifists, who are endangered because of their previous political activities or their refusal to comply with Nazi rules—is often even more serious than that of the Jewish refugees. . . .

To help these victims of Fascism constitutes an act of humanity, an attempt to save important cultural values and, not the least, a gesture of considerable political significance. . . . To allow the condition of these victims to deteriorate further would not only be a heavy blow to all who believe in human solidarity but would encourage those who believe in force and oppression. . . .

The following remarks, which were cast in a more analytical vein, also date from 1935. The manuscript bears the notation "not published."

To the everlasting shame of Germany, the spectacle unfolding in the heart of Europe is tragic and grotesque; and it reflects no credit on the community of nations which calls itself civilized!

For centuries the German people have been subject to indoctrination by an unending succession of schoolmasters and drill sergeants. The Germans have been trained in hard work and made to learn many things, but they have also been drilled in slavish submission, military routine and brutality. The postwar democratic Constitution of the Weimar Republic fitted the German people about as well as the giant's clothes fitted Tom Thumb. Then came inflation and depression, with everyone living under fear and tension.

Hitler appeared, a man with limited intellectual abilities and unfit for any useful work, bursting with envy and bitterness against all whom circumstance and nature had favored over him. Sprung from the lower middle class, he had just enough class conceit to hate even the working class which was struggling for greater equality in living standards. But it was the culture and education which had been denied him forever that he hated most of all. In his desperate ambition for power he discovered that his speeches, confused and pervaded with hate as they were, received wild acclaim by those whose situation and orientation resembled his own. He picked up this human flotsam on the streets and in the taverns and organized them around himself. This is the way he launched his political career.

But what really qualified him for leadership was his bitter hatred of everything foreign and, in particular, his loathing of a defenseless minority, the German Jews. Their intellectual sensitivity left him uneasy and he considered it, with some justification, as un-German.

Incessant tirades against these two "enemies" won him the support of the masses to whom he promised glorious triumphs and a golden age. He shrewdly exploited for his own purposes the centuries-old German taste for drill, command, blind obedience and cruelty. Thus he became the *Fuehrer*.

Money flowed plentifully into his coffers, not least from the propertied classes who saw in him a tool for preventing the social and economic liberation of the people which had its beginning under the Weimar Republic. He played up to the people with the kind of romantic, pseudo-patriotic phrasemongering to which they had become accustomed in the period before the World War, and with the fraud about the alleged superiority of the "Aryan" or "Nordic" race, a myth invented by the anti-Semites to further their sinister purposes. His disjointed personality makes it impossible to know to what degree he might actually have believed in the nonsense which he kept on dispensing. Those, however, who rallied around him or who came to the surface through the Nazi wave were for the most part hardened cynics fully aware of the falsehood of their unscrupulous methods.

A famous cause with which Einstein identified himself in 1935 was the candidacy of Carl von Ossietzky for the Nobel Peace Prize.[8] A crusading German pacifist editor who had opposed German chauvinism even before the First World War, Ossietzky had been released from prison only a short time before Hitler came to power. His prison sentence, imposed under the Weimar Republic, was due to an article which he published in his magazine, *Die Weltbühne,* and in which he criticized the German military budget. Because the Nazis promptly threw Ossietzky into a concentration camp, he became an international symbol of the struggle against Nazism. The campaign to have the Nobel Peace Price awarded to Ossietzky, thus drawing world attention to the struggle against Nazism, was pursued for several years in various countries, among them the United States; the campaign met great difficulties. Moreover, there were other worthy contenders, notably President Masaryk of Czechoslovakia. Ossietzky's backers realized that, because of Ossietzky's extremely precarious condition, it was important to proceed with great caution. They felt that premature publicity about the Peace Prize might well result in greater suffering to him than he was already exposed to—indeed, in his death. (He was then already ill with tuberculosis, the disease which caused his death in 1938.)

It was at Einstein's suggestion that Jane Addams, the American social worker and peace advocate and herself a Nobel Peace Prize winner, proposed Ossietzky as early as 1934. Many noted European intellectuals joined with her, including Thomas and Heinrich Mann, Romain Rolland, Wickham Steed, Lion Feuchtwanger, Arnold Zweig and André Germain. Ossietzky's candidacy was also supported by the American section of the International League for Academic Freedom, of which Einstein was a member, together with John Dewey, Alvin Johnson and many others. Several other organizations adopted similar resolutions. Despite the great caution observed by those who directed the movement, word of its activities leaked into the press. The *New York World-Telegram* carried a story on May 31, 1935. This was followed by another full-page story in the *New Yorker Volkszeitung* on June 15, 1935, and a column in the *New York Post* on June 24, 1935. The news was also reported in the German refugee newspaper published in Prague. Einstein's name was mentioned in all these accounts.

Einstein's own reaction to the publicity is best illustrated by a letter of September 1, 1935, written in response to a request that he personally contact the Nobel Committee:

Your suggestion that I write the Nobel Committee on behalf of Ossietzky, while having much to recommend it, has even more that militates against it:

1. I believe the judges will assume that a proposal coming from German political émigrés is not based on objective motives; such a proposal will, therefore, fail of its intended effect.

2. Through his friends abroad, Ossietzky has let it be known that, were the Nazi rulers to learn that any efforts in his behalf emanated from German émigrés, this would only aggravate his already dreadful existence. If I were to send the Nobel Committee a message, even unofficially, might it not leak out through an indiscretion?

Jane Addams proposed Ossietzky last year, at my suggestion. Such an indirect approach is probably the most promising procedure. I have no way of finding out who among those entitled to propose candidates might be approached with some prospect of success. Should you be able to obtain any reliable information on this score, I would be glad to approach one or two people.

I believe good old Nobel would turn in his grave were he to see the list of those who, over his name, have been praised and rewarded for their efforts in behalf of peace.

Despite misgivings, Einstein *did* write to the Nobel Committee, on October 27, 1935, from Princeton:

Formally speaking, I have no right to propose a candidate for the Nobel Peace Prize. But under the conditions now prevailing, my conscience dictates that I address to you this letter.

In awarding this prize, the Nobel Committee has a unique opportunity to accomplish an act of great historical significance, an act whose repercussions would most likely contribute to a solution of the peace problem. This could be accomplished only by awarding the prize to a man who, by his actions and his agony, is more deserving of it than any other living person: Carl von Ossietzky. To award the Peace Prize to him would instill new life in the cause of pacifism in the very country which, because of the circumstances now prevailing there, constitutes the gravest threat to world peace. Moreover, such a gesture would arouse the conscience of all well-meaning people the world over and inspire them to work for the establishment of a secure international order.

Two days later, on October 29, 1935, the supporters of Ossietzky in America made a tactful move intended to avoid any appearance of rivalry between Masaryk and Ossietzky. They cabled directly to Masaryk that as "admirers of your interest in the promotion of peace [we] venture to ask for your co-operation in bringing to the attention of the Nobel Prize Committee in Oslo the merits of Carl von Ossietzky, who, through his stalwart devotion to the ideals of peace, has given strength and courage to all those who believe in the ideals he is advocating." Although Einstein's name is not among those who signed the cable, this would not necessarily imply that he had any objections to approaching Masaryk.

It is known that Einstein co-operated with the Ossietzky supporters in their efforts to induce other prominent personalities to use their influence with the Nobel Committee in favor of Ossietzky. He personally approached three past Nobel Peace Prize winners: Nicholas Murray Butler, the President of Columbia University; Sir Austen Chamberlain, the former British Foreign Secretary; and Sir Norman Angell, the English author and pacifist. All three declined to act. Chamberlain remarked in his reply that he did not think Nobel had intended the prize for cases of this kind; a member of Nobel's family had told him that Nobel hoped the prize would be awarded in recognition of a definite act contributing to peace, rather than of general championship of peaceful principles. Chamberlain further expressed the opinion that Nobel's executors had often deviated from this line. Angell felt unable to recommend Ossietzky for the 1936 prize since he had already submitted a strong recommendation for Lord Cecil; he regarded the case for granting Lord Cecil the prize as overwhelming. He indicated, however, that he might be able to recommend Ossietzky for next year's prize.

In November 1935, the Nobel Committee decided not to award the Peace Prize for that year. A year later, however, the prize *was* awarded to Ossietzky, despite the protests of the Nazi Government, which, embarrassed by the award, passed a law to make it impossible for Germans to accept any Nobel Prizes in the future. There is evidence that Einstein's activities in behalf of Ossietzky involved considerably more than letter-writing; that his support was, in fact, of major importance in the eventual success of the campaign, even though —or perhaps, because—his role remained virtually unknown to the public.

Einstein remained deeply concerned over the failure of the United States to enter the League of Nations. Declining an invitation to speak before a Newark peace group, Einstein wrote on February 26, 1936:

The nonparticipation of the United States in international political affairs would further weaken the influence of the League of Nations and increase the likelihood of a new world war. If war should actually come, I hardly believe the United States could remain neutral for long, even if she were to abandon the principle of protecting her own maritime traffic.

On the other hand, were the United States to find an appropriate way to become associated with the League, the danger of a new world war would be greatly lessened. Hence, I am convinced that the policy of isolationism, which currently enjoys so much popularity in this country, serves neither the ideals of pacifism nor the cause of America's security.

On March 18, 1936, ten days after Hitler marched into the Rhineland, Einstein, as was, on occasion, his practice, obeyed an impulse to write a public figure who had particularly impressed him. Raymond Leslie Buell, the President of the Foreign Policy Association, had just published a pamphlet, *The Dangerous Year*, in which he criticized the weaknesses of United States foreign policy in the face of increasing German rearmament and Italian and Japanese expansionism. Einstein wrote:

Last night at eleven o'clock I began reading your pamphlet on the present international political situation. I was so fascinated with your presentation that I could not put the pamphlet down until I had finished it at three o'clock this morning. You deserve a great deal of credit for having written it. Your analysis of the various interrelationships is exceptionally lucid, thorough and objective. It would be impossible to overestimate the impact which the pamphlet might, and should, have in the field of political education. I have the greatest admiration for the courageous objectivity and moderation with which you have evaluated the British attitude and criticized the policies of your own country. In this respect your contribution is truly unique.

I admire no less the consistency with which you emphasize the importance of the League of Nations while making no attempt to conceal its sins and weaknesses. If your pamphlet is accorded the attention it deserves, it may well exert a significant and constructive influence on American foreign policy which is bound to have an increasingly important impact upon international developments.

If it is not presumptuous to express any criticism of your study, I should like to indicate two observations. First, I agree with you that Italy, Germany and Japan find themselves in a dilemma because of overpopulation. While these nations are justified in seeking better opportunities for international trade as well as alleviation of population pressure through emigration, both of which can be accomplished by peaceful means, overpopulation does not justify in any way the desire of these countries for territorial expansion. No state has the right to seize foreign territory merely to enable its excess population to emigrate. . . .

My second point concerns the policy of the Allies toward Germany. Germans believe in an unwritten tradition that good faith and compliance with agreements should be practiced only among themselves, but are not extended to foreigners and foreign countries. I have often had occasion to observe this practice, which, incidentally, has become even more pronounced since the World War. The French have long known about it, but the British seem to be curiously unaware of it. Once this practice is well understood, personalities like Clemenceau and Poincaré will, no doubt, be regarded with more sympathy.

A young Canadian of radical views, one of the few who had written Einstein in support of his shift on the question of war resistance, kept up a sporadic correspondence with him. On September 14, 1935, Einstein wrote him:

You speak the language of the Communist catechism, yet there is much truth in what you say. For my part I believe in the possibility of steady social progress. Your characterization of the bourgeoisie seems somewhat stereotyped. . . . The entrepreneurial class is numerically so small that, in any democratic country with a reasonable degree of political maturity, it would have to bow to the majority. The real question is whether such political maturity is attainable. I maintain that, in the long run, the masses cannot be helped unless they achieve political maturity. While you consider the political maturity of the masses a prerequisite to revolution, I suggest that, once the goal of maturity is realized, a revolution will no longer be necessary.

It is true that scientists generally have evidenced but little interest in social and political problems. The reason lies in the unfortunate specialization of intellectual work, which has created a kind of blindness to political and human problems. Thoughtful and responsible people must combat this evil through a patient process of political enlightenment which is also the only effective weapon against Fascism and militarism. No society, whatever its political organization, can in the long run insure its own health except by maintaining political insight and a genuine sense of justice.

On April 20, 1936, Einstein wrote to the same correspondent, who had sent him Romain Rolland's book *Through Revolution Peace:*

I have read a good part of Rolland's book, without really warming up to it. The man is curiously abstract. Words seem to mean more to him than life itself. Of course I agree almost completely with much that he says, yet I am surprised that so sophisticated a man still believes that he may affect the course of events through his declarations.

Your indictment of intellectuals is justified. By immersing themselves in abstract problems most of them have lost sight of mankind's most urgent needs. This explains why, when confronted with political problems, they tend to adopt the unsavory policy of least resistance by escaping entirely into the particular specialty to which their work is devoted. I myself have come to realize how difficult it is to pursue exhausting intellectual work and yet to remain a whole human being. Nonetheless, the scientists, by their honest labor, are contributing more toward removing crippling prejudice than political leaders do. We should not forget that Karl Marx and Lenin also came from the intelligentsia and drew their strength from it. . . .

One of the American educators [9] who visited Einstein at Caputh in 1931 (see p. 140) wrote him five years later to ask his opinion about a peace plan he had devised. Einstein replied on May 18, 1936:

I have thought about your peace plan and have these reservations:

1. Is it possible that governments would be prepared to accept, *a priori*, the decisions of a committee such as the one you suggest? If not, why would the decisions or recommendations of such a

body carry more weight than the opinions of any competent individual?

2. Even if governments were pledged to abide by the committee's decisions, would they keep their word if confronted by strong opposition from within their borders? My answer is no. Without even recalling the various breaches of pledges to the League of Nations, one only need think of the American Civil War. Then, even an intact, recognized central government was unable to prevent a number of states from refusing to comply with the decisions of the Federal government, which they had pledged to do; nor could it prevent them from resorting to arms.

3. It follows that only a world authority, backed by adequate military power, offers any hope of avoiding war. Indeed, even so radical a step would not guarantee full security. But real protection of peace is certainly not attainable with anything less.

During this period, a collection of Einstein's speeches and statements had been published under the title *The World As I See It.* Einstein had an inscribed copy sent to General Jan Christian Smuts, then Minister of Justice (formerly Prime Minister) of the Union of South Africa and a prominent internationalist. In a letter of thanks to Einstein mailed on May 15, 1936, Smuts called attention to the growing intolerance, persecution and dictatorship in the world. He himself, however, was not without hope. He expressed the thought that mankind was not plunging into the night but was, rather, passing through a phase which, while very disheartening, held the promise of daylight beyond. He expected that the forces of justice in human nature would eventually prevail, and mankind would emerge on a higher level of living and thinking. Since he feared that the League of Nations was in danger of foundering, which would present a grave problem to Europe, Smuts suggested that Einstein, whom scientists and thinkers the world over looked to as a great leader, raise his voice and send Europe some message of encouragement, faith and enlightenment "which may help and strengthen those who are laboring for a better world."

Einstein replied on June 24, 1936:

I would gladly follow your kind suggestion were I to have the slightest hope that it might accomplish anything. Our age is far less inclined than the preceding one to listen to intellectuals who have no power behind them and who, to some extent, are themselves responsible for their weakened position since many of them accepted evil compromises. Moreover, since I have expressed my views repeatedly and unequivocally, I would merely be repeating myself.

But I do thank you warmly for the faith and sympathy expressed in your kind letter.

A staff member of the magazine *Current History* asked Einstein's opinion about the following problem: Were there not two kinds of pacifism—the older, idealistic type, now dwindling in strength, and the more current, materialistic approach, based on the premise that war had become unprofitable? Einstein sent an answer on July 9, 1936, without actually replying to the question asked:

I am prepared to join with anyone who is serious about pacifist objectives, even if he is driven by purely utilitarian motives. I am convinced that the British Commonwealth is correct in asserting that only a powerful and well-organized international military force will insure enduring peace. By the same token I consider the American policy of nonparticipation in the solution of international problems an unfortunate mistake. Such aloofness can only increase the danger of war. Besides, once a war has broken out and spread, America is bound to become involved, as she was in the past. To my mind the principal task of American pacifists today is to make these facts known.

Just before the outbreak of the Civil War in Spain, the noted scientist Hans Thirring wrote Einstein from the Tyrol (Austria) about a World Peace Congress called for September 1936 in Geneva. While, he said, he would have welcomed the opportunity of meeting Einstein again, he nevertheless felt that émigrés might best serve the cause by staying in the background as much as possible. Attached to the letter was a report which Thirring had drafted as a member of the Austrian delegation to the congress. The report suggested that peace propaganda not be inseparably bound up with anti-Fascist action. He pointed out that the Fascist regimes were very firmly in the saddle and that dictatorships could not be overthrown peacefully. Therefore, in renouncing the use of force, pacifism necessarily renounced objectives, such as the overthrow of Fascist governments, which were attainable only by force. Thirring further suggested that even Fascist countries might well be interested in exploring peaceful alternatives.

Einstein replied on August 12, 1936, from Glenwood, Saranac Lake, New York:

. . . I have read your remarks about the Peace Congress with interest. So far as I recall, I have not been invited to attend, nor would I do so under any circumstances. I cannot approve of the views which you expressed. While I would agree that such a congress is not the place for an attack on the Fascist type of government, I consider it utterly wrong to invite or even admit people from Fascist countries. And this for two reasons:

1. Such people cannot state their real convictions without needlessly endangering their lives.

2. Fascist governments would arrange to be represented by men completely subservient to them and would make every effort to sabotage the congress and exploit it for propaganda purposes.

I am not in favor of efforts which attempt simply to keep the so-called peace. The only sensible goal today is the creation of an international system of security, unconditionally subordinated to an international authority. It is a question of international power as against the power of individual states. It was a catastrophic blunder on the part of the British not to have seen this in time and to have deserted the French. Now it is too late, and a disastrous war seems unavoidable.

A strange breed of pacifist, you will probably say of me! But I cannot shut my eyes to realities. It is no exaggeration to say that the British and, to some extent, French pacifists are largely responsible for the desperate situation today because they prevented energetic measures from being taken at a time when it would have been relatively easy to adopt them. In vain, I advocated appropriate policies in 1933. But the "Great Men" at that time almost ridiculed the danger of war.

On October 15, 1936, in celebration of the tercentenary of higher education in America, Einstein addressed an Albany convocation of the University of the State of New York, which conferred an honorary degree on him. One paragraph from his speech is of particular interest: [10]

I feel the greatest evil in education is a school which operates primarily through fear, coercion and the artificial authority of teachers. Such methods undermine the healthy spirit, the sincerity and the self-confidence of students; they produce submissive human beings. It is no accident that such schools have been the rule in Germany and Russia. I know that the schools in this country do not operate under these evil conditions, nor do the schools in Switzerland or, probably, in any democratically governed country. It is relatively easy to protect the schools from this worst of all evils: the teacher should be allowed to use as little coercive power as possible, which means that the respect of the student must result from an appreciation of the teacher's human and intellectual qualities.

On March 31, 1937, Einstein gave this statement to the Hunter College (New York City) Chapter of the American Students Union:

The true pacifist is one who works for international law and order. Neutrality and isolation, when practiced by a great power, merely contribute to international anarchy and thus (indirectly) help to bring about situations that can only lead to war.

To a New York mass meeting held on April 18, 1937, in support of the embattled Spanish Republic and addressed also by Thomas Mann, Einstein sent a message through Bishop Francis J. McConnell, explaining that ill health kept him from attending in person:

Let me emphasize above all that I view vigorous action to save freedom in Spain as the inescapable duty of all true democrats. Such a duty would also exist even if the Spanish Government and the Spanish people had not given such admirable proof of their courage and heroism. The loss of political freedom in Spain would seriously endanger political freedom in France, the birthplace of human rights. May you succeed in rousing the public to giving active support. . . . The success of your just and significant cause is very close to my heart.

On October 11, 1937, Einstein sent a message to the international celebration of Founder's Day by the Young Men's Christian Association. The following paragraphs occurred in the message: [11]

. . . The political and economic discord and conflicts of the last few decades have created dangers which even the gloomiest pessimists of the last century could not have anticipated. In those days, the injunctions of the Bible concerning human behavior were accepted by both the faithful and the unfaithful as the unchallenged obligations of the individual and society as a whole. Had any individual failed to acknowledge the quest for objective truth and knowledge as man's highest and eternal aspiration, he would not have been taken seriously.

Yet, today, we must recognize with horror that these pillars of civilized human existence have lost much of their former strength. Nations once highly respected are yielding to tyrants who dare openly to assert that "right" is anything that serves their purpose. They no longer respect the quest for truth for its own sake. Arbitrary rule, oppression, persecution of individuals and of whole communities are openly practiced and tolerated as justifiable and inevitable.

Humanity at large has slowly grown accustomed to these symptoms of moral decay. The elementary reaction in favor of justice and against injustice is sorely missing although, in the long run, this reaction is man's only protection against a relapse into barbarism. I am firmly convinced that man's passionate will for justice and truth has done more to improve social and political conditions than astute political shrewdness, which eventually only breeds general distrust. Can there be any doubt that Moses was a better leader of humanity than Machiavelli? . . .

The November 1937 issue of the *Bulletin*, published by the National Society for the Abolition of Cruel Sports in England, carried a letter Einstein had addressed to the society on August 21, 1937: [12]

I am wholeheartedly in agreement with the views expressed in the pamphlet *Two Similar Pastimes: Sport and War*; indeed, the pamphlet expresses a view which I consider indisputable. Nature has implanted a love of killing into all animals; to exist, they must eat the flesh of other animals. From those animals man is, no doubt, descended. However, man's instinct to kill seems to fade away after he has lived under civilized conditions for thousands of years. Only thus am I able to explain to myself the instantaneous, strong revulsion which I experience in thinking of a hunting party, although I realize it engenders the very opposite reaction in the minds of many of my fellow men whose ancestors have lived under civilized conditions for a shorter period of time.

That such deeply diverse reactions are possible among human beings is nothing less than tragic to my way of thinking. This discrepancy in feeling not only prevails toward the animal world but also in the domain of man's emotional attitude toward his fellow man; the writer of your pamphlet has expressed these ideas extremely well.

The American League against War and Fascism organized a People's Congress for Democracy and Peace, to be held in Pittsburgh, November 26–28, 1937; Einstein endorsed the congress but, at the same time, posed several questions concerning the organization of the League. In reply to Einstein's inquiry whether the League was nonpartisan, its executive secretary stated that while some Communists were active in the League, it was not dominated by the Communist party. Einstein, in a letter of November 15, 1937, was primarily concerned with the strategy of pacifism in a world threatened by Fascism:

It is, in principle, reassuring that a widespread organization, such as yours, exists to advocate the ideals of democracy and pacifism. On the other hand, it must be said that of late pacifists have harmed rather than helped the cause of democracy. This is especially obvious in England, where the pacifist influence has dangerously delayed the rearmament which has become necessary because of the military preparations in the Fascist countries.

It is quite true that any increase in military strength represents a danger to democracy. But if the democracies remain unarmed and defenseless in the face of the bellicose Fascist countries, the danger to democracy will be far greater.

In my view, this whole dilemma results from the rather shortsighted policies which the pacifist organizations have pursued. The supreme goal of pacifists must be the avoidance of war through establishment of an international organization, and not the temporary avoidance of rearmament or involvement in international conflict. In the United States, the pacifist movement played an important part in forcing through Congress the neutrality legislation which has proven so disastrous to the victims of Fascist aggression and may prove to be equally harmful in the future.

In the present world situation, only those countries which have adequate military power can effectively work toward the establishment of international order and security. To close our eyes to these unfortunate facts is nothing less than a crime against the pacifist ideal. . . .

Since rearmament appears inevitable, every effort should be made to prevent excessive concentration of economic power in the hands of private enterprise. It would certainly be preferable to concentrate such power in the hands of the government, through nationalization of those industries which are primarily involved with the armament program.

The main goal of pacifist propaganda should be to support the strongest possible supranational authority for the settlement of international conflicts. But no support should be given to the concept of isolationism which today can only be characterized as the most shortsighted kind of selfishness.

With Hitler's march into Austria on March 21, 1938, the plight of the Jews within reach of the Nazi terror became even more desperate than before. Einstein's close friend, the economist Otto Nathan, sought to persuade him to initiate a broad appeal to the conscience of the world. Einstein was reluctant to do so since he did not believe that such an appeal would be successful; but he then agreed to communicate about some possible action with Professor Felix Frankfurter, then Professor at Harvard Law School at Cambridge and since 1939 a Justice of the U. S. Supreme Court; because of his Austrian-Jewish origin and his well-known close contact with President Roosevelt, he seemed a particularly appropriate person to consult. On April 3, 1938, Einstein addressed the following letter to Frankfurter:

Today I discussed the desperate situation of European Jewry with my friend Professor Nathan. We both feel that Jewish charitable aid is totally inadequate, if only for purely quantitative limitations. The only step that seemed to hold any promise of significantly alleviating the suffering of European Jews would be an effort to rally major non-Jewish, nonpolitical organizations (churches, university professors, teachers, the Red Cross, etc.) in Europe as well as America for a common appeal to the conscience of all men of good will. We believe that if such an appeal could actually be launched, the worst might still be averted at this late hour.

How do you feel about this? Would you care to devote your energies and your experience to such a cause? Would you consult with us? We shall do nothing until we have your reply. If you wish, we shall come to see you.

Frankfurter endorsed the idea in general terms; but since he "hesitated to bring Einstein up to Cambridge," he never arranged to meet with Einstein and Nathan. Instead, he recommended that Einstein approach Charles C. Burlingham, liberal lawyer of New York, who, Frankfurter felt, might serve as an appropriate initial sponsor. On April 9, 1938, Einstein wrote the following memorandum for Burlingham:

The breakdown of the system of collective security has profoundly affected everyone who is seriously concerned with the welfare of mankind. We are painfully aware that this deplorable retrogression in the life of nations can be reversed only by paying a heavy price in human life. Yet, we must recognize that nonpolitical organizations are incapable of solving this urgent problem. It is, rather, the task of governments and of political organizations within individual countries.

We are no less concerned and outraged at being compelled to witness nations, once proud of their civilized heritage, destroy the political and personal rights of a segment of their population—human rights long respected as a matter of course in civilized countries. In the past we, as individuals, and those governments which have preserved the integrity of elementary human values have felt the necessity of adhering to the principle of noninterference in the internal affairs of other countries and have hence believed that they were unable to take any action about this relapse into barbarism, which has posed a serious threat to hard-won traditions everywhere. The question as to whether or not this attitude of noninterference is actually justified is a pre-eminently political issue and, regrettably, can be decided only by political bodies.

Yet, there remains *one* principle which no group of human beings that claims to serve the welfare of mankind can permit to be disregarded: No government has the right to conduct a systematic campaign of physical destruction of any segment of the population which resides within its borders. We must be determined to prevent by every means at our disposal the annihilation of innocent people, whether by force of arms or by systematic denial of livelihood.

Germany has embarked upon such a path of destruction through its inhuman persecution of German and Austrian Jews; in addition, it is availing itself of its military, political and economic power over the smaller countries of Eastern Europe in an effort to destroy their Jewish population as well.

As members of nonpolitical groups, we, both as individuals and as representatives of our groups, are resolved to insist with all the power at our command that the lives of innocent people everywhere be respected and kept inviolate. On this point we do not recognize any principle of noninterference.

Can there be anything more humiliating for our generation than to feel compelled to request that innocent people not be killed?

As a result of Einstein's letter to Burlingham, a meeting of prominent individuals was arranged at the home of Harry Emerson Fosdick, then President of Union Theological Seminary in New York. The meeting actually convened more than a month after Einstein had mailed the letter to Burlingham. Various suggestions for action were discussed, but no further meeting was called, and the whole effort came to nothing.

In a message to a peace meeting held in New York on April 5, 1938, Einstein said: [13]

. . . Many Americans, even pacifists, are thinking and saying: Let Europe fall, she deserves no better; we shall stand aside and have no part in it. I believe such an attitude is not only unworthy of Americans but shortsighted. It is unworthy of a great nation to stand idly by while small countries of great culture are being destroyed with a cynical contempt for justice. Such an attitude is shortsighted even from the point of view of enlightened self-interest. The triumph of barbarism and inhumanity can only lead to a situation in the world in which America herself will be forced to fight, and this under circumstances vastly more unfavorable than most people can possibly anticipate today. . . .

In the year before the outbreak of war in Europe, Einstein prepared a postscript to "The World As I See It" (see p. 111) which was published in 1939 in a collection of credos of eminent men and women: [14]

Reading once again the lines I wrote almost ten years ago, I receive two peculiarly contrasting impressions. What I wrote then still seems essentially as true as ever; yet it all seems curiously remote and strange. How can that be? Has the world changed so profoundly in ten years, or is it merely that I have grown ten years older and my eyes see everything in a changed, dimmer light? What are ten years in the history of mankind? Must not all those forces that determine the life of man be regarded as constant when compared with such a trifling interval? Is my critical sense so fallible that the physiological change in my body during those ten years has been able to influence my concept of life so deeply? It seems clear to me that such considerations cannot explain the change in the emotional approach to the general problems of life. Nor may the reasons for this curious change be sought in my own external circumstances; for I know that these have always played a subordinate part in my thoughts and emotions.

No, something quite different is involved. In these ten years confidence in the stability and even the viability of civilized human society has largely disappeared. One senses not only a threat to man's cultural heritage but also that a lower value is placed upon all that one would like to see protected at all costs.

Conscious man, to be sure, has at all times been keenly aware that life is an adventure, that life must, forever, be wrested from death. In part the dangers were external: one might fall downstairs and break one's neck, lose one's livelihood without fault of one's own, be condemned though innocent, or ruined by calumny. Life in human society meant dangers of all sorts; but these dangers were chaotic in nature, subject to chance. Human society, of which one was a part, seemed as a whole stable. Measured by the ideals of taste and morals, it was decidedly imperfect. But, all in all, one felt at home with it and, except for many types of accidents, comparatively safe in it. One accepted its intrinsic qualities as a matter of course, as the air one breathed. Even standards of virtue, aspiration and practical truth were taken for granted as an inviolable heritage, common to all civilized humanity.

To be sure, the First World War had already shaken this feeling of security. The sanctity of life vanished and the individual was no longer able to do as he pleased and to go where he liked. To lie was made an instrument of politics. The war was, however, widely regarded as an external event, only partly or not at all the result of man's conscious, planned action. It was held to be an interruption of man's normal life from the outside and was universally considered unfortunate and evil. The feeling of security in regard to human aims and values remained, in the main, unshaken.

The subsequent development is sharply marked by political events that are less far-reaching than their socio-psychological background, which it is more difficult to comprehend. First a brief, promising step forward, characterized by the creation of the League of Nations through the grandiose initiative of Wilson, and the establishment of a system of collective security among nations. Then the formation of Fascist states, attended by a series of broken pacts and undisguised acts of violence against individual human beings and against militarily weaker nations. The system of collective security collapsed like a house of cards—a collapse the consequences of which cannot be measured even today. It was a manifestation of weakness of character and lack of responsibility on the part of the leading intellectual groups in the respective countries, and of shortsighted selfishness, which prevented any vigorous counterattack, in the democracies that had outwardly remained intact.

Things grew even worse than a pessimist of deepest insight would have dared prophesy. In Europe, to the east of the Rhine, free exercise of the intellect virtually no longer exists, the population is terrorized by gangsters who have seized power, and youth is poisoned by systematic lies. The pseudo-success of political adventurers has fooled the rest of the world; it becomes apparent everywhere that this generation lacks the strength and force which enabled previous generations to win, in painful struggle and at great sacrifice, the political and individual freedoms of man.

Awareness of this state of affairs overshadows every hour of my present existence, while ten years ago it did not yet occupy my thoughts. It is this that I feel so strongly in rereading what I then wrote.

And yet I know that, all in all, man changes but little, even though prevailing notions make him appear at different times in a very different light, and even though the events of given times, like the present, cause him unimaginable suffering. Nothing of all that will remain but a few pitiful pages in the history books, briefly describing to the youth of future generations the follies of its ancestors.

On January 9, 1939, Einstein wrote the Queen Mother of Belgium asking her aid in obtaining permission for an aged cousin, now in Germany, to settle in Belgium. He took the occasion to philosophize about life, work and the world:

. . . I have been too troubled to write in good cheer. The moral decline we are compelled to witness and the suffering it engenders are so oppressive that one cannot ignore them even for a moment. No matter how deeply one immerses oneself in work, a haunting feeling of inescapable tragedy persists.

Still, there are moments when one feels free from one's own identification with human limitations and inadequacies. At such moments, one imagines that one stands on some spot of a small planet, gazing in amazement at the cold yet profoundly moving beauty of the eternal, the unfathomable: life and death flow into one, and there is neither evolution nor destiny; only being.

The work has proved fruitful this past year. I have hit upon a hopeful trail, which I follow painfully, but steadfastly in company with a few youthful fellow workers. Whether it will lead to truth or fallacy—this I may be unable to establish with any certainty in the brief time left to me. But I am grateful to destiny for having made my life into an exciting experience so that life has appeared meaningful. . . .

Early in 1939 Phi Beta Kappa, the national honor society in America, asked Einstein to speak on the occasion of a campaign to raise money for a "Defense Fund for the Humanities and Intellectual Freedom." Einstein's reply of February 1, 1939, is perhaps as noteworthy for its content as it is for those portions contained in the original draft that were later omitted. In the actual letter sent he pleaded that he was neither an effective speaker nor sufficiently versed in the English language to express himself orally without the danger of misunderstandings. He added, however, some words of praise for the undertaking and concluded:

. . . It is very praiseworthy and politically significant for a body of such high repute to come so energetically to the defense of freedom of speech, teaching and research, at a time when these freedoms are more gravely menaced than in the past. . . .

Omitted, presumably as inappropriate, was a long paragraph opposing, as he had in the past, isolationism as a national policy and further implying America's responsibility for the failure to achieve collective security. Also omitted were these two paragraphs:

Europe today resembles a town in which the thieves and murderers are thoroughly organized while law-abiding citizens are unable to decide whether they should create a police force.

And what about America? For the time being there persists the illusory faith in the possibility of security through isolation, even if Europe, including Great Britain and its empire, should fall victim to new barbarians. However, once the fallacy behind such thinking is recognized by a country as vigorous as America, an effective countermovement will rather quickly develop. There is no time to waste if we are to prevent America from finding herself later in a situation where she has to fight for her life, without allies, against heavy odds, and with doubtful prospects of victory.

Under the chairmanship of the renowned anthropologist Franz Boas and with the participation of many eminent scholars, a Lincoln's Birthday Committee for Democracy and Intellectual Freedom was created as part of a campaign of public enlightenment. The committee submitted a number of provocative questions to forty outstanding intellectual leaders. Here is the full text of both the questions and Einstein's replies, prepared in early February 1939:

Q: How can the scientist insure freedom of research and socially useful application of the fruits of his research?

A: Freedom of research and the socially useful application of its results are dependent upon political factors. This explains why the scientists can exert their influence not as professionals but only as citizens. It further explains why scientists have an obligation to become politically active in the interest of free scientific research. They must have the courage, both as teachers and publicists, to enunciate with clarity their hard-won political and economic convictions. Through organization and collective action, they must attempt to protect both themselves and society from any infringement upon the freedom to speak and the freedom to teach, and they must ever keep a vigilant eye in this field.

Q: How can scientists and educators help to combat racial, religious and other forms of discrimination which violate the letter or spirit of the Declaration of Independence and the Bill of Rights? How can the schools best meet the obligations which rest upon them as fortresses of democracy?

A: Academic freedom and the protection of ethnic and religious minorities constitute the basis of a democracy. To keep this truth alive, and to recognize the significance of the inviolability of individual rights, is the most important task of education. The teacher bears much responsibility because of his wide opportunity for effective action. There is no special method which insures success in these important matters. More important than general knowledge and understanding is the intellectual atmosphere and the example set by the teacher himself.

Q: How can the government most effectively assist the expansion of science and culture?

A: The government can and should protect all teachers against any economic coercion which might influence their thinking. It should foster the publication of good, low-priced books and encourage popular education generally. It should make it possible even for the student who lacks sufficient funds to secure intellectual and professional training in keeping with his talents. Finally, the school system should not be administered by a centralized authority, which tends to enforce conformity, and should be as independent of private capital as possible.

In the summer of 1939 Einstein drafted a message that may well be, physically speaking, his most enduring. For G. Edward Pendray's fabulous Westinghouse publicity coup, the Time Capsule, a stout metal cocoon holding contemporary memorabilia buried during the New York World's Fair, he contributed these lines: [15]

Our age has produced many ingenious minds whose inventions might make our lives much easier. Already, we cross the oceans by the power of machines and avail ourselves of mechanical power which may eventually relieve mankind of all physical drudgery. We have learned to fly, and we communicate with ease from one end of the world to the other by means of electromagnetic waves.

Yet, the production and distribution of goods are completely unorganized. Everyone lives under the shadow of the fear of being eliminated from gainful employment and suffering dire want. Furthermore, there is the spectacle of people living in different countries sporadically killing one another, which is another reason why all those who give any thought to the future live in terror and anguish. All this is due to the fact that the intelligence and character of the masses are incomparably lower than the intelligence and character of the few who produce real values for society.

May posterity be in a position to read this statement with a sense of proud and justified superiority.

Within days of this message, on August 12, 1939, Einstein wrote to the Queen Mother of Belgium from his summer retreat on Long Island:

. . . Reading your sweet note, I felt the many bitter sentiments fading away which have heretofore been indissolubly linked with thoughts of Europe. After six long years of absence, the desire is strong to set foot again on the familiar soil. But I am like an old lady with such a fussy train on her robe that she dare not rise again once she has successfully managed to seat herself. . . .

He wrote of the joys of sailing his boat and of weekly chamber music sessions with neighbors. He was greatly impressed with the way classical music had taken hold in America. "A stranger, able only to observe the noisy surface of this land, would never suspect this."

. . . Except for the newspapers and the countless letters, I would hardly be aware that I live in a time when human inadequacy and cruelty are achieving frightful proportions. Perhaps, someday, solitude will come to be properly recognized and appreciated as the teacher of personality. The Orientals have long known this. The individual who has experienced solitude will not easily become a victim of mass suggestion. . . .

Only ten days earlier, Einstein had signed his name to a letter destined to change the course of history—a letter addressed to President Franklin D. Roosevelt proposing that the United States Government concern itself with the possibilities of atomic fission.

CHAPTER NINE

BIRTH OF THE ATOMIC AGE | 1939-1940

EINSTEIN'S LIFE as a scientist was unusually productive and fulfilling. He was fortunate in being able to concentrate his labors on those fields of scientific endeavors for which his gifts were best suited. He found it possible, as only few have, to devote himself almost exclusively to basic and pure scientific work and to avoid distracting obligations which consume the time and energy of many scholars. He was blessed by his success in increasing man's knowledge of the universe of which man is a part, by living to see his revolutionary scientific speculations confirmed, and by having been recognized, early in life and throughout the scientific world, as one of the giants among men who leave their mark on civilization for all time. And yet, paradoxically enough, the most tragic experience in his life, which he deeply felt, came precisely as a result of his unusually rich and meaningful work as a scientist. It is tragic that the greater insight into the physical world which Einstein's scientific genius helped reveal should have found its first application, not in improving man's welfare, a matter of deepest concern to him, but in the production of a tremendously powerful instrument of destruction; and that he, who all his life strove devotedly for a world without war, should, through an ironic twist of history, have aided in providing the scientific basis for the most serious threat to man's survival: the atomic bomb.

It is still more tragic that Einstein, through his revolutionary work early in life, not only initiated the scientific evolution toward the production of atomic weapons; he lived to play an even more direct role by emphasizing the need for the experimental scientific work which culminated in the dropping of atomic bombs over Hiroshima and Nagasaki in August 1945, causing more than 200,000 casualties—a role he played primarily because of the unique reputation which his scientific achievements had secured for him. The details of the developments which led to the birth of the atomic age will be recorded on the next few pages. An attempt has been made, on the one hand, to evaluate Einstein's historic significance in the dramatic events of those days—to the extent that available documents make this possible—and, on the other, to throw light on the surprisingly casual nature of the initial steps that were taken to promote a technical development of enormous promise which was even then considered to be of utmost military importance.

Basic to an understanding of the early history of the atomic bomb is the realization that the atom is a veritable storehouse of energy, a fact which became manifest after Henri Becquerel's discovery in 1896 of radioactivity in uranium, and the subsequent isolation of radium by Marie and Pierre Curie in 1902.[1] Three years later, in 1905, Einstein astonished the scientific world with his revolutionary equation stating the equivalence of matter and energy, expressed in the famous formula $E = mc^2$ (energy equals mass multiplied by the square of the speed of light). However, the first man-made transformations of matter into energy, which ultimately proved to be a virtual confirmation of Einstein's formula, did not come for about fifteen years, and then only on a minuscule scale.

In the period before and after the First World War, there was considerable speculation as to whether ocean liners might ultimately cross the seas powered by the atomic energy embodied in a single lump of coal or any other like substance. The problem that concerned scientists then was to discover a method to start the release of power and keep it going at a desirable rate. What is now commonly referred to as a "chain reaction," or the self-perpetuating production of energy, was comparatively easy to induce, maintain and control in ordinary fuels and explosives. However, even Einstein himself, who considered the release of atomic energy theoretically possible, did not expect that it would actually be accomplished during his lifetime.

Throughout the twenties and thirties, physicists strove to pull atoms apart by bombarding them with the various kinds of particles that had come to be known. But the most they were able to accomplish was to knock off tiny splinters, producing only fleeting bursts of energy smaller than the energy needed to create them. Most promising of these new particles was the neutron, a particle of proton size, discovered by James Chadwick of England in 1932. Using neutron beams, Enrico Fermi in Italy as well as Irène and Frédéric Joliot-Curie in France produced disintegrations of heavy atoms in 1934, but failed to interpret the process as atomic fission (or the splitting of the atom), which it actually was.

The puzzle did not begin to unravel until December 1938, when two German scientists, Otto Hahn and Fritz Strassmann of the Kaiser-Wilhelm-Gesellschaft in Berlin, identified one of the large fragments, produced in the neutron bombardment of the heavy element uranium, as barium, an element roughly half as heavy as uranium. Hahn sent an advance copy of their epoch-making paper [2] (published in early January 1939) to his long-time colleague Lise Meitner, who, being half-Jewish, had recently fled Nazi Germany and was then living in Sweden. Together with her nephew, Otto R. Frisch (then working with Professor Niels Bohr in Copenhagen), she surmised at once that, in the experiments by Hahn and Strassmann, the uranium atom had in fact been split into two approximately equal parts, thus releasing an enormous amount of energy, a process that came to be known as nuclear fission. Frisch and Meitner prepared a statement to that effect for a scientific journal. Even before its publication in February 1939, its content was conveyed to Bohr, one of the most notable contributors to the world's knowledge of atomic structure. Bohr immediately grasped the vast implications of the discovery and discussed them at a scientific meeting in Washington late in January 1939. The news created a sensation. Several scientists are reported to have left before the end of that meeting and were able to verify the discovery in their laboratories within a few hours; it was learned later that Frisch, in Copenhagen, had already confirmed the discovery.

The most significant aspect of the new discovery was the possibility, discussed by several scientists, that during the process of atomic fission, induced by neutron bombardment, additional neutrons would be emitted, which in turn might cause more atoms to split. If this speculation proved correct, man's ability to produce an atomic chain reaction seemed, at last, within sight. Fermi mentioned the possibility of creating a chain reaction in his discussions with Bohr at the Washington meeting, at the very same time when it was also being considered by other scientists, including Joliot-Curie in Paris. Conclusive proof that additional neutrons could be produced, conducive to the attainment of atomic power and atomic bombs, was not to come for some time. When it did come, it was partly the result of Bohr's conjecture, subsequently confirmed, that only one rare variety or isotope of uranium was readily fissionable.

The intensity of the scientific research induced by these developments may be gauged from the fact that, within less than a year after Hahn's and Strassmann's discovery, more than 100 scientific papers were published on atomic fission.[3] While the scientists were working at high speed, the international situation grew steadily more threatening. In the spring of 1939, Hitler seized Czechoslovakia. The threat of Fascist aggression was most keenly felt by those who were familiar with the nature and ideology of the regimes in Germany, Italy and Spain, and who closely followed political developments in Europe. This was particularly true of many European and refugee scientists in the United States who had escaped from Fascism and were well aware of its real objectives.

The physicists among these scientists, more so perhaps than their American colleagues, immediately grasped the ominous possibilities presented by the new scientific discoveries. They were afraid that a terrible new weapon might be constructed in Germany, where such important work on atomic fission had just been performed. Germany still enjoyed the reputation for great scientific skill which dated from pre-Hitler times. Moreover, it was known that the Nazis were devoting large resources to weapons research. Reports reached the United States that Germany had discontinued the export to all foreign countries of uranium ore from Czechoslovakia, which was now under German control, and that an entire section of the Kaiser-Wilhelm-Gesellschaft of Berlin was engaged in secret work involving atomic research directed toward the achievement of a nuclear chain reaction. Some of the refugee scientists in America were very anxious to accelerate the development of atomic research lest Fascist Germany be able to produce the new weapon ahead of the democratic nations. Outstanding among these scientists were Enrico Fermi, then professor at Columbia University in New York, Leo Szilard, who had worked with Einstein in Berlin and who was now a guest in the physics laboratories of Columbia University, Eugene P. Wigner of Princeton University, Victor F. Weisskopf of the Massachusetts Institute of Technology at Cambridge, and Edward Teller of George Washington University at Washington.

By March 1939, Szilard, Fermi and other scientists had established that, in the process of releasing vast amounts of energy through nuclear fission, extra neutrons were emitted which might be capable of starting a chain reaction. Szilard and Walter H. Zinn, of Columbia University's physics laboratories, completed a paper on that work, dated March 16, 1939, and entitled "Instantaneous Emission of Fast Neutrons in the Interaction of Slow Neutrons with Uranium," which was published in *The Physical Review* of April 15, 1939. At about the same time, George B. Pegram, Dean of Graduate Faculties at Columbia University, at the urging of Szilard and Fermi, addressed a letter to Admiral S. C. Hooper of the United States Navy, wherein he stated "the possibility that uranium might be used as an explosive that would liberate a million times as much energy per pound as any known explosive." Pegram arranged for Fermi to meet representatives of the Navy Department to discuss a practical method of keeping the Navy informed of further scientific developments. Pegram did so although he and Fermi, in common with a number of other scientists, were not yet certain that an atomic chain reaction and the successful construction of an atomic bomb were actually practicable. Pegram stated his reservations in a letter to Hooper, in which he said his own feeling was that the probabilities were against it. "And Enrico himself," says Mrs. Laura Fermi in her book dealing with the life and work of her late husband, "when talking to Admiral Hooper, doubted the relevance of his predictions." [4] The only outcome of the meeting between the Navy and Fermi was that the Navy asked to be kept informed. Later in the spring of 1939, at a scientific meeting in Princeton, Leo Szilard also held informal discussions with the Navy; but on July 10, 1939, Ross Gunn, scientific consultant to the Navy, advised Szilard that the Navy did not intend to pursue the matter at that time.

Of all the scientists involved, it was apparently Szilard who felt the keenest sense of urgency. A man of great creative imagination, he, earlier than others, had come to assume that the construction of an atomic bomb was a technical possibility which might be realized in the foreseeable future. Some of his own calculations had shown great promise. But Fermi had left New York for the summer, and little could be accomplished until his return in the fall, when the schools reopened. Szilard became disturbed at the delay and wondered what could be done. The role he was to play in the subsequent developments is the more remarkable when it is recalled that, at the time, Szilard was an alien in the United States, without any official position, not even enjoying the status of a regular university appointment; he was merely a guest at Columbia University.

It was only at this point, in the early summer of 1939, that Einstein, through Szilard, became involved in the efforts to experiment with the construction of atomic bombs. It would appear that, several years before, Einstein had been very doubtful about the possibility of splitting the atom. At the winter session of the American Association for the Advancement of Science in Pittsburgh in January 1935, reporters asked Einstein whether he thought that scientists would ever be able to transmute matter into energy for practical purposes. In the subsequent newspaper account, which should be considered with caution, Einstein is reported to have replied [5] that he felt almost certain it would not be possible, and to have referred to the vast amount of energy required to release energy from a molecule. "It is," he is reported to have added, "something like shooting birds in the dark in a country where there are only a few birds."

It is possible that Einstein may have learned early in 1939 about the Hahn-Strassmann-Meitner-Frisch work as well as about subsequent publications concerning these developments. It does not appear, however, that he was very optimistic regarding the possibility of a practical application of the new scientific discoveries at an early date. In a statement made in reply to a question submitted to him on the occasion of his sixtieth birthday, March 14, 1939, and published in *The New York Times,* Einstein made the following remarks: [6]

The results gained thus far concerning the splitting of the atom do not justify the assumption that the atomic energy released in the process could be economically utilized. Yet, there can hardly be a physicist with so little intellectual curiosity that his interest in this important subject could become impaired because of the unfavorable conclusion to be drawn from past experimentation.

Szilard's first contact with Einstein in the matter of nuclear fission took place several months later. When he first considered consulting with Einstein about the new scientific discoveries and their implications, he did not contemplate any approach to the United States Government. Szilard recalls that he and Wigner had by this time become very perturbed by the thought that Germany might obtain large quantities of uranium from the Belgian Congo, the chief source of the material. Germany might thus be greatly helped in her research on atomic energy and ultimately in the production of atomic bombs. Szilard and Wigner felt that the Belgian Government should be advised of these eventualities in order that uranium exports to Germany might be halted if Belgium so desired. Szilard knew that Einstein had for years been on friendly terms with Queen Elizabeth of Belgium. When he and Wigner decided to visit Einstein at Nassau Point, Peconic, Long Island, where Einstein was spending the summer, it was, as Szilard has reported, their intention to suggest to Einstein that he communicate with Queen Elizabeth. It is one of the dramatic aspects of the whole atomic development that this visit, with a relatively modest and probably inconsequential purpose, led to events of completely different and, eventually, momentous import. The visit took place around July 15, 1939.

Szilard recalls that Einstein, when told about the possibility of producing a chain reaction, exclaimed, "*Daran habe ich gar nicht gedacht!*" (That never occurred to me.) Szilard reports that Einstein immediately recognized the implications of Germany's access to uranium in the Congo and declared he would be prepared to assist in informing the Belgian Government accordingly. Several approaches to the problem were discussed by the three scientists. Wigner apparently emphasized not only the desirability of advising the Belgian Government through the Queen or the Belgian Ambassador in Washington of the dangers involved in uranium exports to Germany but also the need for large imports of uranium into the United States. Whether recommendations were made as to how to secure such imports or who might be approached on the matter is not known. Einstein is reported to have favored a suggestion, apparently also offered by Wigner, to submit to the State Department a draft of a projected letter to the Queen of Belgium. The letter would be mailed to the Queen only if no objection were raised by the State Department. There is no information available as to whether, at this original meeting, Einstein, Szilard and Wigner considered advising the American Government of the implications of the new scientific discoveries with a view to engaging its interest in promoting or subsidizing further research in the atomic field.

Even before his visit to Einstein, Szilard had discussed the entire problem with a New York friend in the financial world; he had felt that the financial resources of the physics department of Columbia University would not suffice for the additional research contemplated by Fermi and himself and that outside funds would therefore be necessary. Upon Szilard's return to New York from his visit to Einstein, the finance expert informed him that he had consulted with Dr. Alexander Sachs, a well-known economist connected with the New York banking house of Lehman Brothers and sometimes one of President Roosevelt's unofficial advisers. When it was suggested to Szilard that he communicate with Dr. Sachs, he did so, apparently without delay. It was undoubtedly Sachs who recognized the magnitude and significance of the problem and realized that, to obtain results, the matter should be brought to the attention of the White House.[7] He, therefore, suggested to Szilard that Einstein's letter be addressed to President Roosevelt rather than to the Belgian Queen or the Belgian Ambassador. Sachs offered to see to it that the letter would reach the President personally. Writing to Einstein on July 19, 1939, Szilard stated that, although he had seen Sachs only once in his life and had not been able to form an opinion of him, he nonetheless recommended accepting the course of action outlined by him. Szilard added that this recommendation was also supported by Professor Edward Teller, then guest professor at Columbia University, with whom he had consulted. Szilard further suggested that Einstein's projected letter be entrusted to Sachs since he believed that Sachs was in a position to do as he had promised. Szilard enclosed a draft of the letter. Since Sachs was to play an important role during the ensuing months, and since Einstein's letter to Roosevelt was to release a "chain reaction" which possibly no move by any other individual could have effected at that time, Szilard's casually arranged meeting about an all-important matter with a person completely unknown to him, his subsequent confidence in that person on the basis of a single meeting, and Sachs's perception of Roosevelt's capacity for bold decisions are startling incidents in the drama that was to unfold.

While it is not possible to reconstruct all the developments during the two weeks following Szilard's meeting with Sachs, it is known that, during this period, Szilard once again called on Einstein at his Long Island summer home. Since Wigner was out of town, Szilard was accompanied on his second visit by Edward Teller. At this meeting with Szilard and Teller, if not before by phone or mail, Einstein accepted Sachs's suggestion to bring the matter to the attention of the President and to have a letter to Roosevelt transmitted through Sachs. Einstein dictated to Teller the draft of a letter in German which is preserved in his files. This draft contains some of the main points of the history-making communication to Roosevelt that Einstein was eventually to sign. The draft reads as follows:

Of late some work has become known which makes it appear likely that uranium will become an important new source of energy. A recent study by E. Fermi and L. Szilard, as yet unpublished, indicates the probability that the release of energy from uranium by means of a chain reaction will be achieved in the immediate future. Less certain, though not to be ignored, is the possibility that this may facilitate the production of bombs which, while perhaps too heavy to be transported by air, would not be too heavy for ships; and a single such bomb, exploded in a port, might well destroy the port together with its environs.

In this situation it would be advantageous if the Administration maintained continuing contact with the group of physicists in this country who are working on the problem of chain reactions. A possible approach would be for you to entrust a private person, who enjoys your confidence, with the task of creating and maintaining such contact. I understand that Germany has already halted the export of uranium ore; this may perhaps be explained by the fact that the son of Secretary of State von Weizsäcker works as a physicist in the Kaiser Wilhelm Institute in Berlin, where the American studies on uranium ore are now being repeated.

The United States has only low-grade uranium ore. The most important uranium deposits are in the Belgian Congo.

Einstein's draft is an indication of how, in possibly less than a week, the initial modest proposition to write a letter to the Belgian Queen had developed into a meaningful and highly suggestive approach to the President of the United States. Whether Einstein's dictated draft was inspired by the draft which Szilard had prepared after his meeting with Sachs and had mailed to Einstein before his second visit cannot be ascertained. On August 2, 1939, Szilard wrote to Einstein that, in his discussions with Sachs about additional recommendations, K. T. Compton, Bernard Baruch and Charles Lindbergh had been suggested for the position of liaison man between the government and the atomic scientists, the position recommended in Einstein's draft and also in his final letter to Roosevelt. Szilard added that Lindbergh was the "favorite" at the time of writing.

On the basis of Einstein's German draft, Szilard prepared, after a further meeting with Sachs, two English versions of a letter to the President, which he forwarded to Einstein in his letter of August 2, 1939. Einstein favored the shorter of the two Szilard drafts. The letter actually sent to Roosevelt and dated August 2, 1939, reads as follows:

Albert Einstein
Old Grove Road
Nassau Point
Peconic, Long Island
August 2, 1939

F. D. Roosevelt
President of the United States
White House
Washington, D. C.

SIR:

Some recent work by E. Fermi and L. Szilard, which has been communicated to me in manuscript, leads me to expect that the element uranium may be turned into a new and important source of energy in the immediate future. Certain aspects of the situation seem to call for watchfulness and, if necessary, quick action on the part of the Administration. I believe, therefore, that it is my duty to bring to your attention the following facts and recommendations.

In the course of the last four months it has been made probable —through the work of Joliot in France as well as Fermi and Szilard in America—that it may become possible to set up nuclear chain reactions in a large mass of uranium, by which vast amounts of power and large quantities of new radium-like elements would be generated. Now it appears almost certain that this could be achieved in the immediate future.

This new phenomenon would also lead to the construction of bombs, and it is conceivable—though much less certain—that extremely powerful bombs of a new type may thus be constructed. A single bomb of this type, carried by boat or exploded in a port, might very well destroy the whole port together with some of the surrounding territory. However, such bombs might very well prove to be too heavy for transportation by air.

The United States has only very poor ores of uranium in moderate quantities. There is some good ore in Canada and the former Czechoslovakia, while the most important source of uranium is the Belgian Congo.

In view of this situation you may think it desirable to have some permanent contact maintained between the Administration and the group of physicists working on chain reactions in America. One possible way of achieving this might be for you to entrust with this task a person who has your confidence and who could perhaps serve in an unofficial capacity. His task might comprise the following:

a) To approach Government Departments, keep them informed of the further developments, and put forward recommendations for Government action, giving particular attention to the problem of securing a supply of uranium ore for the United States.

b) To speed up the experimental work which is at present being carried on within the limits of the budgets of University laboratories, by providing funds, if such funds be required, through his contacts with private persons who are willing to make contributions for this cause, and perhaps also by obtaining the cooperation of industrial laboratories which have the necessary equipment.

I understand that Germany has actually stopped the sale of uranium from the Czechoslovakian mines which she has taken over. That she should have taken such early action might perhaps be understood on the ground that the son of the German Under-Secretary of State, von Weizsäcker, is attached to the Kaiser Wilhelm

Institut in Berlin, where some of the American work on uranium is now being repeated.

Yours very truly,

A. EINSTEIN

This letter, addressed by the then greatest living scientist to one of the most important political leaders of the world, bearing on dramatically important scientific and military developments and suggesting crucial moves by the American Government, was actually not submitted to President Roosevelt for over two months, during which period the Germans might have made much progress in the search for a nuclear chain reaction. The available documents in Einstein's files and all other sources of information fail to provide an adequate explanation for the delay in transmitting Einstein's communication. In a letter of September 27, 1939, Szilard conveyed to Einstein his impression that the letter "had already been in Washington for some time." But in another letter, dated October 3, 1939, Szilard reported that he and Wigner had called on Sachs, and Sachs admitted still having Einstein's letter in his possession; Sachs explained that he had gained the impression from several telephone conversations with Roosevelt's secretary that it was advisable to see the President at a later time since he was overburdened with work. In his testimony of November 27, 1945, before the Special Committee on Atomic Energy of the United States Senate, Sachs stated that he had not wanted to accept an appointment with the President as long as the President was involved in revising the existing neutrality legislation. However, the neutrality legislation did not become an acute issue until the war broke out in Europe on September 1, 1939, which was more than four weeks after Einstein had signed the letter.

In his letter to Einstein of October 3, 1939, Szilard remarked that he and Wigner had begun to wonder whether it might not become necessary to entrust another person with the mission Dr. Sachs had volunteered to perform. But Sachs did finally see President Roosevelt on October 11, 1939, and submitted to the President Einstein's letter, a more technical memorandum by Szilard, as well as considerable background material. The Szilard memorandum stated that, if fast neutrons could be used, "it would be easy to construct extremely dangerous bombs . . . with a destructive power far beyond all military conceptions." Sachs also submitted to the President a written statement of his own in which he summarized the main problems involved and listed the steps which he thought should be taken by the United States in the matter of further exploring the problem of nuclear fission.

President Roosevelt acted at once. He appointed an "Advisory Committee on Uranium," which was to report to him as soon as possible; a few days later, he addressed the following letter to Einstein:

The White House
Washington

October 19, 1939

MY DEAR PROFESSOR,

I want to thank you for your recent letter and the most interesting and important enclosure.

I found this data of such import that I have convened a board consisting of the head of the Bureau of Standards and a chosen representative of the Army and Navy to thoroughly investigate the possibilities of your suggestion regarding the element of uranium.

I am glad to say that Dr. Sachs will co-operate and work with this committee and I feel this is the most practical and effective method of dealing with the subject.

Please accept my sincere thanks.

Very sincerely yours,

FRANKLIN D. ROOSEVELT

Dr. Albert Einstein
Old Grove Pond
Nassau Point, Peconic
Long Island, New York

The Advisory Committee on Uranium was a three-man committee composed of Dr. Lyman J. Briggs, Chief of the Bureau of Standards, who acted as chairman; Lieutenant Colonel Keith F. Adamson, representing the Army Ordnance Department; and Commander Gilbert C. Hoover, representing the Navy Bureau of Ordnance. The first meeting of the committee, attended by Sachs, Szilard, Fermi, Wigner and Teller, took place on October 21, 1939. As early as November 1, 1939, the committee issued a report to the President which was remarkably positive in its appraisal of the scientific revolution in progress. It spoke of the possibility of producing a chain reaction which could conceivably be used as a source of great atomic energy and as "a possible source of bombs with a destructiveness vastly greater than anything now known." The report suggested that, in view of the fundamental importance of these technological possibilities and their potential military value, a thorough investigation of the subject be made possible; it further stated that such an investigation "is worthy of direct financial support by the government." The further history of the many stages in the development of the atomic bomb is recorded in other publications and need not be repeated. What is of interest here are the few instances when Einstein again intervened.

After the first meeting of the Advisory Committee, other scientists were invited to participate in subsequent consultations. Sachs continued to play a very important role as the representative of the President and, as he himself frequently emphasized, as the individual who maintained contact with Einstein: he consulted with Einstein and presented Einstein's opinions and suggestions to the President or the committee orally or in writing, as circumstances would dictate.[8] It would appear that Sachs frequently took the initiative for accelerating the work of the committee and for inducing it to concentrate its attention on the most urgent measures to be decided upon. During that period, the first winter of the European war, the Advisory Committee was the only group on uranium that had official status.

The first official steps in support of further atomic research, which heretofore had been the concern solely of university laboratories, were very modest: in accordance with the recommendations of the November first report of the Advisory Committee, the government allocated for the study of uranium fission the amount of $6,000 for the period of November 1, 1939, to October 31, 1940 ("during the first critical year of its concern with the uranium program," as Arthur H. Compton describes this year); during the same period, the Carnegie Institution of Washington allocated for uranium studies the sum of $20,000. These figures, particularly when compared to the vast armament expenditures, are minute and would indicate that atomic research was hardly pushed as vigorously as some of its staunchest advocates would have wished. It is possible, although it cannot be stated with certainty, that some of the American scientists, as well as the Army and Navy, did not share the sense of urgency which plagued their European colleagues in American universities. The general atmosphere during that period may help to explain the possible lack of concern: after the conquest of Poland, open warfare was at a minimum, and the hope was entertained in many quarters that the war could be brought to an early end through diplomatic maneuvers and appeasement, and before the United States would herself become involved in hostilities.

Although the Advisory Committee continued to operate, Szilard and Sachs were perturbed at its relatively slow progress and, in February 1940, they decided once again to secure Einstein's intervention. It took the form of another letter from Einstein, dated March 7, 1940. While nominally addressed to Sachs (who apparently helped draft it), the letter was actually intended for the President:

In view of our common concern in the bearings of certain experimental work on problems connected with the national defense, I wish to draw your attention to the development which has taken place since the conference that was arranged through your good offices in October last year between scientists engaged in this work and governmental representatives.

Last year, when I realized that results of national importance might arise out of the research on uranium, I thought it my duty to inform the Administration of this possibility. You will perhaps remember that in the letter which I addressed to the President I also mentioned the fact that C. F. von Weizsäcker, son of the German Secretary of State, was collaborating with a group of chemists working upon uranium at one of the Kaiser Wilhelm Institutes—namely, the Institute of Chemistry.

Since the outbreak of the war, interest in uranium has intensified in Germany. I have now learned that research there is carried out in great secrecy and that it has been extended to another of the Kaiser Wilhelm Institutes, the Institute of Physics. The latter has been taken over by the government and a group of physicists, under the leadership of C. F. von Weizsäcker, who is now working there on uranium in collaboration with the Institute of Chemistry. The former director was sent away on a leave of absence, apparently for the duration of the war.

Should you think it advisable to relay this information to the President, please consider yourself free to do so. Will you be kind enough to let me know if you are taking any action in this direction?

Dr. Szilard has shown me the manuscript which he is sending to the *Physics Review* in which he describes in detail a method for setting up a chain reaction in uranium. The papers will appear in print unless they are held up, and the question arises whether something ought to be done to withhold publication.

I have discussed with Professor Wigner of Princeton University the situation in the light of the information available. Dr. Szilard will let you have a memorandum informing you of the progress made since October last year so that you will be able to take such action as you think in the circumstances advisable. You will see that the line he has pursued is different and apparently more promising than the line pursued by M. Joliot in France, about whose work you may have seen reports in the papers.

The reference to the projected publication of Szilard's findings was obviously made for an important tactical reason. At an earlier stage, Szilard and other prominent atomic scientists had suggested that a collective effort be made to halt further publication of papers which might contain important scientific information. They enlisted the cooperation of Niels Bohr. Their recommendation was a matter of some delicacy: to withhold the results of scientific research conflicted with principles long defended by Szilard and many of his colleagues. Further, they knew that often the only way the creative scientist can protect the priority of his scientific findings is through prompt publication of his results, as Hahn, Strassmann, Meitner and Frisch had only recently done. However, in view of the existing international situation and America's virtually undisguised support of the Allied cause, the support of the National Research Council was sought to help prevent publication of important scientific data "in all fields of military interest." In Western Europe, Bohr had endorsed the proposition, as had the British scientists; French scientists were more hesitant. Eventually, however, there evolved a centrally organized system of voluntary censorship.

On March 15, 1940, Sachs brought Einstein's second letter to the attention of the President, who, on April 5, 1940, proposed an enlarged meeting of the Advisory Committee on Uranium which would include Einstein and others whom Einstein might suggest. Briggs, the chairman of the committee, invited Einstein to participate in such a meeting. Since Einstein was unable to accept the invitation, he addressed, on April 25, 1940, the following letter to Briggs:

I thank you for your recent communication concerning a meeting of the Special Advisory Committee appointed by President Roosevelt.

As, to my regret, I shall not be able to attend this meeting, I have discussed with Dr. Wigner and Dr. Sachs particularly the questions arising out of the work of Dr. Fermi and Dr. Szilard. I am convinced as to the wisdom and the urgency of creating the conditions under which that and related work can be carried out with greater speed and on a larger scale than hitherto. I was interested in a suggestion made by Dr. Sachs that the Special Advisory Committee submit names of persons to serve as a board of trustees for a nonprofit organization which, with the approval of the government committee, should secure from governmental or private sources, or both, the necessary funds for carrying out the work. It seems to me that such an organization would provide a framework which could give Dr. Fermi and Dr. Szilard and co-workers the necessary scope. The preparation of the large-scale experiment and the exploration of the various possibilities with regard to practical applications is a task of considerable complexity, and I think that given such a framework and the necessary funds, it could be carried out much faster than through a loose co-operation of university laboratories and government departments.

As far as can be established, Einstein had no further connection either with the work that preceded the atomic bomb project or with the project itself. The Advisory Committee did not continue much longer as such. When, in June 1940, Roosevelt created the National Defense Research Committee, which was to develop into a very significant organization with regard to America's military preparations, he asked that the Advisory Committee be reorganized, again under the chairmanship of Dr. Briggs, as a subcommittee of the newly created National Defense Research Committee. The President specifically assigned to the new committee the responsibility for research on nuclear problems. "This meant," Professor Karl T. Compton, a member of the new committee, remarked, "reviewing and acting upon the recommendations of Dr. Briggs's committee."

Viewed in historical perspective, it would appear that the decision to use Einstein's unique authority in the attempt to obtain the government's direct participation and financial assistance in atomic research may well have been decisive, since his intervention succeeded in securing the attention of President Roosevelt. The Advisory Committee on Uranium was organized by the President as an immediate result of Einstein's intervention and was the germinal body from which the whole huge atomic effort developed. Whether, without Einstein's intervention, similar developments would have taken place around the same period, and whether the atomic bomb would still have been produced around the time it was produced—that is, before the end of the war—are legitimate questions. Although some scientists, such as Professor Arthur H. Compton and Dr. Vannevar Bush, the Chairman of the National Defense Research Committee, seem to be inclined to answer in the affirmative, there can be nothing more than conjecture on such a question. In many respects, the events leading to the production of the atomic bomb in 1945 are no different from other crucial developments in history. Although these developments would, in essence, have eventually occurred in any event, the specific character and the timing of each individual event are no doubt affected or even determined by the unique actions of specific individuals or, as in the case of the atomic bomb, even by casual incidents that defy explanation. We shall never know with any degree of certainty what would have happened if Szilard had not called on Einstein in July 1939, or if Einstein, in turn, had not been immediately willing to lend his authority to supporting a request to the President of the United States that was partly based on scientific assumptions and speculations.

Even after the creation of the National Defense Research Committee, it took a relatively long time before the government became engaged in nuclear research to the extent the original advocates had hoped for. Actually, it was not until December 6, 1941, the eve of Pearl Harbor, that massive government support was decided upon. A year later, on December 2, 1942, the first self-sustained chain reaction was achieved in Chicago. Ultimately the project was to evolve into the Army Engineers' "Manhattan District." Under the command of General Leslie R. Groves, it grew into one of the great scientific and industrial undertakings in history and eventually produced the first atomic bomb in the world. The first decisive and successful test of an atomic bomb took place in the deserts of New Mexico, at Alamogordo, on July 16, 1945. About three weeks later, on August 6 and 9, 1945, atomic bombs were dropped on the Japanese cities of Hiroshima and Nagasaki.

There is no evidence that Einstein was associated in any way with the actual development of the bomb; nor that he was kept advised either about the work in progress or the scientific research involved; the extraordinarily strict secrecy regulations under which anyone connected with the atomic project, including Einstein's scientist friends, worked and lived make it most unlikely that any news of the project could have reached him. Although, in 1943, he became a consultant to the Navy's Bureau of Ordnance, all available evidence indicates that his services were in no way connected with the construction of the bomb. Members of Einstein's household recall that naval officers and scientists attached to the Navy appeared at his residence in Princeton from time to time and were closeted with him for hours. But the association itself was not kept secret; in fact, publicity pictures were taken of Einstein and Navy personnel. Soon after Einstein had become a consultant to the Navy, Dr. Vannevar Bush, head of the U. S. Office of Scientific Research and Development, asked Einstein also to serve as a consultant to his agency; but Einstein declined the invitation.[9]

Until the first atomic bomb was dropped over Japan, the work on the bomb and its successful completion were exceedingly well-guarded secrets. It seems probable, however, that Einstein, because of his participation in the earliest phase of the project, may have assumed that intense research in the direction suggested by him was being conducted. In the latter part of 1944, partly inspired by discussions with an old scientist friend, he suggested, in a letter to another scientist, that consultations be arranged with the most outstanding scientists in America and the Allied countries, including the Soviet Union; an attempt was to be made in these consultations to bring the collective influence of the scientists to bear upon their respective governments, with a view to establishing an international army and a supranational government. This radical thought, as Einstein himself called it, was but a reiteration of his international aspirations before the advent of German Fascism. Although Einstein remarked in his letter that he was afraid future wars would be "wars of veritable destruction with much greater loss of life than in the present war," there is no indication as to whether he was assailed with specific forebodings about the impact of atomic energy upon humanity or whether his fears resulted from a general understanding of the inevitable, never-ceasing technological refinements in the production of instruments of destruction. Einstein did not pursue his plan; the scientist to whom the letter had been addressed and who knew about efforts of a similar nature being made elsewhere dissuaded him from doing so.

As the production of the bomb came closer to realization, the scientists who had actually been engaged in the atomic project grew profoundly apprehensive about the possibility of its being used for its deadly purpose, as well as about the implications it held for the future of mankind. As early as July 1944, Niels Bohr, who had been smuggled out of Denmark and was secretly working in America, drafted a memorandum on postwar atomic control which he discussed with President Roosevelt the following month.[10] Bohr was convinced that the Soviet leaders should be advised of the existence of atomic weapons. By doing so while the war was still in progress, plans for postwar cooperation might be formulated on a more realistic level. In a second memorandum to President Roosevelt, of March 24, 1945, Bohr suggested that the existing channels of communication among scientists of various countries should be utilized in an attempt to find a solution for the baffling new problems—an approach which appears to be very similar to that which Einstein had considered only a few months earlier. At about the time that Bohr prepared his original memorandum to Roosevelt, the first of several official committees was established to study those problems in the field of atomic energy which the country and the world were expected to face in the years after the war. The Jeffries Report, the first of several such reports, a "document of great historic interest," was submitted as early as November 18, 1944.[11]

In March 1945, Szilard, then working at the Metallurgical Laboratory in Chicago, drafted a remarkably prophetic document in which he predicted the dangers of an atomic arms race, and even discussed the role of intercontinental rockets.[12] He emphasized the unfavorable effect which the existence of an atomic weapon might have on the postwar position of the United States, which "could no longer count on winning a war by outproducing other countries in guns and tanks." Szilard called on Einstein and, without revealing anything except his great concern for the future, once again enlisted Einstein's aid in an effort to obtain an appointment for himself with President Roosevelt. On March 25, 1945, Einstein handed Szilard the following letter of introduction to President Roosevelt:

112 Mercer Str.
Princeton, New Jersey
March 25, 1945

The Honorable Franklin Delano Roosevelt
The President of the United States
The White House
Washington, D. C.

SIR:

I am writing you to introduce Dr. L. Szilard, who proposes to submit to you certain considerations and recommendations. Unusual circumstances which I shall describe further below induce me to take this action in spite of the fact that I do not know the substance of the considerations and recommendations which Dr. Szilard proposes to submit to you.

In the summer of 1939 Dr. Szilard put before me his views concerning the potential importance of uranium for national defense. He was greatly disturbed by the potentialities involved and anxious that the United States Government be advised of them as soon as possible. Dr. Szilard, who is one of the discoverers of the neutron emission of uranium on which all present work on uranium is based, described to me a specific system which he devised and which he thought would make it possible to set up a chain reaction in unseparated uranium in the immediate future. Having known him for over twenty years both from his scientific work and personally, I have much confidence in his judgment, and it was on the basis of his judgment as well as my own that I took the liberty to approach you in connection with this subject. You responded to my letter dated August 2, 1939, by the appointment of a committee under the chairmanship of Dr. Briggs and thus started the government's activity in this field.

The terms of secrecy under which Dr. Szilard is working at present do not permit him to give me information about his work; however, I understand that he now is greatly concerned about the lack of adequate contact between scientists who are doing this work and those members of your Cabinet who are responsible for formulating policy. In the circumstances, I consider it my duty to give Dr. Szilard this introduction and I wish to express the hope that you will be able to give his presentation of the case your personal attention.

Very truly yours,
A. EINSTEIN

The letter, found in President Roosevelt's office after his death, was submitted to President Truman. Truman referred it to James F. Byrnes, who was designated to become Secretary of State, but who, at this point, was a private citizen having no official government status. About six weeks later, on May 28, 1945, when the war in Europe had already ended, Szilard, in the company of two other scientists, finally saw Byrnes at his home in Spartanburg, South Carolina. Byrnes reports that Szilard complained of the inadequate contact between atomic scientists and government policy-makers. According to his own account, Byrnes was "unfavorably impressed" by Szilard's proposals. But, on the other hand, a particularly conscientious historian, who later discussed the Spartanburg meeting with the three participating scientists, came to the conclusion that "at no time did Byrnes impress the scientists with his grasp of the significance of atomic energy." [13] The scientists spent most of the interview talking about the potential use of atomic energy for power, which Byrnes had not known about.

Byrnes found little time to discuss either Szilard's memorandum or his view that the interests of peace might best be served and an arms race avoided by not using the atomic bomb against Japan. Byrnes informed the scientists of a forthcoming meeting of the Interim Committee, which had been appointed by President Truman to advise him on the use of the new atomic weapons.[14]

The Interim Committee, which met on May 31, 1945, was composed of Secretary of War Henry L. Stimson; George L. Harrison, president of the New York Life Insurance Company; James F. Byrnes, serving as the personal representative of President Truman; Undersecretary of the Navy Bard; Assistant Secretary of State Clayton; Vannevar Bush; President Karl T. Compton of the Massachusetts Institute of Technology, who was with the Office of Scientific Research and Development; and President Conant of Harvard University, chairman of the National Research Council. Secretary Stimson, who acted as chairman, recalled that both he and General George C. Marshall, the Army Chief of Staff, had expressed the view that atomic energy must be considered in terms of a new relationship of man to the universe, and not simply in terms of military weapons. Although this weighty thought had been offered as a guide to its considerations, the Interim Committee unanimously recommended on June 1, 1945, that the bomb be used against Japan without prior warning and as soon as possible; and that it be used "on a military installation or war plant surrounded by or adjacent to houses most susceptible to damage." Since Byrnes, as a member of the Interim Committee, participated in this unanimous recommendation, it would appear that the visit Szilard and his two fellow scientists had paid him only a few days before had no effect upon his decision with regard to the bomb.

The Interim Committee was assisted in its work by a scientific panel consisting of four nuclear physicists of the first rank: Arthur H. Compton, Enrico Fermi, Ernest O. Lawrence and J. Robert Oppenheimer. In their official report to the Interim Committee, these scientists stated that they saw "no acceptable alternative to direct military use." However, during the same period, other atomic scientists engaged in several organized efforts to make certain that the bomb not be dropped over a populated area, at least not without considerable advance warning. Szilard, a most determined opponent of using the bomb under any circumstances, participated in several of these attempts. With six other Chicago scientists, headed by the physicist Professor James Franck, he signed a memorandum, submitted to Secretary of War Stimson, advocating that a first demonstration of the new weapon be staged "on a desert or some barren island" in the presence of representatives of all the member states of the United

Nations, and that the bomb not be used unless Japan were first given an ultimatum either to surrender or to evacuate certain regions. The Franck Report,[15] as the memorandum of the seven Chicago scientists —three physicists, three chemists and one biologist—has come to be known, made prophetic remarks about a future race for nuclear armaments which, if no efficient international agreement were achieved, "will be on in earnest not later than the morning after our first demonstration of the existence of nuclear weapons." The opposition, expressed in the report, to the military use of the bomb over Japan was based on the belief that such a precedent would create "an almost insuperable barrier to the establishment of international control of atomic energy." The report emphasized that protection for the human race would have to come from the political organization of the world. Franck also called attention to the "intolerable" conflict among scientists who, having learned about the efforts devoted to peace planning for the future, were pledged to secrecy about the development of atomic weapons and knew "in their hearts that all these plans were obsolete because the future war had an entirely different and a thousand times more sinister aspect than the war which was then being fought."

The atomic scientists, however, were not in agreement on the course of action to be adopted. In a poll taken at the direction of Arthur H. Compton among the scientists at the Metallurgical Laboratory of the University of Chicago in July 1945,[16] 15 per cent of the 150 scientists who had been approached favored full, unlimited military use of the atomic bomb, 46 per cent favored its limited use (which meant a military demonstration in Japan to be followed by renewed opportunity for surrender before full use of the weapon), and 26 per cent wanted an experimental demonstration in the United States before using it militarily; only 13 per cent of the scientists preferred to avoid any military use whatever. It has been pointed out, however, that those four questions, and particularly the second question about "limited use," had been ambiguously phrased and that the real attitude of the 46 per cent of the participants who voted affirmatively on this second question must remain uncertain.

Szilard, who firmly believed that the case against the military use of the bomb on humanitarian and moral grounds should be forcefully stated at the highest level, obtained more than sixty signatures to a last-minute direct petition to President Truman.[17] The language used in the petition expressed opposition to the use of atomic weapons against Japan without suitable warning and without giving her an opportunity to surrender under known conditions. Arthur H. Compton has reported that Szilard's original draft, which called for outright rejection of the use of atomic bombs on moral consideration, had to be rephrased. The more conciliatory position was adopted in an effort to obtain a larger degree of support among the scientists. Szilard's petition, as well as several counterpetitions prepared and signed by other scientists in the course of those crucial weeks, testifies to the diversity of opinion within the scientific community and undoubtedly reflects the great emotional upheaval among the relatively few people who knew about the "secret." Compton forwarded Szilard's petition to Washington on July 17, 1945, the day after the first atomic bomb was successfully exploded at Alamogordo. By then, President Truman and his advisers had already left for the Allied Peace Conference at Potsdam, Germany; and it is not known whether the results of the poll among the Chicago scientists, Leo Szilard's last-minute petition, as well as several other petitions, actually reached President Truman before he made the final decision to drop the atomic bomb over Japan.

There is no evidence that Einstein had any knowledge at all concerning the sentiments and activities of the scientists with regard to the use of the bomb prior to its use over Japan. However, in view of subsequent statements, there can be no doubt he would have strongly supported Professor James Franck and the other Chicago scientists.[18] When news of Hiroshima reached him, Einstein sadly said, "*Oh, weh!*" (Alas!); and when his letter to President Roosevelt became known, he made it clear, as he did on many later occasions, that only the great threat of Germany's possible construction of atomic bombs had caused him to bring the matter to President Roosevelt's attention.

During the remaining ten years of his life, literally until he was fatally striken on April 13, 1955, no issue outside his scientific work engaged his interest and active participation more intensely than the effort to protect mankind from destruction by atomic warfare.

CHAPTER TEN

THE SECOND WORLD WAR | 1939–1945

EINSTEIN HAD JUST PASSED his sixtieth birthday when the Second World War broke out. His situation was quite different from what it had been at the outbreak of the First World War. His impact on the political scene had become very considerable in the intervening years. While, in 1914, his signature under a political statement counted for relatively little, it now commanded wide, often international, attention. He continued to express himself freely on issues which appeared important or crucial although his public statements were less frequent during the war years than before; there were apparently fewer opportunities for expressing his political and social views. Even though the acute threat of war since 1933 had removed him from the ranks of uncompromising pacifists, his deep conviction about the abolition of war had not changed; he hoped, as is evident in a brief note he sent to the Soviet Ambassador in December 1941, that the end of the war might provide mankind with another opportunity to assure a lasting peace through the establishment of an international organization.

In a message to the Atlantic City convention of the New Jersey Education Association on November 10, 1939, he reviewed his philosophy of education. He contrasted the "school of life" with formal schooling: [1]

. . . The school of life is unplanned and chaotic while the educational system operates according to a definite scheme. . . . That explains . . . why education is such an important political instrument: there is always the danger that it may become an object of exploitation by contending political groups. While at school, the student may be taught ominous prejudices from which he may find it difficult to free himself in his later years. The process of education may be so controlled by the state that its citizens will be kept in intellectual bondage. . . .

Einstein then proceeded to outline the four principal tasks of an educational system: the education of character on the basis of specific moral and social values; the development of the student's capacities, both intellectual and physical; the teaching of general knowledge; and the cultivation of special skills. He emphasized that the mere acquisition of facts was not sufficient.

. . . Something more is needed to produce a truly educated person—namely, an ever-present feeling of social responsibility for one's fellow human beings. . . . [Character training] is not accomplished by merely teaching the student pious formulas such as "Thou shalt love thy neighbor as thyself." Stories about so-called model personalities who have allegedly conducted themselves faultlessly are of little value. . . .

In general, a healthy social attitude is acquired, not through being taught, but through experience. The collective spirit can be appreciated only if it is practiced. A student's interest should be stimulated, not by competition which merely encourages the cult of the ego, but by arousing a sense of pleasure in creative work. Only in this way will classmates learn to take a friendly and constructive interest in each other.

What can the schools do to defend democracy? Should they preach a specific political doctrine? I believe they should not. If they are able to teach young people to have a critical mind and a socially oriented attitude, they will have done all that is necessary. Students will then become equipped with those qualities which are prerequisite for citizens living in a healthy democratic society. . . .

The appointment of Bertrand Russell to a teaching position at the College of the City of New York became the subject of considerable controversy in the spring of 1940. Einstein numbered among the many prominent persons who came to Russell's defense. In a communication of March 19, 1940, to Morris Raphael Cohen, Professor Emeritus of Philosophy at City College, Einstein said: [2]

Great spirits have always encountered violent opposition from mediocre minds. The mediocre mind is incapable of understanding the man who refuses to bow blindly to conventional prejudices and chooses instead to express his opinions courageously and honestly.

On April 9, 1940, Nazi Germany's aggression spread farther across Europe: Denmark and Norway were invaded. A month later, the Netherlands, Belgium and Luxemburg were attacked and occupied. During that period, Einstein prepared the following statement: [3]

Nothing is more painful than to witness brute force triumph over precious human values. This, the horrible affliction of our time, is even more distressing than the suffering of individuals. The artistic and intellectual achievements of the Netherlands have enriched all mankind. Its struggles for justice have contributed to the spiritual and political freedom of all men. What made the human atmosphere in Holland so particularly endearing was the perfect blending of tolerance, understanding, humor and genuine co-operation.

Why did the cultural and creative forces in the world fail so completely to prevent these assaults by brute force? The answer is that the principle of collective security has not yet prevailed over obsolete traditions; and once an organism has been weakened, germs will find an opening wedge for disease. Let us hope that, one day, when all this senseless agony has become a thing of the past, a more understanding generation will arise—one that will be able to achieve security based on justice.

The American Association of Scientific Workers made public its position on the war, which was interpreted in certain circles as isolationist and neutralist. On May 22, 1940, seventeen scholars in Princeton, including Einstein, sent the following telegram to President Roosevelt: [4]

The undersigned men of science, residing in Princeton, express their emphatic disagreement with the petition prepared by the American Association of Scientific Workers. We believe that the interests of the United States as well as those of civilization everywhere are placed in imminent danger by totalitarian aggression and that our best national defense consists in assistance to those forces now opposing this aggression.

On June 22, 1940, from the chambers of a Federal judge in Trenton, New Jersey, Einstein, shortly after his examination on his application for American citizenship, participated in a broadcast sponsored by the United States Immigration and Naturalization

Service. The broadcast was part of a series entitled "I Am an American," in which notable immigrants were interviewed. Here are excerpts from Einstein's remarks: [5]

. . . I must tell you that I do not think words alone will solve humanity's present problems. The sound of bombs drowns out men's voices. In times of peace I have great faith in the communication of ideas among thinking men, but today, with brute force dominating so many millions of lives, I fear that the appeal to man's intellect is fast becoming virtually meaningless. . . .

Making allowances for human imperfections, I do feel that, in America, the development of the individual and his creative powers is possible, and that, to me, is the most valuable asset in life. In some countries men have neither political rights nor the opportunity for free intellectual development. But for most Americans such a situation would be intolerable. In this country, it has been generations since men were subject to the humiliating necessity of unquestioning obedience. Here, human dignity has been developed to a point where people would find it almost impossible to endure life under a system in which the individual is only a slave of the state and has neither a voice in his government nor any control over his own way of life. . . .

I gather from what I have seen of Americans since I came here that they are not suited, either by temperament or tradition, to live under a totalitarian system. I believe that many of them would find life not worth living under such circumstances. Hence, it is all the more important for them to see to it that these liberties be preserved and protected. . . .

Science has gone a long way toward helping man to free himself from the burden of hard labor; yet, science itself is not a liberator. It creates means, not goals. It is up to men to utilize those means to achieve reasonable goals. When men are engaged in war and conquest, the tools of science become as dangerous as a razor in the hands of a child. We must not condemn man because his inventiveness and patient conquest of the forces of nature are being exploited for false and destructive purposes. Rather, we should remember that the fate of mankind hinges entirely upon man's moral development. . . .

Anyone who seeks to affect the course of events must have the gift of being able to exert direct influence on men and their activities. . . . Intellectuals often lack the gift of impressing their audiences. Among the outstanding American statesmen, Woodrow Wilson probably provides the clearest example of an intellectual. Yet not even Wilson seems to have mastered the art of dealing with men. At first glance, his greatest contribution, the League of Nations, appears to have failed. Still, despite the fact that the League was crippled by his contemporaries and rejected by his own country, I have no doubt that Wilson's work will one day emerge in more effective form. Only then will the stature of that great innovator be fully recognized. . . .

I am convinced that an international political organization is not only a possibility but an absolute necessity; life on our planet will otherwise become intolerable. The League of Nations failed because its members were unwilling to surrender any part of their sovereignty and because the League itself did not have any executive power. Similarly, a world-state which does not control all the resources of its member states will not be able to ensure peace.

Excessive nationalism is a state of mind which is artificially induced by the prevalent obsession of nations that they must, at all times, be prepared for war. If the danger of war were eliminated, nationalism would soon disappear. Further, I do not accept the thesis that the unequal geographical distribution of raw materials must necessarily lead to war. So long as a nation has access to the resources of other countries which it needs for its industrial development, it will be able to develop its economy adequately. This is clearly demonstrated by the economies of nations such as Switzerland, Finland, Denmark and Norway, which before the war were among the most prosperous countries in Europe. . . . One of the most important functions of an international organization, thus, would be to guarantee the unhampered marketing of raw materials.

Concerning the possibility of creating an international organization, I am far from being optimistic. I merely intended to suggest certain possibilities which might prevent human existence from becoming totally intolerable. Concerning the formation of an international organization, there is probably general agreement that we now seem even further from this goal than we were ten years ago. We would hardly have suffered such a setback if, ten years ago, the democracies had evidenced the same solidarity and readiness for sacrifice they exhibit now in the face of a grave emergency. Solidarity, foresight and the will to sacrifice are, however, most effective *before* an emergency has actually arisen. . . .

I believe that America will prove that democracy is not merely a form of government based on a sound Constitution but is, in fact, a way of life tied to a great tradition, the tradition of moral strength. Today more than ever, the fate of the human race depends upon the moral strength of human beings.

On June 21, 1940, the day before he delivered his remarks for the "I Am an American" broadcast, he sent a note to a close friend on the West Coast which, even more succinctly than the official broadcast, expressed his deep concern during that period: [6]

Since we last met, we have witnessed events more terrible than have been experienced in many a generation. No serious person can fail to be profoundly apprehensive of the future. Each day, it is a wonder to me that the sky, the trees and the birds are still as they have always been.

A noteworthy exchange of letters about the political organization of the world after the war began on August 10, 1940, with the following communication from Professor Harold C. Urey,[7] then at Columbia University, who, six years before, had won the Nobel Prize for the discovery of heavy hydrogen:

There appears to be agreement on one point between the Axis Powers and Great Britain—namely, that it is impossible for the small countries of Europe and the world in general to remain completely independent, maintaining their own tariff walls, their own means of communication and transportation. Hitler regards the present Balkanization of Europe as an impossible situation, and it seems to me that he is entirely right about this. He proposes to solve the problem by conquering Europe, and perhaps all of the world besides, by establishing a *Herrenvolk*, to consist of himself and his friends, a prosperous Germany, and a slave group consisting largely of the rest of the world, including ourselves. We are arming rapidly to prevent ourselves from falling into this last group.

Guns will not defend us against ideas. The democratic countries are fighting with their backs to the wall trying to maintain the status quo. They have no central driving idea for which they are fighting. They are opposed by a group who have what appears to them to be a grand and glorious idea—a new idea in government, totalitarianism—the sacrifice of the individual to the state. Though we cannot perhaps understand it, the men of the Axis Powers to a large extent are sacrificing and dying for what appears to them to be a grand idea, and it seems to me that as long as this situation is maintained they will inevitably win, if not in a military way, then so far as their ideas are concerned.

To fight this thing we must meet it with a definite idea, one for which we also will sacrifice and die if necessary.

Basing his arguments largely upon the great success of our own Federal system and upon this system as it has been used in Canada, Switzerland and Australia, Clarence Streit [American journalist and author] proposes a Federal Union of the democracies of the world, a union organized on a democratic basis to secure the advantages of closer union made necessary by these remarkable advances in transportation and communication. Many people are interested in this idea and regard it as a very important advance. It is something which enables us to form an idea as to what will be done with victory for Great Britain if that is secured—something that extends beyond the immediate war. . . .

I am writing this letter particularly to appeal to you to endorse this Federal Union of the democracies of the world, and to write a statement which can be used for publicity purposes if Streit sees fit. He has asked me to write to all Nobel laureates in the United States proposing this, and this I am doing. I hope very much that you will join us and help in this important campaign from the standpoint of ideas—one that I believe is just as important as any aid which we can give for national defense on the physical side.

I should be very glad to know your decision in this matter. . . .

Einstein replied on August 16, 1940, from Knollwood, Saranac Lake, New York:

Ever since the last war the necessity of establishing an effective political organization of all nations in the interest of security should have become clear to every intelligent person. For some time now, it has been obvious that the traditional concept of neutrality, under present conditions, amounts to a kind of national suicide. The need for a supranational authority equipped with judicial and military power is even more urgent today than it was twenty years ago.

The question is: What can we intellectuals contribute toward the realization of this vitally important goal? We know too well that political decisions are more often the consequence of emotional impulses than of rational thinking. After the last war I was still of the belief that the impact merely of preaching and reasoning could exert considerable influence in molding public sentiment for peace. I no longer believe this. It seems more likely that some of us may be able to exert some influence on people's thinking through the authority which we enjoy because of the blind confidence people have in us. However, the blind confidence in those who have distinguished themselves by intellectual achievements has been greatly undermined due to the fact that, in recent years, brute violence and oppression have triumphed to a degree seldom equaled in history. Hence, if a collective statement is to carry any weight with the general public, it should not be issued merely by a small group of intellectuals, such as the Nobel Prize winners. On the other hand, it will not be possible to achieve agreement by a larger group of people with intellectual authority on a statement that expresses a concise position with regard to the crucial political issues of our time.

To cite an example: In my opinion, it is a fact that America's attitude toward the present war, particularly toward England, is as disastrous as was England's attitude toward the European democracies several years ago: halfhearted and insufficient measures instead of unconditional solidarity. Do you believe that America's intellectual leaders would ever openly subscribe to a policy which was clearly antithetical to the feelings of the average American? I am convinced they would not do so. Rather, they will choose, as they have done in the past, to remain passive while one bulwark of culture and justice after another is being destroyed—passive, that is, until their own turn comes. Intellectuals are cowards, even more so than most people. They have always failed miserably when called upon to fight on behalf of dangerous convictions.

I would be very interested in knowing whether you are really so much more optimistic than I about the possibility of action. The difference between us may be that I have suffered more disappointments in life than you.

Urey wrote again on October 2, 1940, the day after Einstein had become a citizen of the United States:

I was very much interested in your recent letter and did not reply at the time because I wished to see what sort of response I would get from other people in regard to the idea of Union Now of the Democracies. I should say that the results of this letter were entirely in accord with the views that were expressed by you. I also believe that it is impossible to get intellectual people to come out for any controversial issue of this kind unless it is fairly certain that a majority of the people of the country also favor that view. I believe it is true that they will take no courageous stand in matters of this kind. They will not take an interest in political things, believing that they are unimportant compared with their scientific work. I think they are afraid that their scientific colleagues will criticize them for taking an interest in such matters, and they are unwilling to be criticized in that way.

I think the situation is very discouraging. Who will think about those things, and who will try to lead in matters of this kind? We in the United States are repeating all of the mistakes that were made in Germany at the time Hitler came to power; in fact, we have repeated the very mistake that the democracies have made in the whole crisis. It seems to me a "law of nature" that no one can tell anyone else about the threat to all civilization until the threat is at their door. I am sorry that this is the case, but apparently it is. I am only writing you this letter to tell you that this is my conclusion.

Congratulations on becoming a citizen of the United States!

For a dinner of the Common Council for American Unity, held on April 3, 1941, Einstein wrote the following message: [8]

When men are animated by a common purpose, they do not need to have uniform habits or cultural traditions in order to act effectively as a community. The history of America provides the most comprehensive illustration of the validity of this statement.

Yet, it can hardly be said that, even in America, this truth is universally recognized. National and racial prejudices hinder many people from working together at the common task. These prejudices persist partly because we allow them to control our actions even if we are very careful not to talk about them in public. But things that fear the light of day can often be effectively fought and rendered harmless by bringing them into the open. It is precisely in this domain that the work of the Common Council for American Unity has been so successful. Hence, everyone who has the real interests of this country at heart ought to support the efforts of the council.

The struggle of the council against deep-rooted prejudices is even necessary in times of peace; but now, in this period of international complications, its importance is very much increased. Threats from abroad, as well as the subversive activities of internal enemies, have created political tensions serious enough to constitute an actual danger. And while watchfulness and foresight are urgently necessary to safeguard the work of defense, blind suspicion can do great harm. A man's political reliability does not depend on whether he was born on this side of the ocean or on where his forefathers lived. Many refugees are particularly able fighters for the American cause. Every man's contribution should be welcomed once his trustworthiness has been tested and established.

In every segment of the population, responsible persons are to be found who, through their personal connections, can obtain reliable information about individuals. This method, resting as it does upon personal confidence, is the only one by which all those who are competent can be mobilized in the service of the country.

Systematic exclusion of whole groups of the population not only curtails the possibilities for effective action but also creates bitterness. Let us hope that, through efficient organization and dissemination of information, the Common Council may succeed in serving the cause of justice and in increasing the national capacity for action in these times of serious danger from abroad.

Einstein continued to receive letters from pacifists accusing him of having deserted the pacifist cause. On the other hand, soon after the outbreak of war, he received letters from soldiers blaming him for clinging to the pacifist position. His replies to these letters add little to the explanation he had given in 1933. His correspondents were often humble and lonely folk struggling with big personal and political problems. Invariably he replied; tone and content of his letters were thoughtful and kindly, indicating an obvious desire to live up to the manifest trust people placed in him. One such letter, from a student at Missouri University, reached him at Knollwood in the summer of 1941. The student explained that he was facing prison because of his refusal to bear arms. Yet, since he had "never been religious in the conventional form," his conscience would not permit the claim of conscientious objection. "Please write me and let me know that I have one friend in the world!" Einstein replied on July 14, 1941:

My abhorrence of militarism and war is as great as yours. Until about 1933 I advocated conscientious objection. But with the rise of Fascism I recognized that one could not maintain such a point of view except at the risk of allowing the whole world to fall into the hands of the most terrible enemies of mankind. Organized power can be opposed only by organized power. Much as I regret this, there is no other way.

If all the young people in America were to share your beliefs and act as you intend to act, the country would be defenseless against attack and easily delivered into slavery. That is why today every honest man and woman must fight against Fascist tyranny and must temporarily sacrifice a degree of individual liberty.

There are two kinds of pacifism: sound and unsound. Sound pacifism tries to prevent wars through a world order based on power, not through a purely passive attitude toward international problems. Unsound, irresponsible pacifism contributed in large measure to the defeat of France as well as to the difficult situation in which England finds herself today. I urge you to do your share, lest this country make the same mistake!

This is not to imply that militant pacifism is not as important today as ever before. What is important is to make people aware of the fact that peace can be secured only on the basis of a world organization to which the special interests of one's own country are subordinated. The goal must be: security through sacrifice. Had America, after the last war, adopted the policies of Woodrow Wilson, who fought so vigorously for this goal, we would not be facing such terrible problems today. We must learn from the mistakes of the past!

Five months later, on Pearl Harbor Day, December 7, 1941, Einstein dictated a "Message for Germany" over the telephone to a White House correspondent: [9]

This war is a struggle between those who adhere to the principles of slavery and oppression and those who believe in the right of self-determination both for individuals and for nations. Man must ask himself: Am I no more than a tool of the state? Or is the state merely an institution which maintains law and order among human beings? I believe the answer is that, in the last analysis, the only justifiable purpose of political institutions is to assure the unhindered development of the individual and his capacities.

This is why I consider myself particularly fortunate to be an American. America is today the hope of all honorable men who respect the rights of their fellow men and who believe in the principles of freedom and justice.

Einstein's never-ceasing hope that a truly effective international organization to secure peace would come into being is best illustrated by the fact that only three days after America's entry into war, on December 10, 1941, he addressed a note to Maxim Litvinov, Soviet Ambassador to the United States, in which he expressed his conviction that the co-operation of the Soviet Union was indispensable to any effort to build an international peace organization. He wrote to Ambassador Litvinov in Washington as follows:

I hope you will forgive me for approaching you with a brief suggestion which I make under the severe shock of these last few days.

In view of Russia's crucially important position today, could you not see to it that Roosevelt does his utmost to try to effect America's entry into a reorganized League of Nations, one which would be equipped with powerful guarantees? Surely this would strengthen Soviet policy at home as well as contribute toward a settlement with Finland. I believe, in view of the shock which people in this country have just experienced, the moment is most favorable for such action.

Needless to say, this note does not call for a reply.

Litvinov answered Einstein's note on December 18, 1941: [10]

I thank you for your letter. I am sure that after what has happened, there can hardly be a relapse to isolationism in any country.

When discussing postwar problems I shall certainly bear in mind your suggestion.

On December 29, 1941, Einstein was briefly interviewed in Princeton on the occasion of a meeting of the American Physical Society. He believed, he said, that the democracies would win the war, but it would undoubtedly prove costly and require great sacrifices.

After America's entry into the war, Einstein practiced some restraint in public statements which, at times, apparently caused him frustration. In a letter to Otto Lehmann-Russbüldt, his old pacifist friend, he said on September 25, 1942:

. . . I live here in great isolation and keep busy with my work. Although I often am on the right track about things in general, I completely lack the ability to speak convincingly and influence others effectively.

Ely Culbertson, the bridge expert, was a pioneer among proponents of World Government. In July 1942 he sent his carefully worked-out World Federation Plan to Einstein with a request for his "valuable criticism and advice." Einstein replied on August 8, 1942, again from Knollwood, Saranac Lake, New York:

In most respects I consider your plan reasonable and workable, especially your suggestions for the organization of the World Federation. I do not believe, however, that your proposals regarding the treatment of Germany and Japan during the postwar decades are practicable.

Should those countries have armies at their disposal, recruited from their own people, and should they control their own industrial capacity, they would undoubtedly find opportunities, as they did so successfully after the last war, to prepare surreptitiously for new aggression. Few people in this country have any clear understanding of how deeply rooted is the military mentality of certain classes, in Germany and Japan, which identify themselves with the state. You will realize what I mean when you read the enclosed article by the eminent German historian Friedrich Wilhelm Förster, who fought the criminal policies of the ruling classes of his country with extraordinary energy and courage.

An excellent and exhaustive analysis of these characteristics of the ruling classes was also presented by the American economist Thorstein Veblen, in my opinion one of the most remarkable political writers not only in America but in the entire world. You will find this analysis particularly in Veblen's books *The Nature of Peace* (1917) and *Germany and the Economic Revolution* (I am not certain of the title, but you can easily check this). It seems a great pity that this great man is not sufficiently appreciated in his own country.

A year and a half later, in February 1944, Culbertson sent Einstein a copy of his new book, *Total Peace*. He added that he had found Einstein's criticism most valuable. He felt that, in the interim, he had adequately solved the problem of permanent disarmament of Germany (see pp. 288–289 of *Total Peace*) and expressed the hope that he might continue to benefit by Einstein's advice and criticism.[11]

The Jewish Council for Russian War Relief tendered Einstein a testimonial dinner on October 25, 1942. Because poor health kept him from attending, he delivered his address by telephone from Princeton: [12]

I consider this an occasion of greatest importance. As friends of human progress, as Americans, and not least as Jews, we are most keenly interested in giving our utmost to the struggle of the Russian people for freedom.

Let us be clear at the outset. For many years our press has misled us about the efforts and achievements of the Russian people and their government. But today, everybody knows that Russia has promoted and continues to promote the advancement of science with the same zeal as our own country. Moreover, her conduct of the war has made obvious her great achievements in all industrial and technical fields. From rudimentary beginnings, the rate of her development in the last twenty-five years has been so extraordinary that it is virtually without parallel in history. But it would be quite unfair to mention only those accomplishments which are chiefly due to improvements in organization. We must particularly emphasize the fact that the Russian Government has labored more honestly and unequivocally to promote international security than any of the other great powers. Her foreign policy was consistently directed toward this goal until shortly before the outbreak of war, actually up to the time the other powers brusquely excluded her from the European concert, in the days of Czechoslovakia's betrayal. Thus was she driven into the unfortunate pact with Germany; for, by then, it had become obvious that attempts were being made to turn the force of the German attack eastward. Russia, unlike the Western Powers, supported the legitimate government of Spain, offered assistance to Czechoslovakia and was never guilty of increasing the power of the German and Japanese adventurers. Russia, in short, cannot be accused of disloyalty in the field of foreign policy. It seems reasonable, then, to look forward to her powerful and loyal co-operation in devising an effective scheme of supranational security, provided, of course, that she encounters the same degree of seriousness and good will in the other great powers.

Now, a comment on the domestic affairs of Russia. It is undeniable that a policy of severe coercion exists in the political sphere. This may, in part, be due to the necessity of breaking the power of the former ruling class, of protecting the country against foreign aggression and of converting a politically inexperienced, culturally backward people, deeply rooted in the traditions of their past, into a nation well organized for productive work. I do not presume to pass judgment in these difficult matters; but, in the unity of the Russian people against a powerful enemy from without and in the limitless sacrifice and exemplary self-denial of every single individual, I see proof of a strong and universal will to defend what they have won. We should also remember that the achievement of economic security for the individual and the utilization of the country's productive powers for the common good must necessarily have entailed certain sacrifices of personal freedom, a freedom which may have relatively little meaning unless accompanied by a measure of economic security.

Then, let us consider Russia's extraordinary success in fostering the intellectual life of her people. Enormous quantities of the best books are distributed and are eagerly read and studied; and this in a country where until twenty-five years ago cultural education was restricted to the very privileged few. It is difficult even to conceive of such revolutionary changes.

Finally, let me mention a fact of particular importance to us Jews.

In Russia the equality of all national and cultural groups is not merely nominal but is actually practiced. "Equal objectives and equal rights together with equal obligations to society" is not merely an empty slogan but a practice which is realized in everyday life.

So much for Russia as she appears today. Now let us briefly consider her present significance to the United States and the Western Powers. Suppose she too had succumbed to the German hordes, as has almost the whole Continent of Europe. How would this have affected the situation of England and the United States? I am sure it requires very little imagination to realize that we should be in a very bad way. In fact, I believe that, without Russia, the German bloodhounds would have already achieved their goal, or would achieve it very soon.

Thus, it is no more than a dictate of self-preservation that we help Russia in whatever way we can, to the utmost limit of our resources. And, quite apart from this selfish interest, we and our children owe a great debt of gratitude to the Russian people for having experienced such immense losses and suffering. If we wish to retain our self-respect as human beings, we must be conscious of their great sacrifice every hour of our lives.

Let us act accordingly.

The only noteworthy document from the year 1943 deals again with the Soviet Union. To a rally welcoming a Soviet-Jewish delegation visiting the United States, Einstein sent this message: [13]

. . . In these grave times, when so many of our people have been murdered by the Germans, it is of special importance to preserve and cherish the solidarity of the Jewish people. Such solidarity will also serve to deepen co-operation and mutual understanding between the Russian and American peoples. Upon such co-operation and understanding depend not only the victorious conclusion of this war but also the establishment of effective security for all nations against the repetition of acts of violent aggression such as the two we have suffered from Germany in a single generation.

May your delegation elicit, from the American people, the kind of response which is worthy of the ethical ideals our two nations hold in common, and which also expresses our gratitude for Russia's heroic achievement in the struggle against the basest criminals that ever threatened mankind.

To the London *News Chronicle,* which congratulated him on his sixty-fifth birthday and asked for a message for the people of Britain, Einstein cabled on March 13, 1944: [14]

I have greatly admired the fortitude of the English people in their hour of peril and I feel every confidence in the victorious outcome of the war. I do, however, await with mingled hope and fear the postwar period. Might not the German peril, despite its having been averted for the moment, reassert itself if jealousy and strife weaken the Allies after the war? Will the impact of the great losses of this war help us avoid a repetition of the blunders and evil experiences which we suffered from 1918 to 1939? Indeed, it is not enough to hope; we must be firmly resolved to act with this end consistently in view.

Late in May 1944 Einstein issued a statement addressed to a National Wartime Conference, organized in New York by the National Council of Scientific, Professional, Art and White Collar Organizations.[15] The council, under the leadership of Professor Kirtley F. Mather of Harvard University, acted as co-ordinating agency for some seventy-five groups.

I consider it important, indeed urgently necessary, for intellectual workers to build an organization for themselves, both to protect their own economic interests and to secure some measure of influence in the general political field.

As far as the protection of economic interests is concerned, the working class may serve us as a model. Workers have succeeded, at least to some extent, in defending their economic position in society. We can learn from them how the problem of organization may be solved. We can also learn from them that the gravest threat to an organized group, which we must seek to avoid, are internal dissension and splits which impair its strength. Once a split has occurred, the individual groups begin to fight one another, with the result that united action becomes even more difficult.

We can also learn from the experiences of workers that our interests will not be sufficiently protected if we limit ourselves to fighting for immediate economic aims and exclude political objectives and political work. In this respect, even the workers in this country have only just started to become active. The trend towards increasing centralization of production makes it inevitable that the economic and political struggle will become increasingly closely interwoven while the political factor will gain ever greater significance. In the meantime, the intellectual worker, due to his lack of organization, remains less protected against arbitrary and exploitative forces than the members of any other occupational group.

Intellectual workers should unite not only in their own interest but also in the interest of society as a whole. The lack of organization among intellectuals, in part, accounts for the fact that the resources and experience which this group possesses have so rarely been utilized for political purposes in general. Rather, what has almost exclusively determined political decisions in the past were political ambition and the desire for economic advantage, and not professional knowledge and judgment based on objective thinking.

Therefore, an organization of intellectual workers which would influence public opinion through publicity and education would have the greatest significance for society as a whole. For example, a proper task of such an organization would be to defend academic freedom, without which the healthy development of a democratic society is impossible.

At this time, a particularly important task for an organization of intellectual workers would be the fight to establish a supranational political force to protect nations against the possibility of new wars of aggression. I believe, however, that the actual drafting of a specific plan for an international government is not our most urgent job; if the majority of people were firmly resolved to establish an organization to guarantee international security, decisions about the appropriate technical institutions of such an organization should not prove difficult. What the majority of people lack is the conviction, based on clear thinking, that such an organization offers the only means of permanently avoiding catastrophes such as we now witness. Therefore, in my opinion, the most important service an organization of intellectual workers could perform at this historic moment would be to disseminate information on this subject. Only by the vigorous pursuit of these aims can an organization such as has been outlined here achieve internal strength and influence public opinion.

By June 1944 Rome had fallen to the Allies. On June 7, 1944, Einstein addressed a letter to the Italian philosopher and statesman, Benedetto Croce,[16] who at that time had emerged into political prominence for a brief period:

I learned from a soldier in the American Army, who had the good fortune of being able to visit you, that he took it upon himself not to deliver the letter which I had given him for you. My consolation is the thought that you must have incomparably more important matters on your mind just now. I am sure you are full of hopes that your beautiful country will soon be liberated from its evil oppressors, both within and outside its borders. I sincerely hope that, in this period of general confusion, you may have the satisfaction of finding it possible to help your country since you are one of the few who, being nonpartisan, enjoy the confidence of the entire nation. If this should become possible and our beloved Plato could witness your doing so, he would be gratified indeed; in the many centuries that have passed since his death, it has happened but rarely that a nation was guided, as Plato would have wished it, by enlightened philosophers. During all these years he would have noted, undoubtedly with more pride than real satisfaction, that his prediction of cyclical recurrence of governmental systems has again and again been proven correct.

While it does not appear very probable that reason and philosophy will become the guides of men in the near future, they will remain, as they have always been, the most cherished refuge of the selected few. These few constitute the only true aristocracy, an aristocracy which neither oppresses men nor arouses their envy; indeed, this aristocracy cannot even be recognized, except by those who actually belong to it. In no other group is the bond between the living and the dead so alive. Those who live today sense as friends their fellows of past centuries whose works have never lost their charm, their relevance and their quality of personal graciousness. And, finally, any person who really belongs to this aristocracy may be destroyed by other people; but they can never offend him!

Croce replied on July 28, 1944, from Sorrento:

Your letter has touched me deeply, because I vividly remember the long conversation we held in Berlin in 1931, when we were both equally concerned about the danger which threatened European liberty at that time. I had another occasion to recognize the similarity of our feelings and ideals; it was after you had been exiled from your native land, as a result of an intensified attack upon liberty, and we happened to collaborate on a volume of essays on freedom, published in New York four years ago.

You spoke of two theories of Plato. One of these, that of the ideal republic, built on reason and ruled by philosophers, has not only failed to find acceptance but has actually been rejected by modern philosophical thought. The other, which was not peculiar to Plato alone, regarding the cycle of forms through which history must necessarily move, has been retained and indeed illuminated by the complementary theory of the perpetual progress and elevation of mankind in a manner which it pleased your Goethe to describe as a "spiral motion." Herein is the basis of our faith in reason, life and reality.

As for philosophy, it is not worthy of the name unless it is aware not only of its function but also of the limitations of that function; for its chief contributions to human progress are clear thinking and the light of truth. Philosophy is a mental process, which opens a path to practical moral action; although it may inspire such action, it does not claim to take its place. In the realm of action, we humble philosophers should imitate our ancient predecessor, Socrates, who fought as a hoplite [a heavy-armed infantry soldier] at Potidea, or the poet Dante, who fought at Campaldino. But since we cannot all, at all times, be active to this extent, we must at least take part in the even more complex and difficult daily struggle which is waged in the political arena. I too frequent the company, which you so nobly describe, of those who lived before us and left behind the treasure of their philosophical and poetical thought. To dip into their writings in search of spiritual refreshment is to me somewhat of a religious rite. But I must not linger in this purifying immersion; I must step out of it and face the humble and often ungrateful duties which wait to be accomplished in the world around me.

Hence, it is in accord with my ideals and convictions that I am taking part in my country's political struggle today. I could wish I had a greater abundance of strength with which to meet these exigencies, but as it is I give all that which, with considerable effort, I am able to gather. I thank you for the good wishes which you so generously sent to Italy. Italy's sad experience goes back to the collapse which it suffered, along with other countries, after the First World War. In this condition, unreasoning, violent men were able to seize power, not without world-wide approval, and to force Italy into an utterly alien path, one in contradiction to its entire history. Not, since the fall of the Roman Empire, had Italy embraced the insane notion of world conquest. For centuries it practiced or sought after freedom, and freedom was the keystone of its national unification. Nationalism and Fascism grew out of foreign ideas, the only ones which these unreasoning, violent men were able to use in justifying their misdeeds. Indeed, not even ancient Rome was possessed by this madness. The task it had set itself was to pursue that which had been begun by Greece, to create Europe, by giving a code of law to barbarians who had heretofore known no law or, at best, known only a barbaric one.

War is war; it obeys no principle but its own and uses even the noblest ideologies as means to forward its own ends. Every student of history knows this, and every man of intelligence is able to understand it. Once the war is over, the internal struggle for civilization and liberty will have to be waged within every single nation, whether victor or vanquished. All of them have equally suffered from their participation in the war and are now equally alienated from the practices of freedom; for this reason the struggle ahead will be difficult and dangerous. Since wars by their very nature are directed toward the attainment of peace, let us hope and pray that today's statesmen may take thought at once to prevent developments which might make an enduring peace impossible, damage the cause of liberty and pave the way for a new conflict. War cannot be avoided by the use of force; its prevention requires that man's spirit be attuned to peace, concord and the dignity of human labor. "Tongues have power to stay swords," as an old Italian philosopher put it.

I do not wish to bore you with my observations and judgments of the international and particularly the Italian political scene. On the contrary, I should beg your pardon for having taken advantage of your kind and cordial words to set forth my own thoughts on the important questions raised in your letter. *Naturam expelles furca, tamen usque recurret* or, to paraphrase, You may throw nature out the door, but she will come back through the window, and I refer in this case to the incorrigible way a philosopher has of always drawing distinctions and theorizing.

On June 19, 1944, Einstein responded to five questions for a symposium on Science and World Co-operation to appear in the magazine *Free World:* [17]

Q: The advance of science has made impossible a return to the old world of isolationism, to a compartmented world. What is the best way, or the chief way, in which scientists can make their influence felt in an effort to achieve world co-operation?

A: In my view, scientists can best contribute to the attainment of international security by publicly supporting the establishment of a supranational authority equipped with a permanent staff and standing military forces. A collective declaration of this character, by a large number of outstanding intellectuals, becomes all the more necessary when it is realized that, without heavy outside pressure, not a single major power seems inclined to surrender any part of its sovereignty in foreign affairs.

Q: In certain quarters, the view seems to be held that a genuine or "pure" scientist should not concern himself with political issues. Would you care to comment on this view?

A: I believe that every citizen has the duty to express his political views to the best of his ability. A healthy democracy cannot prevail if intelligent and able citizens neglect this duty.

Q: What relationship, if any, do you see between the progress of physics and mathematics and the progress of society?

A: Physics and mathematics are important to society in two quite different respects. First, they serve to stimulate technological development. And, secondly, like all noble cultural efforts, they serve as an effective weapon against the danger that men may succumb to a dreary materialism which, in turn, can lead to the rule of unrestrained selfishness.

Q: What educational measures should be taken to undo the effects of Nazi indoctrination and to redirect the German people into the paths of democracy?

A: It is possible either to destroy the German people or keep them suppressed; it is not possible to educate them to think and act along democratic lines in the foreseeable future.

Chiefly to assist in the re-election of President Roosevelt in the fall of 1944, an Independent Citizens' Committee of the Arts, Sciences and Professions was organized under the leadership of Jo Davidson, the American sculptor. Einstein endorsed the organization in the following statement:

To be effective, an association of intellectuals for political purposes must formulate a clear and firm program of its aims. In my opinion, the two most important objectives today are:

1. To secure peace. To this end the internationalization of military power is indispensable. Unless it is generally recognized that any less radical approach to the security problem can provide only a temporary solution, it will not be possible to mobilize effective pressure for this objective through public opinion. An international association of influential intellectuals who are adequately informed about the dangers to civilization inherent in recent military inventions will be able to exert a direct influence upon responsible political leaders.

2. The second important objective of an association of intellectuals would be, in my opinion, the protection of the individual and society against the overwhelming power of finance capital. To help secure such protection, such an association should attempt to influence legislation and enlighten public opinion on this subject.

A relatively small committee of independent and influential intellectuals should discuss these and related questions until agreement has been reached on the basic program to be adopted by the association.

Einstein also gave Davidson's committee a statement to be used in the Presidential campaign of 1944:

Roosevelt was among the very few individuals who fully recognized the danger confronting America in the prewar period and acted in accordance with his beliefs and with great energy. He further helped to create a feeling of confidence among the Allies. I am convinced that it is of great significance, not only to America, but to the whole course of international developments that the experience of Roosevelt, as well as the confidence he universally enjoys, be utilized in preparing the peace treaties and in promoting reconstruction in the world. Thus, it is my belief that everything possible should be done to insure his re-election.

A longer statement by Einstein in favor of a fourth term for President Roosevelt was made public at a rally of the Independent League for Roosevelt on October 9, 1944, in Trenton, New Jersey: [18]

The coming Presidential election involves one of the most fateful decisions which the American people have ever had to make. Their decision will determine whether the heavy sacrifices America has made for its security will, for the second time, be wasted, and whether our children will be spared the harsh ordeal which the present younger generation has had to suffer.

The next few years must be used to establish peace and guarantee security and protection against any future attempt at aggression. I believe that Roosevelt, Churchill and Stalin are sincere in their efforts to create legal guarantees and a framework of mutual trust which would insure the security of all nations. These men have given evidence that they possess the will, the strength and the moderation needed to carry this task to a favorable conclusion. Further, they have created an atmosphere of confidence among nations without which no work of peace can succeed. We must not endanger the successful completion of their efforts by creating a situation that would bring to an end the era of mutual trust which these three men have inaugurated.

The older among us lived through the fateful days when Wilson's efforts for international security collapsed because his fellow citizens deserted him before the final goal was reached. We must do all in our power to prevent another such failure; we must do so not only in our own interest and in the interest of our children, but also in the interest of all the peoples who have suffered so grievously from German and Japanese aggression.

This is why we should make every effort and use all our influence to insure the re-election of Roosevelt by a large majority.

In the fall of 1944, the Charter for the United Nations was drafted at the Dumbarton Oaks Conference. A number of outside individuals and groups took it upon themselves to inform and enlighten the public about the work of the conference. One of them, the Commission to Study the Organization of Peace, associated with the older League of Nations Association, invited Einstein to be one of the sponsors of a popular campaign for acceptance of the Dumbarton Oaks recommendations.[19] Einstein replied on January 31, 1945:

I shall be glad to become a member of the sponsoring committee for the campaign you intend to organize. I am convinced it is of great importance that the American people be made aware of the great significance of that project. Mutual confidence and organized co-operation among the great powers are the only way to prevent future wars. If we fail in this objective, and nations continue to distrust one another, increased armaments will be inevitable and even preventive wars may well take place within the next few decades.

It also seems important that everyone in this country come to recognize clearly that, without an effective system of international security, the United States, with its great land surface and relatively small population, will be increasingly menaced by the rapid technological development of the weapons of aggression.

When the defeat of Germany became a certainty, Einstein, in a note of March 9, 1945, remarked to the friend on the West Coast to whom he had expressed apprehension and gloom in the early days of the war: [20]

. . . So we have after all lived to witness the breakdown of the terrible evil over there. Perhaps all those horrible happenings will lead to something good in the long run: it might not be altogether illogical to place a statue of the contemptible Hitler in the vestibule of the future palace of world government since he, ironically, has greatly helped to convince many people of the necessity of a supranational organization.

On April 12, 1945, Franklin D. Roosevelt died. The New York German language publication, *Aufbau,* of April 27, 1945, carried a message which Einstein had prepared for a memorial meeting in New York: [21]

. . . It does not often happen that a man who has his heart in the right place also possesses the qualities of political genius and determination without which no individual can have a decisive and lasting influence upon the course of history. President Roosevelt early anticipated the inevitability of later events and saw to it that America was able to resist effectively the grave threat posed by German aggression. To the extent that it was politically feasible, he worked successfully for economic reconstruction and greater economic security of the underprivileged masses. Despite the heavy burdens he had to carry, his sense of humor enabled him to remain intrinsically free and detached, as only few individuals who constantly face the most critical decisions are able to do. He was utterly consistent in the determination to achieve his ultimate objectives. At the same time, he was admirably flexible in surmounting the many obstacles any farsighted statesman will experience, particularly in a country with democratic institutions; for in such a country the authority of even the highest office is always limited.

No matter when this man might have left us, we would have felt that we had suffered an irreplaceable loss. It is tragic that he did not live to lend his unique abilities to the task of finding a solution to the problem of international security. . . . All people of good will feel that with the death of Roosevelt they lost an old and dear friend. May he have a lasting influence on the hearts and minds of men!

CHAPTER ELEVEN

THE THREAT OF ATOMIC WEAPONS | 1945

THE END OF THE NAZI menace to the world, through the military defeat of Germany in May 1945, and the explosion of the atomic bomb over Hiroshima in August 1945, opened a new phase in Einstein's public life. There was no longer any reason for the restraint which he had imposed upon himself in his pacifist activities when Hitler came to power; and the successful use of atomic energy for purposes of mass destruction suddenly presented a problem to the world the full and dreadful implications of which caused Einstein to assume a most active role in the postwar struggle to protect mankind from disaster and annihilation.

The intensity of Einstein's public activities in the early years after the Second World War can only be compared to his sincere devotion to the pacifist movement and the cause of war resistance in the years before 1933. In fact, in the struggle after 1945 to abolish atomic weapons and in the advocacy of world government Einstein accepted leadership and responsibility to an extent he had never done before. He did so because of the immense threat which he was sure atomic weapons presented to mankind and, undoubtedly, also because he was conscious of the role he had played in initiating the work that eventually produced the bomb.

Although the revelation in the official Smyth Report (*Atomic Energy for Military Purposes* [1]) of Einstein's history-making letter to President Roosevelt in August 1939 pushed him again into the limelight, his everyday life followed its accustomed course. He seldom left Princeton, except for summer vacations; his movements were ordinarily limited to walks between his two studies, one in his modest house on Mercer Street, the other in the Institute for Advanced Study which he continued to visit daily even after his formal retirement on April 15, 1945. The steady stream of visitors and correspondence never subsided. His interest in helping to secure Palestine as a homeland for the Jewish people was as strong as ever; he lent support to the Zionist cause whenever he felt it might prove useful, and did so particularly in the years preceding the actual establishment of the State of Israel. He also devoted his active interest to the creation of a Jewish-sponsored university in America, which was later to become Brandeis University. He withdrew from these efforts only when his ideas concerning the academic organization of the new institution met great resistance and when he and his associates in the project became targets of political vilification—among the earliest symptoms of the great wave of reactionary persecution which spread through America during the cold war and against which Einstein emerged as one of the great uncompromising fighters for human freedom and decency.

Einstein always found time for these and many other causes; and none of his many visitors could ever have felt that he had not been given generous opportunity to present and discuss his views and ideas. And yet, throughout it all, Einstein ceaselessly pursued his scientific work, which then, as ever, had first claim upon his interest and which, as always, occupied his thoughts throughout the waking hours of his days. These were years of particularly intense scientific efforts which led, in 1949, to the well-known publication of his last attempt to formulate a unified field theory.[1a]

Einstein's active interest in protecting mankind from an atomic holocaust became evident very soon after the fateful explosions over Japan. About a month after the dropping of atomic bombs on Hiroshima and Nagasaki, a United Press reporter approached Einstein "at his cabin deep in an evergreen forest."

> In my opinion [he said during this interview on September 14, 1945, at Saranac Lake] the only salvation for civilization and the human race lies in the creation of a world government, with security of nations founded upon law. As long as sovereign states continue to have separate armaments and armaments secrets, new world wars will be inevitable.[2]

Earlier that month Robert M. Hutchins, then Chancellor of the University of Chicago, had invited Einstein to attend a conference of physical and social scientists, public officials and other citizens to discuss the problems raised by the existence of atomic bombs.[3] Hutchins quoted from the concluding words of the Smyth Report, to the effect that these "are not technical questions; they are political and social questions, and the answers given to them may affect all mankind for generations. . . . In a free country like ours, such questions should be debated by the people and decisions must be made by the people through their representatives." Einstein replied on September 10, 1945, in much the same words he was to use a few days later in the interview at Saranac Lake:

I thank you for your kind invitation and for the very interesting report on the atomic bomb by Professor Smyth. To my great regret I am unable to take part in the conference for reasons of poor health and because of the pressure of work.

For me the problem is a purely political one. As long as nations demand unrestricted sovereignty we shall undoubtedly be faced with still bigger wars, fought with bigger and technologically more advanced weapons. The most important task of intellectuals is to make this clear to the general public and to emphasize over and over again the need to establish a well-organized world government. They must advocate the abolition of armaments and of military secrecy by individual nations.

Emery Reves, an economist and writer of Hungarian origin, published toward the end of the war a brief, widely noted book, *The Anatomy of Peace*.[3a] In September 1945 he acquainted Einstein with a statement issued by a group of scientists at the Oak Ridge atomic installation in Tennessee recommending that a world security council be made the sole custodian of nuclear power in the world; that all nations agree to thorough inspection of scientific, technical, industrial and military establishments by that agency; and that all scientific and technological advances be reported to it directly and immediately. In Reves's view,[4] these recommendations demonstrated that the scientists

. . . have not thought the political problem through and still abide by old-fashioned internationalism, believing a league of sovereign nation-states capable of maintaining peace between its member states. . . . If the nation-states would do what they ought to do . . . there would be not the slightest danger that the atomic bomb would be used anywhere.

Unfortunately, peace among sovereign powers is a daydream. . . . It can be said with mathematical certainty that if control of atomic energy were to be transferred to the United Nations Security Council, a devastating world war with unlimited use of atomic power would be inevitable. . . .

There is only one way to prevent an atomic war and that is to prevent war. . . . Analyzing all the wars of history . . . I think it is possible . . . to define the one and only condition in human society that produces war. This is the non-integrated coexistence of sovereign powers. . . . Peace is law. Peace between warring sovereign social units . . . can be achieved only by the integration of these conflicting units into a higher sovereignty . . . by the creation of a world government having direct relations with the individual citizen.

Attempts to maintain peace . . . by a league structure such as the San Francisco Organization . . . are pitifully outdated and bound to fail. . . . There is only one way and one way alone to make the United States secure from an attack by atomic bombs. The method is the same that today makes the states of New York and California (nonproducers of atomic bombs) safe from annihilation by the states of Tennessee and New Mexico (producers of atomic bombs).

No group of people today have such influence on the public as do the nuclear physicists. Their responsibility in making political suggestions is tremendous. . . . They should always keep in mind the fundamental thesis Hamilton expressed in *The Federalist:* "To look for a continuation of harmony between a number of independent, unconnected sovereignties, situated in the same neighborhood, would be to disregard the uniform course of human events, and to set at defiance the accumulated experience of ages." . . .

Because Einstein—mistakenly—assumed that Dr. J. Robert Oppenheimer of Los Alamos was one of the signers of the Oak Ridge statement, he forwarded Reves's letter to Oppenheimer, on September 29, 1945, and included a letter of his own. Einstein's letter clearly bore the imprint of Reves's thinking, which closely paralleled ideas Einstein himself had held for years:

Mr. Emery Reves, whom I have known for many years and with whom I have often discussed urgent political problems, has sent me a copy of the statement which you and your colleagues issued for the enlightenment of the public and the government. While I was very much pleased by the candid language and the sincerity of the statement, I was, at the same time, somewhat bewildered by the political recommendations, which I consider inadequate.

The pathetic attempts made by governments to achieve what they consider to be international security have not the slightest effect on the present political structure of the world, nor is it recognized that the real cause of international conflicts is due to the existence of competing sovereign nations. Neither governments nor people seem to have learned anything from the experiences of the past and appear to be unable or unwilling to think the problem through. The conditions existing in the world today force the individual states, out of fear for their own security, to commit acts which inevitably produce war.

At the present high level of industrialization and economic interdependence, it is unthinkable that we can achieve peace without a genuine supranational organization to govern international relations. If war is to be avoided, anything less than such an over-all solution strikes me as illusory.

A few weeks ago, Emery Reves published a short book entitled *The Anatomy of Peace* which, in my opinion, explains the problem as clearly and pertinently as anyone ever has. I have learnt that several men who play an active role in public life are taking steps to make the book known to every American. I urge you and your colleagues to read it and discuss its conclusions. Although it was written before the explosion of the atomic bomb, it contains a solution which is directly applicable to the problem created by this new weapon. I shall be glad to send you a number of copies for distribution or to mail copies directly to you and your colleagues if you send me their addresses. I am convinced that the political part of the statement which you and your colleagues issued would have been formulated differently, had the facts and discussions presented in this book been made known to those who drafted the statement.

I do hope you will forgive my bothering you with this, but the problem is vital and your responsibility great.

This letter reflected the concern Einstein felt at the time about the problems of the atomic bomb and world government. The statement referred to in Reves's and Einstein's letters had, as was already mentioned, been issued by a group of atomic scientists at Oak Ridge, Tennessee, while Dr. Oppenheimer himself was at Los Alamos, New Mexico. Dr. Oppenheimer was in no way connected with the preparation of the statement and had no prior knowledge of it.

Einstein associated himself with nineteen other prominent personages, including Supreme Court Justice Owen J. Roberts and Thomas Mann, in another statement along similar lines which appeared as a letter to the editor in *The New York Times* on October 10, 1945: [5]

The first atomic bomb destroyed more than the city of Hiroshima. It also exploded our inherited, outdated political ideas.

A few days before the force of nature was tried out for the first time in history, the San Francisco Charter was ratified in Washington. The dream of a League of Nations, after twenty-six years, was accepted by the Senate.

How long will the United Nations Charter endure? With luck, a generation? A century? There is no one who does not hope for at least that much luck—for the Charter, for himself, for his work and for his children's children. But is it enough to have peace by luck? Peace by law is what the peoples of the world, beginning with ourselves, can have if they want it. And now is the time to get it.

Everyone knows that the Charter is only a beginning. It does not guarantee peace. Yet the hopeful and passionate words of Dumbarton Oaks and San Francisco created one very real danger: that millions of Americans will relax and believe that by ratification a machinery has been set up to prevent another war.

We think it our duty to warn the American people that this is not so. The Charter is a tragic illusion unless we are ready to take the further steps necessary to organize peace. Coming East from San Francisco, President Truman said in Kansas City: "It will be just as easy for nations to get along in a republic of the world as it is for you to get along in the republic of the United States. Now when Kansas and Colorado have a quarrel over water in the Arkansas River they don't call out the National Guard in each state and go to war over it. They bring a suit in the Supreme Court of the United States and abide by the decision. There isn't a reason in the world why we cannot do that internationally."

These words were historic words, pointing our road to a future far beyond San Francisco.

For thousands of years men have learned that wherever there is government by law there can be peace, and where there is no law and no government human conflicts have been sure. The San

Francisco Charter, by maintaining the absolute sovereignties of the rival nation-states, thus preventing the creation of superior law in world relations, resembles the Articles of Confederation of the thirteen original American republics. We know that this confederation did not work. No league system ever attempted in human history could prevent conflict between its members. We must aim at a Federal Constitution of the world, a working world-wide legal order, if we hope to prevent an atomic war.

It happens that at this anxious moment of our history a small book has been published, a very important book, which expresses clearly and simply what so many of us have been thinking. That book is *The Anatomy of Peace* by Emery Reves. We urge American men and women to read this book, to think about its conclusions, to discuss it with neighbors and friends privately and publicly. A few weeks ago these ideas seemed important but perhaps reachable in the future. In the new reality of atomic warfare they are of immediate, urgent necessity, unless civilization is determined on suicide.

In his last address, which he did not live to speak, Franklin Roosevelt wrote words which were his political testament: "We are faced with the pre-eminent fact that if civilization is to survive we must cultivate the science of human relationship—the ability of peoples of all kinds to live together and work together in the same world, at peace." We have learned, and paid an awful price to learn, that living and working together can be done in one way only—under law. There is no truer and simpler idea in the world today. Unless it prevails, and unless by common struggle we are capable of new ways of thinking, mankind is doomed.

On the letterhead of the Radiation Laboratory of the Massachusetts Institute of Technology, Dr. Daniel Q. Posin, physicist, wrote Einstein on October 21, 1945, as follows: [6]

The scientists of Cambridge, as well as those throughout the world, need help urgently in these days of turmoil and unprecedented tension. What makes the present atomic power situation so full of anguish for all of us is the cruel irony wherein one of the greatest and most joyful triumphs of scientific intellect may bring frustration and death rather than spiritual uplifting and more audacious life. The final total confirmation of your principle $E = mc^2$ should mark the beginning of an era of light; but we stand perturbed and seem to see ahead an impenetrable night. . . .

The scientists of Los Alamos have given voice to some of their thoughts, the scientists of Oak Ridge have also had their say—that which is not restricted; a physicist in Texas has implored scientists to be also conscious citizens; from Chicago have come pleas for freedom and international agreement—there [Samuel King] Allison has indicated an inability to do his life's work in secret; here, at the Massachusetts Institute for Technology, [Norbert] Wiener stands aghast—as though a man in a confused dream—and wonders what we must do, and he protests at scientific meetings the "Massacre of Nagasaki" which makes it easier, for some, to contemplate other massacres; here at the Radiation Laboratory, young scientists meet to protest the May-Johnson bill [for control of atomic energy by the United States Government] and to formulate statements on the obvious need for international control of the atomic bomb and atomic energy. . . .

But these voices, each speaking alone, are not enough. . . .

We propose, therefore, to call a national congress of scientists of very great magnitude in order to derive strength from one another and aid one another in clarifying more specifically our attitudes and resolves. And, therefore, I say we need you here to speak out on the social implications of the era of atomic energy. We feel instinctively that with you here we shall feel inspired to better master our future; we almost feel that it is your duty to help us and eventually the world, not only because yours is at once a humble and a powerful voice, but also because your own work, the mass-energy principle, has in a larger sense led us to this road that has two turnings—and we count on you to help us all travel along the correct path. . . .

Accompanying this letter was an outline for a National Congress of Scientists, scheduled for January 10–12, 1946, anticipating the participation of many eminent scientists besides Einstein. Since the Congress actually never convened, Einstein apparently did not mail the message which he had drafted for the occasion:

Unfortunately I cannot attend your congress. Poor health compels me to limit myself to activities which I can perform at home.

I am sincerely gratified that the great majority of scientists are fully conscious of their responsibilities as scholars and world citizens; and that they have not fallen victim to the widespread hysteria that threatens our future and that of our children.

We must not permit any restrictions on the publication and dissemination of scientific work; this would be exceedingly harmful to the intellectual development of society. It is horrifying to realize that the poison of militarism and imperialism threatens to bring about undesirable changes in the political attitude of the United States at the very moment when this country ought to assume a position of leadership in establishing international security.

Who is the potential enemy that serves as a target of all these maneuvers? Who creates such fear among the American people that they should be obliged to accept permanent military bondage? The answer is that it is the same Russia which, so far, has been the leader in the search for international security and the most loyal supporter of the League of Nations.

What we see at work here is not an expression of the sentiments of the American people; rather, it reflects the will of a powerful minority which uses its economic power to control the organs of political life. This minority does not really fear actual military action by Russia. Rather, they fear the moral influence of a powerful Russia which might undermine and thereby jeopardize their status in society in indirect ways.

Should the government pursue this fateful course, we scientists must refuse to submit to its immoral demands, even if they are backed by legal machinery. There is an unwritten law, that of our own conscience, which is far more binding than any bills that may be devised in Washington. And there are, of course, even for us, the ultimate weapons: non-co-operation and strike.

We justifiably blame German intellectuals for having unconditionally surrendered themselves to the control of an unworthy government. It is right to punish them for the crimes which they committed even though they claim that they were legally compelled to act as they did. I am hopeful that our own intellectuals are determined to avoid similar wrongdoing; the attitude they have thus far adopted justifies such hope.

Einstein added the following postscript to his letter to Posin: "This letter should not be treated confidentially. I am glad to stand up for my convictions." The war being over, Einstein was obviously prepared to lend his authority, with as little restraint as in the past, to causes which were close to his heart. However, this does not mean that he did so indiscriminately. When the American Committee for Spanish Freedom, an organization advocating that the United States break diplomatic and commercial relations with Franco Spain, advised Einstein that it intended to mail out a fund appeal letter over his name, he refused his permission. In his immediate reply of October 1, 1945, he said:

. . . I do not feel justified in making myself a public spokesman for the Spanish cause, although I am convinced that justice is on the side of the Spanish loyalists and that the survival of Fascist Spain seriously endangers international security. I do not possess any firsthand information about the pertinent facts and particularly about those facts mentioned in the news release which you suggest should be attached to the fund appeal letter. It would hence not be honest and, indeed, unwise to use the popularity and advertising value of my name for the purpose of your appeal. Should I allow my name to be used under such conditions, I would very soon lose the confidence which many people have in me and which enables me to exercise some effective influence upon such causes in regard to which I feel justified in voicing an opinion.

Despite this unqualified refusal the committee used Einstein's name as signature on its letters appealing for funds. One of these letters reached Congressman John Rankin, from Mississippi, an ultraconservative politician known for his racist views. On October 25, 1945, Rankin bitterly attacked Einstein on the floor of the House of Representatives: [7]

. . . This foreign-born agitator would have us plunge into another European war in order to further the spread of Communism throughout the world. . . . It is about time the American people got wise to Einstein. In my opinion he is violating the law and ought to be prosecuted. . . . Here is a man using the mail to raise money to propagandize us into breaking relations with Spain, which, as I said, would mean another war probably. . . . I call upon the Department of Justice to put a stop to this man Einstein. . . .

Einstein ignored the attack completely.

In October 1945 Joseph H. Ball, U. S. Senator from Minnesota, introduced into the Senate a bill designed to meet objections voiced against the pending May-Johnson bill (an atomic energy control bill drafted by the War Department). In a statement released on November 5, 1945, Senator Ball said:

I agree with most of the scientists who have expressed themselves on the May-Johnson bill that, as it stands, it is not only undemocratic, in that it creates a gigantic monopoly which would function in complete secrecy, but it is also impractical, because its stringent secrecy and control requirements would slow down rather than speed up fundamental research as well as research on peaceful applications of atomic energy.

This bill [Senator Ball's bill] is an attempt to free research on fundamentals and on industrial applications . . . while retaining the secrecy required for security only on the purely military application of atomic energy. I think that the only sound solution for the United States lies along these lines. . . .

On November 17, 1945, Senator Ball sent Einstein a copy of his bill and said in an accompanying note: [8]

I would appreciate your comments on the bill, and if you think it is a reasonably good answer perhaps you would like to help by writing and getting some of your fellow scientists to write their views to the Special Senate Committee on Atomic Energy headed by Senator Brien McMahon of Connecticut.

Einstein replied to Senator Ball on November 22, 1945:

I very greatly admired your speech before the Cincinnati Foreign Policy Institute on November 9 and your exhaustive analysis of the international security situation. I agree with everything you said. [Ball had advocated strengthening the United Nations organization along world government lines.]

However, as to the proposed bill on the development and control of atomic energy, I am not in complete agreement with you. It is true that the proposals made in your bill are far preferable to the May-Johnson bill. But it seems to me that your bill, should it become law, would make more difficult the solution of the most pressing problem, that of creating the necessary atmosphere of confidence among the great military powers, in order that agreement may be reached on international problems.

Would you consider it possible to postpone the discussion of the legal solution of the atomic problem until an all-out attempt has been made to reach agreement among the three great powers on the subject of atomic energy and, more generally, on the need for imposing limitations on national sovereignty in military matters? It seems to me that adequate legislation on this all-important matter can be achieved only when the international situation has been sufficiently clarified. There cannot be a compromise between a policy of competitive armaments and the concept of a world government guaranteeing security for all nations, as was demonstrated so convincingly in your Cincinnati address.

In his prompt acknowledgment, Ball pointed out that while the McMahon Committee [the Special Committee on Atomic Energy of the U. S. Senate] was likely to move slowly, the Administration was pressing for prompt action. The committee might be receptive to suggestions that legislation be limited to a one- or two-year period. "I am certainly in accord with you," he concluded, "that the United States should make a much stronger effort in the direction of an international understanding than it appears at present to be making."

Earlier in the year, on August 27, 1945, Einstein had spontaneously addressed a letter to Raymond Gram Swing of the American Broadcasting Company, who, because of his daily evening broadcasts during the war, had become one of the best-known American news commentators:

I wish to express my deep gratitude for your systematic endeavor to advise the public about the need for an effective world government.

You were quite correct in pointing out that the occupation of the Pacific islands by American forces alone is a step in the wrong direction, and one that will hinder any future attempts to achieve international security.

But most dangerous of all is the policy of military secrecy and the maintenance of huge organizations which can produce new secret weapons on a national scale. This, too, you have expressed, and very convincingly. You remain one of the few independent persons who have insight into the critical issues of today and exercise great influence on public thought and sentiment. I am astonished that your broadcasts have not had a greater impact on public opinion in the face of the great danger which confronts us and the fateful mistakes of our government.

I hope with all my heart that you may be able to influence the course of events by your courage and sincerity.

Although Einstein's letter bore the postscript "No answer is expected," Swing replied on August 30, 1945: [9]

I am thrilled to have your letter and approbation, which I might say I need, for it seems to me that most of the world goes on as though nothing had happened.

May I ask a favor? When you are back in Princeton would you let me come to see you some Saturday to talk over the implications of atomic energy?

Einstein actually did see Swing in Princeton; as a result, an article appeared in the November 1945 issue of the *Atlantic Monthly*, "Atomic War or Peace," by Albert Einstein as told to Raymond Swing.[10]

The release of atomic energy has not created a new problem. It has merely made more urgent the necessity of solving an existing one. One could say that it has affected us quantitatively, not qualitatively. As long as there are sovereign nations possessing great power, war is inevitable. This does not mean that one can know when war will come but only that one is sure that it will come. This was true even before the atomic bomb was made. What has changed is the destructiveness of war.

I do not believe that the secret of the bomb should be given to the United Nations Organization. I do not believe it should be given to the Soviet Union. Either course would be analogous to a man with capital who, wishing another individual to collaborate with him on an enterprise, starts by giving him half his money. The other man might choose to start a rival enterprise, when what is wanted is his co-operation. The secret of the bomb should be committed to a world government, and the United States should immediately announce its readiness to do so. Such a world government should be established by the United States, the Soviet Union and Great Britain, the only three powers which possess great military strength. The three of them should commit to this world government all of their military resources. The fact that there are only three nations with great military power should make it easier, rather than harder, to establish a world government.

Since the United States and Great Britain have the secret of the atomic bomb and the Soviet Union does not, they should invite the Soviet Union to prepare and present the first draft of a Constitution for the proposed world government. This would help dispel the distrust of the Russians, which they feel because they know the bomb is being kept a secret chiefly to prevent their having it. Obviously, the first draft would not be the final one, but the Russians should be made to feel that the world government will guarantee their security.

It would be wise if this Constitution were to be negotiated by one American, one Briton and one Russian. They would, of course, need advisers, but these advisers should serve only when asked. I believe three men can succeed in preparing a workable Constitution acceptable to all the powers. Were six or seven men, or more, to attempt to do so, they would probably fail. After the three great powers have drafted a Constitution and adopted it, the smaller nations should be invited to join the world government. They should also be free not to join and, though they should feel perfectly secure outside the world government, I am sure they will eventually wish to join. Naturally, they should be entitled to propose changes in the Constitution as drafted by the Big Three. But the Big Three should go ahead and organize the world government, whether or not the smaller nations decide to join.

Such a world government should have jurisdiction over all military matters, and it need have only one other power. That is the power to interfere in countries where a minority is oppressing the majority and, therefore, is creating the kind of instability that leads to war. For example, conditions such as exist today in Argentina and Spain should be dealt with. There must be an end to the concept of non-intervention, for to abandon non-intervention in certain circumstances is part of keeping the peace.

The establishment of a world government should not be delayed until similar conditions of freedom exist in each of the three great powers. While it is true that in the Soviet Union the minority rules, I do not believe that the internal conditions in that country constitute a threat to world peace. One must bear in mind that the people in Russia had not had a long tradition of political education; changes to improve conditions in Russia had to be effected by a minority for the reason that there was no majority capable of doing so. If I had been born a Russian, I believe I could have adjusted myself to this situation.

It should not be necessary, in establishing a world government with a monopoly of authority over military affairs, to change the internal structure of the three great powers. It would be for the three individuals who draft the Constitution to devise ways for collaboration despite the different structures of their countries.

Do I fear the tyranny of a world government? Of course I do. But I fear still more the coming of another war. Any government is certain to be evil to some extent. But a world government is preferable to the far greater evil of wars, particularly when viewed in the context of the intensified destructiveness of war. If such a world government is not established by a process of agreement among nations, I believe it will come anyway, and in a much more dangerous form; for war or wars can only result in one power being supreme and dominating the rest of the world by its overwhelming military supremacy.

Now that we have the atomic secret, we must not lose it, and that is what we would risk doing if we gave it to the United Nations Organization or to the Soviet Union. But, as soon as possible, we must make it clear that we are not keeping the bomb a secret for the sake of maintaining our power but in the hope of establishing peace through world government, and that we will do our utmost to bring this world government into being.

I appreciate that there are persons who approve of world government as the ultimate objective but favor a gradual approach to its establishment. The trouble with taking little steps, one at a time, in the hope of eventually reaching the ultimate goal, is that while such steps are being taken, we continue to keep the bomb without convincing those who do not have the bomb of our ultimate intentions. That of itself creates fear and suspicion, with the consequence that the relations between rival countries deteriorate to a dangerous extent. That is why people who advocate taking a step at a time may think they are approaching world peace, but they actually are contributing by their slow pace to the possibility of war. We have no time to waste in this way. If war is to be averted, it must be done quickly.

Further, we shall not have the secret of the bomb for very long. I know it is being argued that no other country has money enough to spend on the development of the atomic bomb and that, therefore, we are assured of the secret for a long time. But it is a common mistake in this country to measure things by the amount of money they cost. Other countries which have the raw materials and manpower and wish to apply them to the work of developing atomic power can do so; men and materials and the decision to use them, and not money, are all that is needed.

I do not consider myself the father of the release of atomic energy. My part in it was quite indirect. I did not, in fact, foresee that it would be released in my time. I only believed that it was theoretically possible. It became practical through the accidental discovery of chain reaction, and this was not something I could have predicted. It was discovered by Hahn in Berlin, and he himself at first misinterpreted what he discovered. It was Lise Meitner who provided the correct interpretation and escaped from Germany to place the information in the hands of Niels Bohr.[11]

In my opinion, a great era of atomic science cannot be assured by organizing science in the way large corporations are organized. One can organize the application of a discovery already made, but one cannot organize the discovery itself. Only a free individual can make a discovery. However, there can be a kind of organization wherein the scientist is assured freedom and proper conditions of work. Professors of science in American universities, for instance, should be relieved of some of their teaching so as to have more time for research. Can you imagine an organization of scientists making the discoveries of Charles Darwin?

I do not believe that the vast private corporations of the United States are suitable to the needs of the times. If a visitor should come to this country from another planet, would he not find it strange that, in this country, private corporations are permitted to wield so much power without having to assume commensurate responsibility? I say this to stress my conviction that the American government must retain control of atomic energy, not because socialism is necessarily desirable but because atomic energy was developed by the government; it would be unthinkable to turn over this property of the people to any individual or group of individuals. As for socialism, unless it is international to the extent of producing a world government which controls all military power, it might lead to wars even more easily than capitalism because it represents an even greater concentration of power.

To give any estimate as to when atomic energy might be applied for peaceful, constructive purposes is impossible. All that we know now is how to use a fairly large quantity of uranium. The use of small quantities, sufficient, say, to operate a car or an airplane, is thus far impossible, and one cannot predict when it will be accomplished. No doubt, it will be achieved, but no one can say when. Nor can one predict when materials more common than uranium can be used to supply atomic energy. Presumably, such materials would be among the heavier elements of high atomic weight and would be relatively scarce due to their lesser stability. Most of these materials may already have disappeared through radioactive disintegration. So, though the release of atomic energy can be, and no doubt will be, a great boon to mankind, this may not come about for some time.

I myself do not have the gift of explanation which would be needed to persuade large numbers of people of the urgency of the problems that now face the human race. Hence, I should like to commend someone who has this gift of explanation: Emery Reves, whose book *The Anatomy of Peace* is intelligent, clear, brief, and, if I may use the absurd term, dynamic on the topic of war and need for world government.

Since I do not foresee that atomic energy will prove to be a boon within the near future, I have to say that, for the present, it is a menace. Perhaps it is well that it should be. It may intimidate the human race into bringing order to its international affairs, which, without the pressure of fear, undoubtedly would not happen.

This, Einstein's first public statement on the atomic bomb, was widely noted and was reprinted in a number of publications, among them *The New York Times* of October 27, 1945. A few days later, on November 1, 1945, the *Times* published a letter from Einstein in which he expressed regret that his reference to *The Anatomy of Peace* had been omitted from the *Times's* republication of the *Atlantic Monthly* article:

. . . To draw the attention of the American people to this book was one of the main reasons I wrote that article. The vast and complex problems involved in establishing an urgently needed, world-wide organization to prevent an atomic war cannot be sufficiently explained in a short article. I am afraid that some of my statements, without further explanation, may arouse surprise and misunderstanding. I consider it, therefore, in the public interest that this book be called to the attention of the public. It presents, in my opinion, the clearest and most complete analysis of the problem of peace and serves to document the arguments in my article.

The editors of the *Atlantic Monthly* asked Sumner Welles, who had been Under Secretary of State until September 1943, to comment on Einstein's article. Welles's sharp dissent was published in the January 1946 issue under the title "The Atomic Bomb and World Government." He argued that the Soviet Union would never accept the kind of world government envisaged by Einstein, as this would involve the complete destruction of the Soviet system. Further, Welles challenged Einstein's inconsistency in suggesting that the proposed world government be empowered to intervene in countries where a minority is suppressing a majority while he apparently accepted minority rule in Russia. Welles himself strongly favored working toward the ultimate goal of establishing a federal government of the world through the new United Nations although this might require considerable time.

Einstein drafted a reply which, however, was never released for publication. It is here published for the first time: [12]

The importance of the issue obliges me to reply, even though briefly, to the recent remarks by Sumner Welles. Eventualities which depend solely upon the decisions of men should never, in advance, be labeled "impossible." In the sphere of human activity, everything depends on the strength of men's convictions. These convictions must be based upon clear understanding of the prevailing objective conditions which have been affected by the unexpectedly swift and radical technological development of weapons.

Surely, no one can doubt that a war among the great powers

would lead to the destruction of a large part of the world's population, cities and industrial resources. No thoughtful person can fail to be convinced that there is no conceivable cause which could justify so great a sacrifice.

Hence, I should like to raise the following question: Is it really a sign of unpardonable naïveté to suggest that those in power decide among themselves that future conflicts must be settled by constitutional means rather than by the senseless sacrifice of great numbers of human lives? Once such a firm decision has been reached, nothing will be "impossible." And a second decision must necessarily follow, which is, to make certain that no individual nation is able to use its own independent military resources for the purpose of forcing its will upon other nations.

A "sophisticated" person might well comment: We have been working toward the same goal by means of small, patient steps, which, in view of human psychology, is the only possible method. But I, the so-called "idealist," regard this attitude as a fatal illusion. There is no *gradual* way to secure peace. As long as nations have no real security against aggression, they will, inevitably, continue to prepare for war. And, as history has proven conclusively, preparation for war always leads to actual war. When the North American Colonies united and created a central government in Washington, it came about not through a slow process but through a resolute and creative act.

Only such a resolute and creative act can provide a possible solution to the present perilous situation in which the nations of the world find themselves. If we fail to take such action, murderous conflicts are bound to develop which will bring about unimaginable destruction and, eventually, result in the oppression of all by a single power.

Late in November 1945, four scientists at Oak Ridge wrote Einstein a letter which anticipated some of the arguments later published by Sumner Welles. Meetings had been held among them to discuss the problems of atomic energy and peace. In principle, they shared the views Einstein had presented in the *Atlantic Monthly* article, but they felt that the deep economic and social gulf which existed between certain countries precluded the early formation of an effective world government. In the interim, should not the United Nations be utilized? Einstein replied on December 3, 1945: [13]

As to the possibility of establishing world government in the present economic, political and psychological context, the essential point is to what degree individual nations must at the very outset surrender their sovereignty in order to avert the imminent danger of another war. I do not believe the necessary degree of surrender would be as great as you assume. There would be no immediate need for member nations to subordinate their own tariff and immigration legislation to the authority of a world government. In fact, I believe the sole function of a world government should be to have a monopoly over military power, which would make certain that no single nation would ever be in a position to employ, at its own discretion, the troops and military resources stationed within its borders; this could be adequately ensured through a thoroughgoing international rotation of officer and men.

A permanent world court should be established to restrain the executive branch of world government from overstepping its mandate which, in the beginning, should be limited to the prevention of war and war-provoking developments in the member nations. Individual nations should have the right to appeal to this court whenever they feel that illegal acts have been committed against them. The decisions of the court should be based on a carefully framed charter, ratified by all the member nations, in which the powers and duties of the world executive are codified in the most precise language possible.

The freedom of each country to develop economic, political and cultural institutions of its own choice must be guaranteed at the outset, except when developments occur, such as in Argentina and Nazi Germany, which constitute a potential threat to other countries. Each country should also be allowed to maintain its tariff and immigration legislation. (I might add that while I personally do not consider such unlimited freedom desirable, I believe the primary goal, that of achieving military security, can be attained without curtailing the "freedom" of individual nations.)

I hardly believe that the United Nations, as presently constituted, can serve as an effective machinery for implementing world government. Our most immediate concern should be to see to it that agreement favoring the establishment of a world government is reached among the chief military powers. The rest would be merely a matter of procedure.

On December 10, 1945, Einstein delivered an address to a Nobel Anniversary dinner in New York.[14] It has become known under the title "The War Is Won, but the Peace Is Not."

Physicists find themselves in a position not unlike that of Alfred Nobel. Alfred Nobel invented an explosive more powerful than any then known—an exceedingly effective means of destruction. To atone for this "accomplishment" and to relieve his conscience, he instituted his awards for the promotion of peace. Today, the physicists who participated in producing the most formidable weapon of all time are harassed by a similar feeling of responsibility, not to say guilt. As scientists, we must never cease to warn against the danger created by these weapons; we dare not slacken in our efforts to make the peoples of the world, and especially their governments, aware of the unspeakable disaster they are certain to provoke unless they change their attitude toward one another and recognize their responsibility in shaping a safe future. We helped create this new weapon in order to prevent the enemies of mankind from achieving it first; given the mentality of the Nazis, this could have brought about untold destruction as well as the enslavement of the peoples of the world. This weapon was delivered into the hands of the American and the British nations in their roles as trustees of all mankind, and as fighters for peace and liberty; but so far we have no guarantee of peace nor of any of the freedoms promised by the Atlantic Charter. The war is won, but the peace is not. The great powers, united in war, have become divided over the peace settlements. The peoples of the world were promised freedom from fear; but the fact is that fear among nations has increased enormously since the end of war. The world was promised freedom from want; but vast areas of the world face starvation, while elsewhere people live in abundance. The nations of the world were promised liberty and justice; but even now we are witnessing the sad spectacle of armies of "liberation" firing on peoples who demand political independence and social equality, and supporting, by force of arms, those individuals and political parties which they consider best suited to represent their own vested interests. Territorial conflicts and power politics, obsolete as these purposes of national policy may be, still prevail over the essential requirements of human welfare and justice. . . .

The prognosis for our postwar world is not bright. We physicists are not politicians, nor has it ever been our wish to meddle in political affairs. However, we happen to know a few things that the politicians do not know, and we feel it our duty to speak up and remind those in responsible positions that there can be no easy escape into indifference; that there is no time left for petty bargaining and procrastination. The world situation calls for bold action, for a radical change in our approach and our political concepts. May the spirit that moved Alfred Nobel, the spirit of trust and confidence, of generosity and brotherhood among men, triumph over the minds of those whose decisions shape our destiny. Otherwise, our civilization is doomed.

Around this time, a number of intellectuals, including Einstein and other outstanding scientists, were at work on an ambitious project whose aim was to inform the American public of the full import of the atom bomb. The project was to take the form of a low-cost paper-back volume entitled *One World or None.*[15] In December 1945, when the book was already in the final stages, it was decided to invite contributions from Russian scientists. Einstein drafted the following message:

To the President of the Academy of Sciences, Moscow.

The physicists in this country who participated in the creation of the atomic bomb are conscious of their great responsibility, and recognize the inherent danger in this destructive weapon. They have vigorously expressed the conviction, both individually and collectively, that protection against the danger of atomic weapons can only be achieved on an international basis. In our opinion, the world-wide armaments race, which not only stifles scientific progress through the demands of military secrecy, but serves to intensify war fears, will only be eliminated if the traditional military organization is replaced by a supranational military authority which would possess sole control of all offensive arms: a kind of world government in the interest of international security.

To acquaint the public with the urgent necessity of so radical a political transformation, these scientists intend to publish a book that will convey, reliably and forthrightly, the technical facts about the atomic bomb as well as its practical implications. The final chapters of the book will indicate, at least in outline form, the political ways and means of securing peace.

We are well aware that, during the last century, the most powerful initiatives in respect to the creation of international institutions for peace originated in Russia. For that reason alone we should be most eager to have a number of Russian scientists send us statements of their views for inclusion in the book. (A few hundred words should suffice to characterize the situation in general terms and indicate the policies which we should pursue.)

We should be deeply obliged if you would be kind enough to consider this request favorably and interest a few of our Russian colleagues in the project. We are convinced that such a united effort will serve a great and urgent cause.

Evidently a number of hands worked on revising this message, including Dexter Masters, the science publicist and one of the book's two editors. The cable actually sent on December 18, 1945, over Einstein's signature, read as follows:

Those who have worked on the atomic bomb in this country are deeply concerned with the great dangers connected with this weapon. Some of the basic facts of bomb's development and their practical implications with respect to human survival are now being summarized in book to be published here written mainly by scientists from atomic project. The book will also express our feeling that menace of bomb can be removed only by co-operation on international scale through agreement or organization strong enough to deal with the problem as a world problem. We feel that the book will be incomplete without a statement from some of our Russian colleagues, such as Kapitza, Joffe, Kurschatov, Landau or others you might care to designate. In the interest of clarifying and contributing to solution of the problems raised by atomic bomb, we urge you to cable statement of a few hundred words length care of Albert Einstein, Princeton, New Jersey.

When, after several weeks, no reply had been received (although diplomatic and journalistic help had been enlisted), Masters, on January 22, 1946, sent a second cable over his own name, in which he summarized the book chapter by chapter and listed all the contributors. The cable read as follows:

Academy of Science, Moscow—Professor Einstein reports no answer as yet to cable of December 18th urging Soviet scientists to contribute statements to book on atomic bomb being published here. . . . It is still possible to include Soviet statements and book is far enough advanced now so that we can give you fuller information about it. Book is being published in an effort to bring together in one place and on unassailable authority basic facts about atomic bomb and problems of control it poses. Idea of book originated with project scientists, who feel strongly that these facts and problems must be clearly and widely understood by public if support is to be enlisted to help avert atomic arms race. Contributors and chapters line up as follows. Arthur Compton writes brief preface introducing book. Bohr writes foreword telling of possible impact of bomb on society and urging cooperative solution of problem at world level. Shapley and Wigner write chapters about basic physics of nuclear fission, telling in simple language what happens and how project here achieved its results. Young writes realistic analysis of atomic power possibilities. Oppenheimer writes about the bomb itself and what makes it the new and different weapon it is. Ridenour and Condon tell why there are no known defenses against atomic bombs. Seitz, Bethe and Langmuir discuss wide spread of basic knowledge on the subject, tell why there are no real secrets, point out that other countries have both the brains and the capacity to produce bombs and that only joint handling and cooperative approach will stop atomic arms race. Arnold tells of developments in rockets and planes as bomb carriers and, both as General and citizen, urges all steps to rule out war as being now too devastating for mankind to survive. Morrison gives explicit report on results at Hiroshima and examines what would happen if same bomb exploded over New York. Urey reviews all the preceding and emphasizes that, unless nations of world organize to control atomic bomb and other instruments of mass extermination, humanity faces the most dangerous situation it has faced in history. Szilard examines feasibility of mutual inspection procedures under international agency and concludes that such might well work even though no permanent solution. Lippmann discusses Moscow agreement and UNO machinery as important steps in right direction. Einstein writes that inspection, interchange of technical information and other such measures are useful in present crisis, and that more far-reaching measures must also be prepared now, resting on ultimate assumption of military strength by supranational agency.

Book closes with plea by Federation of Atomic Scientists of America for public to keep itself informed on realities of atomic bomb facts and problems and to bring their pressure to bear on proposals aimed at securing world co-operation in controlling bomb. Proceeds of book go to Federation of Atomic Scientists. First printing is 100,000 copies with expected total sales of 500,000. All contributors are hopeful that Soviet scientists will contribute statement or statements of views on any phase of subject to which they want to address themselves. As editor I should like to give assurances that whatever is submitted will be used without change and we will be glad to show whole manuscript to anyone who may be designated here. We are trying to get book on press by end of month and therefore would appreciate knowing soon as possible whether we may count on Soviet contribution. If we can know definitely by January 31 we will hold presses to receive copy until February 10.

It seems to me [Einstein wrote Masters on January 24, 1946] that you have done very well in sending the detailed cable to the Academy in Moscow. Besides serving the interests of the book, the cable also affords an effective means of unofficially gauging the psychological attitudes and reactions of the Soviet Government. . . .

Actually, by the time the second cable was sent, a reply had already been dispatched to Einstein from Moscow (apparently on January 15, 1946):

The Soviet physicists and other scientists of the USSR send their warm greetings for the wish expressed in your telegram to set up the international collaboration to solve the problem of using the atomic energy for the welfare of humanity. The Soviet Science always fought for using of scientific achievements only for the development of human culture and cannot but approve every step of the scientists in this direction. The Soviet scientists ask to express their thanks for their having been invited to take part in the discussion of the book on atomic bomb and we regret that because of technical difficulties they are deprived of the possibility to express their concrete opinion with respect to the facts proposed for publication. As it is possible to see the manuscript only in New York, as you have informed, it is difficult to look through the book in New York, as there are no Soviet physicists in America at the present moment who know well the special questions of the issue, the aim of which is so important and responsible and must not be underestimated.

President of the Academy of Sciences of the USSR, Academician Vavilov.

On January 30, 1946, the Russians sent another cable:

The Academy of Sciences of USSR has sent you a telegram on January 15 which apparently has not reached you. We received your telegram with detailed information about book on atomic bomb only today. Soviet scientists and particularly those pursuing their research in the field of physics express their deep feeling that nuclear energy must be used for the welfare of humanity and not for atomic bombs. We very much regret that it is too late now to send contributions to the book you sponsor and wish it much success. We are convinced that the united efforts of all true scientists will make the achievements of science contribute to the happiness of mankind.

Serghei Vavilov, President, Academy of Sciences of the USSR.

The exchange of cables with the Soviet Academy of Sciences was not mentioned in *One World or None* when it was published. Einstein's own contribution was entitled "The Way Out":

The creation of the atomic bomb has brought the constant threat of sudden annihilation into the life of every city dweller throughout the world. No one can deny that this situation must cease if man is to make even partial claim to his chosen name of *Homo sapiens*. But there is no agreement yet which of the traditional social and political institutions will have to be sacrificed to achieve security.

After the First World War, we were confronted with a contradictory situation in regard to the solution of international conflicts. An International Court of Justice had been established for the peaceful solution of such conflicts on the basis of international law. In addition, the creation of the League of Nations provided a sort of world parliament, a political instrument for securing peace by means of international negotiation; and the nations united in the League had in fact outlawed war as a criminal method of solving international conflicts.

Thus, an illusion of security had been created in the world, one that could not but lead to bitter disappointment. For even the highest court is of no significance unless it has the power to enforce its decisions, and certainly this is no less true of a world parliament. A single country, in possession of sufficient military and economic power, can easily resort to force and destroy at will the entire structure of supranational security, if that security is founded on nothing more substantial than words and documents. Moral authority alone will prove inadequate to the task of securing peace.

The effectiveness of the United Nations is now being tested. It may eventually emerge as the agency of "security without illusion" that we so badly need. But, as of now, it does not possess more than moral authority, which, as I have said, is not sufficient.

The present situation is even more precarious due to a number of other circumstances, only two of which will be mentioned here. First, as long as individual countries are obliged to consider war as a possibility although they officially condemn war, they are forced to train and indoctrinate their citizens, especially the young generation, in such a manner that, in the event of war, the men can be easily converted into an efficient soldiery. To achieve this end, the countries are compelled not only to promote a military atmosphere and cultivate military training but also to inculcate a spirit of patriotism and national vanity which will assure the psychological readiness of the population in the event of war. Such indoctrination will necessarily counteract any endeavor to establish a supranational organization with moral authority.

The second factor which contributes to the threat of war in our time is the development of technology. The fact that modern weapons, in particular the atomic bomb, give considerable advantage to the aggressor nation may well induce even statesmen, who are conscious of their responsibility, to assume the risk of preventive war.

Confronted as we are with this situation, I am convinced there is only *one* way out:

Institutions must be established which will guarantee that any disputes which may arise between individual nations will be solved on a basis of law and under international jurisdiction. A supranational organization must make it impossible for any country to wage war by being able to employ military forces which that nation alone controls.

Only when these two conditions are fully met will we have some assurance that mankind will escape the fate of being disintegrated someday into atoms and swept up into the atmosphere.

In view of the prevailing political mentality, it may seem illusory, even absurd, to hope for such great changes within the next few years. And yet, we cannot hope that those changes can be accomplished in a slow, gradual development; without supranational military security, the forces pushing toward war are irresistible. Even more disastrous than man's lust for power will be his fear of sudden attack—unless we openly and resolutely set ourselves the task to abandon national military power and accept supranational authority.

With all respect for the difficulties of such a task, about *one* thing I have no doubt: *The peoples of the world will solve the problem as soon as they realize that there is no other, or simpler, alternative to the present dilemma.*

I now feel an obligation to say something about the individual steps which might lead to a solution of the problem of security.

1. Mutual inspection, by the leading military powers, of methods and installations used for the production of offensive weapons, together with an exchange of pertinent technical and scientific discoveries, would help, at least for the time being, to counteract the fear and distrust felt by the responsible military and political personalities. Such mutual inspection would further provide a kind of breathing spell during which time more fundamental measures could be prepared. But, even this most preliminary step should be taken in full recognition that it is only a first step leading toward the ultimate goal of denationalizing all military power.

While this first step is necessary in that it paves the way for all successive measures, it is important to realize that, taken alone, it is not sufficient; it does not, for example, exclude the possibility of an arms race nor the temptation to resort to clandestine military preparations.

2. Denationalization can be advanced through exchanges, at a

steadily increasing degree, of the military, scientific and technical personnel of the various nations. Such exchanges should proceed according to a careful plan whose aim would be the systematic conversion of national armies into a supranational military force. Although a national army would seem the last place where nationalistic sentiments could be expected to weaken, an attempt should be made, even within the ranks of national armies, to combat nationalism while, at the same time, a supranational army is being recruited and trained. Further, the exchange of personnel would diminish the danger of surprise attack, as well as help provide the psychological foundation for the internationalization of military resources. During this period, the strongest military powers could draft a charter for an international security organization and for a court of arbitration. This charter would outline the legal basis of the two institutions and stipulate their jurisdiction, powers and limitations with respect to the individual member nations; it would also determine the electoral methods for establishing and maintaining these agencies. Only when agreement on all these points has been reached can there be security against global war.

3. As these agencies begin to function, the vestiges of national armies can either be disbanded or placed under the high command of the supranational authority.

4. With the co-operation of the great powers assured, efforts should be made to recruit possibly all nations into the supranational organization, on an entirely voluntary basis.

This outline may create the impression that the great powers are to be assigned too dominant a role. I have tried, however, to present the problem in such a way that its reasonably early solution may not encounter even more difficulties than are anyhow inherent in the problem. It is, undoubtedly, easier to reach preliminary agreement among the great powers than among *all* nations, both big and small; a body representing all nations would be a hopelessly clumsy instrument for achieving even the most elemental results. The task demands of all nations the utmost wisdom and tolerance. These qualities can only emerge from a keen awareness of the harsh necessities of the situation.

Einstein's files contain a great number of documents that illustrate the care with which he examined the many communications that were sent to him and the many requests that were made of him. It has often been claimed that he was not sufficiently circumspect in giving his support to statements and appeals for various political and public causes and that he never, or only very seldom, withheld his co-operation. But this is not true. Einstein supported what he felt deserved his support, never without having carefully studied the information presented to him or having had a detailed discussion with the person who sought his assistance on behalf of one of the many purposes and personalities for which Einstein publicly announced his concern. Despite the ever-constant, intense preoccupation with his scientific problems and the pressure of other work, he often spent many hours in discussing a political or social problem that had been submitted to him, in order to determine his own position and to ascertain the most effective way to express his interest or support. The following documents, taken from Einstein's files for 1945, provide a few examples of the many requests which he denied and show that, in each individual instance, he carefully indicated the reasons for his negative decision.

In April 1945 a group was formed in Princeton for the purpose of organizing a "League of People" which, by by-passing the authority of existing governments, would attempt "to mobilize men for peace and freedom." In a letter of April 3, 1945, Einstein informed one of the sponsors of his decision not to join the group; although he had lent his support to worthy causes rather freely in the past, this project seemed too crudely conceived. While he agreed that the character of existing governmental institutions was regrettable, he nonetheless did not believe that it was possible to ignore them.

A few weeks later, the National Council of American-Soviet Friendship in New York asked Einstein to sign a message to the American delegation at the San Francisco Conference, which was then debating the final steps leading to the establishment of the United Nations. In the proposed message, the American delegation was blamed for having taken the initiative in seating Argentina, "a country which has rendered so much aid to the Fascist powers during the war," and urged to support the seating of the Polish Provisional Government. Einstein replied on May 3, 1945, that he was unable to sign the message as presently drafted. He would not hesitate to sign it if it contained only a protest against the admission of Argentina. But since "the real circumstances behind the present difficulties concerning Poland" were not sufficiently known to him, he could not say how he would have acted had he had the responsibility of acting on behalf of the United States.

In October of the same year, a pronouncement suggested by the Independent Citizens' Committee of the Arts, Sciences and Professions in New York assailed the creation of a purely American agency for further research on atomic energy which, the committee said, had been recommended in a statement by President Truman while, in the committee's opinion, the only guardian for the free development of scientific inquiry was a United Nations' organization. Einstein, on October 11, 1945, refused to sign this statement. While expressing "wholehearted agreement" with the position of the committee, he considered its suggestion that "the only safe repository for the atomic bomb was the Security Council" to be quite misleading. In his opinion, the Security Council was only a smoke screen behind which the unlimited rivalry of sovereign states was hidden.

A problem which intensely preoccupied Einstein, particularly after 1933, and which became a crucial international issue immediately after the end of the war was the problem of Germany. Einstein was not able to forget even for a moment the unspeakable crimes of the German people; to restore Germany's capacity for evil was an unbearable thought for him. He viewed the military renaissance of Germany with profound apprehension; until the very last hours of his life, he continued to express his unqualified opposition to the Allied-sponsored rearmament of Germany, which he never ceased to consider a formidable threat to world peace.

In September 1945 a communication reached him from California in which the writer contrasted the healthy idealism of the early period of American history with what he considered to be the crass industrial materialism characteristic of American society since about the Civil War. Surprise was expressed that Einstein had been among those who intervened with President Roosevelt regarding experimentation with the atomic bomb; according to the writer, the bomb was not only directed at Japanese and German aggression but "was in fact a conspiracy against the American people as well." In a long letter of September 8, 1945, Einstein replied to the correspondent,[16] who was completely unknown to him, by posing the question: Since it had been known that the Germans were eagerly at work on the production of the atomic bomb, should we have waited until they had completed the work when we would have become their easy prey? He did not believe, he added, that German scientists, under similar circumstances, would have done what many of their American counterparts did; that is, after completion of the bomb, petition the President, in the interest of peace and security in the world, to lift the secrecy surrounding atomic development. It is true, Einstein continued, that the Germans, as emphasized by his correspondent, had great minds and men in their classical period before Prussian might and spirit had undermined the institutions and the spirit of the German people. But the fact remained that the contemporary German mentality had little in common with that of the classical period; the Germans had swallowed the theory that might was right and that the systematic murder of millions of non-Germans was justified in an effort to dominate Europe and possibly the world.

To the British Council for German Democracy, which asked him to send a message of welcome to its forthcoming conference on "the new, growing democratic movement in Germany," Einstein wrote on October 1, 1945:

The content of your letter reminds me of all the lamentable errors the Allies committed after the last war with regard to Germany. At that time, all the so-called liberals of Germany co-operated with the various governments in their attempt secretly to rearm Germany, thus preparing her for a war of revenge. If people with your and your friends' attitude would have their way, the same lamentable comedy will repeat itself. The only policy to pursue would be to weaken Germany's economic power to such a degree that she loses every possibility and hope of engaging in successful international intrigue. If the Ruhr is left to the Germans, the terrible sacrifices of the English-speaking world will have been in vain.

Several months after the end of hostilities, James Franck, an old friend and one of the physicists who had taken a prominent part in expressing the scientists' warnings on the use of the atomic bomb (see p. 306), acquainted Einstein with the draft of an appeal which he and several other refugees from Germany planned to publish. Although it was denied that the purpose of the appeal was to suggest a "soft peace" for Germany, attention was called to the alleged disastrous consequences of the policies which the Allies pursued in Germany at that time; the fear was expressed that "the indifference of American public opinion . . . will permit the creation in the center of Europe of a state of spiritual and physical degeneration which will endanger the peaceful reconstruction of the world." Einstein replied on December 6, 1945:

I certainly could not approve of everything that is presently being done by the Allies in Germany. But I am firmly convinced that it is absolutely indispensable to prevent the restoration of German industrial power for many years. It does not suffice to destroy Germany's present productive capacity; it must be made impossible for the Germans henceforth to enjoy independent authority over the raw material resources which made them so dangerous during the last century.

This is why I firmly object to any attempt from Jewish quarters to reawaken the kind of soft sentimental feelings which permitted Germany to prepare a war of aggression without any interference on the part of the rest of the world—and this long before the Nazis came to power. . . . I do not favor revenge but, rather, a policy of utmost security against the possibility of renewed aggression by the Germans; such security cannot possibly be accomplished through moral persuasion. . . . Should your appeal be circulated, I shall not fail to do whatever I can to oppose it.

James Franck wrote again and pleaded with Einstein to change his mind. Einstein did not yield and sent Franck a final reply on December 30, 1945:

I remember too well the campaign of tears staged by the Germans after the First World War to be fooled by its repetition. The Germans slaughtered several millions of civilians according to a well-thought-out plan. If they had murdered you too, some crocodile tears would undoubtedly have been shed. The few decent people who are among them do not change the picture as a whole. I have gauged from several letters received from over there, as well as from the information supplied by some reliable persons, that the Germans do not feel one iota of guilt or sorrow. . . . Dear Franck, do not involve yourself in this dirty mess! They will first misuse your kindness and then they will ridicule you for being a fool. But if I am unable to persuade you to refrain, I, for one, will certainly not get mixed up in this affair. Should the opportunity present itself, I shall publicly oppose the appeal.

Another physicist, Professor Arnold Sommerfeld, also a long-time friend, sought to restore Einstein's academic position in Germany. Sommerfeld, professor at the University of Munich, tried to prepare the way for an invitation to be extended to Einstein to rejoin the Bavarian Academy from which he had resigned in 1933. The academy was now willing to eliminate from its record the letter which it had addressed to Einstein that year and in which it had suggested his resignation. Would not Einstein be willing to bury the hatchet? "The world may still be out of joint, but we should do our share to put it back in order." Einstein replied on December 14, 1946:

> . . . The Germans slaughtered my Jewish brethren; I will have nothing further to do with them, not even with a relatively harmless academy. I feel differently about the few people who, insofar as it was possible, remained steadfast against Nazism. I am happy to learn that you were among them. . . .

Einstein's firm and consistent determination not to be associated in any way with anything German is revealed in a communication of December 20, 1946, to the Committee for the Science of Peace, in Vienna, Austria. He advised them that he was unable to accept their invitation to serve as honorary chairman of their committee despite his conviction that the committee was playing an important role in restoring a healthy political attitude in Austria. He explained that his decision was prompted by the fact that he had rejected, for reasons of principle, an invitation to assume a similar position in a German peace society. "I find it completely impossible," he wrote, "to participate in a German organization of any kind since the Germans have murdered my Jewish brothers all over Europe and have not made even the slightest attempt to rehabilitate, either morally or materially, the few who have survived."

CHAPTER TWELVE

MILITANCY | 1946

THE YEAR 1946 was indeed "Year 1: Atomic Age," as it was called in a symposium in the magazine *Survey Graphic*. The symposium, which was published in the January 1946 issue, contained this contribution from Einstein:

The weapons of modern warfare have developed to such a degree that, in another World War, the victor would probably suffer not much less than the vanquished. As long as there exist sovereign states, each with its own, independent armaments, the prevention of war becomes a virtual impossibility. I firmly believe that the majority of peoples in the world would prefer to live in peace and security rather than have their particular nation pursue a policy of unrestricted national sovereignty. Mankind's desire for peace can be realized only by the creation of a world government.

To an exceedingly long letter from a correspondent who had served as a commissioned officer in the United States Army, Einstein replied in February 1946 by outlining his concept of the causes of war:

. . . I do not believe many wars are caused by the feeling that injustice was done to one's own country or to one's own class. In fact, I have no doubt that the causes of war are deeply imbedded in human nature. One can say without exaggeration that war is a normal function in the life of primitive people. . . . The pretexts used in justifying wars merely serve to incite the will to fight of those who are not very belligerent.

The tendency toward war is as much a part of man's nature as it is a part of the nature of rivers to inundate their banks from time to time; and just as artificial means are required to avoid inundations, so man must adopt artificial measures to avoid wars. Supranational force, based on supranational law, is the only means to avert hostilities. This is by no means always the same as what a sensitive human being considers to be "justice." I believe that a law is obeyed only when it is based on principles which the people affected consider acceptable in view of the traditions they have developed over a long period of time. However, what is considered acceptable is subject to serious modifications in the course of time. For instance, we today feel that slavery is exceedingly unjust while the most noble spirits in the Greece of ancient times regarded slavery as just. I believe that the people of every single epoch must try to accomplish what *they* consider to be "just.". . .

I am convinced that a policy to prevent wars is an urgent necessity which cannot wait until we have decided whether or not the problem of "justice" permits of a final and lasting solution.

The editors of *Look* magazine asked Einstein to comment on their picture story, "Your Last Chance," published on March 5, 1946. The article stated that the American people had only three alternatives: world conquest, the attempt at self-defense, or an effort to put an end to war. The magazine expressed itself in favor of the third alternative. On February 23, 1946, Einstein wrote: [1]

I was delighted indeed when I read your article about the atomic bomb which presents the grave problem of our time in a dramatic, courageous and inspiring manner. The article seems to me all the more important since any reasonable action with regard to atomic warfare has been made more difficult due to the atmosphere created by the publicity about the Canadian spy affair [Igor Gouzenko, a clerk at the Soviet Embassy, had defected from the Soviet diplomatic service and implicated a number of persons in charges of espionage]. Every possible effort must be made to prevent Congress from passing measures which might tend to cripple the freedom of scientific inquiry and publication, deepen the mutual distrust among the great military powers and give impetus to a competitive arms race.

On March 15, 1946, Einstein was asked to subscribe to an "Appeal to the Peoples of the World" adopted unanimously at a Conference on World Government held at Rollins College, Winter Park,

Florida. The text of the appeal was transmitted to him by telegram,[2] and he agreed to lend his signature without hesitation or delay. Although Einstein himself did not help draft the appeal, it is inserted here as it provides a particularly clear expression of the views he held, both at that time and during the remainder of his life. The appeal also illustrates how soon after the end of hostilities, and with what precision, the steps to be taken toward peace in the atomic age were set forth. Finally, it may help explain the mood of pessimism that afflicted Einstein during the last years of his life; for despite the vision and devotion of many eminent men working in the cause of world peace through world law, he came to believe that little, if any, significant progress had been made in the whole decade following the war. The appeal, issued by the Conference at Rollins College and distributed in some 50,000 copies in the United States and abroad, reads as follows:

1. The atomic bomb and other applications of science and technology to modern warfare have made war so destructive that the outbreak of another major war must be prevented.

2. Atomic secrets cannot be kept for more than a few years by any nation or small group of nations; nor can there be any adequate military defense against a surprise attack capable of paralyzing the country and peoples attacked.

3. There can be no absolute guarantee that peace will be maintained as long as any nation has the sovereign right to decide questions of war and peace for itself.

4. If nations live under the permanent threat of war, each sovereign state will inevitably become more and more totalitarian, thus depriving its citizens of more and more personal liberty.

5. No nation-state can today hope to be strong enough [and] sovereign enough to protect its citizens from war. Twice in one generation the United States has been forced to enter a war which the people wished to avoid.

6. Peace is not merely the absence of war but the presence of justice, of law, of order—in short, of government.

7. World peace can be created and maintained only under world law universal and strong enough to establish justice and prevent armed conflict between nations.

8. The only way by which a people can assure its survival and preserve its liberties is to create with the other peoples a world gov-

ernment, a constitutional federal government, to which shall be delegated the powers necessary to maintain the general peace of the world, based on law and justice.

The United Nations as now constituted is a league of sovereign states. As such it is not a world government and therefore cannot by law prevent armed conflict between nations and establish justice and security. Nevertheless it is the greatest step yet taken by mankind toward world peace. Since the Charter provides for amendments, every effort should be made to transform the United Nations into a world government.

Such objectives cannot, we know, be reached overnight. The difficulty [is one] of building support within each diversity of cultures, governments and institutions among the nations.

But a start must be made. It must be made now. It must be made with the tools at hand. It must be directed, in the first instance, at the removal of the haunting fear and suspicion with which atomic weapons and weapons of similar destructiveness afflict mankind. The United States has the opportunity and duty to take the lead in proposing such constructive measures as are necessary to that end. It is with these considerations in mind that we make the proposals which follow:

We propose that a General Conference of the United Nations be called, as provided in Article 109 of the Charter, to draft amendments which should accomplish the following objectives:

1. That the United Nations be transformed from a league of sovereign states into a government deriving its specific powers from the peoples of the world.

2. That the General Assembly be reconstituted as the legislative branch of the world government in which the citizens of the member states are represented on an equitable basis.

3. That the General Assembly in addition to its present powers shall have power:

A. To make laws prohibiting or otherwise controlling weapons of mass destruction and, so far as necessary for that purpose, regulating the uses of atomic energy.

B. To make laws providing for such inspection as is necessary or appropriate to the execution of the foregoing powers.

C. To provide for appropriate civil and criminal sanctions for the laws enacted pursuant to the foregoing powers.

D. To provide and maintain such police forces as are necessary for law enforcement.

4. That independent judicial tribunals be created with jurisdiction over cases and controversies arising under laws enacted by the General Assembly or involving questions concerning the interpretation of the Charter of the United Nations.

5. That a Bill of Rights be designed for the protection of persons affected by laws enacted by the General Assembly.

6. That the Security Council be reconstituted as the executive branch of the world government with the power:

A. To administer and insure the enforcement of the laws; and

B. Under the direction of the General Assembly, to perform its present functions as defined in the Charter.

7. That the powers not delegated to the General Assembly be reserved to the member states.

We believe these to be the minimum requirements necessary for the creation of a world government capable of averting the catastrophe of another war in the atomic era. The present United Nations Charter does not meet these minimum requirements.

The establishment of a world government representative of the peoples of the world must be accompanied by a broad program of mass education and the free exchange of knowledge among them. Only world government, even in the limited terms here advocated, can bring the peace in which the peoples of the world can mature to the full responsibility by which they can realize their destiny as free men.

Ely Culbertson (see pp. 321, 322) wrote Einstein on April 26, 1946.[3] While affirming the "common objective" of world peace under world law he took issue with some details of the appeal issued by the Rollins College Conference which bore Einstein's signature:

. . . The first point in your program, to transform the UN Assembly into a popular world legislature, is certainly not politically acceptable today. Nor is it necessary for the establishment of a true federative structure. The essence of the federative structure is not a people's congress but a separate central authority able to act within the scope of specific delegated powers and having the means to enforce its decisions.

Such a minimum goal could be achieved by the establishment of just two world laws: No state or its citizens may prepare for aggressive war; and no state or its citizens may wage aggressive war. These laws must be incorporated in the Charter; there must be a court to interpret them. And—most important—these two laws can be established *now*, since they do not require the establishment of world-wide democracy or a severe limitation of national sovereignty.

Culbertson also sent Einstein a copy of his new book, *Must We Fight Russia?* and asked for comment. Einstein replied on May 2, 1946:

I fully approve of the suggestions in your excellent book *Must We Fight Russia?* as well as the statement contained in your letter of April 26. The first question, however, is: What can the American people and the American Government do to bring about the cessation of the competitive arms race which has already started on a big scale between the United States and Russia? In my opinion, the United States should indicate to Russia her willingness to stop the armaments race, to submit to a mutual arms control and, in the event of controversy, to abide by the decisions of a world authority created according to rules which have been mutually agreed upon. To convince the United States of the wisdom of adopting such a program would require the strong pressure of public opinion.

A committee under Dean Acheson [later Secretary of State in President Truman's second administration], with the advice of a group of experts headed by David Lilienthal [later the first chairman of the Atomic Energy Commission], had meanwhile, on March 28, 1946, made a report outlining a policy on atomic energy for the United States. These proposals subsequently became the basis for the so-called "Baruch Plan" submitted by the United States to the United Nations. The plan, which proposed that there be international control and inspection of atomic energy and weapons, was ultimately vetoed by the Soviet Union. The Lilienthal-Acheson proposals, although widely supported, became the subject of keen controversy in—and outside—the United Nations. One attack which appeared in *The Nation* of April 6, 1946, drew Einstein's qualified approval. In a letter dated April 9 and published in *The Nation* of May 11, 1946, Einstein called the article "justified and of a constructive character," but he added: [4]

On the one hand, it is to be highly appreciated that official authorities, even from army quarters, have openly recognized that security can be reached only on the basis of world government. On the other hand, the measures proposed for the interim period do not appear adequate to the task of bringing us nearer to the goal of world government and convincing other nations of the loyal intentions of our foreign policy.

In May 1946 Einstein took an important step: he agreed to serve as chairman of the newly formed Emergency Committee of Atomic Scientists.

As has been pointed out, a number of the scientists who had worked on the bomb project were deeply disturbed about the menace to mankind created by the existence of atomic weapons. They were conscious of the responsibility which the United States had assumed by her decision to drop atomic bombs over Japanese cities. Discussion groups had sprung up at all the major atomic installations, and despite considerable diversity of opinion, many people were agreed that every possible effort should be made to make sure that the survival of the human race be never threatened by atomic weapons.

In the fall of 1945, atomic scientists played an important role in defeating the May-Johnson bill (see p. 345), which would have kept atomic energy under military control. The scientists increasingly felt the need of an informed public opinion to help in the struggles that lay ahead. The general public seemed confused and apprehensive. The atomic problem was too new and too big, its implications almost too terrible to be fully appreciated by the great mass of people. The many articles and books as well as the many speeches and statements on the subject did not sufficiently provide the people with constructive information and advice.

In January 1946 the various scientific groups which had been concerned with this problem merged into the Federation of American Scientists; the informational activities of the Federation were largely discharged through an organization that dated back to the 1945 San Francisco Conference of the United Nations. Representing some sixty civic, labor, religious, professional and educational organizations, it was now called the National Committee on Atomic Information. The work of the committee was limited by several factors, such as the lack of funds. Further, scientists were not always able to spare the time necessary to prepare the kind of articles which would meet the increasing public demand for information, and the task was too great for amateur publicists.

It was against this background and this need that the Emergency Committee of Atomic Scientists was conceived, primarily as a fund-raising and policy-making agency.[5] It was hoped that its board of trustees, all outstanding scientists of great reputation, would command universal respect and wide financial support. As ultimately constituted, Einstein's fellow trustees were Harold C. Urey (as vice-chairman), Hans A. Bethe, Thorfin R. Hogness, Philip M. Morse, Linus Pauling, Leo Szilard and Victor F. Weisskopf. The first action of the committee was a telegram over Einstein's signature to several hundred prominent Americans appealing for contributions. This was done on May 23 and 24, 1946:

Our world faces a crisis as yet unperceived by those possessing the power to make great decisions for good or evil. The unleashed power of the atom has changed everything save our modes of thinking, and thus we drift toward unparalleled catastrophe. We scientists who unleashed this immense power have an overwhelming responsibility in this world life-and-death struggle to harness the atom for the benefit of mankind and not for humanity's destruction.

[Hans A.] Bethe, [Edward U.] Condon, [Leo] Szilard, [Harold C.] Urey and the Federation of American Scientists join me in this appeal and beg you to support our efforts to make Americans realize that mankind's destiny is being decided today—now—this moment.

We need $200,000 at once for a nation-wide campaign to inform the American people that a new type of thinking is essential if mankind is to survive and move toward higher levels.

This appeal is being sent you only after long consideration of the immense crisis we face. I urgently request that you send an immediate check to me as chairman of the Emergency Committee of Atomic Scientists, Princeton, New Jersey. We ask your help in this fateful moment as a sign that we scientists do not stand alone.

The appeal was widely reprinted in the press. On June 4, 1946, Einstein recorded it for the newsreels, with some slight changes:

. . . An effective program of education, so that the public may understand certain scientific facts as well as their significance to society, has been planned. It will reach the American people through the agency of the National Committee on Atomic Information. . . . We ask for public support in this fateful moment, to make it possible for the atomic scientists to live up to their social obligations.

A number of similar appeals were made by the Emergency Committee in the next few months and in the years that followed. While they were ordinarily not drafted by Einstein himself, he was an active participant in the work and deliberations of the committee. He had frequent, sometimes daily, conferences with the executive secretary; he attended many of the trustees' meetings, some of which were held in his home, and played an important role in determining the policy of the committee. In order to profit from Einstein's advice and to facilitate co-operation with him, the organization established an office in Princeton; subsequently, offices were also opened in New York and Chicago. The committee provided substantial financial support not only to the National Committee on Atomic Information in Washington but also to two other organizations: the Association of Scientists for Atomic Education, a group formed by the atomic scientists at Oak Ridge, and The Atomic Scientists of Chicago, the group which had assumed responsibility for the *Bulletin of the Atomic Scientists*. (The bulletin, originally a mimeographed monthly, had developed into a magazine of growing importance.) From this time on, the needs and activities of the Emergency Committee of Atomic Scientists were to have priority over Einstein's other nonscientific activities.

On May 28, 1946, the Columbia Broadcasting System originated a special broadcast on atomic energy. The broadcast, called "Operation Crossroads," emanated from the Coolidge Auditorium of the Library of Congress in Washington. Among many notable participants were Joseph E. Davies, Mrs. Wendell L. Willkie, William O. Douglas, Luther H. Evans, Henry A. Wallace, Archibald MacLeish, Harold C. Urey, Harold L. Ickes and Harold E. Stassen. The following colloquy formed part of this broadcast: [6]

NEWSCASTER ROBERT TROUT: There are many people who . . . while they hope and pray that war can be averted . . . [are] pessimistic about the chances of avoiding war. They say its's just "human nature," and that while mankind may possibly change some old habits of thinking in a million years, there's certainly no chance of changing them in the next five. What about that "you can't change human nature" argument, Dr. Albert Einstein?

EINSTEIN (speaking from Princeton): When you speak of "human nature," what do you mean?

TROUT (from Washington): Why, I suppose the hates and fears and prejudices that make for wars.

EINSTEIN: Then I would say that it is precisely because we cannot change human nature in a million years that we must do what we have to do very quickly in order to prevent the terrible destruction of an atomic war. . . . This "human nature" which makes wars is like a river. It is impossible in geological time to change the nature of the river. But when it continually overflows its banks and destroys our lives and homes, do we sit down and say, "It is too bad. We can't change the river. We can do nothing about it"?

TROUT: No, Dr. Einstein. We get together and build a dam which will keep the river in check.

EINSTEIN: Exactly. And what do we use to build the dam?

TROUT: We use reason, I suppose, our ability to think.

EINSTEIN: That is correct. And this ability to think is also a part of human nature. It is intelligence, which is the ability to learn from experience, to plan ahead. It includes the capacity to give up immediate, temporary benefits for permanent ones. This part of human nature recognizes that a man's security and happiness depend on a well-functioning society; that a well-functioning society depends on the existence and observance of laws; and that men must submit to these laws in order to have peace. It is this reasoning faculty which is responsible for all of man's progress in art, science, agriculture, industry and government.

TROUT: And you believe, Dr. Einstein, that this thinking man can solve our great problem for us?

EINSTEIN: I believe nothing else can. Just as we use our reason to build a dam to hold a river in check, we must now build institutions to restrain the fears and suspicions and greeds which move peoples and their rulers. Such institutions, as have been described by Mr. Stassen and Mr. Douglas, must be based on law and justice. They must have authority over atomic bombs and other weapons, and they must have the power to enforce this authority. To do this is difficult, yes; but we must remember that if the animal part of human nature is our foe, the thinking part is our friend. We do not have to wait a million years to use our ability to reason. It does not depend on time. We are using it every day of our lives. We can and must use it now, or human society will sink into a new and terrible dark age which may last forever.

And further along in the broadcast, prompted by Archibald MacLeish, professor of poetry at Harvard University, Einstein said:

Just as we have changed our thinking in the world of pure science to embrace newer and more useful concepts, so we must now change our thinking in the world of politics and law. It is too late to make mistakes.

The following day, May 29, 1946, Einstein gave a radio address to a Chicago rally of the Students for Federal World Government: [7]

I have been deeply impressed with a talk I had with three students from the University of Chicago. It made me realize that there is indeed a sense of responsibility and initiative at work among the younger generation in this country. These students fully realize that the destiny of their generation will be decided in the next few years. And they are resolved to exert as much influence as they can on the course of events.

Just what is the situation? The development of technology and military weapons has resulted in what amounts to a shrinking of our planet. Economic intercourse between countries has made the nations of the world more dependent upon one another than ever before. The offensive weapons now available leave no spot on earth secure from sudden, total annihilation. Our only hope for survival lies in the creation of a world government capable of resolving conflicts among nations by judicial verdict. Such decisions must be based upon a precisely worded constitution which is approved by all governments. The world government alone may have offensive arms at its disposal. No person or nation can be regarded as pacifist unless they agree that all military power should be concentrated in the hands of a supranational authority, and unless they renounce force as a means of safeguarding their interests against other nations.

Political developments, in this first year since the end of the Second World War, have clearly brought us no closer to the attainment of these goals. The present Charter of the United Nations does not provide either for the legal institutions or the military forces which would be necessary to bring real international security into being. Nor does it take into account the actual balance of power in the world today. Real power is today concentrated in a few hands. It is no exaggeration to say that the solution of the crucial problem depends solely upon the achievement of a far-sighted agreement between this country and Russia. If such an agreement were brought about, these two powers alone would be able to prevail upon all other nations to renounce their sovereignty to the degree necessary for the attainment of universal military security.

Many people say that, in the present circumstances, fundamental agreement between the United States and the Soviet Union is impossible. Such an assertion might be justified had America made a really serious effort in that direction since the end of the war. It seems to me that America has done just the opposite: It was not wise to admit Fascist Argentina into the United Nations over Russia's protest. Further, there was no need to keep on producing more and more atomic bombs and to spend twelve billion dollars in a single year on armaments, when there was no military threat in sight. Nor was there any sense in denying Trieste to Yugoslavia, a former ally who was in real need of this port that has, in fact, little economic significance to Italy, a former enemy country. There is no point in further enumerating all the details which indicate that nothing was done by the United Nations to mollify Russia's distrust. In fact, we have done much toward fostering this distrust which the events of the last several decades make only too understandable.

Enduring peace will come about, not by countries continuing to threaten one another, but only through an honest effort to create mutual trust. One should assume that the desire to bring about decent conditions for mankind on this planet as well as the fear of unspeakable annihilation would render those in positions of responsibility wiser and more dispassionate. But you cannot wait for this to happen, my young friends. You must attempt to galvanize the younger generation into insisting on a farsighted policy of peace. If you do that, you will not only achieve effective protection for yourselves; you will deserve the gratitude of your country and of posterity to a larger degree than any generation before you.

In addition to this broadcast to the Chicago student rally, Einstein was interviewed by Paul Arthur Schilpp, Professor of Philosophy at Northwestern University, and by a student officer of the National Organization of Student Federalists: [8]

Q (by Professor Schilpp): Professor Einstein, what, precisely, is the real difference between world government and the United Nations Organization? . . .

A: By world government I understand an institution whose decisions and rules are binding upon the individual member states . . . In its present form the United Nations does not possess the powers of a world government, because its decisions and judgments have no binding power over the individual member states.

Q (by student leader): . . . My fellow students and I would very much like to know what you think we, the future leaders of the world, can do to achieve a federation of the world such as the original thirteen states achieved in this country 160 years ago.

A: First of all, the younger generation must ascertain what minimal conditions must be met to stop future military threats among the various nations or a combination of nations. The next task would be to spread this knowledge throughout the country. The third task would require the kind of organizational activity that would influence the members of Congress and the individual state assemblies in a way which reflects the will of the people on the subject of peace.

Q (by Professor Schilpp): Do you believe that mutual envy and hatred among nations can be overcome by a world government?

A: No, of course not. But a world government would be able to prevent such natural emotional reactions from leading to acts of violence among nations.

Q (by student leader): Does any other industrial country in the world possess the natural resources and scientific ability to produce atomic weapons?

A: Other countries, undoubtedly, command enough such resources and ability to constitute an unending and intolerable threat to each other.

Q (by Professor Schilpp): From this last answer, Professor Einstein, I take it that you, who know as much as any living person about the threat of atomic bombs to the future of humanity, consider the establishment of real world government an inescapable necessity to be realized at the earliest possible moment.

A: There can no longer be any doubt about its being an absolute necessity. For this reason everything that is done in international affairs must be done from the viewpoint of whether it will advance or hinder the establishment of world government.

On the day of this broadcast, May 29, 1946, Einstein also sent a message to the Soviet Union, to be delivered by a mission visiting that country on behalf of the Jewish Council for Russian Relief:

I welcome this opportunity to send my warmest greetings to my Jewish brethren in Soviet Russia, as well as to the whole Russian people. You have succeeded, at immense sacrifice, in banishing the danger which threatened mankind at the hands of its worst enemies.

May you equally succeed in contributing to the creation of a solid world order in which conflicts are settled by peaceful means on the basis of institutions and principles of law approved and supported by all.

Cord Meyer, youthful spokesman for the new generation of war veterans, had sent Einstein the manuscript of a thoughtful and forceful critique of the Lilienthal-Acheson Report, which was to appear in the July 1946 issue of *The Atlantic Monthly*. He asked for permission to quote from a letter Einstein had sent to *The Nation*, which was readily granted. Einstein added, in a letter dated June 5, 1946: [9]

I fully agree with the arguments and conclusions expressed in your article. Without world government there can be no security, and without security there can be no effective solution concerning the exceptional problem of protection against the atomic bomb.

The Lilienthal Report is gratifying as an official admission of the impossibility of liberating the world from the atomic danger in any way other than through international organization. It would have been even better had the five men bluntly stated that the preservation of state sovereignty in military matters is incompatible with a policy of protection against atomic aggression.

A transition period, as must be realized, poses the same difficulties with regard to the establishment of a world government as it does with regard to the danger of an atomic war. I believe, therefore, that the best minds should be called upon to formulate proposals for the transitory period with respect to the world government project.

In an interview published in the Paris Newspaper *France-Soir*, on June 22, 1946,[10] André Labarthe, a physicist, quoted Einstein as having said that the atomic bomb could have been perfected two years earlier, thus saving mankind a great deal of misery. "The professional soldiers," Einstein is reported to have said, "who today express themselves so loudly and arrogantly, displayed at the outset of the atomic scientific development a skepticism which often acted as a brake on research. Further, the exaggerated application of secrecy, the overly exclusive departmentalization of various scientific and research groups, and the behavior of the co-ordinating officers, who were ignorant of the new scientific discoveries, constituted the major causes of delay." Einstein emphasized the necessarily horrible character of any future war and the need for international co-operation which, he feared, was already being endangered by the secrecy surrounding the atomic bomb. Such secrecy might well increase the Soviet Union's distrust regarding the impartial character of international agreements. In discussing the German problem, Einstein warned against repeating the mistakes made by the Allies after the First World War. He called it childish to believe in the possibility of "evangelizing" Germany and supported the French suggestion that the industrial areas of Germany be politically separated from the rest of the country.

Einstein set forth his views at greater length in an interview with Michael Amrine, published in the Sunday magazine of *The New York Times* of June 23, 1946.[11] Entitled "The Real Problem Is in the Hearts of Men," the article was extensively used by the Emergency Committee of Atomic Scientists in its fund-raising activities. Einstein is quoted as saying:

Many persons have inquired concerning a recent message of mine that "a new type of thinking is essential if mankind is to survive and move toward higher levels."

Often in evolutionary processes a species must adapt to new conditions in order to survive. Today the atomic bomb has altered profoundly the nature of the world as we know it, and the human race consequently finds itself in a new habitat to which it must adapt its thinking.

In the light of this new knowledge, a world authority and an eventual world state are not just *desirable* in the name of brotherhood; they are *necessary* for survival. In previous ages a nation's life and culture could be protected to some extent by the growth of armies in national competition. Today we must abandon competition and secure co-operation. This must be the central fact in all our considerations of international affairs; otherwise we face certain disaster. Past thinking and methods did not succeed in preventing world wars. Future thinking *must* prevent wars.

Modern war, the bomb, and other discoveries present us with revolutionary circumstances. Never before was it possible for one nation to make war on another without sending armies across borders. Now, with rockets and atomic bombs, no center of population on the earth's surface is secure from destruction by a single surprise attack.

America has a temporary superiority in armaments, but it is certain that we have no lasting secret. What nature tells one group of men, she will tell in time to any group interested and patient enough in asking the questions. But our temporary superiority gives this nation the tremendous responsibility of taking the lead in mankind's effort to surmount the crisis.

Being an ingenious people, Americans find it hard to believe that there is no foreseeable defense against atomic bombs. But this is a basic fact. Scientists do not even know of any course of action which promises us any hope of adequate defense. The military-minded cling to old methods of thinking, and one Army department has been surveying possibilities of going underground and, in the event of war, placing factories in places like Mammoth Cave. Others speak of dispersing our population centers into "linear" or "ribbon" cities.

Reasonable men, in considering these new aspects of warfare, refuse to contemplate a future in which our culture would attempt to survive in ribbons or in underground tombs. Neither is there any reassurance in such proposals as keeping a hundred thousand men alert along the coasts scanning the sky with radar. There is no radar defense against the V-2, and should a "defense" be developed after years of research, it is not humanly possible for any defense to be perfect. Should one rocket with an atomic warhead strike Minneapolis, that city would look almost exactly like Nagasaki. Rifle bullets kill men, but atomic bombs kill cities. A tank is a defense against a bullet but there is no defense in science against the weapon which can destroy civilization.

Our defense is not in armaments, nor in science, nor in going underground. Our defense is in law and order.

Henceforth, every nation's foreign policy must be judged at every point by one consideration: Does it lead us to a world of law and order or does it lead us back toward anarchy and death? I do not believe that we can prepare for war and at the same time prepare for a world community. When humanity holds in its hands the weapon with which it can commit suicide, I believe that to put more power into the gun is to increase the probability of disaster.

Remembering that our main consideration is how to avoid this disaster, let us briefly consider international relations in the world today, starting with America. The war which began by Germany using weapons of unprecedented frightfulness against women and children ended with the United States using a supreme weapon which killed thousands at one blow.

Many persons in other countries now regard America with great suspicion, not only because of the bomb but because they fear she will become imperialistic. I was sometimes not quite free from such fears myself. Although other countries might not fear Americans if they knew us as we know one another, as honest and sober neighbors, they also know that even a sober nation can become drunk with victory. If Germany had not been victorious in 1870, what tragedy for the human race might have been averted!

We are still making bombs, and the bombs are making hate and suspicion. We are keeping secrets and secrets breed distrust. I do not say we should now turn loose the secret of the bomb; but are we ardently seeking a world in which there will be no need for bombs or secrets, a world in which science and men will be free?

So long as we distrust Russia's secrecy and she distrusts ours, so long will we walk together to certain doom.

The basic principles of the Acheson-Lilienthal Report are scientifically sound and technically ingenious, but as Mr. Baruch has wisely said, it is a problem not of physics but of ethics. There has been too much emphasis on legalisms and procedure. It is easier to denature plutonium than it is to denature the evil spirit of man.

The United Nations is the only instrument we have to work with in our struggle to achieve something better. But we have used the United Nations and its procedure to outvote the Russians on some occasions when the Russians were right. No, I do not think it is possible for any nation to be right all the time or wrong all the time. In all negotiations, whether over Spain, Argentina, Palestine, food, or atomic energy, so long as we maintain the threat of military power, we are merely clinging to old methods in a world which is changed forever.

No one gainsays that, at times, the United Nations Organization gives great evidence of eventually justifying the fervent hope that millions have in it. But time is not given us to solve the problems science and war have created. Powerful forces in the political world are moving swiftly toward crisis. When we look back to the end of the war—it seems like ten years! Many leaders have clearly expressed the need for world authority and an eventual world government, but actual planning and action to this end have been appallingly slow. . . . Men in high government positions propose defense or war measures which would not only compel us to live in a universal atmosphere of fear but would cost untold billions of dollars and ultimately destroy our free American way of life, even before the actual outbreak of war. . . .

Before the raid on Hiroshima, leading physicists urged the War Department not to use the bomb against defenseless women and children. The war could have been won without it. The decision was made in consideration of possible future loss of American lives; but now we have to consider the possible loss, in future atomic bombings, of *millions of lives*. The American decision may have been a fatal error, for men accustom themselves to thinking that a weapon which was used once can be used again.

Had we allowed other nations to witness the test explosion at Alamogordo, New Mexico, the bomb would have served as an education for new ideas. This would have been an impressive and favorable moment to make considered proposals for world order to end war. Our renunciation of this weapon as too terrible to use would have carried great weight in negotiations and would have convinced the other nations of our sincerity in asking for their co-operation in developing these newly unleashed powers for good and peaceful purposes.

The old type of thinking could raise a thousand objections, in the name of "realism," against such a simple attitude. But such thinking ignores the *psychological realities.* All men fear atomic war. All men hope for benefits from this new power. Between the realities of man's true desires and the realities of the danger confronting man, what do the obsolete "realities" of protocol and military protection amount to?

During the war many persons lost the habit of thinking for themselves, for many had simply to do as they were told. Today such lack of independent thinking would be a great error, for there is much the average man can do about the danger facing him.

This nation once held a great debate concerning the menace of the Axis. Today again, we need a great chain reaction of awareness and communication. Current proposals should be discussed in the light of the basic facts. They should be discussed in every newspaper, in schools, in churches, in town meetings, in private conversations, and among neighbors. Reading about the bomb promotes understanding in the mind, but talk between men can promote feeling in the heart.

Not even scientists completely understand atomic energy, for each man's knowledge is incomplete. Few men have ever seen the bomb. But all men if told a few facts can understand that the bomb—and the danger of war—are very real things, and not something far away. They directly concern every person in the civilized world. We cannot count on generals, senators and diplomats to work out a solution over a period of generations. Perhaps in five years, when several nations will have the bomb, it will be too late to avoid disaster.

Ignoring the realities of faith, good will, and honesty in seeking a solution, we place too much faith in legalisms, treaties and mechanisms. We must begin through the U.N. Atomic Energy Commission to work toward a binding agreement. But America's decision will not be made over a table in the United Nations. Our representatives in New York, Paris and Moscow depend ultimately on decisions made in the village square. To the village squares we must carry the facts of atomic energy. From there must come America's voice.

Believing this to be true, physicists prompted us to form the Emergency Committee of Atomic Scientists, with headquarters at

Princeton, New Jersey, in order to make possible a great national campaign for education on these issues. Detailed planning for world security will be easier when negotiators are assured that there is public understanding of our dilemma. Then our American proposals will not merely be documents about mechanical details or dull, dry statements of one government to another, but they will embody a message to humanity from a nation of human beings.

Science has brought forth this danger, but the real problem is in the minds and hearts of men. We will not change the hearts of other men by mechanical devices; rather we must change *our own* hearts and speak bravely. We must be generous in giving the rest of the world the knowledge we have of the forces of nature, after establishing safeguards against possible abuse. We must not merely be willing, but must be actively eager to submit ourselves to the binding authority necessary for world security. We must realize we cannot simultaneously plan for war and for peace.

When we are clear in heart and mind—only then shall we find courage to surmount the fear which haunts the world.

A Polish journalist,[12] to whom Einstein repeated his views about the necessity of a supranational organization and curtailment of national sovereignty, asked whether Einstein believed in the possibility of re-educating the German nation to an appreciation of democratic values. Einstein replied, on July 23, 1946, that the hardest thing to change in human society are the ideals and values of men. "This is why I am convinced that the aggressive German mentality will not, in the foreseeable future, be changed by education. Only practical measures, i.e., measures that will make it impossible for Germany to launch new wars of aggression, offer any hope of effective protection."

An old correspondent of Einstein's, the painter Albert Merckling in Switzerland, sent him a copy of his pamphlet *Open Letter to Truman, Stalin, Attlee and Bevin,* appealing for peace on earth. On August 25, 1946, Einstein replied as follows:

Thank you for your pamphlet, with which I am in full agreement. It is a strange thing that human affairs, particularly those of great importance, often develop so differently from what a normal person endowed with five senses might have expected. This, I believe, can be explained by the fact that the very qualities which may open the door to leadership are also those that can transform life into a living hell. . . .

Henry A. Wallace, Secretary of Commerce and Former Vice-President of the United States, voiced open opposition to the foreign policy of the Truman Administration. On September 18, 1946, Einstein wrote Wallace:

I cannot refrain from expressing to you my high and unqualified admiration for your letter to the President. You have shown deep appreciation of the factual and psychological situation and real understanding of the fateful consequences of present American foreign policy. Your courageous intervention deserves the gratitude of all of us who regard the present position of our government with grave concern.

Wallace replied on October 7, 1946, after his resignation from President Truman's Cabinet: [13]

I shall treasure your letter of September 18 as one of the most precious which I have received. More than any other individual, you have unloosed certain forces upon the world. It is now up to all of us to see that those forces are diverted to good rather than evil channels. . . .

On various occasions, Einstein identified himself publicly with the struggle for Negro rights. In an article attacking race prejudice, which appeared in the January 1946 issue of *Pageant* magazine,[14] he appealed to men to have the courage to set an example of human quality by word and deed and concluded that there is no greater satisfaction for a just and well-meaning person than the knowledge that he has devoted his best energies to the service of a good cause. In May 1946 he accepted an honorary degree from Lincoln University, a Negro institution in Pennsylvania. On September 22, 1946, the eighty-fourth anniversary of Lincoln's first Emancipation Proclamation, the American Crusade to End Lynching launched a campaign and sent a delegation to President Truman. In support of these efforts Einstein prepared the following letter, which the delegation was to present to the President:

May I wholeheartedly endorse the aims of this delegation, in the conviction that the overwhelming majority of the American people is demanding that every citizen be guaranteed protection against acts of violence. To insure such protection is one of the most urgent tasks for our generation. A way always exists to overcome legal obstacles whenever there is a determined will in the service of such a just cause.

In the fall of 1946, the Association of Philadelphia Scientists arranged a public conference in Philadelphia to acquaint the public with the facts about atomic energy. The Association, which was a chapter of the Federation of American Scientists, arranged the conference in co-operation with the Philadelphia Council of Churches and the Board of Jewish Ministers. Einstein, unable to attend, sent the following message, dated October 30, 1946: [15]

I feel deeply grateful to you, our fellow scientists in Philadelphia, and the religious groups for having united in an effort to emphasize publicly the effect which the atomic bomb and other recently developed means of mass destruction may have upon world security and the fate of humanity. I should have much liked to join you on this important occasion and regret that it will not be possible for me to come to Philadelphia. It is, however, a consolation for me to know that those who attend your conference are able people who are devoted to our common task.

A democracy such as ours must be responsive to public opinion, and public opinion can only be intelligent and powerful if the people are fully informed. What, in essence, is the present situation? Up to now, controversies among nations have been settled by military force, either by war or the threat of war. This is and always was morally wrong. The question of right or wrong can never be decided by force; such a method is neither just nor practical. Now, because of new advances in military technology, the use of force will be even more disastrous in both its physical and moral effect. A new war would mean the destruction of a large part of the population in all the nations involved. This is why we must build an international structure to guarantee security and resolve controversies among nations by peaceful means. To this end, we must be prepared to abandon part of our national sovereignty and transfer it to a world agency. We would deceive ourselves if we were to assume that our objective can be obtained in any other way.

It is important for us to realize that, in this insecure world, the great power currently enjoyed by the United States is likely to engender fear among other nations. We have the obligation, therefore, to convince the rest of the world, by deeds and by words, that we are sincere in our desire for peace and that we do not seek to use our present strength to obtain concessions which would ordinarily not be granted us. For consent thus achieved from other nations would merely sow the seeds of future conflict. . . . We should realize that those nations may have more reason to fear us than we have to fear them. . . .

The Emergency Committee of Atomic Scientists was formally incorporated in the State of New Jersey on August 2, 1946. Einstein was one of the incorporators. The certificate issued by the State of New Jersey listed as purposes of the nonprofit corporation:

1. To advance the use of atomic energy in ways beneficial to mankind.

2. To diffuse knowledge and information about atomic energy and to promote the general understanding of its consequences, to society and to the people of the United States of America, in order that an informed citizenry may intelligently determine and shape its action to serve its own and mankind's best interest.

3. To make such grants in aid or donations . . . as may be necessary or desirable to accomplish the foregoing purposes. . . .

The charter of the Emergency Committee also stated that "no substantial part of its activities shall consist of carrying on propaganda or otherwise attempting to influence legislation."

The committee now expanded its work considerably and launched a campaign far more ambitious than it had earlier in the year. Late in October 1946 this campaign began with a letter from Einstein addressed to a select group of prominent citizens:

I first appealed in the spring of this year for help in bringing to our people an understanding of the revolutionary changes which have occurred in this world through the release of atomic energy. We need now to strengthen our group for the greater task which lies ahead. You have been suggested by a friend as one who shares with American scientists the sense of responsibility and urgency which this great new force has impressed upon our lives. I hope that you will become one of us in this effort to make use of man's ability to understand and solve, while time remains, the central problem of our times.

I have called a full meeting of the Emergency Committee of Atomic Scientists at Princeton, on the 15th, 16th and 17th of November, together with representatives of scientific groups throughout the country associated with this effort. The first two days of this conference will be used by the scientists to reach final agreement on our program of education for survival to be presented to the American public, and on the allotment of responsibilities in administering it. We are mindful that we are faced with a tremendous educational project which must be completed in months rather than in the years or decades usually allowed the learning process. We have learned that $200,000, the sum originally scheduled for our work, is inadequate to the task. The enlarged campaign we are about to undertake will require the expenditure of one million dollars.

On Sunday, November 17, I am inviting a small group of representative citizens from throughout the country to meet with me and my colleagues. I should like you to join us as my guest for luncheon at one o'clock in the dining room of the Institute for Advanced Study in Princeton. At our luncheon Dr. Harold C. Urey of the University of Chicago will present to our guests the program of this committee, lay before you our financial needs, and ask for your support. After luncheon there will be an opportunity for full and frank discussion between guests and scientists. In the late afternoon, Dr. Frank Aydelotte, the Director of the Institute for Advanced Study, and the members of the institute will be our hosts at tea.

It is my earnest hope that you will be with us for luncheon and for the discussion which follows, and that you will then be willing to return to your community to give informed leadership in our drive for public support and understanding. I am inviting to this meeting friends from all parts of the country and I am fully conscious that many will come at great personal inconvenience. However, I do not hesitate to call upon you to share in the sacrifices which time and events have laid upon all thinking men and women. At stake is the fate of our civilization. In these fateful years let us resolve that nothing we can do shall be left undone in this struggle to preserve and hand on to those who come after us the civilization which generations of mankind have built through the centuries. . . .

The actual conference was apparently limited to a single day, November 17, 1946. At the luncheon meeting, which was broadcast, Einstein said: [16]

. . . Our efforts spring from the realization of the grave responsibility which physicists have incurred by creating the atomic bomb. You all know that the development of this fearful weapon of destruction became unavoidable because of the dangerous situation which then existed. The menace was removed when the scientific and engineering work succeeded; but at the same time the success itself created a new and menacing situation which has been an anguish to all of us ever since.

The new element in the situation derives from the fact that national armaments no longer constitute an adequate defense against aggression. While it is still possible to use armaments to threaten others, they can no longer offer us any kind of effective protection. Such protection can be assured only when the present state of international anarchy gives way to reliable supranational guarantees against military attack.

To achieve this is the task of responsible statesmen; on its solution hinges the destiny of our generation and of posterity, not only in America but everywhere. And what can a small group of intellectual workers do toward the attainment of this goal? I do not believe it is an exaggeration to say that we have already with some success embarked on the only promising course. Intellectual workers cannot hope to succeed by directly intervening in the political struggle; but they can see to it that concise information about the situation and the possibilities for successful action be made widely available. By spreading enlightenment they can prevent able statesmen from being impeded in their work by general prejudice and reactionary opinion. It is in support of such a campaign of public enlightenment that the Emergency Committee of Atomic Scientists was formed.

The conference was well attended; the press release listed more than sixty guests, some of them having come from as far as Texas, Arizona, and California. Seven of the eight trustees, all but Linus Pauling, were present. Several trustees spoke at the afternoon symposium on "The Social Task of the Scientist in the Atomic Era." Other speakers were Chester I. Barnard of the Lilienthal-Acheson Committee; Michael Straight, publisher of *The New Republic* and Secretary of the Committee; John Hersey, the novelist; Professor Selig Hecht of Columbia University; and Professor Philip Morrison of Cornell University. Einstein made the following extemporaneous remarks: [17]

I have to say something. I have to contradict the statement of my friend [Harold C.] Urey who said that we had so much time ahead of us to accomplish our task; I rather feel that our time is severely limited. I believe this, not only because our present situation is unique and without precedent in political affairs, but also for the following reasons:

To begin, if we are to have security from the atom bomb and other man-made weapons, we must find a way to prevent war. Unless we are able to do that, you can be sure that, despite all the promises they may make, nations will, in the event of war, employ every means of destruction at their disposal. Further, as long as war remains a possibility, the governments of all nations will continue to arm. This policy of military preparedness makes the abolition of war impossible.

I believe this is the crucial problem that confronts us. Our first task should be to try to communicate to others our conviction that war must be abolished at all costs, and that all other consideration must be of secondary importance.

For instance, I read in the newspapers that there was a great deal of debate in the United Nations as to whether the police force of Trieste itself or the forces of some other country should control the city. Now, in the abstract, such debate is certainly valid, but confronted as we are with the problem of wholesale destruction, it becomes ridiculous. . . .

Without a powerful awareness on the part of the public that we face an emergency situation, in which there can be no halfway solutions, we are surely headed for catastrophe; for when people become preoccupied with war and the preparation for war, they are neither willing nor able to conceive of peaceful alternatives.

This is why we have but little time to make people aware of the fundamental facts of the situation.

This is all I have to say.

At the end of the conference, Einstein and his fellow trustees summed up their views in the following statement:

These facts are accepted by all scientists:

1. Atomic bombs can now be made cheaply and in large number. They will become more destructive.

2. There is no military defense against the atomic bomb and none is to be expected.

3. Other nations can rediscover our secret processes by themselves.

4. Preparedness against atomic war is futile, and if attempted will ruin the structure of our social order.

5. If war breaks out, atomic bombs will be used and they will surely destroy our civilization.

6. There is no solution to this problem except international control of atomic energy and, ultimately, the elimination of war.

The program of the committee is to see that these truths become known to the public. The democratic determination of this nation's policy on atomic energy must ultimately rest on the understanding of its citizens.

The Princeton conference made news from coast to coast. Most of the press comment was favorable, or at least factual. However, the Emergency Committee of Atomic Scientists was to draw criticism from a number of sources in the months to come. The aged Dr. Charles Greeley Abbot of the Smithsonian Institution wrote Einstein in May 1947 that he thought the very idea of world government "chimerical" and considered the committee's activities "a disservice to this nation." He preferred to rely on Theodore Roosevelt's famous dictum: "Walk softly and carry a big stick." [18] Another correspondent quoted a friend who had suggested that the committee's appeals be turned over to the Federal Bureau of Investigation. Expressions of overt opposition, however, were in the minority. The committee continued to collect substantial funds to finance conferences, seminars, publications and similar activities.

On December 4, 1946, Einstein sent this message to Congressman

Robert Hale of Portland, Maine, to be used at a world government meeting in Portland on December 11: [19]

The most hopeful aspect in the present state of international problems is the unmistakable will of the people to achieve security on a supranational basis. The poll in Massachusetts [a referendum in which a large vote was cast in favor of world government] has once again demonstrated this fact most impressively. If, besides this will, there exists a clear evaluation of the situation and the existing opportunities, our goal will surely be achieved. Hence, the significance of the project now under way in Maine: to attempt through public meetings to consolidate the sentiment for peace with a clear understanding of the situation.

Let us admit openly that all these activities are prompted by the general dissatisfaction with the developments since the end of the war. Everyone knows today that the tremendous impact of modern offensive arms has rendered obsolete the old security system based on national armaments; any claim it may have had of providing effective protection against mass destruction of men and vital installations has been made absurd by technological developments. Everyone knows, too, that inexorably the day of doom will approach unless the present state of international anarchy is brought to an end. And, finally, everyone knows that our only salvation lies in the complete renunciation of violence in settling disputes and in the creation of a supranational organization. Such an organization would guard the common interests of all nations by juridical means and would provide security against attack.

Imagine, if you will, that the responsible leaders in America, Russia, and Britain had concluded, as a result of informal consultation on the problem of survival, that a solution could be achieved only on a supranational basis—that is, by the surrender of national military power and by the cessation of war preparations; they had come to recognize that in the present circumstances real international security is paramount, and that establishment of the necessary supranational institutions is basically a technical problem to be solved by objective experts; therefore, they had mutually undertaken to do their utmost to convince the legislative bodies of their respective countries of the need for such action, in the general interest. They had then succeeded in establishing a United Nations whose power and authority would be equal to the task of safeguarding security and yet be sufficiently restricted so as not to threaten the internal development of the member nations.

The legislative assembly of the United Nations would consist of representatives elected on a territorial basis; individual territories would thereby be represented in proportion to their actual significance. The elected representatives would not be like delegates of governments who are obliged to operate under rigid instructions; rather, they would be free men who would vote, by secret ballot, according to their convictions. Such an assembly should have authority to act on its own initiative. Further, I would assume that no nation would find it necessary to demand the right of veto. Such a demand would be absurd; to comply with it would destroy the institution.

Thus far, men have lacked the necessary faith to reach such brave decisions; hence war has remained a possibility, and its specter has, unavoidably, determined many of our actions. Distrust and bitterness have grown. The United States has reached a point where she feels compelled to fortify islands, produce more atomic bombs, and hamper free scientific exchange; the Army demands huge budgets to stimulate research and guides it into specific channels; and youth is being indoctrinated with the spirit of nationalism. All this is done in preparation for the day when the specter may come to life. Unfortunately, these very policies are the most effective way of actually bringing the specter into being.

Developments have taken the same course everywhere. But our responsibility is particularly great, for circumstances have temporarily placed the United States in so powerful a position that our influence on current decisions is of very great significance. In the face of so heavy a responsibility, the temptation to abuse one's power is great and potentially very dangerous.

You cannot simultaneously prevent and prepare for war. The very prevention of war requires more faith, courage and resolution than are needed to prepare for war. We must all do our share, that we may be equal to the task of peace.

To a Nobel Foundation dinner honoring Carl von Ossietzky (see pp. 264–67) on December 10, 1946, Einstein sent this message: [20]

Only someone who lived in Germany during the years following the First World War would be able to understand how hard was the battle that a man like Ossietzky had to fight. Ossietzky knew that defeat had not modified his countrymen's tradition of violence and war. He also knew how difficult, thankless, and dangerous it was to preach sanity and justice to his countrymen who were embittered by the harsh experience of defeat and the demoralizing effect of a long war. In their blindness they repaid him in hatred, persecution, and in causing his slow destruction; they did this even though to have believed him and have acted in his spirit would have meant their own salvation and the salvation of the whole world.

It is to the everlasting credit of the Nobel Foundation that it bestowed its high honor on this humble martyr, and that it is determined to keep alive his memory, and the memory of his work. His work remains all the more meaningful for mankind today since the fatal illusion against which he fought has not been removed by the outcome of the last war. The repudiation of force as a solution to human problems is as much of a task today as it was in his time.

In response to a series of long questions on atomic energy submitted to him by a French journalist,[21] Einstein wrote on December 20, 1946:

In my opinion it would be both unjustified and fatal to grant the military any measure of control over scientific work and scientific publications. Before the Fascist era this kind of interference would not have been tolerated by any government; the general respect for cultural values would have precluded such a possibility in any country.

I am convinced that the policy of inspection alone cannot secure peace. As long as national security is based on national military power, an arms race is unavoidable and no government will be loyal to commitments which involve the mere *restriction* of armaments.

Only by transferring military power to a supranational body, which derives its moral and legal authority from the fact that it genuinely represents the individual member nations, will peace be secured. Peace cannot be achieved by a gradual development; peace requires a decisive, radical step. . . .

Earlier in 1946, a movement was started to improve the living conditions of the 2,500 American conscientious objectors who were still conscripted in Civilian Public Service camps under circumstances which the *Washington Post*, on July 8, 1946, described as "resembling slave labor." In California, a number of conscientious objectors staged a strike. In response to a letter from a conscientious objector in a Federal correctional institution,[22] Einstein, in a letter of December 20, 1946, expressed the "hope that justice will be done to those brave men who stood up for their convictions." He also declared his willingness to sign any petition to the President asking for amnesty for conscientious objectors, but did not feel that he should send the President a personal letter, "for everybody has to keep his political activities within reasonable limits."

CHAPTER THIRTEEN

THE NEED FOR A SUPRANATIONAL ORGANIZATION | 1947

ELEANOR ROOSEVELT and Edgar Ansel Mowrer, the journalist and writer, invited Einstein to join them at a luncheon meeting on January 17, 1947, at which it was planned to discuss problems concerning Germany. Einstein declined the invitation but sent this message on January 9: [1]

. . . The danger of a development similar to that which took place after the First World War is very great indeed. The aggressive mentality of the German people is deep-rooted; the decline of the forces behind this mentality is at best temporary. The problem must be to make Germany economically self-supporting and, at the same time, prevent her from obtaining great political power.

This cannot be accomplished if the Germans are once more allowed to own and exploit their raw materials resources without outside control. And such control depends upon honest co-operation between the United States and Russia.

After the First World War, Franco-British rivalry neutralized the provisions of the Versailles Treaty; the Germans, consequently, found it possible to gain control over enterprises in countries which had been neutral during the war and where the Allies could not interfere. This danger is even greater now. . . . I am convinced that the German problem cannot be handled apart from an attempt to overcome the atmosphere of rivalry and distrust that pervades the international sphere.

Among the scientists who were apprehensive about the military implications of atomic energy was Professor Norbert Wiener of Harvard University, the mathematician and inventor of the term *cybernetics*. Early in January 1947, Wiener withdrew from a symposium on the problems of large-scale calculating machines sponsored by Harvard University and the United States Navy. Wiener stated that under the then prevailing system of military financing, scientific discoveries, by being turned over to the Army and Navy, were moving out of the control of the scientist and into "the hands of people whom he was least inclined to trust with their use." He was afraid that he would be working on a project that might well be used for mass slaughter. The Overseas News Agency directed a number of questions to Einstein on the subject of Wiener's statement. Einstein replied on January 20, 1947: [2]

I greatly admire and approve the attitude of Professor Wiener; I believe that a similar attitude on the part of all the prominent scientists in this country would contribute much toward solving the urgent problem of international security.

Q: The step taken by Professor Wiener is bound to be ineffectual without the co-operation of scientists all over the world. For the first time in history we are confronted with the possibility of a strike of scientists in order to prevent the possibility of mass slaughter. Are you in favor of such a strike? It is unlikely that all scientists would participate in such a move. Hence, they are bound to split up into political factions. Is it not likely that scientists in democratic countries would be more willing to join such a movement than those in totalitarian countries? Would not scientific research suffer if such a movement assumed considerable strength in the democracies while having no support, or very little, in totalitarian countries? Would not such a development give a very important advantage to totalitarian countries?

A: Non-co-operation in military matters should be an essential moral principle for all true scientists, i.e., for all who are engaged in basic research. It is true that it is more difficult for scientists in non-democratic countries to adopt such an attitude; but the fact is that, at present, the non-democratic countries constitute less of a threat to healthy international developments than the democratic nations which, enjoying economic and military superiority, have subjected scholars to military mobilization.

Q: While the principle established at the Nuremberg trials, that an officer, soldier, Gestapo man, etc., who merely obeyed his superior is nevertheless personally responsible for his acts, rather justifies the stand taken by Professor Wiener, the question still arises as to whether the scientists of a nation should feel free to assume such an attitude. Would this not imply that the scientists, rather than the elected representatives of a country, would determine, in the ultimate analysis, the nature of the defense and the war potential of a country?

A: Submission to the law of the land must not be blind. In the event of a conflict, the moral law of conscience takes precedence over one's obligation to the state.

Q: As there has never been an invention which could not be utilized for both constructive and destructive uses, would not all scientific efforts in the long run be affected?

A: The progress of science originates from man's quest for knowledge, and rarely from his pursuit of practical objectives. Science will stagnate if it is made to serve practical goals.

Q: Have scientists the right to adopt such an attitude when the laboratories and all other research facilities are not their personal property? Their work is made possible by universities, institutions and laboratories which are in most cases maintained by public funds.

A: Society should be very anxious to promote scientific research through material aid; but society should not interfere with the research itself since such interference can have only an unfavorable effect upon the scientific work.

Q: Would it not be necessary for the various countries to pass new laws which would make the withholding of scientific information an offense, in order to protect their preparations for defense? I can visualize certain scientists preferring to face imprisonment rather than disclose their knowledge; clearly, no one can compel a man to divulge what is locked up in his mind.

A: Any law stipulating secrecy in the field of basic science would not only do great injury to science, but would harm the development of the country whose legislation would impede the truly productive work of its scientists. Such a nation would actually sabotage the intellectual development of mankind.

When President Truman nominated David Lilienthal as head of the newly created United States Atomic Energy Commission, the nomination met with considerable opposition in the Senate. Einstein supported Lilienthal in a message which was broadcast over a New York station on February 21, 1947: [3]

You all know that the policies of the United States since the end of the war have caused anxiety and distrust throughout the world. The destruction of large Japanese cities without adequate previous warning, the unceasing production of atomic bombs, the Bikini tests, the expenditure of many billions of dollars for military purposes despite the absence of any external threat, the attempt to militarize science—all this has impeded the development of mutual trust among nations which is indispensable to the establishment of a secure peace.

There can be little doubt that the nomination of David Lilienthal to the Atomic Energy Commission has contributed to the easing of prevailing tensions. His work and his personality have engendered confidence throughout the world. It seems to me that the current machinations to prevent confirmation of his nomination have already done considerable harm. Powerful public pressure is necessary to secure Lilienthal's confirmation since otherwise grave international repercussions will be unavoidable.

At this critical juncture everyone must realize that his own fate, and that of his children, depends on the resolute effort of every individual to help attain real peace based on mutual trust.

The fund-raising and educational activities of the Emergency Committee of Atomic Scientists, which were operating vigorously during this period, received considerable attention from the press. The following letter is representative of the letters of solicitation sent out over Einstein's signature:

Through the release of atomic energy, our generation has brought into the world the most revolutionary force since prehistoric man's discovery of fire. This basic power of the universe cannot be fitted into the outmoded concept of narrow nationalism. For there is no secret and no defense; there is no possibility of control of atomic energy except through the aroused understanding and insistence of the peoples of the world.

We scientists recognize our inescapable responsibility to acquaint our fellow citizens with the simple facts of atomic energy and its implications for society. In this lies our only security and our only hope: we believe that an informed citizenry will act for life and not for death.

We need $1,000,000 for this great educational task. Sustained by faith in man's ability to control his destiny through the exercise of reason, we have pledged all our strength and our knowledge to this work. I do not hesitate to call upon you to help. . . .

The magazine *Newsweek,* in its issue of March 10, 1947, devoted almost three pages to "Einstein, the Man Who Started It All," and to the work of the Emergency Committee of Atomic Scientists.[4]

Had I known that the Germans would not succeed in developing an atomic bomb [it quoted Einstein as saying], I would have done nothing for the bomb. [He conceded that atomic energy would have been released sooner or later without his intervention, but] our situation would have been much better if the emergency had not come about so quickly.

It is important to enlighten public opinion on the real situation about the bomb. We can be saved from its consequences only by action on an international scale which will make war and the preparation for war unnecessary and even impossible.

If we [the scientists] can make the public realize the facts and their implications, we have done all that we can. Our committee is attempting to provide the funds needed to reach the public. . . . If we are able to bring the facts to the attention of the American public and of the more influential intellectuals in European countries, it will have some effect. Everybody has to reckon with world opinion. Experience has shown that the Russians, too, are sensitive to it. . . .

The secret of the atomic bomb is to America what the Maginot Line was to France before 1939. It gives us imaginary security; and in this respect it is a great danger.

For a dinner on March 12, 1947, at which *The World Federalist News* presented him with an award, Einstein prepared this message:[5]

Everyone knows how hard it is to bring about co-operation among different organizations, even when they ostensibly serve the same purposes. It is most reassuring, therefore, that such co-operation has been achieved with regard to the proposal for "strictly limited world government." [This refers to an action taken earlier at Asheville, North Carolina, when several world government groups joined to form the United World Federalists, with Einstein as a member of the Advisory Board.] It is also gratifying that you have expressed public recognition for those who have earned our gratitude by devoting themselves to the most important goal of our time. Other important contributions have been made by those who endeavored to enlighten the public, and who have dispassionately examined the possibilities for realizing international security.

The elimination of harmful emotionalism is an important prerequisite to success in international relations, even more so than in other fields of human endeavor. Agreement with Soviet Russia, in particular, depends upon a full appreciation of the difficulties and limitations with which responsible Soviet authorities have to contend. If we fail to understand this, we might easily conclude that the problem of security on a global basis will not be solved in time. Many people who are sincerely dedicated to working for peace privately voice their discouragement and despair over the petty disappointments of everyday political life.

To such expressions of discouragement I know but one reply: There is no alternative. If we wish to escape the threat of disaster, as we all want to, we must eliminate fear and distrust and see to it that the goal of international security takes precedence over all other considerations. Once we accept this formulation, the political problem would then become a purely technical one. Instead of engaging in endless controversy, man would direct his energies to concrete problems which can be solved through practical cooperation by all who are interested. . . . The difficulties which confront us are more psychological than material. I hope that you will succeed in overcoming the traditional national prejudices and that you will do so while there is still time.

In October 1946 the French Delegation to the United Nations submitted a plan for the establishment of International Research Laboratories under the auspices of the United Nations. In consequence, the Secretary-General conducted a broad inquiry among the agencies of the United Nations, as well as other international organizations, and renowned scientists. Einstein's views were sought on March 26, 1947.

Einstein said that the idea of international scientific research, while interesting in principle, had to be considered with great care and caution:

The history of science has shown that great scientific advances are not achieved through organization and planning; new ideas have their origin in the mind of some individual. Hence, the freedom of the individual scholar to pursue his work is the chief prerequisite to scientific progress. An organization is a poor instrument for scientific work, except in certain carefully chosen fields, such as astronomy, meteorology, geophysics and plant geography. Therefore, one should project an international scientific organization with great caution, particularly since an institution of this sort may be brought under the influence of the views of only one or two individuals. There is probably no need more urgent and indispensable than the creation of a great center of sociological studies, under truly international and impartial auspices. At such a center, the ways and means of establishing better understanding among nations should be studied. A method, which might help break the spell of nationalism, should be evolved whereby history is taught without creating in the minds of students an obsession with the past, as has so often been the case. An over-all improvement of relations among the peoples of the world should be the aim of such an institute. Social studies of this nature should be pursued with utmost eagerness, since conditions favoring true international co-operation should be explored first; without such international co-operation, scientific and technical progress can have little meaning for mankind.

For a meeting of an unidentified group that apparently took place in May 1947 Einstein wrote this message: [6]

I am very grateful for the opportunity to send greetings to a gathering of persons devoted to the cause of world law.

I believe that the growing movement toward the establishment of a supranational government constitutes the deepest hope of mankind. I am convinced that only when men everywhere will meet as you are now meeting, that is, as men pledged to a common law, will mankind be able to conquer its despair. . . . With all my heart I believe that the world's present system of sovereign nations can lead only to barbarism, war, and inhumanity, and that only world law can assure progress toward a civilized, peaceful humanity.

As a citizen of Germany, I saw how excessive nationalism can spread like a disease, bringing tragedy to millions. Now, as a citizen of the United States, while appreciating the blessings of a free association of states and peoples in America, I must add in frankness and humility that I recognize indications of the disease of nationalism also in this country. The confidence I have in American democracy compels me to voice this honest warning.

There can be no doubt that world law is bound to come soon, whether by coercion or by peaceful agreement. No other effective defense exists against the modern methods of mass destruction. Should man misuse science and engineering in the service of selfish passion, our civilization is doomed. The nation-state is no longer capable of adequately protecting its citizens; to increase the military strength of a nation no longer guarantees its security.

The present condition of international anarchy, which forces mankind to live under the constant threat of sudden annihilation, has led to a dangerous atomic armaments race. The Emergency Committee of Atomic Scientists is conscious of its serious responsibility to advise the citizens of this country, and of every other country, that nations can no longer think in terms of military power or technical superiority. What one group of men has discovered, other groups of men who pursue knowledge intelligently and patiently will also find out. There are no scientific secrets. Neither can there be any effective defense against aggression on a purely national basis.

The release of atomic energy has created a new world in which old ways of thinking, that include old diplomatic conventions and balance-of-power politics, have become utterly meaningless. Mankind must give up war in the atomic era. What is at stake is the life or death of humanity.

The only military force which can bring security to the world is a supranational police force, based on world law. To this end we must direct our energies.

The Monument Builders of America, a trade association, asked Einstein to suggest an appropriate inscription for the war memorials that were being erected in different parts of the United States. Late in May 1947 Einstein composed this text, which was apparently never used:

We suffered and died that you might be free and that peace with justice might prevail. May you, the living, never forget the responsibility which our sacrifice has imposed upon you.

At the invitation of the Atomic Scientists of Chicago, a conference was held at Lake Geneva, Wisconsin, June 18–22, 1947, to which members of the Federation of American Scientists, the Association of Scientists for Atomic Education at Oak Ridge, the Northern California Association of Scientists, and other affiliated organizations were invited. Apparently, some disagreement on basic policies had already developed within the Emergency Committee of Atomic Scientists. On June 14, 1947, Einstein sent Professor Harold C. Urey a memorandum for possible discussion at the conference. In a note to Urey, to which the memorandum was attached, Einstein said: [7]

I hastened to write down what seemed to me essential in view of the problems confronting us. I am sending it to you, although I feel very strongly that I am not sufficiently informed about our situation and the opinions and intentions of our colleagues. I fear, therefore, that the memorandum may not be useful and, in fact, may be considered trivial and obvious. So I shall certainly understand if you have no use for it at Lake Geneva.

The memorandum:

Assuming there is agreement on a desirable policy for security against war, as well as agreement by the group on what is to be its general sphere of activity, it seems to me both possible and desirable that the Atomic Scientists [Emergency Committee of Atomic Scientists] continue to function as a separate body. At your request, I am setting down a few personal remarks in the hope that they may facilitate discussion:

(a) Aspects of the International Situation

1. Measures which deal with atomic energy are not sufficient to ensure security. Security will be achieved only when war among sovereign states is made impossible.

2. War will be prevented only when military power in the hands of individual nations is abolished and is replaced by the military monopoly of a supranational organization ("supranational government").

3. The member states of the supranational organization must have no veto right against measures and decisions taken by the supranational government in the interest of security.

4. The supranational government must be dependent upon representatives of the *populations,* not the governments of member states; in other words, the representatives must be able to act and vote according to their own convictions, except in those instances when they are specifically instructed by their constituents.

I am convinced that fulfillment of these four conditions is both necessary and sufficient to make wars among the member states impossible and render war preparations superfluous.

The question remains whether, in the broader interest of achieving security, all nations would be willing to accept such far-reaching limitations on their freedom of action. Because of recent developments, many people are inclined to answer this question in the negative. In my view, none of us is able, at this time, to answer it with any certainty. However, I believe that as long as the possibility exists of incorporating *all* nations into a supranational government, we ought to work toward that goal without sacrificing any of the measures which are indispensable to the protection of the member states against aggression.

Should developments in the immediate future indicate that certain nations are unwilling to comply with the minimum requirements for international security, the question will then arise as to whether it is desirable to form a supranational organization that does not include all nations. I believe the answer to this question must be in the negative unless the nations which would belong to the supranational organization enjoy decisive economic and military superiority over the nations which are not part of the organization. . . .

(b) Activities of Our Group [Emergency Committee of Atomic Scientists]

In my opinion, we have been successful in the past because we have been able to inform and influence a group of people who, while not numerous, form part of the government in Washington or are locally influential during Congressional elections. This is the kind of activity which a small committee such as ours can adequately perform. I do not believe we should change our policy and attempt to influence the public at large, except for official declarations in the press, whenever they seem necessary or desirable. . . . If we act within these limited spheres, we do not need to raise large funds, nor do we need to expand our organization. . . .

The Lake Geneva Conference adopted a statement on the responsibilities of scientists, the desirability of the establishment of an international agency for the control of atomic energy, and the need for comprehensive plans for world co-operation. The statement was endorsed and publicized by the Emergency Committee of Atomic Scientists. Simultaneously with this endorsement, the Emergency Committee issued the following statement of its own on June 29, 1947:

A year has passed since the founding of this committee and the publication of our first appeal to reason in the face of the overwhelming threat presented to civilization by the atomic bomb. During this year our hopes for international agreement on control of atomic energy have come to nothing. It is imperative that the American people understand this failure if any constructive solutions are to be arrived at in time.

Can thoughtful and well-informed men any longer expect fruitful agreements to come out of the discussions now going on in the United Nations Atomic Energy Commission? Are the American proposals for the international control of atomic energy fair? Are the Russians to blame for the fact that any agreement is further away than at the initiation of the discussions?

These are questions of varying degree of importance, but the imperative question, the answer to which is a matter of historic necessity, is: "How can we reach a world consensus to abolish in the near future the threat of atomic war and, ultimately, the possibility of war itself?" If we fail to find the answer to this question, the answer to any other question is irrelevant.

All signs indicate that we are failing to meet the challenge. Peoples throughout the world want peace as never before, yet nations prepare feverishly for war. Preparation goes on day and night on both the material and psychological planes. Instead of the "One

World" which men proclaimed a few short years ago, we have come even to the partition of existing nations. The United Nations, in which was invested the hopes of peoples throughout the world, is granted inadequate powers and, indeed, this tribunal is by-passed on matters of primary importance. Militarism is rampant throughout the world. In all history, never in any period of "peace" have so many men been under arms. Even in Great Britain and America, with their great antimilitarist traditions, liberal-thinking men, considering the necessities of the situation, turn to the "realistic" solution. The Prussian disease of which the German and Japanese states have died is beginning to infect the conquerors.

Events during the past year have emphasized the tragic pertinence of our Six Point statement published on November 17, 1946.

Once stockpiles of atomic bombs have been accumulated by two national blocs in a divided world, it will no longer be possible to maintain peace. Thus we have one year less to secure a workable solution to safeguard our civilization.

Why have the year-long discussions in the United Nations Atomic Energy Commission not succeeded? Is this because of incidental and transitory factors which can be remedied by simple measures such as, for instance, the appointment of new personnel to carry on the discussions? The answer is in the negative. The representatives of great states, while striving to safeguard the peace, have fulfilled their traditional duty to place their own nations in the most advantageous position to win the next war. It is useless to proceed further along this path; one cannot prepare for war and expect peace.

This is not to say that war is inevitable. It is to say, however, that the discussions now under way may not make a war less likely and are, in fact, based upon the premise of an anticipated war. What is necessary at this critical time is to determine whether there remains an alternative approach more likely to achieve a peaceful solution.

We believe that there is such an alternative approach. We believe that the problem of atomic energy can no longer be treated as an isolated issue. We had hoped a year ago to achieve a pattern of international control of atomic energy, which could be applied to other spheres of international concern, to implement the creation of a stable world society. To foster this hope today, as we move into a world divided into two armed camps, would be a betrayal of our responsibility.

We believe that the imperative problem of international control of atomic energy must be solved and can only be solved within the context of a general agreement which guarantees a reasonable degree of security to all nations and provides for far-reaching economic and cultural co-operation among nations. Such a settlement is not possible if the respective peoples are concerned exclusively with the security and welfare of their own countries.

Because of the importance of the United States in the world today it is imperative that the American people take an active part in achieving such a world settlement. America must be prepared to mobilize her vast resources on an adequate scale to help the peoples of the world lift the levels of their economic life. All peoples would be expected to make reciprocal sacrifices to achieve great ends. Only bold measures of this kind can produce an atmosphere among nations which makes it possible to discuss constructively the restrictions on national sovereignty necessary to the preservation of peace.

But the American people should understand that there is no easy path to the accomplishment of these great objectives; that, in the long run, the creation of a supranational government, with powers adequate to the responsibility of maintaining the peace, is necessary.

Is this realistic? We believe that nothing less is realistic. We know that the developments of science and technology have determined that the peoples of the world are no longer able to live under competing national sovereignties with war as the ultimate arbitrator. Men must understand that the times demand a higher realism which recognizes that "no man is an island," that our fate is joined with that of our fellow men throughout the world. We must contrive to live together in peace even at the cost of great material sacrifice; the alternative is the death of our society. As we approach what may be the last hour before midnight, the challenge is plainly before us. What will be our response?

Einstein and all the other trustees of the Emergency Committee, except Linus Pauling, were present at the press conference in Princeton at which the statements of the Lake Geneva Conference and the Emergency Committee were made public.[8] Reporters urged the scientists to suggest how soon Russia might succeed in producing an atomic bomb and when atomic war might be expected. Many newspapers reported that Professor Urey estimated it might take the Russians eight to ten years to produce the bomb. Urey's statement made headlines and was often attributed to Einstein himself.

The reaction of the press to the two statements was on the whole respectful. There were, however, important exceptions. The *New York Herald Tribune* of July 1, 1947, carried an editorial, "Scientists Afield," in which it charged the committee with "dangerous misconceptions" and "high contempt for the United Nations. . . . Tearing away at its foundation, they perform no service when they offer in its place nothing more substantial than a long, vague word [supranational government]."

This prompted Einstein and Philip M. Morse, who was then the Acting Executive Director of the committee, to dispatch the following letter to the *New York Herald Tribune:*

Your editorial, "Scientists Afield," of July 1, requires an answer, since it does not represent adequately the standpoint of the Emergency Committee of Atomic Scientists as expressed in our recent statement. You speak of our "expression of high contempt for the United Nations"; . . . this is not an accurate interpretation of our words. We stated that "the United Nations is granted inadequate powers and . . . is by-passed on matters of primary importance." It is common knowledge that Mr. Trygve Lie [then Secretary-General of the United Nations] agrees with this. We stated that "the year-long discussions in the United Nations Atomic Energy Commission [have] not succeeded." Everybody agrees that this is the fact. . . .

Although the *New York Herald Tribune* had not reprinted the committee's statement in its original news story, it eventually published the statement together with the letter signed by Einstein and Morse, as well as a concluding editorial note in which the editors reiterated their previous position.

About two weeks later, on July 15, 1947, Einstein and the Administrative Committee of the Federation of Atomic Scientists joined in a statement urging continued faith in the United Nations.[9] The occasion was the second anniversary of the test explosion at Alamogordo:

Two years ago today the first atomic bomb exploded on the New Mexico desert. During these two years, the Federation of Atomic Scientists, which represents the majority of America's atomic scientists, has persistently affirmed the thesis that there must be one world or none. To this end we have advocated the establishment of international control of atomic energy and all weapons of mass destruction.

Although we knew from the beginning that the task would be difficult, the lack of progress to date has been discouraging. Some people, in fact, have accepted defeat and have actually suggested that United Nations negotiations be abandoned. We, on the other hand, on this second anniversary of the atomic bomb, affirm our belief that the common interests which led to the establishment of the United Nations are more compelling than ever.

We have learned many valuable lessons during the past two years. We now know that the problem of atomic energy cannot be solved apart from the consideration of other issues. At the same time we maintain that human security can never be assured until the world has been made safe for atomic energy. It is necessary to pursue every avenue toward one world, taking full advantage of the opportunities offered by the United Nations and its agencies.

In the following transcript of a broadcast of July 17, 1947, on "The Immediate Need for World Law," the remarks of the interviewers (but not of Einstein) have been abridged: [10]

RAYMOND SWING: Last week a resolution was introduced in the House of Representatives of the Congress by a bipartisan group, calling on the President to take the initiative to strengthen the United Nations into an organization capable of enacting, interpreting and enforcing world law. At the same time a resolution was introduced in the Senate, also by a bipartisan group, calling on the President to take the same initiative in proposing revisions in the structure of the United Nations to strengthen it as an instrument to prevent war and preserve peace. . . . Tonight it is a privilege to hear the opinion on this stirring theme of a man whose credentials to speak about it are peerless. We are sitting tonight in his study at Princeton, and it is my privilege to introduce Dr. Albert Einstein!

Einstein: The resolutions submitted to Congress by a bipartisan group will mark a turning point in international politics, if they find the vigorous support of large sections of the American people.

These resolutions are based on a recognition of certain facts which, although generally known today, are often obscured by political emotionalism.

There is no effective defense against modern methods of mass destruction. Therefore no nation is any longer able to adequately protect its citizens merely through an increase in its military strength. As long as the present condition of international anarchy prevails, all of us will continue to live under the constant threat of sudden annihilation. This is a state of affairs that cannot endure; before long, it must come to an end, either by way of brute force or by peaceful agreement, which inevitably implies a world government.

The use of brute force would result in unimaginable destruction and suffering. To spare mankind such a catastrophe is the main purpose of the present resolutions. The resolutions aim at a fundamental alteration of the United Nations Charter, with a view to an eventual transformation of the United Nations into a world government. Only such a *supra*national, not *inter*national, organization, resting on law and vested with adequate military power to enforce the law, can guarantee the security of the nations of the world.

In considering the situation objectively, anybody can see that the method suggested in the resolutions is the only one that will save us. Of course, the opponents of the resolutions will tell us: Your way of proceeding may be theoretically correct, but in reality it has been proved wholly impracticable. Have not the Russians obstructed all our attempts at organized international co-operation, with regard to the control of atomic energy, and even as far as economic assistance to devastated countries is concerned? Have they not stubbornly insisted on their veto power, which in itself makes the problem of security insolvable?

It is true and becomes more evident every day that the Russians are at present guided in all their decisions by fear and distrust of everything foreign while, before Chamberlain's Munich Pact, they had worked for an international security system more fervently than any other great power. It is not difficult to explain this attitude.

The Soviet experiences with the outer world have never been too good. We must remember the support of the West by anti-Soviet generals during the [Russian] Civil War, the long political and economic boycott against the Soviet Union, the constant propaganda campaign of the foreign press against Soviet Russia. Later on the Russians joined the League of Nations, but then they saw how the Fascist aggressions in Manchuria, in Spain, in Abyssinia, in Austria, were accepted and condoned, how agreements were made with the aggressors. And eventually, when they found themselves excluded from the most crucial European settlements in the first period of the Hitler regime, then, understandably enough, they changed their attitude.

So we have to reckon with the fact that Russia has become xenophobic; she is obsessed by the utopia of isolationism. We may regret this state of affairs, but we must understand its reasons in order to act in a way that will not aggravate the evil. One thing is certain, that threats and intimidation are not a promising method to dispel distrust and to bring a reluctant partner back into the community of nations.

What can America do? What good can we expect from forceful support of the present resolutions [in Congress]? We can show the world that our concern is not the increase of national power but the security of all nations, a demonstration which, unlike other demonstrations, would greatly improve the international atmosphere. We shall encourage all forces striving for a supranational solution of the security problem. We shall repair the damage that has been done to the authority of the United Nations by recent unilateral actions.

In the future the legislative assembly of the United Nations must be composed of men and women who are responsible not to national governments but only to the people who elect them. The decisions of the United Nations in the matter of international security must bind national governments without the restrictive possibility of a veto. If these aims of the present resolutions were reached, the foundations would be laid for a world government to which all the armed forces of the member nations could be and should be subordinated.

It would seem inappropriate and unwise to exert pressure of any kind on those nations which do not yet consider themselves in a position to participate in the new organization. But their nonparticipation should not be allowed to delay the formation of a supranational government. Nor should their consent be purchased by concessions regarding the obligations of member states.

Above all, let us never forget that in human affairs all real and lasting power is ultimately founded on confidence and free consent.

Swing: . . . Now let me make another introduction, of someone who will want to ask Dr. Einstein some questions. . . . Mr. Cord Meyer, President of the United World Federalists. . . .

Meyer: . . . There is a question I would like to ask you, Dr. Einstein. Many people will agree that some form of world government will eventually be achieved by humanity, but the idea that it can be realized by peaceful consent in our time is often ridiculed as hopelessly utopian. What do you think of this point of view?

Einstein: Certainly the establishment of a government able to prevent international war will involve deep changes in nationalistic attitudes and prejudices. Such adjustments in traditional ways of thinking have usually taken place slowly and over a long period of years. But now the existence of atomic weapons and other methods of total destruction leaves us no choice but to accomplish immediately what might otherwise have taken centuries. So long as nations seek protection in competitive armaments, their separate attempts to gain security will merely serve to increase their mutual suspicions.

Soon the preparations for war made by fearful governments will make war itself inevitable. When, within a very few years, rival national blocs possess atomic weapons, fear will destroy the last hope of peace. A world government with powers adequate to guarantee security is not a remote ideal for the distant future. It is an immediate necessity, if our civilization is to continue. It is the condition of the survival of ourselves and of all we value.

Swing: I would also like to ask Dr. Einstein a question that has been put to me a great many times. Do you believe that the Soviet Union is committed by its nature and structure to a form of imperialist expansion which would make it impossible for Russia to join in forming a world government?

EINSTEIN: I think one must draw a distinction between the world as it has been without a world government and the world as it would be if a world government were formed. In a world without a world government, in which rivalry for power is the predominant theme, the tendency of a great power to expand is almost unavoidable. For a great nation which has a great rival is bound to seek to increase its security and to undertake a policy of expansion in the interest of security. Such a policy is really identical with a kind of imperialism.

On the other hand, if there were a world federation and security was no longer based on national power, the security of any one nation would no longer constitute the insecurity of other nations. Then the basis for rivalry would be changed. There would still be rivalry in a world federation, just as there is rivalry in the United States between the East and the South, or between management and labor. But, in a federation, law would be substituted for force, and the rivalries would express themselves through legal channels. The various parts of the federation could not make war on each other.

I believe that the desire for security is the chief motive behind Russian political thinking. I believe it is far stronger than any motive of expansion for the sake of expansion. If the Russians have the invitation to enter a world in which their security is the concern of everyone, they would be fools not to join.

SWING: And wouldn't you call us fools if we failed to invite them to join such a world?

EINSTEIN: Certainly. We have never yet dared to propose to the Russians a system of law which makes them equals before the law instead of rivals for supreme power. I should add that the Russians have never invited us to form such a world either.

But the United States should not wait to be asked. It is the heir of a Western civilization which has long been preoccupied with the art and science of government. If the United States does not take the initiative, no one will.

In a special "Atomic Supplement" to the *Washington Post* of August 3, 1947, Einstein answered these four questions: [11]

Q: A large proportion of our scientific research, particularly atomic research, is dependent on government financing, and hence subject to government direction. Do you see any dangers in this situation?

A: The advancement of scientific research is undoubtedly in the interest of the community as a whole. It is, therefore, necessary and to be welcomed under present-day circumstances that the government assist research through financial support. However, in order that this financial support shall effectively further research, the distribution of these funds must be entrusted to men who, through their life's work, have demonstrated that they possess both the understanding and the interest necessary for this difficult task; political influences should not affect the choice of the responsible men. Scientific research can flourish only if it is pursued for its own sake, without regard to its practical application.

Q: Do you agree with assertions often made that the failure to re-establish the prewar "free community of science" seriously affects American scientific research? Do you agree with the more extreme assertion that the situation, presumably dictated by reasons of national security, actually threatens national security by exerting an adverse effect on research even in atomic weapons?

A: The free publication of scientific findings is an absolute prerequisite to successful research. Partial concealment is harmful, not only to pure science but also to those technical applications which are based on scientific progress. Such concealment will, in the long run, do more harm than good even to the military interests. Regimentation of any kind will further cause the best scientific minds to be repelled.

Q: Does the June 29, 1947, statement by the Emergency Committee of Atomic Scientists [p. 410], of which you are the chairman, mean that you feel that the only goal to strive for is world government and that present negotiations in the United Nations —for control of atomic energy and for other purposes—are necessarily vain and futile?

A: The Emergency Committee of Atomic Scientists is firmly convinced that military security can be achieved only on a supranational basis. It is also convinced that international security is not sufficiently protected by controlling special weapons (e.g., the atomic bomb). No nation will honestly renounce any effective military weapon, as long as it feels compelled to prepare for a possible future war. This is the reason why the Emergency Committee of Atomic Scientists is convinced that the problem of peace and security admits only of a total solution (world government).

Q: The official American policy appears to be to strive with all diligence to negotiate an international atomic control agreement, but, pending such agreement, to continue making as much fissionable material as possible for use, if necessary, in atomic bombs. Do you believe this policy is inherently inconsistent? In the light of your statements that any atomic war would destroy civilization, including our own, do you feel that our continuing manufacture of atomic bomb material is necessary or desirable?

A: The question as to whether the production of atomic bombs is justifiable under the present circumstances is not easily answered. It is essential, however, for the United States to act in such a manner that its intention to solve the problem of security on a supranational basis will be made manifest beyond doubt. Unfortunately, up till now this has not been the case.

A major new peace movement had arisen in England, called the Crusade for World Government; it had as its outstanding exponent Henry C. Usborne, Labor Member of Parliament.[12] Its avowed purpose was to create a new world organization which would replace the United Nations. This was to be accomplished at a People's World Convention in the fall of 1950. Representatives to the convention were to be chosen, during the summer of 1950, through direct elections conducted throughout the world, on the basis of one representative for each one million people. A charter was to be written by 1951, to come into effect when half the nations of the world, or nations representing half the population of the world, had ratified it. The new world organization would have a monopoly of armed forces to be used as a world police force; a monopoly of the processes involved in atomic development and of other scientific discoveries capable of mass destruction; a world food board; and a world bank to create a common world currency and engage in large-scale economic planning. All this would, of course, imply a surrender of sovereignty by the ratifying nations.

More than eighty members of the British Parliament supported the movement, as did many other noted Britons. A number of them actually agreed to stand for election to the Peoples' World Convention. The World Movement for World Federal Government called an international conference in Montreux, Switzerland, August 17–24, 1947. Since Einstein was not able to attend the Montreux Conference, he sent the following message, dated July 31, 1947:

The Montreux Conference, which I regret I cannot attend for reasons of health, will prove of great significance if it calls attention to certain urgent international problems. The most important task before the conference is to reach clear-cut and concrete decisions concerning the character of the projected world government, as well as its constitution and functions. The supranational character of the conference makes it likely that its proposals will impress the various governments and nations much more than local groups could possibly do. May the conference succeed in demonstrating that, under pressure of compelling necessity, differences in national viewpoints can be resolved.

May you further succeed in establishing genuine co-operation among the major national groups, which would allow an effective organization to be created. Such a new body would offer significant and permanent influence to the many adherents of supranational security scattered throughout the world. If this can be accomplished, resistance to the limitation of national sovereignty will not prove as formidable as it may now appear.

The Montreux Conference endorsed the plan for a "Peoples' World Constituent Assembly" in 1950 as well as the proposed charter. Einstein, with twelve others, signed the following appeal:

We, the undersigned, who believe the world is in mortal danger of self-destruction through war, wish to recommend to you as seriously as we can the proposals for a Peoples' World Constituent Assembly to be held in 1950.

Confronted by the means of destruction that are now in the hands of men, all differences of politics, race, and creed are beside the point. The human race as such will cease to exist unless a world government capable of enforcing world law is established by peaceful means. Only in this way can war be averted, and the peace and plenty which we all desire for humanity can be made possible.

The choice is indeed between one world or none.

In September 1947 Usborne visited the United States and was warmly received by public audiences. Plans were made to extend the People's World Convention movement to America, and the Emergency Committee of Atomic Scientists contributed toward defraying the expenses of Usborne's trip. On September 28, 1947, Usborne visited Einstein in Princeton.

In the Spring 1947 issue of *The American Scholar,* Louis N. Ridenour, Dean of the Graduate School at the University of Illinois, published an article entitled "Military Support of American Science, a Danger?" Ridenour, on the whole, discounted the danger for a number of reasons. He felt that the armed services were mindful of the need for basic research, much of which now required large resources, such as only the government could provide. In an era of total war all human activity was related to war and the problem, therefore, was the morality of war as such, rather than a concern with the development of specific weapons. Besides, Ridenour pointed out, secrecy was no longer necessary in most areas, and scientists were under no compulsion to accept government support.

The Summer 1947 issue of the magazine carried a number of favorable and unfavorable reactions to Ridenour's article, including contributions from Aldous Huxley, Vannevar Bush, and Norbert Wiener. Einstein wrote a piece under the title, "The Military Mentality." [13]

The crucial element in our situation seems to be that the problem under discussion cannot be treated as an isolated issue. To begin, one may argue that, today, institutions of learning and research must increasingly be supported by government grants since, for various reasons, private resources are inadequate to the task; but does that mean that it is reasonable to permit the military to distribute the funds raised from the taxpayers for research purposes? Surely, intelligent people will answer this question in the negative. The difficult task of apportioning these funds to best advantage ought clearly to be placed in the hands of men whose training and experience justify the assumption that they have some familiarity with science and scholarship.

If sensible men nevertheless insist that a major share of the funds available for research be distributed through military agencies, then the reasons for such an attitude must be sought in the fact that cultural values have become subordinated to over-all political considerations. We must, therefore, direct our attention to this basic political attitude, as well as its origin and implications. We shall then come to realize that the problem under discussion is but one of many and can only be fully appreciated and adequately judged when viewed within a broader frame of reference.

The attitude we have mentioned is something new in America. It arose under the impact of two world wars, when all resources were concentrated on military goals, thus fostering a predominantly military mentality which was further strengthened by the suddenness of victory. The essential fact which lies behind this mentality is that "naked power"—the phrase so aptly coined by Bertrand Russell—has come to play a much larger role in international relations than any other factor. The mentality of the Germans, who were particularly corrupted by Bismarck's successes, suffered a similar change; in fact, it brought about their complete ruin in less than a hundred years.

I must confess that the foreign policy of the United States since the end of hostilities often irresistibly reminds me of the foreign policy of Germany under Kaiser Wilhelm II. I know that others have independently recognized this painful analogy.

It is characteristic of the military mentality to consider material factors, such as atomic bombs, strategic bases, arms of every description, raw material resources, and the like as important while, at the same time, regarding man himself, his thoughts and aspirations as quite inferior. In its theoretical approach the military mentality bears some resemblance to Marxism. In both, man is minimized as being merely "capacity" or "manpower." Under the impact of this kind of thinking, the goals which normally determine human aspirations simply disappear. To fill the gap, the military mentality makes the possession of "naked power" a goal in itself. This surely is one of the strangest delusions to which man can fall victim.

Today, the existence of the military mentality is more dangerous than ever; for the weapons which are available to aggressor nations have become much more powerful than weapons of defense. This fact will inevitably produce the kind of thinking which leads to preventive wars. Because of the general insecurity resulting from these developments, the civil rights of citizens are being sacrificed to the alleged cause of national interest. Political witch-hunting and governmental interference in many forms, such as official control over teaching, research and the press, appear inevitable and, consequently, do not encounter the kind of popular resistance that might otherwise serve to protect the population. All traditional values are changing and anything which does not clearly serve the utopian goal of militarism is considered inferior.

I see no escape from the present dilemma other than a farsighted, honest, and courageous policy aimed at achieving security on a supranational basis. Let us hope that, while this nation still has the opportunity for leadership, enough men of character will be found to guide its course in this direction. If they are found, problems such as have been discussed today will no longer exist.

Presumably on the occasion of the twentieth anniversary of the execution of Sacco and Vanzetti (August 22, 1927), Einstein issued a statement which apparently appeared in *Die Weltbühne,* then published in East Berlin as a successor magazine to the journal which bore the same name and which, until 1933, was edited by Carl von Ossietzky: [14]

Nothing should be left undone to keep alive in the minds of men the memory of the tragic Sacco and Vanzetti case. It serves to remind us that even the most perfectly planned democratic institutions are no better than the men whose instruments they are. True justice cannot exist unless the people themselves are determined to be just; unless they practice brotherhood, respect the truth, and have the courage to resist blind prejudice and political passion.

Although justice did not prevail in the Sacco-Vanzetti case, the belief in justice was stronger then than it is today. Man's conscience has become dulled by too much horror. This is why the struggle to preserve the dignity of man has become all the more urgent. The symbol embodied in the death of Sacco and Vanzetti must be kept alive by all those who earnestly strive for a better world.

John Dewey, the aged philosopher and teacher, was among those who received, in August 1947, an appeal from the Emergency Committee of Atomic Scientists to contribute to its work. Dewey replied to Einstein and the members of the committee: [15]

I regret not to be able to contribute. I could and would contribute if there were included in your appeals all public statements and instructions given your corps of lecturers concerning a definite movement urging the repeal of the right of veto. I am not naïve enough to suppose the USSR would heed that appeal. But at least there would be reason to hope that the money would not be raised and spent in vain because of any default for which the contributors were primarily responsible.

Einstein replied on September 4, 1947:

I thank you warmly for your kindness in writing to me about the work of this committee. I am in full agreement with your suggestion that our statements and speakers should stress the practical necessity for the repeal of the veto right.

I shall lay your proposal before the next meeting of the trustees, which occurs in October, and hope that they will concur.

Dewey replied on September 7, 1947:

Thank you heartily for your cordial response to my suggestion. I am happy that you concur, and I deeply prize your kind words.

With warm personal regards and appreciation of the great work you are doing.

Ambassador Carlos P. Romulo, head of the Philippine Delegation to the United Nations, sent Einstein a copy of a speech delivered in the General Assembly on September 18, 1947, in which he had urged modification of the veto power in the Security Council as well as stricter observance of General Assembly decisions. On October 16, 1947, Einstein thanked Romulo for sending the speech

which I studied carefully and with which I am in undivided accord. I also appreciated very much the speech you made in the United Nations last year concerning better representation of the people in the Assembly. It seems that the intelligence of the delegates is not always proportionate to the potential influence of the countries they are representing.

On June 5, 1947, in a speech at Harvard University, Secretary of State George C. Marshall proposed the so-called "Marshall Plan" for foreign aid. Later in the year, former Secretary of War Henry L. Stimson asked Einstein to join a committee in support of the Marshall Plan. Einstein replied on November 4, 1947: [16]

As you may imagine, I am unreservedly in favor of supporting Europe in its grave situation. I feel, however, that I cannot advocate the Marshall Plan as it is presently formulated. I believe that such an international action should be undertaken within the framework of the United Nations. This seems particularly necessary since the Marshall Plan is regarded, both inside and outside the United States, as a political scheme directed against the Russian bloc and hence may serve to aggravate existing political tensions.

Another letter of the same period also indicates that Einstein, although critical of much that was happening in the Soviet Union, would not allow his name to be used for any anti-Soviet action which might further increase the existing danger to international peace. In the summer of 1947, Louis Fischer, journalist and author, asked Einstein to issue a public recommendation of his forthcoming book on Gandhi and Stalin. Einstein declined in a letter mailed to Fischer in July 1947:

I have read your book with real interest and feel that the confrontation of Gandhi and Stalin is quite effective. Similarly, I am convinced that your critique of Stalin and the present regime in Russia is justified to a large extent, as is also your suggestion that the Western nations become more self-critical.

On the other hand, I tend to believe that your criticism fails to recognize that the situation in Russia, for internal and external reasons, has been considerably more difficult than conditions in India, which, it should not be forgotten, was confronted with a relatively fair opponent. I also feel that your book is written in a way that is bound further to aggravate the phobia against the Soviet Union; this phobia is anyhow a threat to world peace. An uncritical reader of your volume may become confirmed in his belief that Russia must be suppressed through the intervention of outside forces. I am sure that this is not what you believe yourself; yet, what matters is not only whether a statement is truthful but also at what time such a statement is made public. This is why I cannot assume the responsibility of publicly recommending your otherwise valuable book.

On the occasion of a dinner given for the members of the Security Council and the General Assembly of the United Nations on November 11, 1947, in New York, the Foreign Press Association presented

Einstein with an award for his work in connection with the Emergency Committee of Atomic Scientists. A fellow trustee on the Emergency Committee, Thorfin R. Hogness, came from Chicago to receive the award for Einstein. Senator Warren Austin, Sir Hartley Shawcross and Andrei Vishinsky spoke, and Einstein broadcast the following address from Princeton: [17]

I am most grateful for the award you have conferred upon me and for this appreciation of my modest efforts in a great cause. If my satisfaction is somewhat tempered, it is due to an awareness of the grave and menacing situation in our world which has become a closely knit community facing a common destiny. We all know this; yet how few among us act accordingly. Most people have lost courage and just continue to live their everyday lives; whether frightened or indifferent, they passively observe the ghastly tragicomedy which is being played, for all to see, on the international stage where, under bright lights, actors perform their appointed roles. This is the stage on which the life and death of nations, including our own, is being determined.

It would be another matter if the danger that threatens every one of us were not created by man, who himself has constructed the atomic bomb and other means of mass destruction. It would be another matter if, for example, the world were threatened by a plague. In such an event, conscientious experts would be assembled to devise a sensible plan to combat the epidemic. Once they had agreed upon the proper approach, they would submit their plan to the various governments. The governments would hardly be expected to raise any serious objections and would be able to agree upon the specific measures to be taken. It would certainly never occur to them to attempt to spare their own particular nation while allowing the others to be decimated.

Is our own situation not analogous to the threat of plague? Yet, blinded by passion, people seem unable to recognize the real character of the situation. General fear and anxiety continue to breed hate and engender acts of hate and aggression. The fact that men have become accustomed to war preparations has so corrupted their mentality that objective and humane thinking becomes a virtual impossibility; such thinking will even be regarded as suspect and will be suppressed as unpatriotic.

No doubt, in the opposite camp there are enough people with

sound judgment and a sense of justice who, given the opportunity, would be eager and able to help devise a solution to our very real difficulties. But these people find it hard to engage in such efforts since they have been prevented from meeting with us for informal discussion. I refer, of course, to those people who are used to approaching problems objectively and, hence, are not subject to extreme nationalism and other passions. I consider this enforced isolation of like-minded individuals in both camps one of the main obstacles to finding an acceptable solution of the burning problem of international security.

So long as contact between the two camps is limited to official negotiations, I see little prospect of reaching an intelligent agreement on disarmament. Considerations of personal and national prestige, and the inevitable temptation to harangue the masses of the people, make real progress all but impossible. For these reasons alone, proposals offered by one side are immediately regarded as suspect by the other, if not altogether unacceptable; and back of all official negotiations there is always, even if carefully disguised, the threat of naked power.

The official approach will be successful only after prior discussions of an informal character at which the opposing sides had become convinced of the possibility of reaching a mutually satisfactory solution.

We scientists believe that what we and our fellow men do or fail to do within the next few years will determine the fate of our civilization. We, therefore, consider it our task ceaselessly to spread the truth, to make people aware of what is at stake, and to work not for a policy of appeasement but for understanding and ultimate agreement between peoples and nations.

I like to believe that the foreign journalists working in this country, in conferring the award upon a scientist, were influenced by considerations similar to those which I have just expressed. I hope they may help in gaining general acceptance for that point of view.

While Einstein frequently emphasized the contribution which scientists should have made during the crucial years after the war, he nevertheless rejected the suggestion that the responsibility of the scientist differs from that of any other man. If it were correct that the scientist carried a larger measure of responsibility for political or social events because his research had led to dangerous discoveries such as the atomic bomb, then Newton was also "responsible" because he formulated the law of gravitation; and philologists, by advancing the development of languages, were "responsible" for Hitler's speeches. Certainly, the fear that scientific discoveries might be used for destructive purposes should not in any way induce scientists to abstain from research.

For a student rally in Cleveland, scheduled for Armistice Day, 1947, Einstein recorded this message: [18]

I am very thankful to you for the fact that you are about to engage in energetic public action for the cause of world government. The vital importance of this problem has not as yet been sufficiently recognized by the voters of this country, although considerable progress has been made.

Why do we need a world government? Why do we need it in the near future if unspeakable disaster for all is to be avoided? The answer is: Because technological developments have created a situation in which no corner of the planet is safe from sudden destruction, we must succeed soon and decisively in putting an end to the present state of international anarchy. Modern technology favors the aggressor nation and has rendered ineffective any defense based on national armament. Hence the state of growing nervousness which has been manifest in all international negotiations.

However, even the recognition of the danger does not necessarily mean that adequate action will be taken to remedy the situation. Instead, fear may develop, and fear can lead to acts of hostility.

One may ask: Can we not simply leave the urgent solution of the problem of security in the hands of our government? No, we cannot. A democratic government can make important and fateful decisions only when it knows that it has the unqualified support of the majority of the people. Without strong enlightened popular support, the great and crucial task of creating a supranational authority, based on law, cannot be accomplished.

I am convinced that such a potentially strong will exists among the people all over the world. This will must find expression through an appropriate organization in order to become effective in the political life of the various nations. This is the important and urgent task before you and before all of us.

We should also be conscious of the fact that the citizens of our own nation have a particularly heavy responsibility. It so happens that this nation enjoys a temporary technical and military superiority over other nations. This is why the initiative for the creation of an effective supranational organization must originate in this country. The initiative we are to take must be of such a nature that other nations will become convinced that our efforts are characterized by our concern for the welfare of the larger world community we wish to establish. We must be careful to avoid the suspicion that we intend to pursue a policy of politics based on narrow national self-interest. For progress in human affairs will never be permanent unless it is based on confidence and co-operation.

If your efforts are imbued with this spirit, they cannot fail to be successful.

When Einstein, in his speech to the Foreign Press Association in New York, mentioned the need for "informal discussion and exchange," he was probably thinking of the plan for an international meeting of scientists which had been suggested by Leo Szilard and was then under consideration by the Emergency Committee of Atomic Scientists. Professor Harrison Brown, who was a trustee and the executive Vice-Chairman, of the Emergency Committee, described the project in the following statement: [19]

. . . The plan was initiated by the Emergency Committee of Atomic Scientists in the late fall of 1947. The hope was that we might have an "East-West" conference of scientists to discuss problems of atomic-energy control. This would have been completely extragovernmental, and our decision to attempt to have it was stimulated by the collapse of the atomic-energy negotiations within the United Nations. Preliminary letters were sent to scientists in France, the United Kingdom and the United States, and these were met with considerable enthusiasm. On the basis of this I was asked to approach the Russians. We decided that there would be no point in having such a conference unless Soviet scientists were permitted to participate. We decided to have the conference on the island of Jamaica for the reason that the question of visas would be in British hands and the American participants would require no passports. Einstein approved thoroughly and had agreed to make the journey to Jamaica to participate himself, provided that boat transportation could be secured for him.

I wrote to Secretary of State Marshall, apprising him of the plan. No reply was received from him. I made contact with Mr. Gromyko at the Soviet Delegation headquarters in New York through a Polish attaché at the United Nations who had been approached by Leo Szilard. Mr. Gromyko seemed quite receptive to the idea and relayed the request to the Soviet Union. Two weeks later I was asked by Mr. Gromyko to come to see him, which I did, this time accompanied by a well-known lawyer, Mr. Fowler Hamilton. Mr. Gromyko, in a flowery speech, told me that he had contacted the Soviet scientists and that "they did not wish to participate." In view of this refusal, we cancelled the plans for the meeting.

Two years after the publication of his article on "Atomic War or Peace" in the *Atlantic Monthly* (see p. 347), Einstein published a second article in the same magazine on the same subject. Raymond Swing was again the narrator; the article appeared in the November 1947 issue of the magazine: [20]

Since the completion of the first atomic bomb nothing has been accomplished to make the world safer from the threat of war, while much has been done to increase the destructiveness of war. I am not able to speak from any first-hand knowledge about the development of the atomic bomb since I do not work in this field; but enough has been said by those who do to indicate that the bomb has been made more effective. Certainly, one can envisage the possibility of building a bomb of far greater size, capable of causing destruction over a larger area than heretofore. It is also possible that extensive use could be made of radioactivated gases which would spread over a wide region, causing heavy loss of life without damage to buildings.

In speculating about the modern technology of war, one must consider even other possibilities than atomic bombs. I am doubtful, however, whether bacteriological warfare, for example, presents dangers comparable to those of atomic warfare. Nor do I feel one needs take into account the danger that a chain reaction may be started great enough to destroy part or all of this planet. I dismiss this possibility since, if such a chain reaction could be produced by a man-made atomic explosion, it would already have occurred from the action of cosmic rays which are continually reaching the earth's surface.

But it is not necessary to imagine that the earth may be destroyed like a nova by a stellar explosion to understand fully the growing peril of atomic war and to recognize that another war, should it not be prevented, is likely to cause destruction on a scale never before held possible and, even now, virtually inconceivable, and that not much of the existing civilization would survive it.

In the first two years of the atomic era another phenomenon could be recognized. Although the public has been warned of the horrible nature of atomic warfare, it has done nothing about it and has largely dismissed from its consciousness the existing danger. It is possible that people feel that a danger that cannot be averted or against which every possible precaution has been taken had better be forgotten. . . . I should say, parenthetically, it may be a good thing that this country actually has not taken such precautions; to have done so could have made atomic war more probable since it might convince the rest of the world that we are resigned to it and are preparing for it. On the other hand, nothing has been done to avert war, while much has been done to make atomic war even more horrible than it already was in 1945; there is no excuse, therefore, to ignore the existing great danger.

Let me repeat that nothing has been done to avert war since the completion of the atomic bomb. Despite the proposal for supranational control of atomic energy submitted by the United States to the United Nations, this country has made only a conditional proposition, and this on terms which the Soviet Union is determined not to accept. This has made it possible to blame the failure on the Russians.

But in blaming the Russians, the Americans should not ignore the fact that they themselves have failed to renounce the use of the bomb as a war weapon prior to the achievement of supranational control, and that they will continue to refuse to renounce it if supranational control is not achieved. Thus they have fed the fear of other countries who believe that they, the Americans, will consider the bomb a legitimate part of their arsenal so long as other countries decline to accept the American terms for supranational control.

Americans may be convinced of their determination not to launch an aggressive or preventive war and, therefore, may consider it superfluous publicly to announce that they will not again be the first to use the atomic bomb. But this country has been solemnly urged to renounce the use of the bomb—that is, to outlaw it—and has declined to do so unless the American terms for supranational control are accepted.

I believe that such a policy is a mistake. I realize that there might be a certain military advantage in not renouncing the use of the bomb in that it might be felt that the possession of the bomb by the United States may restrain another country from starting a war in which the United States could possibly use the bomb. But what is gained in one way is lost in another. For by pursuing such a policy, the possibility of reaching an agreement with regard to supranational control of atomic energy is made that much more remote. This may be no military drawback so long as the United States has the exclusive use of the bomb; but the moment another country is able to make atomic bombs in substantial quantities, the United States stands to lose greatly through the absence of an international agreement because of the vulnerability of its concentrated industries and its highly developed urban life.

In refusing to outlaw the bomb while having the monopoly of it, this country suffers in another respect; it demonstrates its failure to return to the ethical standards of warfare which, prior to the last war, were formally recognized. It should not be forgotten that the atomic bomb was produced in this country as a preventive measure to head off its use by the Germans in the event that they might discover it before the end of the war. The policy of bombing civilian centers was initiated by the Germans and adopted by the Japanese. The Allies who responded in kind—and, as it turned out, with greater effectiveness—were morally justified in doing so. But now, without any provocation and without the justification of wanting to have it available for reprisal or retaliation, the refusal of the United States to outlaw the bomb (except for use in retaliation in case of an attack by bombs) is making political capital of its possession. This is hardly justifiable.

I am not saying that the United States should not manufacture and stockpile the bomb, for I believe that it must do so; it must be able, by having bombs itself, to deter other nations from making an atomic attack. But deterrence should be the only purpose of stockpiling bombs. Similarly, I believe that the United Nations should have atomic bombs as soon as it has armed forces and weapons of its own. But it, too, should have the bomb for the sole purpose of deterring an aggressor or preventing a rebellious nation from making an atomic attack. The United Nations should no more use the bomb on its own initiative than the United States or any other country. To maintain a stockpile of atomic bombs and not promise never to initiate its use is to exploit the possession of the bombs for political purposes. It is possible that the United States hopes that this attitude will frighten the Soviet Union into accepting supranational control of atomic energy. But the creation of such fears will only enhance the existing antagonisms and increase the danger of war. I am of the opinion that American policy has ignored the very real virtue of achieving supranational control of atomic energy.

We have emerged from a war in which we had to accept the degradingly low ethical standards of the enemy. But now, instead of feeling liberated from his standards and of feeling free to restore the sanctity of human life and the safety of noncombatants, we are, in effect, making the low standards of the enemy in the last war our own. Thus we are heading in the direction of another war whose standards will be degraded by our own actions.

It may be that the public is not fully aware that, in any future war, atomic bombs will be available in large quantities. The danger created by atomic bombs may be measured by referring to the havoc caused by the three bombs exploded before the end of the last war. The public may also fail to appreciate that, with regard to the damage inflicted in war, atomic bombs have become the most economical form of destruction that can be used on the offensive. If there is another war, bombs will be plentiful and comparatively cheap. Unless the determination not to use atomic bombs is far stronger than can today be noted among American political and military leaders, and on the part of the public itself, atomic warfare will be hard to avoid. Unless Americans come to recognize that they are not stronger because they have the bomb but, rather, have become weaker due to their vulnerability to atomic attack, they are not likely to conduct their policy at Lake

Success [temporary headquarters of the United Nations] or in their relations with Russia in a spirit that furthers understanding.

But I do not mean to suggest that America's failure to outlaw the use of the bomb, except for the purpose of retaliation, has been the sole impediment to reaching an agreement with the Soviet Union over atomic control. For the Russians have made it clear that they will do everything in their power to prevent a supranational government from coming into existence. They not only reject a supranational government in the realm of atomic energy; they reject it sharply in principle. Thus they have spurned in advance any overture which might be made to join a limited world government.

Mr. Gromyko has correctly stated that the essence of the American proposition with regard to atomic weapons is the concept that national sovereignty is not compatible with the atomic era. He declares that the Soviet Union cannot accept this thesis. The reasons given by him are obscure, for they quite obviously are pretexts. But it seems to be true that the Soviet leaders believe they cannot preserve the social structure of the Soviet state within the context of a supranational regime; and the Soviet government is determined to maintain its present social structure.

The Russians may be partly right about the difficulty of retaining their present social structure within the framework of a supranational regime although they may come to realize in time that such a regime is much preferable to remaining outside a world governed by law. But at present they appear to be motivated only by their fears, and one must admit that the United States has greatly contributed to these fears, not only with regard to atomic energy but in many other respects. Indeed, this country has conducted its Russian policy as though it were convinced that fear is the greatest of all diplomatic instruments.

However, the fact that the Russians are striving to prevent the formation of a supranational security system is no reason why the rest of the world should not try to create one. It has been pointed out that the Russians have a powerful and ingenious way of resisting what they do not wish to happen; but once it happens, they can be flexible and accommodate themselves to it. Therefore, it would be well for the United States and other powers not to create a situation which would allow the Russians to veto any attempt toward creating supranational security. They can then proceed with some hope that, once the Russians see they cannot prevent such a regime, they may join it.

Thus far the United States has shown no interest in the security of the Soviet Union. The United States has been interested in her own security, which is characteristic of the struggle for power among sovereign states. But one cannot know in advance what would be the effect on Russia's fears if the American people were to force their leaders to pursue a policy of law in place of the present policy of anarchy in international relations. In a world of law, Russia's security would be equal to our own; and for the American people to endorse this concept wholeheartedly—something that should be possible in a democracy—might work a kind of miraculous change in Russia's thinking.

At present, the Russians have no reason to believe that the American people are not actually supporting a policy of military preparedness, which they regard as a policy of deliberate intimidation. If the Russians would become convinced of a passionate desire on the part of Americans to preserve peace in the one way it can be maintained, namely, by a supranational regime of law, this would undoubtedly help revise Russian calculations about the peril to Russian security resulting from American preparations and intentions. Not until a genuine, convincing offer is made by the United States to the Soviet Union, supported by an aroused American public, will one be entitled to be hopeful about a possible response by Russia.

It may be that the first Russian response would be to reject the world of law. But if, with the passage of time, it became clear to the Russians that such a world was coming into existence without them, and that their own security would be increased by becoming a part of the new organization, their ideas necessarily would change.

I am in favor of inviting the Russians to join a world government authorized to provide security and, if they are unwilling to join, of proceeding to establish supranational security without them. Let me admit immediately that I consider such a course dangerous. If it is adopted, nevertheless, it must be done in such a way as to make it utterly clear that the new regime is not a coalition against

Russia. It must be an organization which, by its composite nature, will greatly reduce the chances of war. It will be more diverse in its interests than any individual state and, therefore, less likely to resort to aggressive or preventive war. Similarly, it will be larger, hence stronger, than any individual nation. It will be geographically much more extensive and thus more difficult to defeat by military means. It will be dedicated to supranational security and will hence be hostile to the concept of national supremacy, which is such a strong factor in fomenting wars.

If a supranational regime is set up without the participation of Russia, its service to peace will depend on the skill and sincerity with which it functions. The desire to have Russia become a part of the regime should, at all times, be manifest and should always be emphasized. It must be clear to Russia, as well as the nations comprising the organization, that no penalty will be incurred when a nation decides not to join it. If Russia does not join at the outset, she must be assured of being welcome if and when she decides to join. Those who create the organization must understand that they are building with the final objective of obtaining Russia's participation.

These observations are necessarily abstract; it is not easy to outline the specific policies which a partial world government must pursue to induce Russia to join. But two prerequisites to her participation seem obvious: The new organization must have no military secrets, and Russia must be free to have observers at every session of the organization when its Constitution is drafted, discussed and adopted, and when its policies are determined. This would demolish the great factory of secrecy where so many of the world's suspicions have been manufactured.

The military-minded person may be shocked by the suggestion of creating a regime that does not maintain any military secrets. He has been taught to believe that important information which is not kept secret might enable a war-minded nation to attempt to conquer the earth. (As to the so-called "secret" of the atomic bomb, I assume that Russia will be able to produce such bombs through her own efforts within a short time.) I admit that there is some risk in not maintaining military secrets. But if a sufficient number of nations pool their resources, they can face such a risk for their security will be greatly increased. And it can be done with greater confidence because of the resultant decline of fear, suspicion and distrust. The tensions created by an ever increasing threat of war in a world based on unlimited sovereignty of individual nations would be replaced by a growing confidence in peace created by the supranational organization. In time, this development might prove so convincing to the Russian people that their leaders would mellow in their attitude toward the West.

Membership in a supranational security system should, in my opinion, not be based on any arbitrary democratic standards. One requirement, however, is necessary: The representatives to the supranational organization—assembly and council—must be elected in each member country by the people themselves through a secret ballot. The elected representatives will hence represent the people and no longer the various governments, which will enhance the pacific nature of the organization.

To require that other democratic criteria be met is, I believe, inadvisable. Democratic institutions and standards are the result of historic developments, and this to an extent not always appreciated in the countries which enjoy such institutions. To decide upon arbitrary standards would only sharpen the ideological differences between the existing systems in the West and the Soviet Union.

But it is not the ideological differences which are now pushing the world in the direction of war. Indeed, if all Western nations were to adopt socialism while at the same time maintaining their national sovereignty, it is quite likely that the conflict of power between East and West would continue to exist. The current passion expressed over economic systems seems to me quite irrational. The question of whether the economic life of America should be dominated by relatively few individuals, as it now is, or whether these individuals should be subject to the control of the state, may be important, but it is not important enough to justify all the passions that are stirred up over this issue.

I should like to see all the nations, which collectively form the supranational security system, pool their military forces, keeping for themselves only a local police force. Then, I should like to see these forces commingled and distributed over the various countries in the same way as the regiments of the former Austro-

Hungarian Empire were formed and used. Then it was appreciated that men and officers coming from one region would serve the purposes of empire better by not being stationed exclusively in their own provinces, which were subject to local and racial bias.

I should like to see the authority of the supranational regime restricted to the field of security although I am not sure as to whether this would be possible. Previous experience may make it desirable to create, in addition, some authority over economic matters since, under modern conditions, economic developments are capable of causing national emergencies which may lead to violent conflicts in capitalist countries. I should like to see the United Nations to be developed into this supranational regime in order to preserve continuity in the search for peace.

I fully recognize the great difficulties involved in establishing a world government, either with or without Russia. I am fully aware of the risks involved. Since I do not believe that it should be permissible for a country, once it has joined the supranational organization, to secede, one of the risks would be the possible outbreak of a civil war. But I also believe that world government is inevitable; the question that remains is: at what price? It will come, I believe, even if there is another world war; however, should it come after such a war, it would be a world government established by the victor, relying on his military power and hence dependent upon the permanent militarization of the human race.

I also believe, however, that world government could come into being through agreement and through the force of persuasion, hence at a low price. But the appeal to reason alone will not be a force sufficient to establish world government. One source of strength of the Communist system in the East is that it has, in some way, the character of a religion and that it inspires emotions similar to those of a religion. Unless the movement for a "peace based on law" gathers the force and zeal of a religious movement, it can hardly hope to succeed. Those who are responsible for the moral education of the human race face a great duty and have a challenging opportunity. The atomic scientists, I believe, have become convinced that they cannot arouse the American people to the truths of the atomic era by logic alone. There must be added the power of deep emotion which is a basic ingredient of religion.

It is to be hoped that not only the churches but the schools, the colleges and the leading organs of public opinion will acquit themselves well of their unique responsibility in this regard.

A month earlier, in the October 1947 issue of the magazine *United Nations World*, Einstein had covered much the same ground in an "Open Letter to the General Assembly of the United Nations": [21]

We are caught in a situation in which every citizen of every country, his children, and his life's work are threatened by the terrible insecurity which reigns in our world today. The progress of technological development has not increased the stability and the welfare of humanity. Because of our inability to solve the problem of international organization, it has actually contributed to the dangers which threaten peace and the very existence of mankind.

The delegates of fifty-five governments, meeting in the Second General Assembly of the United Nations, undoubtedly will be aware of the fact that during the last two years—since the victory over the Axis powers—no appreciable progress has been made either toward the prevention of war or toward agreement in specific fields such as control of atomic energy and economic cooperation in the reconstruction of war-devastated areas.

The United Nations cannot be blamed for these failures. No international organization can be stronger than the constitutional powers given it, or than its component parts want it to be. As a matter of fact, the United Nations is an extremely important and useful institution *provided* the peoples and governments of the world realize that it is merely a transitional system toward the final goal, which is the establishment of a supranational authority vested with sufficient legislative and executive powers to keep the peace. The present impasse lies in the fact that there is no sufficient, reliable supranational authority. Thus the responsible leaders of all governments are obliged to act on the assumption of eventual war. Every step motivated by that assumption contributes to the general fear and distrust and hastens the final catastrophe. However strong national armaments may be, they do not create military security for any nation, nor do they guarantee the maintenance of peace.

There can never be complete agreement on international control and the administration of atomic energy, or on general disarmament, until there is a modification of the traditional concept of national sovereignty. For, as long as atomic energy and armaments are considered a vital part of national security, no nation will give more than lip service to international treaties. Security is indivisible. It can be reached only when necessary guarantees of law and enforcement obtain everywhere, so that military security is no longer the problem of any single state. There is no compromise possible between preparation for war, on the one hand, and preparation of a world society based on law and order on the other.

Every citizen must make up his mind. If he accepts the premise of war, he must reconcile himself to the maintenance of troops in strategic areas like Austria and Korea; to the sending of troops to Greece and Bulgaria; to the accumulation of stockpiles of uranium by whatever means; to universal military training; to the progressive limitation of civil liberties. Above all, he must endure the consequences of military secrecy, which is one of the worst scourges of our time and one of the greatest obstacles to cultural betterment.

If, on the other hand, every citizen realizes that the only guarantee for security and peace in this atomic age is the constant development of a supranational government, then he will do everything in his power to strengthen the United Nations. It seems to me that every reasonable and responsible citizen in the world must know where his choice lies.

Yet the world at large finds itself in a vicious circle since the United Nations powers seem to be incapable of making up their minds on this score. The Eastern and Western blocs each attempt frantically to strengthen their respective power positions. Universal military training, Russian troops in Eastern Europe, United States control over the Pacific islands, even the stiffening colonial policies of the Netherlands, Great Britain and France, atomic and military secrecy—are all part of the old familiar jockeying for position.

The time has come for the United Nations to strengthen its moral authority by bold decisions. First, the authority of the General Assembly must be increased so that the Security Council as well as all other bodies of the United Nations will be subordinated to it. As long as there is a conflict of authority between the

Assembly and the Security Council, the effectiveness of the whole institution will remain necessarily impaired.

Second, the method of representation at the United Nations should be considerably modified. The present method of selection by government appointment does not leave any real freedom to the appointee. Furthermore, selection by governments cannot give the peoples of the world the feeling of being fairly and proportionally represented. The moral authority of the United Nations would be considerably enhanced if the delegates were elected directly by the people. Were they responsible to an electorate, they would have much more freedom to follow their consciences. Thus we could hope for more statesmen and fewer diplomats.

Third, the General Assembly should remain in session throughout the critical period of transition. By staying constantly on the job, the Assembly could fulfill two major tasks: first, it could take the initiative toward the establishment of a supranational order; second, it could take quick and effective steps in all those danger areas (such as currently exist on the Greek border) where peace is threatened.

The Assembly, in view of these high tasks, should not delegate its powers to the Security Council, especially while that body is paralyzed by the shortcomings of the veto provisions. As the only body competent to take the initiative boldly and resolutely, the United Nations must act with utmost speed to create the necessary conditions for international security by laying the foundations for a real world government.

Of course there will be opposition. However, it is by no means certain that the USSR—which is often represented as the main antagonist to the idea of world government—would maintain its opposition if an equitable offer providing for real security were made. Even assuming that Russia is now opposed to the idea of world government, once she becomes convinced that world government is nonetheless in the making her whole attitude may change. She may then insist on only the necessary guarantees of equality before the law so as to avoid finding herself in perennial minority as in the present Security Council.

Nevertheless, we must assume that, despite all efforts, Russia and her allies may still find it advisable to stay out of such a world government. In that case—and only after all efforts have been made in utmost sincerity to obtain the co-operation of Russia and her allies—the other countries would have to proceed alone. It is of the utmost importance that this partial world government be very strong, comprising at least two thirds of the major industrial and economic areas of the world. Such strength in itself would make it possible for the partial world government to abandon military secrecy and all the other practices born of insecurity.

Such a partial world government should make it clear from the beginning that its doors remain wide open to any nonmember—particularly Russia—for participation on the basis of complete equality. In my opinion, the partial world government should accept the presence of observers from nonmember governments at all its meetings and constitutional conventions.

In order to achieve the final aim—which is one world, and not two hostile worlds—such a partial world government must never act as an alliance against the rest of the world. The only real step toward world government is world government itself.

In a world government the ideological differences between the various component parts are of no grave consequence. I am convinced that the present difficulties between the United States and the USSR are not due primarily to ideological differences. Of course, these ideological differences are a contributing element to an already serious tension. But I am convinced that even if the United States and Russia were both capitalist countries—or Communist, or monarchist, for that matter—their rivalries, conflicting interests, and jealousies would result in strains similar to those existing between the two countries today.

The United Nations now, and world government eventually, must serve one single goal—the guarantee of the security, tranquillity and the welfare of all mankind.

Partly in reply to Einstein's Open Letter to the United Nations, the English-language *New Times*, published in Moscow, carried in its issue of November 26, 1947, an Open Letter on "Dr. Einstein's Mistaken Notions," which was signed by Sergei Vavilov, A. N. Frumkin, A. F. Joffe, and A. N. Semyonov, outstanding physicists and chemists as well as members of the Soviet Academy of Sciences: [22]

The celebrated physicist Albert Einstein is famed not only for his scientific discoveries; of late years he has paid much attention to social and political problems. He speaks over the radio and writes in the press. He is associated with a number of public organizations. Time and again he raised his voice in protest against the Nazi barbarians. He is an advocate of enduring peace and has spoken against the threat of a new war, and against the ambition of the militarists to bring American science completely under their control.

Soviet scientists, and the Soviet people in general, are appreciative of the humanitarian spirit which prompts these activities of the scientist, although his position has not always been as consistent and clear-cut as might be desired. However, in some of Einstein's more recent utterances there have been aspects that seem to us not only mistaken but positively prejudicial to the cause of peace which Einstein so warmly espouses.

We feel it our duty to draw attention to this, in order to clarify so important a question as to how most effectively to work for peace. It is from this point of view that the idea of a "world government," which Dr. Einstein has of late been sponsoring, must be considered.

In the motley company of proponents of this idea, besides out-and-out imperialists who are using it as a screen for unlimited expansion, there are quite a number of intellectuals in the capitalist countries who are captivated by the plausibility of the idea, and who do not realize its actual implications. These pacifist and liberal-minded individuals believe that a "world government" would be an effective panacea against the world's evils and a guardian of enduring peace.

The advocates of a "world government" make wide use of the seemingly radical argument that in this atomic age state sovereignty is a relic of the past, that it is, as Spaak, the Belgian delegate, said in the United Nations General Assembly, an "old-fashioned" and even "reactionary" idea. It would be hard to imagine an allegation that is further from the truth.

In the first place the idea of a "world government" and "superstate" are by no means products of the atomic age. They are much older than that. They were mooted, for instance, at the time the League of Nations was formed.

Further, these ideas have never been progressive in these modern times. They are a reflection of the fact that the capitalist monopolies, which dominate the major industrial countries, find their own national boundaries too narrow. They need a world-wide market, world-wide sources of raw materials and world-wide spheres of capitalist investment. Thanks to their domination in political and administrative affairs, the monopoly interests of the big powers are in a position to utilize the machinery of government in their struggle for spheres of influence and their efforts economically and politically to subjugate other countries, to play the master in those countries as freely as in their own.

We know this very well from the past experience of our own country. Under Czarism, Russia, with her reactionary regime, which was servilely accommodating to the interests of capital, with her low-paid labor and vast natural resources, was an alluring morsel to foreign capitalists. French, British, Belgian and German firms battened on our country like birds of prey, earning profits which would have been inconceivable in their own countries. They chained Czarist Russia to the capitalist West with extortionate loans. Supported by funds obtained from foreign banks, the Czarist government brutally repressed the revolutionary movement, retarded the development of Russian science and culture, and instigated Jewish pogroms.

The Great October Socialist Revolution smashed the chains of economic and political dependence that bound our country to the world capitalist monopolies. The Soviet Government made our country for the first time a really free and independent state, promoted the progress of our socialist economy, technology, science and culture at a speed hitherto unwitnessed in history, and turned our country into a reliable bulwark of international peace and security. Our people upheld their country's independence in the civil war, in the struggle against the intervention of a bloc of imperialist states, and in the great battles of the war against the Nazi invaders.

And now the proponents of a "world super-state" are asking us voluntarily to surrender this independence for the sake of a "world government," which is nothing but a flamboyant signboard for the world supremacy of the capitalist monopolies.

It is obviously preposterous to ask of us anything like that. And it is not only with regard to the Soviet Union that such a demand is absurd. After World War II, a number of countries succeeded in breaking away from the imperialist system of oppression and slavery. The peoples of these countries are working to consolidate their economic and political independence, debarring alien interference in their domestic affairs. Further, the rapid spread of the movement for national independence in the colonies and dependencies has awakened the national consciousness of hundreds of millions of people, who do not desire to remain in the status of slaves any longer.

The monopolies of the imperialist countries, having lost a number of profitable spheres of exploitation, and running the risk of losing more, are doing their utmost to deprive the nations that have escaped from their mastery of the state independence which they, the monopolies, find so irksome, and to prevent the genuine liberation of the colonies. With this purpose, the imperialists are resorting to the most diverse methods of military, political, economic and ideological warfare.

It is in accordance with this social behest that the ideologians of imperialism are endeavoring to discredit the very idea of national sovereignty. One of the methods they resort to is the advocacy of pretentious plans for a "world state," which will allegedly do away with imperialism, wars and national enmity, ensure the triumph of universal law, and so on.

The predatory appetites of the imperialist forces that are striving for world supremacy are thus disguised under the garb of a pseudo-progressive idea which appeals to certain intellectuals—scientists, writers and others—in the capitalist countries.

In an open letter which he addressed last September to the United Nations delegations, Dr. Einstein suggested a new scheme for limiting national sovereignty. He recommends that the General Assembly be reconstructed and converted into a permanently functioning world parliament endowed with greater authority than the Security Council, which, Einstein declares (repeating what the henchmen of American diplomacy are asserting day in and day out), is paralyzed by the veto right. The General Assembly, reconstructed in accordance with Dr. Einstein's plan, is to have final powers of decision, and the principle of the unanimity of the Great Powers is to be abandoned.

Einstein suggests that the delegates to the United Nations should be chosen by popular election and not appointed by their governments, as at present. At first glance, this proposal may seem progressive and even radical. Actually, it will in no way improve the existing situation.

Let us picture to ourselves what elections to such a "world parliament" would mean in practice.

A large part of humanity still lives in colonial and dependent countries, dominated by the governors, the troops, and the financial and industrial monopolies of a few imperialist powers. "Popular election" in such countries would in practice mean the appointment of delegates by the colonial administration or the military authorities. One does not have to go far for examples; one need only recall the parody of a referendum in Greece, which was carried out by her royalist-fascist rulers under the protection of British bayonets.

But things would be not much better in the countries where universal suffrage formally exists. In the bourgeois-democratic countries, where capital dominates, the latter resorts to thousands of tricks and devices to turn universal suffrage and freedom of ballot into a farce. Einstein surely knows that in the last Congressional elections in the United States only 39 per cent of the electorate went to the polls; he surely knows that millions of Negroes in the Southern states are virtually deprived of the franchise, or are forced, not infrequently under threat of lynching, to vote for their bitterest enemies, such as the late arch-reactionary and Negrophobe Senator Bilbo.

Poll taxes, special tests and other devices are employed to rob millions of immigrants, migrant workers and poor farmers of the vote. We will not mention the widespread practice of purchasing votes, the role of the reactionary press, that powerful instrument for influencing the masses wielded by millionaire newspaper proprietors, and so forth.

All this shows what popular elections to a world parliament, as suggested by Einstein, would amount to under existing conditions in the capitalist world. Its composition would be no better than the present composition of the General Assembly. It would be a distorted reflection of the real sentiments of the masses, of their desire and hope for lasting peace.

As we know, in the General Assembly and the United Nations committees, the American delegation has a regular voting machine at its disposal, thanks to the fact that the overwhelming majority of the members of the United Nations are dependent on the United States and are compelled to adapt their foreign policy to the requirements of Washington. A number of Latin-American countries, for instance, countries with single-crop agricultural systems, are bound hand and foot to the American monopolies, which determine the prices of their produce. Such being the case, it is not surprising that, under pressure of the American delegation, a mechanical majority has arisen in the General Assembly which votes in obedience to the orders of its virtual masters.

There are cases when American diplomacy finds it preferable to realize certain measures, not through the State Department, but under the flag of the United Nations. Witness the notorious Balkan committee or the commission appointed to observe the elections in Korea. It is with the object of converting the United Nations into a branch of the State Department that the American delegation is forcing through the project for a "Little Assembly," which would in practice replace the Security Council, with its principle of unanimity of the Great Powers that is proving such an obstacle to the realization of imperialist schemes.

Einstein's suggestion would lead to the same result, and thus, far from promoting lasting peace and international co-operation, would only serve as a screen for an offensive against nations which have established regimes that prevent foreign capital from extorting its customary profits. It would further the unbridled expansion of American imperialism and ideologically disarm the nations which insist upon maintaining their independence.

By the irony of fate, Einstein has virtually become a supporter of the schemes and ambitions of the bitterest foes of peace and international co-operation. He has gone so far in this direction as to declare in advance in his open letter that if the Soviet Union refuses to join his newfangled organization, other countries would have every right to go ahead without it, while leaving the door open for eventual Soviet participation in the organization as a member or as an "observer."

Essentially this proposal differs very little from the suggestions of frank advocates of American imperialism, however remote Dr. Einstein may be from them in reality. The sum and substance of these suggestions is that if the United Nations cannot be converted into a weapon of United States policy, into a screen for imperialist schemes and designs, that organization should be wrecked and a new "international" organization formed in its place, without the Soviet Union and the new democracies.

Does Einstein not realize how fatal such plans would be to international security and international co-operation?

We believe that Dr. Einstein has entered a false and dangerous path; he is chasing the mirage of a "world state" in a world where different social, political and economic systems exist. Of course there is no reason why states with different social and economic structures should not co-operate economically and politically, provided that these differences are soberly faced. But Einstein is sponsoring a political fad which plays into the hands of the sworn enemies of sincere international co-operation and enduring peace. The course he is inviting the member states of the United Nations to adopt would lead not to greater international security but to new international complications. It would benefit only the capitalist monopolies, for whom new international complications hold out the promise of more war contracts and more profits.

It is because we so highly esteem Einstein as an eminent scientist and as a man of public spirit who is striving to the best of his ability to promote the cause of peace that we consider it our duty to speak with utter frankness and without diplomatic adornment.

Einstein's reply, which he prepared in December 1947, was published in the February 1948 issue of the *Bulletin of the Atomic Scientists* [22] and was given wide currency by the Emergency Committee of Atomic Scientists:

Four of my Russian colleagues have published a benevolent attack upon me in an open letter carried by *New Times.* I appreciate the effort they have made and I appreciate even more the fact that they have expressed their point of view so candidly and straightforwardly. To act intelligently in human affairs is only possible if an attempt is made to understand the thoughts, motives, and apprehensions of one's opponent so fully that one can see the world through his eyes. All well-meaning people should try to contribute as much as possible to improving such mutual understanding. It is in this spirit that I should like to ask my Russian colleagues, and any other readers, to accept the following answer to their letter. It is the reply of a man who is sincerely trying to find a feasible solution without having the illusion that he himself knows "the truth" or "the right path" to follow. If, in the following, I express my views somewhat dogmatically, I do it only for the sake of clarity and simplicity.

Although your letter, in the main, constitutes an attack upon the nonsocialistic foreign countries, particularly the United States, I believe that behind this aggressive front lies a defensive mental attitude which constitutes an almost unlimited isolationism. This desire to escape into isolationism is not difficult to understand when one realizes what Russia has suffered at the hands of foreign countries during the last three decades—the German invasions with planned mass murder of the civilian population, foreign interventions during the civil war, the systematic campaign of calumnies conducted by the Western press, the West's support of Hitler as an alleged tool to fight Russia. But, however understandable this desire for isolation may be, it constitutes a policy which will prove no less disastrous for Russia than for all other nations; I shall say more about this later on.

The chief object of your attack against me concerns my support of "world government." I should like to discuss this important problem only after having said a few words about the antagonism between socialism and capitalism; for your attitude concerning the significance of this antagonism seems to dominate completely your views on international problems. Considered objectively, the socio-economic problem appears as follows: Technological development has led to increasing centralization of the economic mechanism. This development is also responsible for the fact that in all widely industrialized countries economic power has become concentrated in the hands of relatively few people. These people, in capitalist countries, do not need to account for their actions to the public as a whole; they must, however, do so in socialist countries where they function as civil servants exactly as those who exercise political power.

I share your view that whenever a socialist administration maintains at least halfway adequate administrative standards, a socialist economy possesses advantages that definitely counterbalance its disadvantages. No doubt, the day will come when all nations (insofar as nations, as such, still exist) will be grateful to Russia for having been the first country to demonstrate, despite exceedingly great difficulties, the practicability of a planned socialist economy. I also believe that capitalism, or perhaps we should say the system of private enterprise, will prove unable to check unemployment, which will become increasingly chronic because of technological progress; nor will it be able to maintain a healthy balance between production and the purchasing power of the people.

On the other hand, we should not make the mistake of blaming capitalism for all existing social and political evils, nor of assuming that the very establishment of socialism would be sufficient to cure all the social and political ills of humanity. The danger inherent in such a belief is, first, that it encourages fanatical intolerance on the part of the "faithful," thus turning a feasible form of social organization into a kind of church that brands all those who do not belong to it as traitors or wicked evil-doers. Once this stage has been reached, the ability to understand the actions and convictions of the "unfaithful" vanishes completely. You know, I am sure, from history how much unnecessary suffering has been inflicted upon mankind by those who held such rigid beliefs.

Any government is in itself an evil insofar as it carries within it the tendency to deteriorate into tyranny. However, except for a very small number of anarchists, every one of us is convinced that no civilized form of society can exist without government. In a healthy nation there is a kind of dynamic balance, between the will of the people and the government, which prevents its degeneration into tyranny. It is obvious that the danger of such deterioration is more acute in a country in which the government has authority not only over the armed forces but also over every channel of education and information as well as over the economic existence of every single citizen. I say this merely to indicate that socialism as such cannot be considered as the solution to all social problems but merely as a framework within which such a solution is possible.

What surprises me most in your general attitude, as expressed in your letter, is that you, who are such passionate opponents of anarchy in the economic sphere, with equal passion advocate anarchy, i.e., unlimited sovereignty, in the sphere of international politics. The proposal to curtail the sovereignty of individual states appears to you in itself reprehensible, a kind of violation of a natural right. In addition, you seek to prove that, behind the idea of curtailing sovereignty, the United States is hiding her intention of economic domination and exploitation of the rest of the world without the necessity of going to war. You attempt to justify this indictment by analyzing, in your fashion, certain actions of this government since the end of the last war. You attempt to show that the Assembly of the United Nations is a mere puppet show controlled by the United States and hence by American capitalists.

Such arguments impress me as a kind of mythology; they are not convincing. They make obvious, however, the deep estrangement among the intellectuals of our two countries, which is the result of a regrettable and artificial isolation from one another. If a free exchange of personal views were encouraged and made possible, intellectuals, perhaps more than anyone else, could help to create an atmosphere of mutual understanding between the two nations. Such an atmosphere is a prerequisite to the fruitful development of political co-operation. However, since for the time being we seem to depend on the cumbersome method of "open letters," I should like to indicate briefly my reaction to your arguments.

Nobody would deny that the influence of the economic oligarchy upon all branches of our public life is very powerful. This influence, however, should not be overestimated. Franklin Delano Roosevelt was elected President in spite of the desperate opposition by these very powerful groups, and he was re-elected three times; and this took place at a time when decisions of great consequence had to be made.

Concerning the policies of the American Government since the end of the war, I am neither willing nor qualified to justify or explain them. It cannot be denied, however, that the proposals of the American Government with regard to atomic weapons represented at least an attempt toward the creation of a supranational security organization. If they were not acceptable, they could at least have served as a basis for discussions of a real solution to the problem of international security. It is, indeed, the attitude of the Soviet Government, partly negative and partly dilatory, that has made it so difficult for well-meaning people in this country to use their political influence as they would have wished to, and to oppose the "war-mongers." With regard to the influence of the

United States upon the United Nations Assembly, I wish to say that, in my opinion, it stems not only from the economic and military power of the United States but also from the efforts of the United States and the United Nations to come closer to a genuine solution of the security problem.

Concerning the controversial veto power, I believe that the attempts to eliminate it or to make it ineffective have been caused less by any specific actions of the United States than by the manner in which the veto privilege has been used by the Soviet Union.

Let me come now to your suggestion that the policy of the United States is aimed at obtaining economic domination and exploitation of other nations. Since it is a precarious undertaking to say anything reliable about aims and intentions, let us rather examine the objective factors involved. The United States is fortunate in being able to produce all important industrial products and foods at home in sufficient quantity, and to own the resources for almost all important raw materials. But, because of her tenacious belief in "free enterprise" the United States cannot succeed in keeping the purchasing power of the people in balance with the productive capacity of the country. For these very same reasons, there is a constant danger that unemployment may reach threatening dimensions.

Because of these circumstances, the United States is compelled to emphasize her export trade. Without this trade, she would not be able to keep her productive machinery fully utilized. This condition would not be harmful if exports were balanced by imports of about the same value. Exploitation of foreign nations would then consist in the fact that the labor value of imports would considerably exceed the labor value of exports. However, every effort is being made to avoid such a development of imports since almost every kind of import tends to keep some part of the American productive machinery idle.

This is why foreign countries are not able to pay for the exports from the United States; for in the long run such payment is possible only by means of imports of commodities or services into the United States. Failing this, foreign countries must export gold in payment for their imports, which explains why a large portion of all the gold in the world has come to the United States. On the whole, gold cannot be utilized except for the purchase of foreign commodities, which, for the reasons already stated, is not practicable. There it lies, this gold, carefully protected against theft, a monument to governmental wisdom and to the science of economics! The reasons which I have just indicated make it difficult for me to take very seriously the alleged exploitation of the world by the United States.

However, the situation just described has a serious political facet. The United States, for the reasons indicated, is compelled to ship part of its production abroad. These exports are financed through loans which the United States grants to foreign countries. It is indeed difficult to imagine how these loans can ever be repaid. For all practical purposes, therefore, they must be considered, not as loans, but as gifts which may be used as tools in the arena of power politics. In the light of existing conditions and of what we know about human beings, this, I frankly admit, represents a real danger. Is it not true, however, that we have stumbled into such a state of international affairs that every invention of man's mind and every material good tend to be turned into a weapon and, consequently, become a danger to mankind?

This question brings us to the most important matter, beside which all else appears insignificant indeed. We all know that power politics, sooner or later, will necessarily lead to war, and that war, under present circumstances, would mean the destruction of human beings and material goods on a scale far, far greater than anything that has ever happened in history.

Must our passions and our inherited customs really and inescapably condemn us to destroy one another so thoroughly that there would be nothing left worth conserving? Is it not true that all the controversies and differences of opinion which we have touched upon in our strange exchange of letters are petty and insignificant compared to the objective danger confronting all of us? Should we not do everything in our power to eliminate this danger which threatens all nations alike?

If we persist in holding fast to the concept and practice of unlimited national sovereignty, this can only mean that each country reserves the right to pursue its objectives through the use of force. Under those circumstances, every nation is bound to feel it must prepare for the eventuality of war, which means that each must try with all its might to be militarily superior to every other country. This objective will come to dominate more and more our entire public lives and will poison the minds of our youth long before the catastrophe of war is actually upon us. So long as we retain even a trace of calm reasoning and humanity, we must not tolerate this.

Those considerations alone lead me to advocate the idea of "world government," without any regard to what others may have in mind when they work for the same objective. I advocate world government because I am convinced that there is no other possible way of eliminating the most terrible danger which has ever threatened man. The objective of avoiding total destruction must have priority over any other goal.

I am sure you are convinced that this letter is written with all seriousness and honesty at my command; I trust you will accept it in the same spirit.

In early December 1947 two scientists, a physical chemist and a chemical engineer, addressed a troubled letter to Einstein. Both had taken an active part in a recent meeting of scientists in Princeton (at which the Emergency Committee of Atomic Scientists apparently also participated). They felt that too much time had been wasted at the meeting in futile argument on statements debated many times before. They viewed the conferees as badly frightened, guilt-ridden men who were reluctant to face the moral and political responsibilities of scientists. They took the position that while scientists cannot be held responsible for the evil uses made of their discoveries they must refuse to work on certain developments, including any research on nuclear power. They called on Einstein to lead and participate in an open crusade to that effect. Einstein replied on December 15, 1947: [23]

Needless to say, I fully agree with your basic approach. The only question is whether we can hope that the course you propose will help prevent the threatening disaster.

The discussions held among the physicists at the Princeton Conference did not prove as confused and disappointing as they seemed at first. At the moment, the chief difference of opinion revolves about a question that is indeed hard to answer: Will existing tensions not become further aggravated if we strive now for partial world government without Russia's co-operation? After much hesitation, I am nevertheless in favor of world government even without the participation of the Soviet Union. I believe that the

Russians are more likely to participate when they realize that their opposition which, incidentally, is quite understandable, will not be able to arrest the course of events. Perhaps the fear of being completely isolated may modify their attitude. I must admit, however, that a thoughtful and sincere person might well have an opinion different from my own.

Your proposition concerning the non-participation of scientists in nuclear research contains weaknesses similar to those found in proposals for voluntary disarmament. Disarmament cannot be effective unless all countries participate loyally. If even one nation continues to arm, openly or secretly, the disarmament of the others will involve disastrous consequences. England, France, and the United States had to pay dearly for remaining more or less unarmed from 1925 to 1935; this fact merely served to encourage the arrogance of the Germans. Similarly, your proposition would, if effective, surely lead to a serious weakening of the "democracies." For we must realize that we are probably not able to exert any significant influence on the attitude of our Russian colleagues. Although one might say with some justification that, at present, the Western powers have a military advantage and may hence be more aggressive, one cannot dismiss the *possibility* that a revolutionary step on the part of the Western physicists and engineers, such as suggested by you, might have the effect of driving the Russians into a more aggressive move.

Apart from that, we must first ask ourselves: Would any action by a group as small as the group recently assembled in Princeton have any decisive influence? Would the physicists and engineers necessarily follow our course of action? And assuming they would want to, would they be *free* to do so? To these questions my answer is "no," for the following reasons:

1. Almost all scientists are economically completely dependent.
2. The number of scientists who possess a sense of social responsibility is so small that their "non-participation" would have virtually no effect on the production of armaments.

For these reasons I do not believe that your proposal is, in any sense, practicable; indeed, it is doubtful whether anything of value could be achieved by forcing its adoption.

The following humorous fragment was apparently drafted by Einstein around this time, probably against the background of the exchange of open letters with the Russians and, on the other hand, the Princeton meeting of scientists:

Resolution

We American scientists, after three days of careful consideration, have come to the following conclusions:

We do not know

(a) What to believe;
(b) What to wish for;
(c) What to say; and
(d) What to do.

Appendix

On the basis of an open letter signed by Russian scientists, we may construct a parallel resolution for them:

After careful consideration, and after due consultation with our government, we do know

(a) What not to believe;
(b) What not to wish for;
(c) What not to say; and
(d) What not to do.

On December 29, 1947, Einstein wrote to Otto Lehmann-Russbüldt, one of the leaders of the German peace movement (he was the post-World War I secretary-general of the German League for Human Rights), whose seventy-fifth birthday fell on New Year's Day: [24]

My warmest good wishes for your seventy-fifth! What we have in common with the gods is the futile struggle against stupidity. Where we have the better of them is in that it is given to us to retire honorably one day from the field of battle—and this "retirement" just happens of itself.

Things are going much as they did after 1918, except that there are different actors on the stage. They play as badly as they did then, but the general bankruptcy which threatens will be incomparably worse. Having lost the illusion of free will, one cannot even react in anger.

When you and I arrive in heaven, we shall meet in the haunts of Don Quixote. Meanwhile, good luck!

CHAPTER FOURTEEN

THE STRUGGLE FOR MANKIND'S SURVIVAL | 1948

EINSTEIN'S RELENTLESS EFFORTS for positive action toward the abolition of war reached a certain climax in 1948. It was the last year of America's monopoly in the possession of atomic weapons. It was the year when rumors were rife concerning the possibility of a preventive war, which troubled Einstein deeply and spurred him to assume new responsibilities in the antiwar struggle at home and abroad. It was also the year when he felt compelled to realize that the prospect of achieving speedy and positive results for the movement against war was slim; indeed, that the increasing cold war atmosphere in international relations and the lack of unity among the peace forces at home made concerted and effective action against war more than unlikely. It was a symbolic event that just before the end of the year the Emergency Committee of Atomic Scientists, on which Einstein had served as a devoted chairman, discontinued its work and virtually removed itself from the thinning ranks of fighters against an atomic catastrophe. From now on, Einstein kept more aloof from organizational activities; he seemed a lonely, towering figure even more than before, although no less concerned than he had always been nor less willing to lend his great influence to the cause of peace.

In fact, Einstein had become more articulate in his pronouncements, his position more concise and crystallized on what he believed to be essential and inevitable. He refused more than ever to compromise with what he considered to be the only possible solution of the peace problem: the creation of a genuine world authority. Three statements made in the course of 1948 are perhaps the most characteristic of Einstein's beliefs and feelings in those days: a contribution to a college debaters' handbook on world government, a letter to a Polish scientist refusing support of a plea for international co-operation of scientists, and a letter to the War Resisters' League reaffirming the views which he had held on the subject of individual refusal of military service since 1933.

Einstein's contribution to the college debaters' handbook was prepared in 1948 and entitled "The Fateful Decision." It reads as follows: [1]

This is a time in which men and women are called upon to consider the possibility of the greatest disaster in the history of modern civilization.

All about us we see the wreckage of what were once the great hopes held by mankind for the building of peace. The gulf between East and West, which men of good will have labored to close, is widening daily. Some people voice the belief that no reconciliation is possible and that only another world war can resolve the present conflict. To this, we scientists reply that it is no longer possible to decide any issue by war since atomic warfare can effect no solution but would cause unprecedented death and devastation to both sides.

Times such as ours have always bred defeatism and despair. But there remain, nonetheless, some few among us who believe man has within him the capacity to meet and overcome even the greatest challenges of his time. If we want to avoid defeat, we must wish to know the truth and be courageous enough to act upon it. If we get to know the truth and have courage, we need not despair.

We scientists have ample evidence that the time of decision has come, and that what we do, or fail to do, within the next few years, will determine the fate of our civilization. Man must come to recognize that his fate is linked with that of his fellow men throughout the world. Great ideas have often been expressed in very simple words. In the shadow of the atomic bomb it has become even more apparent that all men are, indeed, brothers. If we recognize and act upon this simple truth, mankind may proceed to a higher level of human development. But should the angry passions of a nationalistic world engulf us any further, we are doomed.

We consider it the task of the scientists to be untiring in their explanation of these truths to the American people that they may understand what is at stake. Equipped with real understanding, the American people will reject war and will want to seek a peaceful solution; they will come to realize that real security in the world can only come through the creation of a supranational body, a government of the world with powers adequate to preserve the peace.

Each of us, whether a scientist who helped make possible the release of atomic energy, or whether a citizen of the nation which first applied that knowledge for war purposes, is responsible for whatever use is made of this tremendous new force in the future: our generation will have to make the most fateful decision in the recorded history of the human race. Our collective determination can ensure that this formidable achievement of man's intellect will, instead of destroying humanity, be utilized for the benefit of future generations. I believe that mankind is capable of reason and courage and will choose the path of peace.

Professor Ignace Zlotowski, a Polish atomic physicist and then a member of the Polish Delegation to the United Nations, submitted to Einstein the draft of an article in which he emphasized the need for close international co-operation among scientists and for international freedom of information in scientific matters. Although Einstein had stood all his life for the closest international co-operation in any field and for unrestricted information in science, he refused to prepare an introduction to the article since he felt it attacked only symptoms of the disease and not the disease itself. Einstein did not want to support recommendations which he was convinced were unfeasible so long as war as such was not abolished. He made his position clear in a letter to Professor Zlotowski dated March 31, 1948:

After careful consideration I do not feel able to write an introduction in support of your article, although I am in complete agreement with many of your ideas. This is the reason for my attitude: I share your view that the restriction of free information in any field of research is a great evil. Such restriction endangers the development of pure and applied science as well as the relations among nations. And this restriction is particularly injurious to the intellectual and economic development of smaller nations.

On the other hand, I am convinced that the restriction of free information is only a symptom of the disease afflicting the world and that this symptom cannot be treated as an isolated phenomenon. So long as nations feel compelled to prepare for war, scientific knowledge and the industrial capacity based thereupon form a part of military preparation, an interrelationship which has not existed in the past to the same extent as it does today. As a consequence, the maintenance of free co-operation and publication in the field of pure and applied science, which is so desirable, can be achieved only if the institution of war and the competitive arms race among nations have been abolished.

In my opinion, this can only be achieved through a supranational organization, a real world government. I am convinced there exists no less radical a solution. However, this crucial problem is not even mentioned in your article, which hence appears to be merely an attack upon the symptoms of war without giving any hope of curing the disease.

I am sure you know how deeply I care about maintaining and encouraging free personal exchange of ideas among scientists and intellectuals of all nations. However, in the present situation, I feel that the main purpose of all such exchanges should be to contribute to the solution of international political problems through a dispassionate discussion of the one existing alternative to war.

In the spring of 1948, Mr. Roy C. Kepler, the Associate Secretary of the War Resisters' League in New York, reminded Einstein of his active participation in the war resisters' movement in the pre-Nazi period. He quoted some of the statements which Einstein had in those days made warmly endorsing the activities of the movement, and asked Einstein to rejoin the movement "in proclaiming the task of war resistance, of nonviolence and world brotherhood." Einstein's reply of August 8, 1948, provides a remarkably concise statement of his basic position: [2]

I can no longer ascertain whether the statement you quoted in your letter was prepared by me in that form for a special occasion or is merely a compilation of various pronouncements made at different times. In any event, it expresses very accurately the views which I held on war resistance in the period from 1918 to the early thirties. Now, however, I feel that the policy I then suggested, concerning the refusal of individuals to participate in war preparations and military activities, is too primitive. These are my reasons:

(1) As long as international anarchy exists and some countries employ forceful means to prevent their citizens from engaging in antimilitaristic activities of any kind, the war resistance movement actually serves to weaken the nations with a more liberal type of government and, indirectly, to support the policies of the existing tyrannical governments. This was particularly true during the pe-

riod of Hitler and Mussolini; to help increase their strength by weakening the defense potential of the democratic countries was all the more unreasonable as the former not only intended to enslave the rest of the world but even to exterminate whole nations.

Antimilitaristic activities, through refusal of military service, are wise only if they are feasible everywhere throughout the world, as was more or less the case in the interwar period, before the advent of Hitler. The situation today with respect to this problem is quite different since, on one hand, individual antimilitarism is impossible in Russia and, on the other hand, the democratic countries have become more aggressive.

(2) I have become convinced that any appeal to individuals to resist the policies of the countries in which they earn their livelihood must necessarily prove ineffectual, except during certain periods of history when the masses are under the influence of a powerful religious hypnosis; only then are many people ready to become martyrs.

(3) For the reasons just mentioned, I now believe that the policy of war resistance does not provide an effective weapon against wars and that a policy directed toward the abolition of international anarchy through the establishment of world government offers greater hope of success. I firmly believe that all responsible men should concentrate their efforts on working toward this goal.

On December 20, 1947, eleven prominent Englishmen declared in a document released in England that all attempts to control atomic energy had been frustrated by the intransigence of the Soviet Union.[3] They felt the peoples of America and Britain would choose war if they had to make the choice between Communism and war. They urged the United States and Great Britain to make one last attempt, at the highest possible level, to secure Soviet participation in a scheme for the control of atomic energy. If the appeal failed, "the freedom-loving powers closely associated with Great Britain and America should act in concert. They should together develop such a predominance of defensive strength, including atomic strength, that no power would dare to challenge them." Among the signers were Bertrand Russell, T. S. Eliot, Lady Violet Bonham Carter, Lord Vansittart and the Reverend Gordon Lang. Lang, a Labor Member of the House of Commons, was the chairman of the Crusade for World Government (see p. 420), an organization in which Einstein was deeply interested.

By cable, Einstein advised Lang of his disagreement with the statement, a dissatisfaction which was also shared by Henry Usborne, the principal driving force behind the Crusade for World Government. Usborne wrote Einstein at length about his disappointment at the statement and particularly at Lang for signing it apparently without consulting his colleagues. While Usborne and the other members of the Crusade considered a world federation the only solution to the danger confronting humanity, Gordon Lang and some of his friends had begun to sympathize with the idea of a European federation. Einstein apparently felt that the controversy should be brought to the attention of the Emergency Committee of Atomic Scientists, which, as was indicated before, had expressed its interest in Usborne's plan. However, since the committee's trustees were not scheduled to meet for several weeks, Einstein emphasized that the views expressed in a letter to Usborne of January 9, 1948, merely represented his personal opinions. The letter is an important document inasmuch as it provides a particularly clear statement of Einstein's position:

1. I believe that the statement issued by Gordon Lang, Lord Vansittart, etc., is harmful indeed and that a statement opposing it is necessary. (It seems that Bertrand Russell's signature was not authorized by him.)

2. I agree with what Cord Meyer [in an article, "Peace Is Still Possible," in *The Atlantic Monthly*, October 1947] says about the Baruch proposals. It is not feasible to abolish one single weapon as long as war itself is not abolished. This can be done only by establishing effective world government.

3. The Russians would have been justified in their rejection of the Baruch proposals had they explained their rejection by genuine considerations and had it been accompanied by constructive and reasonable proposals of their own. Their actual counterproposal of general disarmament without supranational control cannot be taken seriously; and they must have known this.

4. It has become clear to me that the Soviets will categorically reject any supranational institution which would involve inspection of their country by foreigners or which would impose any limitations on their sovereignty. They will adhere to this position as long as they have any hope that this policy may successfully prevent the establishment of an effective supranational organization. This is manifest, for example, in the Open Letter addressed to me by four Russian scientists and recently published in the magazine

New Times [see p. 443]. This Open Letter must be regarded as a semiofficial statement.

5. The following difficult question remains: How can one work vigorously for world government without creating the risk that the result will be a coalition directed against Soviet Russia? It is precisely this question that makes it so difficult for the atomic scientists in this country to reach agreement on a specific and immediate policy.

6. Nevertheless, I myself believe that we should take a vigorous position in favor of world government, even at the risk of temporarily driving Soviet Russia into self-imposed isolation; and, naturally, everything should be done in such a way as to make it easy and attractive for the Russians to change their isolationist attitude. I believe that if this were done intelligently (rather than in clumsy Truman style!), Russia would co-operate once she realized that she was no longer able to prevent world government anyhow.

7. Matters would be considerably simplified if the United States were to adopt an unequivocal and unwavering position in favor of a supranational solution of the security problem. I believe that, in this connection, some criticism from the other side of the Atlantic, especially from England, would prove useful.

You may quote everything I have said in this letter, providing it is made clear that I am speaking only as an individual.

As a result of the controversy created by the statement he had signed, Lang was not re-elected chairman of the Crusade for World Government. Einstein was able to convince the Emergency Committee of Atomic Scientists to continue their support of the Peoples' World Convention movement, as will be shown later in this chapter.

Universal Military Training had by this time become a major political issue in the United States. Einstein was a supporter of the National Council against Conscription and, with twenty other prominent Americans, subscribed to the following statement on "Militarism and Civilization" that served as an introduction to the council's pamphlet, "The Militarization of America," published in January 1948: [4]

Arnold J. Toynbee in his monumental *Study of History* points out that militarism "has been by far the commonest cause of the breakdown of civilizations." The present trend toward military control over American life and institutions should, therefore, be of the deepest concern to every patriotic American. It would be fatuous and suicidal for us to assume that we can adopt ways which have corrupted and destroyed other civilizations, and that we can ourselves escape the same fate.

Militarism leads both to war and to loss of freedom. And there are subtle as well as obvious dangers to a nation which yields its civil functions to military control. The spirit of initiative and inquiry may be sapped even where some of the external trappings of regimentation do not appear. If, for example, the right to differ from the military is not vigorously exercised because of the increased prestige of military men, the theoretical or formal existence of the right will not profit or save our free society.

Because of our deep conviction that America cannot remain democratic if the present trend toward military control of our institutions continues, we join in issuing this report and recommending it for most serious study by our fellow citizens. In listing these numerous illustrations of the expanding influence of the military in America we do not necessarily imply that each of us would be opposed to every activity herein described; but what might be approved or overlooked as an isolated activity cannot be ignored when seen as part of a basically dangerous pattern.

A much-traveled army officer and American Legion official, who had retired to a California ranch, challenged Einstein's opposition to conscription and asked him, in flawless German, to develop his views in greater detail. Einstein replied on January 28, 1948: [5]

Your excellent German encourages me to answer you in the only language in which I feel truly at home.

It is, of course, correct to say that the United States was inadequately armed when she found herself compelled to intervene in the last two great wars; and I am not of the opinion that America should disarm completely in the present circumstances. As a matter of fact, this is not at all likely to happen. On the contrary, I believe the danger lies at present in the possibility that America may totally succumb to that fearful militarization which engulfed Germany half a century ago. Even now, there is real danger that the political power and the power to influence the minds of people will increasingly pass into the hands of the military, which is used to approaching all political problems from the point of view of military expediency. Because of America's present supremacy, the military point of view is forced upon the rest of the world. We should never forget that it is totally unlikely that any country will attack America in the near future, least of all Russia, which is devastated, impoverished and politically isolated.

As far as conscription is concerned, it seems to me totally unjustified at this time, even from a military point of view. Technological developments are such that, in the future, mere manpower will play an increasingly smaller role, as compared to material and machines. Such a situation does not demand a regular but a professional army, composed in the main of technicians. Anyone who has kept in touch with events in Germany knows how profoundly the military drill corrupted the sound political instincts of the people. There is no more effective way of destroying the democratic mentality.

I must, in conclusion, point out that the only hope for a decent future lies in a supranational solution of the security problem. War with atomic bombs and bacteriological weapons means universal annihilation. Since militarization creates a tendency to decide all problems against the background of a possible war and to indoctrinate the people accordingly, it engenders a mentality that makes impossible the only possible solution.

Einstein was among those whose views on Universal Military Training were solicited by Chan Gurney, U. S. Senator from South Dakota and Chairman of the Senate Committee on Armed Services. Einstein's formal statement is dated March 18, 1948, and was read into the *Congressional Record* on March 24, 1948: [6]

I should consider the introduction of compulsory military training necessary and justified only if there existed a threat of hostile invasion into the territory of the United States in the near future. I am convinced that no such threat exists.

I am further convinced that Universal Military Training would be harmful to the welfare and security of our own nation as well as that of the rest of the world; and this for the following reasons:

(a) It would merely tend to accelerate the arms race, increase the tension between the United States and the Soviet Union, and further intensify the danger of war.

(b) It would tend to undermine the democratic spirit of this nation and strengthen and consolidate the influence of the military, which is already perilously strong.

(c) It would impose a heavy and unnecessary economic burden upon the nation by shifting a large part of our productive and human capacity into unproductive channels.

(d) It would inevitably generate that militaristic spirit among the people which, in the past, has become so fatal to many nations.

Eight months after Communism had come to power in Hungary, a Hungarian radio commentator, preparing a talk on what he called "the *rapprochement* between man and man," posed a series of questions which Einstein answered on February 4, 1948.[7] Besides reiterating his belief in the necessity of world government, Einstein said that, as long as adequate measures of war prevention were not adopted, human nature, being what it is, might possibly always tend toward war. Such prevention, he said, would be possible only if the people everywhere were determined to take the necessary steps. Through close co-operation with one another, the smaller countries could effectively contribute to the solution of the security problem, since their governments were not as much exposed to the inducements of imperialist power politics as are the big powers. True peace, Einstein added, cannot be enforced by armaments; this would be tyranny, not peace. There was no doubt that civilization would not survive a new world war; even the preparations for such a war would destroy civilization.

On January 30, 1948, Gandhi, India's great leader for whom Einstein had long felt a deep affection, was assassinated. On February 11, 1948, Einstein issued the following statement for a memorial service in Washington:[8]

Everyone concerned with a better future for mankind must be deeply moved by the tragic death of Gandhi. He died a victim of his own principle, the principle of nonviolence. He died because, in a time of disorder and general unrest in his country, he refused any personal armed protection. It was his unshakable belief that the use of force is an evil in itself, to be shunned by those who strive for absolute justice.

To this faith he devoted his whole life, and with this faith in his heart and mind he led a great nation to its liberation. He demonstrated that the allegiance of men can be won, not merely by the cunning game of political fraud and trickery, but through the living example of a morally exalted way of life.

The veneration in which Gandhi has been held throughout the world rests on the recognition, for the most part unconscious, that in our age of moral decay he was the only statesman who represented that higher conception of human relations in the political sphere to which we must aspire with all our powers. We must learn the difficult lesson that the future of mankind will only be tolerable when our course, in world affairs as in all other matters, is based upon justice and law rather than the threat of naked power, as has been true so far.

Paul Freiherr von Schoenaich, German ex-general, a veteran of the pre-Hitler German peace movement who, after the defeat of Germany, had become president of the revived German Peace Society, wrote Einstein that he had seen his letter to Lehmann-Russbüldt (see p. 457) as well as his Sacco-Vanzetti statement (see p. 424). Schoenaich, recalling with pride the times when he fought shoulder to shoulder with Einstein, asked for guidance on the East-West conflict. Einstein wrote him on February 18, 1948:

The problem of peace and security is indeed far more important than the conflict between socialism and capitalism. Man must first ensure his survival; only then can he ask himself what type of existence he prefers. I fully agree with you that no sincere individual could unconditionally endorse either of the two camps, East or West. The struggle for power is equally repulsive, conducted as it is, both here and there, with the traditional dishonesty of the political craft.

To a correspondent who sharply criticized Einstein's answer to the Soviet scientists charging that he uncritically accepted liberal views and failed to understand the conflict and antagonism between capitalism and socialism, Einstein wrote on March 8, 1948: [9]

I indeed fully agree with your critical remarks with respect to America's foreign policy since the death of Roosevelt. Your criticisms of the liberal viewpoint, however, are less convincing. The meaning of the term *liberal* has become so watered down as to cover the most diverse views and attitudes. Your criticism should not be directed, for example, against Henry Wallace, who is, without doubt, a liberal. On the other hand, when you speak of socialism, it really seems to me that socialism, as I understand it, does not exist anywhere today.

You say that socialism by its very nature rejects the remedy of war. I do not believe that. I can easily imagine that two socialist states might fight a war against each other.

I know very well that a world government may have both good and bad qualities. Nonetheless, it is the only conceivable machinery which can prevent war. I do not believe that a world government would be just in all its decisions; but with technology at its present level, even a poor world government is preferable to none, since our first goal must be to avoid total destruction through war.

I am far from blaming the Soviet Union for the injustices and barbarism of our age. But I am convinced of one thing: If you knew the Soviet Union as well as you do know the United States, you would be no less bitter in your judgment of conditions there than you now are about conditions in this country. What you do not eat does not taste bitter. . . .

Henry Wallace was the author of a book, *Toward World Peace*, scheduled for publication on April 15, 1948. In a statement made public on March 29, 1948, by the National Wallace for President Committee, Einstein had this to say about the book: [10]

This book is as clear, honest and unassuming as its author. If you read it carefully, with detachment and without prejudice, you will have to agree with its fundamental premises—at least that is the only way I can see it. Only men who are above the petty bickering of the day and above selfish interests can save us from the threatening domestic and international situation: Roosevelt and Willkie were such men, and such a man is Henry Wallace.

A New York correspondent approached Einstein (and a number of other prominent persons) with a plan for forming a broad membership organization to combat war hysteria. Einstein replied on March 29, 1948:

Your attempt meets a real need and I am wholeheartedly in favor of it, provided you are able to rally behind it enough people of genuine good will and sufficient influence. It would be important to mobilize people who have not expressed a position in this matter as often as I have. With your kind permission, I shall inform the Emergency Committee of Atomic Scientists about it; I should be obliged if you would inform me whether your meritorious attempt is making headway. To be effective, your appeal to the public must take a courageous stand with regard to the important controversial issues of the moment: Universal Military Training, the draft, the retention of civilian control of atomic energy, as well as a clear exposition of the fact that Russia is not alone responsible for the precarious and dangerous international political situation.

On April 11, 1948, the Emergency Committee of Atomic Scientists issued a third major policy statement, in which it endorsed the concept of world government. The statement represented a compromise among divergent viewpoints, and there is reason to believe that Einstein may have wanted it to be more far-reaching. However, he signed it, as did all his eleven fellow trustees: [11]

I

Two years ago this month the United Nations Atomic Energy Commission was in process of formation. Today, the discussions on international control of atomic energy are about to be adjourned indefinitely, perhaps never again to be resumed. One of the most fateful events in history has passed almost unnoticed. Its importance must be realized: its lesson for mankind must be made clear.

To clarify the importance of the collapse of these discussions, we reiterate here our Six Point Statement published originally on November 17, 1946:

1. Atomic bombs can now be made cheaply and in large number. They will become more destructive.

2. There is no military defense against atomic bombs and none is to be expected.

3. Other nations can rediscover our secret processes by themselves.

4. Preparedness against atomic war is futile and, if attempted, will ruin the structure of our social order.

5. If war breaks out, atomic bombs will be used and they will surely destroy our civilization.

6. There is no solution to this problem except international control of atomic energy and, ultimately, the elimination of war.

Every scientific development in the intervening seventeen months has supported the accuracy of this statement. Yet the negotiations by which international control of atomic energy was to be achieved have collapsed.

II

This is a time for taking stock of reality and facing up to the facts. The most salient fact confronting our civilization is that the hope of One World is frustrated: today two hostile worlds are in full contest, the Eastern bloc headed by the Soviet Union confronts the Western democracies.

Three possible lines of policy are emerging in the West:

1. The first policy is that of preventive war. It calls for an attack upon the potential enemy at a time and place of our own choosing, while the United States retains the monopoly of the atomic bomb. Let us not delude ourselves that victory in such a war would be cheap and easy. At the outset the Russians would occupy all of Europe up to the Atlantic seaboard, from which they could be dislodged only by large-scale bombardment of cities and communication centers. No military leader has suggested that we could force Russian surrender without a costly ground-force invasion of Europe and Asia. Even if victory were finally achieved after colossal sacrifices in blood and treasure, we could find Western Europe in a condition of ruin, far worse than that which exists in Germany today, its population decimated and overrun with disease. For generations, we would have the task of rebuilding Western Europe and of policing the Soviet Union. These would be the result of the cheapest victory we could achieve. Few responsible persons believe in even so cheap a victory.

2. The second possible policy is maintenance of an armed peace in a two-bloc world, which, historically, had always led to war. This course would lead to rebuilding the strength of Western Europe both economically and militarily to a point where, allied with the United States, it would confront the Soviet bloc with overwhelming strength. This would entail tremendous and steadily accelerating armaments expenditures over an indefinite period and enforce a lower standard of living on the people. It might also betray our

moral position by propping up anti-democratic regimes as counterpoise to the Soviet Union. But it could have no termination save in a war begun at a less advantageous moment than a preventive war, thus ending even less favorably.

3. A third possible policy is the drive for world government, which has little support among governments but has growing and powerful support among the peoples of the West. Stripped of the enthusiasm of its friends and the misapprehensions of its enemies, the world government movement looks toward the creation of a supranational authority with powers sufficient to maintain law among nations. Initially and at every step the door would be open to all nations to federate with the supranational authority and submit to its limited jurisdiction.

Is this a hopeless perspective? We think not. The American proposal for international control of atomic energy was accepted in the essentials by the nations outside the Soviet bloc. Through the projected abolition of the veto power in the field of atomic energy it would have had the effect of transferring sovereignty in this field to an international authority. In substance this would have been a world government in a limited sphere.

The first two suggested policies would lead inevitably to a war which would end with the total collapse of our traditional civilization. The third indicated policy may bring about the acceptance by the Soviet bloc of the offer of federation. If they will not accept federation, we lose nothing that has not already been lost. If, as seems probable, the world has a period of armed peace, time and events may bring about a change in the Soviet policy.

We have then the choice of acceptance, in the first two cases, of the inevitability of war, or in the latter case, of the possibility of peace. Confronted by such alternatives we believe that all our constructive lines of action must be in keeping with the need of establishing a Federal World Government.

III

World Government can be achieved, but it cannot be achieved overnight. In the meantime, statesmen must confront today's problems and attempt to solve them, lest there be no civilized world left to govern. The course of events has indicated a growing dependence on armaments, at a time when armaments can no longer be adequate for purposes of national defense, and has also indicated a decreasing use of the processes of negotiation and conciliation.

No serious negotiations are taking place anywhere in the world between the two great powers, the United States and Soviet Russia. Almost everywhere the pattern is the same—total collapse of discussion on the most important problems—in the United Nations Atomic Energy Commission, in Berlin, in Korea.

We hope for discussion and negotiation at the highest governmental level—if need be, in secrecy in the initial stages—keeping in mind at all times the ultimate goal of peace through world government. We understand and share the distaste among democratic people for secret negotiations. But we see no hope under present conditions for any settlement to come out of public negotiations in which each statesman is the prisoner of his national prestige.

This call to negotiation does not mean appeasement. Every member of this committee was opposed to Munich at the time of Munich, and we are equally committed today to the maintenance of the spiritual and physical bounds of freedom throughout the world. This is why we are deeply disturbed by the conversion of Czechoslovakia into a police state. [The Communist party had taken over complete control of the Czech Government on February 25, 1948.]

IV

We make public our position in the belief that, in a democracy, it is the duty of every citizen to contribute to the clarification of issues and to the solution of the great problems which confront all of us. Scientists have a special position in the tragic situation in which mankind exists today. It is through the work of the scientific community that this great menace has come upon humanity and now threatens to destroy our civilization.

We are all citizens of a world community sharing a common peril. Is it inevitable that because of our passions and our inherited customs we should be condemned to destroy ourselves? No one has the right to withdraw from the world of action at a time when civilization faces its supreme test. It is in this spirit that we call upon all peoples to work and to sacrifice to achieve a settlement which will bring peace.

The day after this statement was issued, on April 12, 1948, the Emergency Committee of Atomic Scientists held a dinner in New York in honor of Dr. Edward U. Condon, Director of the United States Bureau of Standards, "as a testimony of the full confidence by his scientific colleagues in his complete integrity and loyalty to American institutions and as a protest against the unwarranted attacks on his loyalty by the House Committee on Un-American Activities." The event was sponsored by 126 leading scientists from all over America, more than half of them members of the American Academy of Science, and nine of them, including Einstein, Nobel Prize winners. The proceeds were to help support the *Bulletin of the Atomic Scientists.* Since he was unable to attend, Einstein sent a message to the dinner in which he said: [12]

In addition to the natural solidarity which has always united all scholars, this gathering is the expression of our unwillingness to accept a policy which, based on vague suspicions, publicly pillories men who, through devoted, selfless work, have made great contributions to the common good. Confidence and loyalty, the indispensable foundation of a healthy society, can flourish only when they are universally practiced.

A Texas correspondent had drawn Einstein's attention to Aldous Huxley's volume *Science, Liberty and Peace* [13] and suggested that Einstein declare in his public utterances "that all conscientious and responsible scientists should refuse to place their scientific skill at the disposal of any government which might use it chiefly for the development of ever more lethal and terrible means of mass-slaughter."

Einstein replied on April 15, 1948:

Although your beliefs are very close to my own, I feel that your proposition does not offer any prospect of success. Most scientists, especially the younger generation, are, for economic reasons, not at all independent. Opposition to the government would lead to complete economic ruin for most of them; therefore, you cannot expect to be successful in urging self-sacrifice on the part of these men. Under such circumstances, a professional oath for scientists, such as suggested by Dr. Huxley, becomes no more than an empty formula. Furthermore, the sacrifice of some persons would be useless if, say, a third or even fewer than a third of the competent scientists failed to participate.

Huxley's message is a kind of theoretical anarchism. We cannot ignore the constant advance of technology. It leads, as he rightly points out, to concentration of economic and political power which, indeed, tends to endanger the political independence of the individual. But our struggle for freedom must go on even under these most difficult conditions. We must realize that we can alter neither men nor the progress of technology.

World Government is not a protection against tyranny; it is protection against the threat of destruction; and existence, after all, must have priority.

On April 27, 1948, in a ceremony at Carnegie Hall, New York, the One World Award Committee, a group dedicated to perpetuating the ideals of the late Wendell Willkie, conferred its One World Award upon Einstein, describing him "as the world's greatest scientist who is devoting his whole life to the goal of world unity and permanent peace." Einstein's statement of acceptance was read for him by Cord Meyer, Jr., president of the United World Federalists: [14]

I am greatly touched by the signal honor which you have chosen to confer upon me. In the course of my long life I have received from my fellow men far more recognition than I deserve, and I confess that a certain sense of shame has always outweighed my pleasure at the recognition given me. But never before has the pain so far outweighed the pleasure as on this occasion. For all of us who are concerned with peace and the triumph of reason and justice must be keenly aware of how small an influence reason and honest good will exert today upon events in the political field. However that may be, and whatever fate may have in store for us, it is nonetheless certain that without the tireless efforts of those who are concerned with the welfare of humanity as a whole, the lot of mankind would be even worse than in fact it now is.

In this time of fateful decisions, we must, above all, impress this fact upon our fellow citizens: Whenever the belief in the omnipotence of physical force dominates the political life of a nation, this force takes on a life of its own and becomes even stronger than the very men who intended to use it as a tool. The proposed militarization of the nation not only immediately threatens us with war; it will also slowly but surely undermine the democratic spirit and the dignity of the individual in our land. The assertion that events abroad are forcing us to arm is incorrect; we must combat this false assumption with all our strength. Actually, our own rearmament, because of its effect upon other nations, will bring about the very state of affairs upon which the advocates of armaments seek to base their proposals.

There is only *one* path to peace and security: the path of supranational organization. Arming on the part of individual nations only contributes to the general uncertainty and confusion without offering any effective protection.

This message, and possibly certain statements of the Emergency Committee of Atomic Scientists, prompted the *Washington Star*, on April 29, 1948, to publish an editorial, "Only a Dream," in which credit was given to Einstein's sincere dedication to the cause of world unity and permanent peace. But the editorial insisted that "the course which he would have us take ignores all of the lessons of our experience. Once before, after World War I, the United States discarded its arms. . . . And in doing so we came within a hair's breadth of losing World War II. We must not do it again. . . . The world government of Dr. Einstein's dreams will have to wait until mankind is ready for it."

A few days later, on May 3, 1948, Ely Culbertson (pp. 321 and 373) sent Einstein a copy of a forceful letter which he had addressed to the editor of the *Washington Star*. "I respectfully disagree with some of Dr. Einstein's concepts of the structure of world government," the letter said. However, "if I had to choose between Einstein's 'dream' of world government and your 'realistic' atomic race now going on between America and Russia, then I would certainly choose Albert Einstein's world government." Culbertson offered his own "ABC Plan for World Peace," subsequently published in the June 1948 issue of *The Reader's Digest* and embodied in concurrent Congressional resolutions sponsored by thirty members of Congress. In a letter to Einstein, Culbertson summarized his proposal for revision of the United Nations Charter: [15]

Revision A establishes two world laws—no state (or its citizens) may prepare for or wage aggressive war. It delegates sovereign powers to the revised Security Council in these two matters.

Revision B provides for full control of the atomic threat and for scheduled disarmament in important weapons on a world level, under supervision of the Security Council.

Revision C establishes a federal armed force, so designed that it is not only effective but is politically acceptable.

I would very much like to explore this matter further with you, and should be very delighted to come to Princeton whenever it would be convenient to you. There are few whose achievements and intelligence I admire so much.

Einstein replied on May 6, 1948:

Thank you very much for your kind letter and for your gallant defense of my views on world government. I have carefully read the exposition of your plan, which was known to me before. In one respect I fully agree with you: The differences in our views on what constitutes a practical approach are not of primary importance and should not be emphasized. What is essential is our mutual conviction that a way must be found to halt the present drift toward war between the United States and the Soviet Union through supranational measures setting up a supranational military force of such strength that an act of aggression would become futile.

You express the conviction that your plan not only offers adequate security but also enjoys the advantage of being more readily acceptable for psychological reasons. I am rather doubtful about both points. Further, I believe that supervision of quantitatively circumscribed national armaments, as you suggest, would in itself create a dangerous source of conflict among the major powers, even if the size of armaments were agreed upon before.

I would never favor any public quarrel over differences of opinion among those groups which are striving essentially for the same goal. On the contrary, we should do our utmost to unify our efforts.

However, I do not believe that a meeting between us would be very profitable since my direct influence upon these groups is very small; and I am, of course, hardly an expert in military matters.

What does seem clear to me, however, is that the actual steps presently being taken by the United States constitute a greater menace to peace than those taken by the Russians. I believe that all of us should be very careful not to contribute further to the artificially created hysteria in present-day America.

In April 1948, Einstein replied to a series of questions submitted by the French journal *Franc-Tireur* on the danger of war and on the subject of East-West relations: [16]

Viewed objectively, there is no reason why another world war should be inevitable. Neither America nor Russia actually seeks world domination, nor does there exist between them any truly grave conflict of vital interests. The real danger lies in the fact that neither of these two great powers has evidenced a sincere willingness to solve the problem of security on a supranational basis. In their effort to make their individual military arrangements as favorable as possible *in the event of war*, both sides are in fact intensifying the crisis at a frightening pace.

The other nations, especially those in Europe, can do much to improve the situation. This can be accomplished by resolute and reasonable criticism of the policies of the two chief adversaries and not by one-sided partisanship. These countries, exhausted and impoverished as they are at present, tend to underestimate their potential moral influence. The responsibility falls mainly on the intellectuals and the press. Public opinion is confused and, with its sense of impending peril, more than ordinarily susceptible to influences, both good and evil.

Fear, hate and, above all, personal cowardice are everywhere the greatest obstacles to an intelligent solution of our problems.

Lewis Mumford, author on modern culture, had written an article, "Atom Bomb, 'Miracle' or Catastrophe," which appeared in the July 1948 issue of *Air Affairs*. He proposed a one-year world armistice; an international congress of scientists at which the United States would reveal the full extent of her atomic armaments, thereby allowing the congress accurately to project the scope of any future conflict; joint United States and Soviet initiative in changing the United Nations into a world government; dismantling of atomic stock piles and biological weapons, once the Soviet Union had declared itself in favor of world government; halting of any further production of atomic energy until a world authority could take over which would control other sources of energy as well; and, finally, control by the United Nations of all international straits and waterways. According to Mumford, both the United States and the Soviet Union had blundered and misconceived their national interests. They must bring about an "open world" or perish within a closed world. The notion of "gradualism" was a fallacy and foreign policy had become "the art of the impossible." Mumford conceded that the chance of his proposal's being acted upon was one in a hundred, but a miracle was the only alternative to catastrophe.

Einstein apparently saw an advance copy of the article, for on May 3, 1948, he wrote Mumford:

I wish to express my full agreement with your general attitude toward the problem of peace. Regarding your proposals I have only two remarks:

1. Under the present circumstances I do not believe that any official step could overcome the Russian Government's fear and distrust of us, unless it was carefully prepared in preliminary unofficial discussions between informed Russians and Americans who do not hold office and would, therefore, be free of official ties.

2. It seems clear to me that the people in the Kremlin rigidly believe that any attempt toward the establishment of a real world government must be prevented by all means. I am confident that this attitude could be changed only by convincing the Russians that a world security organization will be created without them should they persist in their negative attitude regarding participation. The problem is how this can be done without producing the impression that the real goal is a military alliance against Russia.

Mumford's reply was dated May 9, 1948: [17]

I am grateful for your letter of the third. The unofficial approach to the Russians is, I agree, highly important, and the more initiatives we take in that direction the better. As for starting an effective world government without Russia, that seems to me a necessary second step, if the first step—that of convincing the Russians that there is no alternative—fails. But I am reluctant to see the second step put first, since the fact is that our attempts to find common ground so far have been on the basis of solidifying the *status quo:* we have not approached the Russians with proposals looking to a future which would demand changes in our own political and economic purposes, as well as in Russia's. Without such proposals, I doubt that the Kremlin will accept world government without first seeking military domination. The point is that so far the official attitude of the United States has been almost as negative and arbitrary as that of Russia: certainly this was true till we instituted the Marshall Plan. Hence we must take practical steps to demonstrate that world government is not a mask for American domination. But of course you yourself see this danger.

On May 5, 1948, at the General Conference of the Methodist Church in Boston, the Reverend Ralph W. Sockman of New York read the following telegram from Einstein: [18]

At this time, a particularly heavy responsibility weighs on the clergy; on the other hand, you are presented with a unique opportunity to render an invaluable service to the community by providing information and enlightenment to vast sections of the people. And in this you are freer than the press and the radio, whose organs unfortunately are so susceptible to being influenced by political authorities and vested interests.

The United States is at present the most decisive factor in world politics. Politically, militarily and economically, her attitude and decisions largely determine the destinies of nations. Any future war would mean the end of civilized humanity. Under present conditions, a real and lasting peace can no longer be based upon national armaments but solely upon a supranational organization capable of making crucial decisions in matters of international security and equipped with adequate means to enforce these decisions. Without such a world government a pernicious armaments race and eventually war itself is inevitable. Please lend your assistance lest our generation fail in meeting the most fateful problem of our time.

For Dorothy Norman's column in the *New York Post* of May 14, 1948, "A World to Live in," Einstein answered a number of questions: [19]

Q: In the light of the recent statement made by the Emergency Committee of Atomic Scientists to the effect that it looks toward the establishment of a supranational authority—with power sufficient to maintain law among nations—I am wondering how you feel this proposal can be implemented. How would you suggest that the "discussion and negotiation at the highest governmental level" advocated by the committee could be hastened? By the United States taking leadership? Or how else?

A: All men of good will would welcome it if the government of the United States should take the initial step in starting discussion and negotiation at the highest governmental level with Russia, as recommended by the Emergency Committee of Atomic

Scientists. "Leadership" can only be the result of sincere and successful co-operation among nations; one cannot "take" leadership.

Q: The committee's statement refers to the fact that the American proposal for international control of atomic energy, "through its abolition of the veto power in the field of atomic energy," would constitute "world government in a limited sphere." How much further do you think nations should go in abolishing the veto power and establishing world government? Would you say that sovereignty would be given up with respect to matters such as citizenship, migration, customs unions, currency, treasury, the bill of rights, international law, the right to declare war—or anything else on which you may wish to comment?

A: "International control of atomic energy" is one of the functions indispensable to an effective world government. Control of a particular kind of weapon, however, is not synonymous with world government. We can speak of world government only when such an institution is vested with the power and duty to protect the individual nation-states against aggression. It must have supreme sovereignty over them in the field of military security, with no veto to balk it. It need have no duties or prerogatives not immediately connected with the problem of security. If it should prove desirable to enlarge the range of its activities, there is nothing to prevent such a development. To demand at the outset limitations on national sovereignty in excess of the necessary minimum would merely render more difficult a solution of the pressing problem of security.

Q: As I understand it, you would be for inviting Russia to join a federation. Would you be for inviting all nations to join? On a regional basis? Or otherwise? If Russia would not agree to join a federation would you go ahead and create a world government without her?

A: It goes without saying that, if at all possible, Russia should be included in the world federation *from the very outset*. Should this prove impossible, efforts should nonetheless be made to organize the other nations into a world federation, provided that it be done in such a way that Russia were free to join at any time, with all the privileges and duties of the other nations.

Q: Would you attempt to form a world government inside the United Nations? Outside the United Nations?

A: Transformation of the United Nations into a world government is possible and, in my opinion, the most natural course to pursue. However, it would amount to a radical transformation which would hardly differ from the creation of an entirely new organization.

Q: You said that you would make public all information concerning atomic energy. Would you do this with respect to all scientific discoveries and all armament questions? Would you do this irrespective of what Russia would agree to do?

A: Any world government, even if it did not include Russia at the outset, should in my opinion abolish all scientific and military secrecy.

Q: Would you outlaw armaments or disarm? If not, would you care to see quotas established with respect to the various nations, or a federal system worked out with respect to armaments?

A: Military power should be completely and solely in the hands of the world federation.

Q: Would you differentiate as between the democracies, monarchies and dictatorships invited to join the federation? Would you welcome Germany, Japan, Italy, Spain?

A: Once the federation is established, any country that meets the conditions for membership should be free to join.

Q: Would you "outlaw" monarchy or dictatorship within the federation?

A: There should be no interference by the federation with respect to the form of government of the member states.

Q: At what point do you think it would be justifiable to go to war against "preparation for aggression" or "aggression"?

A: National armament by member states of the federation must be prevented by means of inspection and, if necessary, intervention.

Under the title "Looking Ahead" the June 1948 issue of *The Rotarian* reprinted a number of Einstein's recent public statements as well as a specially prepared answer to the following questions: [20]

Q: Do you favor a world state? Why do you think it necessary? Why do you think it practical now?

A: Unlimited national sovereignty implies that every country must be prepared for the eventuality of war. In the present state of technology this means preparing for total mutual annihilation by every possible means. Such preparations, in turn, tend to lead not only to wars but to universal destruction. This is the fatal vicious circle into which we slipped before because of our own negligence and shortsightedness.

Unless we manage to break away from that vicious circle, we are, all of us, doomed. The longer we continue on this catastrophic course, the more difficult it becomes to alter it.

The establishment of law and order in international relations is the only solution. There is little sense in asking whether this is practical or otherwise to our liking. It is really foolish to raise the question as to whether we should perhaps wait a little longer before establishing world government, and meanwhile continue on the same old path. The situation is much the same as it would be with an urgent surgical operation. Every day's delay lessens the patient's chances for survival.

Einstein grew more and more perturbed about the increasing intensity of the cold war and particularly about the possibility of a preventive war, which was then widely discussed. He considered some counteraction necessary. After preliminary discussions, he addressed, on April 1, 1948, a letter to Professor Harlow Shapley of the Harvard College Observatory. Shapley was at that time president of the National Council of the Arts, Sciences and Professions, an organization which Einstein supported. Einstein wrote:

. . . I believe that it is the duty of the leading intellectuals in this country to launch a strong appeal to the American public to mobilize powerful opposition to the development toward a preventive war before irrevocable steps are taken and the course of events can no longer be reversed. In my opinion such an appeal can be effective only if it takes the form of a strong counterattack. What is your opinion about it?

Shapley replied promptly. In a lengthy letter dated April 7, 1948,[21] he made a number of suggestions:

I agree with you completely. There is a crisis and an urgency for action. I continue to hope that a cool rational study and exposition of the situation in the immediate future might be as effective as a passionate appeal to the American people to stop the dangerous trend. The best thing to do, so far as I am concerned, is to assemble a two- or three-day conference in New York City, at which time respected specialists would (perhaps in round-table conferences or through discussions of prepared papers) analyze issues such as the origin of the present crisis, the probable consequences of the prevailing national and international policies, and the changes that are necessary to guarantee security and survival. Our two-day serious conference should be "off record," with no reporters present. But on the evening of the second day we could and probably should have a Madison Square Garden meeting, with radio hookup, at which time we could state dramatically to the American people at least some of the preliminary conclusions of our conference. As alternate to this systematically prepared conference and public meeting, we might plan an earlier considered statement from a selected group of American intellectual leaders. In fact, we might do both.

Shapley referred to the project as a "Construct of Peace" and a "Plan for Survival." His letter also mentioned the fact that efforts were under way to sever the National Council's ties with the Progressive Citizens of America, which was then in the process of merging with the third-party movement headed by former Vice-President Henry Wallace. Wallace's Presidential candidacy, he felt, was "only indirectly useful in the present emergency. The proposed strong counterattack must be as nonpartisan and objective as possible." Einstein wrote Shapley again on April 9, 1948:

I am in full agreement with everything you have said and proposed. The new independent Council of the Arts, Sciences and Professions should be a suitable organization to call the conference you proposed. It is certainly very necessary to avoid any ties with political parties if we are to assemble all the individuals who may be helpful in our efforts toward the main goal, "Action against Militarization of the Nation." And should not the idea of supranational organization of peace and security versus competitive armament be placed at the very center of these efforts?

As far as the program for the conference is concerned, I am in full agreement with you about most of the points you suggest.

However, I am afraid that a discussion on the causes of the present crisis might waste time and create disunity. If this problem were freely discussed, there would not be unanimity of opinion. Possibly an individual, who is both well informed and sufficiently objective, might present to the conference a statement of his own views on that issue, without any further discussion.

Your suggestion to exclude the press from the conference and to publicize only the results of the conference also has my full approval.

The most delicate point, in my opinion, is the question whether or not—assuming it becomes necessary—one should strive for a partial world organization without Russia. We can make an effective stand against the militarization of the nation only if we can offer a concrete alternative. Or does it appear sufficient simply to project the thesis that the present situation does not seem to justify any *increase* in United States armaments?

Early in May, Shapley reported to Einstein that a small steering committee was helping him formulate precise plans for the proposed conference. Shapley asked Einstein to join him and Thomas Mann in issuing the call to the conference and also to prepare a message for the public meeting, which was then planned for Carnegie Hall in New York. Einstein agreed. The conference took place in New York on June 5, 1948, and succeeding days. Several dozen persons attended. Einstein had prepared the following message which was read at the conference:

Since I shall not be able to participate personally in your important discussions, I should like to present my views in a short statement.

You have come together because all of us are greatly disturbed by recent developments. We must not remain inactive at a time when our country is headed toward a conflict with the Soviet Union which would be both unnecessary and disastrous.

There are no problems so vital that a conflict between the United States and the Soviet Union is unavoidable. Even if the two countries were completely cut off from each other because of an earthquake or some similar accident of nature they both could well continue to exist. This is why it should be possible to find a *modus vivendi* through negotiations. As soon as this is accomplished, the road to a permanent solution of the security and peace problem will no longer be blocked.

I had assumed until a little while ago that Soviet apprehension about foreign intervention constituted the main source of existing international tension. However, this opinion seems no longer tenable since our government—twice during the last few weeks—brusquely rejected a Soviet suggestion to enter into direct negotiations in the hope of arriving at an understanding between the two countries.

This attitude of our government seems to be a clear indication that our present policy may lead to a break with the Soviet Union, to a preventive war, although this is not openly admitted. The military victory over Nazi Germany and Japan has given the military excessive influence upon our political life and has strengthened military attitudes which endanger the democratic institutions of our country and the peace of the world. This danger is further increased by our conviction that we enjoy temporary military superiority.

However, the democratic tradition of the American people is still alive, as is their universal desire for a peaceful solution of international problems. We have the duty to make the political will of our people influential and effective, while time remains. I hope that your meeting will help find an effective way of mobilizing public opinion in regard to the all-important political issue of peace.

The public meeting at Carnegie Hall, New York, which took place on June 17, 1948, was attended by about 2,000 people and was presided over by Harlow Shapley. The economist Raymond J. Walsh, the playwright Lillian Hellman and the physicist Philip Morrison spoke. Einstein addressed the meeting by telephone from his home in Princeton:

We are meeting here tonight because of our grave concern about the future. It is not a political meeting in the ordinary sense of the word, even though it is exclusively concerned with political issues.

As the immediate occasion for our meeting we may regard the brusque refusal of our government to agree to the course of direct negotiation offered by Russia. This incident is a grave symptom of the dangerous point which has been reached in American-Soviet relations.

The peoples of the world thirst for peace. The terrible wounds of the last war have not yet healed. Nowhere, not even in countries under totalitarian rule, are governments wholly independent of the will of the people. Everyone knows that in the present state of technology war would mean mass annihilation of men and the products of their labor to an unprecedented degree. How then is it possible that we should once again be faced with the danger of war? How is it possible that, in this country, otherwise normal people are not horrified by the very concept of preventive war although they must know that such a war would threaten their own country with catastrophe? Why are great sacrifices made in giving economic aid to Western Europe at a time when the increasing danger of war paralyzes the spirit of enterprise and hence makes such economic aid illusory?

The answer is simple. Without a supranational organization to make war impossible or, at least, virtually hopeless for the aggressor, governments must seek to make their military position as favorable as possible in the event of war. However, such preparations create so much tension and distrust that sooner or later the war which everyone dreads actually breaks out.

The situation is such that the United States as well as Russia are intent upon controlling as many nations and important military bases as possible so that, in the event of war, each country will have reliable allies and fortifications. Therefore, the actions by one country will always imply a threat to the other and will lead almost automatically to counteractions. Each side suspects the other of seeking to rule the world. Peace, therefore, cannot be secure without a supranational solution which would make national preparations for war not only unnecessary but impossible.

The United States emerged from the war as the strongest military and economic power and, temporarily, is the only country to possess the powerful atomic bomb. Such power imposes a heavy obligation. To a large extent, the United States is responsible for the ominous competitive arms race which has taken place since the end of the war and which has virtually destroyed the postwar prospects for an effective supranational solution of the security problem. Every additional measure of national armament leads us further away from the goal of a secure peace, and every such measure is a nail in the coffin of democratic liberties.

Before we can move toward a solution of the great peace problem we must attempt to recover the mutual confidence which has been lost in the last three tragic years. Only patient and understanding negotiations can help in this situation; we must not pursue a policy of weakness and unjustifiable concessions, but one of fairness and comprehension of the requirements and traditions of other nations.

The policies of a democratic nation depend upon the intelligence and character of every individual citizen. We must make every effort to insure that the great influence our country enjoys today will be of help to all other nations; this alone will make it possible to obtain security for ourselves and to protect our political heritage.

Besides the conference of June 5, a second conference, primarily of representatives of various organizations, took place on June 30. The following day, Shapley wrote Einstein with considerable satisfaction, enclosing the draft of a petition to the President of the United States and the Secretary of State which, Shapley added, had been adopted almost unanimously. Although the petition echoed some of Einstein's thoughts, it failed to achieve the main purpose which had been on Einstein's mind when he originally suggested the action. It had already become clear during the first conference that the majority of the participants were in favor of a relatively narrow statement and did not want to advocate specific, bold action against war itself. The petition which Shapley enclosed read as follows:

Twice this year our government has rejected Soviet offers to enter into direct negotiations aimed at reaching an understanding between the two nations. Such an attitude on the part of our government has many dangers; it may lead to a break with the Soviet Union; it may lead to so-called preventive war, which would be suicidal war. The influence of our military men, encouraged by what is believed to be temporary military superiority, endangers the peace of the world. The cold war, with its militarization program and its attacks on our civil liberties, not only increases the threat of a real war but endangers the democratic institutions of our country.

The democratic tradition, however, is very much alive throughout this land, and the desire for a peaceful solution of the international problem is mounting everywhere.

Realizing that the American people must make their voices heard while there is still time, we, the undersigned

1. Advocate the calling of immediate conferences between the United States and the USSR to reach agreement on basic differences; we also advocate the resumption of conferences between scientific and cultural organizations of the United States and the USSR.

2. Insist that capitalism and communism can and must peacefully coexist. United States–USSR co-operation won the last war, and abandonment of that co-operation led us to the present crisis.

In the coming elections, it is important that the American people judge candidates exactingly by their commitment to promote United States–USSR conferences and to lay the foundations for a *modus vivendi* with the Soviet Union and subsequently for the establishment of a permanent peace.

To carry through the planned mass activity, Shapley pointed out, would require substantial funds. He asked whether Einstein would be willing to invite a group of potential contributors to his home in Princeton. After consultation with his friend Otto Nathan, who had participated in the various proceedings in New York and had kept him advised of the disappointing character of the original meeting and the subseqent discussions with the group and individual members, Einstein replied to Shapley on June 6, 1948, as follows:

I am sure you cannot possibly have any doubt that I have considered it extremely important to pursue most energetically the original objectives of our action: (1) to work against the increasing militarization of the United States; and (2) to try to convince as large a number of people as possible that the unyielding foreign policy of the Truman Administration, which is closely tied to its military program, be replaced by a more constructive and conciliatory attitude in foreign affairs. You no doubt recall that, originally, it was our intention to unite a large number of outstanding intellectuals on a carefully elaborated platform and to bring our action to the attention of the general public over the names of those intellectuals. I am as anxious and willing as I have been ever since I first wrote you to participate in such an action, provided it is carefully and purposefully prepared.

The project as it is now contemplated in the two-point pledge enclosed in your letter limits itself—without recognizable reason—to suggesting negotiations with the Soviet Union. I find it impossible to assume that truly effective action could be based on such a narrow program, not mentioning the fact that similar actions have already been started by several other organizations. I can well imagine that the officers of the National Council of the Arts, Sciences and Professions had their own reasons to consider such a limitation of the program advisable. But I cannot approve of this course of action and do not want to have my signature affixed to the short, two-point pledge, nor do I wish to receive at my house a group of potential donors with the purpose of soliciting funds for the contemplated limited action.

I am very sorry that our original objective has not come closer to being accomplished and that I feel compelled to adopt a negative attitude on the most recent proposal of the National Council. I should like to emphasize once more that I should be only too happy to co-operate wholeheartedly in any action which is in line with our original intentions.

Shapley replied at considerable length. He pointed out that compromise had been necessary, that the brief statement was intended only as a first step, that a fuller program would take careful formulation, that quick action was indicated during the Presidential campaign "when the ears of the policy-makers are most sensitive to the voice of the people." He asked Einstein to reconsider. While Einstein consented to sign the statement, he apparently did not change his basic position, as is evident from his final note to Shapley in mid-July 1948:

Many thanks for your recent letter. I now understand much better in which stages you intend to develop the project. If the "two-item" statement should be distributed as explained in your letter, I shall be glad to have my signature affixed to it. On the other hand, I do not consider it sufficiently justified to receive prospective donors to finance this action. I feel that such an appeal to financially important people should be saved for a more significant project.

Despite all the bustle and marshaling of resources and despite the continuance of an operations or steering committee, nothing seems to have eventuated from this effort. Apparently it became submerged in preparations for the Scientific and Cultural Congress for World Peace held at the Waldorf-Astoria Hotel in New York in March of the following year.

In *The Saturday Review of Literature* of August 7, 1948, Norman Cousins, its editor, published a widely noted editorial, "Don't Resign from the Human Race." [22] Cousins built his argument on the basis of a mock court trial which was called for the purpose of deciding whether the human species had justified its right to survive. After a long and learned discussion by a fictitious prosecutor during which the prosecutor also deals with the concept of world government, Cousins replies to the challenge:

> The only price [man] has to pay for his survival is decision. He has at his command, once he makes the decision to use them, such resources of courage and intelligence as he himself would hardly dare to imagine. No one can foretell what great changes in him may be wrought by crisis—once that crisis is recognized and understood.

"We have nothing to lose but our adolescence," Cousins concluded. His message was all the more calculated to appeal to Einstein as he posed the problem of world government in terms very similar to those so often used by Einstein since the end of the war. On August 4, 1948, Einstein, suggesting that reprints of the editorial be widely distributed, wrote to Cousins:

> Your article "Don't Resign from the Human Race" is really beautiful and impressive. You have been able to present the most important problem of our time in a new and challenging form without antagonizing your readers; most of your readers may, for political reasons, not be able to make an objective appraisal of the international situation. I find it encouraging that men like yourself still exist in our midst.

Harlow Shapley, in his letter to Einstein of July 1, 1948, mentioned that he had received an invitation to attend a World Congress of Intellectuals, to be held late in August in Wroclaw (Breslau), a city in that part of Poland which, before 1939, had belonged to the German-Prussian province of Silesia. Einstein received a similar letter about the same time, and on July 6, 1948, he replied to the French-Polish Organizing Committee:

I much appreciate your kindness in calling my attention to your project to assemble an international congress of scholars in Poland some time in the near future. I have noted with great interest that the congress is to discuss the promotion of a true and genuine peace.

What is particularly important in these days of political hypertension is to consider and appraise our problems in a historical and philosophical perspective. We must have the courage to discuss acute and timely problems without getting lost in the petty political controversies of everyday life. History has taught us that brute force has never led to stable conditions and a satisfactory basis for the solution of the real problems of the world. This is particularly true today, since war in our own time would mean unimaginable destruction on a scale heretofore unknown.

To escape this terrifying danger we must overcome unrestrained national selfishness and stop thinking in terms of brute force. I hope with all my heart that you will succeed in assembling at your important gathering men of open mind and real courage. I also hope that those in power throughout the world will support your efforts, since men will gain confidence in one another only when they strive together for an objective understanding and appreciation of the developments around them.

The relatively small group of representatives from the Western democracies who attended the World Congress of Intellectuals included Einstein's friend Otto Nathan. Einstein had given Nathan a message especially prepared for delivery before the Congress—both of them, in fact, had worked on it with great care. Nathan made many efforts to present this message on behalf of Einstein. However, those in charge of the congress, at which many intemperate remarks were made about the United States, requested that certain passages of the message, particularly those urging the establishment of a supranational organization, be changed or be omitted altogether. Nathan refused to make any changes and insisted on presenting the message to the congress exactly as prepared by Einstein; since this proved impossible, the message was not read at all. Instead, without the prior knowledge of either Einstein or Nathan, Einstein's letter of July 6 to the French-Polish Organizing Committee was officially read to the congress and falsely announced as Einstein's "Message to the Congress." When American newspapers brought the "message" read at Wroclaw to Einstein's attention, he recognized that it bore no resemblance to the statement which he had written and that his letter had been substituted for the message. He declared "that such practices cannot contribute to the creation of an atmosphere of mutual trust" and released through *The New York Times* the real message, which Nathan had been unable to deliver: [23]

We meet today, as intellectuals and scholars of many nationalities, with a deep and historic responsibility placed upon us. We have every reason to be grateful to our French and Polish colleagues whose initiative has assembled us here for a momentous objective: to use the influence of wise men in promoting peace and security throughout the world. This is the age-old problem with which Plato, as one of the first, struggled so hard: to apply reason and prudence to the solution of man's problems instead of yielding to atavistic instincts and passions.

By painful experience we have learned that rational thinking does not suffice to solve the problems of our social life. Penetrating research and keen scientific work have often had tragic implications for mankind. On the one hand, they produced inventions which liberated man from exhausting physical labor, making his life easier and richer; but on the other hand, they introduced a grave restlessness into his life, making him a slave to his technological environment, and—most catastrophic of all—creating the means for his own mass destruction. This is indeed a tragedy of overwhelming poignancy!

However poignant the tragedy is, it is perhaps even more tragic that, while mankind has produced many scholars so extremely successful in the field of science and technology, we have been so inefficient in finding adequate solutions to the many political conflicts and economic tensions which beset us. No doubt, the antagonism of economic interests within and among nations is largely responsible for the dangerous and threatening situation in the world today. Man has not succeeded in developing political and economic forms of organization which would guarantee the peaceful co-existence of the nations of the world. He has not succeeded in building the kind of system which would eliminate the possibility of war and banish forever the murderous instruments of mass destruction.

We scientists, whose tragic destiny it has been to help make the methods of annihilation ever more gruesome and more effective, must consider it our solemn and transcendent duty to do all in our power in preventing these weapons from being used for the brutal purpose for which they were invented. What task could possibly be more important to us? What social aim could be closer to our hearts? That is why this congress has such a vital mission. We are gathered here to take counsel with each other. We must build spiritual and scientific bridges linking the nations of the world. We must overcome the horrible obstacles of national frontiers.

In the smaller units of society man has made some progress toward minimizing sovereignty with its antisocial implications. This is true, for example, of life within cities and, to a certain degree, even of life within individual states. In such communities tradition and education have had a moderating influence and have brought about tolerable relations among the people living within those confines. But in relations among nations complete anarchy still prevails. I do not believe that we have made any real progress in this area during the last few thousand years. All too frequently conflicts among nations are still decided by resort to brute force, by war. The unlimited desire for ever greater power seeks aggressive outlets wherever and whenever a physical possibility offers itself.

Throughout the ages this state of anarchy in international affairs has inflicted indescribable suffering and destruction upon mankind; again and again it has impeded the progress of men, their souls and their well-being. At given times it has almost annihilated whole areas.

However, the desire of nations to be ever prepared for war has still other repercussions upon the lives of men. The power of every state over its citizens has grown steadily during the last few hundred years—no less in countries where the power of the state has been exercised wisely than in those where it has been used for brutal tyranny. The function of the state to maintain peaceful and orderly relations among its citizens has become increasingly complex and extensive largely because of the concentration and centralization of modern industry. In order to protect its citizens from aggression a modern state requires a formidable, expanding military establishment. In addition, the state considers it necessary to educate its citizens for the possibility of war, an "education" that not only corrupts the soul and spirit of the young, but also adversely affects the mentality of adults. No country can avoid this corruption altogether. It pervades the citizenry even in countries which do not harbor outspoken aggressive tendencies. The state has thus become a modern idol whose suggestive power few men are able to escape.

Education for war, however, is a delusion. The technological developments of the last few years have created a completely new military situation. Horrible weapons have been invented, capable of destroying in a few seconds huge masses of human beings and tremendous areas. Since science has not yet found protection from these weapons, the modern state is no longer in a position to prepare adequately for the safety of its citizens.

How, then, shall we be saved?

Mankind can gain protection against the danger of unimaginable destruction and wanton annihilation only if a supranational organization has alone the authority to produce or possess these weapons. It is unthinkable, however, that, under existing conditions, nations would hand over such authority to a supranational organization, unless the organization had the legal right and duty to solve the kind of conflicts which in the past have led to war. Under such a system the function of individual states would be to concentrate more or less upon internal affairs; and in their relations with one another they would deal only with issues and problems which are in no way conducive to endangering international security.

Unfortunately, there are no indications that governments yet realize that the situation in which mankind finds itself makes the adoption of revolutionary measures a compelling necessity. Our situation is not comparable to anything in the past. It is impossible, therefore, to apply methods and measures which, in an earlier age, might have been sufficient. We must revolutionize our thinking, revolutionize our actions and must have the courage to revolutionize relations among the nations of the world. The clichés of yesterday will no longer do today, and will, no doubt, be hopelessly out of date tomorrow. To bring this home to men all over the world is the most important and most fateful social task intellectuals have ever had to shoulder. Will they have enough courage to overcome their own national ties to the extent that is necessary to induce the peoples of the world to change their deep-rooted national traditions in a most radical fashion?

A tremendous effort is indispensable. If it fails now, the supranational organization will be built later, but then it will have to be built upon the ruins of a large part of the world. Let us hope that the abolition of the existing international anarchy will not need to be brought about by a self-inflicted world catastrophe, the dimensions of which none of us can possibly imagine. The time is terribly short. We must act now if we are to act at all.

When Einstein's letter to the Organizing Committee was falsely used as his message, Dr. Julian Huxley, at that time the Director-General of UNESCO, presided over the conference. Nathan had informed him before about the controversies over Einstein's message. Huxley later stated in a letter to Einstein that the "misunderstanding" was not "in any way his fault." In his reply to Huxley of September 18, 1948, Einstein said:

. . . Under the prevailing conditions, it is impossible for the intellectuals of East and West to co-operate for peace and intellectual freedom. I am convinced that our colleagues on the other side of the fence are completely unable to express their real opinions.

In considering plans for a world settlement, Einstein did not limit himself to organizational efforts and conferences. Earlier in the year a San Francisco psychoanalyst of German origin submitted to him a thirteen-page manuscript entitled "A Method to Enforce World Peace." In essence, his plan was as follows: If the Soviet Union refused to join a veto-free, limited world government for the control of atomic energy, the members of such a world government would, after due notice, conduct enforced aerial inspection of the Soviet Union. Einstein replied on April 8, 1948: [24]

First, a brief introductory remark. You instinctively proceed from the premise that the United States seeks supranational organization (world government), while the Soviet Union, being aggressively inclined, is opposed to the idea. I do not believe that such a description does justice to the psychological situation.

As to your proposal, we both agree that only world government can create security. You make the following assumption: if we would seek a solution through the establishment of a world government, while Russia seeks to avoid such a solution, the world government thus created would remain incomplete for the time being.

Since this partial world government does not include Russia, it will soon be compelled to arm to such an extent that Russia would have no chance of a military victory over the world government.

So far we are in agreement. But where your proposal differs from my own is in your proposition that we ought to compel Russia to join before she becomes strong enough to attack the rest of us. The desirability of such a procedure seems debatable. I doubt that it is the proper course to take. If we create conditions under which aggression will look hopeless to the Russians, while membership will appear advantageous, the attitude of the Soviet Union is likely to change and she may choose to join without coercion. It seems that enforced adherence, as you suggest, might be of rather dubious value.

However, as long as it remains uncertain whether the United States actually seeks to bring about real world government, our differences of opinion are academic. Only when partial world government, in the form of a powerful supranational organization, becomes a reality will the question arise as to whether it might be preferable to wait for further developments or to force Russia's entry into world government. Until a partial world government is actually established, the question of coercion should not even be raised since it can only have a harmful effect on the psychological situation.

The author of the plan replied in several further pages of argument, including an approving letter from Bertrand Russell, who at this time apparently favored a preventive war unless Russia agreed to international inspection concerning atomic weapons. Einstein replied on May 28, 1948:

Your letter is logical enough. However, I cannot accept your viewpoint, much less the one expressed by Bertrand Russell. Your approach resembles that of a professional soldier or engineer inasmuch as you seem to oversimplify the psychological reactions to war preparations, especially with regard to the Russians. Their behavior clearly indicates that they are deeply disturbed by the technological advance in warfare and might consent to substantial concessions if this were made easier for them by greater flexibility on our part. I am convinced that Roosevelt would have been able to reach a satisfactory *modus vivendi* with Russia and that the present administration could do the same if it had the sincere will to do so.

The West Coast analyst returned to the argument once again but could not convince Einstein, who replied on September 29, 1948:

Your recent letter has greatly interested me. I fully agree with you that the solution of the security problem by supranational means cannot wait. In the face of Russia's openly negative attitude, there seems to be no alternative but to create an organization without Russia and the countries in the Russian bloc—a rump world government, so to speak. On this point, I know, we also are in agreement.

The question then arises of whether such a rump world government should attempt to compel Russia to join. This would mean war—a "preventive war." Here I disagree with you. You justify your affirmative position with the argument that Russia's relative strength will increase with time, thus putting the rest of the world at a disadvantage. While I admit that this reasoning is correct, I remain unconditionally opposed to a policy of coercion. It reminds me of the man who committed suicide because he was so afraid of death. For moral as well as practical reasons, I should prefer a policy which would seek to create conditions under which the Russians would consider it in their own selfish interest to abandon their separatist attitude. I feel this would become possible if we, for our part, would pursue an appropriate policy. I cannot prove it. I can only say that my instinct compels me to favor such a course of action.

Einstein's interest in Henry Usborne's Peoples' World Convention plan was mentioned before (see pp. 420 ff.). On March 5, 1948, in a round-robin letter to Einstein and a number of other outstanding internationalists, Usborne said: [25]

It's high time now that we received more definite and encouraging news from the American Crusaders. I know that hard work is being done but it's important that the rest of the world should now know about it. Please make haste. It's time you showed your hand and told the world exactly how you plan to conduct your ballot in 1950 so as to send your representatives to Geneva.

As a matter of fact, efforts to promote such a campaign in America were by then well under way. In April a group of federalists in Chicago enlisted the interest of Professor Stringfellow Barr, the liberal educator and historian. Barr succeeded in persuading Mrs. Anita McCormick Blaine of Chicago, a wealthy, great-hearted lady in her eighties, who held advanced political ideas and was committed to the Usborne plan, to finance a conference at which the subject of world government would be thoroughly explored. Barr then issued the following invitation to a number of interested persons:

I am writing you on my own behalf and on that of Mr. Grenville Clark [a retired corporation lawyer and long-time adherent of the world government movement], Dr. Albert Einstein, Mayor Hubert Humphrey [of Minneapolis], Dr. Leo Szilard and Mr. Carl Van Doren.

The plan outlined in the enclosed memorandum seems to us worth carrying out, provided we can devise appropriate means of doing so. The difficulties seem insuperable. Since, however, our country faces grave danger, and since this plan offers a means of educating our people as to the nature of the danger and the difficult steps necessary to avoid it, we have determined to meet and explore possibilities.

We have chosen as a convenient place of meeting Pocono Crest in Pocono Pines, Pennsylvania. We intend to meet at 8 P.M., Friday, June 25, and give ourselves until the afternoon of Sunday, June 27, for our discussions.

Mr. Henry Usborne, Member of Parliament, who initiated the plan in Great Britain, is coming over to be with us in Pocono Pines as our guest.

We hope that after considering the memorandum you will agree with us that a ballot of this sort should be held in America to send able delegates to Geneva, provided a good method of achieving this end can be devised.

P.S. The committee proposes that the conference receive no publicity.

Some forty-five persons (including Cord Meyer, Norman Cousins and Harrison Brown of the Emergency Committee of Atomic Scientists) met at the Pocono Conference under the chairmanship of Professor Barr. All but three voted to support the Usborne plan; a

Continuing Committee, headed by Barr, was set up to draft a long-range campaign. Meanwhile, however, Mrs. Blaine's interest had taken a different course. In early July 1948 she had been persuaded to establish a Foundation for World Government, with an endowment of one million dollars, to be headed by Stringfellow Barr. While support of the Peoples' World Convention movement was not written into the trust agreement, this was one of the main concerns of the new foundation; on July 10, 1948, at the invitation of Harrison Brown, Barr laid the project before the Emergency Committee of Atomic Scientists, presumably in Einstein's presence. The committee subsequently passed the following resolution:

WHEREAS, the Emergency Committee of Atomic Scientists, having explored for two years all means other than world government for making responsible the control of atomic energy, has become convinced that no other method than world government can be expected to prove effective, and that the attainment of world government is therefore the most urgent problem now facing mankind,

Therefore, be it resolved, That the Emergency Committee

1. Heartily endorses the effort now being made to secure American participation in the Crusade for a Peoples' World Convention, sponsored in Britain by the so-called Usborne Committee, as the most promising method now offered for promoting world government;

2. Has today allocated the sum of one thousand dollars as a token of their interest, to be transmitted to the proposed Foundation for World Government; and

3. Has appointed a subcommittee of its members, namely: Dr. Albert Einstein, Dr. Harold C. Urey, Dr. Philip M. Morse and Dr. Harrison Brown, to work closely with the trustees of said foundation, and to explore methods for aiding the work of the trustees, both financially and by all means in the committee's power.

Just how far the Emergency Committee of Atomic Scientists was prepared to go may be judged from Harrison Brown's report to a meeting of the Pocono Continuing Committee "that the Emergency Committee of Atomic Scientists was willing to abolish its existence as a separate fund-raising organization and turn over its complete and well-tested fund-raising mechanism to the foundation, if the latter were successfully established."

But events of a political nature supervened. Mrs. Blaine was an ardent supporter of Henry Wallace's Progressive party candidacy for the Presidency (another foundation trustee, Scott Buchanan, was also a prominent member of the Progressive party); she had expressed the hope that Wallace might eventually be associated with her foundation. But Mrs. Blaine did not make an issue of the matter, and it was agreed that the time to consider such a step was premature. The Wallace movement was then widely suspect of being under Communist influence. This posed a painful dilemma in world government circles. The Foundation for World Government commanded larger funds than had ever been made available for the cause—funds with which major gains might be secured. Yet many federalists believed that a Wallace "taint" would be extremely harmful to the movement. Particularly some members of the Pocono Continuing Committee became nervous. The situation came to a head when the *New York World-Telegram* of September 14, 1948, and other Scripps-Howard newspapers made the story public in a sensational way, under the headline "Angel's Million Assures Wallace Post-Election Job." Mrs. Blaine, in Chicago, had made certain ambiguous statements that seemed to lend support to the story, which was repeated in other papers.

Barr, returning from abroad in the midst of the furor, declined to make a statement although he himself was not a Wallace man. He resigned from the Pocono Committee, which was subsequently disbanded. Mrs. Blaine sought to clarify her position. The United World Federalists promptly dissociated itself from the Foundation for World Government. The Emergency Committee of Atomic Scientists took similar action. It asked the foundation to move from the office where it had been given space by the committee, and the offer of support was withdrawn. It can scarcely be assumed that any of these actions could have pleased Einstein.

As it turned out, Henry Wallace never did have any connection with the Foundation for World Government, even after his defeat at the election of November 1948. In the course of time, amicable relations were restored between the foundation and various world government groups, but despite continuing (if at times faltering) support by the foundation, the Peoples' World Convention movement was all but destroyed in the United States. This may not have displeased some federalists who found the Usborne plan too strong for their taste. To Einstein, however, who had supported the movement as a welcome addition in the struggle for a supranational organization, the turn of events must have meant a severe disappointment.

For the *Cheyney Record*, a student paper of Cheyney State Teachers College, a Negro school in Cheyney, Pennsylvania, Einstein answered these questions in October 1948: [26]

Q: Do you feel that the scientists who gave us the atomic bomb should be held morally responsible for any destruction wrought by the bomb?

A: No. It is true that advances in physics have made possible the application of scientific discoveries for technical and military purposes, which engenders great danger. The responsibility, however, lies with those who make use of these new discoveries rather than with those who contribute to the progress of science—with the politicians rather than the scientists!

Q: Do you feel that race prejudice in the United States is merely a symptom of a world-wide conflict?

A: Race prejudice has unfortunately become an American tradition which is uncritically handed down from one generation to the next. The only remedies are enlightenment and education. This is a slow and painstaking process in which all right-thinking people should take part.

Q: Can mathematics be a tool for the solving of social problems as well as scientific considerations?

A: Mathematics is a useful tool for social science. In the actual solution of social problems, however, goals and intentions are the dominant factors.

Q: Do you feel that democracy can always solve the problems of society?

A: Democracy, taken in its narrower, purely political, sense suffers from the fact that those in economic and political power possess the means for molding public opinion to serve their own class interests. The democratic form of government in itself does not automatically solve problems; it offers, however, a useful framework for their solution. Everything depends ultimately on the political and moral qualities of the citizenry.

Q: Do you feel that a United States of Europe will solve the problem of war?

A: Creation of a United States of Europe is an economic and political necessity. Whether it would contribute to a stabilization of international peace is hard to predict. I believe yes rather than no.

In a letter, of November 25, 1948, to his old friend Maurice Solovine in Paris, Einstein noted with satisfaction the fact that there was resistance in France to the American policy of bringing the Nazis in

Germany back into power, to be used against the "bad" Russians. He added that it was almost unbelievable how little people learn from even the most bitter experience. At about the same time, Einstein sent the following cable to the mathematician Jacques Hadamard in Paris, apparently in reply to Hadamard's request for Einstein's support in his attempt to organize French intellectuals in opposition to allied pro-German policies:

I warmly wish you success with your initiative. In this situation the interests of all men and all nations are served by defending the national interest of France.

It seems especially important, in the wake of this terrible war, that we do not repeat the errors made after the last war, when the disunity among the Allies paved the way for the preparation of the Second World War. We must not forget that this catastrophe could have been avoided if Clemenceau's prophetic warnings had been heeded.

Another cause, also centering in Paris, aroused Einstein's interest at about the same period. In June 1948, during a stay in Paris, Garry Davis, a young American, voluntarily forswore his American citizenship as a gesture of protest against the drift toward war. In September, after the French refused to extend his residence permit, he attracted international attention by setting up living quarters in a tent on the grounds of the Palais de Chaillot, which had been declared international territory because the United Nations General Assembly was meeting there. Davis was taken under the wing of a former colonel from the French underground, Robert Sarrazac-Soulage, whose activities in France were similar to those of Henry Usborne in England. As the epitome of the "little man" rebelling against the fruitless ceremonial of international politics, Davis became to millions a symbol of the struggle for world peace. In November, he and Sarrazac-Soulage created an incident by speaking from the gallery of the United Nations Assembly in favor of the Peoples' World Convention. To a subsequent mass meeting held in Paris, under the auspices of the "Garry Davis Council of Solidarity," Einstein sent this message, dated November 28, 1948:

I feel impelled to pay my respects to Mr. Davis, the youthful war veteran, for the sacrifices he has made on behalf of the general welfare of mankind. By renouncing his citizenship, he made himself a "displaced person," in order to fight for the natural rights of those who are the silent witnesses to the moral decay of our time.

The worst slavery pressing down on mankind today is the militarization of the peoples of the world. This militarization springs from fear of another world war and the mass annihilation it threatens. Unfortunately, the well-meaning attempt to control this situation by the establishment of the United Nations has proved totally inadequate. A supranational organization, if it is to solve the problem of international security, must be both powerful and independent. The establishment of such an organization must not depend upon the initiative of the various governments. Only the unbending will of the peoples of the world is capable of setting in motion the forces required to make such a radical break with old and obsolete political traditions.

I salute your meeting as an earnest effort to serve the most important task of our generation.

Toward the end of 1948 the Emergency Committee of Atomic Scientists ceased being a fully functioning organization and became virtually inactive. While Harrison Brown's offer to turn over the entire machinery of the Emergency Committee to the Foundation for World Government was unquestionably sincere, it may have been motivated, at least in part, by the internal difficulties that had been plaguing the committee for some time.

It was often difficult to assemble the trustees for meetings, and even more difficult to reach full agreement on policy. As Einstein sadly remarked to Joseph H. Schaffner, the committee's original Executive Director and Treasurer: "How can we presume to rescue the American people from their uncertainties if we cannot agree among ourselves?"

Difficulties extended to many areas. Members of the committee differed in their attitude toward the United Nations and in their position toward world government, whether a partial supranational organization was better than none, if a complete world government was not attainable in the near future. There was yet another problem which created difficulties and differences of opinion: by its very nature, the committee was forced to concern itself with essentially political problems, although it should not have done so in view of its charter, which stipulated that "no substantial part of its activities shall consist of carrying on propaganda or otherwise attempting to influence legislation." Furthermore, there were complaints that administrative expenses were too high and that too small a share of the funds was used for educational activities. And although Einstein was able to announce by early 1948 pledges amounting to nearly $400,000, which ultimately totaled considerably more, serious difficulties were at times experienced in fulfilling current financial commitments.[27]

Harrison Brown, the committee's Executive Vice-Chairman during this period, described the situation inside the committee as follows:

> The group failed of its purpose in the sense that it had little long-range impact upon public thought—at least in my opinion. One of the reasons for this was that the general outlook of the individual members of the board varied enormously, and near the end of our days we could not really agree among ourselves as to the next step to take. Einstein played an enormously important role in clarifying certain of our goals. He attempted to reconcile conflicting viewpoints from time to time, but rather unsuccessfully. Einstein himself could not bring himself to agree with the views of certain of the committee members.

As late as September 17, 1948, solicitation letters like the following were still being mailed over Einstein's signature:

> Today every citizen lives in desperate peril. It is not only his own life and that of his loved ones which is menaced. We see the twilight deepening over our great civilization. It is the fate of civilization itself—the edifice of creative thought and heroic labor which countless generations of humankind have built through the ages—about which we are so gravely concerned.
>
> For the two past years we scientists have worked to inform our fellow citizens that the old order has ended—that the emergence of atomic energy upon the world stage has made necessary a reordering of world institutions in order that they may effect the abolition of war. We sought as a first step public support for an agreement upon the international control of atomic energy. But such agreement has failed because of the clash of rival nationalisms. The nations are adrift upon a familiar voyage whose only termination throughout history has been the catastrophe of war.
>
> The challenge civilization faces—we face—is the effective abolition of war. Because the enclosed article by Norman Cousins ["Don't Resign from the Human Race"; see p. 491] is a clear and eloquent statement of the case, I send it to you. I wish that every

citizen of the United States could have the opportunity to read and understand these few pages with their inspired thought and positive conclusion.

Its message to humanity is: "We need not fail. The deepening twilight need not end in darkness and disaster—it can lead to fulfillment and a greater future for humanity. Each of us bears his share of responsibility for the decision which is the historic role of our age to take. We must not fail the challenge—we cannot fail if we but use the vast reserves of intelligence and courage which lie untapped within every human being."

To do our part in meeting this challenge, my colleagues and I have the duty to ask for your further help. We ask today for your continued support of our campaign of education. Help us to ensure that this historic achievement of science—the discovery and development of atomic energy—will be used for the benefit of mankind and not for its destruction.

But on November 10, 1948, Urey, Brown, Hogness, Szilard and Mayer met in Chicago and decided to recommend that as of January 1, 1949, the Emergency Committee of Atomic Scientists become inactive, although it nominally remain in existence. The recommendation was apparently accepted by Einstein and the other trustees. As a result of these developments the *Bulletin of the Atomic Scientists* for December 1948 carried a letter from Einstein in which he made the following remarks:

From the very beginning, one of the important activities supported by the Emergency Committee has been the *Bulletin of the Atomic Scientists*, a magazine founded by the Atomic Scientists of Chicago, three years ago this month, and devoted to public education on atomic issues and related fields.

The developments of the last two years have made it plain that the education of mankind toward a clear understanding of the implications of atomic energy, and full appreciation of the dangers and hopes inherent in new discoveries, is a long-range task which cannot be solved on an emergency basis.

The Editorial Board of the *Bulletin* and the Emergency Committee have agreed that the best way to provide the *Bulletin* with a broader and more permanent basis for the continuation and widening of its activities is through the organization of a permanent sponsoring committee, representative of the American scientific community.

The Emergency Committee wishes the *Bulletin* continued success in its important work, and appeals to all who have in the past supported the *Bulletin* by their donations to the Emergency Committee to continue and strengthen this support by contributions to the *Bulletin.*

Dr. Eugene Rabinowitch, editor of the *Bulletin of the Atomic Scientists* and a close observer of the committee, summed up his impressions of the significance of the Emergency Committee in these words:

Whether the Emergency Committee was a failure depends upon what one expected from it. Some scientists hoped to achieve an immediate revolutionary change in the thinking of all governments, beginning with our own; and this the Emergency Committee certainly was not able to produce. Others saw from the beginning only an off-chance for such a sudden change and assumed that a long education (partly by facts and partly by consistent repetition of their views by scientists) could ultimately bring political relations in the world in harmony with the scientific revolution produced by the liberation of atomic energy. From this point of view (which I share) the Emergency Committee was *not* a failure but contributed significantly to the first steps in this education. What *is* a failure is, to me, the disappointment of most scientists in the absence of quick results and their reluctance to take part in the long pull—which is still needed and will be needed for years to come. I think the Emergency Committee should *not* have been disbanded but should have transformed itself into a more permanent "general staff" of a scientists' movement.

If the Emergency Committee of Atomic Scientists did fail to accomplish some of the high purposes which Einstein and others had envisioned at its inception, surely the failure was not without honor; and the committee had a great, even if not decisive, impact upon public opinion during the active years of its existence. There can be no doubt that Einstein contributed generously and with a deep sense of responsibility to the work of the committee.

On November 24, 1948, Einstein drafted the following Christmas message: [28]

Christmas is the festival of peace. Every year it comes in its own good time. But peace within us and among us can come only by constant effort. This holiday serves as a reminder that all men yearn for peace. Every year it admonishes us to be vigilant against the enemies of peace that slumber inside all of us, lest they cause tragedy not only at Christmastide but throughout the year.

CHAPTER FIFTEEN

TOTAL DISARMAMENT OR NONE | 1949-1950

On March 14, 1949, Einstein was seventy years old. Good wishes poured in from all over the world. The scientific community used the occasion to pay special tribute to Einstein the scientist. Under the auspices of Princeton University and the Institute for Advanced Study in Princeton, three hundred scientists assembled in Princeton to hold a symposium on Einstein's contributions to contemporary science. Professor Isidor I. Rabi of Columbia University, one of the participants in the symposium and himself a Nobel Prize winner in physics, remarked that "this significant celebration of Einstein's seventieth birthday is hardly equalled in the whole history of science, for when was there another man whose contribution was so great? . . . No other man before Einstein, or since, has delved so deeply into our most instinctive concepts of space, time and causality, no one has brought up so much new knowledge and understanding. . . ."Also on the occasion of Einstein's seventieth birthday, the Library of Living Philosophers published a volume, *Albert Einstein: Philosopher–Scientist,* which assembled twenty-five essays on his work. Perhaps the most significant contribution to the volume was prepared by Einstein himself. In his "Autobiographical Notes," he sketched the development of his scientific work and made a few exceedingly interesting remarks about his boyhood and youth.

Little was said in these public testimonials about Einstein's contribution to the world outside the field of science; only one of the twenty-five papers in the large volume attempted to deal with "Einstein's Social Philosophy." Scant tribute was paid to the fact that Einstein was a man who had passionately fought all his life for a better and saner world, one without war and with greater dignity for every human being. When *The New York Times* said, in an otherwise sympathetic editorial of March 14, 1949, that "Einstein has not always been happy in his solutions of the political problems that have bedeviled the world for decades," it voiced the opinion of many who were not sufficiently acquainted with Einstein's basic ideas for the reorganization of man's political, economic and social institutions.

While Einstein's public expressions of his thoughts on contemporary developments became somewhat less frequent during this last period of his life, they continued to be characterized by the same idealism that had inspired him from his early days. If anything, Einstein became increasingly more outspoken and, in the most constructive sense, less tolerant of attitudes which he considered superficial, unrealistic or even detrimental to the fight against war.

On February 18, 1949, Einstein wrote to an Australian pathologist who had appealed to him for "a few words of leadership and hope": [1]

There seems to be no doubt that in all countries power lies in the hands of power-hungry men who practice little restraint when it comes to realizing their ambitions. This is true whatever the form of the political machinery, dictatorial or democratic. Power not only relies on coercion but on subtle persuasion and deception which is accomplished through the educational system and through all the media of public information.

You ask whether self-restraint in research on the part of creative thinkers and scientists might not prevent the further development of the technological means of mass destruction. I do not believe that salvation can be expected even if the scientist should adopt such a policy; and this for the following reasons:

1. Man already possesses technical means generally known and sufficient to bring about his total annihilation.

2. Men really devoted to the progress of knowledge concerning the physical world, men like Faraday or Rutherford, never worked for practical, let alone military, goals. No one could have predicted the applications that flowed from their discoveries.

3. People of technical skill are so numerous and economically so dependent that the individual cannot be expected to refuse employment offered him by the government or by private industry, even if he knows that his work may lead to disaster on a world-wide scale.

One can only hope that there are enough people the world over who possess the intellectual and moral integrity to resist all the nefarious influences brought to bear on them. While it might possibly be helpful to organize such people, the usefulness of such organization tends to be overestimated. What is important is that individuals have the honesty and courage to stand up for their convictions on every occasion.

Five years later, the same correspondent, a Quaker, wrote Einstein again, asking whether he felt sympathetic toward the aims of the Society of Friends and pointing out what seemed to him an inconsistency between the third point and the last sentence of Einstein's letter. The pathologist and his friends felt that employment in all occupations whose aims were destructive should be refused, even at the risk of poverty or imprisonment. Einstein replied, on February 23, 1954:

I feel that the Society of Friends is the religious community which has the highest moral standards. As far as I know, they have never made evil compromises and have always been guided by their conscience. In international life, especially, their influence has been very beneficial and effective.

I see no contradiction in the remarks made in my former letter to you. We cannot expect that the rules applying to a pioneering moral elite will necessarily be emulated by the rank and file.

When H. Runham Brown of the War Resisters' International, with whom Einstein closely co-operated before 1933, asked him to express support for the suggestion that the right to conscientious objection be inserted in the military service laws of Israel, Einstein replied on February 22, 1949:

I should be gratified if the State of Israel were to establish a legal basis for the protection of conscientious objectors. Such a measure would seem to be in harmony with the best Jewish moral traditions. You may feel free to use this statement in any way you consider desirable, although I strongly believe that I have no right, and that it would be presumptuous of me, to attempt to advise people who have safely led our little nation through seemingly insurmountable difficulties.

In March 1949, a Scientific and Cultural Congress for World Peace met in New York City which, to some extent, was a belated result of the efforts made by Einstein and Harlow Shapley in the spring of 1948 to organize a meeting on "Patterns for Survival." [2] Einstein's name was included on the list of more than 500 sponsors, many of whom were unaware or unconcerned that anti-Communists severely attacked the conference for its alleged Communist auspices.

On April 7, 1949, Einstein's friend, the French mathematician and pacifist Jacques Hadamard, cabled from Paris to inquire whether Einstein, who, in his opinion, symbolized the scientists' aspiration for peace, would be willing to send a message to the World Peace Congress. The Congress, the first of a series of such meetings initiated by the Wroclaw Conference in August 1948, was scheduled to take place on April 20. Einstein replied the same day: [3]

I was deeply moved by the address you delivered over the radio on the occasion of my seventieth birthday.

In answer to your cable I must frankly confess that, in view of my experience with the first congress of this kind at Wroclaw last August [see p. 491], and from what I have observed concerning the recent congress in New York, I have the strong impression that this kind of procedure does not really serve the cause of international understanding. The reason is simply that it is more or less a Soviet enterprise and everything is managed accordingly. This in itself would not be so bad if the Russians and the men coming from the countries affiliated with Russia were really free to express their personal opinions rather than having to express what is currently the official Russian point of view. Therefore, most people have the impression that these gatherings constitute "Soviet propaganda," particularly since the speakers from the Western countries are so selected that they do not disturb the over-all pattern of the meetings. So the result of these meetings is that they tend to sharpen the silly controversies and polemics which characterize the international situation of today.

You may be certain that I would gladly lend my name to any endeavor to bring about an honest discussion of the possibilities for reaching understanding and international security.

Einstein did not change his views about the various meetings of the World Peace Congress. When, eighteen months later, Professor Frédéric Joliot-Curie, his French colleague, invited him to attend the meeting of the Congress to be held in Sheffield, England, Einstein replied on November 3, 1950:

. . . I confess that, given the present world situation, I do not believe such manifestations will help the cause of peace. In my opinion, the only way to achieve peace is to strive for the creation of a world government.

Einstein, with Thomas Mann, Professor Emily G. Balch of the Women's International League for Peace and Freedom, the Reverend Edwin Dahlberg and Bishop W. J. Walls, was one of the original sponsors of the Conference on Peaceful Alternatives to the North Atlantic Treaty, which was held in Washington on May 20, 1949. He did not attend the conference. When the conferees sent him three resolutions that had been adopted and asked him to serve as one of five honorary chairmen of a Continuation Committee, he replied on May 27, 1949: [4]

I have carefully studied the three resolutions adopted at the conference. As far as the criticism of the present United States foreign policy is concerned, especially with regard to the Atlantic Pact, I am in full agreement.

Nevertheless, I feel unable to sign the resolutions. In my opinion the proposals offered are not far-reaching enough to solve the problem of international security. That goal can be attained only by creating a world government with authority to settle conflicts on the basis of law and with sufficient strength to enforce its decisions. No less radical a measure will call a halt to the arms race and prevent war. Indeed, I believe that advocacy of such half-measures only serves to divert the public from the real issue.

I feel unable, therefore, to become an honorary chairman or to serve as a member of the Continuation Committee established at the conference.

The writer and poet Christopher La Farge was one of those who had been invited to attend the Washington Conference. He expressed to Einstein the fear that, unless the conference dealt squarely with the question of world government, this all-important cause might be weakened by the dispersion of available energies. Einstein replied on May 13, 1949:

You are right in saying that the creation of a world government is the really important objective toward which we must all work. I have supported the Washington Conference insofar as I consider it most important to oppose the present almost hysterical trend toward complete militarization of this country and an open conflict with Russia. Had the North Atlantic Treaty been organized within the framework of the United Nations, I would have no objection to it.

About this time Einstein recommended for publication in the *Bulletin of the Atomic Scientists* an article written by Professor Herbert Jehle, entitled "For a Universal Morality." Professor Jehle, a physicist and pacifist of German origin, recalling the criticism of those who helped the Nazis in their evil activities, asserted in the article that participation in war preparations posed a challenge to man's conscience under any circumstances. He therefore urged that scientists refuse to participate in war work under any government, democratic or totalitarian. Dr. Eugene Rabinowitch, editor of the *Bulletin*, who had said he would welcome having Jehle's point of view discussed in his journal, decided against publication of this particular article since he felt the issue had not been adequately presented by Jehle. He so advised Einstein, who did not challenge Rabinowitch's decision but made some interesting comments in his letter to him of August 18, 1949:

In a sense Mr. Jehle's position is much more congenial to me than almost anything else that is being published on the subject. I am convinced that ethical judgments cannot be made on the basis of scientific deduction. There is too much discussion of whether the victim is to be hanged or guillotined, while I am deeply convinced he should not be executed at all. So long as the overriding consideration concerns what must be done in order to secure the most favorable strategic position in the event of war, international relations will never improve. If one realizes the implications of war preparations, one is virtually forced to become a rebel in the present circumstances. It becomes no longer possible for such an individual to feel a sense of solidarity with the society upon which one depends both *de facto* and *de jure*. That is what is behind Mr. Jehle's contribution and, since this cannot be said in so many plain words, any pronouncement about these issues will, of necessity, become defective logically! And, after all, to speak more frankly would merely outrage the conformist crowd.[5]

In a letter to Professor Jehle, mailed before receipt of Rabinowitch's letter about his rejection of Jehle's article, Einstein said:

I have read your article several times and feel that it is in complete harmony with my own way of thinking.

I hope that the *Bulletin* will publish the article but doubt that its effect will correspond to its good intentions. To an insane person, the truth appears foolish. He suspects ulterior motives and is indignant at the thought that a "foreigner" should be a better judge of what Americans ought to do. There are, after all, only few who think in supranational terms. Most people are satisfied to find themselves in agreement with the masses.

The majority of the really great scientists in this country have not participated in military work; this is true to a greater extent than was ever the case in Germany. On the other hand, most of the young scientists who have not yet made a reputation have yielded to the almost irresistible political and social pressure. One cannot expect them to be any different since few men are willing to be martyrs unless they are pushed in that direction by a mass movement. Your approach, therefore, is justified since it may help generate such a mass movement.

The predicament from which we suffer is in a sense timeless. Public institutions necessarily function on a rather low moral level, as do the men who stand behind these institutions. The individual is at the mercy of these institutions, the standards of which he must recognize as low if he is conscientious and not bare of any imagination. He is hence forced to accept some compromise, particularly since he must realize that those necessarily imperfect institutions are indispensable.

If those who recognize all these circumstances do not honestly and courageously work for a better world, conditions will continue to deteriorate.

An editor of the student yearbook of Cooper Union, an engineering and art college in New York, posed some questions to Einstein, one of which read as follows: Will not science necessarily be a source of man's eventual destruction? Einstein replied late in December 1949:

It seems to me unreasonable to make science responsible for the lamentable political happenings of the last decades. If destruction comes, then it will be due not to science but to moral degeneration and lack of political organization on a world-wide scale.

Professor Jacques Hadamard, the French mathematician, once again addressed himself to Einstein, soliciting his support (and through him possibly that of others) for an appeal sponsored by a French movement called the "Fighters for Peace and Freedom." The appeal asked that the French Parliament outlaw atomic bombs and that the United Nations order their destruction. Whoever threatened the world with atomic war was to be considered a war criminal. The triumph of law and reason was to be sought through all elected assemblies. Einstein's reply, dated December 29, 1949, was written in French, a language he otherwise never used in his correspondence:

I need hardly assure you that the problem of preventing war, with or without atomic bombs, is of supreme concern to me. It is, indeed, the most important of all international objectives. I must nevertheless tell you that I do not believe the approach proposed by the Fighters for Peace and Freedom stands any chance of success.

So long as security is sought through national armament, no country is likely to renounce any weapon that seems to promise it victory in the event of war. In my opinion security can be attained only by renouncing all national military defense.

Unfortunately, since both the United States and the Soviet Union persist in their mutually stubborn attitude, we cannot expect that either of them will make any constructive peace moves. Only a collective effort on the part of those nations which are militarily weak has any chance of success. I shall gladly use my humble energies in that direction, and I shall seek to enlist allies as far as my limited possibilities permit me to do.

If the nations which are militarily weak join forces, they can put pressure upon the two principal rivals to compose their differences peacefully by accepting the intercession of the United Nations and by pledging to submit to United Nations decisions without reservations.

During his visit to the United States, Pandit Nehru was courageous and resolute enough to declare publicly that India will not under any circumstances join either side. India's economic situation surely is no less precarious than that of the countries of Europe. They can certainly take the same risks as India.

On September 23, 1949, President Harry S. Truman made an announcement which Einstein and many other scientists had long anticipated: the American atomic monopoly was broken; the Soviet Union had detonated an atomic bomb. A month later A. J. Muste, secretary of the pacifist Fellowship of Reconciliation, called to Einstein's attention an article, "Russia's Atomic Bomb," by Dr. Kathleen Lonsdale of the Atomic Scientists' Association of Great Britain. Muste appealed for an "imaginative, creative and venturesome proposal" by scientists to arrest the growing danger of atomic war. Einstein replied on October 31, 1949:

There is no *purely mechanical* solution for the security problem. Also, security cannot be attained through armament but only on the basis of a give-and-take relationship which would make the creation and maintenance of a policy of peaceful co-operation desirable to both parties. Once this course is taken, it would mean the beginning of the development of mutual confidence which alone can make disarmament possible.

We should do our utmost to convince our fellow citizens that it is practically impossible for the Soviets to accept the Baruch Plan. Some of the reasons are convincingly stated in your letter.

Temporary suspension of the production of atomic bombs is, in my opinion, ineffective. On the one hand, nobody abroad would really believe it; on the other, such a single measure would be of little significance as long as the armaments race continues. An especially bad policy, in my opinion, is our economic boycott of Eastern Europe. To give you an example: The United States Government has prevented the shipment of goods (machinery) to Czechoslovakia, which that country had bought in the United States and paid for. One can easily imagine what bitterness such a policy must create in a small, impoverished and war-ravaged country. The American public hardly ever hears of such happenings.

The concatenation is this: No peace without disarmament; no disarmament without confidence; no confidence without mutual and effective economic relations. I cannot help feeling that since the death of President Roosevelt our foreign policy has proceeded in the wrong direction, and there seems to be little prospect at the moment for a shift toward a more reasonable policy.

Freedom of research and publication, and preservation of civil liberties, can be secured only in an atmosphere of genuine peace. Otherwise these freedoms will slowly, but irretrievably, be lost. I do not expect very much even from a concerted effort on the part of the scientists since we are faced with a political and economic, rather than a technical, problem. The American physicists, individually and collectively, have again and again expressed their conviction that it is impossible to attain security through armaments; they have, unfortunately, been unsuccessful in convincing others.

Dr. Lonsdale's article seems to be excellent and meritorious. Its wide dissemination would be very desirable.

Einstein, in those days, did not miss any opportunity to emphasize that world government was the only solution for world peace and to support those who were enlisted in the struggle toward that goal. Henry Usborne, the originator in England of the Peoples' World Convention, stood for re-election for the British House of Commons early in 1950. In reply to a letter received from Lancelot Hogben, the English mathematician, Einstein said on January 19, 1950:

I was very pleased to learn from you that our mutual friend Henry Usborne will be presenting the case for world government to the British public during the campaign for the forthcoming elections. The breathing space which is given us before disaster strikes may prove to be far too short; that is why at this time the struggle for universal law which may save us from universal destruction should take precedence over all domestic issues. It will hearten those in America who give priority to peace rather than to party politics if your fellow citizens will respond to the challenge of the atomic age by disregarding party affiliation and sending to the new Parliament men who are firmly committed to the world-wide movement for federal world government.

As early as 1946 Einstein's friend, the Austrian physicist Hans Thirring, had published details concerning an atomic bomb quite different from the kind of bomb that destroyed Hiroshima and Nagasaki.[6] Instead of utilizing energy from the *fission* of heavy elements, the new bomb would depend on energy liberated in the *fusion* of certain light atoms, notably the isotopes of hydrogen. Late in 1949, when scientific developments had increased the likelihood that bombs of virtually limitless explosive power might be made by this principle, a great behind-the-scenes debate took place in the United States on whether research on the production of the so-called hydrogen bomb should be started. News began to leak out that the United States Government was seriously considering an all-out effort to produce an H-bomb. Like many others, A. J. Muste, for many years one of the leading

American pacifists, was deeply concerned over this development. In writing Einstein an impassioned plea to throw the full weight of his influence against the threatening decision, Muste touched upon a subject on which Einstein was to become increasingly sensitive. On January 23, 1950, Einstein replied: [7]

I sense the sincerity and seriousness of your intentions and well understand that you are making certain suggestions to me in the light of your own views concerning the development of atomic weapons and the present situation in the world. You proceed, however, from false assumptions.

I have never taken part in work of a military-technical nature and have never done research having any bearing upon the production of the atomic bomb. My sole contribution in this field was that, in 1905, I established the relationship between mass and energy, a truth about the physical world of a very general nature, whose possible connection with the military potential was completely foreign to my thoughts. My only contribution with respect to the atomic bomb was that, in 1939, I signed a letter to President Roosevelt in which I called attention to the existing possibility of producing such a bomb and to the danger that the Germans might make use of that possibility. I considered this my duty because there were definite indications that the Germans were working on such a project.

It would, therefore, be quite ridiculous if I were to issue a statement declaring my refusal to participate in armament work. Since the military authorities are well aware of my position, it would never occur to them to invite me to participate in such work.

Concerning the political situation, I do not believe your proposal that the United States refrain from experimenting with the production of hydrogen bombs touches the core of the problem. The fact of the matter is that the people who possess the real power in this country have no intention of ending the cold war. The ruling group in this country has as little sought to avoid a conflict with the Soviet Union as the Russian ruling group has tried to avert such a conflict with the United States. Both groups are exploiting that conflict for their own internal political purposes, in complete disregard of the possible consequences.

This development began immediately after Roosevelt's death. The men in power succeeded in deceiving, intimidating and fanaticizing the public. I do not see how that tiny group of people, who do know about all these circumstances, could possibly stop the disastrous course of events, especially in view of the fact that even the so-called "neutral" nations do not unite to co-operate for the protection of peace on a supranational basis.

I myself have never hesitated to express my opinions freely; I have considered it my duty to do so. However, the voice of an individual is powerless against the shouting of the masses—this has always been so.

A few days later, on January 30, 1950, Muste sent Einstein a telegram in which he mentioned a number of prominent religious leaders and others [8] who were joining him in appealing to Einstein "to use [his] great influence to secure delay hydrogen bomb decision pending thorough public discussion. People must have opportunities to ponder and discuss this life-and-death issue, if United States is to remain democratic nation."

Einstein replied by letter the same day:

Your new proposal seems to me quite impracticable. As long as competitive armament prevails it will be not possible to halt the process in one country. The only possible solution would be an honest attempt to work toward a reasonable agreement with Soviet Russia and, beyond this, for security on a supranational basis.

The following day, January 31, 1950, President Truman announced that the United States would engage in an all-out effort to develop a hydrogen bomb. Two weeks later, on February 13, 1950, Einstein appeared (on film) in a television program dealing with the implications of the hydrogen bomb. The program, conducted by Mrs. Eleanor Roosevelt, also included David Lilienthal and J. Robert Oppenheimer, whose opposition to a crash program on the hydrogen bomb was to play an important role in his elimination as a consultant to the government in Washington four years later. These were Einstein's remarks: [9]

I am grateful to you, Mrs. Roosevelt, for the opportunity to express my convictions on this most important political question.

The belief that it is possible to achieve security through armaments on a national scale is, in the present state of military technology, a disastrous illusion. In the United States, this illusion has been strengthened by the fact that this country was the first to succeed in producing an atomic bomb. This is why people tended to believe that this country would be able to achieve permanent and and decisive military superiority which, it was hoped, would deter any potential enemy and thus bring about the security, so intensely sought by us as well as by the rest of the world. The maxim we have followed these last five years has been, in short, security through superior force, whatever the cost.

This technological as well as psychological orientation in military policy has had its inevitable consequences. Every action related to foreign policy is governed by one single consideration: How should we act in order to achieve the utmost superiority over the enemy in the event of war? The answer has been: Outside the United States, we must establish military bases at every possible, strategically important point of the globe as well as arm and strengthen economically our potential allies. And inside the United States, tremendous financial power is being concentrated in the hands of the military; youth is being militarized; and the loyalty of citizens, particularly civil servants, is carefully supervised by a police force growing more powerful every day. People of independent political thought are harassed. The public is subtly indoctrinated by the radio, the press, the schools. Under the pressure of military secrecy, the range of public information is increasingly restricted.

The arms race between the United States and the Soviet Union, initiated originally as a preventive measure, assumes hysterical proportions. On both sides, means of mass destruction are being perfected with feverish haste and behind walls of secrecy. And now the public has been advised that the production of the hydrogen bomb is the new goal which will probably be accomplished. An accelerated development toward this end has been solemnly proclaimed by the President. If these efforts should prove successful, radioactive poisoning of the atmosphere and, hence, annihilation of all life on earth will have been brought within the range of what is technically possible. The weird aspect of this development lies in its apparently inexorable character. Each step appears as the inevitable consequence of the one that went before. And at the end, looming ever clearer, lies general annihilation.

Is there any way out of this impasse created by man himself? All of us, and particularly those who are responsible for the policies of the United States and the Soviet Union, must realize that, although we have vanquished an external enemy, we have proved unable to free ourselves from the war mentality. We shall never achieve real peace as long as every step is taken with a possible future conflict in view, especially since it becomes ever clearer that such a war would spell universal annihilation. The guiding thought in all political action should therefore be: What can we do in the prevailing situation to bring about peaceful coexistence among all nations? The first goal must be to do away with mutual fear and distrust. Solemn renunciation of the policy of violence, not only with respect to weapons of mass destruction, is without doubt necessary. Such renunciation, however, will be effective only if a supranational judicial and executive agency is established at the same time, with power to settle questions of immediate concern to the security of nations. Even a declaration by a number of nations that they would collaborate loyally in the realization of such a "restricted world government" would considerably reduce the imminent danger of war.

In the last analysis the peaceful coexistence of peoples is primarily dependent upon mutual trust and, only secondarily, upon institutions such as courts of justice and the police. This holds true for nations as well as for individuals. And the basis of trust is a loyal relationship of give-and-take.

And what about international control? Well, it may be useful as a police measure but cannot be considered a prime factor. In any event, it may be wise not to overestimate its importance. The example of Prohibition comes to mind and gives one pause.

Two Canadians, Patricia Plante and Albert A. Shea, and a Hungarian, Paul Esway, in Paris, representing no political party or organization, were so inspired by Einstein's televised statement on the hydrogen bomb that they immediately prepared a petition of support, which was signed by more than 500 people representing forty-seven nationalities. Einstein wrote Shea on March 7, 1950:

I was gratified and encouraged to receive your and your friends' petition as a sign of approval on the part of so many people of different nationalities. I am convinced that those in responsible positions of power would be compelled to change their fatal attitude if the opinions and aspirations of the majority could be effectively and publicly expressed.

On February 1, 1950, Einstein joined Thomas Mann and fourteen others in protesting the punitive action that had been taken against several attorneys who had served as counsel to the defendants in the first of the famous Smith Act trials for alleged conspiracy to overthrow the government by force and violence.[10] The joint statement declared that such acts of judicial censure, imposition of prison sentences and threats of disbarment against legal defenders of political and racial minorities and labor organizations might, if unchallenged, "destroy the right to a fair trial and adequate legal counsel guaranteed by the Constitution."

During the same month, the National Council against Conscription published another study, *Militarism in Education*, introduced with the following statement signed by Einstein and twenty-five others: [11]

In recent months the nation's press has reported an increase in military activity and influence in our American educational institutions. This activity, represented by military subsidy of science departments, expanded military training units, increased use of schools and colleges as recruiting grounds, and military propaganda directed toward students and faculty, has serious implications both for the future of our nation and for world peace.

Already, in some colleges, military subsidy has led to government investigation of the students and faculty directly involved; it has placed some schools in the position of being increasingly dependent upon military funds for their existence. Military training and large military faculties have, in some other schools, tended to bring the discipline and attitudes of West Point or Annapolis into the normally free academic atmosphere of a civilian college.

The desperate need of the world for peace demands leadership commensurate with that need. Such leadership is more likely to come from those whose orientation and training, during their educational career, has been in the spirit of world brotherhood and free inquiry unhampered by narrow military considerations.

In a day when we are told there is no real security short of the abolition of war and the formation of a world society of nations, education must point the way. As UNESCO has pointed out, since wars begin in the minds of men, it is in the minds of men that the defenses of peace must be constructed.

It is therefore important that our fellow citizens should have authoritative information on the military program as it affects our educational institutions. In presenting this report of the expanding military influence in education, we do not necessarily imply that each of us would be opposed to every activity or measure herein described. It is the basic pattern that is dangerous. It is the trend that is wrong and that must be reversed.

Therefore, we join in issuing this report and recommending it for serious study by our fellow citizens and by their servants and representatives in state and national legislatures.

James E. Murray, U. S. Senator from Montana, sent Einstein the text of two articles, "Made in Germany" and "The Road to Peace," which had originally appeared in the magazine *Prevent World War III*, the publication of the Society for the Prevention of World War III. Both articles, which the Senator had inserted in the *Congressional Record*, sharply opposed the remilitarization of Germany, pointing out the historic and continuing German policy of playing East against West. Einstein wrote the Senator on March 7, 1950: [12]

What you have said is the naked truth. I know the Germans well, and I know how right you are on every point. I simply cannot understand how the Western Powers, despite their terrible experiences, can repeat the same mistakes and blunders that they made after the First World War. Responsible Western leaders seem once again to be blinded by their overestimation of the Russian danger, while underestimating the German danger. People like myself cannot make any public statement on this important matter because our views are considered as biased. For this reason I am all the more grateful to you for your lucid analysis of the issues involved.

If a serious attempt were made, I see no reason why it should not be possible to reach an agreement with Soviet Russia; the Soviet Union has nothing to gain from an armed conflict and, no doubt, wants to maintain peace. The Germans, however, with their rigid mentality, know no alternative but to fish in muddy waters, taking skillful advantage of the discord they have fostered between the United States and Soviet Russia.

A Hindu correspondent urged Einstein to emulate Gandhi and practice *ahimsa*—embark on a hunger strike until production of the hydrogen bomb was stopped. Einstein replied on March 24, 1950:

I can well appreciate that the course of action you suggest in your recent letter seems quite natural to you since you are living among people of Indian mentality. But knowing the mentality of the American people, I am quite convinced that the action which you suggest would not have the desired effect. It would, on the contrary, be considered an expression of unpardonable arrogance.

This does not mean that I do not have the greatest admiration for Gandhi and for the Indian tradition in general. I feel that the influence of India in international affairs is growing and will prove beneficent. I have studied the works of Gandhi and Nehru with real admiration. India's forceful policy of neutrality in regard to the American-Russian conflict could well lead to an unified attempt on the part of the neutral nations to find a supranational solution to the peace problem.

On March 4, 1950, Einstein sent the following letter, together with his check for membership dues, to the newly formed Society for Social Responsibility in Science: [13]

I am convinced that your Society for Social Responsibility in Science serves one of the most important causes scientific workers can engage in at this time. Such a society will develop their sense of responsibility and bolster their courage to resist the insidious inducement to accept work associated with mass destruction. Men need to recognize that individual conscience comes before the letter and the intention of the law. This was implicitly acknowledged at the Nuremberg trials.

Since Einstein had not permitted publication of this statement, which he considered too brief, A. J. Muste pleaded with him later to make a public statement on behalf of the society. On July 19, 1950, the following open letter from Einstein to the Society for Social Responsibility in Science was released:

DEAR FELLOW SCIENTISTS:

The problem of how man should act if his government prescribes actions or society expects an attitude which his own conscience considers wrong is indeed an old one. It is easy to say that the individual cannot be held responsible for acts carried out under irresistible compulsion, that he is completely dependent upon the society in which he is living and must therefore accept its rules. But the very formulation of this kind of reasoning makes it obvious to what extent such a concept contradicts our sense of justice.

While external compulsion can, to a certain extent, affect an individual's sense of responsibility, it can never wholly destroy it. In the Nuremberg trials this position was virtually accepted as self-evident. The morality existing in our institutions, as well as our laws and mores in general, are the result of the cumulative efforts of countless individuals throughout the ages to express what they considered to be just. Institutions are, in a moral sense, impotent unless they derive support from the individual's sense of responsibility. That is why any effort to arouse and strengthen this sense of responsibility becomes an important service to mankind.

In our time, scientists and engineers carry a particularly heavy burden of moral responsibility, because the development of military means of mass destruction is dependent upon their work and activities. I feel, therefore, that the formation of the Society for Social Responsibility in Science serves a real need. Through its discussion of the objective problems confronting the scientist, it will make it easier for the individual to clarify his own mind and to arrive at a conclusion concerning his own actions. Moreover, mutual help is essential for those whose situation will become difficult whenever they act according to their conscience.

Trygve Lie, Secretary-General of the United Nations, received a letter from Einstein, dated April 18, 1950, following Lie's proposal for special Security Council sessions at the highest level, a proposal that was to lead to his visit to Moscow a few weeks later. Einstein wrote:

I feel I must wish you luck and success in your great initiative. You are one of the very few who, in the midst of the bewilderment and confusion of our time, has succeeded in keeping his vision clear, and whose urge to be of constructive help remains undeterred by obstacles and narrow allegiances. May your concrete proposals succeed in showing us a way out of the present tension, occasioned as it is more by emotional factors than by material causes, and in providing a solution advantageous to all concerned. Even relatively small successes in the direction of economic co-operation should soon improve and stabilize the political and emotional situation.

I am one of the many whose thoughts accompany you with gratitude and hope.

In June 1950 the National Council against Conscription issued still another study, *America, Russia and the Bomb*, a well-argued plea for total disarmament. Einstein joined fifteen others in sponsoring the publication and subscribing to this introductory statement: [14]

The developments of weapons of mass destruction, together with the armaments race in which the United States and Russia are engaged, have caused wide discussion about the possibility of disarmament and abolition of war. A leading United States Senator [Millard Tydings] has proposed total world disarmament down to rifles. Other proposals have been made in the press and officially through the United Nations.

The peoples of the world are eager for some solution to the problem of war. Their aspirations were expressed in the Atlantic Charter statement: "All of the nations of the world, for realistic as well as for spiritual reasons, must come to abandon the use of force."

Yet, today, the two leading powers, the United States and Russia, are in such disagreement about atomic energy control and disarmament that only a profoundly informed world public opinion and a real will to peace on the part of the people can persuade them to resolve the impasse.

It is therefore important that our fellow citizens should have authoritative information on past and present Russian and American proposals and attitudes concerning disarmament. We recognize that in a complex world all nations must share responsibility for world problems. Neither Russia nor the United States can evade this responsibility. Any attempt to deal with the disarmament impasse must therefore rise above partisanship and nationalism. Nevertheless, because we are Americans and because of the leadership which America may yet provide for world disarmament, we join in sponsoring this report. This does not necessarily imply that each of us would give full and final support to all of the suggestions herein presented for resolving the impasse, but we do believe they will make a contribution to the much-needed public discussion on this issue.

Therefore we join in issuing this report and recommending it for serious study by our fellow citizens and by their servants and representatives in positions of official responsibility.

On June 18, 1950, just a week before the outbreak of the Korean War began, Einstein participated[15] in a documentary broadcast, "Year of Decision," part of a series sponsored by the United Nations under the title "The Pursuit of Peace":

Q: Is it an exaggeration to say that the fate of the world is hanging in the balance?

A: No exaggeration. The fate of humanity is always in the balance, but more truly now than at any known time.

Q: How can we awaken all the peoples to the seriousness of the moment?

A: I believe this question *can* be answered. The remedy doesn't lie in preparing oneself for the possibility of a future war. We must start with the conviction that security against military disaster can be realized only through patient negotiation. We must create a legal basis for the solution of international problems, supported by a sufficiently strong executive agency—in short, a kind of world government.

Q: Is the current atomic armaments race leading to another world war or is it, as some people maintain, a way to prevent war?

A: Competitive armament is not a way to prevent war. Every step in this direction brings us nearer to catastrophe. An armaments race is the *worst* possible method of preventing an open conflict. On the contrary, real peace cannot be reached without systematic disarmament on a supranational scale. I repeat, armament is not only no protection against war, but leads inevitably *to* war.

Q: Is it possible to prepare for war and a world community at the same time?

A: Striving for peace and preparing for war are incompatible with each other, and in our time more so than ever.

Q: Can we prevent war?

A: There is a very simple answer. If we ourselves have the courage to decide in favor of peace, we will *have* peace.

Q: How?

A: By the unshakable determination to reach agreement. This is axiomatic. We are not playing a game. We are in a situation which poses the greatest threat to our survival. Unless we are firmly resolved to settle problems in a peaceful way, we shall never arrive at a peaceful solution.

Q: What is your opinion of the profound changes in our living predicted by some scientists, for example, the possibility of our need to work only two hours a day?

A: We are always the same people. There are no really profound changes. It is not so important whether we work five hours or two. Our problem is social and economic and must be dealt with on the international level.

Q: What would you suggest doing with the supply of atom bombs already stockpiled?

A: Put them into the hands of a supranational organization. During the interval before solid peace is attained we must have some protective power; one-sided disarmament is impossible. It is out of the question. Arms must be entrusted solely to an international authority. There is no alternative to systematic disarmament under a supranational government. We must not consider the problem of security from too technical a point of view. The *will* to peace and the readiness to accept every measure needed to attain this goal are the most important factors.

Q: What can the private individual *do* about the problems of war and peace?

A: He can insist that anyone who runs for office (Congress, for example) give a clear pledge to work for international security and, to this end, for a limitation of national sovereignty. Everybody who is involved in forming public opinion must really understand what is needed and must have the courage to speak out.

Q: United Nations Radio is broadcasting to all the corners of the earth, in twenty-seven languages. Since this is a moment of great danger, what word would you have us broadcast to the peoples of the world?

A: On the whole, I believe that Gandhi held the most enlightened views of all the political men in our time. We should strive to do things in his spirit: not to use violence in fighting for our cause and to refrain from taking part in anything we believe is evil.

In June 1950 Stringfellow Barr, the President of the Foundation for World Government, reminded Einstein of a telegraphic request which Einstein had received a few months earlier for an expression of his support of a great world government demonstration to be held in Cahors, France, on June 24–25, 1950. This event had developed from the work of Robert Sarrazac-Soulage and his Centre de Recherche et d'Expression Mondialiste.[16] In the wake of a tour of the South of France made by Garry Davis in 1949, the French commune of Trouillas had declared itself "world territory." It was reported that the larger towns of Cahors and Figeac, in the Department Lot, followed suit by overwhelming popular vote; that a majority of the towns in the province did so later; and that within a year the "world territories" comprised a belt stretching about hundred miles north of the Spanish border, from the Atlantic to the Mediterranean, and including about three million people. Ultimately the movement is said to have affected about five hundred communities, including the town of Königswinter in Germany.

On June 20, 1950, Einstein replied to Barr: [17]

I did indeed receive the cabled request, but I did nothing about it at the time, simply because I did not know what to do; I feel the same today. Although one has the impression that the senders of the telegram are quite sincere about their proposal, I cannot help but feel it is a "soap bubble." When one advocates such romantic enterprises, one soon ceases to be taken seriously and loses whatever prestige one may have gained.

I have carefully read your report. I could perhaps agree with you, if it were not for the fact that the world situation constitutes such an immediate danger to peace. I believe that if world government were realized, even on the basis of a minimum program, its functions and duties would very soon have to be expanded. Yet I think it would be considerably easier to rally the support of the pertinent groups throughout the world for a minimum program, rather than for a more extensive program including human rights, famine elimination, birth control, etc. I hope that all sensible people will support a minimum program and prevent the dissipation of our potential strength since general annihilation through war threatens the strong and weak alike; indeed it may pose an even more immediate threat to the stronger nations.

These remarks should not be taken as objections insofar as your efforts are aimed at education and enlightenment.

On the occasion of the fifth anniversary of the bombing of Hiroshima and Nagasaki, Norman Cousins, writing in *The Saturday Review of Literature* of August 5, 1950, projected two versions of how the historian of 1960 might evaluate the present. The article, entitled "As 1960 Sees Us," takes the form of two separate accounts. In the first, "The Repudiation of Man," atomic war has ravaged the world; civilization has been destroyed; human nature has changed. Man no longer believes in progress and has not the will to rebuild or create. Cousins chose the image of a doomed ship, a gaping hole in her prow, in which the passengers, rigidly kept apart in the three passenger classes, prove incapable of forgetting their compartmentalization and of joining forces in the work which alone could save them. They fight one another to the end, clawing with one hand as the other clings to a piece of wreckage. The United States, which might have prevented disaster, failed to fulfill her own historic mission.

In the second part of the article, entitled "The Age of Valor," the President of the United States reviews American foreign policy in the light of the Korean War and submits to Congress and the American people new instructions for the American delegates to the United Nations, which would transform that body into a world government. This does not bring the millennium, but it does usher in an age of peace.

On August 2, 1950, Einstein wrote Cousins: [18]

I have read your article and think that it should have a good effect on people. The first part should serve to dampen the romantic attitude toward the present dangerous war adventure; the analogy of a ship in danger is very well done.

In the second part of your article you employ a method which is psychologically most effective. Instead of merely criticizing the foreign policy of the United States, you demonstrate how the reactionary approach of our government plays into the hands of the Soviet Union everywhere, especially with regard to Asia. I was also impressed by the skillful way in which you placed your own proposals, with which I fully agree, in the mouth of the hapless President. It provides a contrast with the actual attitude of our government in a manner which is at once inoffensive and effective. Your implicit criticism has achieved something constructive and necessary.

What I do object to in your article is that you not only fail to oppose the widespread hysterical fear in our country of Russian aggression but actually encourage it. All of us should ask ourselves which of the two countries is objectively more justified in fearing the aggressive intentions of the other. Those who have not thoroughly considered this question with the aid of a world map will, of necessity, lack the objectivity essential to the development of an intelligent political attitude.

As the intensity of the cold war increased, the hostility of the United States toward the Soviet Union became ever more bitter and widespread. Only a small minority of Americans succeeded in not becoming affected by the mounting hysteria. Since Einstein never wavered in his calm and objective analysis of Soviet developments and in the conviction that peace in the world depended on friendly relations with the Soviet Union, he was often subject to political attacks and insinuations.

A frequent correspondent on these problems was Professor Sidney Hook of New York University. Einstein always answered promptly and patiently. Hook wrote in May 1950, referring to two articles published by Einstein in 1934 and 1947 respectively, which had just been republished in a partial collection of Einstein's writings. Hook claimed that while certain passages in these articles were "not formally contradictory, their spirit clearly was." Einstein replied on March 16, 1950, the very day Hook's letter had been received. He denied that the passages cited by Hook contradicted each other and then added:

I have endeavored to understand why the Russian Revolution became a necessity. Under the circumstances prevailing in Russia at the time, I believe that the revolution could have been successfully undertaken only by a resolute minority. A Russian who had the welfare of the people at heart would, under the then existing conditions, naturally co-operate with, and submit to, this minority since the immediate goals of the revolution could otherwise not have been achieved. To an independent person, this must surely have entailed *temporary*, painful renunciation of his personal liberty. But I believe that I myself would have deemed it my duty, and would have considered it the lesser evil, to make this temporary sacrifice. This, however, should not be taken to mean that I approve of the Soviet Government's policy of intervention, both direct and indirect, in intellectual and artistic matters. I view such interference as objectionable, harmful and even ridiculous. I also believe that centralization of political power and limitation of individual freedoms should not exceed the limits determined by such considerations as external security, domestic stability and the requirements of a planned economy. An outsider is hardly in a position to appraise adequately the existing conditions and needs of another country. In any case, there is no doubt that the achievements of the Soviet regime in the fields of education, public health, social welfare and economics are considerable and that the people as a whole have greatly benefited from those achievements.

A correspondent in Massachusetts, a manual worker who considered himself "uneducated," criticized Einstein's alleged optimism concerning the possibility of establishing a world government. In his opinion, world government could come into being only when the masses of the people were sufficiently well informed about that form of government. Such an attitude, he felt, could be realized only under socialism; hence, all attempts at world government would be futile as long as the prevailing political and economic system in the United States remained unchanged. Einstein said in his reply of June 12, 1950, that he had been much interested in his correspondent's remarks and his criticism of certain statements Einstein had made about the intelligence and the character of the masses more than a decade ago. Einstein called the criticism "justified a good deal" and then continued:

Concerning the establishment of a world government, we unfortunately have no time to wait. Unless we are able, in the near future, to abolish the mutual fear of military aggression, we are doomed. Furthermore, however much I may believe in the necessity of socialism, it will not solve the problem of international security. On the contrary, socialism necessarily gives rise to a high concentration of political power in a democracy; and socialist bureaucrats are not less inclined toward acts of aggression than the exponents of private economic power, as it now exists. With respect to the problem of peace and socialism, I have encountered a good deal of what I consider to be unfounded optimism in socialist circles.

To the Committee for Academic Freedom at the University of California, which had asked his support for faculty members dismissed for refusal to sign a new loyalty oath, Einstein wrote on August 3, 1950:[19]

I sympathize fully with your endeavor; at the same time, however, I must face the fact that this endeavor means fighting only the symptoms, while the *disease* itself remains the root of the problem.

The disease stems from the fact that one tries to base the security of the country on national armament rather than on international organization. The result is an increasing militarization of the country, which inevitably leads to the formation of a police state and, in fact, has already done so to a large extent. Unless we concentrate on fighting the underlying causes, we shall never be successful. The ever mounting military rivalry necessarily results in increasing espionage attempts, which in turn call forth countermeasures that destroy the liberties and rights of the individual. In the last analysis, how relatively insignificant is the destruction of academic freedom if it is compared with the military enslavement which forces individuals to sacrifice their lives in actions many of them condemn!

The Società Italiana per il Progresso delle Scienze held its forty-third meeting in Lucca, Italy, in October 1950. Einstein sent this message "On the Moral Obligation of the Scientist": [20]

Let me first thank you most sincerely for your kindness in inviting me to attend the meeting of your society. I should have gladly accepted the invitation if my health had permitted me to do so. Under the circumstances, all I can do is to address you briefly from my home across the ocean. In doing so I have no illusions that I have anything to say which would actually enlarge your insight or your understanding. However, we are living in a period of such great external and internal insecurity, marked by its lack of clear objectives, that the mere confession of our convictions may be useful even if these convictions, as all value judgments, cannot be proven through logical deduction.

At once, the question arises: Should the search for truth—or, more modestly expressed, our efforts to understand the knowable universe through constructive logical thought—be the independent objective of our work? Or should the search for truth be subordinated to other objectives, such as "practical" considerations? Such a question cannot be decided on the basis of logic. Nonetheless, our decision, however arrived at, will have considerable influence upon our thinking and moral judgment, provided that it stems from a deep and unshakable conviction. Let me then make a confession: I believe that the struggle to achieve greater insight and understanding is one of those independent objectives without which a thinking individual could not have a conscious, positive attitude toward life.

It is the very essence of our efforts for greater understanding that, on the one hand, man attempts to encompass the great and complex variety of human experience, while on the other, he looks for simplicity and economy in the basic assumptions. In view of the primitive state of our scientific knowledge, the belief that these two objectives can exist side by side is a matter of faith. However, without such faith I could not have so strong and unshakable a conviction concerning the independent value of knowledge.

The attitude of the man engaged in scientific work, which, in a sense, is a religious attitude, exerts a certain influence upon his whole personality. For, apart from the knowledge which the man of science acquires from accumulated experience and from the rules of logic, theoretically there is no authority whose decisions and statements can claim to be "the truth." This leads to the paradoxical situation of the individual who, having devoted all his strength to objective matters, thereby develops, from a social point of view, into an extreme individualist; and, at least in principle, this individualist has faith in nothing but his own judgment. It is thus quite possible to assert that intellectual individualism and the thirst for scientific knowledge emerged simultaneously in history and have remained inseparable.

It may be thought that the man of science, as sketched in these sentences, is no more than an abstraction which actually does not exist in this world, not unlike the *Homo oeconomicus* of classical economics. However, it seems to me that science, as we know it today, could neither have emerged nor remained alive if men of science had not actually existed for many centuries.

Of course, not everyone who has learned to use tools and methods which directly or indirectly appear to be "scientific" is, in my opinion, a man of science. When I speak of scientists, I refer only to those individuals in whom the scientific mentality is truly alive.

What, then, is the attitude of today's man of science toward contemporary society? Obviously, he is rather proud of the fact that the work of scientists has helped to alter radically the economic life of men by virtually eliminating manual labor. On the other hand, the scientist is distressed by the realization that the result of his scientific labors is a threat to the existence of mankind since his work has fallen into hands of those who blindly exercise political power. He is conscious of the fact that technological methods, made possible by his work, have led to a concentration of economic and, hence, political power in the hands of small minorities which have succeeded in dominating totally the lives of the masses who appear more and more amorphous. Even more serious is the fact that the concentration of economic and political power in fewer and fewer hands has not only made the man of science economically dependent; it has also threatened his independence from within; the shrewd methods of intellectual and psychic influence brought to bear upon the scientist will prevent the development of genuinely independent personalities.

Thus the man of science, as we can observe with our own eyes, suffers a truly tragic fate. In his sincere attempt to achieve clarity and inner independence, he has succeeded, by his sheer superhuman efforts, in fashioning the tools which will not only enslave him but also destroy him from within. He cannot escape being silenced by those who wield political power. When he is a soldier, he must sacrifice his own life and destroy the lives of others, even if convinced of the absurdities of such sacrifices. He is fully aware of the fact that universal destruction is unavoidable since the historical development has led to the concentration of all economic, political and military power in the hands of national states. He also realizes that mankind can be saved only if a supranational system, based on law, is created to eliminate the methods of brute force. However, the man of science has retrogressed to such an extent that he accepts as inevitable the slavery inflicted upon him by national states. He even degrades himself to such an extent that he obediently lends his talents to help perfect the means destined for the general destruction of mankind.

Is there really no escape for the man of science? Must he really tolerate and suffer all these indignities? Is that time forever past when, aroused by his inner freedom and the independence of his thinking and his work, the scientist had the opportunity of enlightening and enriching the lives of his fellow human beings? In placing his work on too intellectual a basis, has he not forgotten about his responsibility and dignity as a scientist? My answer is: While it is true that an inherently free and scrupulous person may be destroyed, such an individual can never be enslaved or made to serve as a blind tool.

If today's man of science could find the time and the courage to reflect honestly and critically about himself and the tasks before him, and if he would then act accordingly, the possibilities for a sane and satisfactory solution of the present dangerous international situation would be considerably improved.

In August 1950, Mark Van Doren, poet and Professor of English Literature at Columbia University, sent Einstein a statement opposing German rearmament. He expressed the hope that many prominent persons would sign. Einstein replied on October 8, 1950:

I have not signed the statement you have sent me although I am in full agreement with its content. The reason is simply that I wish to avoid any impression of disagreeing only with the rearmament of Germany. In reality such rearmament is but a link in the chain of measures our government has followed since Roosevelt's death; such measures may, in my opinion, lead to disastrous consequences in the future.

A somewhat parallel statement on the rearming of Japan was submitted to Einstein in September by A. J. Muste of the Fellowship of Reconciliation. On October 11, 1950, Einstein wrote: [21]

I am, of course, in full agreement with your position. But your attempt seems to me so hopeless that I cannot get myself to participate in it. It seems to me like sending a bottle of sugar water to a chronic alcoholic in the hope of curing him.

The executive secretary of the Paraguayan Academy of the Historical, Political and Social Sciences appealed to Einstein for a reply to the question of what should be the attitude of Latin-American youth in such times of world-wide uncertainty. Einstein replied on October 16, 1950: [22]

I think your question can be unequivocally answered, provided I have properly understood it. Since you addressed me in Spanish, I may be allowed to respond in German. I am confident you will find someone to translate my letter for you.

It is generally agreed that the problem of security can only be solved on a supranational basis. The United Nations, despite its being, at present, a rather weak factor toward stabilization, provides nevertheless a useful beginning in the evolution of an agency which would assume the functions of a limited world government.

In the course of promoting such a development an important task falls to the smaller nations. Instead of continuing to play the role of satellites to the existing major powers, the United States and the Soviet Union, they should join hands, become an independent mediating factor and resolutely oppose any attempt to reduce the United Nations to a mere instrument in the struggle for national power. I have no doubt that India's present attitude can be explained in the light of such considerations. Should India's attitude in time gain the support of the smaller nations, the next few years may bring an end to the perilous condition in which the world finds itself today because of the deepening conflict between the opposing great powers.

Once that is achieved, the next task can be approached in the hope for success: to make an attempt so that the delegates to the United Nations become independent of their respective governments, and that they be responsible solely to the constituents who elect them, and to their own conscience. Only then will they be able to act on behalf of the supranational interests of all.

If the smaller nations join in a policy of united action, I believe they will be able to consolidate supranational relations.

Einstein's mood in that period is well illustrated by a letter which he sent to an unknown physician in Indiana who had complained that his son was about to be inducted into the army although he, the father, had thought that his own five years' service during the Second World War should have assured his son a life of peace. Einstein, whom the physician urged to redouble his efforts in behalf of peace, replied on November 5, 1950:

You are very right in assuming that I am badly in need of encouragement. I have indeed the impression that our nation has gone mad and is no longer receptive to reasonable suggestions. Its whole development reminds me of the events in Germany since the time of Emperor William II: through many victories to final disaster.

In spite of all discouragement, I promise you that I will make use of any opportunity that may be offered me in the attempts to further the people's understanding of existing conditions.

That Henry Usborne's plan for a Peoples' World Convention failed to take hold in the United States, despite the active support of Einstein and many others, has been mentioned before. Nevertheless, the plan did give rise to some noteworthy efforts on a local scale. In North Dakota, the physicist Daniel Q. Posin, who had unsuccessfully promoted a National Congress of Scientists late in 1945, made a dramatic tour of the state with a liberal attorney, Harold Bangert. His activities brought him into difficulties at the North Dakota State College, where he was teaching.[23] More immediately successful was the campaign waged in Tennessee by another liberal, the lawyer Fyke Farmer, who had been instrumental in bringing Usborne to the United States in 1947. As a result of Farmer's efforts, on April 7, 1949, the state legislature of Tennessee enacted a law which authorized the election of three delegates to the Peoples' World Convention. Such an election was actually held in August 1950, with Farmer as one of the successful candidates. (The statute was subsequently repealed.)

The Peoples' World Convention, eventually assembled by Henry Usborne in the Palais Electoral at Geneva on December 31, 1950, with Lord Boyd Orr as honorary president, was, although a valiant gesture, a mere shadow of the great scheme on which such high hopes had been staked in 1947 and 1948. Although there were some 500 "observers," the official elected delegates numbered just three: two from Tennessee, and one from Nigeria. Fyke Farmer presented this message from Einstein:[24]

The mounting danger of a conflict that would cause total annihilation has served to convince the whole world of the necessity of creating a world government. What has been lacking heretofore is a permanent and effective body, truly international in composition, supranational in its thinking, enjoying the confidence of like-minded people throughout the world, and authorized to represent them in pursuit of that great goal. To give birth to such a representative body is the main objective of the Geneva Convention.

The convention must decide the question of whether and to what extent the United Nations may serve as the basis for our efforts. We are convinced that the United Nations will be able to develop into a world government only when the Assembly is no longer composed of delegates appointed by governments, but, instead, of representatives elected directly by the people. Only in this way will the delegates serve the interests of supranational order and security according to their own best judgment.

CHAPTER SIXTEEN

THE FIGHT FOR INTELLECTUAL FREEDOM | 1951-1952

A MAN WHO IS as much an individualist as Einstein was and who, at the same time, recognizes as vividly as he did his dependence upon the community of men cannot fail to have frequent occasions in his life to reflect upon the place and responsibility of the individual in society. There exist many statements which indicate Einstein's deep concern with this difficult problem; he often pondered over the conflict which may arise between the individual's responsibility to himself and his responsibility to the group to which he belongs, and to mankind as a whole. Einstein, who passionately defended the intellectual and moral freedom of the individual, frequently emphasized with equal conviction the obligations which a truly free individual must assume toward the community of which he is an integral part. He never ignored the difficult decisions which the individual in modern society has to make in attempting to comply with the commands of his conscience and, on the other hand, with the just demands of society upon him. Einstein's own attitude on these problems was manifest throughout his public life—from the days when he signed the "Manifesto to Europeans" in 1914, to his active participation in the War Resisters' Movement in the decade after the First World War, to his defiance of the German Academies shortly after the Nazis' advent to power, and to his support of military preparedness against Nazi aggression in the years before the outbreak of war. But at no time did his concern over the intricate relationship between individual freedom and social responsibility assert itself more forcefully than during the last decade of his life.

Various manifestations of Einstein's beliefs on the conflict between individual and social responsibility, particularly concerning the responsibility of the scientist in regard to the production of armaments, have been documented on preceding pages. It is necessary, in addition, to refer to some other pronouncements in which he dealt with the obligations that he believed the struggle against war imposes on all men. Einstein was well aware of the complexity of the concept of freedom; he knew that completely unrestricted "freedom" is impossible in any society and that the protection of human life as well as the gratification of man's economic needs necessarily involve limitations upon man's freedom. What Einstein was primarily concerned with was man's *intellectual* freedom and his unqualified compliance with certain moral and ethical standards.

Sometime in 1951, Einstein drafted the following epigram, which clearly referred to the Nuremberg war crime trials and which may have been destined for a conscientious objector:

There is a curious inconsistency in a government which punishes aliens for *not* following their conscience in a given conflict, while penalizing its own citizens for *following* their conscience in the same kind of conflict. Apparently such a government holds the conscience of its own citizens in lower esteem than that of aliens.

He was more explicit on another occasion. A young German refugee, a veteran and a pacifist, called to Einstein's attention the case of a conscientious objector in Kansas who had been sentenced to a prison term of ten years for refusal of military service. Einstein's reply was dated March 20, 1951: [1]

What we have here is the old conflict between conscience and law. During the Nuremberg trials, the various governments adopted the position that immoral acts cannot be excused on the plea that they were committed on government orders. What constitutes an immoral act can be determined only by one's own individual judgment and conscience. The attitude that moral law takes precedence over secular law is very much in line with people's general sense of right and wrong.

Whenever a person disobeys the law because of his moral convictions, the government considers him a rebel who has breached the law and must be punished. Hence it makes little sense in such cases for the individual in question to appeal to the very officials who are duty-bound to enforce the existing laws.

The conscientious objector is a revolutionary. In deciding to disobey the law he sacrifices his personal interests to the most important cause of working for the betterment of society. In matters of crucial significance this is often the only way to bring about social progress; this is particularly true when the prevailing balance of power precludes the successful utilization of normal legal and political institutions. It was in this sense that the Fathers of the American Constitution specifically acknowledged the people's right to revolution.

Revolution without the use of violence was the method by which Gandhi brought about the liberation of India. It is my belief that the problem of bringing peace to the world on a supranational basis will be solved only by employing Gandhi's method on a large scale.

Einstein's views on the right of the individual to disobey the laws of his country, when these laws compel him to do what in good conscience he is unable to do, were revealed in a moving correspondence with Gene Sharp, a twenty-five-year-old graduate of Ohio State University.[2] Sharp was indicted for defying the draft law and for refusing to report for physical examination and induction; he received a two-year jail sentence. Shortly before the trial, Sharp wrote Einstein to acquaint him with his case and to inquire whether Einstein was willing to write an introduction to the book on Gandhi which Sharp had just completed. Einstein replied on April 2, 1953:

I earnestly admire you for your moral strength and can only hope, although I really do not know, that I would have acted as you did, had I found myself in the same situation. Your manuscript arrived today. I shall read it carefully and prepare some introductory remarks if I sufficiently agree with its contents.

There is a sphere of conflict between the written laws of one's country and the unwritten laws, the existence of which becomes manifest in what we call our conscience. In the event of conflict, the state adheres to the written law; only with great reluctance does it take into account the unwritten law of conscience. But even the state has recognized the duty of the individual to act according to the unwritten law when commands based on national laws are in striking conflict with the laws of his conscience. This principle was unmistakably established in the Nuremberg trials. Such a precedent is a precious tool in the fight against the slavery resulting from the civic duty to kill.

Gene Sharp thanked Einstein "for saying what you did in your letter. It means very much to me. It may also make things somewhat easier on my parents in Ohio, who have found it difficult to understand my position."

A few days later, on April 10, 1953, Einstein wrote again to Sharp advising him that he had read his manuscript "with sincere admiration." He enclosed the following introduction which Sharp was to use in the publication of the manuscript:

This volume reports facts and nothing but facts—facts which have all been published before. And yet, it is a truly significant piece of work which is destined to have a great educational effect. It is the history of the peaceful struggle of the Indian people for liberation under the leadership of Gandhi. Everything that happened took place before the eyes of our generation. What makes the book a highly effective work of art is the selection and organization of the facts here assembled. It is the art of a born historian under whose hands the individual pieces grow into a great picture.

How is it possible that a young man was able to create such a mature piece of work? The author's preface tells us how it was possible. He feels the profound obligation to serve, with all his energies and with unlimited readiness for sacrifice, a purpose which is clearly personified in Gandhi's unique example: to overcome through an awakening of moral strength the danger of self-destruction which confronts mankind as a result of explosive technological developments. The collapse which threatens mankind is characterized in the volume by the words *depersonalization, regimentation, total war,* while its salvation is characterized by the words *personal responsibility, in conjunction with nonviolence and service to human beings in Gandhi's sense.*

I believe the author is completely right in asserting that every human being is compelled to come to a clear decision with regard to this important matter: there is no middle ground.

In the Nuremberg trials the following principle was laid down: Personal moral responsibility cannot be set aside by national laws. Let us hope that we may soon come to the point where the Nuremberg principle will not only be enforced upon citizens of vanquished nations! It is quite possible that Gene Sharp has gained the power to complete this work out of his own inner struggle over these problems. The merits of this work cannot possibly escape anyone who reads it with careful attention.

When Sharp received Einstein's introduction, he wrote that "there are times when a simple 'Thanks' seems hardly enough." A week later, on April 16, 1953, Einstein wrote again. Since he knew that Sharp had not yet found a publisher, he had talked with a friend, the editor-in chief of a publishing house, who would be very glad to be as helpful as possible. He then continued:

I was very much impressed with your letters to the draft board and also with the relatively satisfactory behavior of the board. I am convinced that those letters are a document of real significance which could serve the cause of reason if used in an appropriate way.

After sentencing, Sharp was sent to the Federal Penitentiary in Danbury, Connecticut, from where he wrote Einstein at the end of about six weeks. He expressed himself favorably regarding the prison and life in prison. "I have no regrets," he said, "and feel an inner freedom which comes from knowing that I have done that which is right. The ultimate freedom of man is that which lies within himself. No one can take that from him if he refuses to give it up himself."

Einstein replied immediately, on June 17, 1953, as follows:

I was glad to receive your letter. It shows that there are people everywhere who respect those who follow their conscience. I am glad that you are enjoying your strange situation and are taking it all serenely.

You should not be disappointed that my friend did not succeed in convincing his colleagues to assume the financial risk of publishing your book. The same happened a year ago with another book which involved a much greater financial risk than your book. But my friend made great efforts and was able to find another publisher. You can be sure that he will try even harder in your case.

Einstein also replied immediately to Sharp's mother, who addressed a touching letter to him in which she spoke about her son's extraordinary human qualities and about her other children. Einstein wrote her that her son was "irresistible in his noble sincerity."

Einstein's most striking and most effective public expression concerning intellectual freedom and man's duty, even at the risk of great personal sacrifice, to protect his liberty to speak freely and think for himself, came in connection with the investigation of many political nonconformists by committees of the United States Congress. Since 1947, with the increasing intensity of the cold war, the operations of the Committee on Un-American Activities of the House of Representatives as well as the Subcommittee on Internal Security of the Committee of the Judiciary and the Subcommittee on Investigations of the Committee on Government Operations of the Senate had gained momentum. Many hundreds of Americans, mostly professionals, artists and intellectuals in many fields, were summoned before the committees and questioned about their political beliefs as well as their private and political associations. Those who refused to reply to questions of this character, because they considered them an invasion of the freedom protected by the First Amendment to the Constitution of the United States, faced a jail sentence for contempt of Congress in the event they claimed the protection guaranteed by this amendment; or they faced certain economic ruin if they claimed protection under the Fifth Constitutional Amendment, according to which no witness can be compelled to testify if his testimony might tend to incriminate him. For years, there was much discussion in liberal quarters as to which of these positions constituted the most desirable attitude for witnesses to adopt. William Frauenglass, a Brooklyn teacher, one of the many individuals involved in these investigations, approached Einstein about his case. He was encouraged to do so by a recent statement of Einstein in which he had called himself "an incorrigible nonconformist whose nonconformism in a remote field of endeavor no senatorial committee has as yet felt impelled to tackle." Frauenglass suggested that a statement from Einstein "at this juncture would be most helpful in rallying educators and the public to meet this new obscurantist attack." Einstein replied in a letter of May 16, 1953, which was published in *The New York Times* of June 12, 1953.[3] The letter created a sensation. No other action taken by Einstein in the postwar period focused so much attention on the issue of freedom and intellectual liberty, which he considered so basic to human society, as this much-quoted statement:

Thank you for your communication. By "remote field" I referred to the theoretical foundations of physics.

The problem with which the intellectuals of this country are confronted is very serious. Reactionary politicians have managed to instill suspicion of all intellectual efforts into the public by dangling before their eyes a danger from without. Having succeeded so far, they are now proceeding to suppress the freedom of teaching and to deprive of their positions all those who do not prove submissive, i.e., to starve them out.

What ought the minority of intellectuals to do against this evil? Frankly, I can only see the revolutionary way of non-co-operation in the sense of Gandhi's. Every intellectual who is called before one of the committees ought to refuse to testify, i.e., he must be prepared for jail and economic ruin, in short, for the sacrifice of his personal welfare in the interest of the cultural welfare of his country.

However, this refusal to testify must not be based on the well-known subterfuge of invoking the Fifth Amendment against possible self-incrimination, but on the assertion that it is shameful for a blameless citizen to submit to such an inquisition and that this kind of inquisition violates the spirit of the Constitution.

If enough people are ready to take this grave step they will be successful. If not, then the intellectuals of this country deserve nothing better than the slavery which is intended for them.

P.S. This letter need not be considered "confidential."

Although Einstein knew that his letter to Frauenglass would provoke an explosion of public opinion throughout the world, he attached the postscript that the letter did not need be considered confidential; in other words, he wanted his views on this important issue to be widely known and discussed. So fully did he anticipate a considerable amount of unfavorable reaction that he asked a friend, half in earnest and half jokingly, whether he himself might have to go to jail for having incited disobedience by citizens to the laws of the land. Since this is not the place to recount at any length the repercussions of Einstein's letter, favorable and unfavorable, the remarks in which he himself described the public reaction to the Frauenglass letter may be cited here. In a communication of June 30, 1953, to his Swiss biographer, Carl Seelig, he said:

All the important newspapers have commented in a more or less politely negative tone. This was to be expected since all of them depend heavily on advertising. I received a flood of mail, most of it enthusiastically approving, a minority of it severely critical. Only in a few letters was any attempt made to weigh the argu-

Ich danke Ihnen für Ihre Aufklärungen. Mit dem „remote field“ meinte ich die theoretischen Grundlagen der Physik. —

Das Problem, vor welches sich die Intelligenz dieses Landes gestellt sieht, ist ein sehr ernstes. Es ist den reaktionären Politikern ~~dieses Landes~~ gelungen, durch Vorspiegelung einer äusseren Gefahr das Publikum gegen ~~die~~ alle intellektuellen Bemühungen misstrauisch zu machen. Auf der Basis dieses Erfolges sind sie daran, die freie Lehre zu unterdrücken und die nicht Gefügigen aus allen Stellungen zu verdrängen, d. h. ~~aus~~ auszuhungern.

Was soll die Minderheit der Intellektuellen thun gegen das Übel? Ich sehe offen gestanden nur den revolutionären Weg der Non-cooperation im Sinne Ghandi's. Jeder Intellektuelle, der vor eines der Comité's vorgeladen wird, müsste jede Aussage verweigern, d. h. bereit sein, sich einsperren und wirtschaftlich ruinieren zu lassen, kurz, seine persönlichen Interessen den kulturellen Interessen des Landes zu opfern.

Wenn sich genug Personen finden, die diesen harten Weg zu gehen bereit sind, wird ihnen Erfolg beschieden sein. Wenn nicht, dann verdienen ~~sie eben~~ die Intellektuellen dieses Landes nichts Besseres als die Sklaverei, die ihnen zugedacht ist.

— A. Einstein

Diese Verweigerung ~~dürfte aber nicht~~ ~~gegründet~~ werden auf den bekannten Trick der möglichen Selbstinkriminierung sondern darauf, dass es eines unbescholtenen Bürgers unwürdig ist, sich solcher Inquisition zu unterziehen, und dass diese Art ~~der~~ Inquisition gegen den Geist der Verfassung verstosse.

P. S. Dieser Brief ~~braucht~~ ist nicht als „vertraulich" zu behandeln.

Einstein's original draft of his letter to William Frauenglass, May 16, 1953. (See pages 546–47)

ments carefully. Yet, on the whole, I have the impression that my letter did help somewhat to clear the political air: and I hope it may continue to do so.

One newspaper whose tone was less than "politely negative" was *The New York Times*. In an editorial of June 13, 1953, it blamed Einstein for having urged intellectuals to refuse to testify before Congressional investigating committees, which the *Times* said would be "most unwise. . . . To employ the unnatural and illegal forces of civil disobedience, as Professor Einstein advises, is in this case to attack one evil with another." A reaction to the *Times* editorial was received from an unexpected quarter. In its issue of June 26, 1953, the *Times* carried the following letter from Bertrand Russell: [4]

In your issue of June 13 you have a leading article disagreeing with Einstein's view that teachers questioned by Senator McCarthy's emissaries should refuse to testify. You seem to maintain that one should always obey the law, however bad. I cannot think that you have realized the implications of this position. Do you condemn the Christian Martyrs who refused to sacrifice to the Emperor? Do you condemn John Brown? Nay, more, I am compelled to suppose that you condemn George Washington and hold that your country ought to return to allegiance to Her Gracious Majesty, Queen Elizabeth II. As a loyal Briton, I of course applaud this view; but I fear it may not win much support in your country.

Russell suggested in a brief note to Einstein that he might make use of his letter to the *Times* in any way he liked. Einstein replied to Russell on June 28, 1953:

Your fine letter to *The New York Times* is a great contribution to a good cause. All the intellectuals in this country, down to the youngest student, have become completely intimidated. Virtually no one of "prominence" besides yourself has actually challenged these absurdities in which the politicians have become engaged. Because they have succeeded in convincing the masses that the Russians and the American Communists endanger the safety of the country, these politicians consider themselves so powerful. The cruder the tales they spread, the more assured they feel of their reelection by the misguided population. This also explains why

Eisenhower did not dare to commute the death sentence of the two Rosenbergs, although he well knew how much their execution would injure the name of the United States abroad.

There were several later occasions, in 1954 and 1955, on which Einstein expressed himself on the role of the individual in modern society. Of particular interest is a statement to the Emergency Civil Liberties Committee in which he developed at greater length the basic thoughts that underlay his letter to Frauenglass. In observance of Einstein's seventy-fifth birthday, the committee held a conference in Princeton on "The Meaning of Academic Freedom." [5] The conference took place on March 13, 1954, the eve of his birthday. Einstein did not attend, and declined to accept a floral offering, with these words: "You may bring flowers to my door when the last witch hunt is silenced, but not before." The Emergency Committee submitted several questions to Einstein, who sent these widely quoted answers to the conference:

Q: What is the essential nature of academic freedom and why is it necessary for the pursuit of truth?

A: By academic freedom I understand the right to search for the truth and to publish and teach what one holds to be true. This right also implies a duty; one should not conceal any part of what one has recognized to be true. It is evident that any restriction of academic freedom serves to restrain the dissemination of knowledge, thereby impeding rational judgment and action.

Q: What threats to academic freedom do you see at this time?

A: The threat to academic freedom in our time must be seen in the fact that, because of the alleged external danger to our country, freedom of teaching, mutual exchange of opinions, and freedom of press and other media of communication are encroached upon or obstructed. This is accomplished by creating conditions which people consider a threat to their economic security. Consequently, more and more people avoid expressing their opinion freely, even in their private social life. This is a situation which endangers the survival of a democratic government.

Q: What in your opinion are the special responsibilities of a citizen at this time in the defense of our traditional freedoms as expressed in our Bill of Rights?

A: The strength of the Constitution lies entirely in the determination of each citizen to defend it. Only if every single citizen recognizes his duty to do his share in this defense are the constitutional rights secure. Thus, an obligation is imposed on everyone, and no one must evade this obligation, regardless of the possible risks and dangers to himself and his family.

Q: What in your opinion are the special obligations of an intellectual in a democratic society?

A: In principle, every citizen should be equally responsible for defending the constitutional liberties of his country. The "intellectual" in the broadest sense of the term has, however, an even greater responsibility since, due to his specific training, he is capable of exerting a particularly strong influence on the formation of public opinion. This would explain why those who endeavor to lead us toward an authoritarian government are particularly anxious to intimidate and silence the intellectual. Therefore, under the prevailing circumstances, it is all the more important that the intellectual recognize his particular obligation to society. This should involve the refusal to co-operate with any measure which would violate the constitutional rights of the individual. This refers particularly to all investigations into the private life and political affiliations of a citizen. Whoever co-operates in such inquisitions becomes an accessory to the crime of violating or invalidating the Constitution.

Q: What in your opinion is the best way to help the victims of political inquisitions?

A: It is important for the defense of civil rights that assistance be given to all the victims of these inquisitions who have refused to testify, as well as to all those who, because of these inquisitions, have suffered economic ruin or damage. In particular, it will be necessary to provide legal counsel and to find work for them.

In the summer of 1954, Professor David Spitz of Ohio State University published a paper on civil disobedience.[6] The article defended the right of the citizen, even in the face of existing national laws which required him to act differently, to be loyal to his conscience if, in his considered judgment, disobedience was expected to achieve a greater good than compliance with the law. Einstein wrote to Professor Spitz on October 2, 1954:

Thank you for sending me your penetrating essay; I fully agree with its conclusion. The State may be forced to punish civil disobedience; but the individual should nonetheless follow his conscience if a conflict arises. If individual citizens act differently, not only the State will degenerate, but also the law the State has laid down.

A number of scientists, including Einstein, had become doubtful as to the advisability of continuing publication of the *Bulletin of the Atomic Scientists.* Einstein, moreover, was apparently unhappy with an issue of the *Bulletin* which had been devoted to the problem of civil defense; he seems to have felt that, with the publication of that issue, the scientists had abandoned the principle of opposing war as such, in preference to considerations of how best to prepare for it. Late in 1950 Dr. Eugene Rabinowitch, editor of the *Bulletin,* discussed these problems in a letter to Einstein and, recalling the article by Herbert Jehle (see p. 514) which had been rejected two years before, once more suggested that Einstein himself prepare a presentation of the pacifist point of view for publication in the *Bulletin.* Einstein replied, on January 5, 1951:

I am not what you might call a religious pacifist. Besides, I consider it preferable for men to fight rather than to allow themselves to be butchered without lifting a finger. That was just about the alternative in the case of Hitler Germany. Nor do I favor unilateral disarmament. What I advocate is an armed peace under supranational control.

I will say, however, that in my opinion the present policy of the United States constitutes a more serious obstacle to peace in the world than that of Russia. The current fighting is in Korea, not Alaska. Russia is exposed to a vastly greater threat than the United States, and everyone knows it. I find it hard to understand why people here accept the fable that we are in peril. I can only assume that it is because of their lack of political experience. While the government policy is apparently directed toward preventive war, there is, at the same time, a concerted attempt to make it appear as though the Soviet Union is the aggressor.

I do not intend to write the article which you suggest; I believe an appeal to reason would be utterly futile in the present polluted atmosphere. In the end men will get what they deserve.

The following day, January 6, 1951, Einstein wrote to his old friend, the Queen Mother of Belgium:

DEAR QUEEN:

Your warm greetings pleased me no end and reawakened happy memories. Eighteen harsh years, full of bitter disappointment, have gone by since then. All the more solace and cheer are derived from those few people who have remained courageous and straightforward. It is due to these few that one does not feel oneself altogether a stranger on this earth. You are one of them.

While it proved eventually possible, at an exceedingly heavy cost, to defeat the Germans, the dear Americans have vigorously assumed their place. Who shall bring them back to their senses? The German calamity of years ago repeats itself: people acquiesce without resistance and align themselves with the forces for evil. And one stands by, powerless.

Much as I should like to, it will probably not be given to me to see Brussels again. Because of a peculiar popularity which I have acquired, anything I do is likely to develop into a ridiculous comedy. This means that I have to stay close to my home and rarely leave Princeton.

I am done with fiddling. With the passage of years, it has become more and more unbearable for me to listen to my own playing. I hope you have not suffered a similar fate. What has remained is the relentless work on difficult scientific problems. The fascinating magic of that work will continue to my last breath.

Best wishes from your

A. EINSTEIN

Early in 1951, an article in the *New Republic* discussed the dilemma of the contemporary scientist whose discoveries are utilized for purposes of destruction. Einstein wrote the editor of that magazine on January 31, 1951: [7]

The line of demarcation does not lie between scientists and non-scientists, but between responsible, honest people and the others. Scientists are silent for they have learned that those who are honest people constitute a hopeless minority. The only choice left to them lies between non-co-operation and slavery.

A correspondent in Munich submitted another peace plan to Einstein, for which, with Einstein's help, he intended to collect signatures. Einstein wrote him, on March 30, 1951:

Your remarks bespeak sincerity and good will; but it is hopeless to assume that there are a sufficient number of influential people who will agree on a *detailed* political program, even if vanity and the lust for power could be eliminated.

The goal which seems to me most capable of realization is the abolition of war on a supranational basis. True, so far as justice and reason are concerned, a world government may turn out to be no better than the present governments; but the abolition of war is today a prerequisite to any other fruitful reform. Tyranny and the threat of war are inseparable, especially in the world of today.

The chief obstacle to peace is the desire for greater and greater power on the part of the two countries which have proven most successful in the military sphere: Russia and the United States. Heine once said that an ugly woman has already won half the battle to be virtuous. Similarly, in the political sphere, military impotence is half the battle to achieve a decent policy. All the powerless countries together could become a decisive factor in the world if there were a new Gandhi to utilize the weapon of non-co-operation on a world-wide basis. Since such a policy proved *once* to be successful, why should it not succeed in a much larger area?

Late in March 1951 a California correspondent sent Einstein a lengthy exposition in which he sought to apply the concept of relativity to philosophy. He felt that ideas could be organized into a kind of "periodic table" and concluded that opposites were potentially identical, leading to a formula for measuring tensions between groups. His point of departure in writing was an article in the *Bulletin of the Atomic Scientists*, which, he suggested, took an unjustifiably pessimistic view of social organization. Einstein replied: [8]

You censure Dr. Rabinowitch [editor of the *Bulletin*] because he has recognized and confessed the impotence of all of us. You believe that, through the application of philosophical concepts, you could come closer to a solution of our problems.

However, you seem to forget that no really reliable science exists in the social field and that, consequently, there is no consensus on social concepts and interrelationships. Even if there were a reliable social science, it would be of little help because the influence of sane and benevolent reasoning upon the actions of men is limited.

There are too few people who act reasonably, and their influence for the possible improvement of conditions is too small.

This reply came to the attention of a member of a California law firm who gently chided Einstein for belittling the power of ideas, thereby inviting hopeless lethargy. He felt that such an attitude was a disservice to humanity. Einstein replied on May 16, 1951: [8]

I can understand that you have been displeased with some of the statements I made. But I have never concluded that there is no salvation for mankind. Betterment of conditions the world over is not essentially dependent on scientific knowledge but on the fulfillment of human traditions and ideals. I believe, therefore, that men like Confucius, Buddha, Jesus, and Gandhi have done more for humanity with respect to the development of ethical behavior than science could ever accomplish. You may believe that smoking is bad for your health and nevertheless be a heavy smoker. And this holds true for all the evil impulses that poison life. I do not need to emphasize my respect and appreciation for every possible effort in the direction of truth and knowledge. But I do not believe that the lack of moral and aesthetic values can be counterbalanced by purely intellectual effort. I am sure you will appreciate this point of view.

While Einstein, during this period, frequently expressed his disappointment in the statesmen of the world and in the lack of leadership and courage on the part of intellectuals, he well realized that it would be an error to focus the blame exclusively on the political leaders of the various nations while disregarding the general atmosphere in which they functioned. On July 25, 1951, he wrote to Professor Erwin Schrödinger, the renowned physicist who had left Nazi Germany after 1933 and was then in Dublin, Ireland. Never before, Einstein said in his note to Schrödinger, had such poor actors performed on "that big stage" as now; even if they opened their mouth as wide as possible, the greatest idiot would still recognize that the play was no good. Yet, on the other hand, in a lengthy letter of June 8, 1951, to a correspondent of Brooklyn he said:

You quite obviously have not the slightest idea how people actually function. They are governed by passions among which hatred and shortsighted selfishness are dominant. You assume that the few leading men in politics are alone responsible for all the hardship and difficulties we face while the masses are only interested in what is good and reasonable. Although it is true that the people as a whole are afraid of war, because of their innate psychological structure, they can easily be swayed to any adventure. My colleagues have tried for some time to avert the threatening catastrophe through educational efforts. The attempt was not successful. Those who propagandized against the alleged external enemy have won the support of the masses. Political stupidity has become so widespread that even reasonable people may find it difficult to discover their way back to a saner foreign policy. If people really were as you think they are, they would refuse military service. But there is no inkling of that.

To A. J. Muste of the Fellowship of Reconciliation Einstein wrote on April 11, 1951:

I agree wholeheartedly, in all essential points, with the opinions expressed in the article "The Paranoia Race." [9] I wish to mention, however, that I do not consider it reasonable to compare a disease in the medical sense with the hatred and fear toward Russia which have been instilled in the American people since the death of Roosevelt. It is, of course, incontestable that the arming of individual countries can lead only to war and destruction; not to security. Under present conditions, those countries which have a minimum of armament are most secure. The only reasonable policy the United States could pursue is to declare unconditionally that security in the world depends upon the establishment of a world government which would be open to all nations and would have the duty and power to solve all international conflicts and put an end to colonial oppression.

By the spring of 1951 it had become apparent that the continued existence of the Emergency Committee of Atomic Scientists, even in its inactive state of the past two years, would serve no useful purpose. The trustees were polled on the question of dissolution, and Einstein wrote Harrison Brown on June 12, 1951: [10]

I agree with the proposal that the Emergency Committee of Atomic Scientists be dissolved as soon as possible.

As to the disposition of the funds, I support wholeheartedly the proposal of Dr. Szilard to give the money to the American Friends Service Committee.

When our committee was formed it was undoubtedly our purpose to use our influence to help achieve lasting security in the international field. It is true that the *Bulletin of the Atomic Scientists* tried in the beginning to serve the same purpose, but today it has become no more than a publication of neutral information. Secondly, there are other organizations working for some kind of world government; in this country, the United World Federalists are the group nearest to our aspirations. But I would prefer, according to Szilard's suggestion, to give the money to the Friends, for they have shown by their steadfast efforts through many years a truly supranational attitude, which was manifest long before the present difficult situation arose.

Final dissolution of the Emergency Committee of Atomic Scientists was decided upon at a meeting at Einstein's home on September 8, 1951, and went into effect in November of that year. The suggestion made by Einstein and Szilard concerning the disposition of the funds did not prevail; the assets of the committee were turned over to the *Bulletin of the Atomic Scientists*.

To an artist who had submitted to him a book of anti-war drawings Einstein wrote on August 13, 1951: [11]

I find very real merit in your efforts to counteract the drive toward war through the medium of art. Nothing can equal the psychological effect of real art, neither factual description nor intellectual discussion.

It has often been said that art should not be used to serve political or otherwise practical goals. I have never been able to agree with this point of view. True, it is utterly wrong and disgusting if some specific type of political thought or expression is forced upon the artist. But the artist's own powerful emotional bias has often given birth to truly great works of art. One has only to think of Swift's *Gulliver's Travels* or of Daumier's immortal drawings exposing the corruption in French politics of his time. Our time needs you and your work.

On December 7, 1951, just ten years after Pearl Harbor, Einstein, at his home in Princeton, was interviewed by Edwin Randall of the

American Friends Service Committee as to his views on Universal Military Training.[12] The interview, which was recorded, was intended for radio broadcasting.

Q: What, in your opinion, will be the judgment of other countries—say, Germany, Japan, France, India—if the United States adopts Universal Military Training?

A: If the United States introduces Universal Military Training, it will intensify the conviction everywhere that the problems of the world will, in the future, as in the past, be decided by brute force rather than by a supranational organization.

Q: Do you have a judgment as to the educational effect on young men who take Universal Military Training? Would it militarize their minds?

A: Universal Military Training will greatly contribute to the fostering of a military mentality in the American people and will serve to undermine the democratic spirit, as was the case in Germany after 1870.

Q: Do you believe in Universal Military Training as an effective means to insure peace?

A: In the long run, national armaments do not produce security; they only increase the danger of conflict. The alternative to Universal Military Training is a world government which would act as the exclusive agency through which military power would be stabilized.

Q: A great many people feel that we are making headway with our "get tough" policy. They point to Russian withdrawal from Iran, American intervention in Greece, the Berlin Airlift and Korea as examples of how American strength has succeeded in holding expansionism in check. Why should we give up this system, which seems to be working, for one we have never seen work?

A: The "get tough" policy has largely succeeded in uniting Asia against the West, and the continuation of this policy is likely further to contribute to the dangerous division of mankind into two hostile camps. Temporary successes must not blind us to this danger. The Russian attitude seems to me to be motivated by defensive rather than aggressive considerations.

Q: Is it, in your opinion, at all possible to attain security by the overwhelming military power of any group of nations?

A: International security can be assured only by supranational organization and not by national armaments or alliances. Permanent military superiority is neither desirable nor is it feasible in the long run. If we continue on the road of brute force, the relative size of populations will eventually prove to be the decisive factor.

Q: Is war inevitable?

A: Unless peace is secured by a supranational organization, a general war of annihilation is inevitable. At present the United States, both economically and militarily, is the most powerful nation on earth. Consequently, it is chiefly the foreign policy of the United States which will determine the course of international developments in the immediate future. This fact imposes an enormous responsibility upon us in the present circumstances. Everyone must ask himself in all seriousness: Are we on the right road?

An article, entitled "Culture Must Be One of the Foundations for World Understanding," was prepared by Einstein for the December 1951 issue of the magazine *Unesco Courier:* [13]

In order to grasp the full significance of the Universal Declaration of Human Rights, one should be fully aware of the particular world situation that gave birth to the United Nations and to its daughter institution, UNESCO. The frequency of wars and the resulting chaos during the past half-century have brought home to everybody the fact that, in view of the prevailing level of technological achievements, the security of nations can only be based on supranational measures and institutions. It is widely acknowledged that only the establishment of a world federation can help avoid a conflict which would involve the destruction of all.

As a modest beginning in the development of international order, the United Nations was founded. In fact, this institution is merely an organization of delegates from national governments and not of independent individuals who, guided solely by their personal convictions, represent the populations of the various countries. Moreover, decisions of the United Nations have no binding force on any national government; nor do any concrete means exist by which these decisions can actually be enforced.

The effectiveness of the United Nations is further impaired by the fact that certain nations have been denied membership; their exclusion seriously detracts from the supranational character of the organization. Yet the very fact that international problems are being discussed in the broad light of day favors the possibility of a peaceful settlement of conflicts. The mere existence of such a supranational forum of discussion will tend to accustom the peoples of the world to the idea that national interests must be safeguarded by negotiation rather than by resort to brute force.

I regard this psychological and educational effect as the most valuable feature of the United Nations. World federation presupposes a new kind of loyalty on the part of man, which involves a sense of responsibility that does not stop short at national frontiers. To be truly effective, such loyalty must embrace more than purely political issues. It must be supplemented by mutual understanding among the different cultural groups, and by mutual cultural and economic aid.

Only this kind of approach will re-establish the feeling of confidence that was lost in the psychological wake of war and subsequently replaced by the narrow-minded policy of militarism and power politics. An effective institution for the collective security of nations is impossible without the mutual understanding and trust of the member states.

It was in the pursuit of these cultural objectives that UNESCO was added to the United Nations. It has succeeded, in greater measure than the United Nations, in escaping the paralyzing influence of power politics. Realizing that sound international relations can derive only from populations who have a healthy outlook and enjoy a measure of independence, the United Nations elaborated a Universal Declaration of Human Rights which was adopted by its General Assembly on December 10, 1948. This declaration established a number of universally binding provisions designed to protect the individual, to prevent his economic exploitation, to safeguard his development and to insure the free pursuit of his interest within society.

It is to be welcomed that an avowed and important objective of the organization is to propagate these provisions among all the member states of the United Nations. Accordingly, UNESCO has instituted a third-anniversary celebration for the purpose of drawing attention far and wide to these fundamental aspirations as providing the basis for restoring the political health of the world.

The declaration, which, of necessity, was given the form of a rigid legal document, may give rise to almost endless debate. Such a text cannot possibly take into account the great diversity of conditions of life in all the different countries. It is inevitable, moreover, that the individual provisions of the text will admit of various interpretations. Yet, the general spirit of the declaration is unmistakable and seems altogether appropriate as a generally acceptable basis for future decisions and actions.

It is one thing to give formal recognition to such provisions, but it is another matter to adopt them as a guidepost to action despite the adversities of changing circumstances—a fact which the impartial observer may note particularly from the history of religious institutions. The declaration can exert effective influence only if the United Nations itself demonstrates by its decisions and actions that it actually personifies the spirit of this, its own, declaration.

On January 3, 1952, Einstein again wrote to the Queen Mother of Belgium:

DEAR QUEEN:

It was with pleasure—and embarrassment—that I received your good telegram today. I felt ashamed because I had not yet found words to reply to your most recent and cordial letter. It is now almost twenty years since I was last able to talk and play music with you. How many harsh and difficult times we have lived through in the years between! Saddest of all is the disappointment one feels over the conduct of mankind in general. Younger people may feel little surprise; but, then, they have never known times of calm and reason. Things appeared rather differently to us when we were young. We believed the brutality of former times had been eliminated forever and had yielded to an age of reason and stability. True, in the years between the two world wars sharp disillusionment had set in, but faith in a better future and in a more reasonable attitude of human beings had remained more alive than it is now. People were still inclined to explain catastrophes by ascribing them to the actions of particular individuals.

Now it becomes clear that our only hope lies in the establishment of a world government. It is a slender hope, for our faith in human nature has been so severely shaken. There are those who place their hopes in the operation of machines, because they no longer believe in the free forces of life. Let us hope posterity will have more than a smile of pity for our last hope—provided there is any posterity.

Yet, nature continues to shine in everlasting loveliness and one is so happy with one's precarious existence that the human dilemma is forgotten. One feels reduced to the level of an innocent animal. Dare I hope you share this feeling? Does music still belong in that untouchable sphere? I believe so, so long as one is not a professional musician.

Warmest good wishes for the coming year.

Your
A. EINSTEIN

For Canadian Education Week, March 2–8, 1952, Einstein prepared this message: [14]

The discovery of nuclear chain reactions need not lead to the destruction of mankind, any more than did the invention of matches. But we must do everything in our power to guard against the abuse of such discoveries. In the present stage of technology only a supranational organization, equipped with adequate executive powers, can afford us protection. Only when we realize this fact shall we be willing to make the sacrifices necessary to safeguard mankind. Each one of us will be responsible if the goal is not reached in time. The great danger is that each will wait for the other to act.

Every thinking person must pay tribute to the scientific achievements of our century—even the casual observer who sees only their industrial application. Yet if the fundamental problems of science are kept in mind, recent achievements are less likely to be overrated. It is like riding in a train. As long as we look only at things close to the track, we seem to be rushing along. But when we turn our attention to distant mountain ranges, the scenery seems to change only very slowly. That is the way it is with the great problems of science.

In my opinion it makes little sense to talk either of "our way of life" or that of the Russians. In both cases, we are dealing with a body of traditions and customs that forms no organic whole. Surely it is more appropriate to raise the question which institutions and traditions are harmful to man, and which serve him well; which make life happier, and which add to its sorrows. We should then seek to adopt whatever appears best, irrespective of whether it was accomplished by ourselves or somewhere else in the world.

On March 21, 1952, Einstein responded to a troubled pacifist who, like others, asked for clarification of apparent inconsistencies in Einstein's various statements on pacifism and suggested that he make a public pronouncement about his actual pacifist position. Einstein wrote:

I am indeed a pacifist, but not a pacifist at any price. My views are virtually identical with those of Gandhi. But I would, individually and collectively, resist violently any attempt to kill me or to take away from me, or my people, the basic means of subsistence.

I was, therefore, of the conviction that it was justified and necessary to fight Hitler. For his was such an extreme attempt to destroy people.

Furthermore, I am of the conviction that realization of the goal of pacifism is possible only through supranational organization. To stand unconditionally for this cause is, in my opinion, the criterion of true pacifism.

That same month the French pacifist Jacques Hadamard sent Einstein the draft of an "open letter," this time on the subject of germ warfare. While it did not accuse the United States of conducting germ warfare in Korea, as was then widely charged by the Chinese Government, it did refer to some newspaper accounts to the effect that Washington was engaged in broad research on bacteriological weapons which could spread universal destruction. Did Americans favor such methods? What was the attitude of American science and medicine, in the face of world-wide concern? There were times when one must speak up. Einstein replied on March 26, 1952:

I am indeed the last one to defend this abominable business of armaments, be they atomic or bacteriological weapons. Nor should we be surprised that those who admittedly and systematically work on such horrible things are suspected of using them.

But the guilt for this evil in which we are all so deeply involved does not rest with one side alone. Further, in these times, I do not believe that anything can be achieved by mere declarations. The only solution lies in constructive supranational action aimed at security. The people of Europe could contribute much toward that goal, but for the fact that they believe they need United States support to pursue their miserable policy of colonialism. It must be said, unfortunately, that nowhere except possibly in India is there any influential public opinion that rejects all opportunistic compromise.

Hadamard wrote Einstein in April 1952 that he would like to make Einstein's letter public. The news from Asia was profoundly affecting European public opinion; people who had no part in colonialism were insisting that an International Commission of Inquiry be dispatched to establish the facts on the spot. What did Einstein think and did he have anything to add? Einstein replied on April 19, 1952:

I am sorry, but I cannot permit publication of my private letter to you of March 26. This political propaganda and counterpropaganda, which is actually not based on any proven facts, can only lead to hate and hostility. You must surely know, moreover, that the objective inquiry, which was suggested by the International Red Cross and was to be carried out by the Red Cross organizations of neutral countries, was rejected by the North Korean authorities. I believe that the only way in which supranationally minded intellectuals can effectively promote the good cause is by supporting negotiation, conciliation and a supranational solution of the security problem, but not by taking part in propaganda actions such as this. I feel that, so far, the Quaker organization and the Indian Government have best served supranational interests. I think we must above all abide by the old medical maxim: *Non nocere.*

Requests for a statement against the alleged use of bacteriological weapons in Korea came not only from Jacques Hadamard but from other widely separated quarters; they reached Einstein around the same time and were phrased in almost identical language. On April 1, 1952, Einstein replied to such a communication from the science and mathematics students at the University in the Soviet sector of Berlin; he mentioned with some irony the simultaneity and similarity of the letters received and chided the students for having apparently assumed he would fail to realize that all these communications had originated from a common source. He remarked that the assertions about germ warfare were merely based on some insinuations and continued:

I could not make a statement to the effect that the validity of those allegations had in any way been proven to me. Therefore, you cannot expect me to protest against certain incidents which possibly, and very probably, have never taken place. I am becoming even more skeptical because of the frequency of communications, based on almost identical arguments, that are being sent to me. If you really want to do something for the good of mankind, I suggest that you work for a supranational solution of the security problem, which would inevitably involve the restriction of national sovereignty.

The perennial problem of defining aggression was debated at length by a commission of the United Nations General Assembly early in 1952; the commission decided to place the problem on the agenda of the next General Assembly. Einstein's old colleague, Hans Thirring of Vienna, Austria, prepared a thoughtful memorandum about the issue in which he analyzed the many arguments used in defending or denying the desirability of defining aggression and in which he expressed agreement with the proponents of such a definition. Einstein wrote him on April 12, 1952:

Your detailed essay on defining aggression has, it seems to me, much merit. The fact that an exhaustive definition is not feasible must not prevent a formulation that could serve as a basis for future action by the United Nations (soon, let us hope, to be changed into an organization of greater scope). In any event, such a definition would serve to discourage the use of vague, distorted concepts which are bound to arise in the service of power politics.

To the General Conference of the Methodist Church, which was meeting in San Francisco to consider, among other matters, a Memorial on Sovereignty, Einstein sent this message on April 27, 1952: [15]

Only the creation of a world government can prevent the impending self-destruction of mankind. Whoever recognizes this clearly, but fails to orient his political attitude accordingly, has no right to consider himself a religious person; the atavistic passions of such a person are obviously more powerful than his desire to serve those efforts which all of us, in moments of quiet contemplation, know tend in the right direction.

To his friend Maurice Solovine in Paris, Einstein wrote on May 7, 1952: [16]

In your letter you chastise me for having committed two sins. The first is my uncritical attitude towards the plans put forward for world government. It is true, you do not consider the plans *undesirable,* but rather as being unrealizable in the near future; and you cite good reasons why you believe that they are unrealizable. As one more reason you might very well have expressed the fear that world government might possibly evolve into something even more intolerable and, particularly, more unjust than our present state of anarchy. One has only to consider, for example, the blessings that the United Nations has bestowed upon the people of Korea! But, on the other hand, there is the danger that mankind may utterly destroy itself, a matter that we should certainly not take lightly. Hence we should at least take back, however reluctantly, the word *undesirable.*

As for the word *impossible,* that is another matter. It has a way of changing into the possible in case people will it earnestly enough, even if only out of fear of otherwise remaining in a state of intolerable insecurity. With all our power we must endeavor to bring this will into being. The effort will be worthwhile, even if the goal is not attained; for such an effort will surely have a constructive educational effect since it will be directed against the stupidities and evils of nationalism.

However, you emphasize that young people must first be trained to consider historical events in an objective fashion; only then, you feel, could one hope for progress in the political sphere. But this kind of priority is much like the question of which came first, the chicken or the egg: in other words, we find ourselves in a vicious circle. The political structure is the chicken, and enlightened education is the egg. But, even though we cannot find the loose thread that will unravel the tangled skein, we must keep on trying everywhere and not lose heart.

If all our efforts are in vain and man goes down in self-destruction, the universe will shed no tears.

To an old friend in Italy, Einstein wrote in September 1952: [17]

For my part, I have always tended to solitude, a trait that usually becomes more pronounced with age. It is strange to be known so universally and yet to be so lonely. The fact is that the kind of popularity which I am experiencing pushes the subject into a defensive attitude that leads him into isolation.

We have been obliged to witness tremendous political upheavals, and we shall live through more of them unless we are called away in time. Things always remain essentially the same. Nations continue to fall into the same trap, because atavistic drives are more powerful than either reason or acquired convictions.

The October 1952 issue of the *Bulletin of the Atomic Scientists* was devoted to "American Visa Policy and Foreign Scientists." A number of prominent American scientists were asked to give their views about the increasing difficulties that foreign scholars were experiencing in obtaining permission to respond to the invitations of American groups. Einstein wrote: [18]

The free, unfettered exchange of ideas and scientific findings is as necessary for the sound development of science, as it is in all spheres of cultural life. I do not think there can be the slightest doubt that the interference by political authorities in this country has already done considerable injury to the free exchange of knowledge. Until now, the damage has primarily affected scientific work, but it will soon be felt in all branches of industry as well.

The intrusion of political agencies into the scientific life of our country is especially evident in the denial of permission to American scholars to go abroad as well as to foreign scientists to visit this country. Such petty behavior on the part of a powerful country is only a surface symptom of a much more fundamental ailment.

The interference with the freedom of oral and written communication of scientific results, the widespread political distrust supported by an immense police organization, the anxiety of individuals to avoid anything that might arouse suspicion and thus threaten their economic existence—all these phenomena are merely symptoms although they serve to reveal the grave character of the disease.

In my opinion, the disease proper derives from an attitude which was acquired during the two world wars and which has come to dominate us completely—namely, the belief that we must, in peacetime, organize our whole life and work in such a way as to insure victory in the event of war, since powerful enemies threaten not only our freedom but our very existence.

This attitude serves to explain all the unpleasant facts which we described as "symptoms" a moment ago. Unless rectified, such an attitude, which finds its most prominent expression in the military budget of the United States, will necessarily lead to war and wholesale destruction.

Only after we have overcome this obsession with the policy of preparedness can we devote our attention to the real political problem which confronts us: that of trying to discover how we can best contribute to making life on this shrinking earth more secure and, therefore, more tolerable.

We shall not be able to free ourselves of the many symptoms of the disease unless we are able to conquer the disease itself.

A Hungarian survivor of the Dachau concentration camp, who had emigrated to Australia, asked in referring to the atomic bomb whether Einstein had discarded the old and noble traditions of his profession and had put his conscience and his faith in human ideals in cold storage; was Einstein working for the benefit of the people or had he plotted a revolt against their lives? Einstein took these insinuations seriously and replied on October 1, 1952: [19]

You are mistaken in regarding me as a kind of chieftain of those scientists who abuse science for military purposes. I have never worked in the field of applied science, let alone for the military.

I condemn the military mentality of our time just as you do. Indeed, I have been a pacifist all my life and regard Gandhi as the only truly great political figure of our age.

My name is linked to the atomic bomb in two different ways. Almost fifty years ago I discovered the equivalence of mass and energy, a relationship which served as the guiding principle in the work leading to the release of atomic energy. Secondly, I signed a letter to President Roosevelt, stressing the need for work in the field of the atomic bomb. I felt this was necessary because of the dreadful danger that the Nazi regime might be the first to come into possession of the atomic bomb.

Thus, your letter, as you will no doubt realize, was based on incorrect assumptions.

To a correspondent in England, Einstein wrote on October 9, 1952: [20]

I am a lonely man, as you are, much older than you but probably not much wiser. What we have in common is a deep skepticism about everything we are told by the press, radio, etc., which are considerably worse in the United States than in Old England.

I agree with you with respect to the dangers which would be involved in the creation of a world government. But I believe that these dangers are less significant than the dangers of international anarchy which, in fact, involves the perpetual threat of war. It seems to me that the latter is the most effective means by which government can keep the people in some sort of slavery. I am therefore decidedly in favor of world government.

The reports we receive about Russia are, of course, one-sided and too black. Yet, it seems certain that in spite of her social and economic achievements, her political organization is still considerably more brutal and barbarous than ours. However, it is clear to me that the postwar change in power relations among the nations of the world has resulted in the West's being much more aggressive than the Communist world. Every reasonable person must strive to promote moderation and a more objective judgment.

In a letter dated October 28, 1952, to Leopold Infeld, the Polish physicist who had been his close scientific associate for years, Einstein made the following remarks:

As for these peace efforts [Infeld apparently had asked Einstein to support some action of the Soviet-influenced World Peace Council], I am not able to take part in them; in my view they are more or less propaganda activities connected with the "cold war." Only by a genuine effort on the part of the principal nations to come to terms, and not by a lot of noisy talk in public, can there be any hope for real progress; such talk merely serves as a provocation. I am so often reminded of Heine's poem "The Disputation," which closed with the suggestion that the rabbi and the monk both cut unpleasant figures.

I shall gladly send you the desired photograph and only hope that, as the wind now blows [in Eastern Europe], you will some day not feel the necessity to hide it carefully.

In November 1952 the American Committee for Cultural Freedom asked Einstein for a statement on the purge trial in Prague of Communist leader Rudolf Slansky and other Communist leaders for alleged treason and sabotage. (Slansky and ten others were hanged the following month.) Einstein wrote the committee:

It took Europe many centuries to discard almost completely legal and illegal murder as an instrument of domestic policy. But within the area dominated by present-day Russia the following principle is still proclaimed and followed: The individual can claim neither rights nor protection from the State. The Slansky trial demonstrates once again that the men in power in those countries no longer even pretend the legality of their actions before the nations outside their own domain.

That same month an honor came to Einstein, quite different from the many other honors which the world had offered him over the years. His old friend Chaim Weizmann, first President of the State of Israel, in whose company he had first visited America more than thirty years before, died on November 9, 1952. Following a suggestion first made in the Tel Aviv newspaper *Maariv,* official inquiries were made to ascertain whether Einstein would accept an invitation to become the second President of the new Jewish state. The official exchange began on November 17, 1952, with the following telegram from the Israeli Ambassador in Washington:

Government of Israel has asked me to seek your reaction on a matter of the utmost urgency and importance. Would be grateful if you could receive my deputy, David Goitein, at Princeton at any time tomorrow, Tuesday. Would then like to visit you personally following day to receive your response. Grateful for your cabled reply.

Respectfully,

ABBA EBAN
Ambassador of Israel
Washington

Einstein telephoned Ambassador Eban that night and declined the invitation, of which he apparently had already been informed. Mr. Goitein nevertheless called on Einstein at Princeton the next day, bearing the following letter, dated November 17, 1952:

DEAR PROFESSOR EINSTEIN:

The bearer of this letter is Mr. David Goitein of Jerusalem who is now serving as Minister at our Embassy in Washington. He is bringing you the question which Prime Minister Ben-Gurion asked me to convey to you—namely, whether you would accept the Presidency of Israel if it were offered you by a vote of the Knesset. Acceptance would entail moving to Israel and taking its citizenship. The Prime Minister assures me that in such circumstances complete facility and freedom to pursue your great scientific work would be afforded by the government and people who are fully conscious of the supreme significance of your labors. Mr. Goitein will be able to give you any information that you may desire on the implications of the Prime Minister's question.

I understand the anxieties and doubts which you expressed to me this evening. On the other hand, whatever your answer, I am anxious for you to feel that the Prime Minister's question embodies the deepest respect which the Jewish people can repose in any of its sons. To this element of personal regard, we add the sentiment that Israel is a small state in its physical dimensions but can rise to the level of greatness in the measure that it exemplifies the most elevated spiritual and intellectual traditions which the Jewish people have established through its best minds and hearts both in antiquity and in modern times. Our first President, as you know, taught us to see our destiny in these great perspectives, as you yourself have often exhorted us to do.

Therefore, whatever your response to this question, I hope that you will think generously of those who have asked it and will commend the high purpose and motives which prompted them to think of you at this solemn hour in our people's history.

Yours respectfully,
ABBA EBAN

Einstein's reply, dated November 18, 1952, had already been prepared:

I am deeply moved by the offer from our State of Israel, and at once saddened and ashamed that I cannot accept it. All my life I have dealt with objective matters, hence I lack both the natural aptitude and the experience to deal properly with people and to exercise official functions. For these reasons alone I should be unsuited to fulfill the duties of that high office, even if advancing age was not making increasing inroads on my strength.

I am the more distressed over these circumstances because my relationship to the Jewish people has become my strongest human bond, ever since I became fully aware of our precarious situation among the nations of the world.

Now that we have lost the man who for so many years, against such great and tragic odds, bore the heavy burden of leading us toward political independence, I hope with all my heart that a successor may be found whose experience and personality will enable him to accept the formidable and responsible task.

That same day Einstein received a long and impassioned appeal for acceptance from the editor-in-chief of *Maariv*. "Never," he cabled, "has humanity's age-old dream of entrusting highest sovereignty to the thinker been put to the test. Here, for the first time in known history, is the opportunity." Einstein replied on November 21, 1952: [21]

Frugal *petit bourgeois* that I am, the length of your cable had a downright devastating effect upon me; but it arrived after the fact. Because of an indiscretion, I was prematurely compelled to announce my decision on the issue.

You may imagine how difficult it was for me to decline so touching an offer, coming as it did from my own people. What I said [in my formal declination] accurately reflects my thoughts and feelings. There can be no doubt that I would not have been equal to the task awaiting me there, even though the office, in the main, has but ceremonial character. My name alone cannot make up for these shortcomings.

I also gave thought to the difficult situation that could arise if the government or the parliament made decisions which might create a conflict with my conscience; for the fact that one has no actual influence on the course of events does not relieve one of moral responsibility. I respect the great energy you have devoted to this cause and I am grateful for the confidence which is manifest in your action. But I am convinced I should have done the cause a disservice, had I responded to this tempting and honorable call.

On November 24, 1952, Einstein wrote to a friend: [22]

I was very deeply touched by the offer from my Israeli brothers. But I declined at once with really sincere regret. It is quite true that many a rebel has in the end become a figure of respectability, even a big shot [*Bonze*]; but I cannot bring myself to do so. We shall have to be satisfied, as before, at fuming at the brethren here at home.

To a correspondent in Italy, Einstein wrote on February 11, 1953: [23]

The matter is not quite as simple as you think. In the first place I lack all experience in the field of practical politics. In the second place, as President I should have had to assume moral responsibility for the decisions of others, decisions which I myself could not have affected in the least. Thus, acceptance of the office would quite likely have led to disappointments rather than accomplishments.

It is quite true that our [Israel's] situation has once again become perilous and that we lack all power to check the danger. But when I look at Russia and America, I cannot help wondering whether we [Israel] would behave more sensibly if we were as powerful as they are.

To a friend in England, Einstein wrote on December 27, 1952: [24]

My work keeps me under constant tension, as before, even though imagination and endurance have slackened. That makes one independent of one's personal destiny as well as of political disappointments. Our good America strives successfully to live its own caricature. I can imagine what the more experienced British say about it. Well, as a wiseacre once said: "Experience is the sum of experiences we would rather not have had." Yet it is a good thing to have passed through that school.

CHAPTER SEVENTEEN

TWILIGHT | 1953-1954

EINSTEIN'S LAST FEW YEARS were spent without any significant change in his daily activities and routine. He pursued his scientific work without suffering any decline in his passionate curiosity about the laws that govern the universe; his interest in public affairs remained as keen as his ever-ready desire to support any effort devoted to protecting the individual from unjust exploitation and liberating humanity from the scourge of war; his door remained wide open to anyone who sought his help in the fight for these or related purposes. And yet, shadows had begun to dim the light of his days. The ailment which had been recognized in the Christmas week of 1948 and which was to prove fatal in the spring of 1955 caused frequently serious discomfort; at times, he was forced to interrupt his work. His only sister, who had lived with him during the last twelve years of her life, passed away after years of physical deterioration; the more he was compelled painfully to realize that real help could not be given her, the closer was he drawn to her. Even his scientific work, which for half a century had been a constant source of gratification and fulfillment, caused moments of discouragement in the waning years of his life. After the publication in 1949 of a completely new approach to a unified field theory, the latest and—to him—most hopeful result of twenty-five years of intensive work and thought about a unified theoretical explanation of the universe, he never ceased in his efforts to refine it; and he never lacked imagination for new departures and new avenues of supplementary research. But all these efforts not only failed to yield the coveted verification of his theory; he even came to assume that this ultimate satisfaction would be denied him during his lifetime.

Similar disappointments affected his most cherished hopes and expectations with regard to public affairs. He was deeply perturbed and distressed over the seeming futility of the many efforts to stem the dangerous tides of the time. Because of his unshakable belief in the necessity of creating a supranational organization, he deplored the lack of interest in the establishment of world government, not to say the hostility toward all efforts in this direction. The Soviet Union had not altered its position of complete opposition to the idea of world federalism, a position of which Einstein was well aware from his exchange of letters with Soviet scientists in the winter of 1947 and because of the suppression of his message to the Wroclaw Peace Conference in August 1948. On the other hand, in the United States, the movement for world federalism had lost much of what modest strength it had possessed in the early postwar years; it had become a small and ineffectual group. Those were the years in the United States when the political persecution of all nonconformists was most intense and when the freedom to dissent on the critical political issues of the country was increasingly challenged or denied. Those were also the years when the cold war and the antagonism between East and West grew more bitter month by month and year by year. The increasing danger of a suicidal world conflict only served to strengthen Einstein's conviction that freedom of speech and dissent and political opposition were, if anything, more important than ever before. It was painful to realize that the greater became the need for forceful action against the deadly menace facing the world, the more difficult did it become to organize political opposition for the purpose.

Although Einstein knew well that it was unrealistic to hold any individual nation responsible for the competitive armaments race, he did not ignore that quite frequently specific actions by individual countries or by one of the existing military blocs were likely to aggravate international tensions and to increase the militarization of the world. No other single development in those years disturbed him more deeply than the rearmament of Germany, which he publicly assailed on many occasions; for the last time, he voiced his profound apprehension over German rearmament in his final conversation only several hours before his death. Ever since the end of the war, Einstein had felt that military neutralization of Germany was a prerequisite to peaceful relations between East and West. This is why he so consistently opposed the remilitarization of Western Germany and her incorporation into the military preparations of the Western countries and not, as has sometimes been suggested, because of his own personal feelings toward the country of his birth. His own attitude of complete aloofness from Germany never changed. Several statements from the early postwar period, in which Einstein gave expression to his outraged feelings over the crimes committed by Germany, have already been recorded (see p. 365). Some other pronouncements made in subsequent years may be added here.

Late in 1948, Professor Otto Hahn, one of the two physicists who had made the revolutionary discovery of the splitting of the atom in

1938, informed Einstein that the Kaiser-Wilhelm-Gesellschaft, of which Einstein had been appointed a Director in 1914, was to be reorganized as the Max-Planck-Gesellschaft. Hahn added that both the Board of the Gesellschaft and he himself would consider it an honor and a great satisfaction if Einstein should join as a "Foreign Scientific Member," as some other Jewish scientists, now living outside Germany, had consented to do. Einstein replied on January 28, 1949:

It pains me that I must say "no" to you, one of the few men who remained decent and did what they could during those evil years; but I cannot do otherwise. The crime of the Germans is truly the most abominable ever to be recorded in the history of the so-called civilized nations. The conduct of the German intellectuals—seen as a group—was no better than that of the mob. And even now, there is no indication of any regret or any real desire to repair whatever little may be left to restore after the gigantic murders. In view of these circumstances, I feel an irrepressible aversion to participating in anything which represents any aspect of public life in Germany. I feel certain you will appreciate my position and realize that it has nothing to do with the personal relations between us, which I have always enjoyed.

For the same reasons, explicitly stated, he refused on March 8, 1948, to become an honorary member of a German Association for World Government; on February 18, 1949, to become an honorary citizen of Ulm, the city of his birth; to accept, on December 18, 1952, a similar honor from the city of West Berlin; and on June 19, 1950, to allow the New School for Social Research in New York to establish a scholarship in his name since he felt that the institution did not share his position of strict non-co-operation with public affairs in post-war Germany; and, finally, on February 9, 1953, to accept honorary membership in the German section of the International Organization of Opponents of Military Service. A most characteristic and outspoken refusal was sent to Theodor Heuss, then President of the Federal Republic of Germany (West Germany), who informed Einstein in a lengthy communication of a plan to re-establish the Peace Section of the old Prussian order *Pour le mérite*. Einstein was one of the four members surviving from the pre-Nazi period. Would he be prepared to join should the order be reorganized? Einstein replied in a terse note of January 16, 1951:

I thank you for your letter of January 10, 1951, and the material enclosed. Because of the mass murder which the Germans inflicted upon the Jewish people, it is evident that a self-respecting Jew could not possibly wish to be associated in any way with any official German institution. The renewal of my membership in the *Pour le mérite* order is therefore out of the question.

There were other occasions when Einstein voiced similar sentiments; in fact, he never relented. But he nonetheless made a clear distinction between his own personal feelings of outrage toward the Germans and the objective necessity for Europe and the world to reincorporate Germany into the community of nations. For this reason, he did not criticize the resumption of normal political and diplomatic relations with Germany, nor oppose the help given in the rebuilding of the German economy. But ever since the end of the war, he warned against the restoration of Germany's war-making facilities and urged that her industrial resources which could be used for war purposes be placed under international control. Einstein feared that Germany's military tradition and her desire for revenge and recovery of lost territories would make a rearmed Germany once more a menace to the rest of Europe. In addition, he believed that an understanding between the United States and the Soviet Union could not be brought about unless Germany remained an unarmed territory and her neutrality was jointly guaranteed and enforced by the two major powers.

How seriously Einstein considered the situation created by the rearmament of Germany becomes evident from a letter containing rather unrealistic suggestions, which he addressed on December 31, 1950, to an Indian friend with whom he frequently discussed world affairs and who enjoyed access to high political quarters in his homeland:

It appears very probable to me that the rearmament of Germany and Japan could provoke Russia into a preventive act of aggression which would be the beginning of a world war. This is, of course, well known in Washington and Lake Success [at this period, the site of United Nations headquarters]. Unless the United Nations takes steps to counteract the rearmament of Germany by the Atlantic Treaty, the United Nations themselves will share in the responsibility for the possible outbreak of a world war. Further, any nation which retains membership in the United Nations under such circumstances would bear equal responsibility. I believe, therefore, that India should challenge the United Nations to condemn the remilitarization plan within a specified period of time and should declare that she herself will resign from the United Nations in the event that her challenge goes unheeded.

To a vice-president of *Look* magazine who had sent him a copy of that publication suggesting German rearmament,[1] Einstein wrote on September 9, 1952, that he was not surprised by the attitude of Germany. What he did find surprising was the attitude of the Western nations, which, in spite of their unfortunate experiences in the past, were busily engaged in the dangerous task of restoring German might.

Correspondence developed once more with Professor Sidney Hook of New York University. Professor Hook wrote that he found a position of "unilateral" pacifism unacceptable, a position which, in fact, Einstein had never supported. Einstein replied to Hook on November 12, 1952:

I share your view that given the conditions which have emerged during the last twenty years (and which are not solely attributable to the Russians), no responsible statesman could dare to accept Gandhi's methods without a period of transition. Our only hope for improvement lies in the settlement of some of the existing international conflicts and in the curtailment of competitive armament. The first step, of course, would be the neutralization and demilitarization of Germany. Despite the bad methods used by the Russians, I feel it is completely wrong to consider and treat them as common criminals.

Einstein made similar remarks to a physician from Elizabeth, New Jersey, sometime in 1954. This correspondent suggested that the customary nonaggression pacts be amended by a provision that the contracting powers not only pledge assistance to one another in case of attack, but also commit themselves to assist any nonmember nation in case of aggression by one of the contracting powers. Einstein said he would wish that the suggested change in nonaggression pacts could be made; however, the language of treaties was less significant than the actions of the nations involved. He then continued:

In this respect, the rearmament of Germany is, in my view, an ominous step in the wrong direction. I believe the neutralization of Germany under joint control by the United States and Russia, proposed so convincingly by James P. Warburg, would have been the correct policy to adopt. But his suggestion, unfortunately, has been accorded very little attention.

The last time Einstein was to give written expression to his distress over German remilitarization was shortly before his death. The Jewish Action Committee against German Rearmament (Comité Juif d'Action Contre le Réarmement Allemand), which was located in Paris and to which the mathematician Jacques Hadamard, Einstein's old friend, and many other outstanding men and women belonged, asked Einstein for a statement of support. Einstein replied immediately, on February 8, 1955:

I find it truly incomprehensible that the Western nations, despite their horrible experience with German militarism, have become engaged in the rearmament of Germany. However, Jewish opposition to this insanity will hardly prove effectual even if the majority of Jews were to participate.

Einstein's abhorrence of Prussian and German militarism was profound throughout his life; he frequently gave expression to it privately and publicly. Although for a brief period, during the quasi-revolutionary aftermath of the First World War, he was relatively optimistic about the chances of establishing a peaceful democratic order in Germany, he soon became very apprehensive that the old, evil military masters of Germany would once more gain decisive influence over the basic political decisions in the country. Einstein never doubted that the advent of Nazism to power would give complete rein to German militarism and firmly establish a government whose principal aim would be all-out preparation for war at high speed and at any price. Einstein knew that the Nazi Government would not hesitate to go to war, which it glorified, and would not shrink from employing the most brutal means and weapons in the pursuit of its aggressive policies. Because of this conviction, Einstein felt compelled to change his position toward the War Resisters' movement to support a policy of rearming the non-Fascist nations and, in 1939, to call President Roosevelt's attention to the potential military implications of gaining huge amounts of energy through atomic fission.

Einstein's role in encouraging the efforts which resulted in the production of atomic bombs in 1945 was described in Chapter IX of this volume. When Einstein's initiative in contacting the President became generally known, exaggerated accounts of his part in nuclear research during the war years began to circulate; in some quarters he was even called "the father of the bomb," while pacifists accused him of having betrayed the cause he had served all his life, by helping to get the production of the most murderous weapon under way. To all direct inquiries about his "responsibility" for the existence of atomic bombs, he answered briefly, but always without any equivocation. Only once did such an inquiry cause Einstein to engage in an exchange of several letters. Undoubtedly the fact of its having come from a correspondent in Japan—the country which was the first and only victim of atomic attack—provoked Einstein into discussing, at greater length than he had ever done before, his role in the dramatic developments since 1939.

Einstein had been fond of Japan ever since his visit there in 1922. His friendly feelings are manifest in a message which he sent to Japanese children a number of years after his visit: [2]

In sending this greeting to you, school children of Japan, I may claim a special right to do so; for I have visited your fair land, seen its cities and homes, its mountains and woods, the sources from which Japanese boys draw their love of country. A great book of drawings by Japanese children always lies on my table.

When you receive my message of greeting from across the sea, please try to understand that ours is the first age in history to experience friendly intercourse among the peoples of the world. Formerly, the peoples of different countries lived in ignorance and, indeed, in fear and hatred of one another. Let us hope that the spirit of brotherhood may ever grow in strength! It is in this spirit that I, an old man, send greetings to you, the school children of Japan, in the hope that your generation by its qualities of brotherhood may someday put my generation to shame.

In 1934, in a message to the liberal Japanese magazine *Kaizo*, with which he had entertained friendly relations for many years, Einstein said:

I must not let *Kaizo's* jubilee pass without briefly expressing my joy and gratitude for the wonderful times I spent with Japanese friends twelve years ago. . . .

And in a New Year's message of 1948 for the Japanese newspaper *Asahi*, in which Einstein expounded his well-known position on world government, he mentioned his pleasure at the opportunity to express my gratitude for the generous reception I enjoyed in Japan a quarter of a century ago. I loved the people and country so much that I could not restrain my tears when I had to part from them.

Einstein had some contacts with Japan after the Second World War, even before this message to *Asahi*. On March 3, 1947, he responded to a request for an epitaph for two old acquaintances, Dr. Hayasi Miyake and his wife Miho, of the Surgical Clinic of Kyushu (Fukuoka). It was Dr. Miyake, a physician, who had attended Einstein aboard ship on his trip to the Orient in 1922 (see p. 55). The aged couple—he was almost eighty—were killed in an air raid shortly before the end of the war. Einstein sent these words, now chiseled into a huge granite tombstone in facsimile of his German script:

Here lie Dr. Hayasi Miyake and his wife Miho Miyake. They labored together for the welfare of man and departed together, victims of human folly.

Three months later, on June 2, 1947, Einstein wrote to Morikatsu Inagaki, an old Japanese friend who had served as Einstein's interpreter on his visit to Japan twenty-five years before. Einstein, who, in subsequent years, had occasion to meet Inagaki in Geneva and Princeton, said in his letter:

I was very happy to receive your letter and especially to learn that you have survived those terrible years.

Efforts on behalf of a sensible peace policy are beset with difficulties, mainly because people tend to repeat the same blunders and follies over and over again. This would seem to be the case everywhere. Nonetheless, each of us must do everything within his power. Unless such an effort is made on the part of individuals, things will undoubtedly even worsen.

One might have thought that the danger posed by the incredible development of offensive weapons would engender a radical change in the thoughts and actions of those in responsible positions of leadership. What a vain hope this has proved to be! H. A. Lorentz, the Dutch physicist who died a few years after the First World War, once offered a most appropriate comment: "I am happy that I am a member of a nation that is too small to afford big blunders."

Some five years later Inagaki solicited from Einstein a message to the internationally attended Asian Congress for World Federation, held in Hiroshima November 3–6, 1952. Inagaki was an important organizer of the congress. Einstein's message, dated October 16, 1952, was a virtual reiteration of previous statements on the need for a world government.

The exchanges concerning Einstein's part in the production of the first atomic bombs originated with a letter, dated September 15, 1952, from the editor of *Kaizo*. It was a most polite letter, although not without a note of bitterness.[3]

. . . Recently—that is to say, seven years after the war—the ban on publication of pictures of the destruction wrought by the atomic bomb was lifted; for the first time the Japanese people have come face to face with actual scenes of the catastrophe, vividly showing the most destructive, not to say annihilating, effects of an atomic bomb. Once more the whole Japanese nation has been forcibly reminded of the fruit of its own guilt. . . . Yet we are left with a bewildered feeling as to why science, whose primary aim is to serve the welfare and happiness of mankind, should have been instrumental in producing such horrible results. As a great scientist who played an important role in producing the atomic bomb, you are eminently qualified to relieve the mental anguish of the Japanese people. I therefore venture to ask you the following questions:

1. What is your reaction to photographs showing the destructive effect of atomic bombs?

2. What do you think of the atomic bomb as an instrument of human destruction?

3. The next world war, it is commonly predicted, will be an atomic war. Does this not mean the destruction of mankind?

4. Why did you co-operate in the production of the atomic bomb although you were well aware of its tremendous destructive power?

I know how busy you are with your own research, but I would be most grateful if you were able to reply within the month in order to mitigate the agony of that nation which alone has been exposed to the deadly rays of the atomic bomb.

In case no reply is received from you, I assume you will have no objection to having that fact duly recorded in our magazine.

Einstein replied immediately, on September 20, 1952, specifying that he would assume responsibility only for his German text and not for any Japanese translation which *Kaizo* might prepare: [4]

My participation in the production of the atomic bomb consisted of one single act: I signed a letter to President Roosevelt, in which I emphasized the necessity of conducting large-scale experimentation with regard to the feasibility of producing an atom bomb.

I was well aware of the dreadful danger which would threaten mankind were the experiments to prove successful. Yet I felt impelled to take the step because it seemed probable that the Germans might be working on the same problem with every prospect of success. I saw no alternative but to act as I did, *although I have always been a convinced pacifist.*

I believe that the killing of human beings in a war is no better than common murder; but so long as nations lack the determination to abolish war through common action and find means of solving their disputes and safeguarding their interests by peaceful arrangements according to existing laws, they will continue to consider it necessary to prepare for war. They will feel compelled to engage in the manufacture of even the most detestable weapons in their fear that they may lag behind in the general arms race. Such an approach can only lead to war, and warfare today would mean universal annihilation of human beings.

There is little point, therefore, in opposing the manufacture of *specific* weapons; the only solution is to abolish both war and the threat of war. That is the goal toward which we should strive. We must be determined to reject all activities which in any way contradict this goal. This is a harsh demand for any individual who is conscious of his dependence upon society; but it is not an impossible demand.

Gandhi, the greatest political genius of our time, indicated the path to be taken. He gave proof of what sacrifice man is capable once he has discovered the right path. His work in behalf of India's liberation is living testimony to the fact that man's will, sustained by an indomitable conviction, is more powerful than material forces that seem insurmountable.

Einstein's statement to *Kaizo* apparently did not find a sympathetic reception in some Japanese quarters. Seiei Shinohara, a Japanese pacifist, who had translated Einstein's statement for *Kaizo*, made himself the spokesman of those in Japan who felt dissatisfied with the statement.[5] In a letter of January 5, 1953, written in almost flawless German, Shinohara asked Einstein how he, who considered himself an "absolute" pacifist, had found it possible to write that letter to President Roosevelt in 1939. He described the attitude of his fellow Japanese, who attributed Einstein's seemingly inconsistent conduct not only to his fears that the Germans might have been able to manufacture a similar bomb but also to the fact of his being a Jew, which meant that, consciously or unconsciously, he had been motivated by sentiments of vengeance against the Nazis. If Einstein desired to remain an "absolute pacifist," then, Shinohara felt, he had no alternative but to consider his letter to Roosevelt a regrettable mistake, and one that must never be repeated. Shinohara added that he had often wondered what the great Gandhi would have done had he been in Einstein's place; and he had concluded that Gandhi would not have acted as Einstein had. There were still other reasons why Shinohara was deeply concerned over the problem that had confronted Einstein in 1939:

Because of the resurgence of Japanese armed might under American pressure, the view is being widely expressed that there can be no absolute peace with absolute disarmament, and that the only practical solution would be a relative peace with arms for "just defense" against aggression. Some who adopt this position appear to cite your example in their defense—namely, that even an Einstein, a man recognized as an absolute pacifist, considered it permissible under certain circumstances to participate indirectly in the production of the atomic bomb. There are American correspondents in Japan who go so far as to say that possession and even use of atomic bombs by the United States are compatible with the spirit of world peace, because they consider America to be truly pacifist while the Soviets are now what the Nazis were then.

Einstein replied on February 22, 1953:

Your reproach is well taken from the viewpoint of an absolute, i.e., unconditional, pacifist. But in my letter to *Kaizo* I did not say that I was an *absolute* pacifist, but, rather, that I had always been a

Einstein's original draft of his letter to the editor of the Japanese magazine *Kaizo*, September 20, 1952.

(See page 584)

Meine Beteiligung bei der Erzeugung der Atombombe bestand in einer einzigen Handlung: Ich unterzeichnete einen Brief an Präs. Roosevelt, in dem ~~sich~~ die Notwendigkeit betont wurde, Experimente im Grossen anzustellen zur Untersuchung der Möglichkeit der Herstellung einer Atombombe.

Ich war mir der furchtbaren Gefahr ~~für die Menschheit~~ wohl bewusst, welche das Gelingen dieses Unternehmens für die Menschheit bedeutete. Aber die Wahrscheinlichkeit, dass die Deutschen an demselben Problem mit Aussicht auf Erfolg arbeiten dürften, hat mich zu diesem Schritte gezwungen. Es blieb mir ~~als einem überzeugten~~ nichts anderes übrig, obwohl ich stets ein überzeugter Pazifist gewesen bin. Töten im Kriege ist nach meiner Auffassung um nichts besser als gewöhnlicher Mord. —

Solange aber die Nationen nicht dazu entschlossen sind, durch gemeinsame Aktion den Krieg abzuschaffen und durch friedliche Entscheidungen auf gesetzlicher Basis ihre

~~Angst~~ Konflikte zu lösen und ihre Interessen zu schützen, ~~sind~~ sehen sie sich ~~genötigt~~ (genötigt) sehen sich auf den Krieg vorzubereiten. Sie sind dann genötigt, alle, auch die verabscheuungswürdigsten Mittel ~~vorzubereiten~~ vorzubereiten, um bei einem allgemeinen Wettrüsten nicht überflügelt zu werden. ~~die zur Vernichtung des Gegners führen können.~~

~~Das Verhängnis des immer zwangläufigen Progresses ist ... charakterisiert in der Devise:~~ ~~„Du oder ich“.~~

Dieser Weg führt ~~zum~~ mit Notwendigkeit zum Kriege, der unter den heutigen Verhältnissen allgemeine Vernichtung bedeutet.

Unter diesen Umständen hat die Bekämpfung der Mittel keine Aussicht ~~auf~~ Erfolg. Nur die radikale Abschaffung der Kriege und der Kriegsgefahr selbst kann helfen. Dafür ~~zu~~ soll man arbeiten und dazu entschlossen ~~bereit~~ sein, sich nicht zu Handlungen zwingen zu lassen, die diesem Ziel zuwider ~~sind~~ laufen. Dies ist eine harte Forderung an das Individuum, das sich seiner sozialen Abhängigkeit bewusst ist. Aber es ist keine unerfüllbare Forderung.

Gandhi, der grösste politische Genius unserer Zeit, hat den Weg gewiesen und gezeigt, welcher Opfer ~~ein Volk~~ die Menschen fähig sind, wenn ~~ihnen~~ sie den richtigen Weg ~~gezeigt wird~~ erkannt haben. Sein Befreiungs-Werk für Indien ~~hat~~ ist ein lebendiges Zeugnis dafür, dass der von fester Überzeugung beherrschte Wille stärker ist als scheinbar unüberwindliche materielle Macht.

convinced pacifist. While I am a convinced pacifist, there are circumstances in which I believe the use of force is appropriate—namely, in the face of an enemy unconditionally bent on destroying me and my people. In all other cases I believe it is wrong and pernicious to use force in settling conflicts among nations.

This is why I believe that the use of force was indicated and justified in the case of Nazi Germany. With regard to Russia, it is quite a different matter. In the present conflict between the United States and the Soviet Union it is far from clear which country threatens the existence of the other—indeed, it is even doubtful whether any such threat actually exists. In such a situation I am convinced that an aggressive attitude on the part of either side is unjustified and that, therefore, no other nation has the right to assume a partisan role in the conflict. India's attitude seems to me an exemplary one; I believe that every true Japanese pacifist should seek to appreciate fully the Indian position and should adopt it as a model for Japan.

Shinohara promptly returned to the attack. What was a "convinced" pacifist, he wrote on June 18, 1953, if not an "absolute" pacifist? Hitler, after all, was also convinced that he desired peace. It was regrettable that the atomic bomb, the use of which against Germany Einstein had supported, had, in fact, been dropped on the peaceful people of Hiroshima and Nagasaki rather than on the Germans. Further, Japan would certainly have been compelled to capitulate without being subjected to this weapon of terror. Despite American denials, it was clear that the Japanese had been used as guinea pigs, a conclusion confirmed by the failure of the United States to do anything in behalf of the victims of the two atomic bombs. And now, it appeared that the citizens of the United States were well on the way to surrendering their own cherished liberties.

Shinohara's letter ended with the announcement that he was forwarding Einstein some Japanese color prints in return for an autographed picture Einstein had sent him. Einstein returned the letter to Shinohara with marginal notations. Opposite the charge that he favored use of the bomb against Germany he wrote "No!" In another marginal notation he called attention to the letter he had written only a few days before to William Frauenglass (see p. 546). On the back of one of the pages, returned to Shinohara on June 23, 1953, he wrote:

I am a *dedicated* [*entschiedener*] but not an *absolute* pacifist; this means that I am opposed to the use of force under any circumstances, except when confronted by an enemy who pursues the destruction of life as an *end in itself*. I have always condemned the use of the atomic bomb against Japan. However, I was completely powerless to prevent the fateful decision for which I am as little responsible as you are for the deeds of the Japanese in Korea and China.

I have never said I would have approved the use of the atomic bomb against the Germans. I did believe that we had to avoid the contingency of Germany under Hitler being in *sole* possession of this weapon. This was the real danger at the time.

I am not only opposed to war against Russia but to all war—with the above reservation.

P.S. You should endeavor to form an opinion of others and of their actions only on the basis of sufficient information!

Shinohara replied on June 30, 1953, that he had never meant to hold Einstein responsible for the tragedy of Hiroshima and Nagasaki. He was gratified to know that one of the greatest guardians of America's conscience was as vigilant as ever. Would Einstein be willing to send a message on the occasion of the anniversary of Hiroshima and Nagasaki? Einstein had meanwhile received the color prints, and with his letter of thanks, on July 18, 1953, he sent the following message: [6]

It is good that the memory of the disasters of Hiroshima and Nagasaki is kept alive in the hearts of all men of good will by means of regularly recurrent ceremonies. Yet such memorials will be of real value only if they succeed in strengthening the belief that it is necessary to establish a world government based on peaceful agreement among the nations of the world. This belief must be based on the realization that, in the absence of a supranational authority, war cannot be avoided in the long run and circumstances will ever compel the contending parties to employ the most effective, that is to say, most murderous, weapons of war.

It must be pointed out again and again that any effort to secure peace through military alliances will inevitably lead to war and universal destruction. The greatest danger to the future of mankind lies in man's faith in unworkable methods which are falsely put forward in the name of practical politics.

There was some further correspondence between the two, and Shinohara sent Einstein further gifts. Thanking him, Einstein, in a final letter of July 7, 1954, suggested

that the only comfort which may be derived from the development of atomic weapons is the hope that *this* weapon may act as a deterrent and give impetus to a movement to establish supranational safeguards. Unfortunately, at the present time, the insanity of nationalism seems more powerful than ever before. I shall not send a message to the Hiroshima commemoration ceremonies this year; everyone knows my thoughts on these matters.

At around the same time, Einstein received another communication from Japan which reassured him that, despite his letter to President Roosevelt in 1939, his reputation in Japan had not suffered. The letter came from his old friend Morikatsu Inagaki, who reported on the great unrest in Japan caused by the radioactive fallout due to the recent American H-bomb test and on the increasing ill feeling toward the United States. In transmitting an urgent invitation to Einstein to attend the Congress of the World Federalists scheduled at Hiroshima for the fall of 1954, he said he expressed the wishes of many Japanese whose respect and sympathy for Einstein were "boundless." Einstein replied on July 15, 1954:

I received your recent letter with your urgent invitation. Since, for reasons of health, it is no longer possible for me to undertake long trips, I cannot, to my very real regret, accept your tempting invitation. Moreover, I am very conscious of the fact that I would not be able to say anything that would not be already known to you about the important problem to which our efforts are devoted.

It is reassuring, however, that the Japanese find themselves in the favorable situation of having lost the war; success, particularly in this field, is a very poor teacher. Although the actions of governments in almost all countries, viewed superficially, seem to offer little real hope for an early and intelligent solution of the peace problem, there is actually no basis for pessimism. The methods for wholesale annihilation of human beings that are now available are so formidable that even the most unimaginative person cannot fail to realize the insanity of attempting to resolve conflicts among nations through another world war. In fact, even responsible political leaders have made this unqualified admission in official speeches. The fact that they have thus far failed to draw practical conclusions from this knowledge is merely due to the blind nationalism which exists everywhere and which makes any effort toward reason and planning exceedingly difficult. To bring about a change in this situation is the important task facing the World Federalists. To accomplish such a task will be difficult everywhere, and particularly in those nations which are arrogantly confident in their power and success.

The faint ray of hope which Einstein expressed in this letter to Inagaki became visible from time to time during these last two years of his life. In fact, it appears that, while intellectually he believed that disaster was inevitable unless world government soon became a reality, the instinct for life which exists in every healthy human being led him occasionally to hope that the utter destructiveness of modern weapons might eventually eliminate war itself. On January 12, 1953, Einstein wrote again to the Queen Mother of Belgium to thank her for her customary seasonal greetings:

. . . The strange thing about growing old is that the intimate identification with the here and now is slowly lost; one feels transposed into infinity, more or less alone, no longer in hope and fear, only observing.

One comes to understand that people make life so dreadfully difficult for one another not because of any special reason but because of their immutable heritage. The ancients, especially the Greeks, realized this clearly. Hence, they did not forever seek new remedies for man's salvation. Europeans, by the way, still retain more of this insight than people here, who not only think they know what ought to be but also feel it is their mission to make it come to pass. This state of childlike illusion would be harmless enough were it not linked to such an excess of power.

On May 4, 1953, Einstein accepted an award of one thousand dollars (which he donated to the American Committee for Émigré Scholars) offered by a large New York department store in recognition of constructive nonconformist thinking. His acceptance message was presented to a large luncheon meeting by tape recording: [7]

It gives me great pleasure, indeed, to see the stubbornness of an incorrigible nonconformist warmly acclaimed. To be sure, we are here concerned with nonconformism in a remote field of endeavor [science]; it is a field in which no Senatorial committee has as yet felt impelled to tackle the important task of combating the dangers that threaten the inner security of the uncritical or intimidated citizen.

As for the words of warm praise addressed to me, I shall carefully refrain from disputing them. For who still believes that there is such a thing as genuine modesty? I should run the risk of being taken for no more than an old hypocrite. You will surely understand that I do not find the courage to brave this danger.

To the seventh annual assembly of the United World Federalists in Chicago, June 19–21, 1953, Einstein sent this message, delivered by Norman Cousins:

Strengthening the United Nations requires admission of all nations, irrespective of their internal organization; for averting the danger of war is the supreme and most immediate interest of all.

The extension of the United Nations, to encompass possibly all countries, will create a better basis for disarmament negotiations; hence efforts to increase membership should precede any attempt to solve the problem of disarmament.

An aged lady in Switzerland wrote Einstein a troubled letter in which she sought answers to two questions: Were the exceedingly poor weather conditions, manifest throughout the world in recent years, attributable to atomic explosions? And was there not the danger that our generation, by its attempt to make atomic bombs as effective as possible, might destroy the atmosphere which now protects our planet? Einstein replied on July 4, 1953:

I am sure that, while man's lack of reason is the source of much evil, it is not responsible for the natural catastrophes which you cite. This does not mean that I wish to condone the production of atomic bombs.

Your second question is more difficult to answer. I believe man has the power, or will have it soon, to poison the atmosphere so thoroughly with radioactive substances that all plant and animal life on land would perish. But I am still optimistic enough to believe it likely that man will avert such destruction in time by establishing world government.

It is characteristic of our time that you, I and so many others view such disasters as intolerable mainly because they would also extinguish the pure voice of art. It appears that man's belief in unending progress, so widespread only fifty years ago, has been utterly lost. I nevertheless dare hope that this belief may one day come to life again.

The War Resisters' International, which Einstein had so warmly supported until the Nazi seizure of power in Germany in 1933, re-emerged after the Second World War and again claimed affiliated groups in eighty-six countries. For the conference of its American section, Einstein wrote the following message, dated August 10, 1953: [8]

The War Resisters' League serves an important purpose. There are many persons of independent mind in all countries to whom the saying "War is a crime against humanity" is not an empty phrase. They are people who would rather submit to punishment and social ostracism than act against their conscience.

The existence of such a moral elite is a prerequisite to any fundamental change in public opinion, a change which, under existing circumstances, is absolutely essential if humanity is to survive.

The War Resisters' League is important because the spirit of fellowship within its ranks helps to ease the paralyzing sense of loneliness and isolation that may assail even men of courage and resolution. It offers moral support to them in the fulfillment of what they know to be their duty.

Einstein's letter to William Frauenglass had awakened memories of Henry David Thoreau's famous essay "On the Duty of Civil Disobedience," which was said to have had a profound influence on Gandhi. In answer to a member of the Thoreau Society who asked for his views on the essay, Einstein replied on August 19, 1953: [9]

I have never read anything by Thoreau, nor am I acquainted with his life history. There are, and have been many, although not enough, people of independent moral judgment who considered it their duty to resist evil even when it was sanctioned by state laws.

It may well be that Thoreau has in some way influenced Gandhi's thought. But it should not be forgotten that Gandhi's development resulted from extraordinary intellectual and moral forces in combination with political ingenuity and a unique situation. I think that Gandhi would have been Gandhi even without Thoreau and Tolstoi.

Martin Agronsky, Washington correspondent of the American Broadcasting Company, was eager to do a film interview with Einstein on the atomic bomb and world crisis; in a lengthy letter, he set forth his arguments in favor of such a film, chief of which was his belief that now, after the explosion of a hydrogen bomb by the Russians (August 12, 1953), another determined appeal to reason was essential. Agronsky also told the story of the mother who tried to calm her little girl, since she had been frightened by an atomic bomb drill in school. It was true, the mother admitted, that such a bomb might wipe out the whole family, but "don't you think it would be best, since we all love each other so much, if all of us, you, Daddy and me, could go to heaven together?" "Yes," said the little girl, "it would be nice if all of us were to go to heaven together, but, Mommy, I did so want to grow up!" Einstein wrote Agronsky on September 13, 1953:[10]

The combination of fear and arrogance which prevails in this country prevents the formation of sane opinion. This applies to people of influence as well as the general public. And unscrupulous politicians only exploit and aggravate the situation.

As far as atomic weapons are concerned, I do not know more about them than any intelligent man in the street; and he knows enough to develop a reasonable attitude in such matters. If he were in the right frame of mind, he would realize that security can be achieved only on an international basis and not through armaments and military alliances. He would not tolerate a foreign policy which not only fails to strengthen but systematically weakens the United Nations.

Nor am I able to agree that the public and the Congress are ignorant about the magnitude of the danger. They fail to draw the necessary conclusions from this knowledge because they do not realize that the other side is no less interested in a peaceful solution of the security problem than we ourselves are. In the current psychological situation, the "other side" is looked upon as a kind of devil, and all attempts to come to an agreement with him are considered hopelessly utopian.

For these reasons I am definitely *not* of the opinion that the danger of war can be eliminated without world government. Without such a concrete safeguard the arms race and, ultimately, world war are inevitable. To "outlaw" anything is of no value. We know from long experience—the Briand-Kellogg Pact, the agreement to protect civilian populations in wartime, etc.—that without safeguards such obligations, however honestly intended, are not honored in the event of war. If the principle of "all or nothing" ever applies, it applies in this case.

I hope these remarks will make it clear to you why I feel unable to comply with your request for an interview, despite my earnest will to please you.

To the Jewish Peace Fellowship in New York, Einstein wrote on September 21, 1953:

Mere praise of peace is easy, but ineffective. What is needed is active participation in the fight against war and everything that leads to it.

The distinguished lawyer and pacifist Grenville Clark had convened the first postwar World Government Conference, under the leadership of Supreme Court Justice Owen Roberts, in October 1945, at Dublin, New Hampshire. In 1948 he widely circulated a plan for a settlement with the Soviet Union. In 1953, in a booklet *A Plan for Peace*, Clark projected a comprehensive scheme for transforming the United Nations into a world government through revision of the U.N.'s Charter. The plan envisioned general and universal disarmament, membership of all nations without the right to secede, the establishment of a World Peace Force on a quota basis, abolition of the veto, and representation in the General Assembly on a population basis, though with an upper limit. Einstein wrote Clark on September 25, 1953: [11]

I have read your proposals for an attempt to make the United Nations into an organization strong and effective enough to solve the international problem of peace and security. In particular, I believe that your proposals concerning the election of representatives to the General Assembly are very wise. The potential influence of each particular nation would be determined by the size of its population. At the same time, it would prevent the development of dangerous rivalries among the great powers by introducing an upper limit for the number of their representatives.

I hope that your work will gain the recognition and influence it deserves.

A California correspondent, to whom Einstein, more than ten years before, had sent a note explaining the change in his views about the pacifist movement after the Nazis' conquest of power, inquired whether, in the fight against war, love could be substituted for fear without reference to religious terminology. Einstein replied on November 9, 1953: [12]

My remark about the necessity of using force was made at the time of the Nazi threat of world domination. I saw no alternative for the rest of the world. But in all cases where a reasonable solution of difficulties is possible, I favor honest co-operation and, if this is not possible under prevailing circumstances, Gandhi's method of peaceful resistance to evil.

I am not of the opinion that one should make use of the concept of God in striving for a better world. This, it seems to me, is incompatible with the integrity of a modern cultured person. History shows, moreover, that each party believes, or tries to make others believe, that God is on its side. This makes reasonable understanding and behavior even more difficult. Patient and honest educational work in favor of a moral and enlightened attitude is, in my opinion, the only way to a happier life.

Early in November 1953, James R. Newman, a lawyer and mathematician, sent Einstein a memorandum in which he suggested that new official proposals for the international control of atomic energy were in order and that, in this connection, the problem of inspection might prove less formidable than had been thought. Newman also sought Einstein's participation in a proposed symposium, "What Is Science?" Einstein, on November 5, 1953, drafted this reply to Newman, which, however, was never mailed: [13]

I have read your proposals with intense interest. You have demonstrated that the problem, viewed objectively, is not as difficult as generally described. At the conclusion you emphasize that the main obstacles are psychological, and this seems to me entirely correct. These obstacles have increased alarmingly during the last six years, owing to mistakes made on both sides. Things have reached the point where a proposal coming from one side will not even receive objective consideration by the other.

Any action, if it is to have some prospect of success, must originate with those who are still regarded as neutral. Such proposals, however, rather than being of a technical nature, should emphasize concrete measures calculated to remove conditions which certain nations regard as a threat to them; such measures would be the total disarmament of Germany and of Russia's Balkan satellites or the surrender of air bases of purely aggressive character. If such measures prove unfeasible, I see no prospect that disarmament efforts of a purely military character will succeed.

Both sides should, by tangible acts of renunciation, try to create an atmosphere of confidence in each other's peaceful intentions. If they are not willing to do so and if each side aims only at maximum military "security," then disaster will be inevitable. Compared to the importance of this matter, the question of whether or not I should write an article for your symposium seems of very little significance. I believe one should publish only when one feels the need to do so, which means, objectively speaking, when one has something of value to say. I do not feel that this is the case at present.

The letter actually sent to Newman was dated November 16, 1953, and read as follows:

I have thought very much about your letter. I had even prepared an answer to it some days ago but discarded it afterward. I do not know whether your arguments for an essential simplification of the inspection mechanism would be convincing to the experts. Moreover, I am convinced that even the best proposal which comes from one side will be automatically rejected by the other. The grim danger that confronts us can, as I see it, be averted only if each side is willing voluntarily to renounce certain positions considered by the other side to constitute an immediate menace. Further, it will be necessary to agree to create buffer zones under the control of both.

Since it appears, however, that neither side is prepared to take steps of this kind, I cannot see any possibility of a solution. Reasonable propositions are not likely to meet with a favorable reception.

Concerning your proposed publication, I cannot promise to write a foreword, for I cannot assume in advance that I would agree with the opinions of the people who will prepare the articles. Your eagerness for my co-operation is based on an exaggerated opinion of the importance of my scientific convictions, which are, in all essential points, in opposition to the convictions of most contemporary physicists. I have found that the best way to be sincere without seeming to function as a professional troublemaker is to keep "mum." It is my intention to follow this easy road.

A Hindu student at the University of Rochester, New York, wrote Einstein of his despair over the atmosphere of fear spreading throughout the world. "Since the death of Gandhi," he wrote, "I have looked upon you as the only person whom fear does not touch." Einstein replied on December 2, 1953: [14]

My opinions conform completely with yours and could not have been better expressed than you have done. It has been my experience, however, that in order to be convinced by sound arguments one has to be so constituted as to be susceptible to them and independent of mass suggestion. You must not be surprised, therefore, when your American friends disagree with you.

I wish to offer but one remark to your arguments. You write that your American friends "perhaps rightly" say that they are afraid to drop their arms. It is true, of course, that they cannot *suddenly* drop their arms, after all the policies that have been adopted against Russia in the last six years. The goal can be reached only by a gradual process which little by little will undo those policies, thereby creating a state of mind akin to mutual trust.

The War Resisters' League in New York paid its respect to Einstein for his letter to William Frauenglass and reported that some one hundred pacifists had committed themselves to follow his advice if they were summoned before a Congressional committee. The League inquired whether Einstein, despite his semiretirement, might not be persuaded to address a meeting on McCarthyism under the sponsorship of the most respectable religious and peace organizations. Einstein replied on January 29, 1954: [15]

You know well how close I feel to your organization. I share your belief in the need for united action by all the organized forces that have unmistakably demonstrated their unconditional opposition to the present totalitarian tendencies in our society. As a preliminary step and before any public action is taken, leaders of those organizations should be approached. It should not be difficult to bring them together in an effort to find out whether a common platform can be decided upon which is clear and radical enough to serve the purpose. After such preparation a public meeting sponsored by all of them might have some influence on shaping public opinion in this important matter.

As far as I am concerned, I find it best to adhere to the convictions I have repeatedly expressed. I am convinced it would not be in the interest of the cause were I to engage in direct political action, such as speaking before assemblies or sending messages to them. If I should do so, I would be regarded more as a political partisan than simply as an individual with a social conscience and certain convictions on public issues. Hence I am convinced that it is better for me not to participate in meetings, quite aside from the fact that it would be physically impossible for me to accept all worthy invitations or to make a reasonable selection among them.

In November 1953 Einstein agreed to accept an award from the Decalogue Society of Lawyers in Chicago. The group wrote him about the ambitious plans it was making for the patriotic dinner that was to serve as the occasion. Since he could not attend in person, would he agree to record his message on sound film and would half an hour be enough time? Einstein replied on December 6, 1953:

Your letter scared me a little, because it seems to me that my concept of a message is very different from yours; like the difference between a fly and an elephant. What I have written down is not more than a modest and short speech of acceptance, about the length of two pages, for my brain is not like the brain of a lawyer, a preacher or a politician!

When my elder son was twelve years old he told me complainingly while we were hiking together: "I don't know what's the matter with me. When we have to write a composition in school, some of my classmates write long and beautiful stories about the subject. But with me it always happens that I finish so quickly!" It seems that I inherited this quality from my son.

Einstein's message on "Human Rights," dated December 5, 1953, was played back before the Decalogue Society on February 20, 1954: [16]

You are assembled today to devote your attention to the problem of human rights. You have decided to offer me an award on this occasion. When I learned about it, I was rather saddened by your decision. How unfortunate is an organization which cannot produce a more suitable candidate upon whom to confer such a distinction!

In a long life I have devoted all my faculties to reach a somewhat deeper insight into the structure of physical reality. Never have I made any systematic effort to ameliorate the fortunes of men, to fight injustice and oppression, or to improve the traditional forms of human relations. The only thing I did was this: At long intervals I have publicly expressed opinions on such conditions in society which I considered to be so bad and unfortunate that silence would have made me feel guilty of complicity. It is true that there have been more and more such instances in recent years; but that is certainly not my fault.

The existence and validity of human rights is not written in the stars. It was enlightened men who, in the course of history, conceived and taught the ideals concerning the conduct of human beings toward one another; they also developed concepts about the most desirable structure of society. These same ideals and convictions, which derived from the experience of history as well as from the craving for beauty and harmony, usually have in theory been readily accepted by men, but have at all times been trampled upon by the same people under the pressure of their animal instinct. History is replete with the struggle for human rights, an eternal struggle in which final victory always eludes us. Yet to tire in that struggle would mean to bring about the destruction of society.

Today, when we speak of human rights, we are essentially referring to the protection of the individual against arbitrary infringement by other individuals or by the government; the right to work and to adequate earnings from work; freedom of discussion and teaching; adequate participation of the individual in the formation of his government. Although these rights have nowadays gained theoretical recognition, they are, in fact, subject to greater abuse than ever before. This is being brought about through the use of tricky legal maneuvers.

There is, however, one human right which, although infrequently mentioned, seems destined to become very important: the individual's right and obligation to abstain from participating in those activities which he considers wrong or pernicious. The most important case of such nonparticipation is the refusal of military service. I know of instances where, for this very reason, individuals of unusual moral strength and integrity have come into conflict with organs of the state. The Nuremberg trials of German war criminals gave tacit recognition to the principle that criminal actions cannot be excused on the plea that they were committed on government orders; conscience was judged to supersede the authority of the law.

In our own days the struggle is primarily waged for freedom of political conviction and discussion, as well as for freedom of research and teaching. The fear of Communism has led to policies that expose our country to ridicule by the rest of civilized mankind. How long shall we tolerate power-hungry politicians who try to generate a fear of Communism in order to gain political advantage? Sometimes it seems that the people of today have lost their sense of humor to such a degree that the French saying, "Ridicule kills," has lost its validity.

The problems which were touched upon in the last paragraph of Einstein's statement to the Decalogue Society occupied him very frequently. He always distinguished between the internal political conditions in the Soviet Union, of which he was often extremely critical, and the attitude of the West toward Russia, which he frequently assailed. He did so quite emphatically in his reply of January 14, 1954, to an eleven-page letter received from a correspondent in New York who was unknown to him and who suggested in his letter that the American government, "in order to safeguard its military advantage, must demand unquestioned obedience from its citizens." Einstein wrote:

I fully agree with your critical remarks on the regime in the Soviet Union. Considerably more could be added to what you said about conditions there, such as the mendacity of the political trials, which almost give the appearance of legalized murder, the complete denial of civil rights to the individual and to political minorities, and the deliberate distortion of truth for political purposes which is done much more frequently than in other nations.

But all this cannot be used as a justification for what takes place in our country under the slogan of the "fight against Communism." The "Communist menace" is being used here by reactionary politicians as a pretext to mask their attack on civil rights. The population is too misguided, and the intellectuals too intimidated, to be capable of effectively defending their Constitutional rights. Moreover, the politicians are primarily motivated by the immediate personal advantages which they hope to gain; their activities are either not at all, or only to a small extent, influenced by considerations of what they often know ought to be done. We have come a long way toward the establishment of a Fascist regime. The similarity of general conditions here to those in the Germany of 1932 is quite obvious. What might happen if, in addition, the dreaded economic depression were actually to take place! And why, one wonders, are the British not afraid of their Communists?

A journalist who was born in Russia, had lived and worked in Austria until the beginning of the semi-Fascist regimes there, and who had since been a correspondent for foreign newspapers in Paris, submitted to Einstein a lengthy memorandum with a passionate plea for action against the threat of a new world war. The scheme prepared by the journalist proposed the organization of a co-operative bank, whose purpose would have been to make loans for industrialization and improvement of living conditions in those countries where such efforts were most needed. Every individual throughout the world, through a small deposit, could become a voting member of the co-operative bank; governments would have no influence, and war—so the idealistic author of the scheme hoped—would be abolished as a result of the betterment of human conditions. Einstein, who was assigned a central role in the journalist's scheme, studied the memorandum carefully and replied on February 28, 1954: [17]

What you suggest seems to be a kind of Point Four program on a supranational co-operative basis. You seem to assume that the establishment of such an organization would end the exploitation of country by country and would, thereby, eliminate the danger of war.

If man were justified in assigning to himself the title of *Homo sapiens*, an organization such as the one which you suggest could possibly be established. However, man being what he is, such a plan is not feasible. The individual participants in the suggested organization would hardly derive any advantage from it. In this respect, it would differ considerably from the co-operative which you use as an analogy. Further, the organization, as soon as its operations were successful, would be subject to the same degenerative developments which, over a period of time, afflict all organizations, since degeneration comes about through power and success.

If it were possible to induce the peoples of the world to act rationally and in their own interest, many possibilities would exist for solving the problems facing mankind. Let me cite the example of birth control: since in this case the individual would act in his own interest, it should be relatively easy to introduce birth control, thereby avoiding the threat of overpopulation. But this has not been possible. It is difficult to induce even intellectuals to act reasonably from the point of view of their own interests, even when they are confronted with great dangers.

I do not believe that any human problem can be solved through frontal attack. Only by a gradual process of education and by many piecemeal efforts can we hope slowly to bring about real improvement of human conditions.

On March 28, 1954, two weeks after his seventy-fifth birthday, Einstein wrote to the Queen Mother of Belgium:

DEAR QUEEN:

Once again you have thought of me in such a friendly way on this strange occasion. Actually, unless an individual has already departed, he automatically turns seventy-five without any particular effort. But, having reached that stage, he feels bewildered and awkward since he is quite incapable of proving himself worthy of the many demonstrations of affection—especially when he has, through no will of his own, become a kind of legend in his own lifetime. All manner of fable is being attached to his personality, and there is no end to the number of ingeniously devised tales. All the more do I appreciate and respect what is truly sincere.

And then, I have become a kind of *enfant terrible* in my new homeland, due to my inability to keep silent and to swallow everything that happens there. Besides, I believe that older people who have scarcely anything to lose ought to be willing to speak out in behalf of those who are young and who are subject to much greater restraint. I like to think it may be of some help to them.

Strange that science, which in the old days seemed rather harmless, should have evolved into a nightmare that causes everyone to tremble. And fear is the worst counsel of all. Swords still fail to register the slightest inclination to be beaten into plowshares. This time, however, the European seems more hesitant to be drawn into a disaster. Let us hope this remains so!

And now, it occurs to me that one should guard against lapsing into the loquacity of old age. Warmest thanks and best wishes.

Your
A. Einstein

Late in March 1954 A. J. Muste of the Fellowship of Reconciliation submitted to Einstein an appeal titled "Time to Reflect," which was to serve as the basis for a petition to the President. Einstein wrote on April 6, 1954: [18]

I appreciate fully the motives behind your suggestion. But I cannot participate in this petition. Such a small-scale effort by a few private persons will not have the slightest influence on the behavior of people who have already made up their mind and who, for all practical purposes, lack the freedom to change their attitude. Only powerful political agencies can influence the course of events. I do not find it reasonable to do anything merely to satisfy one's personal urge. Reason alone has no effect, even if it speaks convincingly and with the voice of angels.

A voice from the past spoke to Einstein in the person of Carlo Winteler, member of a Swiss family with whom Einstein had lived during his school years and into which his sister Maja had married.

Winteler, like so many others who corresponded with Einstein, was profoundly dismayed at the turn of world events; his letter was written soon after the radioactive fallout produced by the American testing of a hydrogen bomb had afflicted twenty-three Japanese fishermen in the South Pacific. Einstein wrote on April 10, 1954:

You are quite right in suggesting that this dangerous toy is in unreliable hands—the hands of men to whom the daily political struggles are more important than the survival of man and other living matter. Even the intellectuals have, in part, become corrupted; as a group, they most likely are powerless to influence the course of events, and the shouting of shortsighted men drowns out whatever they may say.

My one hope is that the less powerful nations may band together and thus force an international solution; but by no means do I overestimate the realization of that hope. Unfortunately, the most farsighted among the people in this country have been so intimidated by the pseudo-patriotic pressures to which they have been exposed that their scope for effective action has been greatly reduced. I realize none of this sounds very hopeful, but there seems little point in deluding oneself.

Despite the failure of Usborne's original plan (see p. 420), a World Council for the Peoples' World Convention, of which Einstein was an international sponsor, was still active in Paris. The council was actively engaged in working for a United Nations Charter revision conference in 1955. Einstein was asked by the council to participate in an international seminar in Florence which was to consider whether the establishment of world government should be attempted through a United Nations reform or rather through an unofficial Peoples' Convention.[19] On April 21, 1954, Einstein advised the World Council that he was unable to attend the meeting at Florence; he wanted, however, to discuss in writing those issues on which he felt agreement should be possible among the participants in the seminar. He later authorized the following statement to be published in the *Bulletin of the World Council:*

I consider most sensible the establishment of a small group to discuss the problem of how an effective organization of supranational interests may be brought into being. I believe that the United Nations should be strengthened by inserting the provision that members of the Assembly no longer be responsible to their governments, but rather that they be locally elected and responsible to no one. However, if the Security Council should be continued as a representation of governments, its members should no longer enjoy the right to veto. At the present stage it may be premature to discuss further details concerning the desirable reorganization of the United Nations. On no account should the efforts to secure a reform of the United Nations be dominated by one of the existing power blocs. Only if these efforts maintain a neutral character will they tend to strengthen the position of those countries that have adopted a neutral attitude toward the rivalries of the big nations.

Any such efforts should be limited to the creation and strengthening of a supranational authority and should, on the whole, be neutral concerning the internal affairs of the various countries.

In short, the *sole objective* of our efforts should be to promote the establishment of a truly supranational authority. Only in this way will we avoid the wasteful dispersion of energies.

To the end of his days Einstein continued to reply to everyone who approached him about an important problem. The following letter, dated April 29, 1954, went to a Brooklyn man who had submitted an elaborate peace plan for which he actually sought a United States patent:

I have read your paper from cover to cover. I find it in harmony with the thinking of all reasonable and honest men and women. Its style is simple and lucid.

The question, however, is: How does one activate people who are tired, harassed and also lazy? It is like the founding of a new religion. It almost never succeeds, and *if* it does succeed, one is at a loss to know why.

The people who are leading us to destruction sometimes make speeches which reveal quite clearly that they do not lack the proper insight. In the final analysis, however, every man acts according to the pressure of his personal situation and in his own interests.

I myself express openly what I think. But I know that does not mean that I could create a popular movement such as Gandhi was able to do. You can be sure that nothing can be achieved solely by preaching reason.

At around this time, the case of Dr. J. Robert Oppenheimer created a public sensation. Oppenheimer, the Director of the Institute for Advanced Study in Princeton (of which Einstein had been the first member in 1933) and, during the war, one of the most important officials of the Manhattan District Project (which produced the first atomic bomb), was barred in December 1953 from further work for the United States Atomic Energy Commission because he was allegedly a "poor security risk." The May 1954 issue of the *Bulletin of the Atomic Scientists* devoted a large section to the case and included statements from a number of outstanding scientists. Einstein's contribution was limited to a single sentence:

The systematic and widespread attempt to destroy mutual trust and confidence constitutes the severest possible blow against society.

During the same period, Einstein replied to a correspondent in New York who had written him about the Oppenheimer case:

It is best not to be too excited. Fear and stupidity have generally been the origin of most human actions. We can only continue to strive for honesty and independence of thought.

Professor Anton J. Carlson, physiologist at the University of Chicago, wrote Einstein twice, suggesting that he co-sponsor a letter to President Eisenhower on the menace of atomic, hydrogen and cobalt bombs. Professors Kirtley Mather, Harlow Shapley, Linus Pauling and Michael Heidelberger were mentioned as having collaborated on the letter. Since Einstein, with Leo Szilard, had given the original impetus that led to the manufacturing of the atomic bomb, would it not be fitting if the two of them now urged measures to eliminate the deadly menace of nuclear warfare? Einstein replied on May 3, 1954: [20]

The facts should make it clear to any normal person that a competitive arms race based on the testing of atomic weapons can only lead to general destruction. It requires no particular scientific perspicacity to see this, and I can therefore see no reason why I should help teach this truth to the President.

This is why I did not answer your first letter and why I am not willing to participate in your enterprise.

On June 7, 1954, Einstein sent a message to the annual Assembly of the United World Federalists in which he said:

The events of the last few years have made it very clear that the only way to avoid general disaster is the way of a supranational organization of peace. The surrendering of unlimited sovereignty is a small price to pay for the survival of mankind. I am optimistic enough to believe that the time is not far off when even the most conventionally conditioned minds will understand that protection cannot be sustained by large armaments.

Linus Pauling wrote Einstein about a new organization, Everybody's Committee to Outlaw War, and enclosed a pamphlet in which Einstein was quoted. Einstein replied on June 8, 1954: [21]

I surely do not need to assure you that, in principle, I am wholeheartedly on your side. I believe, however, that in the present situation a mere declaration to outlaw war would be quite ineffective. Even if it were possible to create a mass movement around this slogan, it is clear that competitive armament and the danger of war cannot be prevented without a world government which has sufficient power and independence. Hence, I am unwilling to endorse the statement you sent me. I believe, moreover, that all efforts should be directed toward the great goal of world government; this the World Federalists are trying to do, although, regrettably, not vigorously enough.

The commanding officer of the United States Naval Air Training Center in Jacksonville, Florida, advised Einstein that under a program "to enhance the morale of its personnel" buildings were to be named for "appropriate and outstanding people and famous Naval engagements." Would Einstein grant permission for a building used for the administration of the Aviation Electrician's Mate School to be named "Einstein Hall"? Einstein replied on July 12, 1954: [22]

I thank you very much for your kind intention. I am very sorry that, because of my pacifist convictions, I am unable to give my consent. It must be recognized that, so long as the problem of lasting peace is not solved on a supranational basis, military preparations will be unavoidable. But since it is my conviction that a solution to this problem must be found in any event, and since I consider it most important that this view be widely disseminated, I believe it my duty to avoid anything that might produce an opposite psychological effect.

To a Philadelphia correspondent, apparently a conscientious objector, Einstein wrote on July 23, 1954: [23]

. . . To oppose the law for moral reasons entails great sacrifice; therefore, I do not feel justified in advising you. I believe that the war resisters' movement constitutes an elite of men whose main significance is that they activate and maintain people's awareness of the inhumanity of war. They urge that the duty to participate in organized murder be not recognized, even when this duty is required by the government. I have no right to demand sacrifices of others when I myself did not have the opportunity to make them.

As Einstein had done in many other instances, he felt the need to let Dag Hammarskjöld, Secretary-General of the United Nations, know how favorably impressed he was by a public address delivered by him. Hammarskjöld discussed the value of knowledge. He wondered whether those who fear knowledge do not actually fear change. We should, Hammarskjöld believed, have the courage and possess the humility to accept change and not act as if we had lost the conviction of the value of knowledge. "We must act with undiminished faith in freedom of thought, freedom of research, freedom of speech—in full knowledge of the dangers involved in the changes we set in motion, but also of our responsibility to give that change creative direction." One of these changes, Hammarskjöld felt, was the growing interdependence of nations which "has made this world of ours in many respects one world. . . ." Yet, he continued, while this interdependence of nations had already made world organization necessary, the diversity of nations made world government still impossible. He suggested a middle road: a world organization which would respect the sovereignty of nations and would inevitably evolve into a world community which "for our civilization is the only alternative to disaster." He expressed his belief that attempts to achieve such a world community were already manifest in an intricate system of international agreements and in the development of international law.

Einstein wrote Hammarskjöld on October 2, 1954, as follows: [24]

I cannot refrain from expressing my sincere admiration for your address on the occasion of the Columbia University Bicentennial

Celebration. In the wake of so much mendacity and hypocrisy, your lucid and honest remarks were a welcome relief. I consider it fortunate that a man such as yourself has been entrusted with the most important and difficult position which you now occupy.

Hammarskjöld replied on November 9, 1954, in excellent German:

I can think of no more welcome echo to my address at the Celebration of Columbia University than the letter which you sent me on that occasion. It was my intention to present a vigorous and unequivocal declaration on behalf of those ideals and principles that constitute the only possible background and the only possible atmosphere for the work of a man who, like you, is one of the pioneers of mankind. While my position compels me to proceed with a certain amount of caution, it also imposes upon me an obligation to lend my unqualified support to those ideals. It is not easy to strike a just balance between what I should like to say and do, in order to live up to this obligation, and what I am able to do without creating difficulties for the organization which I was appointed to serve.

I should like to express myself more simply and concretely: I am only too well aware that, when I feel an obligation to express myself in general terms, there is the danger that the people will fail to hear what I actually intend to say. Therefore, it is a truly deep satisfaction for me to know that you not only understood what I tried to communicate to the large audience at the Columbia University Celebration, but that you also approve of what I said. Such understanding, especially coming from you, is meaningful to me beyond words.

At times I ask myself whether the ideals of intellectual liberalism are strong enough to affect the mass civilization of our day or, even more, to survive it. Yet, such doubts should not excuse us from the task of continuing our efforts toward the realization of those ideals. The man in public office has the duty to give wholehearted support to the man in science in every possible way.

I very much hope that I may one day be accorded the privilege of making your personal acquaintance.

The War Resisters' League inquired whether it might reprint the Einstein-Freud exchange *Why War?* Einstein consented on October 13, 1954: [25]

I gladly give you permission to reprint my correspondence with Freud, which took place in 1932 at the invitation of the League of Nations. Since that time, circumstances concerning the problems dealt with in the correspondence have undergone considerable change. All responsible men agree that peaceful coexistence is essential to the survival of the human race, but thus far no responsible leader has proven himself courageous enough to act in accordance with this belief. The delusion that security can be gained by stockpiling armaments is as prevalent as ever. Hence it is highly desirable that every attempt be made to make people aware of the necessity of a supranational organization for the maintenance of peace, and to enlist their energies in that direction.

You may use the above remarks in your proposed publication. I should, however, not like to write the introduction suggested by you, since the main purpose of my brief contribution in the little volume was to persuade Freud to overcome his reluctance to appear in the political marketplace.

Late in 1954 Einstein wrote to Joseph Lewis, dean of American freethinkers:

I thank you for your courtesy in sending me your booklet, *An Atheist Manifesto*.

In my younger years all of us intellectuals thought a happier age for mankind would be ushered in when kings and emperors who reigned "by the grace of God" were abolished. There is no doubt that they did constitute a great evil. Well, they *have* been rather radically abolished, but mankind does not seem to be much better off. Demagogues and clever professional politicians soon came to serve as effective substitutes.

Superstition and priest rule are grave evils, and it is good that you are waging such a resolute and skillful campaign against them. Yet I could not avoid a wry smile in reading your booklet. True, this form of evil must and should be fought; but when victory is at hand—and it is certain in the long run—it will be more than ever apparent that the source of mankind's afflictions is to be found in its own innate heritage.

Well, we must struggle and educate, even when the goal is believed to be unrealizable; for without active resistance on the part of those endowed with vision and relative freedom things would be far worse.

Jules Moch, one-time French Minister of the Interior and Delegate to the United Nations Disarmament Commission for many years, discussed the alternative of disarmament versus atomic annihilation in a book, *La Folie des Hommes,* published in an English translation in 1955 under the title *Human Folly: To Disarm or Perish?* Einstein wrote an introduction for it late in December 1954. He mailed it with a brief note of January 1, 1955, in which he said that he had greatly enjoyed Moch's book: [26]

The title of this book is well calculated virtually to compel men of good will to come to grips with its contents. On the other hand, it may arouse incorrect expectations about the nature of the work. This very much needed volume offers much more than merely a critical analysis of the events of the past ten years in international affairs. It is the work of a man who, in almost unique fashion and with a specialized knowledge which under present conditions is particularly hard to come by, has devoted the whole of his strength to the search for a solution to the perilous situation which threatens the survival of humanity. He reports that his efforts, which have received the support of the French and British governments and which, after difficult negotiations, have been partially successful, have brought us that much nearer to the goal of peace and security. He gives evidence that the respective positions of East and West on the disarmament question, which at first appeared irreconcilable, have come so much closer to a *rapprochement* that an honest agreement appears attainable.

The book is divided into two parts. The first part gives an objective description of the military-technical situation brought about by the development of the atomic bomb. The importance of such an objective description is very great, for it cannot be denied that the present dangerous situation has led to such a thorough *Gleichschaltung* of the organs of public information (press, radio, education) that the ordinary citizen is unable adequately to evaluate the technical situation, or the political role over the past decade of the United States and the Soviet Union, which are the two principal antagonists. The author attributes the conduct of these two countries to the shocking impact of the two world wars. Such understanding is essential if the psychological barriers which at present prevent the formation of reasonable attitudes are to be overcome. The second part of the book throws light on the complex and laborious attempts which have been made in an effort to reach agreement on the question of disarmament. Here, too, the author, writing with admirable objectivity, helps to clarify the position taken by the two antagonists and discusses the possibility of arriving at a reconciliation.

If I am permitted to insert here a comment of my own, it is this: I believe the psychological effect of the two world wars has been such that the attitude of the various nations, even in times of peace (or partial peace, as the case may be), is dominated by one consideration, and that is to pursue a policy which will insure that, in the event of war, the position of one's own nation shall be as favorable as possible. But the adoption of such an attitude not only makes a real peace impossible but necessarily aggravates tensions and eventually leads to catastrophe. Those who do not believe in the possibility of attaining a lasting and secure peace, or who lack the courage to join the struggle to make it a reality, are helping to make the world ripe for destruction.

Toward the end of this period, Einstein issued one more statement implicitly dealing with the problem of intellectual freedom in America which so often occupied his thoughts in those years. The statement, terse and blunt, acquired wide publicity and probably achieved its intended purpose: to arouse and focus public opinion on a problem which Einstein considered to be of crucial significance. Einstein's statement was published in the magazine *The Reporter* of November 18, 1954: [27]

You have asked me what I thought about your articles concerning the situation of scientists in America. Instead of trying to analyze the problem, I should like to express my feeling in a short remark: If I were a young man again and had to decide how to make a living, I would not try to become a scientist or scholar or teacher. I would rather choose to be a plumber or a peddler, in the hope of finding that modest degree of independence still available under present circumstances.

Einstein knew, of course, that any plumber or peddler who voiced political dissent would not have been secure from political persecution and that, on the other hand, any intellectual who conformed to the prevailing political philosophy would not become a victim of the witch hunt. What he obviously meant was that the plumber and the peddler were independent in their work, while it was precisely in the sphere of their professional activities that the independence of intellectuals had become endangered or even jeopardized.

Einstein's warning had a great effect. *The Reporter* said it was grateful for the shock Einstein had produced since shocks of this kind were needed. More important than the honorary membership which the Plumbers' Union conferred upon him was the fact that large parts of the American press felt compelled to discuss the underlying problem of intellectual freedom. Such was Einstein's unique position in society that a brief and somewhat frivolous statement which, had it come from almost anyone else, would probably have been ignored, brought a crucial social and political issue into the center of public discussion.

CHAPTER EIGHTEEN

THE THREAT OF UNIVERSAL ANNIHILATION | 1955

EINSTEIN BECAME ILL in the fall of 1954 and was bedridden for several weeks. He pursued his scientific work whenever he felt well enough to do so and continued to attend to the many demands that came to him through the mail; but, for a prolonged time, he was hardly accessible to visitors. Occasional remarks in his letters indicate that he frequently experienced physical distress and severe pain, but his mind remained as alert and receptive as ever. He felt better toward the end of that year. By the beginning of 1955, he was able to resume a more normal routine, but he was to live only three and a half months.

When he died on April 18, 1955, several pages of mathematical equations lay on the table at his bedside. They were the pages on which he had been working when he was stricken several days before. He had asked to have them brought to him, but, as he remarked the evening before his death, whenever he tried to resume the interrupted work, severe pain would force him to lay the pages aside. Thus, to the very last, did he strive to increase man's knowledge of what he once had called the secrets which nature is hiding through the dignity of her very existence. He remained to the end equally interested in his nonscientific pursuits. Indeed, the accident of events during the last few months of his life provided him with an opportunity to express once more his views on various social and political issues which had occupied him often during his life.

At the beginning of the year, on January 2, 1955, he acknowledged New Year's greetings from the Queen Mother of Belgium:

DEAR QUEEN:

Your telegram illustrates the virtue that has been described as characteristic of your trade—punctuality. More than that, it is an expression of that warmth of human feeling which is so seriously neglected in our age of mechanization. I am ever aware of this quality in you when reading of your public activities. It must require a great deal of courage and independence, especially from one in your position, with its peculiar restraints on freedom of action.

When I look at mankind today, nothing astonishes me quite so much as the shortness of man's memory with regard to political developments. Yesterday the Nuremberg trials, today the all-out effort to rearm Germany. In seeking for some kind of explanation, I cannot rid myself of the thought that this, the last of my fatherlands, has invented for its own use a new kind of colonialism, one that is less conspicuous than the colonialism of old Europe. It achieves domination of other countries by investing American capital abroad, which makes those countries firmly dependent on the United States. Anyone who opposes this policy or its implications is treated as an enemy of the United States. It is within this general context that I try to understand the present-day policies of Europe, including England. I tend to believe that these policies are less the result of a planned course of action than the natural consequence of objective conditions.

Such thoughts are likely to come to one's mind when one delves into the writings of the dreamers and thinkers of the past. I am particularly taken with Lichtenberg. Now, with so many years behind me, the man makes an ever greater impression on me. I know no one else who so plainly hears the grass grow.

Enough now for this New Year. My warmest greetings and fondest wishes.

Your
A. EINSTEIN

To an English friend Einstein wrote on February 5, 1955: [1]

And yet, to one bent by age death will come as a release; I feel this quite strongly now that I have grown old myself and have come to regard death like an old debt, at long last to be discharged. Still, instinctively one does everything possible to delay this last fulfillment. Thus is the game which nature plays with us. We may ourselves smile that we are like that, but we cannot free ourselves of the instinct to which we are all subject.

A letter from Belgium offered Einstein an opportunity of restating his position on world government. He used the occasion to re-emphasize the necessity of trying to convince the peoples of the world, especially the population of the major powers, that only the creation of a supranational organization would secure world peace. The Belgian correspondent, Dr. Balle-Helaers, a Brussels physician, advised Einstein of a project which would establish an organization of intellectuals in the widest sense of the term. The purpose of the organization would be to defend the right of the scientist to complete independence in his research and to unrestricted dissemination of the results of his work. Apparently upon the suggestion of his friend, the Queen Mother of Belgium, Einstein was asked to send a message to the newly formed Belgian Committee. On February 15, 1955, he replied to Professor Gueben, a physicist of Liège, Belgium, who seems to have been one of the initiators of the organization:

I received today a letter from Dr. Balle-Helaers in Brussels, who informed me of plans to form a Belgian organization which would disseminate reliable information concerning the dangers and probable effects arising from the development of nuclear physics. Unless I misunderstood the letter, the information would be disseminated not only to the experts interested in this field but also to the public at large; the organization also plans to seek the co-operation of similar organizations in other countries. Because of the dangers resulting from the development of nuclear weapons, I feel that such an organization would fulfill an important need in bringing the opinions of intelligent, non-political persons into the open. Most important is that an effort be made to educate the general public at large, for reasons which Bertrand Russell has recently expressed with characteristic clarity. He said that the abolition of atomic weapons, which constitute such a menace to mankind, can be accomplished only by the abolition of war itself. This, however, will not be possible except within the framework of an organization composed of all nations which possess sufficient power to make and enforce the necessary decisions.

Indispensable to the formation of such an organization that would make war a virtual impossibility is the existence of a united public opinion in all important countries which would be so powerful that all governments would be compelled to renounce a measure of their sovereignty.

The last time Einstein was to express his belief in the right of the individual to be guided by his conscience, even at the risk of punishment, came less than two months before his death. A correspondent from Philadelphia (Pennsylvania) suggested that a statement of Supreme Court Justice William O. Douglas was in conflict with a frequent observation of Einstein concerning the principle of the supremacy of man's conscience over existing laws—a principle recognized by implication in the Nuremberg trials. The correspondent excused his inquiry by explaining that he, "an average citizen with no formal schooling," was not capable of solving such a difficult problem himself. Einstein replied on February 21, 1955:

In questions involving basic morality, "formal schooling" does not help much since it is impossible, in this area, to make fundamental decisions which would be binding on all citizens.

Justice Douglas makes his decisions as a jurist. I suppose that he holds the following position: The state can and must force its citizens (i.e., the people living within its boundaries) to respect its laws, but the state cannot force citizens (i.e., inhabitants) of foreign countries to do likewise.

I, on the other hand, make decisions of this character merely as a human being. I believe that an individual should act according to his conscience even if such action should contravene the law of the land. I believe he should do so even if he knows he will be subject to punishment by the authorities of the state.

This attitude best corresponds to my own sense of morality. But, to a certain extent, my attitude can also be justified on an objective basis: blind obedience to those state laws which we regard as immoral serves only to impede the struggle to improve such immoral laws.

On March 8, 1955, Einstein wrote to Dr. Walter G. Muelder, Dean of Boston University, commenting on Muelder's University Lecture, "The Idea of the Responsible Society," which a Hindu friend had sent him: [2]

Although I am rather unfamiliar with religious terminology, I fully endorse all the demands which you make of the community, the state, and the individual. I was particularly impressed by the fact that you did not limit yourself to abstract pronouncements which usually leave too much room for interpretation. Through the use of concrete examples you have made clear exactly what you mean. For this everyone who is earnestly concerned with the goal of achieving a better and more humane attitude among men should be grateful to you.

I have no knowledge of the degree of unity among the religious organizations mentioned in your little book or to what extent they are in agreement on basic questions; nor do I know whether they are sufficiently independent to be able to assert their common viewpoint in their respective countries. However, I do believe that in the present dangerous situation all such unions of genuine supranational character are especially valuable; through advice and criticism, they can exert a sound influence in actual instances, and their voice will be listened to with trust and respect by all men of good will.

The individual feels quite hopeless and helpless in the face of powerful organizations in public life, most of which are short-sighted and, indeed, objectionable. Besides, the prophet has never been accepted in his own country. He is regarded as a heretic or even a traitor and, in times of general emotional stress, is treated accordingly. An international group is somewhat better protected against such attacks.

On March 11, 1955, only a few days before his seventy-sixth birthday and little more than a month before his death, Einstein sent what was to be his final letter to his royal friend in Belgium:

DEAR QUEEN:

Your letter made me extremely happy. It indicates that we are in agreement on basic political questions. Although everyone realizes that, given the present state of affairs, any serious military conflict —indeed, even the very act of preparing for a *possible* military conflict—will necessarily lead to universal destruction, governments cannot bring themselves to adopt an attitude of good will and understanding and, instead, continue to pursue a policy of shrewdness and mutual threats.

I must confess that the exaggerated esteem in which my lifework is held makes me feel very ill at ease. I feel compelled to think of myself as an involuntary swindler. If one attempts to do anything about this, one succeeds only in making matters worse.

The little Reklam book [the name of a German publishing house] which I sent you will help to acquaint you with Lichtenberg. He was professor of physics at Göttingen [Germany] (eighteenth century?), an eccentric with a touch of true genius which found expression in immortal fragments of thought. Of his longer pieces, the "Letter from the Earth to the Moon" is particularly delightful. There is a little story about the latter that runs like this: Question: Which is the more useful, the sun or the moon? Answer: The moon, of course; it shines when it is quite dark while the sun shines only when it is light anyhow. In an oblique way this quaint error also shows up in the Bible story of creation.

With warmest wishes,

Your
A. Einstein

To A. J. Muste of the Fellowship of Reconciliation Einstein wrote on March 12, 1955: [3]

I found your critical articles quite convincing, in particular, the criticism of Thirring's proposal. On the other hand, I believe that your suggestion for immediate unilateral disarmament is not acceptable. A genuine solution of the security problem presupposes the existence of a certain degree of mutual confidence among the parties concerned; mere procedural provisions do not constitute an adequate substitute. The building of confidence requires consistent action with that end in mind. An example of such action would have been the demilitarization of Germany, achieved in co-operation with Russia. But what was actually done, both in the case of Germany and that of East Asia, was in almost every instance just the opposite of what might have created confidence.

Einstein's emphatic statements to a Japanese publication and to friends in Japan concerning the role which he had played in initiating research on atomic explosives in 1939 had not become widely known. Inquiries on the subject were frequent. The last request, to which Einstein replied, for clarification of his letter to President Roosevelt came, significantly enough, from Germany. The writer of the letter, Professor Max von Laue, was one of the few German physicists for whom Einstein felt real friendship and with whom, except for the war years, he never lost contact. Einstein replied on March 19, 1955:

Princeton. 11 III. 55

Liebe Königin!

Ihr Brief hat mich ausserordentlich gefreut. Er zeigt mir Übereinstimmung in den grundsätzlichen politischen Dingen. Trotzdem alle sehen, dass ein ernsthafter militärischer Konflikt unter den heutigen Bedingungen zur Vernichtung aller führen muss ja schon die Vorbereitung auf auf einen möglichen militärischen Konflikt, kann man sich nicht dazu entschliessen Schlauheit und gegenseitige Bedrohung durch wohlwollendes Verständnis zu ersetzen.–

Ich muss gestehen, dass die mir entgegengebrachte übertriebene Wertschätzung meiner Lebensarbeit, mir viel Unbehagen bereitet. Ich komme mir vor wie ein unfreiwilliger Hochstapler. Es ist so schwierig, etwas dagegen zu thun, ohne das Übel noch zu vergrössern.

Das hässliche Reklam-Büchlein, das ich Ihnen sandte, wird Ihnen den Lichtenberg näher bringen. Er war Physikprofessor in Göttingen (18. Jahrhundert), sehr original mit wahrhaft genialen Anwandlungen, die sich in unsterbliche Gedankensplitter verdichteten. Von den längeren Sachen ist der Brief der Erde an den Mond besonders ergötzlich. Über den letzteren gibt es folgendes Histörchen. Frage: Wer ist nützlicher, die Sonne oder der Mond? Antwort: natürlich der Mond; er leuchtet, wenn es sonst ganz finster ist, während die Sonne nur scheint, wenn es ohnehin hell ist. In verschleierter Form zeigt sich dieser drollige Irrtum auch in der biblischen Schöpfungsgeschichte.

Mit herzlichen Wünschen

Ihr A. Einstein

Einstein's last letter to the Queen Mother of Belgium, March 11, 1955.
(See page 619–20)

My action concerning the atomic bomb and Roosevelt consisted merely in the fact that, because of the danger that Hitler might be the first to have the bomb, I signed a letter to the President which had been drafted by Szilard. Had I known that that fear was not justified, I, no more than Szilard, would have participated in opening this Pandora's box. For my distrust of governments was not limited to Germany.

Unfortunately, I had no share in the warning made against using the bomb against Japan. Credit for this must go to James Franck. If they had only listened to him!

Shortly before Laue's inquiry was received, an even more fundamental question about Einstein's responsibility for the existence of the atomic bomb was raised. Professor Jules Isaac, a French historian of advanced years, sent Einstein a recently published article, "Atomic War or Coexistence," and asked whether Einstein should not have had the foresight to predict the possible dangerous technological "consequences of his equations" when he first published the Relativity Theory in 1905. Professor Isaac further posed the question as to whether scientists, as a group, should not, long ago, have sought ways of averting the catastrophic developments which would result from their discoveries.[4] Einstein replied on February 28, 1955:

I have read your illuminating pamphlet with great interest, as well as the straightforward letter which you attached to the essay on the history of our people.

One cannot avoid the feeling that one ought to do something to avert the threatening doom. Such action may possibly appear more promising to you than it does to me; for I live in one of the two prime centers of political fever. Things have reached a point where only a handful of people are left with whom one can enjoy a quiet talk. Fear, hatred, and petty personal concerns dominate the actions of everyone, driving nations and men, including scientists, toward the final catastrophe. One can no longer ascertain who does the driving and who is driven. Virtually everyone is aware that the alternative is either a secure peace on a supranational basis or universal doom. But when men are given even the slightest chance of acting in accordance with this knowledge, they fail to do anything; they are victims of the very social pressure to which they themselves have contributed. I suppose this has always been the case, but never before have the consequences been of such global scope.

Now you seem to believe that I, poor fellow that I am, by discovering and publishing the relationship between mass and energy, made an important contribution to the lamentable situation in which we find ourselves today. You suggest that I should then, in 1905, have foreseen the possible development of atomic bombs. But this was quite impossible since the accomplishment of a "chain reaction" was dependent on the existence of empirical data that could hardly have been anticipated in 1905. But even if such knowledge had been available, it would have been ridiculous to attempt to conceal the particular conclusion resulting from the Special Theory of Relativity. Once the theory existed, the conclusion also existed and could not have remained concealed for any length of time. As for the theory itself, it owes its existence to the efforts to discover the properties of the "luminiferous ether"! There was never even the slightest indication of any potential technological application.

For me, as for Bertrand Russell, the question is whether those few scholars of sufficiently wide reputation, courage and selflessness can do anything effective now.

From California came a communication whose purpose was to acquaint Einstein with a book which its author had prepared as an introduction to the "Philosophy of Planetary Universalism." Einstein, asked to comment, replied early in April 1955: [5]

Human beings would be extremely fortunate if they were capable of conducting themselves as you suggest. But they are no more able to do so than a tiger is able to become a vegetarian. Nevertheless, during every waking hour, we must strive to achieve the unattainable.

The *Firing Line*, a publication prepared and distributed by the National Americanism Commission of the American Legion, devoted an entire issue to the United World Federalists. Many of the individuals prominent in the organization of the United World Federalists were listed and characterized by indicating their affiliation with organizations or causes which, by implication, were considered unpatriotic by the American Legion. Einstein was among those so listed and characterized. The United World Federalists advised him by letter that they bitterly resented the implied charge of being subversive, that they had decided to institute action to bring about a retraction of these allegations, and that they would appreciate his suggestions concerning the action to be taken. On the back of the letter, Einstein drafted a reply in longhand, which was mailed on April 5, 1955:

Having read the article in the *Firing Line,* I wish to make a few remarks about it. I firmly believe that, by defending ourselves against the characterization as "subversives," we would give tacit recognition to the validity of such a concept.

We should make it very clear that we consider the current usage of this vague concept by official and nonofficial agencies as damaging and unworthy of the traditions of the United States. Moreover, we should lend emphatic support to the thesis that the danger of universal annihilation can be averted only through the creation of a supranational organization. Any attempt to retard or impede this development, so urgently needed, is "subversive" in the true sense of the word.

This letter was mailed eight days before Einstein was fatally stricken. It so happened that, outside his professional work, his two last actions in life involved the two nonscientific problems which had been closest to his heart for the major part of his adult years: the abolition of war and the establishment in Palestine of a homeland for the Jewish people, for whom Einstein felt an ever deepening loyalty.

The antiwar project which occupied Einstein during the final weeks of his life and to which he gave his signature in his final days was initiated by Bertrand Russell with the following letter from Richmond, Surrey, England, dated February 11, 1955: [6]

DEAR DR. EINSTEIN:

In common with every other thinking person, I am profoundly disquieted by the armaments race in nuclear weapons. You have on various occasions given expression to feelings and opinions with which I am in close agreement. I think that eminent men of science ought to do something dramatic to bring home to the public and governments the disasters that may occur. Do you think it would be possible to get, say, six men of the very highest scientific repute, headed by yourself, to make a very solemn statement about the imperative necessity of avoiding war? These men should be so diverse in their politics that any statement signed by all of them would be obviously free from pro-Communist or anti-Communist bias. I have had a letter from Joliot-Curie which I found encouraging since the fact that he is a Communist and I am not did not prevent agreement on this matter. I expressed my own feelings in a broadcast ["Man's Peril from the Hydrogen Bomb," on December 23, 1954, over the British Broadcasting Corporation], of which I enclose a reprint.[7] This has evoked a surprisingly favorable response in this country, but in other countries, other voices are needed. I do not know personally any of the American atomic scientists, but I read their *Bulletin* monthly with interest and usually with agreement. I am sure that there are many of them who are anxious to find some way of preventing atomic disaster. Do you know any way of securing effective action from any of these men?

There are certain points that seem to me important. First: It would be wholly futile to get an agreement prohibiting the H-Bomb. Such an agreement would not be considered binding after war has broken out, and each side on the outbreak of war would set to work to manufacture as many bombs as possible. Second: It is important not to be sidetracked by the peaceful uses of atomic energy. These will become important when war ceases to be probable, but until then their importance is comparatively negligible. Third: In any attempt to avoid atomic war the strictest neutrality is to be observed. There must be no suggestion of seeking advantage for either side or of preferring either side. Everything must be said from the point of view of mankind, not of this or that group. For this reason, among others, it would be a good thing if some are known Communists and others known anti-Communists. Fourth: The thing to emphasize is that war may well mean the extinction of life on this planet. The Russian and American governments do not think so. They should have no excuses for continued ignorance on the point. Fifth: Although the H-Bomb at the moment occupies the center of attention, it does not exhaust the destructive possibilities of science, and it is probable that the dangers from bacteriological warfare may before long become just as great. This reinforces the general proposition that war and science can no longer coexist.

Joliot-Curie apparently pins his faith to a large international conference of men of science. I do not think this is the best way to tackle the question. Such a conference would take a long time to organize. There would be difficulties about visas. When it met, there would be discussions and disagreements which would prevent any clear and dramatic impression upon the public. I am convinced that a very small number of very eminent men can do much more, at any rate in the first instance.

My own belief is that there should be an appeal to neutral powers. I should like to see one or more of the neutral powers appointing small commissions of their own nationals to draw up a report as to the probable effects of war on neutrals as well as belligerents. I should like to see such a commission composed of, say, six members: a nuclear physicist, a bacteriologist, a geneticist, an authority on air warfare, a man with experience of international relations derived from work in the United Nations, and a chairman who should be not a specialist but a man of wide culture. I should like their report to be published and presented to all governments of the world, who should be invited to express their opinion on it. I should hope that in this way the impossibility of modern war might come to be generally acknowledged. Neutral nations are more likely to consider such a scheme favorably if they know that there is important support for it in countries which are not neutral.

I should be very glad to know your opinion on these various matters.

With warmest good wishes,

Yours very sincerely,
BERTRAND RUSSELL

Einstein replied within the week, on February 16, 1955:

DEAR BERTRAND RUSSELL:

I agree with every word in your letter of February 11. Something must be done in this matter, something that will make an impression on the general public as well as on political leaders. This might best be achieved by a public declaration, signed by a small number of people—say, twelve persons whose scientific attainments (scientific in the widest sense) have gained them international stature and whose declarations will not lose any effectiveness on account of their political affiliations. One might even include men who, like Joliot, are politically labeled provided they were counterbalanced by men from the other camp.

The neutral countries ought to be well represented. For example, it is absolutely vital to include Niels Bohr, and surely there is little doubt that he would join. Indeed, he might even be willing to visit you beforehand and take part in formulating the text of the document to be signed. He might also be helpful in proposing and enlisting signatories.

I hope you will consent to my sending your letter to a few people here in America, men I think may prove useful to the project. The choice is particularly difficult. As you probably know, this country has been ravaged by a political plague that has by no means spared scientists.

I suggest that the text to be offered for signature should be composed by at most two or three people—indeed, preferably by you alone—but in such a way as to insure in advance that there will be full agreement on the part of at least a few of the signers. This will make it easier for the others to sign without offering time-consuming amendments. Of course, we should also obtain signatures from Russia, which should not prove too difficult. In this respect, my colleague L. Infeld, professor at the University of Warsaw, could possibly be of help.

Here in America, in my opinion, Whitehead and Urey should be considered. We should try to see to it, however, that half the signatories are citizens of neutral countries, because that will impress the "hotheads" (*Kriegerischen*) and emphasize the neutral character of the whole project.

With warmest regards,

Yours,
A. EINSTEIN

Russell wrote again on February 25, 1955:

DEAR EINSTEIN:

Thank you for your letter of February 16. I am very glad to find that you and I are in such agreement. I think you are right in suggesting that we should first make sure of two signatories in addition to yourself and me, and that we should then send the draft to selected persons. I should like to leave to you, or to you and Bohr, the choice of such persons, as you know the scientific world much better than I do. I am interested that you think Niels Bohr would be prepared to come and see me. I do not know where he is at present. I made his acquaintance in Copenhagen before the war and found him a very sympathetic personality. I am entirely willing that you should show my letter to anybody that you think may help. In your letter you mentioned Whitehead and Urey. I do not know what Whitehead you are alluding to. Before attempting to draw up a draft for submission to a small number of eminent men of science, I should like to have your opinion as to the best scope for such a document. My own feeling is that after pointing out, briefly and soberly, the universal suicidal folly of a thermonuclear war it should go on to suggest that governments which are uncommitted should approach both sides in an attempt to get them simultaneously to agree that war cannot serve the purpose of either. I think this important, not only because it may succeed, but also because it suggests a possible line of action. I find many people paralyzed by inability to think of anything that could be done; and I do not think we should rest content with pointing out the horrors of war, but should suggest practical steps toward preventing it.

I have been in touch with Nehru and have submitted to him verbally a suggestion which is made explicit in the enclosed draft. This draft, which will be signed by a number of Members of Parliament, is about to be submitted to Mrs. Pandit. Nehru has expressed himself as very favorable to its suggestions, and it seems probable that he will do something along the lines that are suggested. For the moment, the memorandum remains private and nothing must be said about what the Indian Government may do, but I think there is good reason to hope that the outcome may be such as we can welcome.

A declaration by a small number of eminent men such as you and I have in mind runs parallel with any action that the Indian Government may take, and may help the Indian Government to act vigorously.

I shall be glad to hear your opinion on the above points.

Yours very sincerely,
BERTRAND RUSSELL

Accompanying this letter was a memorandum Russell had drawn up on February 15, 1955, to be submitted to Mme. Pandit, High Commissioner for India, by the "Group for World Government." It follows closely the ideas Russell had outlined in his first letter to Einstein of February 11, 1955:

If a great war occurs, nuclear weapons will certainly be employed. A great war with nuclear weapons means, at the lowest estimate, appalling disaster and, not improbably, extinction of all life on our planet.

A great war must, therefore, be prevented.

Neither bloc in the East-West tension can be the first to renounce war, since this would give a diplomatic advantage to the opposing bloc.

Only uncommitted governments can approach both blocs without incurring the odium of appeasement.

Among such, India occupies a special position both on account of its large population and because of friendly relations, on the one hand, with China and, on the other hand, with the other nations of the British Commonwealth.

For this reason, India has the opportunity to do a supreme service to mankind for which no other nation is equally fitted.

India could further the realization that the avoidance of a great war is imperative by some such measure as the following:

The appointment by the government of a commission of six members: 1) a nuclear physicist; 2) a bacteriologist; 3) a geneticist; 4) a man with knowledge of air warfare; 5) a man with experience in international relations; 6) a chairman who should be not a specialist but a man of wide culture.

These men should collect evidence, each in his own province, and should draw up a report pointing out the probable sufferings, not only of belligerents, but also of neutrals.

This report should be published and presented to all the powers with a request for their opinions upon it.

It might in this way become possible to induce both blocs simultaneously to renounce war as an instrument of policy.

If this were achieved, further steps in conciliation would quickly follow.

Einstein wrote Russell again on March 4, 1955, this time in English:

DEAR BERTRAND RUSSELL:

I have written to Niels Bohr and suggested that he get in touch with you. I hope he will do so very soon. I have not written to any colleagues in the United States, being conscious that I am not quite clear about the role you intend for them to play, and also for the reason that such a step is, in some respects, irreversible. It seems to me that to avoid any confusion you should regard yourself as the dictator of the project and give orders. I should be grateful to hear how Niels Bohr has reacted and if you have come to an agreement on the fundamental points.

I am sorry that I was not aware that your old friend Whitehead had passed away. You reminded me of the fact in a beautiful, diplomatic way.

I think that it would be highly desirable to have Albert Schweitzer join our group. His moral influence is very great and worldwide. If you find it advisable I shall write him as soon as you have given me a clear description of the proposed activities of the group.

Expecting orders, I am, with hearty wishes and in admiration,

Yours sincerely,
ALBERT EINSTEIN

Einstein's letter to Niels Bohr, at the Institute for Theoretical Physics in Copenhagen, was dated March 2, 1955:

DEAR NIELS BOHR:

Don't frown like that! This has nothing to do with our old controversy on physics, but rather concerns a matter on which we are in complete agreement. Bertrand Russell recently wrote me a letter, of which I enclose a copy. He seeks to bring together a small group of internationally renowned scholars who would join in a statement to all nations and governments warning of the perilous situation created by atomic weapons and the arms race. This declaration is to coincide with political action initiated by the neutral countries.

Bertrand Russell knows and desires that I write you. Of course, he is well aware that you could greatly aid the project because of your influence, your experience and your personal relationships with outstanding people; indeed, he realizes that your counsel and active participation are virtually indispensable to the success of the project.

The proposed action of the scholars is *not* to be limited to representatives of neutral countries, although the choice of participants should demonstrate clearly the absence of political partisanship. Unless I misinterpret Russell's purpose, he seeks to do more than merely emphasize the existing danger in the world; he proposes to *demand* that the governments publicly acknowledge the necessity for renouncing the use of military force as a means of solving international disputes.

Should you approve of the plan in principle, would you be kind enough to communicate with Bertrand Russell and advise him that you are disposed to participate? The two of you could then decide which individuals would be most desirable as participants. Among those over here, I have been thinking of Urey, Szilard, and James Franck, but there probably should not be too many physicists. I am ready to write to anyone whom the two of you consider suitable, but I am reluctant to undertake the initial (and irrevocable) step until I know your feelings in the matter.

In America, things are complicated by the likelihood that the most renowned scientists, who occupy official positions of influence, will hardly be inclined to commit themselves to such an "adventure." My own participation may exert some favorable influence abroad, but not here at home, where I am known as a black sheep (and not merely in scientific matters).

Much will be gained if you can reach agreement with Bertrand Russell on the main points. For the time being there is no need to write me at all.

With warmest regards,

Yours,
ALBERT EINSTEIN

Russell's final letter was dated April 5, 1955:

DEAR EINSTEIN:

I have been turning over in my mind, and discussing with various people, the best steps for giving effect to the feeling against war among the great majority of the men of science. I think the first step should be a statement by men of highest eminence, Communists and anti-Communists, Western and Eastern, about the disasters to be expected in a war. I enclose a draft of such a statement, and I very much hope that you will be willing to sign it. I enclose also a list of those whom I am asking to sign.[8] If sufficient signatures are obtained, I think the next step should be an international scientific congress which should be invited by the signatories to pass a resolution on the lines of the draft resolution which I enclose. I hope that in this way both governments and public opinion can be made aware of the seriousness of the situation.

On the whole, I have thought that it was better at this time to approach only men of science and not men in other fields, such as Arnold Toynbee, whom you mentioned. Scientists have, and feel they have, a special responsibility, since their work has unintentionally caused our present dangers. Moreover, widening this field would make it very much more difficult to steer clear of politics.

Yours sincerely,
BERTRAND RUSSELL

Einstein replied promptly, on April 11, 1955:

DEAR BERTRAND RUSSELL:

Thank you for your letter of April 5. I am gladly willing to sign your excellent statement. I also agree with your choice of the prospective signers.

With kind regards,
A. EINSTEIN

The signatures on this letter and on Russell's statement were Einstein's last two signatures. Two days later he was fatally stricken. In the preface of this book, Russell tells the dramatic circumstances in which he learned of Einstein's death. He was traveling by air from one congress in Rome to another in Paris, when the pilot of the airplane made the announcement. When he reached Paris, he found Einstein's letter agreeing to sign the statement.

Russell made the statement public in London on July 9, 1955. In reading it to the press, Russell prefaced it with these remarks of his own:

The accompanying statement, which has been signed by some of the most eminent scientific authorities in different parts of the world, deals with the perils of a nuclear war. It makes it clear that neither side can hope for victory in such a war and that there is a very real danger of the extermination of the human race by dust and rain from radioactive clouds.

It suggests that neither the public nor the governments of the world are adequately aware of the danger. It points out that an agreed prohibition of nuclear weapons, while it might be useful in lessening tension, would not afford a solution, since such weapons would certainly be manufactured and used in a great war in spite of previous agreements to the contrary.

The only hope for mankind is the avoidance of war. To call for a way of thinking which shall make such avoidance possible is the purpose of this statement.

The first move came as a collaboration between Einstein and myself. Einstein's signature was given in the last week of his life. Since his death I have approached men of scientific competence both in the East and in the West, for political disagreements should not influence men of science in estimating what is probable, but some of those approached have not yet replied. I am bringing the warning pronounced by the signatories to the notice of all the powerful governments of the world in the earnest hope that they may agree to allow their citizens to survive.

The declaration itself, which closely followed Russell's address over the British Broadcasting Corporation of December 23, 1954, read as follows: [9]

In the tragic situation which confronts humanity, we feel that scientists should assemble in conference to appraise the perils that have arisen as a result of the development of weapons of mass destruction, and to discuss a resolution in the spirit of the appended draft.

We are speaking on this occasion, not as members of this or that nation, continent or creed, but as human beings, members of the species man, whose continued existence is in doubt. The world is full of conflicts; and, overshadowing all minor conflicts, the titanic struggle between Communism and anti-Communism.

Almost everybody who is politically conscious has strong feelings about one or more of these issues; but we want you, if you can, to set aside such feelings and consider yourselves only as members of a biological species which has had a remarkable history, and whose disappearance none of us can desire.

We shall try to say no single word which should appeal to one group rather than to another. All, equally, are in peril, and, if the peril is understood, there is hope that they may collectively avert it.

We have to learn to think in a new way. We have to learn to ask ourselves, not what steps can be taken to give military victory to whatever group we prefer, for there no longer are such steps; the question we have to ask ourselves is: What steps can be taken to prevent a military contest of which the issue must be disastrous to all parties?

The general public, and even many men in positions of authority, have not realized what would be involved in a war with nuclear bombs. The general public still thinks in terms of the obliteration of cities. It is understood that the new bombs are more powerful than the old, and that, while one A-bomb could obliterate Hiroshima, one H-bomb could obliterate the largest cities, such as London, New York and Moscow.

No doubt in an H-bomb war great cities would be obliterated. But this is one of the minor disasters that would have to be faced. If everybody in London, New York and Moscow were exterminated, the world might, in the course of a few centuries, recover from the blow. But we now know, especially since the Bikini test, that nuclear bombs can gradually spread destruction over a very much wider area than had been supposed.

It is stated on very good authority that a bomb can now be manufactured which will be 2,500 times as powerful as that which destroyed Hiroshima.

Such a bomb, if exploded near the ground or under water, sends radioactive particles into the upper air. They sink gradually and reach the surface of the earth in the form of a deadly dust or rain. It was this dust which infected the Japanese fishermen and their catch of fish.

No one knows how widely such lethal radioactive particles might be diffused, but the best authorities are unanimous in saying that a war with H-bombs might quite possibly put an end to the human race. It is feared that if many H-bombs are used there will be universal death—sudden only for a minority, but for the majority a slow torture of disease and disintegration.

Many warnings have been uttered by eminent men of science and by authorities in military strategy. None of them will say that the worst results are certain. What they do say is that these results are possible, and no one can be sure that they will not be realized. We have not yet found that the views of experts depend in any degree upon their politics or prejudices. They depend only, so far as our researches have revealed, upon the extent of the particular expert's knowledge. We have found that the men who know most are the most gloomy.

Here, then, is the problem which we present to you, stark and dreadful and inescapable: Shall we put an end to the human race; or shall mankind renounce war? People will not face this alternative because it is so difficult to abolish war.

The abolition of war will demand distasteful limitations of national sovereignty. But what perhaps impedes understanding of the situation more than anything else is that the term *mankind* feels vague and abstract. People scarcely realize in imagination that the danger is to themselves and their children and their grandchildren, and not only to a dimly apprehended humanity. They can scarcely bring themselves to grasp that they, individually, and those whom they love are in imminent danger of perishing agonizingly. And so they hope that perhaps war may be allowed to continue provided modern weapons are prohibited.

This hope is illusory. Whatever agreements not to use the H-bombs had been reached in time of peace, they would no longer be considered binding in time of war, and both sides would set to work to manufacture H-bombs as soon as war broke out, for, if one side manufactured the bombs and the other did not, the side that manufactured them would inevitably be victorious.

Although an agreement to renounce nuclear weapons as part of a general reduction of armaments would not afford an ultimate solution, it would serve certain important purposes.

First: Any agreement between East and West is to the good in so far as it tends to diminish tension. Second: The abolition of thermonuclear weapons, if each side believed that the other had carried it out sincerely, would lessen the fear of a sudden attack in the style of Pearl Harbor, which at present keeps both sides in a state of nervous apprehension. We should, therefore, welcome such an agreement, though only as a first step.

Most of us are not neutral in feeling, but, as human beings, we have to remember that, if the issues between East and West are to be decided in any manner that can give any possible satisfaction to anybody, whether Communist or anti-Communist, whether Asian or European or American, whether white or black, then these issues must not be decided by war. We should wish this to be understood, both in the East and in the West.

There lies before us, if we choose, continual progress in happiness, knowledge and wisdom. Shall we, instead, choose death, because we cannot forget our quarrels? We appeal, as human beings, to human beings: Remember your humanity and forget the rest. If you can do so, the way lies open to a new paradise; if you cannot, there lies before you the risk of universal death.

RESOLUTION

We invite this congress [to be convened], and through it the scientists of the world and the general public, to subscribe to the following resolution:

"In view of the fact that in any future world war nuclear weapons will certainly be employed, and that such weapons threaten the continued existence of mankind, we urge the governments of the world to realize, and to acknowledge publicly, that their purposes cannot be furthered by a world war, and we urge them, consequently, to find peaceful means for the settlement of all matters of dispute between them."

Besides Russell and Einstein, eight scientists had signed the declaration at the time of its release. They were Percy W. Bridgman and Hermann J. Muller of the United States; Cecil F. Powell and Joseph Rotblat of England; Frédéric Joliot-Curie of France; Leopold Infeld of Poland; Hideki Yukawa of Japan; and Max Born of Germany, whose name was inadvertently omitted at the time of release. A letter transmitting the endorsement of Linus Pauling was received soon afterward, making a total of eleven, of whom all but Rotblat and Infeld were Nobel Prize winners.

Only two of the signers offered any reservations. Muller wanted it understood that "an agreement to renounce nuclear weapons as part of a general reduction of armaments" be taken to mean "a concomitant balanced reduction of all armaments." Joliot-Curie made the reservation that "governments should renounce war as a means of settling differences between states," which was construed as preserving the right of internal revolution. Joliot-Curie also specified that "limitations of national sovereignty should be agreed to by all, and be in the interests of all." [10]

Russell sent copies of the declaration to President Dwight D. Eisenhower of the United States, Premier Nikolai A. Bulganin of the Soviet Union, Prime Minister Anthony Eden of the United Kingdom, President René Coty of France, Chairman Mao Tse-tung of the People's Republic of China, and Prime Minister Louis S. St. Laurent of Canada. These were the heads of states whom Russell considered to be primarily concerned with nuclear armaments.

The Russell-Einstein Manifesto, unlike the Nicolai-Einstein Manifesto of more than forty years before, received widespread and generally favorable publicity throughout the world. Official notice was taken in the United States, Britain, Canada and the Vatican.[11] The first of a number of similar declarations, it came during a particularly threatening period of the cold war; it was released just a week before the first Summit Conference of France, Great Britain, the Soviet Union and the United States met at Geneva, and less than a month before the United Nations Conference on the Peaceful Uses of Atomic Energy convened, also in Geneva. The ultimate significance of the statement must await the verdict of history.[12]

Einstein did not live to witness these developments. He died on April 18, 1955, a week after he had given his signature to the declaration and not quite three months before it was made public. This, however, was not his last action in public affairs. His final act concerned the future of Israel.

This is not the place to discuss in any detail Einstein's single-minded and unqualified identification with the fate of the Jewish people. Once he had, a man of over forty and already world famous, become convinced that the survival of the Jews as a recognizable, independent cultural group depended on the establishment of their own national homeland, he never wavered in this belief, nor in his ever-present willingness to lend a helping hand, wherever he felt it might be useful. Long before Israel acquired statehood and the conflict with the Arab world erupted into warfare, Einstein had emphasized, as had many others, that peaceful coexistence between Arabs and Jews was a prerequisite to the healthy development of a Jewish home in Palestine. It is this thought which preoccupied him when he wrote the very last lines he was ever to write.

Einstein recognized the implications of the Arab-Jewish problem not only from the point of view of the State of Israel but in a much wider context. Toward the end of 1954, he discussed the question at length with Zvi Lurie, a prominent member of the Jewish Agency in Israel. He stressed that the Jewish people, who had themselves suffered so much from discrimination and oppression, should fully appreciate the necessity of pursuing a policy of freedom, democracy and equality for the Arab minority in Israel. He summarized his views in a letter of January 4, 1955, to Zvi Lurie:

We [the State of Israel] must adopt a policy of neutrality concerning the international antagonism between East and West. By adopting a neutral position, we would not only make a modest contribution to the curtailment of the conflict in the world as a whole, but would, at the same time, also facilitate the development of sound, neighborly relations with the various governments in the Arab world.

The most important aspect of our policy must be our ever-present, manifest desire to institute complete equality for the Arab citizens living in our midst, and to appreciate the inherent difficulties of their present situation. If we pursue such a policy, we shall gain loyal citizens and, even more, we shall, slowly but surely, improve our relations with the Arab world. In this respect, the Kibbutz movement is an excellent example. The attitude we adopt toward the Arab minority will provide the real test of our moral standards as a people.

Two months later, on March 8, 1955, Einstein discussed the Arab question in a letter to his Indian friend (see p. 578):

Of course, I regret the constant state of tension existing between Israel and the Arab states. Such tension could hardly have been avoided in view of the nationalistic attitude of both sides, which has only been intensified by the war and its implications. Worst of all has been the policy of the new Administration in the United States [the Eisenhower Administration], which, due to its own imperialist and militaristic interests, seeks to win the sympathy of the Arab nations by sacrificing Israel. As a consequence, the very existence of Israel has become seriously imperiled by the armament efforts of her enemies. This man Dulles is a real misfortune! While pretending to serve the cause of peace, he in fact threatens everybody, hoping thereby to achieve his imperialist aims without becoming involved in a "big" war. Such a policy is not only morally objectionable but will prove dangerous to the United States in the long run. How few people realize this! In a surprisingly brief time, they have come to accept this shortsighted militaristic point of view.

When Einstein was asked by the Israeli Consul in New York whether he would make a statement, on the occasion of the forthcoming anniversary of Israel's independence, about the cultural and scientific accomplishments of Israel, with particular reference to the peaceful uses of atomic energy, he sent this reply on April 4, 1955:

I should very much like to assist the cause of Israel in the difficult and dangerous conditions prevailing today. The question is how this can be done most effectively. I believe the public would hardly be impressed by an address merely on the cultural and scientific achievements of Israel, of which the development of atomic energy for peaceful uses is rather a special and relatively minor aspect. In view of the fact that the Israeli-Arab difficulties are so much more on the public mind, I do not consider the subject of Israel's cultural and scientific developments as having particular relevance at this time.

I feel, therefore, that to make any impact on public opinion, such an address should attempt to appraise the political situation. In fact, I tend to believe that a somewhat critical analysis of the policies of the Western nations with regard to Israel and the Arab states might be most effective. I realize that it is easier for me to offer such remarks than for someone officially connected with Jewish organizations.

To make sure that such an address will be meaningful, I should wish to prepare it carefully in co-operation with responsible Israeli officials. Of course, I do not know in advance whether such cooperation would yield agreement between them and myself, but I believe an attempt should be made, without further delay and loss of precious time.

As a result of Einstein's suggestions, the Israeli Ambassador Abba Eban and Consul Reuven Dafni called on him at Princeton a few days later, on April 11. After their visit Einstein started drafting the planned address, which was to be delivered over a television and radio network. Since he felt the need for further consultations, he met again, on April 13, with the Israeli Consul. The notes Einstein made on that occasion are not available. He was fatally stricken two hours after the visit. During the four remaining days of his life, he frequently expressed concern over his delay in writing the address; although he ordered the notes to his bedside, in the hope of continuing to write, at his death he left only the one page ending with an unfinished sentence which he had drafted just before he was stricken: [13]

I speak to you today not as an American citizen and not as a Jew, but as a human being who seeks with the greatest seriousness to look at things objectively. What I seek to accomplish is simply to serve with my feeble capacity truth and justice at the risk of pleasing no one.

At issue is the conflict between Israel and Egypt. You may consider this a small and insignificant problem and may feel that there are more serious things to worry about. But this is not true. In matters concerning truth and justice there can be no distinction between big problems and small; for the general principles which determine the conduct of men are indivisible. Whoever is careless with the truth in small matters cannot be trusted in important affairs.

This indivisibility applies not only to moral but also to political problems; for little problems cannot be properly appreciated unless they are understood in their interdependence with big problems. And the big problem in our time is the division of mankind into two hostile camps: the Communist World and the so-called Free World. Since the significance of the terms *Free* and *Communist* is in this context hardly clear to me, I prefer to speak of a power conflict between East and West, although, the world being round, it is not even clear what precisely is meant by the terms *East* and *West*.

In essence, the conflict that exists today is no more than an old-style struggle for power, once again presented to mankind in semireligious trappings. The difference is that, this time, the development of atomic power has imbued the struggle with a ghostly character; for both parties know and admit that, should the quarrel deteriorate into actual war, mankind is doomed. Despite this knowledge, statesmen in responsible positions on both sides continue to employ the well-known technique of seeking to intimidate and demoralize the opponent by marshaling superior military strength. They do so even though such a policy entails the risk of war and doom. Not one statesman in a position of responsibility has dared to pursue the only course that holds out any promise of peace, the course of supranational security, since for a statesman to follow such a course would be tantamount to political suicide. Political passions, once they have been fanned into flame, exact their victims . . .

Here the hand that changed the world, and yet, in so many ways, could not change it, faltered and wrote no more.

Einstein's unfinished draft of his proposed address for Israel's Independence Day, 1955; this was the last writing of his life. (See pages 640, 642)

Ich spreche zu Euch heute nicht als ein amerikanischer Bürger und auch nicht als Jude sondern als ein Mensch, der in allem Ernst danach strebt, die Dinge objektiv zu betrachten. Was ich anstrebe, ist einfach, mit meinen schwachen Kräften der Wahrheit und Gerechtigkeit zu dienen auf die Gefahr hin, niemand zu gefallen.

Zur Diskussion steht der Konflikt zwischen Israel und Aegypten. – ein kleines und unwichtiges Problem, werdet ihr denken, wir haben grössere Sorgen. So ist es aber nicht. Wenn es sich um Wahrheit und Gerechtigkeit handelt, gibt es nicht die Unterscheidung zwischen kleinen und grossen Problemen. Denn die allgemeinen Gesichtspunkte, die das Handeln der Menschen betreffen, sind unteilbar. Wer es in kleinen Dingen mit der Wahrheit nicht ernst nimmt, dem kann man auch im grossen Dingen nicht vertrauen.

Diese Unteilbarkeit gilt aber nicht nur für das Moralische sondern auch für das Politische; denn die kleinen Probleme können nur richtig erfasst werden, wenn sie in ihrer Abhängigkeit von den grossen Problemen verstanden werden.

Das grosse Problem präsentiert sich gegenwärtig als Trennung der Menschenwelt in zwei feindliche Lager die sogenannte free world und die kommunist World. Da es mir wenig klar ist, was hier unter free und communist zu verstehen ist, will ich lieber von einem Machtstreit zwischen Ost und West reden, obwohl es wegen der Kugelgestalt der Erde auch nicht recht klar ist, was man da unter West und Ost zu verstehen hat.

Es ist im Grunde nur ein Machtstreit alten Stiles, der wie frühere Kämpfe um die Macht den Menschen in halb-religiöser Verhüllung dargeboten wird. Dieser Machtstreit hat aber durch die Entwicklung der Atomwaffe einen gespenstischen Charakter angenommen. Jede Partei weiss nämlich und gibt es auch zu, dass unsere Menschheit verloren ist, wenn der Streit in einen wirklichen Krieg ausartet. Trotzdem wird von den verantwortlichen Staatsmännern auf beiden Seiten der Streit in altgewohnter Weise auf den Versuch gegründet, den Gegner durch Entwicklung überlegener militärischer Machtmittel einzuschüchtern und mürbe zu machen. Dabei muss man allerdings Krieg und Untergang riskieren. Aber den einzig versprechenden Weg der übernationalen Sicherung einzuschlagen wagt kein verantwortlicher Staatsmann, weil dies seinen sicheren politischen Tod bedeuten würde. Denn die allenthalben entfachte politische Leidenschaft verlangt ihre Opfer.

EDITORS' NOTE

IN EDITING EINSTEIN's literary contributions to the struggle for the abolition of war, we were confronted by a number of difficult problems. When the work was started, shortly after Einstein's death, it was hoped that the bulk of the pertinent material had been preserved in his files. It was soon realized that this was not the case. Einstein himself was not greatly concerned with a systematic collection of his papers and correspondence; only in the last few decades of his life was sufficient attention paid to the preservation of the many important documents and letters that crossed his desk. In addition, Einstein wrote many of his letters in longhand without preparing copies for his files; and, finally, some of the material which had accumulated in the years before his emigration to the United States was lost or stolen when the Nazis ransacked his home in 1933.

Although a thorough and conscientious effort has been made to assemble from all parts of the world the material needed to document Einstein's lifelong devotion to the cause of peace, we cannot be certain whether some important documents may not be missing; some material, particularly letters written in longhand during the earlier periods of Einstein's life, may be long in coming to light. Similarly, while we were able to locate and utilize articles and statements by or about Einstein in many American and foreign periodicals and newspapers, there may be published material which did not come to our attention. Einstein made his writings available to outstanding journals as well as small and obscure publications, some of which have long since been discontinued; hence, the task of locating material was often very difficult. However, despite possible omissions, we are convinced that Einstein's basic position and thoughts on war and peace, at different stages of his life, are adequately documented in this volume; it is unlikely that any additional material which may become available at a later date will necessitate a change in the interpretation of Einstein's views based on the writings here assembled.

Many of the documents in this volume have been published before, but the publications in which they appeared are widely scattered and often virtually inaccessible. Most of Einstein's letters, however, are made public here for the first time. Wherever sources are not indicated, the material was made available by the Estate of Albert Einstein, which is the custodian of Einstein's literary possessions. Except for rare instances, Einstein prepared all his scientific work, correspondence and public statements in German, the only language in which he felt at home and which he fully mastered: his style, not always even, is often impressive for its simplicity and, at times, its eloquence. The necessity of translating the material into English posed not only the intricate problems which translation always presents; we were also faced with the difficulty that many documents had previously been published in English translations which did not, in our opinion, do justice to Einstein's German originals. The question arose as to whether new translations should be prepared in such instances. We hesitated to do so since some translations had been reprinted time and again and since the existence of different versions of a given document is confusing.

We carefully weighed the arguments in favor of new translations against the objections which might be raised; we realized that a distinction should be made between the material in the earlier and in the later chapters of the volume. Since translations of material dating from Einstein's European years had as a rule been prepared without his knowledge or express approval, we felt justified in offering new translations of those passages which, in our opinion, did not render adequately the content of the original texts. With regard to the many documents that had accumulated during Einstein's years in the United States, we were faced with a very different situation. Living in an English-speaking country, Einstein was now more immediately concerned with the translation of his writings since it was in English that his pronouncements and writings were frequently presented to the public or to his correspondents, while the original German texts remained unknown.

Even during Einstein's years in America some of his statements appeared in print, or were presented to audiences, in English versions which he had not seen before. He was meticulous, however, about material which he considered of particular importance or which might affect public opinion. In such instances, he would take great pains with the English version of every sentence he had written and would patiently argue with the translator about individual passages or even specific words. He might have given the same detailed attention to the translation of all his writings had the sheer volume not made it impracticable. For Einstein took great care in composing the many expressions of his thoughts and beliefs; except for routine correspondence, he prepared careful longhand drafts of every letter and every manuscript, remarking frequently about the labor of writing, which did not always come easily to him.

The translations that emerged in his American years from the hands of different friends are of unequal value. Frequently they are awkward or do not present an accurate version of Einstein's original text. We were, therefore, confronted with the question of whether even published English translations which Einstein himself had implicitly approved by affixing his signature or permitting publication should be subject to revision. In those instances, the decision was particularly difficult since we were aware that doubts might be expressed as to whether we were entitled to make even the slightest change in any English translation that had actually been released by Einstein himself. After careful consideration, however, we decided to revise such translations when we thought it necessary in the interest of a more faithful English rendering of Einstein's writings. Close personal association with Einstein justifies the belief that he would have wished us to exercise such judgment in preparing a permanent record of his opinions and activities on war and peace.

Except in relatively few instances where the original text was not available, we were governed by Einstein's manuscripts in revising existing translations. We were, at all times, guided by the desire to establish an English version of Einstein's material which would accurately display the meaning and spirit of his thoughts and which would, at the same time, achieve a certain unity of the language through which he could communicate with the English-speaking world. We regret that it was necessary in many instances to create an additional English version besides one or several translations published before in that language. Whenever a previous translation was revised, the "Notes" to the chapters record the fact; it proved impossible, however, to annotate every individual change. We hope that the translations here assembled, which were prepared with the utmost care, may in time come to be considered the most authentic English versions of Einstein's writings.

A third problem that confronted the editors should be mentioned. While it was the purpose of this volume to let Einstein speak for himself, it would have been impossible to dispense with all editorial comment. It was necessary to prepare connecting tissues linking the individual documents and letters, to explain their background and the context in which they originated, and to outline the general contours of the specific periods in history. We were anxious to limit the editorial comment to what appeared indispensable to an understanding of the material. Information and documents not directly related to the problem of peace were included only when it seemed essential to a fuller appreciation of Einstein's activities and opinions on the issue of a world without war; but we resisted the temptation to reproduce many documents of great interest which, although bearing on Einstein's general political and social views, did not seem to contribute to the purpose of the book. We also refrained from incorporating many interesting communications which Einstein received over the years. In the interest of making Einstein's responses to such communications more intelligible, we paraphrased their content but republished them only in rare and special instances.

We were privileged to receive helpful assistance in various ways. We are grateful to a large number of individuals as well as organizations, newspapers and magazines here and abroad for making material available and providing important information. Miss Charlotte Pomerantz has made a large contribution by providing keen and intelligent analysis of the material and great editorial skill in the final revision of the manuscript. Miss Helene Dukas, who was Einstein's secretary for almost three decades and who, since his death, has been one of the trustees and the archivist of his literary estate, assembled all the pertinent material from his files and provided help and assistance based on her rich experience and long, devoted service. Her co-operation was indispensable to the accomplishment of our task.

OTTO NATHAN
HEINZ NORDEN

New York, August 1960

NOTES

Einstein's personal files, made available by the Estate of Albert Einstein, were a principal source of the documents reproduced in this volume. Additional material was derived from both published and unpublished sources which are acknowledged in these notes. Certain major source books are referred to by the following abbreviations:

MW — *Mein Weltbild*, by Albert Einstein, edited by Carl Seelig, Europa Verlag, Zurich, 1953. This is the principal German-language collection of Einstein's shorter pieces. It is an expanded edition of a collection with the same title published in Holland by Querido-Verlag, Amsterdam, in 1934. (The 1934 edition is referred to as MWI.)

TWAISI — *The World As I See It*, by Albert Einstein, translated by Alan Harris, new abridged edition, Philosophical Library, New York, 1949. Based on MWI.

IAO — *Ideas and Opinions*, by Albert Einstein, revised by Sonja Bargmann, Crown Publishers, Inc., New York, 1954. Based largely on MW.

OOMLY — *Out of My Later Years*, by Albert Einstein, Philosophical Library, New York, 1950.

TFAW — *The Fight against War*, by Albert Einstein, edited by Alfred Lief, John Day Pamphlet No. 20, The John Day Co., New York, 1933.

SCHILPP — *Albert Einstein: Philosopher-Scientist*, edited by Paul Arthur Schilpp, The Library of Living Philosophers, Second Edition, Tudor Publishing Co., New York, 1951.

FRANK — *Einstein—Sein Leben und seine Zeit*, by Philipp Frank, Paul List Verlag, Munich, 1949.

SEELIG — *Albert Einstein: Eine dokumentarische Biographie*, by Carl Seelig, Europa Verlag, Zurich, 1954.

Chapter I

1. The statement by Maurice Solovine is from a personal communication to Otto Nathan.

2. Einstein's letters to Paul Ehrenfest were made available by his widow, Tatjana Ehrenfest.

3. The Manifesto to the Civilized World was written by Hermann Sudermann (see p. 33) and promoted by Matthias Erzberger, one of the leaders of the Catholic Centrist party and the Reich's wartime propaganda chief (assassinated after the war). Passages from it, as well as the entire Manifesto to Europeans, are here translated directly from Georg Friedrich Nicolai's *Die Biologie des Krieges,* published by Orell Füssli, Zurich, 1916, with a foreword by Romain Rolland. An American edition, translated by Constance A. and Julian Grande, was published by the Century Co., New York, 1918, as *The Biology of War.* It is, according to Nicolai, identical with an English edition published by Dent and Co., London; Nicolai also mentions some other foreign-language editions: Swedish, Tidens Förlag, Stockholm; Danish, Steen Hasselbalch, Copenhagen; French, Säuberlin and Pfeiffer, Vevey (Switzerland); and Finnish, Werner Söderström, Porvoo. The Manifesto to Europeans, in the Grande translation, is reprinted in TFAW, p. 5. Most of it, in the same translation, also appears in an article, "War and Men of Science," by Ilse Bry and Janet Doe, *Science,* November 11, 1955.

4. The fact that Wilhelm Förster signed both manifestos was confirmed in a personal communication by Förster's son, the professor of pedagogy and pacifist Friedrich Wilhelm Förster, now living in New York, who adds the detail that refusal of French friends, after the war, to shake his old father's hand hastened his father's death. Nicolai's comments on the failure of his manifesto are translated from his book, Buek's from his unpublished article written in 1955 and quoted by permission of *The Nation,* for which it was prepared.

5. A bibliography of Einstein's scientific writings is given in *A Bibliographical Checklist and Index of the Writings of Albert Einstein,* edited by Boni, Russ and Laurence, Pageant Books, New York, 1960.

6. The account of Nicolai's wartime ordeal is drawn from a small book he published soon after August 1918, *Warum Ich aus Deutschland ging—Offener Brief an denjenigen Unbekannten, der die Macht hat in Deutschland,* Benteli A. G., Bümplitz-Berne. Nicolai served for a time at the German Army post in Graudenz, and this fact apparently served as a basis for garbled accounts that he was incarcerated in the military fortress in that town which appear in a preface to the American edition of *The Biology of War,* and also in *Contre la guerre avec Einstein,* by Maurice Lecat, published by F. Ceuterick, Louvain, 1931.

7. The quotation is from del Vayo's book *The Last Optimist,* Viking Press, New York, 1950, p. 88.

8. A principal source for the activities of the Bund Neues Vaterland and Einstein's connection with it was a pamphlet by Otto Lehmann-Russbüldt, the group's secretary-general until 1927, *Der Kampf der Deutschen Liga für Menschenrechte, vormals Bund Neues Vaterland, für den Weltfrieden,* 1914–1927, Hensel & Co. Verlag, Berlin, 1927, a copy of which was made available by Mr. Alfred Lief. Schücking's observations (p. 9) and data on Einstein's connection with the Hague peace effort (p. 11) are from transcripts of documents in the Ernst Reuter-Archiv, Berlin-Zehlendorf, which conducted a special search of its files for this volume. Other sources were Richard Barkeley, *Die Deutsche Friedensbewegung,* 1870–1933, Hammerich & Lesser, Hamburg, 1948, a copy of which was made available by Kurt R. Grossmann, Lehmann-Russbüldt's successor as secretary-general of the German League for Human Rights, from 1927 to its suppression by the Nazis in

1933, and Grossmann's article, "Peace Movements in Germany," in the *South Atlantic Quarterly*, July 1950, pp. 292 ff. Messrs. Lehmann-Russbüldt and Grossmann also both were kind enough to contribute their personal recollections of this period.

9. The account of Einstein's early wartime activities was provided by Dr. Franziska Baumgartner-Tramer of Berne, Switzerland. Portions of it were published by her in the Berne newspaper *Der Bund*, July 10, 1955.

10. Einstein's letter to Lorentz is translated from the handwritten original in the *Algemeen Rijksarchief*, The Hague, Holland.

11. Einstein's letter to Rolland is translated from a German copy made available by Alfred Lief, who obtained it directly from Rolland. (A different translation appears in TFAW, p. 8.) At the bottom of this transcript Rolland added a handwritten note about Einstein's visit to Vevey described on pp. 14–18.

12. Rolland's letter as well as those on the following pages are translated from the originals and reproduced by permission of Madame Marie Romain Rolland. In a postscript Rolland mentioned a recent report on French camps for German prisoners of war by a Swiss lieutenant colonel, De Marval, a delegate to the International Red Cross. Apparently the report was highly favorable to the French camps, for Rolland added that he wished the Swiss officer could lecture in Germany. Since he had a brother in the German Army, his testimony would not be suspect. Rolland was obviously aware of atrocity stories that were then circulating in Germany.

13. Rolland's diary entry is translated from Romain Rolland, *Journal des années de guerre 1914–1919* (Paris, 1952), p. 510, by permission of Éditions Albin Michel and Madame Marie Romain Rolland.

14. Einstein's letters to Lorentz of November 13, 1916, and April 3, 1917, are translated from the originals in the *Algemeen Rijksarchief*, The Hague, Holland.

15. Einstein's letter is translated from a transcript provided by Madame Marie Romain Rolland.

16. The scientist from a neutral country mentioned in the letter to Hiller is Lorentz. Einstein related this incident on a number of other occasions.

17. In the manuscript from which Einstein's address to the student leaders is translated, the last two paragraphs are lightly crossed out, hinting that they may not have been delivered. The circumstances of this incident and the letter to Max Born are taken from SEELIG, p. 212. Einstein's statement that the incident took place "a little less than twenty-five years ago" would put it late in 1919, but that seems unlikely, since the Constitutional Assembly convened in Weimar early in 1919.

18. Martha Eva Parker-Prochownik, a neighbor of the Einsteins during the early twenties, in a personal communication to Otto Nathan, asserted that Einstein joined the German Social Democratic party, attended meetings and took part in discussions. His attitude indicated, she said, that he regarded it as his personal obligation to give as much time and effort as possible to "help bridge the gulf between workers of brain and brawn," as he allegedly put it. Members of Einstein's household, however, feel certain that he never joined the Social Democratic or any other political party.

19. His views about socialism were particularly clearly expressed in his article "Why Socialism?" in *Monthly Review*, May 1949.

Chapter II

1. In his letter to Ehrenfest cited in Note 5 below, Einstein had

inquired: "Have you perchance heard anything about the British eclipse expedition?" Lorentz wired him on September 22, 1919: "Eddington found star displacement at rim of sun, preliminary measurement between nine-tenths of a second and twice that value, regards." During his subsequent visit to Holland in October 1919 Einstein learned further details. In a letter to his mother from Leiden he wrote: "Yesterday I attended a session of the Academy, with Ehrenfest and Lorentz. Lorentz spoke on General Relativity and the findings of the British expeditions—to please me, of course. The final results are now in and signify *precise corroboration of my theory*."

2. The British scientist was Dr. Robert W. Lawson, who spent the war years at the Radium Institute in Vienna, Austria, and was in 1919 working at the Physics Laboratory of the University of Sheffield. The letter, which is reproduced with Dr. Lawson's permission, was relayed to Einstein by Arnold Berliner, long-time editor of *Die Naturwissenschaften*, and Einstein's friend.

3. The Rolland manifesto appears in his book *The Forerunners*, translated by Eden and Cedar Paul, Allen and Unwin, London, 1920. According to Alfred Lief, 138 intellectual workers in various countries had signed it by the end of 1919.

4. The entire correspondence between Einstein and Lorentz concerning the study group is translated from the original handwritten letters in the *Algemeen Rijksarchief*, The Hague, Holland.

5. Einstein's remarks about staying in Germany are translated from one of his letters to Ehrenfest of which Ehrenfest sent a transcript to Lorentz. The transcript, dated September 21, 1919, is in the *Algemeen Rijksarchief*, The Hague, Holland. At the end of his transcript Ehrenfest added this note: "I was deeply ashamed when I received this letter. But then I was also filled with warm and joyful pride over this wonderful man! If one could only relieve him of his financial worries! The Nobel Prize?"

6. Einstein wrote to Ehrenfest on October 5, 1919 (*Algemeen Rijksarchief*, The Hague, Holland), that he had been to the Dutch Embassy in Berlin that day. He asked his friends to expedite his travel permit at The Hague. Apparently Heike Kamerlingh Onnes, another professor of physics in Holland and Nobel Prize winner, as well as Lorentz and Ehrenfest were instrumental in the success of these efforts. In subsequent letters Einstein repeatedly apologized for the trouble he had caused. Einstein accepted the offer to join the faculty of the University of Leiden, apparently made on December 21, 1919, in his letter to Lorentz of January 12, 1920.

7. The excerpt is translated from a copy of the original handwritten letter, which Professor Max Born made available.

8. The German classical philologist was Ulrich von Wilamowitz-Möllendorff.

9. The letter was made available by Carvallo's son-in-law, Julius W. Schulein, of New York.

10. Details concerning the attacks on Einstein are to be found in FRANK and SEELIG, and in the pamphlet by Lehmann-Russbüldt (*op. cit.*, p. 100), who reports the statement quoted in the text, which was made by a student in a public meeting. The learned society was the *Arbeitsgemeinschaft deutscher Naturforscher*, and Lorentz' letter was dated September 3, 1920.

11. The friend in China (Tientsin) was Dr. Franz Rusch, of Eichstätt, Bavaria. Einstein's letter is translated from a two-part memoir which Dr. Rusch published in the *Abensberger Tagblatt/Neustätter Zeitung*, September 17 and 19, 1955.

12. The Tobenkin interview, which includes an interesting account of Einstein's home life, is reproduced by permission of the *New York Post*. A slightly different version appears in TFAW, p. 9.

13. Einstein's visits to Austria and Czechoslovakia are described at length in FRANK. The visit to Amsterdam is discussed in Lehmann-Russbüldt's pamphlet. The letter to Ehrenfest was received in Leiden on February 12, 1921.

14. The Alderman was Bruce Falconer, who was charged with anti-Semitism by some of his colleagues. Aldermanic President Fiorello H. La Guardia, later to become Mayor of New York, tried to smooth the affair over but apparently without success. The story is found in *The New York Times*, April 6, 1921.

15. It was on the occasion of his visit to Princeton that Einstein coined the famous saying *Raffiniert ist der Herrgott, aber boshaft ist er nicht*.

16. Einstein's farewell speech to America is translated from MWI, p. 50.

17. Details concerning the Franco-German *rapprochement* efforts are taken from Lehmann-Russbüldt's pamphlet, already cited, and from still another pamphlet of the German League for Human Rights, also by Lehmann-Russbüldt, *Die Brücke über den Abgrund*, Verlag Neues Vaterland, E. Berger u. Co., Berlin (probably 1922).

17a. The young attorney who had been introduced to Einstein by Professor Langevin was Raymond de Rienzi of Paris.

18. Solovine's recollections are from the letter cited in Chap. I, Note 1.

19. Einstein's letter is translated from a copy made available by Mme. Marie Romain Rolland.

20. Einstein's recollections of Rathenau are from a letter dated February 2, 1943, to Johanon Twersky of the Hebrew Teachers College in Roxbury, Massachusetts.

21. The letter about the Rathenau memorial service is in Einstein's hand and signed by him. A number of corrections in it suggest that it may have been a draft. On the other hand, it may never have been sent.

22. The letter to Solovine is translated, with due permission, from a facsimile of the original in *Albert Einstein—Lettres à Maurice Solovine*, Gauthier-Villars, Paris, 1956.

23. The letter to Planck is translated from SEELIG, pp. 213 f.

24. Einstein's appearance at the 1922 *No More War*-demonstration is described in Kurt Grossmann's article, "Peace Movements in Germany" (see Chap. I, Note 8).

25. Author of the reparations plan was Arnold Rechberg. In his reply to Einstein, Lord Haldane enclosed a copy of a lukewarm reaction he had received from Sir Basil Blackett, the British treasury's permanent adviser on reparations problems.

26. *Die Friedensbewegung*, edited by Kurt Lenz and Walter Fabian, C. A. Schwetschke u. Sohn, Berlin, 1922. The present translation is revised from TFAW, p. 17.

27. The excerpt from the letter to Solovine is translated from the collection edited by Solovine; see Note 22, above.

28. The autograph note is translated from the original, in the Burndy Library, Norwalk, Connecticut, a copy of which was made available by Mr. Bern Dibner, Director.

Chapter III

1. Einstein's original letter of acceptance of the appointment to the League's Committee on Intellectual Co-operation is translated from the German original in FRANK, p. 328. Another translation is in TFAW, p. 14.

The official name of the committee was apparently changed in 1926 to "International Committee on Intellectual Co-operation," but the later usage was not uniform, and the two names were officially used interchangeably.

2. Gilbert Murray's recollections of Einstein's service on the committee were especially prepared for this volume.

3. The friend through whom Einstein sent word to Comert about his intention to withdraw was Hermann Struck, a painter.

4. The paper on the "Internationalism of Science" is published in German in MW, p. 82, from which this is a new translation. A different English translation appears in TWAISI, p. 50, and IAO, p. 83. In both MW and IAO the paper is dated "shortly after the war," but it was probably prepared several years later.

5. Einstein's resignation from the committee is incorrectly quoted in German in FRANK, p. 328. An English version is given in TFAW, p. 14. The present translation is from the original holograph letter.

6. Gilbert Murray's letters are reproduced by his special permission.

7. Einstein's explanation of his resignation in *Die Friedenswarte* is taken from *The New York Times*, June 28, 1923, and TFAW, p. 14.

8. A fragment of Einstein's statement to the Berlin mass meeting for entry into the League is given in TFAW, p. 15. The present translation is from the manuscript. Einstein's participation in this meeting is documented in Otto Lehmann-Russbüldt's pamphlet cited in Chap. I, Note 8, p. 105.

9. The Einstein-Lorentz correspondence cited through much of this chapter is translated and abstracted from the original holograph letters in the *Algemeen Rijksarchief*, The Hague, Holland. Einstein's acceptance to attend meetings of the Solvay Congress is dated April 12, 1926.

10. Einstein's letter to Mme. Curie is translated from SEELIG, p. 210.

11. At the bottom of Sir Eric Drummond's letter, Einstein simply noted: "*Zustimmend beantwortet am* 25.VI." (Answered in the affirmative on June 25.) Apparently he kept no copy of his acceptance, which may have been written by hand, as were many of Einstein's letters.

12. Einstein's note to Weizmann is translated from the original holograph in the Weizmann Archives, Rehovoth, Israel.

13. A major source for Einstein's activities on the Committee on Intellectual Co-operation is the official minutes of that body which were examined at the Woodrow Wilson Memorial Library in New York.

14. The excerpt from the letter to Solovine is translated from the collection credited in Chap. II, Note 22.

15. The inquiry on *Les États-Unis d'Europe sont-ils réalisables?* came from Maurice d'Hartoy of Paris, initiator of a number of surveys under the title *Les Grandes enquêtes françaises et internationales*.

16. The statement in the *Welt am Abend* is taken, considerably revised, from TFAW, p. 26.

17. The Russian-German society was named Kulturtechnik Ost, which defies translation.

18. The South American encounter with Otto Buek is taken from the unpublished article by Buek credited in Chap. I, Note 4.

19. *The New York Times* interview of May 17, 1925, was with Herman Bernstein. It is reprinted here with slight revisions. The last paragraph appears in TFAW, p. 15.

20. Einstein's New Year's statement, published in the *New York Evening Post* and *Philadelphia Public Ledger*, is reproduced by special permission of the *New York Post*.

It is slightly revised from the German manuscript.

21. The letter by Julien Luchaire of October 24, 1925, is from a sizable collection of photostatic reproductions of original documents in the files of UNESCO, made available through the assistance of Dr. Luther H. Evans, its former Director-General.

22. Einstein's speech on the Institute for Intellectual Co-operation appears in German in MW, p. 85. Identical English translations appear in TWAISI, p. 52, and IAO, p. 86. The present version is virtually a new translation. (Einstein apparently wrote a piece on the same subject for the February 1926 issue of the French journal *L'Europe nouvelle*.) In a letter to his wife of January 17, 1926, Einstein says he was, besides Luchaire, the only speaker at the banquet. "I should like to see any other mortal with such poor French and so little oratorical skill try it, unless he were favored by a kind of mass suggestion! And all I had was an outline in German. . . ."

23. Others who sent contributions to the *Liber Amicorum* of Romain Rolland were President Masaryk of Czechoslovakia, Sigmund Freud, Stefan Zweig, Richard Strauss, John Haynes Holmes, Waldo Frank, Upton Sinclair, H. G. Wells, Rabindranath Tagore, Mahatma Gandhi, and many more. The present translation is from manuscript. Another copy provided through the courtesy of Mme. Rolland shows a minor change in the last paragraph and also omits the final clause of the last sentence.

24. Details about the Brussels Congress for a United States of Europe in June 1926 are taken from Otto Lehmann-Russbueldt's history of the German League for Human Rights, p. 114 (see Chap. I, Note 8).

25. Einstein's letter to Lorentz of September 13, 1927, is the only one in the file at the *Algemeen Rijksarchief*, The Hague, that is typewritten.

26. The article attributed to the *Berliner Tageblatt* is translated from an imperfect typescript, dated only as to the year, 1927.

Chapter IV

1. Einstein's election to the board of the German League for Human Rights is recorded in the group's journal, *Die Menschenrechte*, Vol. III, No. 1, January 31, 1928, made available by Mr. Kurt Grossmann.

2. The letterhead of the *No More War Movement* gives the following "Declaration Signed by Members": "War is a crime against humanity. I am therefore determined: 1. Not to support or take part in any war, international or civil. 2. To work for total disarmament, the removal of all causes of war, and the establishment of a new social and international order based on the pacifist principle of co-operation for the common good."

3. The letter soliciting a contribution to *Records of Progress* was signed by Dr. Rudolf Broda, President of the League for the Organization of Progress, and then a faculty member at Antioch College. In a handwritten note at the bottom of the mimeographed letter Broda reminded Einstein "of your collaboration (1914) on our weekly, *Die Menschheit*." This weekly, published first in Switzerland and then in Germany, was the official organ of the League for the Organization of Progress from 1914–1922 (according to the League's letterhead). Files of it are scanty. If Einstein actually contributed to it as early as 1914, this might imply that he took a public position on political affairs even before the Nicolai Manifesto (see Chapter I, pp. 4–8). Neither Mr. Kurt Grossmann nor Professor Friedrich Wilhelm Förster (both of whom were close to *Die Menschheit*, the latter a regular contributor) nor other sources in Germany were able

to recall or document anything Einstein had written for *Die Menschheit.*

4. Everling headed the *Schutzkartell Deutscher Geistesarbeiter* (Protective League of German Intellectual Workers). The socialist-oriented group was the *Gewerkschaft Deutscher Geistesarbeiter* (Trade-Union of German Intellectual Workers). The third group, the *Arbeitsgemeinschaft der Freien Geistigen Berufe* (Conference of Free Intellectual Professions), tended to go along with the *Schutzkartell.* Labor Minister Braun's unsuccessful candidate was Professor Theodor Brauer of Karlsruhe. Everling was appointed to the ILO Committee in 1931 as a representative of the *Conféderation Internationale des Travailleurs Intellectuels,* which his group had joined, presumably for that purpose. Einstein's file on this matter numbers more than forty documents, and the conscientious attention he gave it refutes—at least for himself—the criticism that the famous members of the committee were unwilling to attend to administrative details. In several of the documents, conferences are mentioned that were held at his bedside. To a friend (Mrs. Margarete Lebach), Einstein wrote on June 28, 1928: "The pace of my convalescence is in inverse ratio to the number of physicians and other persons who interested themselves on behalf of my decrepit corpse." (Item No. 47, Sale No. 1744, Parke-Bernet Galleries, Inc., New York, 1957.)

5. The Armistice Day statement is translated from *Die Menschenrechte,* Vol. III, No. 8, November 11, 1928, made available by Mr. Kurt Grossmann.

6. Some of the papers delivered at the International Conference on Modern Methods of Warfare and the Protection of Civil Populations (in Frankfurt) and the declaration drafted by Langevin were published in a booklet, *Chemical Warfare,* Williams and Norgate, London, 1930, which was made available by Mr. Alfred Lief. This booklet lists Einstein, with 115 others, as a member of a General Council. The conference documents, according to a footnote in *Die Menschenrechte,* May 31, 1930, appeared in German under the title *Die modernen Kriegsmethoden und der Schutz der Zivilbevölkerung,* Endries, Cannstatt; *und Der kommende Giftgaskrieg,* by Dr. Gertrud Woker, Oldenburg Verlag, Leipzig. A paper by Barthelemy de Ligt, delivered at the conference but not published in *Chemical Warfare,* appeared in *Die neue Generation,* February 1929.

7. The oft-cited statement for *Die Wahrheit* appears in TFAW, p. 26. The present translation is slightly revised from an Einstein manuscript. Einstein's Dutch correspondent was Jacob ter Meulen; his letter to ter Meulen was dated July 12, 1930.

8. For the publication of Einstein's original Unified Field Theory see *The New York Times,* February 3 and April 8, 1929, *The Times* (of London), February 4, 1929, *Scientific Monthly,* Vol. 28, and *Observatory,* Vol. 52.

9. Einstein's participation in the Trotsky committee is documented in *Die Menschenrechte,* Vol. IV, No. 4/5, April 20, 1929, made available by Mr. Kurt Grossmann.

10. The contents of the appeal sponsored by the Friends of the Soviet Union are not known in detail.

11. The secretary of the Reichstag Investigating Committee was Dr. Berthold Widmann. Its chairman was Dr. Bell, a member of the Catholic Center party. They were the editors of the five-volume work *Völkerrecht im Weltkrieg.* Dom Norbert Nieuwland wrote Einstein (January 2, 1929) that he himself had been captured by the Germans at Dinant on August 23, 1914, where German troops had shot 674 civilians, the old-

est eighty-eight years of age and the youngest three weeks old.

12. The statement to Paul Hutchinson, editor of the *Christian Century*, is taken from TFAW, p. 19.

13. The Jakubowski appeal, with Einstein's facsimile signature, appears in *Die Menschenrechte*, Vol. IV, No. 7/8, July 25, 1929, made available by Mr. Kurt Grossmann. Further details of the case are taken from a memoir on the German League for Human Rights which Mr. Grossmann drew up for the orientation of the United States Government in 1942, and which Einstein confirmed to be correct.

14. *The Spanish Farm* was published in the United States by the Dial Press. The correspondent was Erich Leyens of Wesel, Germany.

15. The letter from the Transocean News Agency does not mention that Einstein's answers were to be published in *The New York Times*. The translation here given is new, from the original manuscript. *The New York Times* omitted the questions, ran the answers as a connected story.

16. The invitation to the World Congress for International Peace through Religion came from F. Siegmund-Schultze, editor of the quarterly *Die Eiche*.

17. The manuscript of the second statement on science and war bears the notation "Sept. 30–March 31." Its occasion has not been established.

18. The German version of the disarmament manifesto appears in *Die Menschenrechte*, Vol. V, No. 5/6, July 20, 1930, made available by Mr. Kurt Grossmann.

19. The letter about Mrs. Schwimmer appears in TFAW, p. 24. The present translation is a revised version from the German manuscript.

20. The minutes of the Geneva Committee, in which Einstein's remarks are recorded, were revised here for the sake of clarity.

21. Alfred Lief, in TFAW, p. 16, gives a version of Einstein's remarks on education to the Committee on Intellectual Co-operation as a direct quotation. The quotation concludes with a reference to the lamentable lack of co-operation "among savants working in the various branches of science. . . . They always have microscopes before their eyes."

22. The letter to Dufour-Feronce appears in German in MW, p. 70. Virtually identical English translations appear in TWAISI, p. 54, and IAO, p. 84. In IAO this letter is erroneously assigned to the year 1923.

23. The statement on the tenth anniversary of the League of Nations appears in German in FRANK, p. 329, in English in TFAW, p. 15 (the version here given). It was made for the *Völkermagazin*, Berlin, February 13, 1930. The statement that follows is translated from SEELIG, p. 209.

24. The German text of "The World As I See It" appears in MW, p. 7. Three different translations appear in TFAW, p. 20 (in part), TWAISI, p. 1, and IAO, p. 8. It is also reprinted in *Living Philosophies*, Simon and Schuster, New York, 1931; and in *I Believe*, Allen and Unwin, London, 1940. The English version of the excerpts in the text has been revised.

25. The colloquy with Tagore was published in *The American Hebrew*, September 11, 1931.

26. The Manifesto of the Joint Peace Council is translated from the original German text.

27. The message of greeting to America is here offered in a new translation from the original holograph in the possession of Mrs. Joseph Schaffner, New York. Another translation, appearing in TFAW, p. 32, and presumably the one actually broadcast, is attributed to Mrs. Einstein.

28. Details of Einstein's stay in New York are from his diary and from *The New York Times*.

29. Einstein's speech before the New History Society is available in no less than five English versions. The one here given, with rather extensive stylistic changes, is from TFAW, p. 34. The version which Mrs. Schwimmer sent Einstein on December 28, 1930, for authentication was somewhat shorter. The New History Society issued its own version, and others appeared in *The New York Times*, December 21, 1930, and *The World Tomorrow*, January 1931.

30. Rolland's reply to H. Runham Brown's inquiry is reproduced by permission of Mme. Marie Romain Rolland.

31. Einstein's statement about the Remarque film, also mentioned in his diary, is translated from *Die Menschenrechte*, Vol. VI, No. 3, March 20, 1931, made available by Mr. Kurt Grossmann.

32. The first of the two answers to Upton Sinclair appears (in a different translation) in TFAW, p. 28.

33. The German text of Einstein's article "My First Impressions in North America" is published in MW, p. 51, from which the present translation was prepared. A different English version appears in TWAISI, p. 37, and IAO, p. 3. The last paragraph, which alone is republished in the text, appears, in still a different translation, in TFAW, p. 33, where it is identified as having been released by the McNaught Syndicate, on March 29, 1931.

34. The answer from the *Yale Daily News* quiz is taken from *The New York Times*, February 3, 1931.

35. Einstein's address to the students of the California Institute of Technology is given here in a new translation from the original German manuscript. Another translation was distributed by the Associated Press and published in *The New York Times*, February 17, 1931.

36. The Chicago train platform speech is translated from the original German manuscript. Another translation was published in TFAW, p. 39. The delegation was organized by Lola Maverick Lloyd, a pacifist whom Mrs. Schwimmer had commended to Einstein.

37. Details of Einstein's stay in New York on March 4, 1931, are from the *New York World-Telegram* of the same date and *The New York Times*, March 5, 1931. The text of Einstein's shipboard remarks is revised from TFAW, pp. 40/41.

38. The interview with George Sylvester Viereck is taken, with slight stylistic changes, from TFAW, p. 37, where it is described as having been released by Universal Service in January 1931.

Chapter V

1. Einstein's intervention in the case of the anti-Jewish Arab rioters is mentioned in TFAW, p. 26.

2. Einstein's letters in the Pekurinen case are here translated from manuscript. Differing translations are given in TFAW, p. 27. The dates there also differ from those on Einstein's carbons.

3. An abbreviated version of the letter to *Politiken* appeared in the Dutch pacifist journal *Bevrijding*, January 1931, of which a translation appears in TFAW, p. 29. The letter is reproduced by permission of *Politiken*.

4. The offer to set up an Einstein Fund was made by H. Runham Brown in a letter addressed to Einstein in New York, dated December 29, 1930.

5. The money raised in Chicago is mentioned in TFAW, p. 29.

6. Miss Helene Dukas, Einstein's secretary, recalled Masaryk's handwritten letter and suggested the probable reason for its disappearance.

7. The communications in the Mooney-Billings case are published, with some inaccuracies, in TFAW, pp. 27–28.

8. Einstein's intervention in the Sufflay case is documented in *Die Menschenrechte,* Vol. 6, No. 5, June 2, 1931.

9. The German text of Einstein's speech on the Gumbel case appears in MW, p. 25. Slightly differing English versions appear in TWAISI, p. 5, and IAO, p. 28. The present version is comprehensively revised.

10. The colleague to whom Einstein's letter about Gumbel was addressed was Professor Gustav Radbruch of Heidelberg University. It appears in the issue of *Die Menschenrechte,* cited in Note 8 above. Portions of this letter appear in a different translation in TFAW, p. 29. It is there credited to the *Berliner Tageblatt,* April 1931, while the copy in Einstein's files, which differs from the published versions, is dated November 28, 1930.

11. Einstein's statement appeared in *The World Tomorrow,* June 1931. It is reproduced here by permission of *The Christian Century,* with which *The World Tomorrow* merged in 1934. The present translation, from the German original, differs greatly from that given in TFAW, p. 41.

12. The Swiss militia statement was sponsored by the Bund der Kriegsdienstgegner, the German section of the War Resisters' International. In giving his consent, Einstein blamed the French statesman Paul Boncour for reviving this "catastrophic" trend. Other signers of the statement were Otto Lehmann-Russbüldt, Robert Pohl, Franziskus Strasmann, Helene Stöcker, Paula Hans, Ludwig Quidde, Arnold Kalisch and Lida Gustava Heymann. It was printed in *The New World,* July 1931; *Time and Tide,* July 4, 1931; *International Disarmament Notes,* July 29, 1931; and no doubt elsewhere.

13. A. Fenner Brockway's interview with Einstein is reproduced by his permission.

14. The statement on the Kellogg League is from TFAW, p. 42.

15. The message to the Lyons meeting is given in German in an official mimeographed release, which was used to revise slightly the English version given in TFAW, p. 42. The major portion of the German text also appears in *Die Menschenrechte,* Vol. VI, No. 8, August 20, 1931.

16. The Dixmude statement was sent to Jan De Bondt on August 8, 1931. The German text of the statement is given in MW, p. 69. Two different English versions appear in TFAW, p. 44, on the one hand, and in TWAISI, p. 65, and IAO, p. 110, on the other. The present version is comprehensively revised.

17. After rejection by the *Vorwärts,* Einstein sent the article to the *Fackel,* which was a radical publication and which published the article.

18. The German text of *The Nation* article appears in MW, p. 77. The English version that appeared in *The Nation* is included in TFAW, p. 46. Another English version appears in TWAISI, p. 61, and IAO, p. 98 (a few slight differences between the two). The present version represents a revision. The article is reproduced by permission of *The Nation.*

19. The collection of Einstein's antiwar statements was later published as TFAW, edited by Alfred Lief. Einstein had granted permission for it on January 2, 1931. Einstein withdrew permission only for the search of his files, not for the collection itself, which appeared in 1933.

20. The translation of the statement to the Bund der Kriegsdienstgegner is from manuscript and differs from the English version given in TFAW, p. 48.

21. The German text of *The New York Times* article appears in MW, p. 73. Most of *The New York Times* version is reprinted in TFAW, p. 49. Slightly differing versions appear in TWAISI, p. 57, and IAO, p. 95. The

TWAISI version includes the final paragraph about Bauer's book. The present version is comprehensively revised from the German manuscript.

21a. The precise date of the letter to Rocco is not known. The German original is published in MW, p. 24. Slightly different translations appear in TWAISI, p. 31, and IAO, p. 30. The present version is a new translation from the German original.

22. Since Einstein never relinquished his Swiss citizenship, he held dual citizenship from about 1919 to 1933, when he was simultaneously citizen of Switzerland and Germany, and again from 1940 on, when he was citizen of Switzerland and the United States.

23. The excerpts from *Liberty* magazine are reproduced by permission of Lorraine Lester, a co-proprietor of that magazine. Einstein had asked Viereck to arrange the meeting with Rockefeller since he intended to urge a change in the rules of the Rockefeller Foundation regarding their scholarship program for scholars from overseas. Einstein felt these rules were discriminatory against young scholars who had not yet achieved a permanent position in their home countries. Rockefeller wrote to Einstein later that he and his family had greatly enjoyed his visit and that he would discuss with the officers of the Rockefeller Foundation the problem of scholarships which Einstein had commented upon.

24. *The Crisis* statement was reprinted in *The New York Times,* January 19, 1932, and is reproduced here by permission of *The Crisis.*

25. Although it has not been definitely established, this is in all probability the address Einstein delivered in Whittier. This is also indicated by his diary notes of January 18, 1932: "Quaker meeting in near-by town to the south on Disarmament Conference with a brief address from me." The German text appears in MW, p. 79, with an English version in TWAISI, p. 63, and IAO, p. 100. The present translation is a revised version.

26. Excerpts from Einstein's speech at the Schurman dinner appeared in *The New York Times,* January 26, 1932. The present translation is from manuscript.

27. The German text of the speech to the Los Angeles University of International Relations appears in MW, p. 72. Three prior English translations are available: by Professor William B. Munro, in *World Affairs Interpreter,* Summer 1932, a quarterly published by the Los Angeles University of International Relations; in TFAW, p. 56; and in TWAISI, p. 55, and IAO, p. 102 (identical). The present version is new.

28. The excerpts from the Santa Barbara message are slightly revised, with the help of the German manuscript, from the version given in TFAW, p. 57.

29. The German text of the boycott speech appears in MW, p. 61, where the speech is erroneously described as having been delivered before German pacifist students in 1930. This attribution also appears at the head of the English translation in IAO, p. 93, while Alfred Lief, who gives another translation in TFAW, p. 57, indicates correctly time and place of the address. These two translations differ markedly (the IAO translation also appears in TWAISI, p. 44). The version of the excerpts in the text is new. *The New York Times* printed excerpts from this speech on February 28, 1932.

Chapter VI

1. Einstein's files contain another transcript of the German press conference which was submitted to him by the War Resisters' International and which forms the basis for the report given in TFAW, p. 60. Einstein, however, made certain cuts in this tran-

script. As he stated in a letter to H. Runham Brown on June 17, 1932: "I have rather freely revised the report of the press conference, insofar as it deals with me. The version submitted to me contained many misunderstandings and obscurities for which I may have been partly responsible." For the translation in the text, Einstein's own version was used.

2. Romain Rolland's comments and impressions are from transcripts of his diaries kindly made available by Mme. Marie Romain Rolland. The translations are reproduced here by Mme. Rolland's permission.

2a. The excerpts from *Pictorial Review* are reproduced here by permission of Hearst magazines, the present owners of the copyright of *Pictorial Review*.

3. Catchpool's interview was published in the British Quaker Journal, *The Friend*, issue of August 12, 1932. The article, entitled "Sunday Afternoon with Professor Einstein," is reproduced by permission of that magazine.

4. The International Congress against Imperialist Wars was probably the largest and most ambitious event of its kind. Barbusse appended a report to his letter to Einstein of September 11, 1932, in which an attendance of 2,191 delegates was claimed—1,041 without party affiliations, 830 Communists, 291 Social Democrats, 24 Independent Socialists and 10 Dissident Communists. Shaw (England) and Wells (Germany) apparently did not join the international sponsoring committee, but the letterhead lists, in addition to the names mentioned on p. 177, the following personalities: Victor Margueritte, Félicien Challaye, Paul Signac (France); Frantz Masereel (Belgium); Henriette Roland-Holst (Holland); Valle Inclan, Commandant Franco (Spain); Havelock Ellis, Bertrand Russell (England); Charlotte Despard (Ireland); Karl Krauss (Austria); Michael Karolyi (Hungary); Dobrogheanu Gherea (Rumania); Martin Andersen Nexö (Scandinavia); General Augusto Sandino (Latin America); Sen Katayama (Japan); Jean Devanny (Australia). The account mentioned on page 181 is by Kurt Grossmann and appeared in the October 1932 issue of the independent pacifist journal *Die Friedenswarte*.

5. The letter to Solovine is translated by permission of Gauthier-Villars, Paris.

6. The original of the letter to Weizmann is in the Weizmann Archives, Rehovoth, Israel.

7. The excerpts from Freud's letter to Viereck are reproduced by permission of Sigmund Freud Copyrights Ltd., London.

8. The German text of this letter to Freud appears in MW, p. 64, where it is attributed to "1931 or early 1932." (The editor of MW states that Einstein and Freud met twice briefly in Berlin.) An English translation, here revised, appears in TWAISI, p. 46, and IAO, p. 104.

9. The translations of the Einstein and Freud letters that make up *Why War?* were prepared by Stuart Gilbert. They are here reproduced by special permission of UNESCO, the successor agency to the International Institute of Intellectual Co-operation which published the pamphlet containing the two letters. UNESCO made much background information available. Leon Steinig, a major figure in initiating this correspondence, and a member of the staff of the United Nations Secretariat, was also very helpful.

10. The Berlin newspapers published by the publisher to whom Einstein's statement on freedom of the press was addressed were *Die Welt am Abend* and *Berlin am Morgen*.

11. Einstein's statement on the Herriot proposals was given to the *Internationaler Pressedienst "Co-operation,"* Berlin.

12. The *Reichsbanner* statement is translated from Item No. 639, listed in the catalogue for Auction No. 59, conducted on May 21–22, 1957, by Karl und Faber, Munich, Germany. It is described as a signed holograph "ca. 1932."

13. The German text of Einstein's reply to the patriotic American women appears in MW, p. 55. One English version appears in TFAW, p. 63, another in TWAISI, p. 42, and IAO, p. 7. This is a new translation.

14. No date has been established for Einstein's statement on sending women to the front, here revised from a translation in IAO, p. 108 (German text, MW, p. 66).

15. Parts of the address to the students of the California Institute of Technology appear in OOMLY, p. 215. This is a new translation from the manuscript.

16. This statement is translated from a manuscript identified only as "Pasadena, 1932–33, probably for a pacifist youth meeting or journal."

17. The American educator was Carl J. Rautzenberg of Santa Monica, California.

18. The resolution adopted by the New Jersey legislature was sponsored by Assemblyman Frank M. Travaline, Jr. Credit is due Alfred Lief for making this document available.

19. This letter, addressed to a friend—Mrs. Margarete Lebach—is given in part in Item No. 51 of the catalogue of Sale No. 1744, conducted on March 26, 1957, by the Parke-Bernet Galleries, New York.

20. The German text of Einstein's declaration appears in MW, p. 105. The English text given by Miss Seeley appears in TWAISI, p. 81, and IAO, p. 205. This is a revision.

21. About Einstein's dual citizenship, see Chap. V, Note 22.

22. Mrs. Lola Maverick Lloyd, who had organized the train platform reception for Einstein two years before (see Chap. IV, Note 36), was also concerned with this event, of which she wrote an account in the magazine *Unity*, according to her daughter, Jessie Lloyd O'Connor.

23. Mr. Alfred Lief made available material on the Waldorf reception. The New York Public Library has a sizable volume of clippings, entitled "Professor Albert Einstein Visits New York City, March 15, 1933." This scrapbook contains *The New York Times* clipping of Einstein's statement, of March 24, 1933, on the raid made on his summer home. The dispatch is credited to Universal Service.

24. The author to whom Einstein's letter was addressed was Joseph Merory, an engineer of Vienna, Austria.

Chapter VII

1. Abraham Flexner, the American educator who conceived and organized the Institute for Advanced Study, first discussed Einstein's membership in it with him in Pasadena early in 1932, then at Oxford in the spring, and finally at Caputh near Berlin in the summer of that year. See Abraham Flexner, *An Autobiography*, Simon and Schuster, New York, 1960, pp. 250–52.

2. Einstein's exchanges with the two German academies are given in full in MW, p. 105 ff. Identical translations appear in TWAISI, p. 81 ff., and IAO, p. 205 ff. The excerpts here presented have been revised.

2a. Thomas Mann's brother was Heinrich Mann, also a great German writer.

3. The statement for the *Biosophical Review* appeared in a "peace issue" of that quarterly, Vol. 3, No. 1, fall 1933, as a letter to the editor, Dr. Frederick Kettner.

4. Einstein's friendship with the Belgian royal couple went back several years; the friendship was particularly close with Queen Elizabeth. In

a letter from Brussels to his wife in 1931 Einstein kept referring to the royal family as "the Kings"—as though they were a family named King. "I went across to the station . . . to telephone the Kings. It was quite tedious because the line was always busy. . . . At 3 o'clock I drove out to the Kings, where I was received with touching warmth. These two people are of a purity and kindness seldom found. First we talked for about an hour. Then an English woman musician arrived, and we played quartets and trios (a musical lady-in-waiting was also present). This went on merrily for several hours. Then they all went away and I stayed behind alone for dinner with the Kings—vegetarian style, no servants. Spinach with hard-boiled eggs and potatoes, period. (It had not been anticipated that I would stay.) I liked it very much there, and I am certain the feeling is mutual." King Albert, in his reply to Einstein, did not use the term *the Belgian Government*, but rather *Les Gouvernants belges*. As a constitutional monarch he may have had to be cautious in speaking officially for his government. King Albert's letter was written in French. The English translation is inserted here with the approval of his widow.

5. Both *The New York Times* and the *New York Herald Tribune* carried, on September 10, 1933, stories on Einstein's letter to Nahon stating that it had been published the preceding day in *La Patrie humaine*. The Press Service of the International Antimilitaristic Commission of September 7, however, puts publication at August 18, which is the more likely date. Acknowledgment for this reference as well as for documentation of the reaction of the War Resisters' International (p. 232) is made to Alfred Lief. Not quite a year later, on May 2, 1934, Alfred Nahon wrote Einstein to advise him that, after careful consideration, he had come to agree with Einstein's modified position on war resistance and was now in a French military prison because he had not reported for service on time.

6. Lord Ponsonby's letter is translated from the German original and reproduced here by permission of his son.

7. The excerpts from Romain Rolland's diary are translated from a transcript made available by Mme. Marie Romain Rolland; they are reproduced with Mme. Rolland's permission.

8. The interview with Lania, excerpts from which are reproduced by permission of the Newspaper Enterprise Association, appeared in the *New York World-Telegram* on September 19, 1933, datelined that same day at Le Coq-sur-mer, when Einstein had already been in England ten days. The excerpts from the interview have been slightly revised.

9. The translation of the Albert Hall speech follows on the whole that given in *The New York Times*, October 4, 1933, reprinted (without the first and last paragraphs) in OOMLY, p. 148. Some revisions have been made as a result of comparison with the German manuscript, which does *not* contain the three paragraphs dealing with young scientists pursuing their studies in lighthouses. These remarks, which Einstein must have interpolated and which actually have no connection with the rest of the speech, are probably the reason why it bears the otherwise inappropriate title "Science and Civilization" in OOMLY. In a perceptive article on Einstein in *The American Scholar*, Summer 1947, his former collaborator Leopold Infeld refers to this passage: "Once he wrote that the position of lighthouse keeper would be suitable for a scientist, because it would give him much leisure for thinking and working. I tried to explain to him

that only two or three men in the world could work scientifically under such conditions, that almost everyone needs association in his work. Einstein listened, but it was not easy for him to see my point. Indeed, he is the only scientist who could be content as a lighthouse keeper." (Reproduced by permission of *The American Scholar*.) See also SEELIG, p. 241.

10. Although so marked in manuscript, the "second draft" of Einstein's Albert Hall speech may not have been intended for that purpose at all—there is a reference in it to "the reader." The introduction to the Friends of Europe pamphlet based on it (*Friends of Europe Publications*, No. 4) is susceptible to the interpretation that *it* represents the text of the speech, which was certainly *not* the case, though the pamphlet does contain some material from the speech.

Chapter VIII

1. The address at the Nobel dinner is here translated from the German manuscript. Another translation, presumably the one Einstein actually read, is given in *The New York Times*, December 19, 1933, together with a picture of the four guests of honor, Einstein looking most uncomfortable in a full-dress suit.

2. Einstein's contribution to the brotherhood broadcast, over the National Broadcasting Company's national network, was read by Dr. John H. Finley.

3. The speech before the Progressive Education Association is here presented in a new translation from the German manuscript. Two different translations have previously appeared, in OOMLY, p. 207 (under the title "The Schools and the Problem of Peace"), and in IAO, p. 57 (under the title "Education and World Peace").

4. All but the first two paragraphs of the *Polity* article, which is reproduced here with major editorial changes based on the original German manuscript, are reprinted in OOMLY, p. 209. A story on this article appeared in the *New York Sun*, January 9, 1935.

5. A report on the student "strikes" for peace appeared in *The New York Times*, April 13, 1935. It mentions a Princeton meeting, presumably of that date, which was addressed by Norman Thomas, and quotes a single sentence from the statement sent to Temple University.

6. The interview with R. M. Bartlett is reproduced here with some editorial changes.

7. This speech was broadcast over the Columbia Broadcasting System, under the sponsorship of the American Christian Committee for German Refugees and the Emergency Committee in Aid of Political Refugees from Nazism. This is a new translation from the original German manuscript. *The New York Times* carried a story on the speech on October 23, 1935.

8. Many details concerning the Ossietzky campaign were provided through the co-operation of Hilde Walter (a former associate of Ossietzky and one of the most active fighters in his behalf) from documents in the International Institute for Social History, Keizersgracht 64, Amsterdam. Among others who were active in the campaign were Otto Nathan, Professor Werner Hegemann and Gustav Hartung (to whom Einstein's letter of September 1, 1935, was addressed). The column in the *New York Post* of June 24, 1935, was Ludwig Lore's "Behind the Cables." Einstein's letter to the Nobel Committee appears to have been first published (in German) in a small book, *Carl von Ossietzky*, by Kurt Singer and Felix Burger (a pen name for Kurt Grossmann), Europa Verlag,

Zurich, 1937. Originally scheduled to be published in 1936, it was apparently delayed so as not to prejudice the success of the Ossietzky campaign. Grossmann also included the letter in an article, "*Albert Einstein und die Deutsche Liga für Menschenrechte*," that appeared in *Die Menschenrechte*, the revived organ of that group, March–June 1955. In both of these publications the Einstein letter is erroneously dated October 27, 1936.

9. The American educator was Carleton Washburne, Superintendent of the Winnetka Public Schools, Winnetka, Illinois.

10. Identical translations of Einstein's Albany address appear in OOMLY, p. 31, and IAO, p. 59. The paragraph here given has been revised from the German manuscript.

11. The message for the Young Men's Christian Association is published in OOMLY, p. 9. This is a revised translation from the German manuscript.

12. The translation of Einstein's letter to the National Society for the Abolition of Cruel Sports is revised from the German original. The issue of the *Bulletin*, in which the letter was published, was made available by Mrs. Bertram Lloyd, whose late husband was the chief founder and Honorary Secretary of that group.

13. The message for the meeting of April 5, 1938, is identified on the German manuscript only as being for "a meeting for peace and democracy."

14. The postscript to *The World As I See It* was originally published in *I Believe*, Simon and Schuster, New York, 1939, and Allen and Unwin, London, 1940, and is here slightly revised from the German manuscript. It is reprinted in OOMLY, p. 6. The version published in England differs in a few respects from the American publication.

15. Identical translations of the message for the Time Capsule appear in OOMLY, p. 11, and IAO, p. 18. This is a new translation from the German manuscript.

Chapter IX

1. The review of the background of atomic fission as well as the events described in this chapter are based on Einstein's files and on various other sources, chief among which are the following: the so-called Smyth Report: Henry DeWolf Smyth, *Atomic Energy for Military Purposes*, Princeton University Press, Princeton, 1945, originally an official government document; Henry L. Stimson with McGeorge Bundy, *On Active Service in Peace and War*, Harper & Brothers, New York, 1948; Selig Hecht, *Explaining the Atom*, enlarged edition with additional chapters by Eugene Rabinowitch, Viking Press, New York, 1954, a book for which Einstein had words of praise; Carl Seelig, *Helle Zeit–Dunkle Zeit, In Memoriam Albert Einstein*, Europa Verlag, Zurich, 1956; Arthur Holly Compton, *Atomic Quest*, Oxford University Press, New York, 1956. Important information, both orally and in writing, was received from Dr. Leo Szilard, Dr. Alexander Sachs, and Professor Niels Bohr. Professor Peter G. Bergmann, Einstein's assistant for several years, reviewed the passages on science in the chapter.

2. The Hahn-Strassmann paper was published in *Die Naturwissenschaften*, January 15, 1939, the Meitner-Frisch communication in *Nature*, February 1939. See also Otto Hahn, "The Discovery of Fission," *Scientific American*, February 1958.

3. Dr. L. A. Turner reviewed the early literature on atomic fission in the *Review of Modern Physics*, January 1940.

4. The quotations are from Laura Fermi, *Atoms in the Family*, The University of Chicago Press, Chicago, 1954. Pegram's letter to Admiral

Hooper is reproduced in full on pp. 162–63 of that book.

5. Einstein's interview in Pittsburgh is reported in *The Literary Digest* of January 12, 1935.

6. The translation of Einstein's reply to *The New York Times*, March 14, 1939, is revised from the original German manuscript.

7. Details concerning Sachs's involvement are discussed at length in his testimony, *Background and Early History Atomic Bomb Project in Relation to President Roosevelt*, before the Special Senate Committee on Atomic Energy, on November 27, 1945 (Seventy-ninth Congress, First Session, pursuant to S. Res. 179). (See also *The New York Times*, November 28, 1945.) Thanks are due Dr. Sachs, who permitted scrutiny of his private papers.

8. Compton discusses Einstein's and Szilard's intervention and the activities of the Advisory Committee on pp. 27–30 of his book, *Atomic Quest*. Compton's evaluation is summarized in the following statement (p. 29): "In retrospect it is evident that the effect of the appointment of the government's Advisory Committee on Uranium was to retard rather than to advance the development of American uranium research." Dr. Vannevar Bush said in a personal communication: "I would not go as far as Dr. Compton goes. There was a great deal of scientific activity at the time of Einstein's letter, and I do not believe the letter, or the Advisory Committee, affected it much one way or the other."

9. With respect to his invitation to Einstein to become a consultant to the Office of Scientific Research and Development, Dr. Bush says: "I took the step at the urging of some of Einstein's friends. I do not remember whether he accepted or not. I did not know of any relationship of his with the Navy, and he did not mention it to me in a letter or otherwise. I do know that he did not become active in OSRD." The facts about Einstein's association with the Navy were provided by Miss Helene Dukas, Einstein's secretary.

10. Niels Bohr published parts of his memorandum of July 3, 1944, in *Open Letter to the United Nations*, June 9, 1950, J. H. Schultz Forlag, Copenhagen. This document also contains passages from his second memorandum to President Roosevelt on the same general subject, dated March 24, 1945. See also Alice Kimball Smith, "Behind the Decision to Use the Atomic Bomb: Chicago 1944–45," *Bulletin of the Atomic Scientists*, October 1958, p. 292.

11. About the early, remarkably wise and farsighted reports concerning the new atomic age and pertinent activities among scientists, see particularly Alice Kimball Smith, *op. cit.*, pp. 289–293. The quotation characterizing the Jeffries Report is from Mrs. Smith's article.

12. Excerpts from Szilard's memorandum were published in the *Bulletin of the Atomic Scientists*, December 1947. The memorandum is also mentioned by Mrs. Fermi, *op. cit.*, p. 243, A. H. Compton, *op. cit.*, p. 241, and by Mrs. Alice Kimball Smith, *op. cit.*, p. 293. About the Spartanburg visit of Szilard and the two other scientists, see James F. Byrnes, *All in One Lifetime*, Harper & Brothers, New York, 1958, p. 284, and Alice Kimball Smith, *op. cit.*, p. 296. Mrs. Smith is the historian who discussed the Spartanburg meeting with the three scientists.

13. The most comprehensive and meticulous account concerning the background of the decision to use the atomic bomb is given by Mrs. Alice Kimball Smith in the article mentioned before, from which the quotation about Mr. Byrnes's lack of understanding of atomic energy is taken. Mrs. Smith was able to use the files which the various committees de-

posited at the University of Chicago Library, and to interview most of those who participated in the pertinent discussions and activities. The books by Stimson, A. H. Compton and Mrs. Fermi likewise deal with the subject. See also Henry L. Stimson, "The Decision to Use the Atomic Bomb," *Harper's Magazine*, February 1947; James F. Byrnes, *Speaking Frankly*, Harper & Brothers, New York, 1947; *Memoirs by Harry S Truman*, Vol. I, Doubleday and Company, Garden City, 1955; Louis Morton, "The Decision to Use the Atomic Bomb," *Foreign Affairs*, January 1957; and Byrnes, *All in One Lifetime*, *loc. cit.*

14. About the work and deliberations of the Interim Committee, see the publications listed in the preceding note, particularly *Atomic Quest* by Arthur H. Compton, who was a member of the Scientific Panel, and Alice Kimball Smith, *op. cit.* The unanimity of the Interim Committee's recommendation was not entirely maintained since, almost four weeks after it was made, one member—Undersecretary of the Navy Ralph Bard—notified Secretary Stimson that he dissented from the third point of the recommendation, viz., that the bomb be used without prior warning; he urged that two or three days' warning be given the Japanese.

15. The so-called Franck Report, drawn up by a "Committee on Social and Political Implications" in Chicago, was published in the *Bulletin of the Atomic Scientists*, May 1, 1946. Mrs. Alice Kimball Smith (*op. cit.*, p. 299) identifies the signers, in addition to Franck and Szilard, as Donald Hughes, Joyce Stearns, Eugene Rabinowitch, Glenn Seaborg, and J. J. Nickson.

16. The poll which A. H. Compton asked Farrington Daniels to conduct at Chicago on July 12, 1945, is described in the *Bulletin of the Atomic Scientists*, February 1948, and by Mrs. Alice Kimball Smith, *op. cit.*, pp. 303 ff.

17. Szilard's petition has never been published in toto. The discussion in the text about this last-minute action by Szilard is based on Compton's *Atomic Quest*, pp. 241–42, and Alice Kimball Smith, *op. cit.*, pp. 303 and 307. See also Leo Szilard, "A Personal History of the Atomic Bomb," *University of Chicago Round Table*, No. 601 (September 25, 1949). About counterpetitions and other activities among scientists, see also the publications by Compton and Smith.

18. On Einstein's opposition to the use of the bomb, see Virgil S. Hinshaw, Jr., in Schilpp, p. 656. Hinshaw, who talked to Einstein in May 1949, reports as follows: "Einstein flatly challenges the wisdom of having used the bomb over Japan."

Chapter X

1. The excerpts from the message to the science teachers section of the New Jersey Education Association, meeting at Atlantic City, are from a translation in the files; the German original is not available.

2. Einstein's comment on the Russell case is from *The New York Times*, March 19, 1940.

3. The occasion for which the statement on the Netherlands invasion was written has not been established. This translation is from the German manuscript.

4. The telegram from the seventeen Princeton faculty members is from *The New York Times*, May 23, 1940.

5. Einstein's interlocutor on the "I Am an American" broadcast, which went out over a National Broadcasting Company network, was Marshall Dimock, Second Assistant Secretary of the United States Department of Labor. The script has been revised,

following a fragmentary German manuscript.

6. The friend on the West Coast was Dr. Gabriel Segall, a physician in Los Angeles, California, whom Einstein met in January 1931. They soon became friends.

7. Professor Urey's letters are reproduced by his special permission. Einstein's letter to Urey has been revised from the German manuscript.

8. The English version of the message to the Common Council for American Unity, which is from Einstein's files, was revised from the German manuscript.

9. The identity of the White House correspondent to whom the Pearl Harbor Day message was given has not been established. Miss Helene Dukas, Einstein's secretary, recalls that it was to be broadcast in German and that she read it over the telephone in that language. This translation is from the German manuscript.

10. Litvinov's reply to Einstein is reproduced by special permission of the Soviet Embassy in Washington.

11. Excerpts from Culbertson's letters to Einstein are reproduced by special permission of the executors of the Culbertson estate, Bruce E. Culbertson and Albert H. Morehead.

12. Excerpts from Einstein's address to the Jewish Council for Russian War Relief were given in *The New York Times*, October 26, 1942. The translation here given is revised from the German original manuscript in Einstein's files.

13. The message to the Soviet-Jewish delegation is slightly revised from a translation in the Einstein files.

14. The cable to the London *News Chronicle* is slightly revised from a translation in the Einstein files.

15. Excerpts from the message to the National Wartime Conference (June 2 and 3, 1944) are to be found in *The New York Times*, May 29, 1944. The version here given represents a revision of the text appearing in the Proceedings of the Conference and reprinted in OOMLY, p. 179. It is erroneously dated 1945 in that collection.

16. The person whom Einstein had asked to be the messenger of his letter was an acquaintance in the United States armed forces in Italy who apparently preferred to keep Einstein's original letter to Croce (a copy of which is not available) to himself. The exchange was published in pamphlet form in Italy (*Lettera a B. Croce e Risposta del Croce*, Laterza, Bari, 1944). Croce's reply, which is reproduced here by permission of his daughter, Alida Croce, was especially translated for this volume by Frances Frenaye, whose kindness is gratefully acknowledged. The book to which both Einstein and Croce contributed and to which Croce refers is *Freedom, Its Meaning*, edited by Ruth Nanda Anshen (Harcourt, Brace and Co., New York, 1940). Einstein's contribution to that volume is reprinted in OOMLY, p. 12.

17. Einstein's answers are translated from the original German manuscript in Einstein's files, and are reproduced by permission of *World Events Magazine, Inc.*

18. The statement for the Trenton rally appeared in *The New York Times*, October 10, 1944. This statement as well as the two statements for the Davidson Committee are here translated from manuscript.

19. The invitation to Einstein to become a member of a committee to sponsor the acceptance of the Dumbarton Oaks recommendations for a United Nations Charter was signed by William Allen Neilson, Chairman of the Executive Committee of the Commission to Study the Organization of Peace.

20. The letter to the friend on the West Coast was again addressed to the physician Dr. Gabriel Segall in

Los Angeles, to whom Einstein had written before; see Note 6 above.

21. Einstein's statement on Roosevelt's death is reproduced by permission of *Aufbau*. It was previously published in German in MW, p. 254.

Chapter XI

1. See Chap. IX, Note 1.

1a. Albert Einstein, *The Meaning of Relativity*, Third Edition, Princeton, 1950 (see also the Fifth Edition, prepared by Einstein and published after his death in 1956).

2. The Saranac Lake interview appeared in *The New York Times* on September 15, 1945.

3. Dr. Hutchins' invitation was dated September 5, 1945. The subsequently organized group became the Committee to Frame a World Constitution.

3a. Emery Reves, *The Anatomy of Peace*, Harper & Brothers, New York, 1945.

4. Excerpts from Emery Reves's letter to Einstein are reproduced by special permission of Mr. Reves.

5. Additional signers of the letter in *The New York Times* were J. W. Fulbright, Claude Pepper, Elbert D. Thomas, the Right Rev. Henry St. George Tucker, the Rev. Edward A. Conway, S.J., Louis Finkelstein, Mortimer J. Adler, Charles G. Bolte, Gardner Cowles, Jr., Dorothy Canfield Fisher, Albert D. Lasker, Cord Meyer, Christopher Morley, Carl Van Doren, Mark Van Doren, Walter F. Wanger, Robert J. Watt.

6. Excerpts from Dr. Posin's letter to Einstein are reproduced by special permission of Dr. Posin. Einstein's answer is translated from manuscript.

7. U. S. Congress, *Congressional Record*, Vol. 91, Part 8, 79th Congress, 1st Session, p. 10049.

8. Excerpts from former Senator Ball's letters to Einstein are reproduced by his special permission. The May-Johnson bill would have kept atomic energy under military control. Its passage was thwarted by spontaneously organized efforts of the atomic scientists that resulted in additional public hearings at which Leo Szilard, among others, testified.

9. Swing's letter is reproduced by his special permission.

10. Einstein's article has been slightly revised; Mr. Swing had no part in the revision.

11. Einstein is in error on a minor point in the *Atlantic Monthly* article. Lise Meitner did not "escape from Germany to place the information [about atomic fission] in the hands of Niels Bohr." She was already in Sweden at the time (see p. 288).

12. Einstein's reply to Welles is translated from manuscript.

13. The four scientists were John L. Balderston, Jr., Dieter M. Gruen, W. J. McLean, and David B. Wehmeyer. Einstein's reply to them has been revised, following the original German text.

14. Einstein's Nobel Anniversary speech appeared in *The New York Times* on December 11, 1945; in OOMLY, p. 200; and in IAO, p. 115. It was prepared by Einstein's friend, the historian Erich Kahler, whom Einstein told what he wanted to say. The version presented here is revised from the original text.

15. *One World or None*, edited by Dexter Masters and Katharine Way, with a foreword by Niels Bohr and an introduction by Arthur H. Compton, was published by the McGraw-Hill Book Co., New York, in 1946. Contributors, besides Einstein, were Philip Morrison, Harlow Shapley, Eugene P. Wigner, Gale Young, J. Robert Oppenheimer, General H. H. Arnold, Louis N. Ridenour, Edward U. Condon, Frederick Seitz, Hans Bethe, Irving Langmuir, Harold Urey, Leo Szilard, Walter Lippmann, and the Federation of American Scientists. Einstein's con-

tribution is presented here in a revised text, following the German manuscript. Several passages here retained were added by Dexter Masters with Einstein's approval. Einstein's draft cable to the Soviet Academy is translated from manuscript. The version actually sent may have carried the signatures of several other prominent scientists. Mr. Masters was very helpful in reconstructing this entire incident.

16. The name of the correspondent was Mrs. Millicent Bingham of San Francisco.

Chapter XII

1. Einstein's letter to *Look*, published in that magazine on April 16, 1946, and reproduced here by permission of the magazine, is slightly revised.

2. The telegram from Rollins College was signed by George C. Holdt, Director of the Conference.

3. The excerpt from Culbertson's letter is reproduced by special permission of the executors of the Culbertson estate, Bruce E. Culbertson and Albert H. Morehead. Einstein's reply is slightly revised.

4. The article in *The Nation*, upon which Einstein commented, was by I. F. Stone and entitled "Atomic Pie in the Sky."

5. Much assistance in documenting Einstein's role in the Emergency Committee of Atomic Scientists was provided by Harold L. Oram of New York, who directed its fund-raising activities; Professor Harrison Brown of the California Institute of Technology, who served as its major executive officer in the later stages; the staff of the *Bulletin of the Atomic Scientists* in Chicago, and particularly its editor, Dr. Eugene Rabinowitch; and Robert Rosenthal, Curator of Special Collections of the University of Chicago Library, where the papers of the committee are deposited. In addition to Messrs. Oram and Brown, as well as other individuals mentioned in this and later chapters, the following persons deserve major credit for the work of the committee: Lily Payson, Assistant Secretary-Treasurer; Eileen Fry of Mr. Oram's staff, who served as Executive Secretary with an office in Princeton and whose untimely death in 1948 was a severe blow to the group; Joseph Halle Schaffner, the original Executive Director and Treasurer; and Ernest Everet Minett, who served in a similar capacity in Chicago. This list is not complete. A history of the Emergency Committee of Atomic Scientists remains to be written. The background of the American Federation of Scientists is described in two articles by John A. Simpson, "The Scientists as Public Educators," *Bulletin of the Atomic Scientists*, September 1947; and "The Federation of American Scientists," *ibidem*, January 1948. The original trustees of the Emergency Committee included Robert F. Bacher, who later withdrew because of his appointment to the United States Atomic Energy Commission.

6. Einstein's remarks for the "Operation Crossroads" broadcast are reproduced from the script, by permission of the Columbia Broadcastng System, Inc.

7. An English version of Einstein's radio address to the Chicago student rally appears in OOMLY, p. 138, under the title "Toward a World Government." (See also *The New York Times*, May 30, 1946.) The version here given has been revised from the German manuscript.

8. The student leader in the radio interview was Foster Parmelee, Secretary-Treasurer of the National Organization of Student Federalists.

9. Cord Meyer's article on the Lilienthal-Acheson proposals was published in *The Atlantic Monthly*, July 1946, under the title "What Are the Chances?" and as part of a tripartite

symposium (with David Lilienthal and Henry DeWolf Smyth), "Stopping the Atomic Armament Race." Meyer quoted only the last sentence from Einstein's letter to *The Nation* (p. 374). Einstein's letter to Meyer was reproduced in *The Atlantic Monthly*, September 1946. The following year Einstein wrote a brief preface for Meyer's book, *Peace or Anarchy*.

10. The excerpts from Labarthe's interview with Einstein are reproduced by permission of *France-Soir*.

11. Einstein's interview with Michael Amrine, which is republished here by permission of *The New York Times*, was circulated by the Emergency Committee of Atomic Scientists in pamphlet form under the title *Only Then Shall We Find Courage* (together with an article from the *American Scholar* by Christian Gauss, "Is Einstein Right?"). Slight stylistic revisions were made in the text of the interview. A German version was published in *Aufbau*, September 20 and 27, 1946.

12. The Polish journalist was Michael Hofman.

13. Wallace's reply to Einstein is reproduced by his special permission.

14. Einstein's article on the Negro question in *Pageant* magazine, January 1946, is reprinted in OOMLY, p. 132. For his address at Lincoln University, see *The New York Times*, May 4, 1946.

15. The message to the Philadelphia conference, reproduced here with slight stylistic revisions, is from a translation in the Einstein files.

16. Einstein's broadcast at the Princeton Conference of Atomic Scientists was over the facilities of the National Broadcasting Company. His remarks, reproduced by special permission of NBC, are here translated from the German manuscript.

17. Einstein's extemporaneous remarks at the symposium are from a privately printed transcript, which is marked "confidential" and copyrighted in Einstein's name. Einstein made these remarks in English, which was rare for him to do. They have been edited from the printed transcript. In a report on the conference to A. J. Muste of the Fellowship of Reconciliation, Helen Beardsley of Los Angeles, who proposed that the committee include in its program the cessation of the manufacture of atomic bombs, quoted Einstein as follows in the ensuing discussion: "Making peace is a psychological problem. But you have this dilemma. You want to make peace and you want to prepare for war. You cannot serve these two masters. You cannot prepare for peace and for war at the same time. It is psychologically impossible."

18. Dr. Abbot's protest to Einstein is from the files of the Emergency Committee of Atomic Scientists in the University of Chicago Library.

19. Einstein's message to the Portland meeting is translated from the German manuscript. Another translation in the Einstein files was reprinted in the *Rotarian*, June 1948, together with several other statements by Einstein.

20. Einstein's statement on Ossietzky is translated from the German manuscript. Another translation is published in OOMLY, p. 241.

21. The French journalist was Robert Jean Longuet, a great-grandson of Karl Marx.

22. The conscientious objector was Igal Roodenko, who was at the time in the Federal Correctional Institution at Sandstone, Minnesota.

Chapter XIII

1. Einstein's reply to Mrs. Roosevelt's invitation has been slightly revised.

2. The questions about Professor Wiener's attitude were posed by Jacob Landau, Managing Director of the

Overseas News Agency. Einstein's replies, here translated from the German manuscript, are reproduced by permission of Mr. Landau's executors.

3. Einstein's remarks about Lilienthal's nomination, here revised from the German manuscript, were made over radio station WMCA and are reproduced by its special permission. See also *The New York Times*, February 22, 1947.

4. Excerpts from the story in *Newsweek* are reproduced by special permission of that magazine. Reprints of this story were circulated by the Emergency Committee of Atomic Scientists.

5. Einstein's message to *The World Federalist News* dinner, here revised from the German manuscript, is reproduced by special permission of the custodian of the defunct *World Government News,* Stewart M. Ogilvy.

6. Einstein's message to the unidentified meeting is from an English manuscript bearing corrections in Einstein's handwriting. It was made available by Mr. Harold Oram, who dates it May 12, 1947. The meeting was allegedly a gathering of members of the bar, organized by the Emergency Committee of Atomic Scientists.

7. Einstein's memorandum to Urey for the Lake Geneva meeting is translated from the German manuscript. In his accompanying note Einstein wrote: "I am sending you my text in German, knowing that Szilard or somebody else may translate it for you."

8. The press release accompanying the publication of the Emergency Committee's statement announced the election of Harrison Brown and Frederick Seitz as trustees of the committee.

9. Einstein's joint statement with the Federation of American Scientists was published in the *Bulletin of the Atomic Scientists,* September 1947. See also *The New York Times,* July 16, 1947, and July 20, 1947.

10. The broadcast on "The Immediate Need for World Law" was over the facilities of the American Broadcasting Company and is reproduced by its special permission.

11. Einstein's answers to the *Washington Post,* slightly revised from the original German manuscript, are reproduced by special permission of that newspaper.

12. For information about the Peoples' World Convention movement, acknowledgment is made to Henry C. Usborne, Professor Stringfellow Barr, and especially Harris Wofford, Jr. Mr. Wofford's as yet unpublished book, *A Cold War Odyssey: Story of the Foundation for World Government,* provided much useful background information not only for this chapter but for the next one as well. Mr. Wofford's manuscript has been used by his permission. The term "Peoples' World Convention" was used chiefly in America; in England it was usually "Peoples' World Constituent Assembly." The "Crusade for World Government" in England was actually sponsored by the "British Parliamentary Committee," which numbered as many as 200 Members of Parliament. The appeal Einstein signed is from a widely distributed pamphlet, *Crusade for World Government: The Plan in Outline*. Einstein's cosigners were Gerhard Domagk, Robert Hutchins, Kerstin Hesselgren, John Steinbeck, Lord Beveridge, Hu Shih, Yehudi Menuhin, Jaques Maritain, Sir John Boyd Orr, Thomas Mann, Sarvapalli Radhakrishnan and Roberto Rosselini. The World Movement for World Federal Government, in Paris, comprised some thirty-five organizations in sixteen countries. Einstein's message to the Montreux Conference is translated from the German manuscript.

13. The Ridenour article and the entire symposium about it were reprinted in the *Bulletin of the Atomic Scientists,* August 1947. Einstein's reply also appears in OOMLY, p. 212, and IAO, p. 132. The version here given has been comprehensively revised from the German manuscript.

14. The Sacco-Vanzetti statement, apparently solicited by Fyke Farmer, a lawyer of Nashville, Tennessee, is translated from the German manuscript. Publication in the *Weltbühne* is inferred from the correspondence with General von Schoenaich (see p. 468).

15. The correspondence with John Dewey was made available through the courtesy of Mr. Harold Oram and is reproduced by special permission of Mrs. John Dewey.

16. Einstein's reply to Stimson's invitation was actually addressed to Robert P. Patterson, who was Stimson's successor as Secretary of War.

17. Einstein's address to the Foreign Press Association appeared in the *Bulletin of the Atomic Scientists,* December 1947, and also in OOMLY, p. 204. The present translation is from the German manuscript, except for the last paragraph which is reproduced here from the text of the address, as distributed to the press. See also *The New York Times,* November 12, 1947.

18. Einstein's message to the Cleveland rally is translated from the original German manuscript and considerably revised from the translation used by Einstein. See also the *Cleveland News,* November 11, 1947. Participating in the rally were students from Western Reserve University, Case Institute of Technology, Fenn College, John Carroll University and the Cleveland School of Art.

19. Harrison Brown's account of the proposed Jamaica meeting is from a personal communication which is reproduced here by his special permission. For another approach to the settlement of the East-West conflict at about this same time, see Leo Szilard's "Letter to Stalin," in the *Bulletin of the Atomic Scientists,* December 1947.

20. Einstein's second article in *The Atlantic Monthly* is reprinted in OOMLY, p. 190, and IAO, p. 123. A German version was published in *Aufbau,* December 12, 1947. Einstein's article has been slightly revised; Mr. Swing had no part in the revision.

21. Einstein's "Open Letter to the General Assembly" is reproduced by special permission of H. G. Jacobsohn, Chairman of the Board of *World Events* magazine, which took over the *United Nations World.* It appears in OOMLY, p. 156. See also *The New York Times,* September 23, 1947.

22. The exchange between Einstein and the Soviet scientists also appears in OOMLY, p. 161, and IAO, p. 134. Einstein's reply has been revised from the original German manuscript.

23. The two scientists were Arthur M. Squires and Cuthbert Daniel of New York City.

24. Mr. Lehmann-Russbüldt provided a copy of Einstein's handwritten letter to him.

Chapter XIV

1. "The Fateful Decision," here revised, is from *World Government: The Twenty-second Annual Debate Handbook,* published by the National University Extension Association, 1948, and is reprinted by special permission of Professor Bower Aly, University of Missouri, editor of the series.

2. Einstein's letter to the War Resisters' League in New York is translated from a longhand draft in his files; the English translation actually mailed was an abridged version of the original.

3. The document of the eleven Englishmen was published in *The Times* (of London) on December 22, 1947. It was also reported in the American press; see, for example, the *New York Herald Tribune,* December 21, 1947. Einstein's letter to Usborne has been slightly revised from the handwritten German draft. The source of Einstein's statement that Russell's signature was unauthorized has not been established, but from Russell's letter referred to on p. 497 it appears that Russell at this time did favor a show of force toward Russia. In a round-robin letter to Einstein on February 16, 1948, Usborne mentioned that Lang was not present at the meeting at which he failed of renomination as chairman of the Crusade for World Government, and that he subsequently declared he would not have accepted it.

4. Einstein's fellow sponsors of the report by the National Council against Conscription were Gould Beech, Anton J. Carlson, Donald J. Cowling, Henry Hitt Crane, Edwin T. Dahlberg, George C. Danfield, Kermit Eby, Dorothy Canfield Fisher, Reuben Gustavson, J. Thomas Heistand, W. H. Jernagin, Julius Mark, Cord Meyer, Jr., William J. Miller, Arthur Morgan, Chat Paterson, James G. Patton, Paul E. Scherer, Ray Lyman Wilbur and Robert Wilson.

5. The army officer and American Legion official was F. F. Fletcher of Imperial, California.

6. Einstein's statement opposing Universal Military Training is published in U. S. Congress, Senate, Committee on Armed Services, Hearings before the Committee . . . on Universal Military Training, Washington, D. C., Government Printing Office, 1948, p. 267.

7. The Hungarian journalist was Török Sàndor of the Literary Section of the official Hungarian Radio (*Magyar Rádió*).

8. Einstein's statement on Gandhi's assassination has been revised from the German text.

9. The correspondent criticizing Einstein was John Dudzik of New York City.

10. Wallace's book was published by Reynal & Co., New York.

11. A copy of the Emergency Committee's statement was made available by Harold Oram of New York; slight editorial changes have been made in the interest of clarity. Three new names were given as trustees in the press release accompanying this statement: Reuben G. Gustavson, Chancellor of the University of Nebraska, Joseph E. Mayer of the University of Chicago, and Hermann J. Muller of the University of Indiana. Bethe's name was no longer listed.

12. The translation of Einstein's statement for the Condon dinner is slightly revised from the German original.

13. Huxley's book was published by the Oxford University Press in 1947. Einstein's correspondent was Armin F. Doneis of Pharr, Texas.

14. Einstein's One World Award speech appears in OOMLY, p. 146, and IAO, p. 146. See also *The New York Times,* April 28, 1948. A few stylistic changes have here been made.

15. Excerpts from Ely Culbertson's letter are reproduced by permission of his executors, Bruce E. Culbertson and Albert H. Morehead. Einstein's reply has been slightly revised.

16. Einstein's answers to the questions submitted by *Franc-Tireur* were published in its issue of April 6, 1948, and are reproduced here with permission by *Paris-Jour,* the successor of *Franc-Tireur.*

17. Mumford's reply to Einstein is reproduced by Mumford's permission.

18. Einstein's message to the Methodist Conference appears in *Zion's Herald,* Vol. 126, p. 453, and in the Journal of the 1948 General

Conference of the Methodist Church, May 5, 1948 (Eighth Day), p. 306. It is reproduced by permission of Ralph Stoody, Executive Director, Commission on Public Relations and Methodist Information of the Methodist Church.

19. Einstein's answers appeared in Dorothy Norman's column on May 21 and 24, 1948, and are reproduced by her permission and that of the *New York Post*. The answers have been slightly revised from the German original.

20. Einstein's answer to the questions from *The Rotarian* is here translated from the German text. It is reproduced by permission of Karl K. Krueger, editor. The collection published by *The Rotarian* also included the message to the Portland meeting (p. 395), the address to the Foreign Press Association (p. 426), and the reply to the Soviet scientists (p. 449).

21. Excerpts from Professor Shapley's letters are reproduced by his permission. No useful purpose would be served in listing the many persons and groups involved in the fruitless effort. Einstein's message to the conference and his address to the meeting at Carnegie Hall are translated from the German texts. The information about the Carnegie Hall meeting is from a report in *The New York Times* of June 18, 1948.

22. The excerpts from Norman Cousins' article are reproduced by his permission. He was very helpful concerning other matters relating to this period.

23. Einstein's message to the Wroclaw Congress appeared in *The New York Times*, August 29, 1948. The same issue of *The New York Times* carried Einstein's letter to the Organizing Committee in the version read to the congress. This version apparently constituted a poor retranslation into English of a previous translation of Einstein's original English letter. The real message was reprinted in the *Bulletin of the Atomic Scientists*, September 1948; in OOMLY, p. 152; and in IAO, p. 147. Both the letter and the message are here slightly revised from the German originals.

24. Einstein's letters to the San Francisco analyst, Dr. Walter W. Marseille, are translated from the German in which they were written.

25. The excerpts from Usborne's round-robin letter are reproduced by his permission. Messrs. Henry C. Usborne, Stringfellow Barr, and Harris Wofford, Jr. (the junior trustee of the Foundation for World Government and the person who originally suggested the idea of a foundation to Mrs. Blaine), were all generous in providing information on which the account of these incidents is based. The invitation to the Pocono Conference and the resolution of the Emergency Committee of Atomic Scientists are taken from Stringfellow Barr's privately printed *Final Report on the Pocono Conference*. The quotation describing Brown's report (p. 500) is taken, with Mr. Wofford's permission, from his unpublished *A Cold War Odyssey: Story of the Foundation for World Government*, which was an important source on related matters as well (Garry Davis, Sarrazac-Soulage, Leo Szilard). Among others who attended the Pocono Conference were Mortimer Adler, G. A. Borgese, Richard Bolling, Scott Buchanan, Mrs. J. L. Blair Buck, Clifford Dancer, Alan Cranston, James Martin, Robert Redfield and James P. Warburg. Instrumental in persuading Mrs. Blaine to endow the foundation were, in addition to Wofford, Barr and Usborne, the following: Steven Benedict, Leo Szilard, Harold Urey and William Byron. Besides Einstein, the following signed the resolution of the Emergency Committee (p. 500): Urey, Brown, Morse, Seitz, Hogness and Mayer.

Brown succeeded Barr as chairman of the Pocono Continuing Committee before it was dissolved.

26. Surprisingly enough, only three of Einstein's answers seem to have been published in the *Cheney Record*, February 1949.

27. The statement that the Emergency Committee had collected almost $400,000 appears in a solicitation of funds, signed by Einstein, in the *Bulletin of the Atomic Scientists*, January 1948. Details of the committee's difficulties are exhaustively documented in its files, now deposited in the University of Chicago Library. The committee's necessity to avoid any concern with political problems resulted from the fact that tax exemption had been granted the donors of contributions to the committee and that tax exemption implies the obligation not to engage in political propaganda or attempts to influence legislation. Harrison Brown's and Eugene Rabinowitch's comments on the Emergency Committee are from personal communications, dated April 25, 1957, and August 19, 1957, respectively, and reproduced by their permission. The solicitation letter of September 17, 1948 (p. 505), is from the files of the New York Public Library. The recommendation to inactivate the committee was made in a letter from Brown to the trustees on November 15, 1948.

28. The purpose for which the Christmas message was written has not been established.

Chapter XV

1. The pathologist was Alton R. F. Chapple of the Hornsby & District Hospital at Hornsby, Australia. Einstein's first letter has been slightly revised.

2. The Scientific and Cultural Congress for World Peace was held at the Waldorf-Astoria Hotel, New York, March 25–27, 1949, under the auspices of the National Council of the Arts, Sciences and Professions.

3. Einstein's letter to Hadamard has been slightly revised.

4. Einstein's letter to the Committee on Peaceful Alternatives has been slightly revised. Despite considerable effort, no further details concerning the conference and its resolution have been established.

5. Dr. Rabinowitch wrote to the editors on August 19, 1957: ". . . I asked Einstein whether he would not himself consider an article for the *Bulletin* giving a really strong statement of the point of view of conscientious objectors. . . . Einstein answered this saying that he did not feel like writing such an article. Denying being a nonresister, he said that under proper conditions he would be in favor of resisting aggression by force; but that he saw the real danger of war in the growth of militarism in America rather than in [the] aggressive intention of the Soviet Union."

6. Thirring's exposition of the hydrogen bomb appeared in *Die Geschichte der Atombombe*, Neue Oesterreichische Zeitungs-und Verlagsgesellschaft, Vienna, 1946. An article about it appeared in the *Bulletin of the Atomic Scientists*, March 1950.

7. Einstein's letters to Muste have been slightly revised from the German originals. Mr. Muste helped in clarifying his exchanges with Einstein.

8. The names mentioned in Muste's telegram were Clarence Pickett, Paul Scherer, Charles Iglehart, Douglas Steere, Phillips Elliot and John Haynes Holmes.

9. Einstein's remarks on Mrs. Roosevelt's television program are reproduced by permission of Elliot Roosevelt, producer of the program. They are reprinted in IAO, p. 159, and in the *Bulletin of the Atomic Scientists*, March 1950. The *New York*

Post of February 13, 1950, used its entire front page for this banner headline: "Einstein Warns World: Outlaw H-Bomb or Perish." See also *The New York Times* of the same date. Einstein's German text appears in MW, p. 97, and has been used in revising the present version.

10. In addition to Einstein and Mann, the signers of the letter on behalf of the attorneys were Cameron Chesterfield Alleyn, Earl B. Dickerson, Olin Downes, Thomas Emerson, N. K. Harris, John A. Kingsbury, Robert S. Lynd, Carey McWilliams, Kirtley Mather, Philip Morrison, Linus Pauling, Walter Rautenstrauch, I. F. Stone and Colston E. Warne.

11. Research and preparation for the pamphlet *Militarism in Education* are credited to John M. Swomley, Jr., Director of the National Council against Conscription. Einstein's co-signers were A. C. Baugher, A. D. Beittel, Harold A. Bosley, Louis Bromfield, Pearl S. Buck, J. R. Cunningham, Harold D. Fasnacht, John E. Flynn, George Willard Frasier, Laurence M. Gould, Samuel J. Harrison, Robert J. Havighurst, Nelson P. Horn, Gerald Kennedy, William J. Millor, Joy Elmer Morgan, Alonzo F. Myers, Morgan S. Odell, Max C. Otto, James G. Patton, Pitirim A. Sorokin, Harold Taylor, William P. Tolley, Charles J. Turck and Roscoe L. West.

12. Einstein's letter to Senator Murray has been slightly revised.

13. Einstein's letters to the Society for Social Responsibility in Science have been slightly revised from the German originals. The open letter was published in *Science* of December 22, 1950, and is reproduced by permission of Graham DuShane, editor of *Science*. It was reprinted in IAO, p. 26. The German text appears in MW, p. 15.

14. Research and preparation for *America, Russia and the Bomb* are again credited to John M. Swomley, Jr., Director of the National Council against Conscription. Einstein's co-signers were Harold A. Bosley, Charles F. Boss, Jr., Louis Bromfield, Charles S. Johnson, William Appleton Laurence, Benjamin E. Mays, William J. Millor, Joy Elmer Morgan, Alonzo F. Myers, Glenn Randall Phillips, William T. Scott, Pitirim A. Sorokin, Charles J. Turck, James G. Vail and Robert Wilson.

15. Einstein's remarks on the broadcast "Year of Decision" have been slightly revised and are reproduced by permission of Brad Simpson, program director, Mutual Broadcasting System, Inc. They appear in IAO, p. 161. See also *The New York Times*, June 19, 1950.

16. The remarks about the *Mondialiste* movement are based upon a manuscript by Harris Wofford, *A Cold War Odyssey: Story of the Foundation for World Government*.

17. Einstein's letter to Barr has been slightly revised.

18. Einstein's letter to Cousins has been slightly revised from the German original.

19. Einstein's letter to the Committee for Academic Freedom has been slightly revised from the German original.

20. An English translation of Einstein's statement to the Italian society was published in the UNESCO publication *Impact of Science and Technology*, Vol. I (1950), No. 3–4, as well as in the December 1951 Newsletter of the Society for Social Responsibility in Science, and in the *Bulletin of the Atomic Scientists*, February 1952. This is a revised translation which was prepared from the German original, published in the *Physikalische Blätter*, 1952, No. 5.

21. Einstein's letter to Muste has been slightly revised.

22. Einstein's statement to the Paraguayan Academy is reproduced by

permission of Benigno Riquelme Garcia, its Executive Secretary. In December 1956 Sr. Riquelme advised that the statement was to be published in the first issue of the *Revista Nacional de Cultura*. It is here translated from the German.

23. Posin recorded his experiences in a book, *I Have Been to the Villages*, apparently published by himself in 1948 at Fargo, North Dakota. The present account of Posin's and Farmer's efforts is based on Harris Wofford's manuscript, *A Cold War Odyssey: Story of the Foundation for World Government*. Elected with Farmer as delegates from Tennessee were J. B. Avery and W. A. Harwell. (See *The New York Times*, December 27, 1950.) The Tennessee statute provided for compensation to the delegates, if fifteen other states adopted similar statutes. According to the British Crusade for World Government, twenty-two American states did adopt resolutions favoring world government, but the Tennessee delegates had to pay their own way, and only Senator Harwell was with Farmer in Geneva. The Nigerian delegate was Professor Iyo Ita.

24. Einstein's statement, which apparently had a number of other subscribers, including Usborne, has been revised from the German text. Following the symbolic meeting of December 31, 1950, which was adjourned *sine die*, disagreements developed among those in attendance, and Usborne and the British MPs with him withdrew. Farmer and his group apparently formed one continuing committee, while a World Council for the Peoples' World Convention (see p. 605), with headquarters in Paris, was set up with Usborne's blessings. Neither of these groups regained the impetus once mustered, but the British Parliamentary Group for World Government, with some 160 MPs, continues, with Usborne as Honorary Secretary. Mr. Usborne was very helpful in clarifying this background.

Chapter XVI

1. The conscientious objector was Robert Michener, a Quaker, and Einstein's correspondent was Gerhard Nellhaus of Cambridge, Massachusetts. The case was reported in the *Catholic Worker*, March 1951.

2. The letters to Gene Sharp of April 2, 10 and 16, and June 17, 1953, have been slightly revised. The letter from Sharp's mother, Mrs. P. W. Sharp, was dated April 28, 1953, and came from her home in Dayton, Ohio. Sharp's last communication to Einstein was dated November 6, 1953, and was mailed from the Federal Penitentiary in Danbury, Connecticut. Sharp was released on parole from prison after having served about nine and a half months. He resumed work in peace organizations and did research on the problem of nonviolence. He was unable to find a publisher in America for the book to which Einstein had contributed an introduction. In the fall of 1959, Sharp, who gave permission to reproduce excerpts from his letters, reported that the book was to be published in India. The friend with whom Einstein discussed Gene Sharp's manuscript was Saxe Commins, editor-in-chief of Random House, Inc., New York City.

3. The version of the Frauenglass letter which *The New York Times* published omitted the reference to the Fifth Amendment at the beginning of the fourth paragraph of the letter. *The New York Times* of June 12, 1953, carried a statement of Frauenglass to the effect that the revision of the letter, by deleting Einstein's statement about the Fifth Amendment, had taken place at his request. While Einstein probably consented to the

revision requested by Frauenglass, possibly without realizing that the changed version was to be released for publication, his position as stated in the original letter never changed. In all subsequent publications, English and German, the complete letter was used; see IAO, p. 33, and MW, p. 26. Einstein was very familiar with the origins and history of the Fifth Amendment in England and in the United States. He was well aware of its significance. He recognized it as a means for self-protection but did not feel that in the prevailing political climate it was a suitable weapon to fight the Congressional investigating committees and protect intellectual freedom. The letter to Seelig is translated from MW, p. 234. In December 1953, Albert Shadowitz, a scientist and a witness before the McCarthy Permanent Subcommittee on Investigations of the Senate Committee on Government Operations, based his refusal to testify on the First Amendment. He repeatedly stated that he so acted after personal consultation with Einstein, with the latter's full agreement and approval. In April 1954, Emanuel J. Fried, a Buffalo labor leader, refused to testify before the House Committee on Un-American Activities and sent Einstein a statement of his reasons. Einstein wrote him: "I am convinced that you did the right thing and fulfilled your duty as a citizen."

4. Bertrand Russell's letter to *The New York Times* is reproduced by that newspaper's permission.

5. For the conference of the Emergency Civil Liberties Committee, see *The New York Times*, March 12 and 14, 1954.

6. Professor Spitz's article, entitled "Democracy and the Problem of Civil Disobedience," was published in the June 1954 issue of *The American Political Science Review*.

7. The article was "Scientists and the Great Debate," by A. G. Mezerik, in the *New Republic* of February 5, 1951. Einstein's letter was addressed to Michael Straight.

8. The letters to the California correspondent, who was Merlin M. Paine of San Diego, and the California lawyer, who was John M. Cranston of San Diego, have been slightly revised.

9. "The Paranoia Race" by Dr. Alexander D. Mebane appeared in the quarterly *American Perspective*, Summer 1950. Muste sent Einstein a condensed version of the article intended for publication in his journal *Fellowship*.

10. The letter concerning dissolution of the Emergency Committee is from the committee's files in the University of Chicago Library.

11. The artist is Si Lewen of New York. His book, *The Parade*, was published by H. Bittner Co., New York, 1957. Einstein's letter, here slightly revised, is used by Mr. Lewen's permission.

12. The interview on Universal Military Training has been slightly revised from the German text. It was printed, in different sequence, in the *Christian Century*, December 19, 1951, and also in a special reprint of the section on Universal Military Training in that issue. It is here reproduced by permission of Mr. Randall and the *Christian Century*.

13. The article in *Unesco Courier* is reprinted in IAO, p. 163, and is republished here with Unesco's permission. It is revised from the German text.

14. The statement for Canadian Education Week appears in IAO, p. 65, the German text, used in the present revision, in MW, p. 100. It is reproduced with the permission of Harold Morrison of the Canadian Press.

15. The statement to the Methodist Conference is slightly revised from the German text.

16. The letter to Solovine is translated from *Lettres à Maurice Solovine* by permission of the publisher, Gauthier-Villars, Paris.

17. The old friend in Italy was Signora Ernesta Marangoni of Pavia.

18. The article for the visa symposium of the *Bulletin of the Atomic Scientists* was reprinted in IAO, p. 166, under the title "Symptoms of Cultural Decay." The German text, used in the present revision, appears in MW, p. 88. It is there erroneously attributed to the September 1952 issue of the *Bulletin of the Atomic Scientists*.

19. The Hungarian refugee was Mr. A. Steiner, who sent his letter from Lane Cove in New South Wales, Australia.

20. The correspondent in England was T. E. Naiton of Bradford, Yorkshire. The letter has been slightly revised.

21. Apparently there was a leak concerning the Israeli bid to Einstein, for he refused to comment when queried about it by *The New York Times* on November 16, 1952. On the morning of November 18 Ben-Gurion's secretary in Jerusalem still officially denied that the Prime Minister had sent Einstein an official invitation (as was technically true). Confirmation that Eban's effort had been unsuccessful came later in the day. (See *The New York Times*, November 19, 1952.) The first paragraph of Eban's letter, here reproduced by his permission, has apparently not been published before, but the remainder was published in the Israeli press. Einstein's letter of declination, here translated from the German, also appears in SEELIG, p. 233. The editor of *Maariv* was Azriel Carlebach.

22. The friend to whom this letter was addressed was the painter Josef Scharl.

23. The correspondent in Italy was Federico Steinhaus of Mesano (Bolzano).

24. The friend in England was Gertrud Warschauer, the widow of a Berlin rabbi.

Chapter XVII

1. The issue of *Look* magazine was dated September 23, 1952.

2. Einstein's message to Japanese school children is here translated from the German text in MW, p. 29. Another translation (in two slightly different versions) appears in TWAISI, p. 22, and IAO, p. 17. The precise date of this message has not been established, but it was probably a number of years after Einstein's Japanese visit, since he speaks of himself as an "old man."

3. The letter from *Kaizo* was signed by Katusu Hara, its editor-in-chief. The letter is here slightly shortened.

4. The German text of the message to *Kaizo* appears in MW, p. 59. The English version here given differs both from the translation in IAO, p. 165, and from another translation in Einstein's files.

5. Excerpts from Mr. Shinohara's letters are reproduced by his permission. His assistance in documenting this correspondence is gratefully acknowledged.

6. As Shinohara advised Einstein on September 7, 1953, the message was published on August 6 of that year in the Japanese newspaper *Yomiuri-Shimbun*, Japan's third-largest daily.

7. The award was presented by Miss Dorothy Shaver, president of Lord & Taylor. Einstein's speech of acceptance appears in IAO, p. 33.

8. The message to the War Resisters' League has been slightly revised from the German text. In a league leaflet of October 11, 1953, the last two paragraphs of Einstein's message were transposed.

9. The letter on Thoreau appears in the *Thoreau Society Bulletin*, No.

45, Fall 1953. Einstein's letter was addressed to Professor Walter Harding, the society's secretary-treasurer.

10. Einstein's letter to Martin Agronsky has been slightly revised from the German text. The excerpts from Mr. Agronsky's letter are reproduced with his permission.

11. Grenville Clark's book, *A Plan for Peace*, was published by Harper Brothers, New York. In some of his work Clark was associated with Louis B. Sohn of the Harvard Law School. Einstein's letter has been revised.

12. The correspondent in California was John J. Moore of Pasadena. Einstein's letter to him has been slightly revised. His earlier letter was dated March 30, 1942.

13. Einstein's letters to James R. Newman have been slightly revised. *What Is Science?* was published by Simon and Schuster, New York, in 1955.

14. Einstein's letter to the Hindu student, Mr. Sudhir P. Pandya, has been slightly revised.

15. Einstein's letter to the War Resisters' League has been slightly revised.

16. Einstein's address to the Decalogue Society, reprinted in IAO, p. 34, is here reproduced by permission of the *Decalogue Journal*, where it first appeared. The present version has been revised from the original German text.

17. The Paris journalist who prepared the lengthy peace plan on a cooperative basis was Georg Maranz.

18. Einstein's letter to Muste has been slightly revised.

19. The letter from the World Council for the Peoples' World Convention was signed by Jacques Savary, who pointed out that one of the organizers of the Florence meeting was Mrs. Elizabeth Borgese Mann, the daughter of Thomas Mann.

20. Einstein's letter to Carlson has been slightly revised.

21. Einstein's letter to Pauling has been slightly revised.

22. Einstein's letter to the Navy captain has been slightly revised from the German text.

23. Einstein's letter to the Philadelphia correspondent, Mr. H. Lawrence Ross, has been slightly revised.

24. The Hammarskjöld correspondence was in German. The translation of Mr. Hammarskjöld's letter is used by his permission.

25. The letter to the War Resisters' League has been slightly revised. Apparently the league was unable to avail itself of Einstein's permission to reprint the exchange with Freud.

26. Jules Moch's *Human Folly* was published by Victor Gollancz, London. Einstein's introduction, which has been revised from the original German draft, is reproduced by permission of the publisher.

27. Einstein's letter to *The Reporter* is reproduced, with some minor changes, by permission of the magazine.

Chapter XVIII

1. The friend in England was again Gertrud Warschauer, the widow of a Berlin rabbi.

2. Einstein's letter to Dr. Muelder, here slightly revised, is reproduced by his permission and that of the *Boston University Graduate Journal*, where it first appeared in April 1955. Dr. Muelder's lecture was delivered on December 9, 1954, and was published in pamphlet form by the Boston University Press, 1955. Excerpts from it appeared in the *Boston University Graduate Journal*, January 1955.

3. The letter to A. J. Muste is slightly revised from the original draft in German.

4. Professor Jules Isaac's letter came from Aix-en-Provence, France. The article of which he sent a copy to

Einstein was published in the July 1954 issue of *La Revue socialiste*.

5. The California correspondent was M. Matarisvan of Los Angeles.

6. Bertrand Russell's correspondence with Einstein is reproduced by Lord Russell's permission.

7. Russell's BBC broadcast appeared in *The Listener*, December 30, 1954, and was reprinted in leaflet form by the Friends Peace Committee, London.

8. The list of proposed signatories included the following names: Lord Adrian, H. J. Bhaba, Niels Bohr, Max Born, Alexander Haddow, Otto Hahn, Leopold Infeld, Frédéric Joliot-Curie, Li Sze-kuang, Wolfgang Pauli, C. F. Powell, Karl Manne Siegbahn, Dimitri V. Skobeltzyn, Harold C. Urey and Hideki Yukawa. Not mentioned on the list were three scientists who, however, signed the statement: Bridgman, Muller and Pauling.

9. The declaration appeared in *The New York Times*, July 10, 1955, with Russell's preliminary statement, and, of course, in many other newspapers throughout the world. It was reprinted in America by the War Resisters' League in leaflet form.

10. In covering the release of the declaration, *The New York Times* reported (July 10, 1955) that some of the signatories who had been approached had been "unwilling to sign because they held official posts, but were sympathetic. Professor Dimitri V. Skobeltzyn of Moscow gave a friendly but noncommittal reply. Others, including China's Professor Li Sze-kuang, did not answer." The Associated Press report on the same day:

> Refusing to sign . . . were six Nobel Prize winners—Otto Hahn and Max Born of Germany [this is in error, since Born's name was omitted only by inadvertence, as has been stated], Niels Bohr of Denmark [see below], Wolfgang Pauli of Switzerland, Karl Manne Siegbahn of Sweden and Lord Adrian of Britain.
>
> Others who declined to sign were Dr. Homi J. Bhaba of India, President of the United Nations Atomic Energy Conference scheduled in Geneva August 8–20, Soviet Academician Dimitri V. Skobeltzyn, who has helped plan the conference, [and] Professor Alexander Haddow of Britain.
>
> The appeal was ignored by two American Nobel Prize winners, Chancellor Arthur H. Compton of Washington University in St. Louis and Professor Harold C. Urey of the University of Chicago.

Russell had been in touch with Bohr, on March 8, 1955. In a reply of March 23, 1955, Bohr voiced doubt whether such a declaration would have the desired effect, especially with respect to free access to vital information, which Bohr deemed essential. He also feared that the declaration might impede the forthcoming United Nations Conference, but said he was giving much thought to the proposal and hoped he might reach a more considered opinion. Both Urey and Compton were heard from on July 10, 1955 (*The New York Times*, July 11, 1955). Urey said he refused to sign because he felt the appeal was "futile" and "obvious" and there was no practical way to implement it outside of what present governments were already doing. Compton said he approved the general objectives of the appeal but could not support it in detail. He gave the first public inkling that another similar declaration was in the making. This second statement grew from a meeting of Nobel Prize winners at Lindau at Lake Constance, Germany (such meetings had been held there annually since 1951) and was made public on July 15, 1955, only six days after the Russell-Einstein declaration. Apparently it was conceived quite independently. Its full text reads:

> We who sign this appeal are scientists from many countries, of several races, of different creeds, unconnected in politics. Our association is that we have all been privileged to be awarded Nobel Prizes.
>
> Our appeal is to all men everywhere. We must recognize that ours is a common fate, that if we are to live, it can only be as brothers. The alternative is that we will die.
>
> We have given freely a lifetime to the service of science. Science, we hold, is a way to a fuller life for mankind. But we have learned with horror that science has also provided man with the instruments for self-destruction.
>
> In an all-out war the earth can be made so radioactive that whole nations will be destroyed. Many men and women of neutral countries also might be killed.
>
> If the major powers engage in war, where is the assurance that such an all-out struggle will not develop?
>
> A nation that engages in an all-out war thus invites self-destruction and endangers the whole world.
>
> We do not deny that at present the peace of the world may be maintained by the fear of these deadly weapons. Still we feel that it is self-deception for governments to think over a long period that the fear of these weapons will prevent war from occurring. Fear and tension have too frequently produced war. Likewise, it is self-deception to believe that minor conflicts can always be settled by the use of traditional weapons. In extreme need, no warring nation will deny itself the use of any weapon that scientific techniques can provide.
>
> The independent nations must bring themselves to the decision by which they voluntarily renounce force as the last political recourse. If they are not prepared to do this, they will cease to exist.

Listed among the eighteen signers of this statement were Born, Muller and Yukawa, who had also signed the Russell-Einstein statement, as well as Compton and Hahn, who had not. Other signers were Fritz Lippmann and Wendell Stanley of the United States; Frederick Soddy of England; Hans von Euler and Georg von Hevesy of Sweden; Paul Mueller and Leopold Ruzicka of Switzerland; Hermann Staudinger, Kurt Adler, Adolf Butenandt, Gerhard Domagk, Werner Heisenberg and Richard Kuhn of Germany (according to *The New York Times*, July 16, 1955). Einstein probably knew that this second declaration was being discussed among some of the scientists who eventually signed it; details, however, were not known to him.

11. In praising the Russell-Einstein declaration as a "noble appeal," *L'Osservatore Romano*, reflecting the Vatican viewpoint, expressed astonishment that it should have evoked a greater response than similar appeals by the Pope, and complained that it "spoke of the 'biological species' [man] in the same way as the director of a zoological garden would say that the heat was excessive for his polar bears or that there was not enough water for his seals or exotic ducks" (*The New York Times*, July 12, 1955).

12. Lord Russell's efforts gave rise to a series of conferences of scientists of the kind he had projected. The first one, small and improvised, was held in London, August 3–5, 1955, on the eve of the United Nations Conference on Peacetime Uses of Atomic Energy. The second, which Russell was unable to attend, was held at Pugwash, Nova Scotia, July 6–11, 1957, with the Canadian-American financier Cyrus Eaton as host. It was attended by twenty-two scientists from ten nations, including Japan, China, Poland and the Soviet Union. Among those present were four signers of the Russell-Einstein declaration. The Pugwash Conference (with two abstentions) issued a statement and three committee reports, which were subsequently supported in a resolution of the Presidium of the Soviet Academy of Sciences and by a statement by 196 Soviet scientists. (*Bulletin of the Atomic Scientists*, September and November 1957. For a debate between Russell and one of his critics, see *Bulletin of the Atomic Scientists*, April 1958.) Further "Pugwash" conferences were held in 1958 and 1959.

13. Einstein's intention to make a public statement on the anniversary of Israel's statehood led to strange rumors and speculations after his death. It was suggested that one page bearing notes which Einstein had allegedly made about his discussions with Messrs. Eban and Dafni had been stolen at the hospital, although careful investigations did not yield any confirmation of that assumption. On May 1, 1955, *The New York Times* published a lengthy article about Einstein's consultations with the Israeli officials, which was based on information provided by Mr. Reuben Dafni, the Israeli Consul. Included in the article was a "reconstruction" of Einstein's proposed address prepared by the Israeli Consulate allegedly upon the basis of Einstein's own notes. The "reconstruction" was completely unauthorized by those charged with the responsibility for Einstein's literary estate. Since Einstein left but the one page inserted in the text, it was impossible to "reconstruct" the address as he himself might have drafted it. The reconstruction was possibly based on notes made by Messrs. Eban and Dafni at the meeting with Einstein, as well as on suggestions offered to Einstein by these two Israeli officials.

INDEX